Thinking in Writing
Rhetorical Patterns and Critical Response
Fourth Edition

Donald McQuade
University of California, Berkeley

Robert Atwan
Series Editor, The Best American Essays

Boston   Burr Ridge, IL   Dubuque, IA   Madison, WI
New York   San Francisco   St. Louis
Bangkok   Bogotá   Caracas   Lisbon   London   Madrid   Mexico City
Milan   New Delhi   Seoul   Singapore   Sydney   Taipei   Toronto

McGraw-Hill

A Division of The McGraw·Hill Companies

THINKING IN WRITING: RHETORICAL PATTERNS AND CRITICAL RESPONSE

This book is printed on acid-free paper.

1 2 3 4 5 6 7 8 9 0 DOC/DOC 9 0 9 8 7

ISBN 0–07–045983–5

Editorial director: *Phillip A. Butcher*
Sponsoring editor: *Tim Julet*
Marketing manager: *Lesley Denton*
Project manager: *Amy Hill*
Production supervisor: *Lori Koetters*
Designer: *Michael Warrell*
Photo research coordinator: *Sharon Miller*
Compositor: *Shepherd Incorporated*
Typeface: *10/12 Palatino*
Printer: *R. R. Donnelley & Sons Company*

Library of Congress Cataloging-in-Publication Data

Thinking in writing / [edited by] Donald McQuade, Robert Atwan.—4th
  ed.
    p. cm.
  Includes index.
  ISBN 0–07–045983–5 (acid-free paper)
  1. College readers. 2. Report writing—Problems, exercises, etc.,
  3. English language—Rhetoric—Problems, exercises, etc.
  I. McQuade, Donald. II. Atwan, Robert.
  PE1417.T478 1998
  808'.042—dc21   97–25635

http://www.mhhe.com

About the Editors

Donald McQuade is professor of English at the University of California, Berkeley, where he has served as Dean of Undergraduate and Interdisciplinary Studies and as the founding director of the Center for Theater Arts. Professor McQuade teaches writing, American literature, and American studies at Berkeley and has coordinated the English department's writing program. One of the founding members of the Council of Writing Program Administrators, he served as the 1991 Chair of the Conference on College Composition and Communication as well as on the executive committee of the teaching of writing division of the Modern Language Association. His publications include *The Territory of Language: Linguistics, Stylistics, and the Teaching of Composition, Student Writers at Work* and (with Robert Atwan) *Popular Writing in America, The Writer's Presence,* and *Edsels, Luckies, and Frigidaires: Advertising the American Way.* He served as the guest curator of an exhibition entitled "Advertising America" at the Smithsonian Institution's Cooper-Hewitt Museum, as the general editor of the revival of the Modern Library series, and as the general editor of and a contributing editor to *The Harper American Literature.* He has contributed chapters to the *Columbia Literary History of the United States* and to *Redrawing the Boundaries.* He is currently preparing an edition of Frederick Winslow Taylor's *Principles of Scientific Management* and writing on issues of efficiency in twentieth century American culture.

Robert Atwan is the founder and series editor of *The Best American Essays,* which has appeared annually since 1986. His writing has appeared in many national periodicals, including the *New York Times,* the *Los Angeles Times,* the *Atlantic Monthly,* the *National Review,* the *Kenyon Review,* the *Iowa Review, Denver Quarterly,* and *Image* as well as in professional journals and critical collections on the essay. He has edited a number of anthologies on both popular culture and classic literature, including *Bedside Hollywood,* the two-volume *Chapters Into Verse: Poetry in English Inspired by the Bible,* and *Divine Inspiration: The Life of Jesus in World Poetry.* He is also an editor of *The QPB Reader's Shakespeare.* Among his many books devoted to college composition, communication, and literature are: *The Harper American Literature, One Hundred Major Modern Writers, American Mass Media, Why We Write, Enjoying Stories, Writing Day by Day, Effective Writing for the College Curriculum, Ten on Ten,* and *Left, Right, and Center.* He also edits two series of college anthologies featuring recent nonfiction, *Our Times* and *America Now.* He has served as a consultant to national writing assessments, the Library of America, the National Endowment for the Humanities, and several writing awards programs. He has taught courses on writing, advanced composition, and literary nonfiction at Rutgers University and Seton Hall University. He lives in Milton, Massachusetts.

for
Max Anthony Maxwell

Contents

Preface xv

Acknowledgments xvii

Introduction **"Learning to Write Is Learning to Think"** 1

Four Methods of Brainstorming 3

1. Exploring Words 3

Betty Edwards Left and Right 8
"Words and phrases concerning concepts of left and right permeate our language and thinking."

Nancy Mairs On Being a Cripple 9
"'Cripple' seems to me a clean word, straightforward and precise."

2. Making Metaphors 11

Edward Hoagland Turtles 13
"Baby turtles in a turtle bowl are a puzzle in geometrics."

Annie Dillard The Stunt Pilot 15
"The plane moved every way a line can move, and it controlled three dimensions, so the line carved massive and subtle slits in the air like sculptures."

3. Observation and Inference 18

Ian Frazier Making Marks 22
"I look at what is under and around my feet more often than is common, probably because of all the time I spent as a boy searching for four-leaf clovers and arrowheads and rifle shells and golf balls."

4. Abstract and Concrete 26

Joan Didion On Morality 29
"I have been trying to think . . . in some abstract way about 'morality,' a word I distrust more every day, but my mind veers inflexibly toward the particular."

Developing Ideas 31

Chapter 1 **Narration** 33

Elements of Narration 33
Choice of Detail 34

Duration   34

Clear Sense of Direction   36

Sequential Development   37

Elements of Literary Narrative   37

Point of View   37

Voice   38

Dialogue   38

Maya Angelou   Graduation   40

"Finding my seat at last, I was overcome with a presentiment of worse things to come. Something unrehearsed, unplanned, was going to happen, and we were going to be made to look bad."

E. B. White   Once More to the Lake   52

"I watched him, his hard little body, skinny and bare, saw him wince slightly as he pulled up around his vitals the small, soggy, icy garment. As he buckled the swollen belt suddenly my groin felt the chill of death."

Judith Ortiz Cofer   American History   59

"El Building was like a monstrous jukebox, blasting out salsas from open windows as the residents, mostly new immigrants just up from the island, tried to drown out whatever they were currently enduring with loud music. But the day President Kennedy was shot, there was a profound silence in El Building. . . ."

Maxine Hong Kingston   No Name Woman   67

"Whenever she had to warn us about life, my mother told stories that ran like this one, a story to grow up on. She tested our strength to establish realities."

▲▼   Thematic Pair: Giving in to Pressure   79

Langston Hughes   Salvation   80

"Suddenly the whole room broke into a sea of shouting, as they saw me rise. Waves of rejoicing swept the place. Women leaped in the air. My aunt threw her arms around me. The minister took me by the hand and led me to the platform."

George Orwell   Shooting an Elephant   83

"And suddenly I realized that I should have to shoot the elephant after all: The people expected it of me and I had got to do it; I could feel their two thousand wills pressing me forward, irresistibly."

Chapter 2   **Description   91**

Purposes   91

Objective and Subjective Description   92

Steps in Writing Effective Description   94

Mary Gordon   More Than Just a Shrine: Paying Homage to the Ghosts of Ellis Island   97

"The minute I set foot upon the island I could feel all that it stood for: insecurity, obedience, anxiety, dehumanization, the terrified and careful deference of the displaced."

N. Scott Momaday   A First American Views His Land   103

"The Native American's attitudes towards this landscape have been formulated over a long period of time, a span that reaches back to the end of the Ice Age. The land, this land, is secure in his racial memory."

Virginia Woolf   Death of a Moth   113

"It was as if someone had taken a tiny bead of pure life and decking it as lightly as possible with down and feathers, had set it dancing and zigzagging to show us the true nature of life."

Gretel Ehrlich   Time on Ice   117

"Here, at the top of the world. Clouds sweep down so low the landscape appears flattened, as if Earth were clamped by a vise. I sleep on water, walk on water, dream on water—albeit frozen."

▲▼   Thematic Pair: What We Wear   126

Jamaica Kincaid   Biography of a Dress   127

"My skin was not the color of cream in the process of spoiling, my hair was not the texture of silk and the color of flax, my eyes did not gleam like blue jewels in a crown, the afternoons in which I sat watching my mother make me this dress were not cool, and verdant lawns and pastures and hills and dales did not stretch out before me. . . ."

James Agee   Overalls   137

". . . a new suit of overalls has among its beauties those of a blueprint: and they are a map of the working man."

Chapter 3   **Exemplification   143**

Examples Help Make Ideas Clear and Convincing   143

Selecting Examples   145

Organizing Examples   146

Ishmael Reed   America: The Multinational Society   147

"When I heard a schoolteacher warn the other night about the invasion of the American educational system by foreign curriculums, I wanted to yell at the television set, 'Lady, they're already here.'"

Michiko Kakutani   The Word Police   152

"The politically correct lion becomes the 'monarch of the jungle,' new-age children play 'someone at the top of the heap,' and the Mona Lisa goes down in history as Leonardo's 'acme of perfection.'"

Ruth Schwartz Cowan   Less Work for Mother?   158
*"The vacuum cleaner, General Electric announced in 1918, is better
than a maid: it doesn't quit, get drunk, or demand higher wages."*

Alice Walker   In Search of Our Mothers' Gardens   168
*"For these grandmothers and mothers of ours were not Saints, but
Artists; driven to a numb and bleeding madness by the springs of
creativity in them for which there was no release."*

▲▼   Thematic Pair: Negotiating Public Space   178

Edward T. Hall   The Arab World   179
*". . . most Americans follow a rule, which is all the more binding
because we seldom think about it, that can be stated as follows: as soon
as a person stops or is seated in a public place, there balloons around
him a small sphere of privacy which is considered inviolate."*

Brent Staples   Just Walk on By: A Black Man Ponders
His Ability to Alter Public Space   188
*"She cast back a worried glance. To her, the youngish black man—a broad
six feet two inches with a beard and billowing hair, both hands shoved
into the pockets of a bulky military jacket—seemed menacingly close."*

Chapter 4   **Definition   195**

Lexical Definitions   196
Stipulative Definitions   197
Extended Definitions   198

Herbert Gans   The Underclass   200
*"America has a long history of insults for the 'undeserving' poor. In
the past they were bums, hoboes, vagrants and paupers; more recently
they have been culturally deprived and the hard-core poor. Now they
are the 'underclass.' "*

Thomas Sowell   We're Not Really "Equal"   204
*"'Equality' is one of the great undefined terms underlying much
current controversy and antagonism. This one confused word might
even become the rock on which our civilization is wrecked. It should be
worth defining."*

Perri Klass   Ambition   208
*"Especially in women, ambition has often been seen as a profoundly
dislikable quality; the word 'ambitious' linked to a 'career woman'
suggested that she was ruthless, hard as nails, clawing her way to
success on top of the bleeding bodies of her friends."*

Nancy Gibbs   When Is It Rape?   213
*"In court, on campus, in conversation, the issue turns on the elasticity
of the word 'rape,' one of the few words in the language with the power
to summon a shared image of a horrible crime."*

▲▼   Thematic Pair: Language and Prejudice   226

Gloria Naylor   A Question of Language   227
"I was later to go home and ask the inevitable question that every black parent must face—'Mommy, what does 'nigger' mean?'"

Alleen Pace Nilsen   Sexism in Language   231
"Most parents are amused if they have a daughter who is a tomboy, but they are genuinely distressed if they have a son who is a sissy."

Chapter 5   **Classification   239**

When to Use Classification   240
How to Use Classification   241
Partition/Binary Classification   242
Classification as Structure   242

Judith Viorst   Friends, Good Friends—and Such Good Friends   244
"There are medium friends, and pretty good friends, and very good friends indeed, and these friendships are defined by their level of intimacy."

Russell Baker   The Plot Against People   250
"Inanimate objects are classified into three major categories—those that don't work, those that break down and those that get lost."

David Cole   Five Myths about Immigration   253
"Growing up, I was always taught that we will be judged by how we treat others. If we are collectively judged by how we have treated immigrants—those who appear today to be 'other' but will in a generation be 'us'—we are not in very good shape."

Donald Hall   Four Kinds of Reading   258
"It is worth asking how the act of reading became something to value in itself, as opposed for instance to the act of conversation or the act of taking a walk."

▲▼   Thematic Pair: Understanding Human Behavior   263

Desmond Morris   Territorial Behavior   264
"In the broadest sense, there are three kinds of human territory: tribal, family, and personal."

John Holt   Three Kinds of Discipline   273
"We hear constantly that children will never do anything unless compelled to by bribes or threats. But in their private lives, or in extracurricular activities in school. . . . they often submit themselves willingly and wholeheartedly to very intense disciplines, simply because they want to learn to do a given thing well."

Chapter 6   **Comparison and Contrast   279**

Determining a Basis for Comparison   280

Selecting Points of Comparison   281

Establishing a Main Idea   282

Planning an Essay of Comparison   282

Developing an Essay of Comparison:
Three Methods   283

Bruce Catton   Grant and Lee: A Study in
Contrasts   286
*"They were two strong men, these oddly different generals, and they
represented the strengths of two conflicting currents that, through
them, had come into final collision."*

Suzanne Britt   Neat People versus Sloppy People   291
*"I've finally figured out the difference between neat people and sloppy
people. The distinction is, as always, moral."*

Karen Horney   Fear and Anxiety   294
*"When a mother is afraid that her child will die when it has only a
pimple or a slight cold we speak of anxiety; but if she is afraid when the
child has a serious illness we call her reaction fear."*

E. J. Dionne, Jr.   How Liberals and Conservatives Are
Failing America   297
*"We are suffering from a false polarization in our politics, in which
liberals and conservatives keep arguing about the same things when the
country wants to move on."*

▲▼   Thematic Pair: Language and Gender   307

Deborah Tannen   How Male and Female Students Use
Language Differently   308
*"The classroom is a different environment for those who feel
comfortable putting themselves forward in a group than it is for
those who find the prospect of doing so chastening, or even
terrifying."*

John Mack Faragher   Pioneer Diaries of Women and
Men   315
*"Despite similarity in content, there was a notable difference in the
style of men's and women's writing."*

Chapter 7   **Analogy and Extended Metaphor   323**

Explaining by Means of Analogy   324

The Visual Impact of Analogy   325

Analogy as a Means of Discovery   325

Lewis Thomas   The Attic of the Brain   327
"Forget whatever you feel like forgetting. From time to time, practice not being open, discover new things not to talk about, learn reserve, hold the tongue."

Mark Twain   Reading the River   332
"Now when I had mastered the language of this water, and had come to know every trifling feature that bordered the great river as familiarly as I knew the letters of the alphabet, I had made a valuable acquisition. But I had lost something, too."

Plato   The Allegory of the Cave   336
"And now, I said, let me show in a figure how far our nature is enlightened or unenlightened. . . ."

Katha Pollitt   Feminism at the Crossroads   341
"So perhaps the real way feminism will resolve its indecisiveness at the crossroads is that it will continue to debate and hesitate and try both roads at once until one day it sees that in fact the crossroads has disappeared."

▲▼   Thematic Pair: Television as a Drug   348

Marie Winn   TV Addiction   349
"Let us consider television viewing in the light of the conditions that define serious addictions."

Pete Hamill   Crack and the Box   353
"Why, for God's sake? Why do so many millions of Americans of all ages, races, and classes choose to spend all or part of their lives stupefied?"

Chapter 8   **Cause and Effect   361**

Four Ways to Organize a Cause-and-Effect Essay   362
Seven Common Errors   364

Amy Cunningham   Why Women Smile   367
"Despite all the work we American women have done to get and maintain full legal control of our bodies, not to mention our destinies, we still don't seem to be fully in charge of a couple of small muscle groups in our faces."

Laurence Steinberg   Bound to Bicker   374
"Even in the closest of families, parents and teenagers squabble and bicker surprisingly often—so often, in fact, that we hear impassioned recountings of these arguments in virtually every discussion we have with parents or teenagers."

Stephen Jay Gould   Of Crime, Cause, and Correlation   380
"Have a healthy respect for simple answers; the world is not always a deep conundrum fit only for consideration by certified scholars."

Patricia Williams   Hate Radio   387

"As I listened to a range of such programs what struck me as the most unifying theme was not merely the specific intolerance on such hot topics as race and gender, but a much more general contempt for the world, a verbal stoning of anything different."

▲▼   Thematic Pair: The Global Future   396

Sir Frederick Hoyle   The Next Ice Age   397

"The conclusion is that the present sequence of ice ages has scarcely begun. There are hundreds of ice ages still to come."

Carl Sagan   The Warming of the World   404

"The solution to these problems requires a perspective that embraces the planet and the future. We are all in this greenhouse together."

Chapter 9   **Process Analysis   411**

Two Kinds of Process Analysis   411

Steps in Process Analysis   414

Three Stages in the Writing Process   414

Michael Anania   Starting   416

"There is something intimate, however painful, about trying to start your car on a bitter cold morning."

Ernest Hemingway   When You Camp Out, Do It Right   420

"Men have always believed that there was something mysterious and difficult about making a pie. Here is a great secret. There is nothing to it."

Yogi Ramacharaka   The Complete Breath   424

"Avoid a jerky series of inhalations, and strive to attain a steady continuous breath."

Lars Eighner   On Dumpster Diving   429

"I learned to scavenge gradually, on my own. Since then I have initiated several companions into the trade. I have learned that there is a predictable series of stages a person goes through in learning to scavenge."

▲▼   Thematic Pair: On the Writing Process   441

Kurt Vonnegut   How to Write with Style   442

"The writing style which is most natural for you is bound to echo the speech you heard when a child."

Donald M. Murray   The Maker's Eye   447

"Writers must learn to be their own best enemy. They must accept the criticism of others and be suspicious of it; they must accept the praise of others and be even more suspicious of it."

Chapter 10   **Argument and Persuasion   453**

The Difference Between Argument and
Persuasion   453

Argument   453

    Claims   455

    Reasoning Pattern   456

    Organization: Constructing an Argument   460

Persuasion   461

    What Is Persuasion?   461

    The Three Types of Persuasion   462

    Identifying with Your Audience   463

Five Classics   466

Jonathan Swift   A Modest Proposal   467

*"I have been assured by a very knowing American of my acquaintance
in London, that a young healthy child well nursed is at a year old a
most delicious, nourishing, and wholesome food, whether stewed,
roasted, baked, or broiled. . . ."*

Thomas Jefferson   The Declaration of
Independence   476

*"We hold these truths to be self-evident, that all men are created
equal. . . ."*

Elizabeth Cady Stanton   Declaration of Sentiments and
Resolutions   481

*"We hold these truths to be self-evident: that all men and women are
created equal. . . ."*

John F. Kennedy   On Being Inaugurated President of the
United States   486

*"And so, my fellow Americans, ask not what your country can do for
you; ask what you can do for your country."*

Martin Luther King, Jr.,   I Have a Dream   491

*"I have a dream that my four little children will one day live in a
nation where they will not be judged by the color of their skin, but by
the content of their character."*

Three Brief Arguments on Current Issues:
Free Speech on Campus   496

Nat Hentoff   Should This Student Have Been
Expelled?   497

*"Anyway, there was no physical combat. Just words. Awful words, but
nothing more than speech. (Nor were there any threats.)"*

Vartan Gregorian   Free Speech? Yes. Drunkenness?
No.   502
"The day when drunkenness was romanticized, when racial or sexual
harassment could be winked at, condoned or considered merely in poor
taste has long passed."

Gun Control   507

Sandra S. Froman   Armed and Safe   508
"No matter how many gun control laws are enacted, criminals will
always get guns."

Senator Campbell's Rebuttal   511

Tom Campbell   Armed and Dangerous   514
"Would it seriously be argued that seat belts are a bad idea because
they don't prevent all traffic deaths?"

Ms. Froman's Rebuttal   517

The Death Penalty   521

Edward I. Koch   Death and Justice: How Capital
Punishment Affirms Life   522
"The execution of a lawfully condemned killer is no more an act of
murder than is legal imprisonment an act of kidnapping."

David Bruck   The Death Penalty: A Response to Edward
I. Koch   528
"He suggests that we trivialize murder unless we kill the murderers.
By that logic, we also trivialize rape unless we sodomize rapists."

Glossary   535

Permissions Acknowledgments   543

Index   549

Preface

What is "Thinking in Writing"?

The purpose of this book can be stated quite simply: to introduce students to the basic, time-tested procedures for clear thinking and effective writing. More specifically, *Thinking in Writing* responds to both the growing concern for the cognitive development of first-year students and the apparent professional interest in combining a systematic introduction to rhetoric with the actualities of the writing process.

The operating principle built into the design and content of the book is that thinking and writing should be seen as interrelated processes, which stimulate and reinforce each other. The book proceeds on the assumption that clear thinking can best be accomplished when thoughts are put down in writing, and that effective writing, in turn, can best be achieved when the writer recognizes the underlying rhetorical patterns that structure the thinking process.

Thinking in Writing demonstrates in accessible language how familiar rhetorical structures can stimulate the production of thoughts to the point where they will do students the most good—as words on paper. From there, once students can see, read, and rethink their thoughts, they will find themselves better able to practice with greater confidence the skills, structures, and strategies that will help them shape and extend those thoughts into coherent and convincing essays.

The book's organization reflects what is essentially a traditional approach to rhetoric, reactivated within the context of the most distinguished theoretical and pedagogical work being done in the fields of composition and cognitive studies. In this respect, the introductions and exercises in *Thinking in Writing* continuously highlight the interconnectedness—in fact, the simultaneity—of thinking and writing. We have accentuated this overriding interest in the relation of rhetoric to the overlapping processes of thinking and writing throughout the book.

What's New in the Fourth Edition?

The fourth edition of *Thinking in Writing* (the first appeared in 1980) introduces many new features. We have redesigned the book to stimulate even more productive classroom discussion and to prompt more effective writing. Some of the major added features are:

- A new general introduction that unfolds the writing process in greater detail and clearly shows students how thinking and writing are connected. The introduction now incorporates several popular brainstorming strategies from the earlier editions, including such sections as "Exploring Words," "Making Metaphors," "Observation and Inference" as well as "Abstract and Concrete." Each of these sections now includes passages and short essays with new exercises.
- Revised chapter introductions that provide in-depth coverage of essential rhetorical, compositional, and cognitive procedures.
- A thematically arranged pair of selections, with corresponding exercises, concludes each chapter. This new feature will allow instructors to focus on a specific rhetorical pattern and at the same time explore how different writers handle a similar topic. The "Argument and Persuasion" chapter now contains three pairs of short arguments on three current issues as well as an eight-page, four-color portfolio of advertisements, tracing the historical shifts in the persuasive strategies used to make women the subjects and objects of commercial appeals.
- Newly designed sets of questions that follow each selection. These questions call for more concentrated attention on two important activities: class discussion and writing.

In addition to these new features, *Thinking in Writing* retains its accessible blend of classic and contemporary selections that represent an appealing cross-disciplinary spread. Also retained and improved are the glossary and the lists of "Additional Rhetorical Strategies" that follow each selection; these list conveniently highlight the realistic mixture of rhetorical patterns that characterize most good writing.

The Need for Thinking in Writing

This book will have succeeded if students view clear-headed thinking and effective writing as far more manageable, more "do-able" activities than they may now be inclined to consider them. Thinking, after all, is a basic need—"reason's need," Hannah Arendt calls it. And writing, too, is a need—a powerful social and cultural one. Neither activity should feel particularly strange to anyone; we use practically all of the rhetorical procedures discussed and demonstrated in this book within and beyond the thinking and writing we do each day in college and university settings. To be sure, learning to write well requires the conscious mastery of these time-honored rules and procedures. That is an educational fact that nearly everyone who wants to learn how to write must face. But the act of writing doesn't begin with the mastery of basic compositional skills. It begins, quite simply, with something far more fundamental and broadly human: the stubborn itch to think for ourselves and the corresponding urge to say and write something that means something.

Acknowledgments

As was the case with the previous editions of *Thinking in Writing*, our work on this revision has benefited greatly from the solid advice and generous encouragement of our colleagues across the country. We would especially like to acknowledge the incisive and judicious reviews of

> Michael Berberich, Galveston College
> Lynn Z. Bloom, University of Connecticut
> Santi Buscemi, Middlesex County College
> Michael Cochran, Sante Fe Community College
> Michael Daly, Glendale Community College
> Daniel Grubb, Indiana University of Pennsylvania
> Pam Narney, Northern Virginia Community College
> Judy Pearce, Montgomery College
> Beverly A. Ricks, University of Akron
> Virginia Steamer, Dundalk Community College
> Richard Sax, Madonna College
> Michael E. Terry, John Wood Community College
> Billy W. Tucker, Cisco Junior College
> Gordon Van Ness, Longwood College
> Robert Viau, Georgia College

We would also like to thank the following colleagues for their careful readings and useful suggestions on earlier editions: Joseph Boles, Northern Arizona University; Terry Engebretsen, Idaho State University; John Fleming, West Valley College; Stephen Gurney, Bemidji State University; Robert Keefe, University of Massachusetts–Amherst; D. G. Kehl, Arizona State University; George Miller, University of Delaware; and Betty Park, Bucks County Community College.

Many friends and colleagues have had and continue to have considerable influence on the shape of *Thinking in Writing*, and we are grateful to them as well. Among them are: David Bartholomae, Trudy Baltz, William Berry, Janet Brown, Ken Bruffee, Frank D'Angelo, Rosemary Deen, David Follmer, Richard Garretson, Lynn Goldberg, Sarah Hubbard, John Jamison, Jane Jubilee, the late Betsy Kaufman, Richard Larson, Frank Lortscher, Robert Lyons, Elaine Maimon, Gerard McCauley, Christine Pellicano, Marie Ponsot, Jack Roberts, David Rothberg, Sharon Shaloo, the late Sandra Schor, the late Mina Shaughnessy, Nancy Sommers, David Speidel, Rockwell Stensrud, Liza Stern, Ruth Stern, Judith Summerfield, William Vesterman, John Walker, and Harvey Wiener.

We would also like to acknowledge the many people at McGraw-Hill who have contributed to revising this edition of *Thinking in Writing*. We are grateful to Tim Julet for his thoughtful contributions to the project as well as his confidence in it. Amy Hill has managed the revision with great skill, tact, and professionalism. We would also like to acknowledge the assistance of Brian Conzachi, who has served as a first-rate copyeditor.

David Elderbrock, Richard Mikita, and Christopher Motley brought inestimable intelligence, imagination, and energy to this project in its earlier editions. Alix Schwartz contributed outstanding research, unfailingly good judgment, as well as remarkable pedagogical skill and editorial assistance in every phase of this revision. We believe that *Resources for Thinking in Writing*, prepared by Greg Mullins of the University of California, Berkeley, is an outstanding work of criticism in itself. Also filled with thoroughly engaging and carefully articulated pedagogical insight, Greg Mullins's *Resources for Thinking in Writing* will serve as an invaluable aid for helping students to think in writing more effectively.

Helene Atwan and Susanne McQuade have continued most generously to take time from their own busy lives to encourage and assist us. Thanks, too, to Emily and Gregory Atwan as well as Christine and Marc McQuade for their presence and patience. Finally, though it may seem odd, we would like to thank each other—for helping to maintain the strength of friendship throughout yet another collaboration.

"Learning to Write Is Learning to Think"

Thinking in Writing is designed to help you overcome two of the most frustrating obstacles to effective and productive writing: getting ideas and turning them into a paper. Students often complain that it takes them an unendurably long time to think of "something to say" to begin writing, and that once they've finally begun, they discouragingly "run out of things to say" very quickly. For many students, the act of writing becomes a physically and mentally exhausting cycle of getting started and getting stuck.

This book—through its methods and models—offers a practical approach to the ever-difficult task of finding ideas and developing them in composition. A large part of the problem we all face in trying to write fluently and intelligently is not how we think or how we write, but rather how we handle the continuous interplay between both activities while composing. If your tendency is to wait patiently for ideas to come fully expressed and "paper ready," you will sooner or later come to view composition as a kind of mental torture. You may never get started. On the other hand, if your tendency is to slap down whatever ideas come into your head without paying attention to the structural patterns that can be generated from them, your compositions will always remain haphazard and undeveloped—a mental torture to your readers.

Clearly, if you're the type of person who likes to see solid results after spending a reasonable amount of time at your desk writing, you need to become conscious of how the interaction of thinking and writing can remarkably improve your motivation and momentum. You need to learn how to extend and develop ideas by seeing how small segments of writing contain the germ of larger organizational units. You need to see how a thought pattern can lead to an essay structure, how single words and metaphors can sometimes shape an entire piece of writing. And, most importantly, you need to trust your own intelligence, to relax into your own eloquence.

The main instructional principle of this book can be stated quite simply: we think most rigorously and productively when we make the effort to put our thoughts down in writing, and we write most fluently

1

and maturely when we recognize the underlying patterns of our thinking. In the chapters that follow, thinking and writing will be considered as interrelated mental processes that stimulate and reinforce each other. So closely intertwined are these two indispensable human activities that writer and educator Carlos Baker claims quite simply: "Learning to write is learning to think."

In one respect, this book runs counter to a deeply rooted idea about the relationship between thought and language. We are accustomed to consider thinking as a kind of internalized, preparatory activity and writing as its external, finished expression. Our very language constantly reinforces this venerable notion; we speak quite casually of "expressing an idea" or "putting our thoughts into words." The assumption, of course, is that our thoughts and ideas truly exist in some formidable fashion *before* they exist in words. This may be so. But the question we should be in the habit of asking ourselves when we write is: Do we really know what we want to say before we actually say it? For the purposes of this book we want to encourage students to consider this question from a practical point of view. What are the benefits of working as though thinking were not a preparatory activity but rather one that can and does proceed *simultaneously* with writing? In other words, what are the benefits of learning to do our thinking *in* writing?

Obviously, anyone who tries to think about thinking is on shaky ground. Though human beings have been having thoughts for presumably well over two million years, no one really knows for certain exactly what thinking is. This book does not intend to come up with a solution to that ultimate philosophical problem. But just as we can ride a bicycle without being able to say exactly how we do it, so too we can think—and sometimes do so incessantly—without knowing precisely how it happens. Throughout this book, thinking will be considered not in an abstract, theoretical fashion, but in a concrete, operational way. It will also be regarded as a wide-ranging mental activity that includes far more than the power of logical reasoning. To be sure, reasoning is one of the principal types of thinking (it will be treated at some length in the chapter on argument and persuasion) and is usually what we first think of when we think about thinking. Yet cognitive behavior encompasses a broad spectrum of activities. Surely we are thinking when we discover interrelations between dissimilar ideas; when we find resemblances in seemingly disparate things; when we perceive sequential patterns; when we move back and forth between our observations and inferences or between the abstract and the concrete, the general and the specific; when we recognize similar ideas within different contexts; when we sift relevant points from extraneous material, and so on. Quite clearly, our capacity to think involves many different operations, just as does our ability to walk, see, or feel.

In this introduction we will examine four methods of generating ideas and bring them to the point where they can be shaped and expanded into composition. These methods of brainstorming involve (1) contemplating words and their associations; (2) experimenting with metaphors; (3) proceeding from observations to inferences; and (4) moving back and forth between an abstract and a concrete vocabulary. These are not peculiar forms of thinking but mental processes we use all of the time, though usually without being aware of them. Since learning to write is learning to think, to become more aware of your thought processes is to take a major step in developing proficiency in composition.

FOUR METHODS OF BRAINSTORMING

1. Exploring Words

No matter what we are going to write about—whether our subject is required or inspired—we begin with words. Though this may sound fairly obvious, we often forget just how important a part words play in the way we perceive a subject, in the way we generate ideas about a subject, and in the way we continue to think about that subject throughout each stage of composition. Words are not simply handy building blocks to be fitted into their proper places. They are, rather, powerful agents that continuously shape and reshape our thinking and writing.

In any composition, certain words will be worked harder than others. These are the ones that help carry our composition from the exploratory phase, through to its starting point, and on to revision and completion. They are the words—simple or complex, idiomatic or formal—that trigger our thoughts about a subject and help give our initial ideas solidity and purpose. As we begin to consider a subject, any subject, we necessarily start to encounter all sorts of words. These may be, as they frequently are, the given words of an assigned topic ("Discuss your attitude toward capital punishment"); or words that form in our minds as we randomly imagine various subjects we might write about ("the neighborhood I grew up in," "a teacher who has meant a great deal to me"); or words that spontaneously pop up as we jot down notes in a diary or journal ("Why did I find the film tonight so depressing?"). Whatever we want to write about, no matter how visual or nonverbal it seems at first, words will automatically attach themselves to our subject and become inseparable from our thinking about it.

Thinking carefully about words can be especially helpful in the difficult, formative stages of composition—getting a line on our subject and getting started. The subjects that come to us at first, even those we're assigned, are usually too general and unwieldy for the practical purposes of composition. Before we can start writing about them, we need to bring them down to manageable proportions and find some point or points of entry. Though many of the rhetorical strategies discussed in the following chapters can help us isolate a subject and start writing about it, a more fundamental way to begin is simply to identify certain words and take our lead from their definitions and associations. We can do this by paying attention to two types of meaning—*denotative* and *connotative*.

The denotative value of a word is its primary dictionary definition—what Fowler's *Dictionary of Modern English Usage* calls "its barest adequate definition." Its connotative value, on the other hand, includes the word's entire range of public and private associations. Imagine words as tiny solar systems with concentric circles of meaning that radiate out from basic definitions, through middle spheres of publicly accepted connotations, to outer orbits of private associations. Thus, a word like *work* would have at its core the denotative sense *exertion or effort directed to produce or accomplish something,* but its meaning would spread outward through cultural connotations suggesting the value of work in our civilization (*work* as *job;* as a category opposed to *unemployment;* as a *work of art;* and so on), to our private associations (*work* as a *series of meaningless tasks* or as a *rewarding career,* and so on). Generally speaking, the wider the range of a word's denotations and connotations, the more complex and powerful the word. (This, of course, has nothing to do with the word's surface difficulty; *healthy,* for example, is a far more powerful word than *salubrious.*) Even words we often use interchangeably can exist within different systems of denotation and connotation: *home* suggests more than *house; modern* has a wider range of associations than *recent.*

For many writers, the compilation of a word list is an essential first step in the writing process. Though such a list will usually contain some degree of private and random associations (a few of which may lead to something promising), we should be concerned mainly with setting down as many of the principal terms related to our subject as possible. Many words will suggest themselves almost automatically; others will come to mind as we notice the relationships between various words in the list. Once assembled, our list will provide us with much more than a catalog of inert terms. It will give us a special vocabulary of terms that will take an active role in our composition, the words we will be working with.

Suppose you are asked to write an essay describing your "favorite place on earth." If you're like most people, a single place doesn't automatically pop into your mind. You need to reflect on the topic, to run some favorite places through your memory until you hit on the right one. Instead of relying on visual pictures and memory alone, however, you might try putting down thoughts just as they come to you. Here's what one Boston, Massachusetts student, given that assignment, came up with:

My dorm room—just kidding! Too bad the assignment isn't LEAST favorite places.

My old bedroom at home—I really miss the privacy.

Fanueil Hall—where we used to hang out.

Annie's basement—we had the best parties there.

Our town swimming pool—where I finally learned how to swim and where I met Adam!

Blue Hill Reservation—great hiking in the fall.

Coming to a stop at this point, the student looked over her list and asked herself which one of these places brought back the warmest memories. She decided to write about her old bedroom, the place she now missed most. Constructing this list also helped her get her essay started. She realized that what made her miss her bedroom most was the privacy she had there, a luxury she no longer had at college. In her essay she wondered whether contrast alone makes us think more favorably of one place instead of another. If she were actually writing the essay in her old bedroom, she asked herself, would she have selected it as her favorite place? She thought not.

Such associative word lists can be used for all types of papers, not only personal essays. Suppose, for example, that you've been asked to write a short argumentative paper explaining your position on capital punishment.

The assignment, naturally, requires that you do more than say whether you are for it or against it. You are not being asked to vote on the subject, but to articulate as persuasively as you can what you think about the issue and why you think the way you do. It is possible that you have very strong feelings about the subject, yet have never really thought your ideas out past the slogan state of "It's wrong to take a life" or "An eye for an eye and a tooth for a tooth." Like most vital terms, *capital punishment* comes to us embedded in a web of meanings, many of which are strongly connected to various religious beliefs and social philosophies. Making a list of some of the words suggested by the subject and some of their associations may not alter your feelings about capital punishment, but it will set up an intricate circuitry of related ideas that can spark your thinking throughout all phases of your writing.

For example, if you begin by looking up *capital punishment* in a dictionary in order to fix the term's rock-bottom meaning, you will find something like the following: "punishment by death for a crime; death penalty." That seems straightforward—but is it? People often use *capital punishment* and *death penalty* interchangeably, but what about the connotations of these terms? *Capital punishment* sounds legal, emotionally detached; *death penalty* sounds harsher, more violent. You might speculate whether advocates for one or another favor one or another term. You might want to consider the differences between a punishment and a penalty—that one (a punishment) is something we *receive,* whereas the other (a penalty) is something we *pay.* But this is just a start. As you think (on paper) about the terms *capital punishment* and *death penalty,* the following train of associations might easily be jotted down:

prisons	parole
crime	rehabilitation
retribution/revenge	cruel and unusual punishment
judgment	
jury system	death row
Is the death penalty a deterrent to crime?	electric chair/gas chamber/firing squad
Life sentences—are they any better?	social classes/minorities treated unequally

Plenty of other words, phrases, and questions may suggest themselves, but this list gives an adequate illustration of how a pool of related words can be formed.

Within this pool, some terms will spark more connections and ideas than others: they will become your *working words.* For example, you might think about the associations (and misassociations) of such complex words as *revenge* or *retribution* in the same way that Betty Edwards investigates the terms *left* and *right* (see below). Thinking carefully about a word like *deterrence* may lead you to consider whether capital punishment can actually prevent crime—a process of thinking that may in turn lead to the type of cause-and-effect analysis outlined later in this book (see pp. 361–366). Or you might want to take such a closely linked pair of terms as *penalty* and *punishment* and see what makes them tick by applying the kind of comparative analysis that the psychiatrist Karen Horney uses to distinguish between *fear* and *anxiety* (see p. 294). But whatever words you select to work with, and whatever writing strategy they may help lead you to, your complete list will come in handy throughout the process of composition. It will provide you with a tangible cluster of closely related terms and concepts—a working vocabulary for thinking about your subject—that you can draw on for incentive at any time.

Your word list in itself, moreover, represents a preliminary exercise in *thinking in writing,* one that helps you get your composition flowing. You jot down a word, and that makes you think of a closely related word; that process, in turn, suggests an interesting connection (call it an "idea") that you may not have made if you hadn't set the two words down in writing. And as you quickly jot down the connection, you may think of another closely associated word or phrase. Your word list expands; it grows into a work sheet that is actually a verbal picture of your thinking. Surely this is a better method for getting started than scratching your head, sipping coffee, sharpening pencils, and staring at a blank sheet of paper or monitor screen. Not only have you begun to think actively about your subject, but you have also started to write about it—perhaps not in complete sentences and paragraphs, but at least in words, phrases, and fragments. Not all of these, of course, will be useful, finally, but some will carry you into the more consecutive writing you'll do later on. What is most important is that you now have something working for you on paper: a special set of related terms to think with and to think about, to write with and to write about.

Throughout the earliest stages of composition, writing is primarily an intellectual process of extension. We put a little bit down on paper, and we attempt to go on from there to say more. Only after we get enough written do we need to begin worrying about such matters as style, sequence of points, clarity, logical consistency, persuasiveness, and so on. As we try to get started, however, it helps to view writing as a kind of mental stretching. Experienced writers know from countless pages of practice how a few key points can be expanded intelligently into a well-formulated and fluent composition. Less experienced writers produce work frequently marked by choppiness, abrupt stops, dead ends, and premature conclusions mainly because they quickly "run out of things to say."

One of the most important lessons to learn about composition is that ideas don't generate writing as readily as writing generates ideas. To write productively we don't need to keep coming up with new ideas so much as we need to get the most mileage out of the ideas we already have on paper. That is why starting out with a work sheet of key words makes sense: by enlarging the scope of our working vocabulary, we gain insights and make connections that will help us generate more writing about our subject than we may at first have thought possible.

As we explore our subject, then, it pays to consider carefully the words that first come to mind, checking their denotative meanings and listing their range of connotations. Words on paper seem to be more constructive, or conducive to composition, than the same words in our heads. Hence, many experienced writers, even if they already have a clear idea of what they want to say, still perform these preliminary verbal operations either in rough phrase-outline or in such lists as the preceding ones. We can also discover working words in diaries or journals and through prewriting exercises in which we spontaneously jot down whatever enters our minds as we think about a subject. In the brief selections that follow, we will see how a few writers find their working words and put them to use. We will begin by showing how key words can activate a writer's thinking at the start of composition and even become the principal subject of an essay.

In a popular and influential study of how the right side of the brain (the right hemisphere) can stimulate our visual imagination, Betty Edwards, an art teacher and author of *Drawing on the Right Side of the Brain* (1979), explores our responses to the basic words *right* and *left*. Her research is based on the neurological fact that we use both the right and left sides of the brain for thinking, but that the two hemispheres process information differently. The right hemisphere also controls movements of the left side of the body, while the left controls the right side. Note how Betty Edwards uses etymology and associations to establish her point about right-hand bias. After reading this selection, you can practically reconstruct her word and association list.

Betty Edwards

Left and Right

Words and phrases concerning concepts of left and right permeate our language and thinking. The right hand (meaning also the left hemisphere) is strongly connected with what is good, just, moral, proper. The left hand (therefore the right hemisphere) is strongly linked with concepts of anarchy and feelings that are out of conscious control—somehow bad, immoral, dangerous.

Until very recently, the ancient bias against the left hand/right hemisphere sometimes even led parents and teachers of left-handed children to try to force the children to use their right hands for writing, eating, and so on—a practice that often caused problems lasting into adulthood.

Throughout human history, terms with connotations of good for the right hand/left hemisphere and connotations of bad for the left hand/right hemisphere appear in most languages around the world. The Latin word for left is *sinister,* meaning "bad," "ominous." The Latin word for right is *dexter* from which comes our word "dexterity," meaning "skill" or "adroitness."

The French word for "left"—remember that the left hand is connected to the right hemisphere—is *gauche,* meaning "awkward," from which comes our word "gawky." The French word for right is *droit,* meaning "good," "just," or "proper."

In English, "left" comes from the Anglo-Saxon lyft, meaning "weak" or "worthless." The left hand of most right-handed people is in fact weaker than the right, but the original word also implies lack of moral strength. The derogatory meaning of "left" may reflect a prejudice of the right-handed majority against a minority of people, who were different, that is, left-handed. Reinforcing this bias, the Anglo-Saxon word for "right," *reht (riht)* meant "straight" or "just." From *reht* and its Latin cognate *rectus* we derived our words "correct" and "rectitude."

These ideas also affect our political thinking. The political right, for instance, admires national power, is conservative, resists change. The political left, conversely, admires individual autonomy and promotes change, even radical change. At their extremes, the political right is fascist, the political left is anarchist.

In the context of cultural customs, the place of honor at a formal dinner is on the host's right-hand side. The groom stands on the right in the marriage ceremony, the bride on the left—a nonverbal message of the relative status of the two participants. We shake hands with our right hands; it seems somehow wrong to shake hands with our left hands.

Under "left-handed," the dictionary lists as synonyms "clumsy," "awkward," "insincere," "malicious." Synonyms for "right-handed," however, are "correct," "indispensable," and "reliable." Now, it's important to remember that these terms were all made up when languages began by some persons' left hemispheres—the left brain calling the right bad names! And the right brain—labeled, pinpointed, and buttonholed—was without a language of its own to defend itself.

Sometimes the words we use are closely tied up with our own lives and identities. In using certain words in a personal essay, we may be less attentive to their strict definition than to their private connotations. Note how Nancy Mairs, one of contemporary literature's accomplished essayists, explains in the following passage why she prefers to describe herself as a "cripple" rather than choose a different, less negative, term.

Nancy Mairs

On Being a Cripple

The other day I was thinking of writing an essay on being a cripple. I was thinking hard in one of the stalls of the women's room in my office building, as I was shoving my shirt into my jeans and tugging up my zipper. Preoccupied, I flushed, picked up my book bag, took my cane down from the hook, and unlatched the door. So many movements unbalanced me, and as I pulled the door open I fell over backward, landing fully clothed on the toilet seat with my legs splayed in front of me: the old beetle-on-its-back routine. Saturday afternoon, the building deserted, I was free to laugh aloud as I wriggled back to my feet, my voice bouncing off the yellowish tiles from all directions. Had anyone been there with me, I'd have been still and faint and hot with chagrin. I decided that it was high time to write the essay.

First, the matter of semantics. I am a cripple. I choose this word to name me. I choose from among several possibilities, the most common of which are "handicapped" and "disabled." I made the choice a number of years ago, without thinking, unaware of my motives for doing so. Even now, I'm not sure what those motives are, but I recognize that they are complex and not entirely flattering. People—crippled or not—wince at the word "cripple," as they do not at "handicapped" or "disabled." Perhaps I want them to wince. I want them to see me as a tough customer, one to whom the fates/gods/viruses have not been kind, but who can face the brutal truth of her existence squarely. As a cripple, I swagger.

But, to be fair to myself, a certain amount of honesty underlies my choice. "Cripple" seems to me a clean word, straightforward and precise. It has an honorable history, having made its first appearance in the Lindisfarne Gospel history in the tenth century. As a lover of words, I like the accuracy with which it describes my condition: I have lost the full use of my limbs. "Disabled," by contrast, suggests any incapacity, physical or mental. And I certainly don't like "handicapped," by whom I can't imagine (my God is not a Handicapper General), in order to equalize chances in the great race of life. These words seem to me to be moving away from my condition, to be widening the gap between word and reality. Most remote is the recently coined euphemism "differently abled," which partakes of the same semantic hopefulness that transformed countries to "undeveloped" to "underdeveloped," then to "less developed," and finally to "developing" nations. People have continued to starve in those countries during the shift. Some realities do not obey the dictates of language.

Mine is one of them. Whatever you call me, I remain crippled. But I don't care what you call me, so long as it isn't differently abled, which strikes me as pure verbal garbage designed, by its ability to describe anyone, to describe no one. I subscribe to George Orwell's thesis that "the slovenliness of our language makes it easier for us to have foolish thoughts." And I refuse to participate in the degeneration of the language to the extent that I deny that I have lost anything in the course of this calamitous disease; I refuse to pretend that the only differences between you and me are the various ordinary ones that distinguish one person from another. But call me "disabled" or "handicapped" if you like. I have long since grown accustomed to them; and if they are vague, at least they hint at the truth. Moreover, I use them myself. Society is no readier to accept crippledness than to accept death, war, sex, sweat, or wrinkles. I would never refer to another person as a cripple. It is the word I use to name only myself.

In these opening paragraphs of a longer essay, Mairs offers her readers a superb demonstration of a writer at work. Notice that as she reflects on the choice of possible words to describe herself, she not only provides us with the nuances of those terms, but introduces us at the same time to the way her mind works. It is a perfect example of someone thinking *in* writing.

Brainstorming Exercises

1. Start with a common word that is important to you (e.g., love, community, basketball, friend, home). Then build a word list in which you jot down words and concepts suggested by your original word. When you've reached the end of associations, go back over the list to try to discover how various associations link up.

2. Think of a common word that has powerful political or cultural associations. Using a dictionary and a thesaurus, jot down its range of meanings. You might also consult a dictionary of etymology or slang (readily found in most reference libraries). Use this information to construct a word list from which you develop the idea for an essay.

2. Making Metaphors

We saw above how a little preliminary work with the denotative and connotative meanings of words can help us get a fix on a subject. In this section, we'll look at another procedure for exploring a subject and bridging that always difficult gap between having an idea and getting a paper started—the making of metaphors. Like our key words, our metaphors perform at the most fundamental level of the writing process, supplying us with sets of associated terms and concepts that we can draw on throughout our composition.

Metaphor comes from a Greek word meaning *transfer* and is the classical term for the process by which we find resemblances between different kinds of things or ideas. When we see or think of something as though it were like something else, when we discover the similar in the dissimilar, we are using metaphor. We use metaphors all the time: for some students, school may seem to be *a factory,* their courses *a grind,* their social life *a bad joke;* years later, they consider their college days to have been *a picnic,* courses *a breeze,* their social life *a continuous riot.* Our everyday speech is packed with metaphors, many of which we use unconsciously—we don't, for example, realize that we are using a metaphor when we speak of someone's death as "a tragedy." We also tend in our everyday conversations to make up metaphors on the spot: we may say of a clumsy dancer that he moves with all the grace of "a drunken left tackle." Metaphor is sometimes distinguished from simile, in that metaphor works by implicit comparison ("Her mind is a computer"), whereas simile works by the explicit connection of *like* or *as* ("Her mind is like a computer"). Though at times the difference between the two rhetorical figures can be significant, simile, as Aristotle said, usually differs from metaphor "only in the way it is put." (For convenience, metaphor will be used in this book to cover both kinds of rhetorical procedures.)

It is common to think of metaphor as merely stylistic decoration. When we complain of "flowery language," we are usually referring to a highly metaphorical style. However, as we work closely with metaphor, we should remember that it is not simply a cosmetic device, but a potentially powerful mental act that underlies all discourse and pervades all rhetorical strategies and structures. Metaphor does, of course, play a vital part in enlivening the surface of our prose, but it can also function structurally at much deeper levels of thinking and writing. By allowing us to form images and concepts of one thing in terms of another, metaphor helps us to see new connections that can frequently lead to unexpected insights. Far from being merely a special kind of stylistic ornament or a poetic addition to prose, it is rather an irreducible part of language itself. We can neither write nor think without it.

Making metaphors—perceiving similarity in dissimilar things—represents one of the supreme activities of human intelligence. Aristotle regarded metaphor as a "sign of genius" and "the greatest thing by far." Certainly the ability to make metaphors proficiently is a sure sign of a verbally creative person. But metaphors play an important role in less individually creative areas of thought as well. We are frequently relying on metaphor to express key ideas or concepts even when we think we're being quite literal. Nearly all of the abstract terms we use every day had their origins in metaphor (*idea* comes from an ancient Greek term meaning "the shape or blueprint a craftsman uses to begin work with"). Many of these terms still carry with them some vestiges of their figurative roots. The word *idea,* for example, still conveys the sense of something being in its planning stage, something not yet implemented ("That looks like a good idea, but will it work?").

Everyday speech abounds with metaphorical expressions. In their book *Metaphors We Live By* (1980), George Lakoff and Mark Johnson convincingly demonstrate how ordinary figurative expressions structure many of our everyday concepts and thus affect not only how we think about something, but also how we may even experience it. For example, much of our ordinary use of the word *argument* refers explicitly to war, a verbal habit that can easily be observed by considering a few common expressions:

Your claims are *indefensible.*

He *attacked* every weak point in my argument.

His *criticism* was right on target.

I *demolished* his argument.

I've never *won* an argument with her.

You disagree? Okay, *shoot!*

If you use that *strategy,* he'll *wipe you out.*

He *shot down* all of my arguments.

And these are merely a few. What Lakoff and Johnson want us to see is not just that we talk about arguments in terms of war or violent contests, but that many of the things we do in arguing are partially structured by the concept of war. So pervasive are such figurative expressions in our language that we could take practically any abstract concept and list a cluster of commonly related metaphors that give it shape and substance. Such clusters will conveniently show how important a role metaphor plays (note the theatrical metaphor) in our everyday thinking.

Entire books have been devoted to the philosophical, literary, and linguistic significance of metaphor. Here, for simplicity, we will divide metaphor into two basic types, according to how they are commonly used in writing:

Stylistic Metaphors One of the values of metaphor, Aristotle claimed, is that it "gives style clearness, charm, and distinction as nothing else can." It is difficult to find examples of good writing that are not interlaced with perceptive and well-chosen metaphors. When N. Scott Momaday wants to describe what the Oklahoma landscape is like in the dry heat of summer, he writes that "the prairie is an anvil's edge." Or when John Updike wants to show how perfect the beer can was before our technology "improved" it, he writes that it was "as beautiful as the clothespin, as inevitable as the wine bottle, as dignified and reassuring as the fire hydrant." Such metaphors ripple across the surface of sentences like well-toned muscle, giving the writing strength and vigor. But good metaphors do more than perk our attention and make us sensitive to a writer's style. They also make us see things in new ways—the unfamiliar in the familiar, the familiar in the strange. To see the summer prairie as an "anvil's edge" is to see it with a freshness and immediacy not soon forgotten.

Here is how one of America's finest prose stylists, the essayist Edward Hoagland, uses a profusion of metaphors to describe the behavior and appearance of turtles. See how many metaphors you can identify (not all of them are introduced by "like" or "as"):

Edward Hoagland

Turtles

Turtles cough, burp, whistle, grunt and hiss, and produce social judgments. They put their heads together amicably enough, but then one drives the other back with the suddenness of two dogs who have been conversing in tones too low for an onlooker to hear. They pee in fear when they're first caught, walking hundreds of yards within the confines of their pen, carrying the weight of that cumbersome box on legs which are actually positioned for walking. They don't feel that the contest is unfair; they keep plugging, rolling like sailorly souls—a bobbing, infirm gait, a brave, sea-legged momentum—stopping occasionally to study the lay of the land. For me, anyway, they manage to contain the rest of the animal world. They can stretch out their necks like a giraffe, or loom underwater like an apocryphal hippo. They browse on lettuce thrown on the water like a cow moose which is partly submerged. They have a penguin's alertness, combined with a build like a Brontosaurus when they rise up on tiptoe. Then they hunch and ponderously lunge like a grizzly going forward.

Baby turtles in a turtle bowl are a puzzle in geometrics. They're as decorative as pansy petals, but they are also self-directed building blocks, propping themselves on one another in different arrangements, before upending the tower. The timid individuals turn fearless, or vice versa. If one gets a bit arrogant he will push the others off the rock and afterwards climb down into the water and cling to the back of one of those he has bullied, tickling him with his hind feet until he bucks like a bronco. On the other hand, when this same milder-mannered fellow isn't exerting himself, he will stare right into the face of the sun for hours. What could be more lionlike? And he's at home in or out of the water and does lots of metaphysical tilting. He sinks and rises, with an infinity of levels to choose from; or, elongating himself, he climbs out on the land again to perambulate, sits boxed in his box, and finally slides back in the water, submerging into dreams.

Extended Metaphors These are extended expressions of resemblance around which paragraphs and entire compositions can be constructed. An extended metaphor can therefore be a strategic element for expository writing: it allows us to find a structure and to extend the context for a subject in ways otherwise closed to us.

Metaphors can be particularly useful in helping us to explore a subject and discover an angle of approach. As we compile a list of words and phrases associated with our subject or jot down sentences spontaneously in a notebook, we will undoubtedly turn up metaphors—some commonplace, some original, some flashy, some with structural possibilities. Pursuing the implications of promising metaphors may provide us with a point of entry into our composition, and possibly, if the metaphor is rich enough, an organizational pattern for our entire essay.

For example, suppose you are asked to write a paper on advertising's influence on American life. You compile a set of working words and associations. Your list includes some of the products and services promoted through advertising—foods, clothes, drugs, appliances, transportation, cigarettes, cosmetics, household products, and so on. You decide to confine your attention to transportation, and then compile another list of closely related words and phrases. You know more about cars, say, than other types of transportation, so you choose to focus on automobile advertising. As you think about what cars mean in our lives, you come up with additional terms, such as *independence, expense, fun, mobility, driving, status, commuting, pollution.* In this cluster of terms, you notice a word that suggests a promising range of meaning—mobility. Americans, you know, are considered a highly mobile people, and American society depends enormously on automobiles. You observe that the -*mobile* part of *automobile* itself suggests mobility and recall that there is even a gasoline called "Mobil." But *mobile,* you realize as you reflect on the word, also suggests status: sociologists often talk of "upward mobility." In this word, then, there is a metaphor that might offer an entry into your subject. You think of the vast quantity of automobile advertising that appeals to the customer's desire for both types of mobility—physical (travel) and social (status). If you pursue it further, you may find that the metaphor associates itself closely with a popular expression, "going places," which also conveys both physical and social mobility. The implications of this metaphor could lead you to an opening paragraph such as this:

> Americans like to think of themselves as a highly mobile people—both on the road and in society—and no popular art confirms this national characteristic more emphatically than advertisements for automobiles. In common speech, "going places" has long implied a social as well as a geographic destination.

The rest of the paper might demonstrate how advertisements for cars try to influence consumers to buy something that is both an object of luxury and a practical source of transportation.

Metaphors can also exert a continuing presence in our composition by actively guiding our thoughts while we write. Some of the resemblances we come across in the preliminary sketching out of our ideas will take us further than merely an opening paragraph. Should we then decide to stick to one of these key resemblances and organize our entire composition around it, we would be using an extended structural metaphor.

A fine example of an extended metaphor occurs in Annie Dillard's essay "The Stunt Pilot," an appreciation of a spectacular Washington state aerobatic performer named David Rahm. Like Hoagland, Dillard is one of America's finest essayists. As she observes Rahm perform at an air show, she begins to see his aerobatic stunts in artistic terms. Here is how she describes her impression of Rahm's performance:

Annie Dillard

The Stunt Pilot

For the end of the day, separated from all other performances of every sort, the air show director had scheduled a program titled "David Rahm." The leaflet said that Rahm was a geologist who taught at Western Washington University. He had flown for King Hussein in Jordan. A tall man in the crowd told me Hussein had seen Rahm fly on a visit the king made to the United States; he had invited him to Jordan to perform at ceremonies. Hussein was a pilot, too. "Hussein thought he was the greatest thing in the world."

Idly, paying scant attention, I saw a medium-sized, rugged man dressed in brown leather, all begoggled, climb in a black bi-plane's cockpit. The plane was a Bücker Jungman, built in the thirties. I saw a tall, dark-haired woman seize a propeller tip at the plane's nose and yank it down till the engine caught. He was off; he climbed high over the airport in his bi-plane, very high until he was barely visible as a mote, and then seemed to fall down the air, diving headlong, and streaming beauty in spirals behind him.

The black plane dropped spinning, and flattened out spinning the other way; it began to carve the air into forms that built wildly and musically on each other and never ended. Reluctantly, I started paying attention. Rahm drew high above the world an inexhaustibly glorious line; it piled over our heads in loops and arabesques. It was like a Saul Steinberg fantasy; the plane was the pen. Like Steinberg's contracting and billowing pen line, the line Rahm spun moved to form new, punning shapes from the edges of the old, Like a Klee line, it smattered the sky with landscapes and systems.

The air show announcer hushed. He had been squawking all day, and now he quit. The crowd stilled. Even the children watched dumbstruck as the slow, black bi-plane buzzed its way around the air. Rahm made beauty with his whole body; it was pure pattern, and you could watch it happen. The plane moved every way a line can move, and it controlled three dimensions, so the line carved massive and subtle slits in the air like sculptures. The plane looped the loop, seeming to arch its back like a gymnast; it stalled, dropped, and spun out of it climbing; it spiraled and knifed west on one side's wings and back east on another; it turned cartwheels, which must be physically impossible; it played with its own line like a cat with yarn. How did the pilot know where in the air he was? If he got lost, the ground would swat him.

Rahm did everything his plane could do: tailspins, four-point rolls, flat spins, figure eights, snap rolls, and hammerheads. He did pirouettes on the plane's tail. The other pilots could do these stunts too, skillfully, one at a time. But Rahm used the plane inexhaustibly, like a brush marking thin air.

His was pure energy and naked spirit. I have thought about it for years. Rahm's line unrolled in time. Like music, it split the bulging rim of the future along its seam. It pried out of the present. We watchers waited for the split-second curve of beauty in the present to reveal itself. The human pilot, Dave Rahm, worked in the cockpit right at the plane's nose; his very body tore into the future for us and reeled it down upon us like a curling peel.

Like any fine artist, he controlled the tension of the audience's longing. You desired, unwittingly, a certain kind of roll or climb, or a return to a certain portion of the air, and he fulfilled your hope slantingly, like a poet, or evaded it until you thought you would burst, and then fulfilled it surprisingly, so you gasped and cried out.

The oddest, most exhilarating and exhausting thing was this: he never quit. The music had no periods, no rests or endings; the poetry's beautiful sentence never ended; the line had no finish; the sculptured forms piled overhead, one into another without surcease. Who could breathe, in a world where rhythm itself had no periods?

It had taken me several minutes to understand what an extraordinary thing I was seeing. Rahm kept all that embellished space in mind at once. For another twenty minutes I watched the beauty unroll and grow more fantastic and unlikely before my eyes. Now Rahm brought the plane down slidingly, and just in time, for I thought I would snap from the effort to compass and remember the line's long intelligence; I could not add another curve. He brought the plane down on a far runway. After a pause, I saw him step out, an ordinary man, and make his way back to the terminal.

In this passage from "The Stunt Pilot" Annie Dillard manages to convey not only her awe of Rahm's breathtaking aerobatics, but the artistic nature of his "stunts"—something most people might not have noticed. Though she momentarily makes her comparison explicit—that David Rahm is like "any fine artist"—she drives home her central point by maintaining the similarity between Rahm's performance and artistic expression throughout the passage: Rahm is like such modern artists as Saul Steinberg and Paul Klee; he uses his plane "like a brush marking thin air"; the plane's movements resemble the lines of a drawing or sculpture. Once she has constructed her core comparison (that the pilot is an "artist"), she then expands on it in observation after observation, inviting us to see Rahm as a painter, composer, poet, dancer, and sculptor all in one. Such powerful extended metaphors as hers can make us see and think about the world in unexpected ways.

Brainstorming Exercises

1. Choose any common subject (such as money, politics, love, or luck) and write down as many metaphors you can think of that are associated with it. What do your metaphors suggest about your subject? Do you find any patterns?

2. Using Annie Dillard's "The Stunt Pilot" as a model, think of someone whose abilities impress you and find a core comparison that will successfully convey why. Then, in notes, take your core comparison and see how far you can extend it.

3. Observation and Inference

Effective writing invariably develops out of thinking carefully about a subject—preparing something intelligent and interesting to say about it. Neither thinking nor writing is by any means restricted to a rigid and unalterable sequence of activities. The precise nature of either process can vary widely, depending on the writer's subject, purpose, audience, and experience.

We will now examine one basic and very practical procedure writers can use to form an idea about a subject—namely, moving from observation to inference, from paying close attention to what exists around us to making judgments based on those observations. Making an observation involves more than simply perceiving an object or event; it requires us to notice something distinctive about it. For example, seeing a sofa in a room does not qualify as an observation, though noticing dog hair on a sofa does. Drawing inference from an observation involves discovering something about what we can't immediately see from what we can see. If we were to assume that the owners of the sofa also have a dog, we would be drawing an inference.

There are at least three advantages to be gained from learning how to make the leap from observation to inference, from one level of thinking to another. Basing our inferences upon solid observations helps us, first, to progress from what we are sure we know to what we do not yet know; second, to acquire lively, yet disciplined, habits of thinking and writing; and, third, to strengthen our confidence that what we finally decide to say about a subject will be both incisive and distinctively our own.

We write best when we know what we are talking about. Perhaps the surest way to increase our knowledge of a subject is to make observations about it. Nearly all forceful thinking and writing are grounded in observing—in regarding something attentively, considering it carefully, or inspecting it systematically. Observation is basic to all inquiry, from the scientist's analysis of the data gathered during an experiment to the poet's expression of the insights emerging from an intense personal experience. Yet most of us do not pause long enough to observe closely. Consider, for example, the most prominent building on campus. How carefully have we ever observed it? How much, finally, do we really know about it? How specific could we be if asked to describe it to someone who's never seen it? To know the world around us is to observe it carefully. Observation begins with first-hand acquaintance, with using our senses to extend the limits of what we know.

Observation, as we alluded to before, is not simply passive awareness of something perceived ("That is a sofa"). It is, rather, a deliberate mental activity; we probe a subject in order to discover as much as possible about it. For example, observing a football game can be much more satisfying than simply following the ball. So, too, reading a novel can involve a good deal more than merely keeping an eye on the plot. Practice in observation gradually educates us to be more selective—to know what to look for, to find the most meaningful aspects of what is being observed, and to note the relationships that bind the parts into a whole.

Just as important as observation to our intellectual lives is inference. Most talk, whether private or public, is regularly informed by these two processes. We also encounter patterns of observation and inference constantly in our reading. For example, we routinely infer from newspaper reports of what politicians have said how they are likely to vote on a particular issue. So, too, as readers of literature, we regularly draw inferences about, say, the main character's values and prejudices from the novel's dialogue and action.

Our observations provide us with the facts from which we draw inferences. There are different kinds of facts. *Private facts* are those that can be experienced only by the individual involved (the fact of a backache, of enjoyment in the taste of fruit, and the like). There are also *public facts*, those that the world at large has agreed to (the meaning of hour, meter, kilogram). Then there are *scientific facts*, the principles of physics, mathematics, biology, and so on—theories that are regarded as facts but are always subject to modification. Finally, there are *primary facts*, those about which there can be no disagreement (for example, the number of fingers on a hand, the number of cars parked in our driveway). Primary facts are indisputable. If a primary fact is something known with certainty, then it must finally have a demonstrable, observable existence.

Any writer considering any subject has a responsibility to provide convincing, factual evidence to support each assertion. And all writers, whatever their purpose or point of view, rely on essentially three sources of knowledge: *direct observation,* the data gathered from firsthand experience; *recollection,* the remembrance of what was once observed; and *testimony,* the reports of what others have observed or recalled. The quality of each observation depends on how familiar we are with the subject at hand. First-semester biology students, for example, may well have some initial difficulty deciding on what to focus on and what inferences to draw as they watch a classmate dissect a frog. But in the end, careful observation should provide us with a good deal of manageable information: perceptions that are concrete, limited, and verifiable. If, for example, we apply these criteria to the observations we make while conducting a laboratory experiment, reading a textbook, or even walking down the street, we will discover that observation suggests a pattern in our thinking, a movement toward greater lucidity and eventually toward converting that understanding into an idea about a subject.

Our thinking normally follows a pattern of observation and inference—moving from what we perceive of an experience through our senses to what is suggested by that experience. Based on our observations, we draw inferences about a subject. As noted earlier, to draw an inference is to make a statement about what is still uncertain on the basis of what is certain. To take one example, let us suppose that we are driving through a small coastal community in Florida. We observe extensive damage to the roads, homes, and shops in town. From its location, as well as from the lingering signs of rain and diminishing winds, we infer, reasonably enough, that the community has been hit by a hurricane. We generalize on the basis of our observations (the weather conditions, the damage done) and then we infer what we have not observed directly (the hurricane). In this, and in all other instances, inference takes us beyond what is present, beyond what can be immediately seen.

Inference is speculative, adventurous thinking. It involves making statements about what is absent based on what is present. For example, nearly all detective work depends on moving from observation to inference. By carefully examining the evidence in a case, detectives can infer a great deal about, for example, the date and time of a crime, the criminal's motive, and perhaps even the culprit's identity. The pattern of our own thinking in writing, when we are deliberate about it, is quite similar to the investigative procedures of a detective. We, too, combine numerous fragmentary observations into some sort of generalized whole from which we draw inferences in order to arrive at an idea about the problem or subject in question. And we should remember that the accuracy of our inferences depends on the thoroughness of our observations.

We always run the risk of making mistakes in our thinking when we move from observable facts to inferences drawn from these facts; that is, from the certain to the uncertain. Accordingly, we ought to be aware of how our own background, temperament, interests, prejudices, and special training may influence the inferences we draw. Consider, for example, how our political beliefs might affect the way we think about what we've seen while driving through a torn-down district of an inner city. So, too, we should be sure to base our inferences on a sufficient number of careful observations. In effect, we should train ourselves to draw inferences that can be tested for accuracy and thoroughness. To do so will both broaden and strengthen the core of information created by our observations.

But how does working with observation and inference help us write better? Moving from observation to inference is one fundamental method writers can use to form an idea about a subject. But what do we mean when we talk about having an idea about a subject? And how, exactly, can observation and inference help us form that idea? To have an idea about a subject is to come to a conclusion about it, however tentative. Like a hypothesis, an idea about a subject is a proposition—a provisional conclusion—that must be proven. Raising the question of how we form an idea is equivalent to asking how we reach a particular conclusion, no matter how tentative it might be.

An expository essay introduces our tentative conclusion about a subject and then proceeds to clarify and verify—to explain and offer evidence to support—the point that we want to make. If, for example, we were writing about the end of affirmative action programs, our principal tasks would be to explain and prove our idea about this subject: say, that these programs offer America its best source of human diversity for the decades ahead. Ultimately, expository writing does not explain a subject as much as it explains our idea about a subject.

Suppose that you have been asked to write an essay on the popularity of running in America. Using the procedure outlined earlier, you jot down a list of the words closely associated with the subject: *exercise, health, satisfaction, getting in shape, marathon, shoes, shorts, sweat suits, expenses.* Thinking of the expenses of running may well lead you to consider the extent to which big business is involved in the sport: advertising, retail chains of specialty shops, and so on. The phrase *big business,* though rather vague, might make you pause and consider how such a simple recreational activity has been transformed into an enormous commercial enterprise: newsletters, magazines, books, documentaries, heavily promoted marathons, clothing, and a bagful of special equipment. These observations may lead you to think about running in a new way. While we all have heard a great deal about the benefits of running, perhaps few of us have ever considered its full costs. You are gradually settling on a subject: the escalating costs of running. You might even come up with a title: "The Complete Cost of Running."

But before you can form a precise idea about the cost of running, you must learn enough about the subject. You do this by combining direct observation of runners with some basic research on what has been written about the physical, psychological, and economic advantages and disadvantages of the activity. You compile testimony on the common injuries (shin splints, torn tendons, broken ankles, and so on) as well as the rising number of accidents involving runners (hit by cars on poorly lit roads, attacked by dogs, and so on). You piece together this basic information and infer that there are greater risks to running than most devotees would suspect. Your own observations and the inferences you draw from them carry you closer to your idea—your tentative conclusion. From watching so many people actually waddle around a track in European-designer outfits and day-glo sneakers, you infer, among other things, that running is steadily becoming more enterprise than exercise. It would now be reasonable to shape an idea: that such factors as higher prices for more "required" equipment, as well as greater risk of accident, have raised the *personal cost* of running to an unprecedented level.

Our work—our responsibility to our audience—does not stop once we have put together an idea. We are further obligated to test the idea with additional observation. In this instance, we would need to follow through by analyzing and validating each of our inferences. We can measure the quality of our inferences by placing them on a scale ranging from solid *judgment* (the ability to make reasonable decisions and to perceive relationships among even incomplete observations) to mere *opinion* (the kind of inference we have invested with nothing more than emotion or will). Inferences based on judgment aid us not only in getting hold of an idea, but also in evaluating its soundness. As soon as we've worked out our idea and tested it thoroughly, we'll be in a much stronger position to convince our audience of its validity.

Many of our finest writers are acute observers of the world. Some, like the award-winning nonfiction author, Ian Frazier, might even be called obsessive observers. As the following essay so persuasively shows, Frazier can't seem to stop himself from making observations, whether he's looking for arrowheads on an Ohio lawn, noticing shoe prints on New York subway cars, or finding skunk tracks in rural Montana. For Frazier, the tracks creatures leave are precious phenomena, and the inferences he makes from his shrewd observations range—as he puts it—from the mundane to the fantastical.

Ian Frazier

Making Marks

Tracks, of mountain lions or mailmen, are more than just marks on the ground. When I lived in New York City, I liked to walk in the park right after a snowfall. For a few hours the new snow held tracks—of rats, pigeons, squirrels, dogs, and the sewing machine tracks of sparrows. Always, someone had been there already on cross-country skis. Within a day or so, other tracks, most of them human, would cover the parks so thoroughly that it seemed not a square foot remained untouched, while the snow took on the complicated texture of a sheet of metal struck by millions of blows. On sloppy days there I sometimes studied the floors of subway cars, their dingy linoleum a palimpsest of shoe tracks, of treads and lugs and zigzag patterns, of lightning streaks and logos and brand names. Many shoes print advertisements beneath them with every step. Not only are there a lot more of us on the planet than in former times, but nowadays we make different marks on it with our feet.

I look at what is under and around my feet more often than is common, probably because of all the time I spent as a boy searching for four-leaf clovers and arrowheads and rifle shells and golf balls. One summer evening back then, in suburban Ohio, I suggested to my brothers that we go look for arrowheads on a newly seeded lawn. They agreed, we strolled over, and within a few minutes my sister Suzan picked up a perfect arrowhead about two inches long. It was shaped like a poplar leaf, and its flint was a dark gray marked with flecks and swirls of white. I could hardly have been more excited if she had found a piece of spaceman's antenna made from an element unknown on earth. The numen of this piece of stone—I snatched it from her immediately—overwhelmed me. The shaft it had once been attached to, the unknowable circumstances that had deposited it there, the chipped fingernails of the hand that had made it, all swirled around me in a romantic infinitude of suggestion. It drove me nuts that she had spotted it and I hadn't. Maybe simply because of this, I have kept my eyes to the ground ever since. At the rate of about once a decade, I have found arrowheads, a hide scraper, and what may be a tool for arrow making. I've also found money, mushrooms, pencils, love notes. Mostly, though, what I find are tracks.

Arrowheads and tracks are similar, in a way. Both are relics; both imply motion and direction. Both are larger in what they conjure for the imagination than in their actual physical reality. The bear track still filling with water at a wet place on the trail hits the imagination, inflaming speculation; the sight of the bear herself around the next bend registers in the gut and nerve endings and adrenal glands—no speculation is involved. I have to say, most of the time I prefer to speculate. I watch the track filling with water, my mind veers to speculation, and I retreat to a more comfortable spot to pursue it.

Of the places where I've lived in Montana, the most remote was in a neighborhood among foothills of fir and lodgepole pine—prime mountain lion habitat. Not long after I'd moved there, the people across the way told me that they'd heard a mountain lion scream, and that something had clawed one of their goats. Hiking logging roads through the woods, I began to see mountain lion tracks; they're like dog or coyote tracks but rounder, more elegant and catlike. The animal always traveled alone, keeping to a single wheel rut, cruising along like a car in the express lane. Even when it cut its foot and marked the same red spot in the snow for miles, the pace of the tracks hardly varied.

I never saw the lion itself, and it assumed the predictable configuration of spirit lion in my mind. Then, on a logging road not nearby, when my thoughts were on the river I was hoping to fish and whether or not the vehicle I was driving would make it there, suddenly broadside across the road in front of me was a mountain lion. I stopped, quietly opened the door, and slid from the car. Still the lion watched, an expression of mild curiosity on its face. I took a step toward it. It turned and lopingly ran, gawky as a teenager. I had never seen a big cat run like that—unimpeded, without a wall or bars to stop it. It jumped the shoulder of the road and disappeared. The last I saw was the question mark of its tail moving along above the weeds. Somehow, the tail alone was more evocative of the lion than clear sight of the animal itself had been. On the hard gravel road, the lion's paws had left not a whisper of a track. I paced back and forth, longing for a replay button, telling myself over and over that I'd seen what I'd seen, flummoxed at how undocumented the experience had been. I wanted a receipt; I wanted a track.

Of course, if there had been tracks, I would have just stared at them and day-dreamed until the experience began to resemble something I'd made up. Then maybe the real lion would have come back and leaped on me in irritation at my preferring the imaginary to the real. It's like the time I was tracking a deer on an icy path with an overlay of light snow; the tracks showed the deer putting down each foot carefully, skidding a bit now and then. At a sudden steep decline, I saw that its feet had gone completely out from under in a fall that had sent it sliding. I was imagining this wipeout, enjoying a chuckle, when my own feet slipped. I landed hard, skidded, and wound up at the bottom not far from the sitzmark of the deer.

Now I live in Montana in a small city—the richest place for tracks so far. It has the expected city-country wildlife, the usual encirclement of raccoon tracks around the garbage cans. Skunks enter houses through pet doors; a friend came into her kitchen early one morning and found a skunk eating from her cat's bowl. Skunk tracks—the hind feet with elongated digits, like simian hands—cross the snow in our front yard. Coyotes yip and howl from the bare hillsides east of town, so I assume the ubiquitous dog tracks I see are not all made by dogs. I haven't seen mountain lion tracks, although a few years ago the local paper ran a photo of a mountain lion curled up in a window well in town. That deer browse along the back alley from compost pile to compost pile does not surprise me, nor that their tracks continue along the chainlink fence by the elementary school. As human enterprise takes up more and more of the landscape, animals will certainly remain in it, at large if not exactly wild. Probably developers will one day build them semiofficial housing of their own.

As in New York, most of the tracks here are human. But here the numbers are fewer, and individuality doesn't get trampled out. I know of course the tracks of my own family—the thin, wavy lines of tread on my wife's rain boots, the flat sole and heel of her cowboy boots, my daughter's ice skate cross hatching in the backyard, the thick zigzag tread of what my three-year-old son calls his "big-heavy boots." Because my profession is solitary and I work at home, I live for the mail. I quickly learned to identify the track of the mailman. The soles of our mailman's shoes have regularly spaced short spikes in the shape of hemispheres, which leave crisp concave holes like holes in a tea biscuit.

No one else around here wears such a shoe. His neat tracks proceeding door-to-door up our street in new snow depict the hopefulness and civic rectitude I have always associated with the mail. One day I happened to meet him on the front stoop, and I asked about his shoes. He told me that they were his special winter shoes, that no others were as good on snow and ice, that after he started wearing them he hadn't fallen once, that he recommended them highly. He told me where I could buy a pair and how much they cost. As far as relating goes, we far outdid the usual between mailman and addressee.

I regret that birds don't leave tracks in the air. The fact that only man-made things—fireworks and tracer bullets and jet planes—leave any sign of their airborne passage seems somehow wrong. It would be cool if peregrine falcons, say, left streaks in the sky as they came down on their prey. The sky above certain parts of rivers would be hung with the feathery hover marks of kingfishers. You wouldn't want too many, like a graffiti scratched in the windows of subway cars; but a few would be nice. Because of the medium, they would quickly fade.

Once after a snowstorm had piled new powder everywhere, a squirrel jumped onto a telephone wire behind our house. As he bounded along the wire, his feet knocked snow loose each time they came down. Against the bright blue sky the snow he dislodged fell in vertical white lines, a blue-and-white bar code indicating squirrel; nothing else would have set the snow falling in that particular way. The lines were most distinct a step or two behind him. Farther behind they merged into a glittering curtain, and farther still they had already vanished in the sky.

Some tracks are gone like that, in an instant. But a track is a mark, and like all marks it can exist independent of time. Geographic circumstances can preserve a track for a minute or a week or unknown millions of years. Among my favorites are some dinosaur tracks 200 million years old. Two dinosaurs made them—one a large, plant-eating dinosaur, and the other a smaller, meat eating dinosaur that came after it across a patch of calcareous mud, possibly in pursuit. Mud hardened, geology ensued, and eventually the tracks wound up in the dinosaur wing of the American Museum of Natural History in New York City. Whenever I get a chance, I revisit them there. No other tracks provoke me to fantasize the way these do. To begin with, they're sort of messy, with ragged edges and muddy flourishes: I imagine the squish of the big feet going in, the suck of them coming out. The dinosaurs that made these tracks were as real as the dented taxicab that brought me. Trying to summon them, I imagine that through some time travel miracle I actually come upon the dinosaurs in a muddy place 50 yards or so up ahead; and I imagine that when I do I am disappointed. I am always disappointed when I see what made the tracks I am fantasizing about. These two wouldn't be Dinosaur; they would just be a couple of individual dinosaurs—muddy-footed, maybe with nicks in their hide and missing teeth—mortal beings lit by the same ordinary sunlight as I am. Picturing them as slightly disappointing, almost boring, somehow brings them closer. Tracks let you do that, let you approach the fantastic by way of the mundane. A track is a place where the fantastic and the mundane coincide.

Observation and inference are an elementary, and therefore invaluable, means to extend and enrich our knowledge. Understanding how the mind moves between observation and inference is essential for cultivating lively, productive habits of thinking *in* writing. Awareness of this process also helps develop a disciplined mind, one that can suspend judgment while inquiry continues. Finally, knowing something more about the workings of our own minds may well be one of the most significant and enduring satisfactions in our lives.

Brainstorming Exercises

1. Advertisements have become so much a part of our surroundings that we too often take them for granted. Choose a pictorial ad from your favorite newspaper or magazine and observe it carefully. Jot down your observations. Ask yourself why the advertiser used exactly the illustration featured. What can you infer about the advertiser's use of the particular image? (For example, why would a tobacco company spend millions of dollars developing and promoting the image of Joe Camel? Why would they believe their image will appeal to so many young people?) Study the ad you select in detail; make notes of your inferences.
2. Yogi Berra once said that "you can observe a lot just by lookin'." Observe carefully the room, desk, office, or workplace of someone you don't know well. After making detailed notes of the place, use your observations to draw some conclusions (inferences) about the character of its occupant.

4. Abstract and Concrete

The words *abstract* and *concrete* are conventionally used to describe a writer's style. On the simplest level, the terms refer to word choices. *Concrete words* denote what can be perceived by the senses, what is practical and tangible in our experience. *Abstract words* point to ideas, to the theoretical, to whatever is removed from sense experience. For nearly all of us, thinking swings naturally between the abstract and the concrete, between ideas and their confirmation in sense experience. This movement is such a basic mental activity that we often pay little attention to it and neglect to practice it in our writing. All of us would agree, however, that effective writing ought to balance the abstract and the concrete, that we ought to support each abstract statement with enough concrete details for our readers to hold on to as they follow the course of our thinking in an essay. To trace how writing moves back and forth between the concrete and the abstract is to chart one of the basic patterns of thinking that leads to ideas and makes writing possible.

Much of our thinking consists of partially formed abstractions, of loosely formed ideas about subjects that would require further thinking and an accumulation of evidence to make our ideas at all convincing. Rarely, however, are we pressed to push our thinking beyond this point. The media help make this so, supplying much of what we need to know in order to talk casually about the subjects that are in the public eye. Suppose, for example, that we were asked to write an essay on some aspect of the Oklahoma City bombing. How easy would it be to write a first-rate essay on such a subject? Nearly all of us carry around some vague, media-sponsored version of the horrifying events that occurred in a place that to most of us is no more than a name. But despite the saturation coverage of the political and legal issues involved, our thinking about the victims of the disaster probably would not be very specific at all. To think in *specific* terms is to be explicit, to be definite in what we say about a subject. Few of us, for example, would ever need to know the actual dimensions of the federal office building or its exact floor plans. Nonetheless, we undoubtedly could write about the bombing in *general* terms—that is, we could make broad statements about the events there as indicative of the potentially hazardous world we live in, comparing the bombing with other similar acts of terrorism or discussing it in terms of the increasing threats to individuals in contemporary life. Yet little, if any, of our thinking about the bombing would be *concrete*—tied directly to immediate sense experience. Unless we were at the scene, our knowledge of the tragedy is restricted to what we watched, read, or heard about through the media. Our knowledge of such events thus remains finally abstract, far removed from the stark reality of what occurred.

What we know about an event like the terrorist attack in Oklahoma City demonstrates how much of our thinking consists of hazy abstractions and indirect experience—of how much ours is a *mediated* world. To come to know something in such an imprecise way may explain why we so often seem uncomfortable thinking in abstractions and why we have so much difficulty making our writing more concrete. But exactly what do we mean by abstract and concrete writing, and how does moving from one to the other help us to form ideas?

Our writing may be described as concrete when we record our observations of objects and behavior in the world around us. Anything that can be perceived immediately by the senses is *concrete:* a pear, a truck, a pizza, a shoe. Most often, concrete words are learned in the presence of the object or behavior described. We first understood the meaning of *giraffe*, for example, by seeing a picture of one in a book or on television, or by observing one at a zoo. We need not reflect on concrete words to understand them; they are confirmed immediately through the senses. As we have previously seen, to form an idea about a subject is to come to a conclusion about it—however tentative that conclusion might be. To write concretely about an idea is to use sense experience to explain and prove what we want to say.

Concrete writing is strengthened by specificity. To be *specific* is to state something explicitly, to be particular and definite. Suppose we had witnessed a robbery in our local supermarket and had been asked by the police to write a report on what had taken place. In this case, our writing would most likely be concrete: we saw this; we heard that. It would also be specific as soon as our description was more exact: "The thief was a young white male, approximately twenty years old and about six feet tall. He wore faded blue jeans, a light-green sweatshirt, and black, high-top sneakers. He was slim and frail-looking, with a lean face and a large, crescent-shaped scar on his left cheek. He had a handlebar mustache and short, red, curly hair. He nervously fingered his rimless glasses each time he ordered the manager to do something. . . ." All of the discernible features of the thief's appearance and behavior—taken together—make this passage concrete.

The origin of the word *abstract* tells us a great deal about its meaning and the role it plays in our thinking and writing. *Abstract* can be traced to the Latin word meaning "to remove, to draw out, to pull away." As an adjective, *abstract* refers to whatever is not subject to direct observation and therefore not instantly understood. Such words as *dignity, honesty*, and *love* can be described as abstract because they cannot be understood directly through the senses. Instead, we rely primarily on our past experiences and social conditioning—on the associations abstract words carry—to grasp what they mean. As a verb, *abstract* extends the Latin definition by including also "to consider theoretically"—that is, to think of a quality or an attribute without reference to a particular object or example. In this sense, such words as *motion, dryness,* and *cold* may be considered to be abstractions—thoughts apart from things.

Abstractions refer to whatever we cannot apprehend with our senses. Such words as *hatred, freedom, justice,* and *peace* express states of mind or concepts. For example, we cannot see, hear, or smell freedom. Because abstractions do not point to objects or actions, we should try to be as concrete and specific as possible whenever we use them. Our meaning will be much clearer if we place abstractions in a context of sense experience. Consider the alternatives: popular and sentimental definitions ("Happiness is . . . ," "Friendship is . . .") or the flabby and ineffectual sentences swelling so many recent self-help books. The following passage shows how dangerously easy it is to trade on abstractions:

Love means giving and sharing as well as accepting, and not being stand-offish, defensive, and defiant. In evaluating our capacity to develop relationships, to endure frustration, and to give, consider whether you can admit to biases, prejudices, and weaknesses. Can you accept the loss of a relationship and still persevere, entering into other mutually rewarding relationships?

Openness, honesty, and integrity create strong relationships. Unwillingness to admit to failings or unpleasant emotions generates problems. Fearing rejection, people sometimes hesitate to express the most powerful of emotions—love.

Piling up so many unsupported abstractions obviously limits the impact of this and any similar piece of writing. We should remember that our abstractions must always be able to withstand the test of concrete illustration. When we return our thinking about a subject from the abstract to the concrete, we increase the likelihood that our abstractions will gain expressive power both for ourselves and for those who read or listen to us.

It also helps us to consider abstraction as a process. To abstract is really to engage in a method of selection. When we abstract from something, we single out some part of our experience, some quality or attribute of it. We experience the world around us, to quote the philosopher William James, as a "blooming, buzzing confusion." To identify one element out of the whole is to abstract it from the whole. In many ways the process of abstraction in thinking is similar to that of lens focusing in photography. From the vast concrete scene in front of them, photographers focus on someone or something and try to highlight their subject's essential characteristics. In doing so, they relegate whatever else remains in their field of vision to the fringe of the photograph. Our minds work in much the same way. As we shape an idea in our thinking, our words move through a similar pattern of field and focus, of concrete and abstract.

The American novelist and essayist Joan Didion is often praised for her ability to move between abstract and concrete expression. In the opening passage of an "assigned" essay on the subject of morality (not only student writers get assigned topics), Didion describes the process of her thinking as she tries to tackle a difficult concept. Acknowledging that her mind "veers inflexibly toward the particular," she pursues the private associations that lurk behind her interpretation of this complex abstraction.

Joan Didion

On Morality

As it happens, I am in Death Valley, in a room at the Enterprise Motel and Trailer Park, and it is July, and it is hot. In fact, it is 119°. I cannot seem to make the air conditioner work, but there is a small refrigerator, and I can wrap ice cubes in a towel and hold them against the small of my back. With the help of the ice cubes I have been trying to think, because the *American Scholar* asked me to, in some abstract way about "morality," a word I distrust more every day, but my mind veers inflexibly toward the particular.

Here are some particulars. At midnight last night, on the road in from Las Vegas to Death Valley Junction, a car hit a shoulder and turned over. The driver, very young and apparently drunk, was killed instantly. His girl was found alive but bleeding internally, deep in shock. I talked this afternoon to the nurse who had driven the girl to the nearest doctor, 185 miles across the floor of the Valley and three ranges of lethal mountain road. The nurse explained that her husband, a talc miner, had stayed on the highway with the boy's body until the coroner could get over the mountain from Bishop, at dawn today. "You can't just leave a body on the highway," she said. "It's immoral."

It was one instance in which I did not distrust the word, because she meant something quite specific. She meant that if a body is left alone for even a few minutes on the desert, the coyotes close in and eat the flesh. Whether or not a corpse is torn apart by coyotes may seem only a sentimental consideration, but of course it is more: one of the promises we make to one another is that we will try to retrieve our casualties, try not to abandon our dead to the coyotes. If we have been taught to keep our promises—if, in the simplest terms, our upbringing is good enough—we stay with the body, or have bad dreams.

I am talking, of course, about the kind of social code that is sometimes called, usually pejoratively, "wagon-train morality." In fact that is precisely what it is. For better or worse, we are what we learned as children: my own childhood was illuminated by graphic litanies of the grief awaiting those who failed in their loyalties to each other. The Donner-Reed Party, starving in the Sierra snows, all the ephemera of civilization gone save that one vestigial taboo, the provision that no one should eat his own blood kin. The Jayhawkers, who quarreled and separated not far from where I am tonight. Some of them died in the Funerals and some of them died down near the Badwater and most of the rest of them died in the Panamints. A woman who got through gave the Valley its name. Some might say that the Jayhawkers were killed by the desert summer, and the Donner Party by the mountain winter, by circumstances beyond control; we were taught instead that they had somewhere abdicated their responsibilities, somehow breached their primary loyalties, or they would not have found themselves helpless in the mountain winter or the desert summer, would not have given way to acrimony, would not have deserted one another, would not have *failed.* In brief, we heard such stories as cautionary tales, and they still suggest the only kind of "morality" that seems to me to have any but the most potentially mendacious meaning.

In reflecting on the word *morality*, Didion's mind gravitates toward particular instances of the concept. But note that she doesn't abandon abstractions entirely, because her examples are intended to serve another, larger point. Yet she remains uncomfortable with abstractions. What makes her writing especially effective is the honest way it enacts a natural thought-process. We never feel that she is giving a hollow speech about Morality. As she does her thinking *in* writing, she illustrates one of the important ways the human mind works, as it continually swings between abstract concepts and concrete experience.

Brainstorming Exercises

1. Using Joan Didion's passage on "morality" as a model, consider another complex abstract topic—for example, justice, love, family values, happiness, integrity. After you select a concept, jot down underneath the word the concrete instances of it that come into your mind.
2. One student looks at a tree on campus and says "tree." Another looks at the same tree and says "oak tree." And another, observing the same tree, recognizes it as a "white oak." Consider the different responses. Can one be said to be more concrete? Does a student who recognizes a car in the parking lot as a 97 Acura Integra have a more concrete experience of it than another student who notices only an automobile?

DEVELOPING IDEAS

As we said at the start, *Thinking in Writing* is designed to help students overcome two frustrating obstacles to composition: getting ideas and turning them into successful papers. In this introduction, we have covered four methods of brainstorming, four ways of using basic mental processes to come up with ideas for writing. As you practice these methods, you will undoubtedly discover the procedures that work best for you, and you may even find interesting ways of combining all four.

But once you've come up with an idea for a paper, what then? An idea is hardly an essay. How do you develop a key word or metaphor into several pages? How do you build upon your observations? How do you sustain an idea?

The ten chapters of this book cover the fundamental methods of developing and arranging our ideas. These methods all relate to the subject of rhetoric, one of the world's oldest academic disciplines. The terms *rhetoric* and *rhetorical* are sometimes used today in a negative sense, suggesting an exaggerated or insincere style of language. But the primary definition of *rhetoric* is: the art of using language effectively in speech or writing. The earliest rhetoric textbooks go back thousands of years. Among other matters, they taught students "invention" and "arrangement"—that is, discovering ideas for writing and then developing or arranging them in the clearest and most coherent fashion. Though rhetoricians or writing teachers may use different terminologies, the various ways of organizing ideas are often referred to as "patterns."

In this book we will introduce you to a number of the traditional rhetorical patterns writers have used for centuries to develop their ideas effectively and persuasively. At first, we will examine some of the patterns writers typically rely on when they describe or narrate something. For example, the way we relate the sequence of events in a story will make a large difference in its telling: do we start at the end and work our way to the beginning? Do we start in the middle? Do we proceed in strict chronological order? For a novelist or screenwriter, these are crucial questions.

We then turn to seven key patterns of expository writing, the kind we do when we are attempting to explain or analyze something. You will learn in these chapters how to develop papers or paragraphs by: providing examples and evidence that support general statements, defining complex or significant terms, breaking down a topic into its major parts, discovering resemblances and differences, constructing analogies, describing processes, and investigating the relationship of causes and effects. In the final chapter, you will be introduced to the logical and emotive strategies of effective argument and persuasion.

It is important to note that each of these chapters emphasizes the connections between thinking and writing. In order to construct the sequence of a narrative we must think narratively; to build a convincing case for a cause or position we must provide clear and consistent reasons. The patterns of our writing will duplicate the patterns of our thinking.

CHAPTER 1

Narration

W e want to tell someone what happened to us as we waited hours in line to register for classes. We try to explain to our roommate exactly how the Astros scored thirteen runs in the fifth inning. A friend who left the party just before the police arrived wants us to tell her everything she missed. All of these situations call for a basic thought process we use every day—narration.

Narration is a way of telling what happened. We use it for a wide variety of practical and creative purposes: to tell a joke, to provide autobiographical information, to write history, to record a laboratory experiment, to make a journal entry, to put the details of an accident on an insurance form, to tell a story (either true or fictional), to report a news event, and so on. But no matter how many different ways we may use narration, we are generally performing a single operation: linking a succession of events together into a meaningful sequence.

Elements of Narration

The most elementary type of narration merely relates a series of events: "and then . . . and then . . . and then." Though this may work well for children's stories, accident reports, and some banal movies—where all that matters is "what happens next"—a simple string of loosely related events narrated in a strict chronological sequence can be monotonous and uninformative. When using narration in expository writing, we should try to avoid the formula "*A* happened, then *B* happened, then *C* happened. . . ." Instead of merely relating one event followed by another, we should try constructing a sequence of interdependent events in which one thing *leads* to another. To do this effectively requires, first, a skillful selection of *details;* second, control of the time sequence, or *duration;* third, a clear sense of *direction;* and fourth, a logical *development.*

Paying close attention to these four elements can bring clarity and coherence to most narratives. Let's take a fairly ordinary, though complex, writing occasion. Suppose you are e-mailing a letter to a close friend and want to report how you are getting along at school. You have a lot to say on the subject—some of it optimistic, some of it pessimistic; some of it about your courses, some of it about your social life—and you feel the need to put your thoughts across clearly, effectively, succinctly.

33

Since most of your account will be rooted in personal experience, cover a fairly long stretch of time, and involve a relatively complex succession of events, you'll probably find yourself instinctively choosing a narrative format to convey your autobiographical message. You have a rough idea of what you want to say but before you begin to write, you may want to think about some of your options. You can do this conveniently by considering *detail, duration, direction,* and *development.*

Choice of Detail

Most subjects, especially those based on personal experiences, are made up of innumerable details, ranging from the highly memorable and unique to the trivial and easily forgotten. From the mass of details that cluster around and form our subject, we must select those most appropriate to our general purpose. If you want to say in your letter how surprised you were to find you really do have mathematical ability, you can do this by relating the sequence of anxieties you experienced while waiting for your grade and the amazement you felt when it turned out to be an A. Or, if you want to convey how tiresome the freshman orientation lecture series was, you might give a blow-by-blow account of how you got yourself through it: toying with a pencil, doodling, gazing out the window, glancing at your watch—details that may seem insignificant in themselves, yet will unmistakably convey your intended effect. The choice of details is crucial. We can never recount everything that happened (which is one reason why life and art are two different things), so we must carefully select only those events and actions which matter, either because of their intrinsic importance or because of what they represent. A good rule in narration is to try to make every detail relevant, to make each one contribute in some way to the overall narrative effect. (In George Orwell's "Shooting an Elephant," notice how the narrator enhances the impact of the final scene by paying special attention to numerous minute details.)

Duration

In narration, no matter what sort of subject we are considering, we will be handling the passage of time. Since we usually have a limited time in which to tell our story, we must find ways of scheduling narrative events so that we can cover our subject in a much shorter time than the events we are writing about actually occupied. In other words, we have to make chronological time fit comfortably into narrative time. We do this, of course, by eliminating a large number of details, by compressing others, and by subordinating some parts of the action to others more relevant to our purpose. Narrative, however, is flexible and allows us to work with different rates of time in different ways. In some instances (relating the precise movements of an acrobat's stunt or the play of expressions on a lover's face), we may want to prolong a split-second phenomenon for many pages. Our narrative durations will generally depend on our expository purpose or the dramatic effect we want to achieve.

In your e-mail to a friend you may be able in five or six pages to tell about events that occurred over a period of two to three months. To do this adequately requires a careful management of time. If your subject involves a long succession of complex events, you can divide your narrative into a series of related episodes. You can, for example, talk about your anxieties on the first day of school, move from there to the pleasure you felt in running into an old high school friend in the cafeteria, and then proceed to an account of a class you particularly enjoy. Or you may compress time in another way. You may choose to narrate one continuous episode and focus on it in such a way that it alone conveys the impression you want to give of your life at college. A few pages on getting up in the morning and getting to biology class can be done in a narrative fashion that lucidly portrays in miniature everything you want to say about life at school.

Strict chronological order may at first suggest itself as the most natural way to proceed with narration. But there are other ways to construct a narrative. We can begin at the end, then move to the beginning and proceed from there (as do many news reports), simply reversing the normal sequence. Or we can begin *in medias res* ("in the middle of things") in the fashion of much literature. (Stephen Crane's *The Red Badge of Courage,* for example, begins on the eve of a battle and flashes back to the days before the hero's enlistment.) Or we can begin at the beginning, move quickly to the end, and then supply the middle portions. In short, our narrative chronology—the time scheme we devise for the purposes of our composition—can take whatever sequence we wish to give it. We can begin at any time we want to. You can start your letter by recalling how you felt on the eve of an examination, flash back to your decision to apply to college, and then return to a straightforward chronological order that takes you up to the day of your letter. You should be careful, however, not to put too heavy a strain on your narrative (as well as your reader) by moving back and forth in time unnecessarily or by constructing a more elaborate narrative sequence than your subject and purpose actually call for.

Regulating our time scheme involves more than carving out and reordering selected episodes from whatever stretch of time we are considering. It means controlling smaller elements of composition as well—especially those having to do with tense sequence and words related to time. Most narrative is organized around the past tense ("When Ms. Long passed out the math midterm and I saw the first question, I thought *I* would pass out."), though we may occasionally mix in the present tense, as do many storytellers, to create dramatic immediacy. Because verbs play such a vital part in all types of narration, we should be particularly attentive to the consistency and coordination of tenses. We need to make sure that tenses follow each other in a logical sequence and are not shifted indiscriminately: "As I *walked* into the classroom and *saw* the questions on the board, I suddenly *realized* that I *had studied* all the wrong chapters last night and I thought: 'I *will* flunk this test for sure.' "

In well-regulated narration, we need to rely on many familiar words having to do with time: *now, then, when, no sooner had . . . , previously, meanwhile, afterward, just, since,* and so on. These words can be thought of as the glue which holds narrative together. They help keep our narrative from getting into a monotonous "and then . . . and then" rhythm. They also allow for the proper subordination of events, as in the following:

> *No sooner* had I sat down than I looked at all the questions on the board *again* and *this time* realized that they were intended for another section. *When* the instructor handed out our test questions, I saw *at once* that I had studied not only the right material but exactly the right material. I got an A on the test and *since then* have had more confidence in statistics than I ever thought I'd have. *Now,* when I think about how much I worried all those weeks *before* the test, I want to laugh at myself for being so intimidated by mere numbers. *During* the last few weeks of classes, I've been something of an ace on the subject. In fact, *after* the last class yesterday, our instructor asked me if I'd be interested in attending a special workshop to study the election returns. The workshop doesn't start *until* next week, so in the *meantime* I'm brushing up on sampling methods.

As this example shows, organizing the relation of events syntactically by means of time words can add strength and purpose to our narratives.

Clear Sense of Direction

One of the effects of well-articulated narrative is a sense of forward movement. We normally say of a well-told story that it "flowed," that it "carried us right along." One of the best means of achieving this "flow" or forward movement when composing narrative is to begin with and maintain a clear sense of direction. (In "Salvation," p. 80, for example, Langston Hughes sustains a forceful, steady movement by always keeping his narrative purpose clear.) So that our audience will feel our narrative is definitely going somewhere, we should avoid clogging it with extraneous details and unnecessary digressions. Our direction need not be explicitly stated. In your letter, for example, the narrative may move step by step toward a single event—the A on the math exam—which dramatically shows (rather than tells) that you think your decision to attend Silas Marner University was the right one after all. A clear sense of direction will help us maintain the steady forward movement through a succession of events that is one of the strengths of narrative.

Sequential Development

Effective narrative moves along not just sequentially but *consequentially*. In other words, it develops: *A* leads to *B*, which leads to *C*, which leads to *D*, and so on in a closely linked chain. When constructing a narrative, we should aim to make each step in our sequence follow necessarily (or, as Judith Ortiz Cofer does in "American History," p. 59, at least with a high degree of probability) out of the preceding step. Suppose you want to tell your friends how you have grown more independent since you started school. The *direction* of your narrative would point toward this new sense of independence, while the *development* of your narrative would show how that independence was cumulative, built up out of a succession of connected experiences—living away from home, managing your own affairs, arranging your own schedules, and so on. If narrative direction is concerned with where we are going, narrative development is concerned with how we are getting there. Development gives the forward movement of our narrative orderly progression and logical connectedness. Two common mistakes in composing narratives involve development: one is overlooking or misplacing a critical step in our sequence, thus disrupting the entire chain; the other is inserting a totally arbitrary item into the narrative sequence, thus rendering the entire series improbable.

Elements of Literary Narrative

Point of View

Narration implies a narrator, someone who relates the narrative, who tells the story. Our choice of narrator often determines the point of view from which events will be perceived. In your letter about school, you would most likely narrate events in the first-person singular—the "I" would be yourself. But you could also—in playfulness, irony, or satire—invent an "I" that was not identical to yourself and then tell your own story from the invented point of view. Either way, the "I" would still occupy a central position in the narrative. But it is possible, too, to create an "I" who relates a story in which he or she plays merely a peripheral role. (In F. Scott Fitzgerald's *The Great Gatsby*, for example, the narrative "I" belongs to Nick Carraway, a young man who presents himself as someone not central to the main action of the novel.)

The third-person singular provides us with another point of view, a relatively objective one common to many forms of expository narration. It is even possible to use it in autobiography; you may, for example, write an essay in which you look at yourself from a distance ("Three months ago, Sheila was a timid, dependent young woman with no clear sense of what she wanted to do in life. Now . . .."). Though expository writing generally works within a much narrower range of narrative viewpoints than does fiction or poetry, we should think clearly about our narrative vantage point before we begin to write. The first-person narrative "I" comes to mind almost automatically, but it may not always be the most effective way to proceed.

Voice

Once we decide who will narrate our composition, we then have to create a voice that will characterize the narrator and establish the dominant *sound* of our narrative. The narrative voice is what our audience literally hears, and in some cases it can exert a more powerful influence than our message or logic. (Consider how many advertisers identify their product with a warm, intimate voice rather than with the coaxing pitch of a salesperson.) A narrative voice is not always a simple thing to put down on paper; it is not enough merely to sound "natural." When we try to create a narrative voice, we should remember that our own speaking voice is largely a complex interweaving of word choice, tone, speech cadences, dialect, and idioms. If we want to create a voice in writing—even our own—we need to listen carefully to how both our voice and other voices sound. In most expository narration, however, the voice we use will not be a mimicry of a "real" individual voice, but a carefully regulated educated voice that retains enough personality to sound authentic and sheds just enough of its idiosyncrasy to be broadly communicative.

Dialogue

We frequently need to incorporate conversation and dialogue into expository narration. News reports, for example, often include quotations and dialogue to enhance the on-the-spot quality of the account and, more important, to record significant comments. In our narrative writing, we should introduce dialogue economically and judiciously, taking special care that it sounds authentic, relates to our main action, and advances the narrative. Dialogue can either be direct ("I think you have a pretty solid chance of getting accepted to medical school four years from now if you keep up your work," she said) or indirect (She told me that she thought I had a pretty solid chance of getting accepted to medical school four years from now if I keep up my work). If we want to write factual narrative, we should be sure we are reporting quotations and dialogue accurately.

There is a tendency in writing to make dialogue sound artificial and stiff. Paying close attention to *how* people talk, not just to what they are talking about, can help us—with practice, of course—write natural-sounding dialogue. The more authentic our dialogue sounds, the more we can rely on quotations alone to characterize speakers, and the less we have to depend upon the monotony of "he said . . . she said," or, worse, such strained variations as "he replied . . . she retorted."

The following selections illustrate a number of ways we can work with narrative structures in our compositions. Some further characteristics of expository narration will be covered in the chapter on "Process Analysis."

Graduation

Maya Angelou

Maya Angelou (b. 1928) is widely recognized as one of the great voices of contemporary African American literature. "Graduation" is excerpted from I Know Why the Caged Bird Sings *(1970), the first of her five autobiographical novels, which trace the life story of a black American woman in the twentieth century. Her story resonates for a broad spectrum of readers; as Angelou explains, "I speak to the black experience but I am always talking about the human condition—about what we can endure, dream, fail at and still survive."*

For Angelou, who was born Marguerite Johnson, the act of writing autobiography necessitates moving from "an 'as told to' to an 'as remembered' state." She describes her writing process in this way: "Every morning I wake up, usually about 5:30 and try to get to my work room. I keep a little room in a hotel. Nothing on the walls, nothing belonging to me, nothing." She quits for the day no later than 2:00, but never before she has written to the end of an incident from her past. "I will write to a place that's safe. Nothing will leak away now; I've got it. Then at night I'll read it and try to edit it."

The children in Stamps[1] trembled visibly with anticipation. Some adults were excited too, but to be certain the whole young population had come down with graduation epidemic. Large classes were graduating from both the grammar school and the high school. Even those who were years removed from their own day of glorious release were anxious to help with preparations as a kind of dry run. The junior students who were moving into the vacating classes' chairs were tradition-bound to show their talents for leadership and management. They strutted through the school and around the campus exerting pressure on the lower grades. Their authority was so new that occasionally if they pressed a little too hard it had to be overlooked. After all, next term was coming, and it never hurt a sixth grader to have a play sister in the eighth grade, or a tenth-year student to be able to call a twelfth grader Bubba. So all was endured in a spirit of shared understanding. But the graduating classes themselves were the nobility. Like travelers with exotic destinations on their minds, the graduates were remarkably forgetful. They came to school without their books, or tablets or even pencils. Volunteers fell over themselves to secure replacements for the missing equipment. When accepted, the willing workers might or might not be thanked, and it was of no importance to the pregraduation rites. Even teachers were respectful of the now quiet and aging seniors,

---

[1]Stamps: A town in southwestern Arkansas—Eds.

and tended to speak to them, if not as equals, as beings only slightly lower than themselves. After tests were returned and grades given, the student body, which acted like an extended family, knew who did well, who excelled, and what piteous ones had failed.

Unlike the white high school, Lafayette County Training School distinguished itself by having neither lawn, nor hedges, nor tennis court, nor climbing ivy. Its two buildings (main classrooms, the grade school and home economics) were set on a dirt hill with no fence to limit either its boundaries or those of bordering farms. There was a large expanse to the left of the school which was used alternately as a baseball diamond or basketball court. Rusty hoops on swaying poles represented the permanent recreational equipment, although bats and balls could be borrowed from the P.E. teacher if the borrower was qualified and if the diamond wasn't occupied.

Over this rocky area relieved by a few shady tall persimmon trees the graduating class walked. The girls often held hands and no longer bothered to speak to the lower students. There was a sadness about them, as if this old world was not their home and they were bound for higher ground. The boys, on the other hand, had become more friendly, more outgoing. A decided change from the closed attitude they projected while studying for finals. Now they seemed not ready to give up the old school, the familiar paths and classrooms. Only a small percentage would be continuing on to college—one of the South's A & M (agricultural and mechanical) schools, which trained Negro youths to be carpenters, farmers, handymen, masons, maids, cooks and baby nurses. Their future rode heavily on their shoulders, and blinded them to the collective joy that had pervaded the lives of the boys and girls in the grammar school graduating class.

Parents who could afford it had ordered new shoes and readymade clothes for themselves from Sears and Roebuck or Montgomery Ward. They also engaged the best seamstresses to make the floating graduating dresses and to cut down secondhand pants which would be pressed to a military slickness for the important event.

Oh, it was important, all right. Whitefolks would attend the cere- [5] mony, and two or three would speak of God and home, and the Southern way of life, and Mrs. Parsons, the principal's wife, would play the graduation march while the lower-grade graduates paraded down the aisles and took their seats below the platform. The high school seniors would wait in empty classrooms to make their dramatic entrance.

In the Store I was the person of the moment. The birthday girl. The center. Bailey[2] had graduated the year before, although to do so he had had to forfeit all pleasures to make up for his time lost in Baton Rouge.

---

[2]Bailey: Her brother; they help out in their grandmother's store—Eds.

My class was wearing butter-yellow piqué dresses, and Momma launched out on mine. She smocked the yoke into tiny crisscrossing puckers, then shirred the rest of the bodice. Her dark fingers ducked in and out of the lemony cloth as she embroidered raised daisies around the hem. Before she considered herself finished she had added a crocheted cuff on the puff sleeves, and a pointy crocheted collar.

I was going to be lovely. A walking model of all the various styles of fine hand sewing and it didn't worry me that I was only twelve years old and merely graduating from the eighth grade. Besides, many teachers in Arkansas Negro schools had only that diploma and were licensed to impart wisdom.

The days had become longer and more noticeable. The faded beige of former times had been replaced with strong and sure colors. I began to see my classmates' clothes, their skin tones, and the dust that waved off pussy willows. Clouds that lazed across the sky were objects of great concern to me. Their shiftier shapes might have held a message that in my new happiness and with a little bit of time I'd soon decipher. During that period I looked at the arch of heaven so religiously my neck kept a steady ache. I had taken to smiling more often, and my jaws hurt from the unaccustomed activity. Between the two physical sore spots, I suppose I could have been uncomfortable, but that was not the case. As a member of the winning team (the graduating class of 1940) I had outdistanced unpleasant sensations by miles. I was headed for the freedom of open fields.

10   Youth and social approval allied themselves with me and we trammeled memories of slights and insults. The wind of our swift passage remodeled my features. Lost tears were pounded to mud and then to dust. Years of withdrawal were brushed aside and left behind, as hanging ropes of parasitic moss.

My work alone had awarded me a top place and I was going to be one of the first called in the graduating ceremonies. On the classroom blackboard, as well as on the bulletin board in the auditorium, there were blue stars and white stars and red stars. No absences, no tardiness, and my academic work was among the best of the year. I could say the preamble to the Constitution even faster than Bailey. We timed ourselves often: "WethepeopleoftheUnitedStatesinordertoform- amoreperfectunion. . . ." I had memorized the Presidents of the United States from Washington to Roosevelt in chronological as well as alphabetical order.

My hair pleased me too. Gradually the black mass had lengthened and thickened, so that it kept at last to its braided pattern, and I didn't have to yank my scalp off when I tried to comb it.

Louise and I had rehearsed the exercises until we tired out ourselves. Henry Reed was class valedictorian. He was a small, very black boy with hooded eyes, a long, broad nose and an oddly shaped head. I had admired him for years because each term he and I vied for the best grades in our class. Most often he bested me, but instead of being disappointed I was pleased that we shared top places between us. Like many southern Black children, he lived with his grandmother, who was as strict as Momma and as kind as she knew how to be. He was courteous, respectful and softspoken to elders, but on the playground he chose to play the roughest games. I admired him. Anyone, I reckoned, sufficiently afraid or sufficiently dull could be polite. But to be able to operate at a top level with both adults and children was admirable.

His valedictory speech was entitled "To Be or Not to Be." The rigid tenth-grade teacher had helped him write it. He'd been working on the dramatic stresses for months.

The weeks until graduation were filled with heady activities. A group of small children were to be presented in a play about buttercups and daisies and bunny rabbits. They could be heard throughout the building practicing their hops and their little songs that sounded like silver bells. The older girls (nongraduates, of course) were assigned the task of making refreshments for the night's festivities. A tangy scent of ginger, cinnamon, nutmeg and chocolate wafted around the home economics building as the budding cooks made samples for themselves and their teachers.

In every corner of the workshop, axes and saws split fresh timber as the woodshop boys made sets and stage scenery. Only the graduates were left out of the general bustle. We were free to sit in the library at the back of the building or look in quite detachedly, naturally, on the measures being taken for our event.

Even the minister preached on graduation the Sunday before. His subject was, "Let your light so shine that men will see your good works and praise your Father, Who is in Heaven." Although the sermon was purported to be addressed to us, he used the occasion to speak to backsliders, gamblers and general ne'er-do-wells. But since he had called our names at the beginning of the service we were mollified.

Among Negroes the tradition was to give presents to children going only from one grade to another. How much more important this was when the person was graduating at the top of the class. Uncle Willie and Momma had sent away for a Mickey Mouse watch like Bailey's. Louise gave me four embroidered handkerchiefs. (I gave her crocheted doilies). Mrs. Sneed, the minister's wife, made me an undershirt to wear for graduation, and nearly every customer gave me a nickel or maybe even a dime with the instruction "Keep on moving to higher ground," or some such encouragement.

Amazingly the great day finally dawned and I was out of bed before I knew it. I threw open the back door to see it more clearly, but Momma said, "Sister, come away from that door and put your robe on."

20   I hoped the memory of that morning would never leave me. Sunlight was itself young, and the day had none of the insistence maturity would bring it in a few hours. In my robe and barefoot in the backyard, under cover of going to see about my new beans, I gave myself up to the gentle warmth and thanked God that no matter what evil I had done in my life He had allowed me to live to see this day. Somewhere in my fatalism I had expected to die, accidentally, and never have the chance to walk up the stairs in the auditorium and gracefully receive my hard-earned diploma. Out of God's merciful bosom I had won reprieve.

Bailey came out in his robe and gave me a box wrapped in Christmas paper. He said he had saved his money for months to pay for it. It felt like a box of chocolates, but I knew Bailey wouldn't save money to buy candy when we had all we could want under our noses.

He was as proud of the gift as I. It was a soft-leather-bound copy of a collection of poems by Edgar Allan Poe, or, as Bailey and I called him, "Eap." I turned to "Annabel Lee" and we walked up and down the garden rows, the cool dirt between our toes, reciting the beautifully sad lines.

Momma made a Sunday breakfast although it was only Friday. After we finished the blessing, I opened my eyes to find the watch on my plate. It was a dream of a day. Everything went smoothly and to my credit. I didn't have to be reminded or scolded for anything. Near evening I was too jittery to attend to chores, so Bailey volunteered to do all before his bath.

Days before, we had made a sign for the Store, and as we turned out the lights Momma hung the cardboard over the doorknob. It read clearly: CLOSED, GRADUATION.

25   My dress fitted perfectly and everyone said that I looked like a sunbeam in it. On the hill, going toward the school, Bailey walked behind with Uncle Willie, who muttered, "Go on, Ju." He wanted him to walk ahead with us because it embarrassed him to have to walk so slowly. Bailey said he'd let the ladies walk together, and the men would bring up the rear. We all laughed, nicely.

Little children dashed by out of the dark like fireflies. Their crepe-paper dresses and butterfly wings were not made for running and we heard more than one rip, dryly, and the regretful "uh uh" that followed.

The school blazed without gaiety. The windows seemed cold and unfriendly from the lower hill. A sense of ill-fated timing crept over me, and if Momma hadn't reached for my hand I would have drifted back to Bailey and Uncle Willie, and possibly beyond. She made a few slow jokes about my feet getting cold, and tugged me along to the now-strange building.

Around the front steps, assurance came back. There were my fellow "greats," the graduating class. Hair brushed back, legs oiled, new dresses and pressed pleats, fresh pocket handkerchiefs and little hand-bags, all homesewn. Oh, we were up to snuff, all right. I joined my comrades and didn't even see my family go in to find seats in the crowded auditorium.

The school band struck up a march and all classes filed in as had been rehearsed. We stood in front of our seats, as assigned, and on a signal from the choir director, we sat. No sooner had this been accom-plished than the band started to play the national anthem. We rose again and sang the song, after which we recited the pledge of alle-giance. We remained standing for a brief minute before the choir direc-tor and the principal signaled to us, rather desperately I thought, to take our seats. The command was so unusual that our carefully re-hearsed and smooth-running machine was thrown off. For a full minute we fumbled for our chairs and bumped into each other awk-wardly. Habits change or solidify under pressure, so in our state of ner-vous tension we had been ready to follow our usual assembly pattern: the American national anthem, then the pledge of allegiance, then the song every Black person I knew called the Negro National Anthem. All done in the same key, with the same passion and most often standing on the same foot.

Finding my seat at last, I was overcome with a presentiment of[30] worse things to come. Something unrehearsed, unplanned, was going to happen, and we were going to be made to look bad. I distinctly re-member being explicit in the choice of pronoun. It was "we," the gradu-ating class, the unit, that concerned me then.

The principal welcomed "parents and friends" and asked the Bap-tist minister to lead us in prayer. His invocation was brief and punchy, and for a second I thought we were getting on the high road to right action. When the principal came back to the dais, however, his voice had changed. Sounds always affected me profoundly and the princi-pal's voice was one of my favorites. During assembly it melted and lowed weakly into the audience. It had not been in my plan to listen to him, but my curiosity was piqued and I straightened up to give him my attention.

He was talking about Booker T. Washington, our "late great leader," who said we can be as close as the fingers on the hand, etc. . . . . Then he said a few vague things about friendship and the friendship of kindly people to those less fortunate than themselves. With that his voice nearly faded, thin, away. Like a river diminishing to a stream and then to a trickle. But he cleared his throat and said, "Our speaker tonight, who is also our friend, came from Texarkana to deliver the commencement address, but due to the irregularity of the train schedule, he's going to, as they say, 'speak and run.' " He said that we understood and wanted the man to know that we were most grateful for the time he was able to give us and then something about how we were willing always to adjust to another's program, and without more ado—"I give you Mr. Edward Donleavy."

Not one but two white men came through the door off-stage. The shorter one walked to the speaker's platform, and the tall one moved to the center seat and sat down. But that was our principal's seat, and already occupied. The dislodged gentleman bounced around for a long breath or two before the Baptist minister gave him his chair, then with more dignity than the situation deserved, the minister walked off the stage.

Donleavy looked at the audience once (on reflection, I'm sure that he wanted only to reassure himself that we were really there), adjusted his glasses and began to read from a sheaf of papers.

35   He was glad "to be here and to see the work going on just as it was in the other schools."

At the first "Amen" from the audience I willed the offender to immediate death by choking on the word. But Amens and Yes, sir's began to fall around the room like rain through a ragged umbrella.

He told us of the wonderful changes we children in Stamps had in store. The Central School (naturally, the white school was Central) had already been granted improvements that would be in use in the fall. A well-known artist was coming from Little Rock to teach art to them. They were going to have the newest microscopes and chemistry equipment for their laboratory. Mr. Donleavy didn't leave us long in the dark over who made these improvements available to Central High. Nor were we to be ignored in the general betterment scheme he had in mind.

He said that he had pointed out to people at a very high level that one of the first-line football tacklers at Arkansas Agricultural and Mechanical College had graduated from good old Lafayette County Training School. Here fewer Amen's were heard. Those few that did break through lay dully in the air with the heaviness of habit.

He went on to praise us. He went on to say how he had bragged that "one of the best basketball players at Fisk sank his first ball right here at Lafayette County Training School."

40   The white kids were going to have a chance to become Galileos and Madame Curies and Edisons and Gauguins, and our boys (the girls weren't even in on it) would try to be Jesse Owenses and Joe Louises.

Owens and the Brown Bomber were great heroes in our world, but what school official in the white-goddom of Little Rock had the right to decide that those two men must be our only heroes? Who decided that for Henry Reed to become a scientist he had to work like George Washington Carver, as a bootblack, to buy a lousy microscope? Bailey was obviously always going to be too small to be an athlete, so which concrete angel glued to what county seat had decided that if my brother wanted to become a lawyer he had to first pay penance for his skin by picking cotton and hoeing corn and studying correspondence books at night for twenty years?

The man's dead words fell like bricks around the auditorium and too many settled in my belly. Constrained by hard-earned manners I couldn't look behind me, but to my left and right the proud graduating class of 1940 had dropped their heads. Every girl in my row had found something new to do with her handkerchief. Some folded the tiny squares into love knots, some into triangles, but most were wadding them, then pressing them flat on their yellow laps.

On the dais, the ancient tragedy was being replayed. Professor Parsons sat, a sculptor's reject, rigid. His large, heavy body seemed devoid of will or willingness, and his eyes said he was no longer with us. The other teachers examined the flag (which was draped stage right) or their notes, or the windows which opened on our now-famous playing diamond.

Graduation, the hush-hush magic time of frills and gifts and congratulations and diplomas, was finished for me before my name was called. The accomplishment was nothing. The meticulous maps, drawn in three colors of ink, learning and spelling decasyllabic words, memorizing the whole of *The Rape of Lucrece*[3]—it was for nothing. Donleavy had exposed us.

We were maids and farmers, handymen and washerwomen, and[45] anything higher that we aspired to was farcical and presumptuous.

Then I wished that Gabriel Prosser and Nat Turner had killed all whitefolks in their beds and that Abraham Lincoln had been assassinated before the signing of the Emancipation Proclamation, and that Harriet Tubman had been killed by that blow on her head and Christopher Columbus had drowned in the *Santa Maria*.

It was awful to be a Negro and have no control over my life. It was brutal to be young and already trained to sit quietly and listen to charges brought against my color with no chance of defense. We should all be dead. I thought I should like to see us all dead, one on top of the other. A pyramid of flesh with the whitefolks on the bottom, as the broad base, then the Indians with their silly tomahawks and teepees and wigwams and treaties, the Negroes with their mops and recipes and cotton sacks and spirituals sticking out of their mouths. The Dutch children should all stumble in their wooden shoes and break their necks. The French should choke to death on the Louisiana Purchase (1803) while silkworms ate all the Chinese with their stupid pigtails. As a species, we were an abomination. All of us.

---

[3]*The Rape of Lucrece:* A long narrative poem published by Shakespeare in 1594; it is 1,855 lines long and memorizing the entire poem would be an extraordinary feat—Eds.

Donleavy was running for election, and assured our parents that if he won we could count on having the only colored paved playing field in that part of Arkansas. Also—he never looked up to acknowledge the grunts of acceptance—also, we were bound to get some new equipment for the home economics building and the workshop.

He finished, and since there was no need to give any more than the most perfunctory thank-you's, he nodded to the men on the stage, and the tall white man who was never introduced joined him at the door. They left with the attitude that now they were off to something really important. (The graduation ceremonies at Lafayette County Training School had been a mere preliminary.)

50   The ugliness they left was palpable. An uninvited guest who wouldn't leave. The choir was summoned and sang a modern arrangement of "Onward, Christian Soldiers," with new words pertaining to graduates seeking their place in the world. But it didn't work. Elouise, the daughter of the Baptist minister, recited "Invictus,"[4] and I could have cried at the impertinence of "I am the master of my fate, I am the captain of my soul."

My name had lost its ring of familiarity and I had to be nudged to go and receive my diploma. All my preparations had fled. I neither marched up to the stage like a conquering Amazon, nor did I look in the audience for Bailey's nod of approval. Marguerite Johnson, I heard the name again, my honors were read, there were noises in the audience of appreciation, and I took my place on the stage as rehearsed.

I thought about colors I hated: ecru, puce, lavender, beige and black.

There was shuffling and rustling around me, then Henry Reed was giving his valedictory address, "To Be or Not to Be." Hadn't he heard the whitefolks? We couldn't *be*, so the question was a waste of time. Henry's voice came out clear and strong. I feared to look at him. Hadn't he got the message? There was no "nobler in the mind" for Negroes because the world didn't think we had minds, and they let us know it. "Outrageous fortune"? Now, that was a joke. When the ceremony was over I had to tell Henry Reed some things. That is, if I still cared. Not "rub," Henry, "erase." "Ah, there's the erase." Us.

Henry had been a good student in elocution. His voice rose on tides of promise and fell on waves of warnings. The English teacher had helped him to create a sermon winging through Hamlet's soliloquy. To be a man, a doer, a builder, a leader, or to be a tool, an unfunny joke, a crusher of funky toadstools. I marveled that Henry could go through with the speech as if we had a choice.

[4]Written by the British poet William Ernest Henley (1849–1903)—Eds.

I had been listening and silently rebutting each sentence with my[55] eyes closed; then there was a hush, which in an audience warns that something unplanned is happening. I looked up and saw Henry Reed, the conservative, the proper, the A student, turn his back to the audience and turn to us (the proud graduating class of 1940) and sing, nearly speaking,

> "Lift ev'ry voice and sing
> Till earth and heaven ring
> Ring with the harmonies of Liberty . . ."

It was the poem written by James Weldon Johnson. It was the music composed by J. Rosamond Johnson. It was the Negro national anthem. Out of habit we were singing it.

Our mothers and fathers stood in the dark hall and joined the hymn of encouragement. A kindergarten teacher led the small children onto the stage and the buttercups and daisies and bunny rabbits marked time and tried to follow:

> "Stony the road we trod
> Bitter the chastening rod
> Felt in the days when hope, unborn, had died.
> Yet with a steady beat
> Have not our weary feet
> Come to the place for which our fathers sighed?"

Each child I knew had learned that song with his ABC's and along with "Jesus Loves Me This I Know." But I personally had never heard it before. Never heard the words, despite the thousands of times I had sung them. Never thought they had anything to do with me.

On the other hand, the words of Patrick Henry had made such an impression on me that I had been able to stretch myself tall and trembling and say, "I know not what course others may take, but as for me, give me liberty or give me death."

And now I heard, really for the first time: 60

> "We have come over a way that with tears
> has been watered,
> We have come, treading our path through
> the blood of the slaughtered."

While echoes of the song shivered in the air, Henry Reed bowed his head, said "Thank you," and returned to his place in the line. The tears that slipped down many faces were not wiped away in shame.

We were on top again. As always, again. We survived. The depths had been icy and dark, but now a bright sun spoke to our souls. I was no longer simply a member of the proud graduating class of 1940; I was a proud member of the wonderful, beautiful Negro race.

Oh, Black known and unknown poets, how often have your auctioned pains sustained us? Who will compute the lonely nights made less lonely by your songs, or the empty pots made less tragic by your tales?

If we were a people much given to revealing secrets, we might raise monuments and sacrifice to the memories of our poets, but slavery cured us of that weakness. It may be enough, however, to have it said that we survive in exact relationship to the dedication of our poets (include preachers, musicians and blues singers).

Additional Rhetorical Strategies

Description (paragraphs 2, 9); Example (throughout).

Discussion Questions

1. What qualities characterize the black community of Stamps, Arkansas, in 1940, when this story takes place? Point to specific actions recounted in this autobiographical episode that illustrate each of the qualities you name. What are young Marguerite's values, and where did she learn them? (The author was named Marguerite Johnson at birth; she took on the name Maya Angelou upon her debut as a dancer in her early twenties.)
2. Who is the subject, the agent, of the first five paragraphs of this essay? Why does Angelou withhold the use of the identity of the main character (and narrator) of this essay until paragraph 6? What does she accomplish before she brings young Marguerite to center stage, figuratively speaking?
3. How are the two white men who attend the graduation ceremony characterized? How does Angelou effect a contrast between them and the members of the black community? Look not only at the words Angelou chooses, but also at the shifts in tone throughout the essay.
4. What are the implications of Marguerite's realization about Patrick Henry in paragraph 59? Look back throughout the essay and find examples of other white men whose words Marguerite has memorized and otherwise taken to heart. What is it about the graduation that enables her to realize the importance of her own cultural history, to listen for the first time to the words of the "Negro national anthem"?

Essay Questions

1. Compare and contrast "Graduation" with "In Search of Our Mothers' Gardens" (p. 168). What role do the "unknown poets"

(paragraph 63) play in the lives of each of these pivotal African American writers? Explore the sources of strength—cultural, familial, and personal—upon which each author draws.

2. Angelou writes of a momentous occasion in the life of a young person—graduation from high school—that becomes memorable for an entirely unexpected reason. Write an essay in which you narrate an occasion that had an unexpected outcome. We often learn the most when our expectations are not fulfilled; if this was true in your case, be sure to convey the lesson you learned from the experience.

Once More to the Lake

E. B. White

Few writers of the twentieth century are as well regarded and beloved as E. B. White (1899–1985). Many children who delighted in Stuart Little *(1945),* Charlotte's Web *(1952), and* The Trumpet of the Swan *(1970) grew up to be college students whose compositions showed the salutary effects of* The Elements of Style *(1959), and adults whose enjoyment of the* New Yorker *would never have been possible had not E. B. White begun contributing essays to that fledgling magazine when it was barely a few months old.*

White is known for his unaffected, deceptively informal essays, in which not a word is out of place. His New Yorker *pieces, collected in* The Essays of E. B. White *(1977), often begin with a small incident that takes on much larger implications. "Once More to the Lake" will give you a good idea of the style and strategies that made White famous.*

Upon receiving the National Medal for Literature in 1971—only one of countless awards he was to receive in his lifetime—White wrote, "I have always felt that the first duty of a writer was to ascend—to make flights, carrying others along if he could manage it. . . . Only hope can carry us aloft . . . only hope and a certain faith. . . . This faith is a writer's faith, for writing itself is an act of faith, nothing else. And it must be the writer, above all others, who keeps it alive—choked with laughter, or with pain."

One summer, along about 1904, my father rented a camp on a lake in Maine and took us all there for the month of August. We all got ringworm from some kittens and had to rub Pond's Extract on our arms and legs night and morning, and my father rolled over in a canoe with all his clothes on; but outside of that the vacation was a success and from then on none of us ever thought there was any place in the world like that lake in Maine. We returned summer after summer—always on August 1st for one month. I have since become a salt-water man, but sometimes in summer there are days when the restlessness of the tides and the fearful cold of the sea water and the incessant wind that blows across the afternoon and into the evening make me wish for the placidity of a lake in the woods. A few weeks ago this feeling got so strong I bought myself a couple of bass hooks and a spinner and returned to the lake where we used to go, for a week's fishing and to revisit old haunts.

I took along my son, who had never had any fresh water up his nose and who had seen lily pads only from train windows. On the journey over to the lake I began to wonder what it would be like. I wondered how time would have marred this unique, this holy spot—the coves and streams, the hills that the sun set behind, the camps and the paths behind the camps. I was sure that the tarred road would have found it out and I wondered in what other ways it would be desolated. It is strange how much you can remember about places like that once you allow your mind to return into the grooves that lead back. You remember one thing, and that suddenly reminds you of another thing. I guess I remembered clearest of all the early mornings, when the lake was cool and motionless, remembered how the bedroom smelled of the lumber it was made of and of the wet woods whose scent entered through the screen. The partitions in the camp were thin and did not extend clear to the top of the rooms, and as I was always the first up I would dress softly so as not to wake the others, and sneak out into the sweet outdoors and start out in the canoe, keeping close along the shore in the long shadows of the pines. I remembered being very careful never to rub my paddle against the gunwale for fear of disturbing the stillness of the cathedral.

The lake had never been what you would call a wild lake. There were cottages sprinkled around the shores, and it was in farming country although the shores of the lake were quite heavily wooded. Some of the cottages were owned by nearby farmers, and you would live at the shore and eat your meals at the farmhouse. That's what our family did. But although it wasn't wild, it was a fairly large and undisturbed lake and there were places in it which, to a child at least, seemed infinitely remote and primeval.

I was right about the tar: it led to within half a mile of the shore. But when I got back there, with my boy, and we settled into a camp near a farmhouse and into the kind of summertime I had known, I could tell that it was going to be pretty much the same as it had been before—I knew it, lying in bed the first morning, smelling the bedroom, and hearing the boy sneak quietly out and go off along the shore in a boat. I began to sustain the illusion that he was I, and therefore, by simple transposition, that I was my father. This sensation persisted, kept cropping up all the time we were there. It was not an entirely new feeling, but in this setting it grew much stronger. I seemed to be living a dual existence. I would be in the middle of some simple act, I would be picking up a bait box or laying down a table fork, or I would be saying something, and suddenly it would be not I but my father who was saying the words or making the gesture. It gave me a creepy sensation.

We went fishing the first morning. I felt the same damp moss covering the worms in the bait can, and saw the dragonfly alight on the tip of my rod as it hovered a few inches from the surface of the water. It was the arrival of this fly that convinced me beyond any doubt that everything was as it always had been, that the years were a mirage and there had been no years. The small waves were the same, chucking the rowboat under the chin as we fished at anchor, and the boat was the same boat, the same color green and the ribs broken in the same places, and under the floor-boards the same fresh-water leavings and debris—the dead hellgrammite, the wisps of moss, the rusty discarded fishhook, the dried blood from yesterday's catch. We stared silently at the tips of our rods, at the dragonflies that came and went. I lowered the tip of mine into the water, tentatively, pensively dislodging the fly, which darted two feet away, poised, darted two feet back, and came to rest again a little farther up the rod. There had been no years between the ducking of this dragonfly and the other one—the one that was part of memory. I looked at the boy, who was silently watching his fly, and it was my hands that held his rod, my eyes watching. I felt dizzy and didn't know which rod I was at the end of.

We caught two bass, hauling them in briskly as though they were mackerel, pulling them over the side of the boat in a businesslike manner without any landing net, and stunning them with a blow on the back of the head. When we got back for a swim before lunch, the lake was exactly where we had left it, the same number of inches from the dock, and there was only the merest suggestion of a breeze. This seemed an utterly enchanted sea, this lake you could leave to its own devices for a few hours and come back to, and find that it had not stirred, this constant and trustworthy body of water. In the shallows, the dark, water-soaked sticks and twigs, smooth and old, were undulating in clusters on the bottom against the clean ribbed sand, and the track of the mussel was plain. A school of minnows swam by, each minnow with its small individual shadow, doubling the attendance, so clear and sharp in the sunlight. Some of the other campers were in swimming, along the shore, one of them with a cake of soap, and the water felt thin and clear and unsubstantial. Over the years there had been this person with the cake of soap, this cultist, and here he was. There had been no years.

Up to the farmhouse to dinner through the teeming, dusty field, the road under our sneakers was only a two-track road. The middle track was missing, the one with the marks of the hooves and splotches of dried, flaky manure. There had always been three tracks to choose from in choosing which track to walk in; now the choice was narrowed down to two. For a moment I missed terribly the middle alternative. But the way led past the tennis court, and something about the way it lay there in the sun reassured me; the tape had loosened along the backline, the alleys were green with plantains and other weeds, and the net (installed in June and removed in September) sagged in the dry noon, and the whole place steamed with midday heat and hunger and emptiness. There was a choice of pie for dessert, and one was blueberry and one was apple, and the waitresses were the same country girls, there having been no passage of time, only the illusion of it as in a dropped curtain—the waitresses were still fifteen; their hair had been washed, that was the only difference—they had been to the movies and seen the pretty girls with the clean hair.

Summertime, oh summertime, pattern of life indelible, the fade-proof lake, the woods unshatterable, the pasture with the sweetfern and the juniper forever and ever, summer without end; this was the background, and the life along the shore was the design, the cottages with their innocent and tranquil design, their tiny docks with the flagpole and the American flag floating against the white clouds in the blue sky, the little paths over the roots of the trees leading from camp to camp and the paths leading back to the outhouses and the can of lime for sprinkling, and at the souvenir counters at the store the miniature birch-bark canoes and the post cards that showed things looking a little better than they looked. This was the American family at play, escaping the city heat, wondering whether the new-comers in the camp at the head of the cove were "common" or "nice," wondering whether it was true that the people who drove up for Sunday dinner at the farmhouse were turned away because there wasn't enough chicken.

It seemed to me, as I kept remembering all this, that those times and those summers had been infinitely precious and worth saving. There had been jollity and peace and goodness. The arriving (at the beginning of August) had been so big a business in itself, at the railway station the farm wagon drawn up, the first smell of the pine-laden air, the first glimpse of the smiling farmer, and the great importance of the trunks and your father's enormous authority in such matters, and the feel of the wagon under you for the long ten-mile haul, and at the top of the last long hill catching the first view of the lake after eleven months of not seeing this cherished body of water. The shouts and cries of the other campers when they saw you, and the trunks to be unpacked, to give up their rich burden. (Arriving was less exciting nowadays, when you sneaked up in your car and parked it under a tree near the camp and took out the bags and in five minutes it was all over, no fuss, no loud wonderful fuss about trunks.)

Peace and goodness and jollity. The only thing that was wrong[10] now, really, was the sound of the place, an unfamiliar nervous sound of the outboard motors. This was the note that jarred, the one thing that would sometimes break the illusion and set the years moving. In those other summertimes all motors were inboard; and when they were at a little distance, the noise they made was a sedative, an ingredient of summer sleep. They were one-cylinder and two-cylinder engines, and some were make-and-break and some were jump-park, but they all made a sleepy sound across the lake. The one-lungers throbbed and fluttered, and the twin-cylinder ones purred and purred, and that was a quiet sound too. But now the campers all had outboards. In the day-time, in the hot mornings, these motors made a petulant, irritable sound; at night, in the still evening when the afterglow lit the water, they whined about one's ears like mosquitoes. My boy loved our rented outboard, and his great desire was to achieve singlehanded mastery over it, and authority, and he soon learned the trick of choking it a little (but not too much), and the adjustment of the needle valve. Watching him I would remember the things you could do with the old one-cylinder engine with the heavy flywheel, how you could have it eating out of your hand if you got really close to it spiritually. Motor boats in those days didn't have clutches, and you would make a landing by shutting off the motor at the proper time and coasting in with a dead rudder. But there was a way of reversing them, if you learned the trick, by cutting the switch and putting it on again exactly on the final dying revolution of the flywheel, so that it would kick back against compression and begin reversing. Approaching a dock in a strong following breeze, it was difficult to slow up sufficiently by the ordinary coasting method, and if a boy felt he had complete mastery over his motor, he was tempted to keep it running beyond its time and then reverse it a few feet from the dock. It took a cool nerve, because if you threw the switch a twentieth of a second too soon you could catch the flywheel when it still had speed enough to go up past center, and the boat would leap ahead, charging bull-fashion at the dock.

We had a good week at the camp. The bass were biting well and the sun shone endlessly, day after day. We would be tired at night and lie down in the accumulated heat of the little bedrooms after the long hot day and the breeze would stir almost imperceptibly outside and the smell of the swamp drift in through the rusty screens. Sleep would come easily and in the morning the red squirrel would be on the roof, tapping out his gay routine. I kept remembering everything, lying in bed in the mornings—the small steamboat that had a long rounded stern like the lip of a Ubangi, and how quietly she ran on the moonlight sails, when the older boys played their mandolins and the girls sang and we ate doughnuts dipped in sugar, and how sweet the music was on the water in the shining night, and what it had felt like to think about girls then. After breakfast we would go up to the store and the things were in the same place—the minnows in a bottle, the plugs and spinners disarranged and pawed over by the youngsters from the boy's camp, the Fig Newtons and the Beeman's gum. Outside, the road was tarred and cars stood in front of the store. Inside, all was just as it had always been, except there was more Coca-Cola and not so much Moxie and root beer and birch beer and sarsaparilla. We would walk out with a bottle of pop apiece and sometimes the pop would backfire up our noses and hurt. We explored the streams, quietly, where the turtles slid off the sunny logs and dug their way into the soft bottom; and we lay on the town wharf and fed worms to the tame bass. Everywhere we went I had trouble making out which was I, the one walking at my side, the one walking in my pants.

One afternoon while we were there at that lake a thunderstorm came up. It was like the revival of an old melodrama that I had seen long ago with childish awe. The second-act climax of the drama of the electrical disturbance over a lake in America had not changed in any important respect. This was the big scene, still the big scene. The whole thing was so familiar, the first feeling of oppression and heat and a general air around camp of not wanting to go very far away. In midafternoon (it was all the same) a curious darkening of the sky, and a lull in everything that had made life tick; and then the way the boats suddenly swung the other way at their moorings with the coming of a breeze out of the new quarter, and the premonitory rumble. Then the kettle drum, then the snare, then the bass drum and cymbals, then crackling light against the dark, and the gods grinning and licking their chops in the hills. Afterward the calm, the rain steadily rustling in the calm lake, the return of light and hope and spirits, and the campers running out in joy and relief to go swimming in the rain, their bright cries perpetuating the deathless joke about how they were getting simply drenched, and the children screaming with delight at the new sensation of bathing in the rain, and the joke about getting drenched linking the generations in a strong indestructible chain. And the comedian who waded in carrying an umbrella.

When the others went swimming my son said he was going in too. He pulled his dripping trunks from the line where they had hung all through the shower, and wrung them out. Languidly, and with no thought of going in, I watched him, his hard little body, skinny and bare, saw him wince slightly as he pulled up around his vitals the small, soggy, icy garment. As he buckled the swollen belt suddenly my groin felt the chill of death.

Additional Rhetorical Strategies

Comparison and Contrast (throughout); Description (throughout).

Discussion Questions

1. What is the effect on White of revisiting the lake he last visited as a child? What seems to be the effect of this same visit on his son? What might cause the difference in their perspectives?
2. Look at White's use of repetition in this essay, on the level of words, sentences, and images. How does this stylistic repetition reinforce the meaning of his essay? Explore the motif of doubling throughout the essay.
3. Examine White's use of metaphor in "Once More to the Lake." In what ways are the metaphors unusual? Do you notice any similarities among the different metaphors he uses?

4. Even the smallest details in White's essay contribute to the overall effect. Try replacing any seemingly insignificant word with another, similar word, and describe the differences it makes. In the second sentence of paragraph 5, for instance, what difference would it make to change the phrase "the dragonfly" to "a dragonfly"? And what difference would it make if you were to change the last word in paragraph 11 from "pants" to "shoes," a word more commonly found in such contexts? Try this exercise with other words in the essay.

5. In paragraph 2, White refers to the lake as "this holy spot." In what way might it be considered "holy"? What other references or allusions to religion or spirituality do you notice in the essay? How would you characterize the religious philosophy implied in this essay?

6. Discuss the ending of the essay. Why does White feel the "chill of death" when his son pulls on a pair of wet swim trunks? Does the theme of death come out of nowhere in this essay about the continuation of life, or are the two themes somehow linked? How? Looking back over the essay a second time, do you find any early clues that death is a theme in the essay?

Essay Questions

1. Write an essay in which you explore change versus stasis in "Once More to the Lake," or an essay in which you reflect on White's use of the lake versus the ocean.

2. Write a narrative essay in which you bring the details alive by appealing to your reader's five senses, and by choosing your words well. Note that almost nothing described by White in this essay is exotic or remarkable in itself: almost everyone has felt the sting of carbonated soda in his or her nose, or unpacked a car. It's White's careful attention to stylistic details that makes these commonplace feelings and actions strike us as fresh and real.

American History

Judith Ortiz Cofer

Judith Ortiz Cofer (b. 1952) was born in Puerto Rico and raised in the United States. She earned her B.A. from Augusta College and her M.A. from Florida Atlantic University. She is an accomplished poet, essayist, and novelist whose publications include the book of poetry Terms of Survival *(1987), a novel,* The Line of the Sun *(1984), the autobiographical* Silent Dancing: A Partial Remembrance of a Puerto Rican Childhood *(1990), and the collections* An Island Like You: Stories of the Barrio *(1995) and* The Latin Deli *(1993), from which the following essay is taken.*

In the prologue to The Latin Deli, *Cofer tells of a time when she was too busy being a teacher and a parent to find time to devote to the writing she longed to do. She decided to wake up early and write before her family awakened, but the first morning the plan failed because she turned off the alarm and fell back to sleep. "The second day I set two clocks, one on my night table, as usual, and one out in the hallway. I had to jump out of bed and run to silence it before my family was awakened and the effort nullified. This is when my morning ritual that I follow to this day began. I get up at five and put on a pot of coffee. Then I sit in my chair and read what I did the previous day until the coffee is ready. I take fifteen minutes to drink two cups of coffee while my computer warms up—not that it needs to—I just like to see it glowing in the room where I sit in semidarkness, its screen prompting "ready": ready whenever you are. When I'm ready, I write."*

I once read in a *Ripley's Believe It or Not* column that Paterson, New Jersey, is the place where the Straight and Narrow (streets) intersect. The Puerto Rican tenement known as El Building was one block up from Straight. It was, in fact, the corner of Straight and Market; not "at" the corner, but *the* corner. At almost any hour of the day, El Building was like a monstrous jukebox, blasting out *salsas* from open windows as the residents, mostly new immigrants just up from the island, tried to drown out whatever they were currently enduring with loud music. But the day President Kennedy was shot, there was a profound silence in El Building, even the abusive tongues of viragoes, the cursing of the unemployed, and the screeching of small children had been somehow muted. President Kennedy was a saint to these people. In fact, soon his photograph would be hung alongside the Sacred Heart and over the spiritist altars that many women kept in their apartments. He would become part of the hierarchy of martyrs they prayed to for favors that only one who had died for a cause would understand.

On the day that President Kennedy was shot, my ninth grade class had been out in the fenced playground of Public School Number 13. We had been given "free" exercise time and had been ordered by our P.E.

teacher, Mr. DePalma, to "keep moving." That meant that the girls should jump rope and the boys toss basketballs through a hoop at the far end of the yard. He in the meantime would "keep an eye" on us from just inside the building.

It was a cold gray day in Paterson. The kind that warns of early snow. I was miserable, since I had forgotten my gloves and my knuckles were turning red and raw from the jump rope. I was also taking a lot of abuse from the black girls for not turning the rope hard and fast enough for them.

"Hey, Skinny Bones, pump it, girl. Ain't you got no energy today? Gail, the biggest of the black girls who had the other end of the rope yelled, "Didn't you eat your rice and beans and pork chops for breakfast today?"

5   The other girls picked up the "pork chop" and made it into a refrain: "pork chop, pork chop, did you eat your pork chop?" They entered the double ropes in pairs and exited without tripping or missing a beat. I felt a burning on my cheeks, and then my glasses fogged up so that I could not manage to coordinate the jump rope with Gail. The chill was doing to me what it always did, entering my bones, making me cry, humiliating me. I hated the city, especially in winter. I hated Public School Number 13. I hated my skinny flat-chested body, and I envied the black girls who could jump rope so fast that their legs became a blur. They always seemed to be warm while I froze.

There was only one source of beauty and light for me that school year. The only thing I had anticipated at the start of the semester. That was seeing Eugene. In August, Eugene and his family had moved into the only house on the block that had a yard and trees. I could see his place from my window in El Building. In fact, if I sat on the fire escape I was literally suspended above Eugene's backyard. It was my favorite spot to read my library books in the summer. Until that August the house had been occupied by an old Jewish couple. Over the years I had become part of their family, without their knowing it, of course. I had a view of their kitchen and their backyard, and though I could not hear what they said, I knew when they were arguing, when one of them was sick, and many other things. I knew all this by watching them at mealtimes. I could see their kitchen table, the sink and the stove. During good times, he sat at the table and read his newspapers while she fixed the meals. If they argued, he would leave and the old woman would sit and stare at nothing for a long time. When one of them was sick, the other would come and get things from the kitchen and carry them out on a tray. The old man had died in June. The last week of school I had not seen him at the table at all. Then one day I saw that there was a crowd in the kitchen. The old woman had finally emerged from the house on the arm of a stocky middle-aged woman whom I had seen there a few times before, maybe her daughter. Then a man had carried out suitcases. The house had stood empty for weeks. I had had to resist the temptation to climb down into the yard and water the flowers the old lady had taken such good care of.

By the time Eugene's family moved in, the yard was a tangled mass of weeds. The father had spent several days mowing, and when he finished, I didn't see the red, yellow, and purple clusters that meant flowers to me from where I sat. I didn't see this family sit down at the kitchen table together. It was just the mother, a red-headed tall woman who wore a white uniform—a nurse's, I guessed it was; the father was gone before I got up in the morning and was never there at dinner time. I only saw him on weekends when they sometimes sat on lawn chairs under the oak tree, each hidden behind a section of the newspaper; and there was Eugene. He was tall and blond, and he wore glasses. I liked him right away because he sat at the kitchen table and read books for hours. That summer, before we had even spoken one word to each other, I kept him company on my fire escape.

Once school started I looked for him in all my classes, but P.S. 13 was a huge, overpopulated place and it took me days and many discreet questions to discover that Eugene was in honors classes for all his subjects; classes that were not open to me because English was not my first language, though I was a straight A student. After much maneuvering I managed "to run into him" in the hallway where his locker was—on the other side of the building from mine—and in study hall at the library, where he first seemed to notice me but did not speak; and finally, on the way home after school one day when I decided to approach him directly, though my stomach was doing somersaults.

I was ready for rejection, snobbery, the worst. But when I came up to him, practically panting in my nervousness, and blurted out: "You're Eugene. Right?" He smiled, pushed his glasses up on his nose, and nodded. I saw then that he was blushing deeply. Eugene liked me, but he was shy. I did most of the talking that day. He nodded and smiled a lot. In the weeks that followed, we walked home together. He would linger at the corner of El Building for a few minutes then walk down to his two-story house. It was not until Eugene moved into that house that I noticed that El Building blocked most of the sun and that the only spot that got a little sunlight during the day was the tiny square of earth the old woman had planted with flowers.

I did not tell Eugene that I could see inside his kitchen from my[10] bedroom. I felt dishonest, but I liked my secret sharing of his evenings, especially now that I knew what he was reading, since we chose our books together at the school library.

One day my mother came into my room as I was sitting on the windowsill staring out. In her abrupt way she said: "Elena, you are acting 'moony.' " *Enamorada* was what she really said—that is, like a girl stupidly infatuated. Since I had turned fourteen and started menstruating my mother had been more vigilant than ever. She acted as if I was going to go crazy or explode or something if she didn't watch me and nag me all the time about being a señorita now. She kept talking about virtue, morality, and other subjects that did not interest me in the least. My mother was unhappy in Paterson, but my father had a good job at the blue jeans factory in Passaic, and soon, he kept assuring us, we would be moving to our own house there. Every Sunday we drove out to the suburbs of Paterson, Clifton, and Passaic, out to where people mowed grass on Sundays in the summer and where children made snowmen in the winter from pure white snow, not like the gray slush of Paterson, which seemed to fall from the sky in that hue. I had learned to listen to my parents' dreams, which were spoken in Spanish, as fairy tales, like the stories about life in the island paradise of Puerto Rico before I was born. I had been to the Island once as a little girl, to grandmother's funeral, and all I remembered was wailing women in black, my mother becoming hysterical and being given a pill that made her sleep two days, and me feeling lost in a crowd of strangers all claiming to be my aunts, uncles, and cousins. I had actually been glad to return to the city. We had not been back there since then, though my parents talked constantly about buying a house on the beach someday, retiring on the island—that was a common topic among the residents of El Building. As for me, I was going to go to college and become a teacher.

But after meeting Eugene I began to think of the present more than of the future. What I wanted now was to enter that house I had watched for so many years. I wanted to see the other rooms where the old people had lived and where the boy I liked spent his time. Most of all, I wanted to sit at the kitchen table with Eugene like two adults, like the old man and his wife had done, maybe drink some coffee and talk about books. I had started reading *Gone with the Wind*. I was enthralled by it, with the daring and the passion of the beautiful girl living in a mansion, and with her devoted parents and the slaves who did everything for them. I didn't believe such a world had ever really existed, and I wanted to ask Eugene some questions, since he and his parents, he had told me, had come up from Georgia, the same place where the novel was set. His father worked for a company that had transferred him to Paterson. His mother was very unhappy, Eugene said, in his beautiful voice that rose and fell over words in a strange, lilting way. The kids at school called him the Hick and made fun of the way he talked. I knew I was his only friend so far, and I liked that, though I felt sad for him sometimes. Skinny Bones and the Hick, was what they called us at school when we were seen together.

The day Mr. DePalma came out into the cold and asked us to line up in front of him was the day that President Kennedy was shot. Mr. DePalma, a short, muscular man with slicked-down black hair, was the science teacher, P.E. coach, and disciplinarian at P.S. 13. He was the teacher to whose homeroom you got assigned if you were a trouble-maker, and the man called out to break up playground fights, and to escort violently angry teenagers to the office. And Mr. DePalma was the man who called your parents in for a "conference."

That day, he stood in front of two rows of mostly black and Puerto Rican kids, brittle from their efforts to "keep moving" on a November day that was turning bitter cold. Mr. DePalma, to our complete shock, was crying. Not just silent adult tears, but really sobbing. There were a few titters from the back of the line where I stood, shivering.

"Listen," Mr. DePalma raised his arms over his head as if he were[15] about to conduct an orchestra. His voice broke, and he covered his face with his hands. His barrel chest was heaving. Someone giggled behind me.

"Listen," he repeated, "something awful has happened." A strange gurgling came from his throat, and he turned around and spit on the cement behind him.

"Gross," someone said, and there was a lot of laughter.

"The president is dead, you idiots. I should have known that wouldn't mean anything to a bunch of losers like you kids. Go home." He was shrieking now. No one moved for a minute or two, but then a big girl let out a "yeah!" and ran to get her books piled up with the others against the brick wall of the school building. The others followed in a mad scramble to get to their things before somebody caught on. It was still an hour to the dismissal bell.

A little scared, I headed for El Building. There was an eerie feeling on the streets. I looked into Mario's drugstore, a favorite hangout for the high school crowd, but there were only a couple of old Jewish men at the soda bar, talking with the short order cook in tones that sounded almost angry, but they were keeping their voices low. Even the traffic on one of the busiest intersections in Paterson—Straight Street and Park Avenue—seemed to be moving slower. There were no horns blasting that day. At El Building, the usual little group of unemployed men were not hanging out on the front stoop, making it difficult for women to enter the front door. No music spilled out from open doors in the hallway. When I walked into our apartment, I found my mother sitting in front of the grainy picture of the television set.

She looked up at me with a tear-streaked face and just said: "Dios[20] mío," turning back to the set as if it were pulling at her eyes. I went into my room.

Though I wanted to feel the right thing about President Kennedy's death, I could not fight the feeling of elation that stirred in my chest. Today was the day I was to visit Eugene in his house. He had asked me to come over after school to study for an American history test with him. We had also planned to walk to the public library together. I looked down into his yard. The oak tree was bare of leaves, and the ground looked gray with ice. The light through the large kitchen window of his house told me that El Building blocked the sun to such an extent that they had to turn lights on in the middle of the day. I felt ashamed about it. But the white kitchen table with the lamp hanging just above it looked cozy and inviting. I would soon sit there, across from Eugene, and I would tell him about my perch just above his house. Maybe I would.

In the next thirty minutes I changed clothes, put on a little pink lipstick, and got my books together. Then I went in to tell my mother that I was going to a friend's house to study. I did not expect her reaction.

"You are going out *today?*" The way she said "today" sounded as if a storm warning had been issued. It was said in utter disbelief. Before I could answer, she came toward me and held my elbows as I clutched my books.

"*Hija*, the president has been killed. We must show respect. He was a great man. Come to church with me tonight."

25   She tried to embrace me, but my books were in the way. My first impulse was to comfort her, she seemed so distraught, but I had to meet Eugene in fifteen minutes.

"I have a test to study for, Mama. I will be home by eight."

"You are forgetting who you are, *Niña*. I have seen you staring down at that boy's house. You are heading for humiliation and pain." My mother said this in Spanish and in a resigned tone that surprised me, as if she had no intention of stopping me from "heading for humiliation and pain." I started for the door. She sat in front of the TV, holding a white handkerchief to her face.

I walked out to the street and around the chain-link fence that separated El Building from Eugene's house. The yard was neatly edged around the little walk that led to the door. It always amazed me how Paterson, the inner core of the city, had no apparent logic to its architecture. Small, neat, single residences like this one could be found right next to huge, dilapidated apartment buildings like El Building. My guess was that the little houses had been there first, then the immigrants had come in droves, and the monstrosities had been raised for them—the Italians, the Irish, the Jews, and now us, the Puerto Ricans, and the blacks. The door was painted a deep green: *verde*, the color of hope. I had heard my mother say it: *Verde-Esperanza*.

I knocked softly. A few suspenseful moments later the door opened just a crack. The red, swollen face of a woman appeared. She had a halo of red hair floating over a delicate ivory face—the face of a doll—with freckles on the nose. Her smudged eye makeup made her look unreal to me, like a mannequin seen through a warped store window.

30   "What do you want?" Her voice was tiny and sweet-sounding, like a little girl's, but her tone was not friendly.

"I'm Eugene's friend. He asked me over. To study." I thrust out my books, a silly gesture that embarrassed me almost immediately.

"You live there?" She pointed up to El Building, which looked particularly ugly, like a gray prison with its many dirty windows and rusty fire escapes. The woman had stepped halfway out, and I could see that she wore a white nurse's uniform with "St. Joseph's Hospital" on the name tag.

"Yes. I do."

She looked intently at me for a couple of heartbeats, then said as if to herself, "I don't know how you people do it." Then directly to me: "Listen. Honey. Eugene doesn't want to study with you. He is a smart boy. Doesn't need help. You understand me. I am truly sorry if he told you you could come over. He cannot study with you. It's nothing personal. You understand? We won't be in this place much longer, no need for him to get close to people—it'll just make it harder for him later. Run back home now."

I couldn't move. I just stood there in shock at hearing these things₃₅ said to me in such a honey-drenched voice. I had never heard an accent like hers except for Eugene's softer version. It was as if she were singing me a little song.

"What's wrong? Didn't you hear what I said?" She seemed very angry, and I finally snapped out of my trance. I turned away from the green door and heard her close it gently.

Our apartment was empty when I got home. My mother was in someone else's kitchen, seeking the solace she needed. Father would come in from his late shift at midnight. I would hear them talking softly in the kitchen for hours that night. They would not discuss their dreams for the future, or life in Puerto Rico, as they often did; that night they would talk sadly about the young widow and her two children, as if they were family. For the next few days, we would observe *luto* in our apartment; that is, we would practice restraint and silence—no loud music or laughter. Some of the women of El Building would wear black for weeks.

That night, I lay in my bed, trying to feel the right thing for our dead president. But the tears that came up from a deep source inside me were strictly for me. When my mother came to the door, I pretended to be sleeping. Sometime during the night, I saw from my bed the streetlight come on. It had a pink halo around it. I went to my window and pressed my face to the cool glass. Looking up at the light I could see the white snow falling like a lace veil over its face. I did not look down to see it turning gray as it touched the ground below.

Additional Rhetorical Strategy

Description (paragraphs 6–7).

Discussion Questions

1. What is the significance of the title, "American History"? Where else (besides the title) does this phrase appear? What events recounted in this essay would normally be studied by future students of American history? What events would be overlooked in the textbooks on this topic?

2. How do the personal events of the narrator's life relate to the main public event recounted in this narrative: the death of President Kennedy? Trace the back-and-forth motion of this essay as it considers the public and the private spheres. Where are the sites of overlap between the two? What did the United States (and the world) lose on that day in 1963? What did Elena lose?

3. What can you infer from this essay about the lives of Puerto Rican immigrants? In paragraph 1, Cofer refers obliquely to "whatever they were currently enduring." What specific problems might she be referring to? What does she gain by leaving this ambiguous?

4. In paragraph 11, the narrator compares her parents' dreams and memories to "fairy tales." What is the significance of this analogy?

5. Elena feels like she has become part of the family of the Jewish couple into whose kitchen window she can see. She also keeps the southern boy, Eugene, company from her fire escape (without his knowledge). Similarly, Elena's parents' "talk sadly about the young widow [of the Irish American Kennedy] and her two children, as if they were family" (paragraph 37). What is the significance of all these virtual families whose members cannot, at least within the scope of the essay, connect in any more tangible way? What are the forces that keep the "family" members of different ethnicities separate? What in the essay brings them together, and suggests that in some figurative sense they are all really part of the same family after all?

Essay Questions

1. In paragraph 11, Elena reveals that her mother has reacted strongly to the onset of her menstrual cycle. Similarly, Maxine's mother, in "No Name Woman," takes the same event in her daughter's life cycle as an opportunity to teach her some lessons crucial to an adult woman. Write an essay comparing and contrasting these two female coming-of-age stories. What does each narrator learn upon becoming a woman?

2. Write an essay exploring the relationship between public events and the private lives that usually don't get recorded in the history books. What noteworthy public events have occurred during your lifetime? Where were you when they occurred? How did they affect you, then and since? To what extent did these events capture the essence of life for you at the time of the occurrence?

No Name Woman

Maxine Hong Kingston

"No Name Woman" is the first chapter of Maxine Hong Kingston's (b. 1949) autobiographical narrative, The Woman Warrior: Memoirs of a Childhood among Ghosts *(1976), which won the prestigious National Book Critics Circle Award for nonfiction. From this piece it is clear that Kingston writes to make sense of her place in the world. As she has said, "I have no idea how people who don't write endure their lives."*

Born in Stockton, California to immigrant Chinese parents, Kingston uses her writing to explore her identity, not quite Chinese but not quite American either. She fleshes out the bare-bones narratives her mother gives her, and although none of the versions they individually offer might be factual, taken collectively the stories are profoundly true.

As you read along, pay special attention to the shifts in this narrative: the shifts in time, the shifts from one version of the story to another, the shifts from insights about the no-name aunt to insights about Maxine. At the heart of her writing is the belief that one cannot understand the present without first understanding the past, and the structure of her essay bears out this belief.

The Woman Warrior *was followed in 1980 by* China Men, *an autobiographical work that takes up the lives of the men in her family, and later by the novel* Tripmaster Monkey: His Fake Book *(1989). Kingston currently teaches literature and creative writing at the University of California at Berkeley.*

"You must not tell anyone," my mother said, "what I am about to tell you. In China your father had a sister who killed herself. She jumped into the family well. We say that your father has all brothers because it is as if she had never been born.

"In 1924 just a few days after our village celebrated seventeen hurry-up weddings—to make sure that every young man who went 'out on the road' would responsibly come home—your father and his brothers and your grandfather and his brothers and your aunt's new husband sailed for America, the Gold Mountain. It was your grandfather's last trip. Those lucky enough to get contracts waved good-bye from the decks. They fed and guarded the stowaways and helped them off in Cuba, New York, Bali, Hawaii. 'We'll meet in California next year,' they said. All of them sent money home.

"I remember looking at your aunt one day when she and I were dressing; I had not noticed before that she had such a protruding melon of a stomach. But I did not think, 'She's pregnant,' until she began to look like other pregnant women, her shirt pulling and the white tops of her black pants showing. She could not have been pregnant, you see, because her husband had been gone for years. No one said anything.

We did not discuss it. In early summer she was ready to have the child, long after the time when it could have been possible.

"The village had also been counting. On the night the baby was to be born the villagers raided our house. Some were crying. Like a great saw, teeth strung with lights, files of people walked zigzag across our land, tearing the rice. Their lanterns doubled in the disturbed black water, which drained away through the broken bunds. As the villagers closed in, we could see that some of them, probably men and women we knew well, wore white masks. The people with long hair hung it over their faces. Women with short hair made it stand up on end. Some had tied white bands around their foreheads, arms, and legs.

5   "At first they threw mud and rocks at the house. Then they threw eggs and began slaughtering our stock. We could hear the animals scream their deaths—the roosters, the pigs, a last great roar from the ox. Familiar wild heads flared in our night windows; the villagers encircled us. Some of the faces stopped to peer at us, their eyes rushing like searchlights. The hands flattened against the panes, framed heads, and left red prints.

"The villagers broke in the front and the back doors at the same time, even though we had not locked the doors against them. Their knives dripped with the blood of our animals. They smeared blood on the doors and walls. One woman swung a chicken, whose throat she had slit, splattering blood in red arcs about her. We stood together in the middle of our house, in the family hall with the pictures and tables of the ancestors around us, and looked straight ahead.

"At that time the house had only two wings. When the men came back we would build two more to enclose our courtyard and a third one to begin a second courtyard. The villagers pushed through both wings, even your grandparents' rooms, to find your aunt's, which was also mine until the men returned. From this room a new wing for one of the younger families would grow. They ripped up her clothes and shoes and broke her combs, grinding them underfoot. They tore her work from the loom. They scattered the cooking fire and rolled the new weaving in it. We could hear them in the kitchen breaking our bowls and banging the pots. They overturned the great waist-high earthenware jugs; duck eggs, pickled fruits, vegetables burst out and mixed in acrid torrents. The old woman from the next field swept a broom through the air and loosed the spirits-of-the-broom over our heads. 'Pig.' 'Ghost.' 'Pig,' they sobbed and scolded while they ruined our house.

"When they left, they took sugar and oranges to bless themselves. They cut pieces from the dead animals. Some of them took bowls that were not broken and clothes that were not torn. Afterward we swept up the rice and sewed it back up into sacks. But the smells from the spilled preserves lasted. Your aunt gave birth in the pigsty that night. The next morning when I went up for the water, I found her and the baby plugging up the family well.

"Don't let your father know that I told you. He denies her. Now that you have started to menstruate, what happened to her could happen to you. Don't humiliate us. You wouldn't like to be forgotten as if you had never been born. The villagers are watchful."

Whenever she had to warn us about life, my mother told stories[10] that ran like this one, a story to grow up on. She tested our strength to establish realities. Those in the emigrant generations who could not reassert brute survival died young and far from home. Those of us in the first American generations have had to figure out how the invisible world the emigrants built around our childhoods fit in solid America.

The emigrants confused the gods by diverting their curses, misleading them with crooked streets and false names. They must try to confuse their offspring as well, who, I suppose, threaten them in similar ways—always trying to get things straight, always trying to name the unspeakable. The Chinese I know hide their names; sojourners take new names when their lives change and guard their real names with silence.

Chinese Americans, when you try to understand what things in you are Chinese, how do you separate what is peculiar to childhood, to poverty, insanities, one family, your mother who marked your growing with stories, from what is Chinese? What is Chinese tradition and what is the movies?

If I want to learn what clothes my aunt wore, whether flashy or ordinary, I would have to begin, "Remember Father's drowned-in-the-well sister?" I cannot ask that. My mother has told me once and for all the useful parts. She will add nothing unless powered by Necessity, a riverbank that guides her life. She plants vegetable gardens rather than lawns; she carries the odd-shaped tomatoes home from the fields and eats food left for the gods.

Whenever we did frivolous things, we used up energy; we flew high kites. We children came up off the ground over the melting cones our parents brought home from work and the American movie on New Year's Day—*Oh, You Beautiful Doll* with Betty Grable one year, and *She Wore a Yellow Ribbon* with John Wayne another year. After the one carnival ride each, we paid in guilt; our tired father counted his change on the dark walk home.

Adultery is extravagance. Could people who hatch their own[15] chicks and eat the embryos and the heads for delicacies and boil the feet in vinegar for party food, leaving only the gravel, eating even the gizzard lining—could such people engender a prodigal aunt? To be a woman, to have a daughter in starvation time was a waste enough. My aunt could not have been the lone romantic who gave up everything for sex. Women in the old China did not choose. Some man had commanded her to lie with him and be his secret evil. I wonder whether he masked himself when he joined the raid on her family.

Perhaps she encountered him in the fields or on the mountain where the daughters-in-law collected fuel. Or perhaps he first noticed her in the marketplace. He was not a stranger because the village housed no strangers. She had to have dealings with him other than sex. Perhaps he worked an adjoining field, or he sold her the cloth for the dress she sewed and wore. His demand must have surprised, then terrified her. She obeyed him; she always did as she was told.

When the family found a young man in the next village to be her husband, she stood tractably beside the best rooster, his proxy, and promised before they met that she would be his forever. She was lucky that he was her age and she would be the first wife, an advantage secure now. The night she first saw him, he had sex with her. Then he left for America. She had almost forgotten what he looked like. When she tried to envision him, she only saw the black and white face in the group photograph the men had had taken before leaving.

The other man was not, after all, much different from her husband. They both gave orders: she followed. "If you tell your family, I'll beat you. I'll kill you. Be here again next week." No one talked sex, ever. And she might have separated the rapes from the rest of living if only she did not have to buy her oil from him or gather wood in the same forest. I want her fear to have lasted just as long as rape lasted so that the fear could have been contained. No drawn-out fear. But women at sex hazarded birth and hence lifetimes. The fear did not stop but permeated everywhere. She told the man, "I think I'm pregnant." He organized the raid against her.

On nights when my mother and father talked about their life back home, sometimes they mentioned an "outcast table" whose business they still seemed to be settling, their voices tight. In a commensal tradition, where food is precious, the powerful older people made wrongdoers eat alone. Instead of letting them start separate new lives like the Japanese, who could become samurais and geishas, the Chinese family, faces averted but eyes glowering sideways, hung on to the offenders and fed them leftovers. My aunt must have lived in the same house as my parents and eaten at an outcast table. My mother spoke about the raid as if she had seen it, when she and my aunt, a daughter-in-law to a different household, should not have been living together at all. Daughters-in-law lived with their husbands' parents, not their own; a synonym for marriage in Chinese is "taking a daughter-in-law." Her husband's parents could have sold her, mortgaged her, stoned her. But they had sent her back to her own mother and father, a mysterious act hinting at disgraces not told me. Perhaps they had thrown her out to deflect the avengers.

20 She was the only daughter; her four brothers went with her father, husband, and uncles "out on the road" and for some years became

western men. When the goods were divided among the family, three of the brothers took land, and the youngest, my father, chose an education. After my grandparents gave their daughter away to her husband's family, they had dispensed all the adventure and all the property. They expected her alone to keep the traditional ways, which her brothers, now among the barbarians, could fumble without detection. The heavy, deep-rooted women were to maintain the past against the flood, safe for returning. But the rare urge west had fixed upon our family, and so my aunt crossed boundaries not delineated in space.

The work of preservation demands that the feelings playing about in one's guts not be turned into action. Just watch their passing like cherry blossoms. But perhaps my aunt, my forerunner, caught in a slow life, let dreams grow and fade and after some months or years went toward what persisted. Fear at the enormities of the forbidden kept her desires delicate, wire and bone. She looked at a man because she liked the way the hair was tucked behind his ears, or she liked the question-mark of a long torso curving at the shoulder and straight at the hip. For warm eyes or a soft voice or a slow walk—that's all—a few hairs, a line, a brightness, a sound, a pace, she gave up family. She offered us up for a charm that vanished with tiredness, a pigtail that didn't toss when the wind died. Why, the wrong lighting could erase the dearest thing about him.

It could very well have been, however, that my aunt did not take subtle enjoyment of her friend, but, a wild woman, kept rollicking company. Imagining her free with sex doesn't fit, though. I don't know any women like that, or men either. Unless I see her life branching into mine, she gives me no ancestral help.

To sustain her being in love, she often worked at herself in the mirror, guessing at the colors and shapes that would interest him, changing them frequently in order to hit on the right combination. She wanted to look back.

On a farm near the sea, a woman who tended her appearance reaped a reputation for eccentricity. All the married women blunt-cut their hair in flaps about their ears or pulled it back in tight buns. No nonsense. Neither style blew easily into heart-catching tangles. And at their weddings they displayed themselves in their long hair for the last time. "It brushed the backs of my knees," my mother tells me. "It was braided, and even so, it brushed the backs of my knees."

At the mirror my aunt combed individuality into her bob. A bun[25] could have been contrived to escape into black streamers blowing in the wind or in quiet wisps about her face, but only the older women in our picture album wear buns. She brushed her hair back from her forehead, tucking the flaps behind her ears. She looped a piece of thread, knotted into a circle between her index fingers and thumbs, and ran the double strand across her forehead. When she closed her fingers as if she were making a pair of shadow geese bite, the string twisted together catching the little hairs. Then she pulled the thread away from her skin, ripping the hairs out neatly, her eyes watering from the needles of pain. Opening her fingers, she cleaned the thread, then rolled it along her hairline and the tops of the eyebrows. My mother did the same to me and my sisters and herself. I used to believe that the expression "caught by the short hairs" meant a captive held with a depilatory string. It especially hurt at the temples, but my mother said we were lucky we didn't have to have our feet bound when we were seven. Sisters used to sit on their beds and cry together, she said, as their mothers or their slave removed the bandages for a few minutes each night and let the blood gush back into their veins. I hope that the man my aunt loved appreciated a smooth brow, that he wasn't just a tits-and-ass man.

Once my aunt found a freckle on her chin, at a spot that the almanac said predestined her for unhappiness. She dug it out with a hot needle and washed the wound with peroxide.

More attention to her looks than these pullings of hairs and pickings at spots would have caused gossip among the villagers. They owned work clothes and good clothes, and they wore good clothes for feasting the new seasons. But since a woman combing her hair hexes beginnings, my aunt rarely found an occasion to look her best. Women looked like great sea snails—the corded wood, babies, and laundry they carried were the whorls on their backs. The Chinese did not admire a bent back; goddesses and warriors stood straight. Still there must have been a marvelous freeing of beauty when a worker laid down her burden and stretched and arched.

Such commonplace loveliness, however, was not enough for my aunt. She dreamed of a lover for the fifteen days of New Year's, the time for families to exchange visits, money, and food. She plied her secret comb. And sure enough she cursed the year, the family, the village, and herself.

Even as her hair lured her imminent lover, many other men looked at her. Uncles, cousins, nephews, brothers would have looked, too, had they been home between journeys. Perhaps they had already been restraining their curiosity, and they left, fearful that their glances, like a field of nesting birds, might be startled and caught. Poverty hurt, and that was their first reason for leaving. But another, final reason for leaving the crowded house was the never-said.

30   She may have been unusually beloved, the precious only daughter, spoiled and mirror-gazing because of the affection the family lavished on her. When her husband left, they welcomed the chance to take her back from the in-laws; she could live like the little daughter for just a while longer. There are stories that my grandfather was different from other people, "crazy ever since the little Jap bayoneted him in the

head." He used to put his naked penis on the dinner table, laughing. And one day he brought home a baby girl, wrapped up inside his brown western-style greatcoat. He had traded one of his sons, probably my father, the youngest, for her. My grandmother made him trade back. When he finally got a daughter of his own, he doted on her. They must have all loved her, except perhaps my father, the only brother who never went back to China, having once been traded for a girl.

Brothers and sisters, newly men and women, had to efface their sexual color and present plain miens. Disturbing hair and eyes, a smile like no other, threatened the ideal of five generations living under one roof. To focus blurs, people shouted face to face and yelled from room to room. The immigrants I know have loud voices, unmodulated to American tones even after years away from the village where they called their friendships out across the fields. I have not been able to stop my mother's screams in public libraries or over telephones. Walking erect (knees straight, toes pointed forward, not pigeon-toed, which is Chinese-feminine) and speaking in an inaudible voice, I have tried to turn myself American-feminine. Chinese communication was loud, public. Only sick people had to whisper. But at the dinner table, where the family members came nearest one another, no one could talk, not the outcasts nor any eaters. Every word that falls from the mouth is a coin lost. Silently they gave and accepted food with both hands. A preoccupied child who took his bowl with one hand got a sideways glare. A complete moment of total attention is due everyone alike. Children and lovers have no singularity here, but my aunt used a secret voice, a separate attentiveness.

She kept the man's name to herself throughout her labor and dying; she did not accuse him that he be punished with her. To save her inseminator's name she gave silent birth.

He may have been somebody in her own household, but intercourse with a man outside the family would have been no less abhorrent. All the village were kinsmen, and the titles shouted in loud country voices never let kinship be forgotten. Any man within visiting distance would have been neutralized as a lover—"brother," "younger brother," "older brother"—115 relationship titles. Parents researched birth charts probably not so much to assure good fortune as to circumvent incest in a population that has but one hundred surnames. Everybody has eight million relatives. How useless then sexual mannerisms, how dangerous.

As if it came from an atavism deeper than fear, I used to add "brother" silently to boys' names. It hexed the boys, who would or would not ask me to dance, and made them less scary and as familiar and deserving of benevolence as girls.

But, of course, I hexed myself also—no dates. I should have stood[35] up, both arms waving, and shouted out across libraries, "Hey, you!"

Love me back." I had no idea, though, how to make attraction selective, how to control its direction and magnitude. If I made myself American-pretty so that the five or six Chinese boys in the class fell in love with me, everyone else—the Caucasian, Negro, and Japanese boys—would too. Sisterliness, dignified and honorable, made much more sense.

Attraction eludes control so stubbornly that whole societies designed to organize relationships among people cannot keep order, not even when they bind people to one another from childhood and raise them together. Among the very poor and the wealthy, brothers married their adopted sisters, like doves. Our family allowed some romance, paying adult brides' prices and providing dowries so that their sons and daughters could marry strangers. Marriage promises to turn strangers into friendly relatives—a nation of siblings.

In the village structure, spirits shimmered among the live creatures, balanced and held in equilibrium by time and land. But one human being flaring up into violence could open up a black hole, a maelstrom that pulled in the sky. The frightened villagers, who depended on one another to maintain the real, went to my aunt to show her a personal, physical representation of the break she made in the "roundness." Misallying couples snapped off the future, which was to be embodied in true offspring. The villagers punished her for acting as if she could have a private life, secret and apart from them.

If my aunt had betrayed the family at a time of large grain yields and peace, when many boys were born, and wings were being built on many houses, perhaps she might have escaped such severe punishment. But the men—hungry, greedy, tired of planting in dry soil, cuckolded—had been forced to leave the village in order to send food-money home. There were ghost plagues, bandit plagues, wars with the Japanese, floods. My Chinese brother and sister had died of an unknown sickness. Adultery, perhaps only a mistake during good times, became a crime when the village needed food.

The round moon cakes and round doorways, the round tables of graduated size that fit one roundness inside another, round windows and rice bowls—these talismans had lost their power to warn this family of the law: A family must be whole, faithfully keeping the descent line by having sons to feed the old and the dead who in turn look after the family. The villagers came to show my aunt and lover-in-hiding a broken house. The villagers were speeding up the circling of events because she was too shortsighted to see that her infidelity had already harmed the village, that waves of consequences would return unpredictably, sometimes in disguise, as now, to hurt her. This roundness had to be made coin-sized so that she would see its circumference: Punish her at the birth of her baby. Awaken her to the inexorable. People who refused fatalism because they could invent small resources insisted on culpability. Deny accidents and wrest fault from the stars.

After the villagers left, their lanterns now scattering in various di-₄₀ rections toward home, the family broke their silence and cursed her. "Aiaa, we're going to die. Death is coming. Death is coming. Look what you've done. You've killed us. Ghost! Dead Ghost! Ghost! You've never been born." She ran out into the fields, far enough from the house so that she could no longer hear their voices, and pressed herself against the earth, her own land no more. When she felt the birth coming, she thought that she had been hurt. Her body seized together. "They've hurt me too much," she thought. "This is gall, and it will kill me." With forehead and knees against the earth, her body convulsed and then relaxed. She turned on her back, lay on the ground. The black well of sky and stars went out and out forever; her body and her complexity seemed to disappear. She was one of the stars, a bright dot in blackness, without home, without a companion, in eternal cold and silence. An agoraphobia rose in her, speeding higher and higher, bigger and bigger; she would not be able to contain it; there would be no end to fear.

Flayed, unprotected against space, she felt pain return, focusing her body. This pain chilled her—a cold, steady kind of surface pain. Inside, spasmodically, the other pain, the pain of the child, heated her. For hours she lay on the ground, alternately body and space. Sometimes a vision of normal comfort obliterated reality: She saw the family in the evening gambling at the dinner table, the young people massaging their elders' backs. She saw them congratulating one another, high joy on the mornings the rice shoots came up. When these pictures burst, the stars drew yet further apart. Black space opened.

She got to her feet to fight better and remembered that old-fashioned women gave birth in their pigsties to fool the jealous, pain-dealing gods, who do not snatch piglets. Before the next spasms could stop her, she ran to the pigsty, each step a rushing out into emptiness. She climbed over the fence and knelt in the dirt. It was good to have a fence enclosing her, a tribal person alone.

Laboring, this woman who had carried her child as a foreign growth that sickened her every day, expelled it at last. She reached down to touch the hot, wet, moving mass, surely smaller than anything human, and could feel that it was human after all—fingers, toes, nails, nose. She pulled it up on to her belly, and it lay curled there, butt in the air, feet precisely tucked one under the other. She opened her loose shirt and buttoned the child inside. After resting, it squirmed and thrashed and she pushed it up to her breast. It turned its head this way and that until it found her nipple. There, it made little snuffling noises. She clenched her teeth at its preciousness, lovely as a young calf, a piglet, a little dog.

She may have gone to the pigsty as a last act of responsibility: She would protect this child as she had protected its father. It would look after her soul, leaving supplies on her grave. But how would this tiny child without family find her grave when there would be no marker for her anywhere, neither in the earth nor the family hall? No one would give her a family hall name. She had taken the child with her into the wastes. At its birth the two of them had felt the same raw pain of separation, a wound that only the family pressing tight could close. A child with no descent line would not soften her life but only trail after her, ghostlike, begging her to give it purpose. At dawn the villagers on their way to the fields would stand around the fence and look.

45   Full of milk, the little ghost slept. When it awoke, she hardened her breasts against the milk that crying loosens. Toward morning she picked up the baby and walked to the well.

Carrying the baby to the well shows loving. Otherwise abandon it. Turn its face into the mud. Mothers who love their children take them along. It was probably a girl; there is some hope of forgiveness for boys.

"Don't tell anyone you had an aunt. Your father does not want to hear her name. She has never been born." I have believed that sex was unspeakable and words so strong and fathers so frail that "aunt" would do my father mysterious harm. I have thought that my family, having settled among immigrants who had also been their neighbors in the ancestral land, needed to clean their name, and a wrong word would incite the kinspeople even here. But there is more to this silence: They want me to participate in her punishment. And I have.

In the twenty years since I heard this story I have not asked for details nor said my aunt's name; I do not know it. People who comfort the dead can also chase after them to hurt them further—a reverse ancestor worship. The real punishment was not the raid swiftly inflicted by the villagers, but the family's deliberately forgetting her. Her betrayal so maddened them, they saw to it that she would suffer forever, even after death. Always hungry, always needing, she would have to beg food from other ghosts, snatch and steal it from those whose living descendants give them gifts. She would have to fight the ghosts massed at crossroads for the buns a few thoughtful citizens leave to decoy her away from village and home so that the ancestral spirits could feast unharassed. At peace, they could act like gods, not ghosts, their descent lines providing them with paper suits and dresses, spirit money, paper houses, paper automobiles, chicken, meat, and rice into eternity— essences delivered up in smoke and flames, steam and incense rising from each rice bowl. In an attempt to make the Chinese care for people outside the family, Chairman Mao encourages us now to give our paper replicas to the spirits of outstanding soldiers and workers, no matter whose ancestors they may be. My aunt remains forever hungry. Goods are not distributed evenly among the dead.

My aunt haunts me—her ghost drawn to me because now, after fifty years of neglect, I alone devote pages of paper to her, though not origamied into houses and clothes. I do not think she always means me well. I am telling on her, and she was a spite suicide, drowning herself in the drinking water. The Chinese are always very frightened of the drowned one, whose weeping ghost, wet hair hanging and skin bloated, waits silently by the water to pull down a substitute.

Additional Rhetorical Strategies

Description (paragraphs 4, 5, 21); Cause and Effect (paragraphs 9, 38–39); Example (throughout).

Discussion Questions

1. In a quest to understand her aunt, and herself, Maxine creates several different versions of the story of "No Name Woman." Identify each version. Then determine the nature of the "ancestral help" (paragraph 22) Maxine gleans from each version. At the end of the story, Kingston suggests that the aunt functions as a double for Maxine, who fears being pulled down as a "substitute." Doubles function in fiction to illuminate the main character, both by comparison and contrast. Discuss the insights we gain about Maxine, and the insights she gains about herself, thanks to this story about her aunt.

2. Maxine's mother has a very different reason for telling her version of the nameless aunt's story. What is her motive? Why does she tell the story at this particular time, to this particular audience, and in this particular way? Is it accurate to characterize Maxine's mother's version as the "truth," in opposition to Maxine's versions, which are speculative? Why or why not?

3. Examine the importance of language, and more specifically naming, in this piece. What is the significance of the fact that the aunt is nameless? of the fact that the aunt protects the name of the father of her child? of the fact that she will never have a "family hall name" (paragraph 44)? What is the significance of the fact that the "population . . . has but one hundred surnames" (paragraph 33)? Why do the immigrant Chinese take "false names," and why are their children always trying to "name the unspeakable" (paragraph 11)? How might a consideration of the project of writing "No Name Woman" itself enhance your discussion of these issues?

4. "No Name Woman" is the first chapter of Kingston's autobiography. Autobiographies are generally recognized as nonfiction. How can you reconcile this genre with the presence of such things as ghosts and multiple speculative versions of events in "No Name Woman"? How would you characterize Kingston's project, and the kind of truth she seeks to establish about her own life?

Essay Questions

1. Compare and contrast "No Name Woman" and "More Than Just a Shrine" (p. 97), in terms of their authors' relations to their ancestors. In neither case is the identification uncomplicated. Explore Kingston's and Gordon's mixed feelings towards the ghosts of their ancestors.

2. In an analytical essay, discuss the significance of circles in "No Name Woman." Be sure to look not only at literal circles (and their symbolic significances) but also at circular patterns in the structure of the essay itself. How does this examination of circles enrich your reading of the essay as a whole?

Thematic Pair: Giving in to Pressure

▲▼ Salvation

Langston Hughes

Langston Hughes (1902–1967) was a key figure in the Harlem Renaissance, a time of unprecedented artistic and intellectual achievement among black Americans. Dubbed "the Poet Laureate of Harlem" by Carl Van Vechten, Hughes was also an innovative and prolific fiction writer, dramatist, journalist, translator, playwright, and autobiographer. His writing helped to bring the experiences, culture, and language of African Americans into the mainstream of American literature.

Hughes was sometimes criticized for depicting blacks in a less than ideal light. He answered these criticisms in this way: "Certainly, I personally knew very few people anywhere who were wholly beautiful and wholly good. . . . Anyway, I didn't know the upper-class Negroes well enough to write much about them. I only knew the people I had grown up with, and they weren't people whose shoes always shined, who had been to Harvard, or who had heard of Bach. But they seemed to me good people too." Hughes was the first black American to earn his living solely from his writing and public lectures. Part of the reason for his success was the love and acceptance he received from average black people.

The following essay, "Salvation," is taken from one of his two autobiographies, The Big Sea *(1940).*

I was saved from sin when I was going on thirteen. But not really saved. It happened like this. There was a big revival at my Auntie Reed's church. Every night for weeks there had been much preaching, singing, praying, and shouting, and some very hardened sinners had been brought to Christ, and the membership of the church had grown by leaps and bounds. Then just before the revival ended, they held a special meeting for children, "to bring the young lambs to the fold." My aunt spoke of it for days ahead. That night I was escorted to the front row and placed on the mourners' bench with all the other young sinners, who had not yet been brought to Jesus.

My aunt told me that when you were saved you saw a light, and something happened to you inside! She said you could see and hear and feel Jesus in your soul. I believed her. I had heard a great many old people say the same thing and it seemed to me they ought to know. So I sat there calmly in the hot, crowded church, waiting for Jesus to come to me.

The preacher preached a wonderful rhythmical sermon, all moans and shouts and lonely cries and dire pictures of hell, and then he sang a song about the ninety and nine safe in the fold, but one little lamb was left out in the cold. Then he said: "Won't you come? Won't you come to Jesus? Young lambs, won't you come?" And he held out his arms to all us young sinners there on the mourners' bench. And the little girls cried. And some of them jumped up and went to Jesus right away. But most of us just sat there.

A great many old people came and knelt around us and prayed, old women with jet-black faces and braided hair, old men with work-gnarled hands. And the church sang a song about the lower lights are burning, some poor sinners to be saved. And the whole building rocked with prayer and song.

Still I kept waiting to *see* Jesus.   5

Finally all the young people had gone to the altar and were saved, but one boy and me. He was a rounder's son named Westley. Westley and I were surrounded by sisters and deacons praying. It was very hot in the church, and getting late now. Finally Westley said to me in a whisper: "God damn! I'm tired o' sitting here. Let's get up and be saved." So he got up and was saved.

Then I was left all alone on the mourners' bench. My aunt came and knelt at my knees and cried, while prayers and song swirled all around me in the little church. The whole congregation prayed for me alone, in a mighty wail of moans and voices. And I kept waiting serenely for Jesus, waiting, waiting—but he didn't come. I wanted to see him, but nothing happened to me. Nothing! I wanted something to happen to me, but nothing happened.

I heard the songs and the minister saying: "Why don't you come? My dear child, why don't you come to Jesus? Jesus is waiting for you. He wants you. Why don't you come? Sister Reed, what is this child's name?"

"Langston," my aunt sobbed.

"Langston, why don't you come? Why don't you come and be 10 saved? Oh, Lamb of God! Why don't you come?"

Now it was really getting late. I began to be ashamed of myself, holding everything up so long. I began to wonder what God thought about Westley, who certainly hadn't seen Jesus either, but who was now sitting proudly on the platform, swinging his knickerbockered legs and grinning down at me, surrounded by deacons and old women on their knees praying. God had not struck Westley dead for taking his name in vain or for lying in the temple. So I decided that maybe to save further trouble, I'd better lie, too, and say that Jesus had come, and get up and be saved.

So I got up.

Suddenly the whole room broke into a sea of shouting, as they saw me rise. Waves of rejoicing swept the place. Women leaped in the air. My aunt threw her arms around me. The minister took me by the hand and led me to the platform.

When things quieted down, in a hushed silence, punctuated by a few ecstatic "Amens," all the new young lambs were blessed in the name of God. Then joyous singing filled the room.

15   That night, for the first time in my life but one—for I was a big boy twelve years old—I cried. I cried, in bed alone, and couldn't stop. I buried my head under the quilts, but my aunt heard me. She woke up and told my uncle I was crying because the Holy Ghost had come into my life, and because I had seen Jesus. But I was really crying because I couldn't bear to tell her that I had lied, that I had deceived everybody in the church, that I hadn't seen Jesus, and that now I didn't believe there was a Jesus anymore, since he didn't come to help me.

Additional Rhetorical Strategies

Cause and Effect (paragraph 11); Analogy (paragraph 13).

Discussion Questions

1. What is the status of the title of this piece? If we are to take it ironically, where does the gap that creates irony lie? What is the usual definition of the word "Salvation"? What, if anything, is the young protagonist actually saved from?
2. What is the pivotal event that the title and the first sentence seem to anticipate? What is the actual pivotal event that is narrated in the course of the essay?
3. How does the character of Westley function in this story? One way to think about this question is to imagine the story without him. What role does he play in the resolution of the narrator's dilemma? How does he help the reader understand the main character better?
4. Analyze the metaphor Hughes employs in paragraph 13. What is the effect of comparing the church to an ocean? What other metaphorical language do you find in this essay, and what effect does it have?

Essay Questions

1. Who is the narrator of this piece? Is it the young Langston Hughes or the adult Langston Hughes or a mixture of the two? Give specific examples based on a close reading of the diction and syntax of this piece to support your answer. What difference would the age of the narrator make to an interpretation of this story?
2. Hughes writes in paragraph 7, "I kept waiting serenely for Jesus." His faith is so strong at this point in the essay that it brings him perfect serenity. By the end of the essay he is crying into his pillow, and it is clear that he no longer has either faith or serenity. Write an essay about what he has gained in exchange for his childhood faith. Given the brevity of Hughes' essay, you may have to draw upon your own knowledge about the trade-offs we experience as we mature, and what is lost and gained in the process.

▲▼ Shooting an Elephant

George Orwell

One of the leading British novelists and essayists of the twentieth century,
George Orwell (1903–1950) was deeply affected by the social and political
conditions of his time. His works are particularly concerned with ques-
tions of human freedom and justice. His best known novels, Animal
Farm *(1946) and* Nineteen Eighty-Four *(1949), depict totalitarian*
worlds that bear a frightening resemblance to our own; for this reason, his
novels are still relevant, and still widely read today.

Of course, he would not still be read today if his prose did not stand
the test of time. In one of his most famous essays, "Politics and the En-
glish Language," Orwell argues that "the fight against bad English is not
frivolous and is not the exclusive concern of professional writers." To
write clearly it is necessary to think clearly, and "to think clearly is a nec-
essary first step towards political regeneration." It is plain that Orwell's
political goals and his standards for writing are interconnected. And in his
own writing he adheres to, indeed exceeds, the standards he sets for others.
In another essay, entitled "Why I Write," Orwell writes that "Good prose
is like a windowpane."

In "Shooting an Elephant," Orwell tells about an incident he wit-
nessed while serving as a police officer in Burma. As you read the essay
that follows, note the clarity of Orwell's prose, which opens a window on
the scene he describes.

In Moulmein, in Lower Burma, I was hated by large numbers of people—the only time in my life that I have been important enough for
this to happen to me. I was subdivisional police officer of the town,
and in an aimless, petty kind of way anti European feeling was very
bitter. No one had the guts to raise a riot, but if a European woman
went through the bazaars alone somebody would probably spit betel
juice over her dress. As a police officer I was an obvious target and was
baited whenever it seemed safe to do so. When a nimble Burman
tripped me up on the football field and the referee (another Burman)
looked the other way, the crowd yelled with hideous laughter. This
happened more than once. In the end the sneering yellow faces of
young men that met me everywhere, the insults hooted after me when I
was at a safe distance, got badly on my nerves. The young Buddhist
priests were the worst of all. There were several thousand of them in
the town and none of them seemed to have anything to do except stand
on street corners and jeer at Europeans.

All this was perplexing and upsetting. For at that time I had already made up my mind that imperialism was an evil thing and the
sooner I chucked up my job and got out of it the better. Theoretically—
and secretly, of course—I was all for the Burmese and all against the
oppressors, the British. As for the job I was doing, I hated it more

bitterly than I can perhaps make clear. In a job like that you see the dirty work of Empire at close quarters. The wretched prisoners huddling in the stinking cages of the lockups, the grey, cowed faces of the long-term convicts, the scarred buttocks of the men who had been flogged with bamboos—all these oppressed me with an intolerable sense of guilt. But I could get nothing into perspective. I was young and ill-educated and I had had to think out my problems in the utter silence that is imposed on every Englishman in the East. I did not even know that the British Empire is dying, still less did I know that it is a great deal better than the younger empires that are going to supplant it. All I knew was that I was stuck between my hatred of the empire I served and my rage against the evil-spirited little beasts who tried to make my job impossible. With one part of my mind I thought of the British Raj[1] as an unbreakable tyranny, as something clamped down, in *saecula saeculorum*,[2] upon the will of prostrate peoples; with another part I thought that the greatest joy in the world would be to drive a bayonet into a Buddhist priest's guts. Feelings like these are the normal by-products of imperialism; ask any Anglo-Indian official, if you can catch him off duty.

One day something happened which in a roundabout way was enlightening. It was a tiny incident in itself, but it gave me a better glimpse than I had had before of the real nature of imperialism—the real motives for which despotic governments act. Early one morning the subinspector at a police station the other end of town rang me up on the phone and said that an elephant was ravaging the bazaar. Would I please come and do something about it? I did not know what I could do, but I wanted to see what was happening and I got on to a pony and started out. I took my rifle, an old .44 Winchester and much too small to kill an elephant, but I thought the noise might be useful *in terrorem*.[3] Various Burmans stopped me on the way and told me about the elephant's doings. It was not, of course, a wild elephant, but a tame one which had gone "must."[4] It had been chained up, as tame elephants always are when their attack of "must" is due, but on the previous night it had broken its chain and escaped. Its mahout,[5] the only person who could manage it when it was in that state, had set out in pursuit, but had taken the wrong direction and was now twelve hours' journey away, and in the morning the elephant had suddenly reappeared in the town. The Burmese population had no weapons and were quite helpless against it.

---

[1]Raj: The British administration
[2]saecula saeculorum: Forever and ever (Latin)
[3]In terrorem: as a warning (Latin)
[4]"Must": Sexual arousal
[5]mahout: Keeper (Hindi)

It had already destroyed somebody's bamboo hut, killed a cow, and raided some fruit stalls and devoured the stock; also it had met the municipal rubbish van and, when the driver jumped out and took to his heels, had turned the van over and inflicted violences upon it.

The Burmese subinspector and some Indian constables were waiting for me in the quarter where the elephant had been seen. It was a very poor quarter, a labyrinth of squalid bamboo huts, thatched with palm-leaf, winding all over a steep hillside. I remember that it was a cloudy, stuffy morning at the beginning of the rains. We began questioning the people as to where the elephant had gone and, as usual, failed to get any definite information. That is invariably the case in the East; a story always sounds clear enough at a distance, but the nearer you get to the scene of events the vaguer it becomes. Some of the people said that the elephant had gone in one direction, some said that he had gone in another, some professed not even to have heard of any elephant. I had almost made up my mind that the whole story was a pack of lies, when we heard yells a little distance away. There was a loud, scandalized cry of "Go away, child! Go away this instant!" and an old woman with a switch in her hand came round the corner of a hut, violently shooing away a crowd of naked children. Some more women followed, clicking their tongues and exclaiming; evidently there was something that the children ought not to have seen. I rounded the hut and saw a man's dead body sprawling in the mud. He was an Indian, a black Dravidian[6] coolie, almost naked, and he could not have been dead many minutes. The people said that the elephant had come suddenly upon him round the corner of the hut, caught him with its trunk, put its foot on his back, and ground him into the earth. This was the rainy season and the ground was soft, and his face had scored a trench a foot deep and a couple of yards long. He was lying on his belly with arms crucified and head sharply twisted to one side. His face was coated with mud, the eyes wide open, the teeth bared and grinning with an expression of unendurable agony. (Never tell me, by the way, that the dead look peaceful. Most of the corpses I have seen looked devilish.) The friction of the great beast's foot had stripped the skin from his back as neatly as one skins a rabbit. As soon as I saw the dead man I sent an orderly to a friend's house nearby to borrow an elephant rifle. I had already sent back the pony, not wanting it to go mad with fright and throw me if it smelled the elephant.

The orderly came back in a few minutes with a rifle and five cartridges, and meanwhile some Burmans had arrived and told us that the elephant was in the paddy fields below, only a few hundred yards away. As I started forward practically the whole population of the

---

[6]Dravidian: A large Indian group

quarter flocked out of the houses and followed me. They had seen the rifle and were all shouting excitedly that I was going to shoot the elephant. They had not shown much interest in the elephant when he was merely ravaging their homes, but it was different now that he was going to be shot. It was a bit of fun to them, as it would be to an English crowd; besides they wanted the meat. It made me vaguely uneasy. I had no intention of shooting the elephant—I had merely sent for the rifle to defend myself if necessary—and it is always unnerving to have a crowd following you. I marched down the hill, looking and feeling a fool, with the rifle over my shoulder and an ever-growing army of people jostling at my heels. At the bottom, when you got away from the huts, there was a metalled road and beyond that a miry waste of paddy fields a thousand yards across, not yet ploughed but soggy from the first rains and dotted with coarse grass. The elephant was standing eight yards from the road, his left side toward us. He took not the slightest notice of the crowd's approach. He was tearing up bunches of grass, beating them against his knees to clean them and stuffing them into his mouth.

I had halted on the road. As soon as I saw the elephant I knew with perfect certainty that I ought not to shoot him. It is a serious matter to shoot a working elephant—it is comparable to destroying a huge and costly piece of machinery—and obviously one ought not to do it if it can possibly be avoided. And at that distance, peacefully eating, the elephant looked no more dangerous than a cow. I thought then and I think now that his attack of "must" was already passing off; in which case he would merely wander harmlessly about until the mahout came back and caught him. Moreover, I did not in the least want to shoot him. I decided that I would watch him for a little while to make sure that he did not turn savage again, and then go home.

But at that moment, I glanced round at the crowd that had followed me. It was an immense crowd, two thousand at the least and growing every minute. It blocked the road for a long distance on either side. I looked at the sea of yellow faces above the garish clothes—faces all happy and excited over this bit of fun, all certain that the elephant was going to be shot. They were watching me as they would watch a conjuror about to perform a trick. They did not like me, but with the magical rifle in my hands I was momentarily worth watching. And suddenly I realized that I should have to shoot the elephant after all: The people expected it of me and I had got to do it; I could feel their two thousand wills pressing me forward, irresistibly. And it was at this moment, as I stood there with the rifle in my hands, that I first grasped the hollowness, the futility of the white man's dominion in the East. Here was I, the white man with his gun, standing in front of the unarmed native crowd—seemingly the leading actor of the piece; but in reality I was only an absurd puppet pushed to and fro by the will of those yellow faces behind. I perceived in this moment that when the white man turns tyrant it is his own freedom that he destroys. He becomes a sort of hollow, posing dummy, the conventionalized figure of a sahib. For it is the condition of his rule that he shall spend his life in trying to impress the "natives," and so in every crisis he has got to do what the "natives" expect of him. He wears a mask, and his face grows to fit it. I had got to shoot the elephant. I had committed myself to doing it when I sent for the rifle. A sahib has got to act like a sahib; he has got to appear resolute, to know his own mind and do definite things. To come all that way, rifle in hand, with two thousand people marching at my heels, and then to trail feebly away, having done nothing—no, that was impossible. The crowd would laugh at me. And my whole life, every white man's life in the East, was one long struggle not to be laughed at.

But I did not want to shoot the elephant. I watched him beating his bunch of grass against his knees, with that preoccupied grandmotherly air that elephants have. It seemed to me that it would be murder to shoot him. At that age I was not squeamish about killing animals, but I had never shot an elephant and never wanted to. (Somehow it always seems worse to kill a *large* animal.) Besides, there was the beast's owner to be considered. Alive, the elephant was worth at least a hundred pounds; dead, he would only be worth the value of his tusks, five pounds, possibly. But I had got to act quickly. I turned to some experienced-looking Burmans who had been there when we arrived, and asked them how the elephant had been behaving. They all said the same thing: He took no notice of you if you left him alone, but he might charge if you went too close to him.

It was perfectly clear to me what I ought to do. I ought to walk up to within, say, twenty-five yards of the elephant and test his behavior. If he charged, I could shoot; if he took no notice of me, it would be safe to leave him until the mahout came back. But also I knew that I was going to do no such thing. I was a poor shot with a rifle and the ground was soft mud into which one would sink at every step. If the elephant charged and I missed him, I should have about as much chance as a toad under a steamroller. But even then I was not thinking particularly of my own skin, only of the watchful yellow faces behind. For at that moment, with the crowd watching me, I was not afraid in the ordinary sense, as I would have been if I had been alone. A white man mustn't be frightened in front of "natives"; and so, in general, he isn't frightened. The sole thought in my mind was that if anything went wrong those two thousand Burmans would see me pursued, caught, trampled on, and reduced to a grinning corpse like that Indian up the hill. And if that happened it was quite probable that some of them would laugh. That would never do. There was only one alternative. I shoved the cartridges into the magazine and lay down on the road to get a better aim.

10   The crowd grew very still, and a deep, low, happy sigh, as of people who see the theatre curtain go up at last, breathed from innumerable throats. They were going to have their bit of fun after all. The rifle was a beautiful German thing with cross-hair sights. I did not then know that in shooting an elephant one would shoot to cut an imaginary bar running from ear-hole to ear-hole. I ought, therefore, as the elephant was sideways on, to have aimed straight at his ear-hole; actually I aimed several inches in front of this, thinking the brain would be further forward.

When I pulled the trigger I did not hear the bang or feel the kick—one never does when a shot goes home—but I heard the devilish roar of glee that went up from the crowd. In that instant, in too short a time, one would have thought, even for the bullet to get there, a mysterious, terrible change had come over the elephant. He neither stirred nor fell, but every line of his body had altered. He looked suddenly stricken, shrunken, immensely old, as though the frightful impact of the bullet had paralyzed him without knocking him down. At last, after what seemed a long time—it might have been five seconds, I dare say—he sagged flabbily to his knees. His mouth slobbered. An enormous senility seemed to have settled upon him. One could have imagined him thousands of years old. I fired again into the same spot. At the second shot he did not collapse but climbed with desperate slowness to his feet and stood weakly upright, with legs sagging and head drooping. I fired a third time. That was the shot that did it for him. You could see the agony of it jolt his whole body and knock the last remnant of strength from his legs. But in falling he seemed for a moment to rise, for as his hind legs collapsed beneath him he seemed to toward upward like a huge rock toppling, his trunk reaching skywards like a tree. He trumpeted, for the first and only time. And then down he came, his belly towards me, with a crash that seemed to shake the ground even where I lay.

I got up. The Burmans were already racing past me across the mud. It was obvious that the elephant would never rise again, but he was not dead. He was breathing very rhythmically with long rattling gasps, his great mound of a side painfully rising and falling. His mouth was wide open. I could see far down into caverns of pale pink throat. I waited a long time for him to die, but his breathing did not weaken. Finally, I fired my two remaining shots into the spot where I thought his heart must be. The thick blood welled out of him like red velvet, but still he did not die. His body did not even jerk when the shots hit him, the tortured breathing continued without a pause. He was dying, very slowly and in great agony, but in some world remote from me where not even a bullet could damage him further. I felt I had got to put an end to that dreadful noise. It seemed dreadful to see the great beast lying there, powerless to move and yet powerless to die, and not even to be able to finish him. I sent back for my small rifle and poured shot after shot into his heart, and down his throat. They seemed to make no impression. The tortured gasps continued as steadily as the ticking of a clock.

In the end I could not stand it any longer and went away. I heard later that it took him half an hour to die. Burmans were bringing dahs[7] and baskets even before I left, and I was told they had stripped his body almost to the bones by the afternoon.

Afterwards, of course, there were endless discussions about the shooting of the elephant. The owner was furious, but he was only an Indian and could do nothing. Besides, legally I had done the right thing, for a mad elephant has to be killed, like a mad dog, if its owner fails to control it. Among the Europeans opinion was divided. The older men said I was right, the younger men said it was a damn shame to shoot an elephant for killing a coolie, because an elephant was worth more than any damn Coringhee coolie. And afterwards I was very glad that the coolie had been killed; it put me legally in the right and it gave me a sufficient pretext for shooting the elephant. I often wondered whether any of the others grasped that I had done it solely to avoid looking a fool.

Additional Rhetorical Strategies

Example (paragraph 1); Description (paragraph 4); Persuasion (throughout).

Discussion Questions

1. What is "enlightening" about the "tiny incident" Orwell recounts in this narrative (paragraph 3)? What does he learn about himself? What larger lessons does he learn about imperialism?
2. Examine the various places in the essay where Orwell reports conflicting urges. Do the internal conflicts he describes near the beginning of the essay bear any relation to the central internal conflict of the story, which he resolves by shooting the elephant?
3. There is almost no dialogue in this essay. Orwell narrates the events through his own eyes, and in his own voice. What is the effect of this stylistic decision? At the end of the essay the author wonders "whether any of the others grasped that I had done it solely to avoid looking a fool." What does this statement tell us about his relationship with the other Europeans? Is this a reflection of the "utter silence that is imposed on every Englishman in the East" (paragraph 2)? How does Orwell's virtual isolation affect the style of his writing?
4. How would you characterize the relationship between the younger Orwell, who shoots the elephant, and the older Orwell, who writes

[7]Dahs: Large knives

about it? Which one seems to be narrating the piece? How can you tell? What is the effect of this narrative decision?

5. Why do you think Orwell describes the dead Dravidian coolie and the death throes of the elephant in such detail? Is there some implied parallel being drawn between the two scenes? To what effect? What is the effect of ending the story not with Orwell's revelation but instead only after the protracted death of the elephant?

Essay Questions

1. In the second paragraph Orwell writes "at that time I had already made up my mind that imperialism was an evil thing." If he already knows this, why write the essay, or—to put it another way— what does he learn about imperialism from the incident with the elephant? Write an essay in which you chart the character development that the narrator undergoes in the course of the essay.

2. Choose a small incident from your life and narrate it in such a way that its larger meaning becomes apparent to your reader. Use Orwell's essay as a model and an inspiration, to the extent possible given the relevance of his rhetorical strategies to your own story. The best essays about personal experience often result from choosing an incident whose significance the writer does not completely comprehend before beginning to write the essay; let the process of writing help you discover the meaning of an incident that seemed full of complex but vague significance to you when you experienced it.

Exploring Connections: Questions Linking the Thematic Pair

1. Both Langston Hughes and George Orwell write of a time when they acted against their consciences because of overwhelming pressure from those around them. Compare and contrast the two situations. Does it make a difference, for instance, that Hughes' pressure comes from his friends and family? What were their respective motivations for bowing to social pressures? Also, compare the lessons they learned from these experiences.

2. In each of these essays, a very small incident is found to have global implications: Hughes' experience unmasks religion and Orwell's unmasks imperialism. Write an essay in which you narrate a seemingly simple event from your own life that turned out to have wider implications. One good way to increase your chances of writing an interesting essay in response to this question is to choose an incident whose meaning you don't quite understand. In the process of writing the essay you may learn something, and some of the excitement of discovery is almost certain to come through the page and touch your reader.

CHAPTER 2

Description

Nearly all of the writing we will ever want or be asked to do will include some description. Writers use description to create a picture in words of a person, place, object, or state of mind. In our media-oriented society, descriptive writing invariably competes with painting, film, and especially photography as a means of transmitting a mental image or impression of the world around or inside us. Yet description in writing also allows for metaphor, for using words in distinctive combinations to create images that we could never see in a painting, film, or photograph. Words provide us, in effect, with an open-ended opportunity to think about thinking and to recreate the world in our own terms. Descriptive writing also helps develop our thoughts into clear sequences and invariably adds liveliness and specificity to our prose.

Description appears frequently in expository writing—primarily to reinforce the effects created by other rhetorical techniques. It may be used, for example, to create a setting for narration, to make a definition livelier, to strengthen an account of cause and effect, to make an illustration more specific, to flesh out an explanation of a process, to make a classification clearer, or to deepen the impact of a particularly striking comparison or analogy. But as we'll see in the selections that follow, description can also serve as the dominant rhetorical strategy in an entire essay.

Purposes

The nature and purpose of an essay determine how central or subordinate a role description will play in our thinking and writing. Suppose that you have been asked to write an essay in which you discuss the one room you regard as the center of your life at home. From among several possibilities, you choose to focus on the kitchen. Although you may well want to tell your readers about the important events that happen there (that is, to use narration), you might first want to create an accurate picture of what the kitchen looks like. Describing in detail the physical appearance of the room, its contents, and perhaps even some of the people who regularly use it would help your audience recreate the special liveliness you associate with the kitchen. You could, for example, lead your readers around the room, describing each of its features in enough detail and in clear enough sequence for them to capture a vivid sense of the distinctive sights, sounds, smells, and activities identified with it. To do so would be to rely on description as the key rhetorical element in the success of such an essay.

In addition to portraying verbally the physical characteristics of a person, place, or object, description can also be used to recreate an idea, an emotion, a quality, or a mood. In the case of the kitchen, your description might include attention to the ways in which the mood in the kitchen changes at various times of the day and the year. Think of the extended description you could write focusing on the kitchen in the midst of the daily routines that distinguish, say, breakfast from lunch and dinner, or of the richness of detail associated with such special occasions as a birthday, Thanksgiving, and the New Year. Your efforts to describe an abstraction like the "holiday spirit" of a room depend finally on your ability to gather concrete illustrations of it. In this instance, you could undoubtedly point to the number of visitors at the house, the variety of food served, the smell of special cooking, the pile of dishes in the sink, and so on. (For a thorough discussion of this procedure for thinking in writing, see "Abstract and Concrete," in the Introduction, p. 26.) In all such instances—whether we are picturing something concrete (the furniture or appliances in the kitchen) or something abstract (the spirit in the room during a holiday)—the process of writing an effective description remains essentially the same. We should start with an overview of whatever we want to describe. We should then proceed to select the most striking and significant details and develop them in an intelligible sequence that produces the effect we intended to create.

Objective and Subjective Description

Basically, there are two kinds of description: objective and subjective. Although descriptive prose falls somewhere between these extremes, combining both in some distinctive proportion, it is useful to keep the following general distinctions in mind. *Objective description* is primarily factual, omitting any attention to the writer. *Subjective description* includes attention to both the subject described and the writer's reactions to it. For example, you could objectively describe the cost of traveling air coach from Los Angeles to New York as $249; writing subjectively, you might say that the price of the trip was "a great bargain." The focus in the first is on the fact, in the second on the way the writer responds to the fact. Or, you might objectively describe a particular automobile as a 1956 cream and gold DeSoto with a push-button transmission and long fins for rear fenders. A more subjective description might add that the car is an "enormous chunk of nostalgia." (For a masterly blending of objective and subjective description, see Virginia Woolf's "The Death of a Moth," p. 113.) Purpose and audience determine whether we ought to use primarily objective or primarily subjective description. Before deciding which form is the more appropriate for an essay, we should ask ourselves, "What is this description being used for?" and "Who is going to read it?"

Writers use objective description whenever they want to make an impartial presentation of observable facts. Objective description is impersonal prose, as literal and matter-of-fact as possible. The following passage exemplifies the essential features of an objective description:

> The kitchen table is rectangular, seventy-two inches long and thirty inches wide. Made of a two-inch-thick piece of oak, its top is covered with a waxy oilcloth patterned in dark red and blue squares against a white background. In the right corner, close to the wall, a square blue ceramic tile serves as the protective base for a brown earthenware tea pot. A single white place mat has been set to the left of the tile, with a knife and fork on either side of a white dinner plate. On the plate are two thick pieces of chicken.

The emphasis here is quite clearly on the presentation of information. Observable facts are conveyed in a detached tone of voice and in simple, relatively short sentences. The focus in the passage is on the objects, not on the writer's responses to them. Accordingly, the sentences rely on nouns and adjectives, rather than verbs, to carry the description. Equal attention is paid to each item in the description. Also, the writer concentrates on the *denotative meaning* of words—that is, on their dictionary meanings. While the passage involves several sense impressions (the objects have particular shapes and tactile properties, and a few even convey odors), the sense of sight dominates this objective description—and most others as well. Objective description reminds us of the need for the visual element in writing. Yet there is a static quality to this kind of description. The objects are described as simply "being there"— as though they were reflected in a mirror.

Besides being the substance of most scientific and technical writing, objective description is also a distinguishing feature of professional brochures, catalogs, and reports. In college life, objective description appears most frequently in textbooks, encyclopedias, reference books, science papers, departmental course guides, and in the classified ads that crowd the back pages of student newspapers and the walls of campus bookstores.

Writers use subjective description whenever they want to convey their personal interpretations of an object, place, person, or state of mind. In subjective description, there is as much emphasis on the writer's feelings as there is on what is being described. Since subjective description is impressionistic, it is likely of depend on strong verbs, forceful modifiers, and graphic figures of speech—language that signals the writer's feelings about what is being described. Though it may lack some of the technical precision of objective description, it usually makes a more immediate and dramatic appeal to our senses. Here is a subjective description of that same kitchen table:

> Our lives at home converged around the kitchen table. It was a magnet that drew our family together. Cut from the toughest oak, the table was sturdy, smooth, and long enough for my mother, my two sisters, and me to work or play on at the same time. Our favorite light-blue ceramic tile, stationed in the right corner, was the table's sole defense against the ravages of everything from a steaming tea pot to the latest red-hot gadget from the Sears catalogue. More often than not, however, the heat would spread quickly beyond the small tile and onto the checkered oilcloth, which just as quickly exuded a rank odor. Yet no matter how intensely the four of us competed for elbow room at the table, none dared venture near the lone dinner place arranged securely to the left of the tile. There was no telling when HE would get home from work, but, when he did, he expected things to be ready. He liked to eat right away—chicken mostly—two thick pieces in the middle of his plate for openers.

The description in this passage is relational—that is, the objects described are controlled by the significance the writer attaches to them. Each object is described as being more than simply "out there." Unlike the previous illustration, in which a neutral tone of voice prevails, this sample of subjective description projects a real sense of a speaker in each sentence, a personal voice that mixes facts and feelings. Accordingly, the language used is more evocative, richer in suggestion than in precision. No numbers, for example, are mentioned. The verbs, nouns, adjectives, and figures of speech depend on *connotation*—the range of associations and implications extending far beyond dictionary meanings—for their effect. Hence, it is not unusual to see a greater variety of sentence structure in subjective than in objective description. The writer invariably works with fewer details, but tries to do much more with each of them. Subjective description is a staple of autobiography, drama, fiction, and poetry. It also marks certain types of expository writing, especially the informal or personal essays featured in magazines and newspapers. (N. Scott Momaday's essay "A First American Views His Land" offers an outstanding example.)

Steps in Writing Effective Description

We can increase the likelihood that we will write successful description, whether objective or subjective, if we keep in mind a fairly simple sequence for our thinking and writing. First, we must observe the object, person, or scene carefully. The fundamental role of descriptive writing is to make our readers *see*. Yet while description is primarily visual—

we create word pictures—we should not ignore the power of language to make readers hear, taste, smell, and even touch our subject as well. Moreover, when we set out to recreate our sense impressions, we invariably will help move our thinking and writing from that level to the point where we can draw inferences. (See "Observation and Inference," in the Introduction, p. 26.)

Our second task—once we have observed our subject carefully—is to choose the most appropriate and evocative details. This is perhaps our most important decision when writing description. More often than not, we will have far more details to select from than we can possibly use. By focusing on the uniqueness of our subject, we should be able to decide which significant details are needed to make the subject as vivid as possible for our audience. If, for example, you wanted to drop off your car at the garage and leave a note for the mechanic explaining what is wrong with it, you would obviously need to be more specific than writing simply, "It doesn't start easily." So, too, you need not describe the car's exterior if you are concerned about the motor's not running. It is the quality, not the quantity, of details that counts. Keeping your purpose and audience in mind will undoubtedly help you decide which details will have the greatest impact in your sentences.

Having selected the most appropriate details, we then need to make sure, especially in a subjective description, that what we say about one detail will be clear enough so that when we move on to the next our readers will not forget those already discussed. The way to avoid this potential problem is to begin the description with a brief overview. (In our earlier case, the kitchen table "was a magnet that drew our family together.") Each detail will then contribute to what may be called the essay's *dominant impression*—the most important point we intend to convey. In the essay describing the kitchen, the dominant impression might be summarized in the family's locating "stability" in the objects and activities identified with the kitchen table. Or, to take another example, suppose you were walking in a thick woods early on a May morning. The scene may have been so pleasant that you wished to write to a friend to report what it was like. Having observed the scene carefully, you would make each of the details selected work toward establishing the dominant impression: the freshness of the morning. (Gretel Erhlich's "Time on Ice," p. 117, is an excellent example of creating a dominant impression in description.)

In writing description, we need to pay as much attention to the sequence of details as to the details themselves. The simplest way to secure the most memorable sequence of details is to present them as the eye discovers them arranged in space. This *spatial order* might progress, for example, from top to bottom or left to right (or vice versa) when describing a person or an object, respectively. When picturing a scene, however, an order of near to far (or vice versa) may prove most effective. There are several standard alternative sequences for developing description: from general to specific, from small to large, and from most common to most unusual feature, or vice versa. We could also begin with an overview of the subject to be described and then gradually focus on its outstanding feature. Whichever sequence we choose to develop, we ought to remember to work with an order natural enough to be followed easily by our audience.

Our point of view—where we stand literally and figuratively in relation to our subject—plays a large role in determining the extent and intensity of a description. Consider, for example, how different a description of a police station could be, depending on the writer's point of view: that of the victim, the accused, the arresting officer, the desk sergeant, the lawyer, or the parents. Generally speaking, the closer we bring our audience to the person, place, object, or state of mind, the greater the number of precise details needed to portray the subject adequately. Whether our point of view is fixed (for example, standing in one spot to describe a room) or moving (describing, say, what we see as we raft down the Colorado), we should either maintain a consistent point of view throughout the essay or alert readers to any shifts in perspective (for example, moving a description of a house from the outside to the inside). A consistent point of view helps unify descriptive writing.

Description stabilizes and enriches our thinking and writing. It not only places our ideas in a clearer context but also adds specificity to our sentences. It thickens our writing. When it works well, description strengthens our thinking by converting random sense impressions into a coherent series of interrelated details. Descriptive writing falters when we simply pile up loosely connected details. When we do this, we invariably run the risk of boring, if not confusing, our readers. We ought, instead, to manage the details of our description with care, choosing those that are best suited to our purpose and audience. Writing effective description is challenging work, but when we succeed at it, we make our prose more precise, realistic, immediate, and engaging.

More Than Just a Shrine: Paying Homage to the Ghosts of Ellis Island

Mary Gordon

Mary Gordon (b. 1949) received her B.A. from Barnard College in 1971. She has taught creative writing at community colleges and at Amherst College. When asked about her teaching methods, Gordon replies, "You cannot teach people to have an interesting mind. You cannot give them an ear. You can teach them craftsmanly tricks and give them some kind of self-criticism. You can make them see that writers are real people, too."

Her novels, including Final Payments *(1978),* The Company of Women *(1981),* Men and Angels *(1985), and* The Other Side *(1989), deal in a complex way with the lives of just such "real people," the working class people among whom she was born and raised. She has also published essays (*Good Boys and Dead Girls and Other Essays, *1991), short stories (*Temporary Shelter, *1987), and novellas (*The Rest of Life: Three Novellas, *1993). The subject matter and the impeccable style of her written work have earned her both a wide popular audience and the praise of critics.*

Gordon reports that she doesn't compose on a typewriter. She drafts her short stories, novels, and essays in longhand, on narrow lines in bound notebooks imported from England. "I have a fetish about my writing tools," she says. "I cannot work without these notebooks and my special, fine-point, felt-tip pens." Her careful attention to detail and to nuances in thinking and writing are amply illustrated in the following essay, "More Than Just a Shrine."

I once sat in a hotel in Bloomsbury[1] trying to have breakfast alone. A Russian with a habit of compulsively licking his lips asked if he could join me. I was afraid to say no; I thought it might be bad for détente. He explained to me that he was a linguist, and that he always liked to talk to Americans to see if he could make any connection between their speech and their ethnic background. When I told him about my mixed ancestry—my mother is Irish and Italian, my father a Lithuanian Jew—he began jumping up and down in his seat, rubbing his hands together and licking his lips even more frantically.

"Ah," he said, "so you are really somebody who comes from what is called the boiling pot of America." Yes, I told him, yes I was, but I quickly rose to leave. I thought it would be too hard to explain to him the relation of the boiling potters to the main course, and I wanted to get to the British Museum. I told him that the only thing I could think of that united people whose backgrounds, histories and points of view were utterly diverse was that their people had landed at a place called Ellis Island.

[1]Bloomsbury: A fashionable section of London.

I didn't tell him that Ellis Island was the only American landmark I'd ever visited. How could I describe to him the estrangement I'd always felt from the kind of traveler who visits shrines to America's past greatness, those rebuilt forts with muskets behind glass and sabers mounted on the walls and gift shops selling maple sugar candy in the shape of Indian headdresses, those reconstructed villages with tables set for 50 and the Paul Revere silver gleaming? All that Americana—Plymouth Rock, Gettysburg, Mount Vernon, Valley Forge—it all inhabits for me a zone of blurred abstraction with far less hold on my imagination than the Bastille or Hampton Court. I suppose I've always known that my uninterest in it contains a large component of the willed: I am American, and those places purport to be my history. But they are not mine.

Ellis Island is, though; it's the one place I can be sure my people are connected to. And so I made a journey there to find my history, like any Rotarian traveling in his Winnebago to Antietam to find his. I had become part of that humbling democracy of people looking in some site for a past that has grown unreal. The monument I traveled to was not, however, a tribute to some old glory. The minute I set foot upon the island I could feel all that it stood for: insecurity, obedience, anxiety, dehumanization, the terrified and careful deference of the displaced. I hadn't traveled to the Battery and boarded a ferry across from the Statue of Liberty to raise flags or breathe a richer, more triumphant air. I wanted to do homage to the ghosts.

5   I felt them everywhere, from the moment I disembarked and saw the building with its high-minded brick, its hopeful little lawn, its ornamental cornices. The place was derelict when I arrived; it had not functioned for more than 30 years—almost as long as the time it had operated at full capacity as a major immigration center. I was surprised to learn what a small part of history Ellis Island had occupied. The main building was constructed in 1892, then rebuilt between 1898 and 1900 after a fire. Most of the immigrants who arrived during the latter half of the 19th century, mainly northern and western Europeans, landed not at Ellis Island but on the western tip of the Battery at Castle Garden, which had opened as a receiving center for immigrants in 1855.

By the 1880s the facilities at Castle Garden had grown scandalously inadequate. Officials looked for an island on which to build a new immigration center because they thought that on an island immigrants could be more easily protected from swindlers and quickly transported to railroad terminals in New Jersey. Bedloe's Island was considered, but New Yorkers were aghast at the idea of a "Babel" ruining their beautiful new treasure, "Liberty Enlightening the World." The statue's sculptor, Frédéric Auguste Bartholdi, reacted to the prospect of immigrants landing near his masterpiece in horror; he called it a "monstrous plan." So much for Emma Lazarus.[2]

---

[2]Emma Lazarus: American poet (1849–1887) whose sonnet "The New Colossus" ("Give me your tired, your hungry . . .") is inscribed on the pedestal of the Statue of Liberty.

Ellis Island was finally chosen because the citizens of New Jersey petitioned the Federal Government to remove from the island an old naval powder magazine that they thought dangerously close to the Jersey shore. The explosives were removed; no one wanted the island for anything. It was the perfect place to build an immigration center.

I thought about the island's history as I walked into the building and made my way to the room that was the center in my imagination of the Ellis Island experience: the Great Hall. It had been made real for me in the stark, accusing photographs of Louis Hine and others who took those pictures to make a point. It was in the Great Hall that everyone had waited—waiting, always, the great vocation of the dispossessed. The room was empty, except for me and a handful of other visitors and the Park Ranger who showed us around. I felt myself grow insignificant in that room, with its huge semicircular windows, its air, even in dereliction, of solid and official probity.

I walked in the deathlike expansiveness of the room's disuse and tried to think of what it might have been like, filled and swarming. More than 16 million immigrants came through that room; approximately 250,000 were rejected. Not really a large proportion, but the implications for the rejected were dreadful. For some, there was nothing to go back to, or there was certain death; for others, who left as adventurers, to return would be to adopt in local memory the fool's role, and the failure's. No wonder that the island's history includes reports of 3,000 suicides.

Sometimes immigrants could pass through Ellis Island in mere[10] hours, though for some the process took days. The particulars of the experience in the Great Hall were often influenced by the political events and attitudes on the mainland. In the 1890s and the first years of the new century, when cheap labor was needed, the newly built receiving center took in its immigrants with comparatively little question. But as the century progressed, the economy worsened, eugenics became both scientifically respectable and popular and World War I made American xenophobia seem rooted in fact.

Immigration acts were passed; newcomers had to prove, besides moral correctness and financial solvency, their ability to read. Quota laws came into effect, limiting the number of immigrants from southern and eastern Europe to less than 14 percent of the total quota. Intelligence tests were biased against all non-English-speaking persons and medical examinations became increasingly strict, until the machinery of immigration nearly collapsed under its own weight. The Second Quota Law of 1924 provided that all immigrants be inspected and issued visas at American consular offices in Europe, rendering the center almost obsolete.

On the day of my visit, my mind fastened upon the medical inspections, which had always seemed to me most emblematic of the ignominy and terror the immigrants endured. The medical inspectors, sometimes dressed in uniforms like soldiers, were particularly obsessed with a disease of the eyes called trachoma, which they checked for by flipping back the immigrants' top eyelids with a hook used for buttoning gloves—a method that sometimes resulted in the transmission of the disease to healthy people. Mothers feared that if their children cried too much, their red eyes would be mistaken for a symptom of the disease and the whole family would be sent home. Those immigrants suspected of some physical disability had initials chalked on their coats. I remembered the photographs I'd seen of people standing, dumbstruck and innocent as cattle, with their manifest numbers hung around their necks and initials marked in chalk upon their coats: "E" for eye trouble, "K" for hernia, "L" for lameness, "X" for mental defects, "H" for heart disease.

I thought of my grandparents as I stood in the room; my 17-year-old grandmother, coming alone from Ireland in 1896, vouched for by a stranger who had found her a place as a domestic servant to some Irish who had done well. I tried to imagine the assault it all must have been for her; I've been to her hometown, a collection of farms with a main street—smaller than the athletic field of my local public school. She must have watched the New York skyline as the first- and second-class passengers were whisked off the gangplank with the most cursory of inspections while she was made to board a ferry to the new immigration center.

What could she have made of it—this buff-painted wooden structure with its towers and its blue slate roof, a place *Harper's Weekly* described as "a latter-day watering place hotel"? It would have been the first time she'd have heard people speaking something other than English. She would have mingled with people carrying baskets on their heads and eating foods unlike any she had ever seen—dark-eyed people, like the Sicilian she would marry 10 years later, who came over with his family, responsible even then for his mother and sister. I don't know what they thought, my grandparents, for they were not expansive people, nor romantic; they didn't like to think of what they called "the hard times," and their trip across the ocean was the single adventurous act of lives devoted after landing to security, respectability and fitting in.

15   What is the potency of Ellis Island for someone like me—an American, obviously, but one who has always felt that the country really belonged to the early settlers, that, as J. F. Powers wrote in "Morte D'Urban," it had been "handed down to them by the Pilgrims, George Washington and others, and that they were taking a risk in letting you live in it." I have never been the victim of overt discrimination; nothing I have wanted has been denied me because of the accidents of blood. But I suppose it is part of being an American to be engaged in a somewhat tiresome but always self-absorbing process of national definition. And in this process, I have found in traveling to Ellis Island an impor-

tant piece of evidence that could remind me I was right to feel my differentness. Something had happened to my people on that island, a result of the eternal wrongheadedness of American protectionism and the predictabilities of simple greed. I came to the island, too, so I could tell the ghosts that I was one of them, and that I honored them—their stoicism, and their innocence, the fear that turned them inward, and their pride. I wanted to tell them that I liked them better than the Americans who made them pass through the Great Hall and stole their names and chalked their weaknesses in public on their clothing. And to tell the ghosts what I have always thought: that American history was a very classy party that was not much fun until they arrived, brought the good food, turned up the music, and taught everyone to dance.

Additional Rhetorical Strategies

Cause and Effect (paragraphs 7, 10–11); Definition (paragraph 15); Narration (throughout).

Discussion Questions

1. In this descriptive essay, Gordon describes both what she actually sees on Ellis Island, as a tourist visiting the site in the twentieth century, and what she imagines the nineteenth-century immigrants saw when they landed there. How do the present-day details evoke the past? Identify the moments of transition between the two different time periods. What strategies besides imagination does Gordon employ to help her summon up a description of a past scene? Look closely at the concrete details she describes, the bricks and the lawn and the windows. How does a vision of the past come to inhere in these physical objects?

2. How does Gordon define what it means to be an American? Where does Gordon stand in relation to that definition? In what ways would she characterize herself as an American, and to what extent does she stand outside, or define herself in opposition to that definition? Look especially at the last paragraph and also at the "boiling pot" metaphor when framing your answer.

3. In paragraph 3, Gordon describes the American landmarks she has *not* visited: "rebuilt forts with muskets behind glass and sabers mounted on the walls and gift shops selling maple sugar candy in the shape of Indian headdresses. . . ." What is the status of such descriptions? What is the effect of this concrete description of the details of what is ostensibly a "zone of blurred abstraction"? Now look at the essay as a whole and analyze the interplay of concrete detail and abstract thought. How and where do the two intersect, and to what effect?

4. Gordon reports Frédéric Auguste Bartholdi's horrified reaction to the idea of immigrants landing near the Statue of Liberty with a good measure of irony. What other tonal shifts do you notice in this essay?

Essay Questions

1. Write an essay describing a place, relying both on your five senses and on your imagination, memory, research, or other methods of conjuring up a vision of the place that has dimensions beyond the here and now. You might, as Gordon has done, describe the place as it looked at an earlier time, from the perspective of people who are no longer alive. Or you might decide to imagine what the place might look like at some time in the distant future. Feel free to think of other options for adding an imaginative dimension to your description.

2. Gordon describes Ellis Island as a place that functioned, among other things, to draw a distinction between the legitimate Americans and the interlopers. In the days since her ancestors came to the United States, the ethnic groups that make up her heritage—the Italians and the Irish—have become assimilated, and different groups have replaced them as the targets of discrimination. Choose a place where the line between insiders and outsiders is drawn today, and describe it in a way that captures the feeling of ostracism. The place you choose need not be as well known as Ellis Island; choose a local place—for example a classroom, social service office, or teen hangout—where you find discrimination in action.

A First American Views His Land

N. Scott Momaday

N. Scott Momaday (b. 1934), whose Kiowa name is Tsoai-talee, was born in Oklahoma and raised on Navajo, Apache, and Jemez Pueblo Indian reservations. He earned his B.A. in political science from the University of New Mexico, and his M.A. and Ph.D. from Stanford University. He taught at the Berkeley and Santa Cruz campuses of the University of California and at New Mexico State University, before becoming a member of the faculty at Stanford. He is also a Kiowa tribal dancer and a chronicler of Native American experience.

N. Scott Momaday's publications include his first novel, the Pulitzer Prize-winning House Made of Dawn *(1968), and the nonfiction works* The Journey of Tai-Me *(1967) and* The Way to Rainy Mountain *(1969), in which he recounts the experiences of his tribe and family. The essay that follows first appeared in* National Geographic *magazine in July 1976.*

First Man
behold:
the earth
glitters
with leaves;
the sky
glistens
with rain.
Pollen
is borne
on winds
that low
and lean
upon
mountains.
Cedars
blacken
the slopes—
and pines.[1]

One hundred centuries ago. There is a wide, irregular landscape in what is now northern New Mexico. The sun is a dull white disk, low in the south; it is a perfect mystery, a deity whose coming and going are inexorable. The gray sky is curdled, and it bears very close upon the earth. A cold wind runs along the ground, dips and

---

[1]The poem that appears throughout the essay is drawn from Momaday's book, *The Gourd Dancer* (1976).

spins, flaking drift from a pond in the bottom of a ravine. Beyond the wind the silence is acute. A man crouches in the ravine, in the darkness there, scarcely visible. He moves not a muscle; only the wind lifts a lock of his hair and lays it back along his neck. He wears skins and carries a spear. These things in particular mark his human intelligence and distinguish him as the lord of the universe. And for him the universe is especially *this* landscape; for him the landscape is an element like the air. The vast, virgin wilderness is by and large his whole context. For him there is no possibility of existence elsewhere.

Directly there is a blowing, a rumble of breath deeper than the wind, above him, where some of the hard clay of the bank is broken off and the clods roll down into the water. At the same time there appears on the skyline the massive head of a long-horned bison, then the hump, then the whole beast, huge and black on the sky, standing to a height of seven feet at the hump, with horns that extend six feet across the shaggy crown. For a moment it is poised there; then it lumbers obliquely down the bank to the pond. Still the man does not move, though the beast is now only a few steps upwind. There is no sign of what is about to happen; the beast meanders; the man is frozen in repose.

Then the scene explodes. In one and the same instant the man springs to his feet and bolts forward, his arm cocked and the spear held high, and the huge animal lunges in panic, bellowing, its whole weight thrown violently into the bank, its hooves churning and chipping earth into the air, its eyes gone wide and wild and white. There is a moment in which its awful, frenzied motion is wasted, and it is mired and helpless in its fear, and the man hurls the spear with his whole strength, and the point is driven into the deep, vital flesh, and the bison in its agony staggers and crashes down and dies.

This ancient drama of the hunt is enacted again and again in the landscape. The man is preeminently a predator, the most dangerous of all. He hunts in order to survive; his very existence is simply, squarely established upon that basis. But he hunts also because he can, because he has the means; he has the ultimate weapon of his age, and his prey is plentiful. His relationship to the land has not yet become a moral equation.

5   But in time he will come to understand that there is an intimate, vital link between the earth and himself, a link that implies an intricate network of rights and responsibilities. In some unimagined future he will understand that he has the ability to devastate and perhaps destroy his environment. That moment will be one of extreme crisis in his evolution.

The weapon is deadly and efficient. The hunter has taken great care in its manufacture, especially in the shaping of the flint point, which is an extraordinary thing. A larger flake has been removed from each face, a groove that extends from the base nearly to the tip. Several hundred pounds of pressure, expertly applied, were required to make these grooves. The hunter then is an artisan, and he must know how to use rudimentary tools. His skill, manifest in the manufacture of this artifact, is unsurpassed for its time and purpose. By means of this weapon is the Paleo-Indian hunter eminently able to exploit his environment.

Thousands of years later, about the time that Columbus begins his first voyage to the New World, another man, in the region of the Great Lakes, stands in the forest shade on the edge of a sunlit brake. In a while a deer enters into the pool of light. Silently the man fits an arrow to a bow, draws aim, and shoots. The arrow zips across the distance and strikes home. The deer leaps and falls dead.

But this latter-day man, unlike his ancient predecessor, is only incidentally a hunter; he is also a fisherman, a husbandman, even a physician. He fells trees and builds canoes; he grows corn, squash, and beans, and he gathers fruit and nuts; he uses hundreds of species of wild plants for food, medicine, teas, and dyes. Instead of one animal, or two or three, he hunts many, none to extinction as the Paleo-Indian may have done. He has fitted himself far more precisely into the patterns of the wilderness than did his ancient predecessor. He lives on the land; he takes his living from it; but he does not destroy it. This distinction supports the fundamental ethic that we call conservation today. In principle, if not yet in name, this man is a conservationist.

These two hunting sketches are far less important in themselves than is that long distance between them, that whole possibility within the dimension of time. I believe that in that interim there grew up in the mind of man an idea of the land as sacred.

> *At dawn*
> *eagles*
> *lie and*
> *hover*
> *above*
> *the plain*
> *where light*
> *gathers*
> *in pools.*
> *Grasses*
> *shimmer*
> *and shine.*
> *Shadows*
> *withdraw*
> *and lie*
> *away*
> *like smoke.*

"The earth is our mother. The sky is our father." This concept of na-10 ture, which is at the center of the Native American world view, is familiar to us all. But it may well be that we do not understand entirely what that concept is in its ethical and philosophical implications.

I tell my students that the American Indian has a unique investment in the American landscape. It is an investment that represents perhaps thirty thousand years of habitation. That tenure has to be worth something in itself—a great deal, in fact. The Indian has been here a long time; he is at home here. That simple and obvious truth is one of the most important realities of the Indian world, and it is integral in the Indian mind and spirit.

How does such a concept evolve? Where does it begin? Perhaps it begins with the recognition of beauty, the realization that the physical world *is* beautiful. We don't know much about the ancient hunter's sensibilities. It isn't likely that he had leisure in his life for the elaboration of an aesthetic ideal. And yet the weapon he made was beautiful as well as functional. It has been suggested that much of the minute chipping along the edges of his weapon served no purpose but that of aesthetic satisfaction.

A good deal more is known concerning that man of the central forests. He made beautiful boxes and dishes out of elm and birch bark, for example. His canoes were marvelous, delicate works of art. And this aesthetic perception was a principle of the whole Indian world of his time, as indeed it is of our time. The contemporary Native American is a man whose strong aesthetic perceptions are clearly evident in his arts and crafts, in his religious ceremonies, and in the stories and songs of his rich oral tradition. This, in view of the pressures that have been brought to bear upon the Indian world and the drastic changes that have been effected in its landscape, is a blessing and an irony.

Consider for example the Navajos of the Four Corners area. In recent years an extensive coal-mining operation has mutilated some of their most sacred land. A large power plant in that same region spews a contamination into the sky that is visible for many miles. And yet, as much as any people of whom I have heard, the Navajos perceive and celebrate the beauty of the physical world.

15   There is a Navajo ceremonial song that celebrates the sounds that are made in the natural world, the particular voices that beautify the earth:

> *Voice above,*
> *Voice of thunder,*
> *Speak from the*
> *dark of clouds;*
> *Voice below,*
> *Grasshopper voice,*
> *Speak from the*
> *green of plants;*
> *So may the earth*
> *be beautiful.*

There is in the motion and meaning of this song a comprehension of the world that is peculiarly native, I believe, that is integral in the Native American mentality. Consider: The singer stands at the enter of the natural world, at the source of its sound, of its motion, of its life. Nothing of that world is inaccessible to him or lost upon him. His song is filled with reverence, with wonder and delight, and with confidence as well. He knows something about himself and about the things around him—and he knows that he knows. I am interested in what he sees and hears; I am interested in the range and force of his perception. Our immediate impression may be that his perception is narrow and deep—vertical. After all, "voice above . . . voice below," he sings. But is it vertical only? At each level of his expression there is an extension of his awareness across the whole landscape. The voice above is the voice of thunder, and thunder rolls. Moreover, it issues from the impalpable dark clouds and runs upon their horizontal range. It is a sound that integrates the whole of the atmosphere. And even so, the voice below, that of the grasshopper, issues from the broad plain and multiplicity of plants. And of course the singer is mindful of much more than thunder and insects; we are given in his song the wide angle of his vision and his hearing—and we are given the testimony of his dignity, his trust, and his deep belief.

This comprehension of the earth and air is surely a matter of morality, for it brings into account not only man's instinctive reaction to his environment but the full realization of his humanity as well, the achievement of his intellectual and spiritual development as an individual and as a race.

In my own experience I have seen numerous examples of this regard for nature. My grandfather Mammedaty was a farmer in his mature years; his grandfather was a buffalo hunter. It was not easy for Mammedaty to be a farmer; he was a Kiowa, and the Kiowas never had an agrarian tradition. Yet he had to make his living, and the old, beloved life of roaming the plains and hunting the buffalo was gone forever. Even so, as much as any man before him, he fitted his mind and will and spirit to the land; there was nothing else. He could not have conceived of living apart from the land.

In *The Way to Rainy Mountain* I set down a small narrative that belongs in the oral tradition of my family. It indicates something essential about the Native American attitude toward the land:

"East of my grandmother's house, south of the pecan grove, there is buried a woman in a beautiful dress. Mammedaty used to know where she is buried, but now no one knows. If you stand on the front porch of the house and look eastward towards Carnegie, you know that the woman is buried somewhere within the range of your vision. But her grave is unmarked. She was buried in a cabinet, and she wore a beautiful dress. How beautiful it was! It was one of those fine buckskin dresses, and it was decorated with elk's teeth and beadwork. That dress is still there, under the ground."

20 It seems to me that this statement is primarily a declaration of love for the land, in which the several elements—the woman, the dress, and this plain—are at last become one reality, one expression of the beautiful in nature. Moreover, it seems to me a peculiarly Native American expression in this sense: that the concentration of things that are explicitly remembered—the general landscape, the simple, almost abstract nature of the burial, above all the beautiful dress, which is wholly singular in kind (as well as in its function within the narrative)—is especially Indian in character. The things that are *not* explicitly remembered—the woman's name, the exact location of her grave—are the things that matter least in the special view of the storyteller. What matters here is the translation of the woman into the landscape, a translation particularly signified by means of the beautiful and distinctive dress, an *Indian* dress.

When I was a boy, I lived for several years at Jemez Pueblo, New Mexico. The Pueblo Indians are perhaps more obviously invested in the land than are other people. Their whole life is predicated upon a thorough perception of the physical world and its myriad aspects. When I first went there to live, the cacique, or chief, of the Pueblos was a venerable old man with long, gray hair and bright, deep-set eyes. He was entirely dignified and imposing—and rather formidable in the eyes of a boy. He excited my imagination a good deal. I was told that this old man kept the calendar of the tribe, that each morning he stood on a certain spot of ground near the center of the town and watched to see where the sun appeared on the skyline. By means of this solar calendar did he know and announce to his people when it was time to plant, to harvest, to perform this or that ceremony. This image of him in my mind's eye—the old man gazing each morning after the ranging sun—came to represent for me the epitome of that real harmony between man and the land that signifies the Indian world.

One day when I was riding my horse along the Jemez River, I looked up to see a long caravan of wagons and people on horseback and on foot. Men, women, and children were crossing the river ahead of me, moving out to the west, where most of the cultivated fields were, the farmland of the town. It was a wonderful sight to see, this long procession, and I was immediately deeply curious. I wanted to investigate, but it was not in me to do so at once, for that racial reserve, that sense of priority that is deep-seated in Native American culture, stayed me, held me up. Then I saw someone coming toward me on horseback, galloping. It was a friend of mine, a boy of my own age. "Come on," he said. "Come with us." "Where are you going?" I asked casually. But he would not tell me. He simply laughed and urged me to come along, and of course I was very glad to do so. It was a bright spring morning, and I had a good horse under me, and the prospect of adventure was delicious. We moved far out across the eroded plain to the farthest fields at the foot of a great red mesa, and there we planted two large fields of corn. And afterward, on the edge of the fields, we sat on blankets and ate a feast in the shade of a cottonwood grove. Later I learned it was the cacique's fields we planted. And this is an ancient tradition at Jemez. The people of the town plant and tend and harvest the cacique's fields, and in the winter the hunters give to him a portion of the meat that they bring home from the mountains. It is as if the cacique is himself the translation of man, every man, into the landscape.

I have not forgotten that day, nor shall I forget it. I remember the warm earth of the fields, the smooth texture of seeds in my hands, and the brown water moving slowly and irresistibly among the rows. Above all I remember the spirit in which the procession was made, the work was done, and the feasting was enjoyed. It was a spirit of communion, of the life of each man in relation to the life of the planet and of the infinite distance and silence in which it moves. We made, in concert, an appropriate expression of that spirit.

One afternoon an old Kiowa woman talked to me, telling me of the place in Oklahoma in which she had lived for a hundred years. It was the place in which my grandparents, too, lived; and it is the place where I was born. And she told me of a time even further back, when the Kiowas came down from the north and centered their culture in the red earth of the southern plains. She told wonderful stories, and as I listened, I began to feel more and more sure that her voice proceeded from the land itself. I asked her many things concerning the Kiowas, for I wanted to understand all that I could of my heritage. I told the old woman that I had come there to learn from her and from people like her, those in whom the old ways were preserved. And she said simply: "It is good that you have come here." I believe that her word "good" meant many things; for one thing it meant *right*, or *appropriate*. And indeed it was appropriate that she should speak of the land. She was eminently qualified to do so. She had a great reverence for the land, and an ancient perception of it, a perception that is acquired only in the course of many generations.

It is this notion of the appropriate, along with that of the beautiful,[25] that forms the Native American perspective on the land. In a sense these considerations are indivisible; Native American oral tradition is rich with songs and tales that celebrate natural beauty, the beauty of the natural world. What is more appropriate to our world than that which is beautiful:

At noon
turtles
enter
slowly

into
the warm
dark loam.
Bees hold
the swarm.
Meadows
recede
through planes
of heat
and pure
distance.

Very old in the Native American world view is the conviction that the earth is vital, that there is a spiritual dimension to it, a dimension in which man rightly exists. It follows logically that there are ethical imperatives in this matter. I think: Inasmuch as I am in the land, it is appropriate that I should affirm myself in the spirit of the land. I shall celebrate my life in the world and the world in my life. In the natural order man invests himself in the landscape and at the same time incorporates the landscape into his own most fundamental experience. This trust is sacred.

The process of investment and appropriation is, I believe, preeminently a function of the imagination. It is accomplished by means of an act of the imagination that is especially ethical in kind. We are what we imagine ourselves to be. The Native American is someone who thinks of himself, imagines himself in a particular way. By virtue of his experience his idea of himself comprehends his relationship to the land.

And the quality of this imagining is determined as well by racial and cultural experience. The Native American's attitudes toward this landscape have been formulated over a long period of time, a span that reaches back to the end of the Ice Age. The land, *this* land, is secure in his racial memory.

In our society as a whole we conceive of the land in terms of ownership and use. It is a lifeless medium of exchange; it has for most of us, I suspect, no more spirituality than has an automobile, say, or a refrigerator. And our laws confirm us in this view, for we can buy and sell the land, we can exclude each other from it, and in the context of ownership we can use it as we will. Ownership implies use, and use implies consumption.

But this way of thinking of the land is alien to the Indian. His cultural intelligence is opposed to these concepts; indeed, for him they are all but inconceivable quantities. This fundamental distinction is easier to understand with respect to ownership than to use, perhaps. For obviously the Indian does use, and has always used, the land and the available resources in it. The point is that *use* does not indicate in any real way his idea of the land. "Use" is neither his word nor his idea. As an

Indian I think: "You say that I *use* the land, and I reply, yes, it is true; but it is not the first truth. The first truth is that I *love* the land; I see that it is beautiful; I delight in it; I am alive in it."

In the long course of his journey from Asia and in the realization of[30] himself in the New World, the Indian has assumed a deep ethical regard for the earth and sky, a reverence for the natural world that is antipodal to that strange tenet of modern civilization that seemingly has it that man must destroy his environment. It is this ancient ethic of the Native American that must shape our efforts to preserve the earth and the life upon and within it.

> *At dusk*
> *the gray*
> *foxes*
> *stiffen*
> *in cold;*
> *blackbirds*
> *are fixed*
> *in white*
> *branches.*
> *Rivers*
> *follow*
> *the moon,*
> *the long*
> *white track*
> *of the*
> *full moon.*

Additional Rhetorical Strategies

Narration (paragraphs 2–3, 7, 22); Definition (paragraphs 4, 8, 29); Cause and Effect (paragraphs 4, 12); Process Analysis (paragraph 6); Example (paragraphs 14, 17); Comparison and Contrast (paragraphs 28–29).

Discussion Questions

1. Who is the "First American" of the title? What evidence might you give for the idea that the title refers to the Paleo-Indian in New Mexico? How might you support the idea that the title refers to the Native American in the region of the Great Lakes at the time of Columbus? How might you construct an argument that the first American is Momaday himself?
2. Momaday has woven a poem from his book *The Gourd Dancer* into this essay. Where else do you find evidence that Momaday is a

poet? What specific instances of poetic language can you identify in
the prose portions of his essay?

3. What does the author gain from the tremendous time span covered
by the essay? How does it further his purpose to begin his essay
with a scene that takes place "One hundred centuries ago"? How is
this expansive time frame relevant to the Native American philosophy Momaday describes in this piece? How would you characterize
that philosophy?

4. How would you characterize the structure of this essay? Look at
each of the narratives and poems that Momaday embeds in his
prose, and identify how each functions. Are the connections among
ideas more often explicit or implicit in this piece?

5. To whom does Momaday refer in paragraph 28 when he writes "In
our society as a whole"? Why does he use the first-person plural
possessive, instead of the third person? What effect does it have on
you as a reader to see him including himself in this analysis of
modern American society?

Essay Questions

1. Analyze one of the stories or poems that Momaday has embedded
in this essay. What meaning can you infer from the fact that the location of the buried woman has been forgotten, for instance? Or
what do you make of the "Shadows" that "withdraw/and
lie/away/like smoke"? Choose just one of the stories or poems on
which to base your essay, and ask yourself as many questions
about it as you can, to get you started on an interpretation.

2. Choose some key words from Momaday's essay, and define
them—and explore their connotations—from the point of view of a
Native American and a European American. Some words you
might choose for the basis of your essay include "investment"
(paragraph 11), "appropriation" (paragraph 26), and "use" (paragraph 29). Use these definitions as a jumping-off place for a discussion of the similarities and differences between the Native American and European American world views, as represented here by
Momaday.

Death of a Moth

Virginia Woolf

One of the most innovative and influential twentieth-century novelists, Virginia Woolf (1882–1941) experimented with and succeeded in perfecting the "stream of consciousness" technique, which she used to explore the problem of personal identity in her later novels: Mrs. Dalloway *(1925),* To the Lighthouse *(1927), and* The Waves *(1931). She is also known for her works of nonfiction, including the seminal feminist work,* A Room of One's Own *(1920) and two volumes of critical essays under the title* The Common Reader.

Woolf devoted her life to writing and publishing, and her thoughts ran often to questions of the role and nature of literature. Of literature in general she once wrote, "Art is being rid of all preaching: things in themselves: the sentence in itself beautiful: multitudinous seas; daffodils that come before the swallow dares. . . ." Speaking more specifically of the essay form, she wrote, "Somehow or other, by dint of labor or bounty of nature, or both combined, the essay must be pure—pure like water or pure like wine, but pure from dullness, deadness, and deposits of extraneous nature." As you read her essay below, note the extent to which Woolf adheres to the ideal she has set forth in these passages from her Writer's Diary.

Moths that fly by day are not properly to be called moths; they do not excite that pleasant sense of dark autumn nights and ivy-blossom which the commonest yellow-underwing asleep in the shadow of the curtain never fails to rouse in us. They are hybrid creatures, neither gay like butterflies nor sombre like their own species. Nevertheless the present specimen, with his narrow hay-coloured wings, fringed with a tassel of the same colour, seemed to be content with life. It was a pleasant morning, mid-September, mild, benignant, yet with a keener breath than that of the summer months. The plough was already scoring the field opposite the window, and where the share had been, the earth was pressed flat and gleamed with moisture. Such vigour came rolling in from the fields and then down beyond that it was difficult to keep the eyes strictly turned upon the book. The rooks too were keeping one of their annual festivities; soaring round the tree tops until it looked as if a vast net with thousands of black knots in it had been cast up into the air; which, after a few moments sank slowly down upon the trees until every twig seemed to have a knot at the end of it. Then, suddenly, the net would be thrown into the air again in a wider circle this time, with the utmost clamour and vociferation, as though to be thrown into the air and settle slowly down upon the tree tops were a tremendously exciting experience.

The same energy which inspired the rooks, the ploughmen, the horses, and even, it seemed, the lean bare-backed downs, sent the moth fluttering from side to side of his square of the windowpane. One could not help watching him. One was, indeed, conscious of a queer feeling of pity for him. The possibilities of pleasure seemed that morning so enormous and so various that to have only a moth's part in life, and a day moth's at that, appeared a hard fate, and his zest in enjoying his meager opportunities to the full, pathetic. He flew vigorously to one corner of his compartment, and, after waiting there a second, flew across to the other. What remained for him but to fly to a third corner and then to a fourth? That was all he could do, in spite of the size of the downs, the width of the sky, the far-off smoke of houses, and the romantic voice, now and then, of a steamer out at sea. What he could do he did. Watching him, it seemed as if a fibre, very thin but pure, of the enormous energy of the world had been thrust into his frail and diminutive body. As often as he crossed the pane, I could fancy that a thread of vital light became visible. He was little or nothing but life.

Yet, because he was so small, and so simple a form of the energy that was rolling in at the open window and driving its way through so many narrow and intricate corridors in my own brain and in those of other human beings, there was something marvelous as well as pathetic about him. It was as if someone had taken a tiny bead of pure life and decking it as lightly as possible with down and feathers, had set it dancing and zigzagging to show us the true nature of life. Thus displayed one could not get over the strangeness of it. One is apt to forget all about life, seeing it humped and bossed and garnished and cumbered so that it has to move with the greatest circumspection and dignity. Again, the thought of all that life might have been had he been born in any other shape caused one to view his simple activities with a kind of pity.

After a time, tired by his dancing apparently, he settled on the window ledge in the sun, and, the queer spectacle being at an end, I forgot about him. Then, looking up, my eye was caught by him. He was trying to resume his dancing, but seemed either so stiff or so awkward that he could only flutter to the bottom of the windowpane; and when he tried to fly across it he failed. Being intent on other matters I watched these futile attempts for a time without thinking, unconsciously waiting for him to resume his flight, as one waits for a machine, that has stopped momentarily, to start again without considering the reason of its failure. After perhaps a seventh attempt he slipped from the wooden ledge and fell, fluttering his wings, on to his back on the window sill. The helplessness of his attitude roused me. It flashed upon me that he was in difficulties; he could no longer raise himself; his legs struggled vainly. But, as I stretched out a pencil, meaning to help him to right himself, it came over me that the failure and awkwardness were the approach of death. I laid the pencil down again.

The legs agitated themselves once more. I looked as if for the enemy against which he struggled. I looked out of doors. What had happened there? Presumably it was midday, and work in the fields had stopped. 5 Stillness and quiet had replaced the previous animation. The birds had taken themselves off to feed in the brooks. The horses stood still. Yet the power was there all the same, massed outside indifferent, impersonal, not attending to anything in particular. Somehow it was opposed to the little hay-coloured moth. It was useless to try to do anything. One could only watch the extraordinary efforts made by those tiny legs against an oncoming doom which could, had it chosen, have submerged an entire city, not merely a city, but masses of human beings; nothing, I knew, had any chance against death. Nevertheless after a pause of exhaustion the legs fluttered again. It was superb this last protest, and so frantic that he succeeded at last in righting himself. One's sympathies, of course, were all on the side of life. Also, when there was nobody to care or to know, this gigantic effort on the part of an insignificant little moth, against a power of such magnitude, to retain what no one else valued or desired to keep, moved one strangely. Again, somehow, one saw life, a pure bead. I lifted the pencil again, useless though I knew it to be. But even as I did so, the unmistakable tokens of death showed themselves. The body relaxed, and instantly grew stiff. The struggle was over. The insignificant little creature now knew death. As I looked at the dead moth, this minute wayside triumph of so great a force over so mean an antagonist filled me with wonder. Just as life had been strange a few minutes before, so death was now as strange. The moth having righted himself now lay most decently and uncomplainingly composed. O yes, he seemed to say, death is stronger than I am.

Additional Rhetorical Strategies

Analogy (paragraph 1); Narration (paragraphs 2, 4, 5).

Discussion Questions

1. Woolf first refers to the moth as "the present specimen." What do these words suggest about her attitude at this point? Does her attitude remain the same throughout the essay? What particular words convey her stance vis-à-vis the moth? Look even at the seemingly most insignificant parts of speech, such as the pronouns.

2. How would you characterize the narrator's interactions with the moth? Of what significance is it that when she touches the insect, she does so not with her finger but with a pencil?

3. Suppose Woolf had written a purely objective description of the moth and its death. In what respects would it differ from this description?

4. What is the relation between the scene outside the window and the scene within the windowpane? How has the scene beyond the window changed as the moth starts to die? What significance, implicit or explicit, does Woolf attach to these changes? What keeps the fields and the birds from becoming irrelevant?

Essay Questions

1. It sometimes happens that a seemingly insignificant event such as the death of a moth becomes the occasion for more profound reflection. Think back on your own experience, and choose one such incident that caused you to think about the far-reaching questions we sometimes ask ourselves, about, for example, our commitment to jobs or schoolwork, our relationship with another person, our mortality, the meaning of our existence. Write an essay describing the incident, making its significance clear to your reader.
2. Speaking about the informal writing she does in her diary, Woolf expresses her belief that "the habit of writing thus for my own eye only is good practice. It loosens the ligaments. Never mind the misses and the stumbles. Going at such a pace as I do I must make the most direct and instant shots at my object, and thus have to lay hands on words, choose them and shoot them with no more pause than is needed to put my pen in the ink." If you don't already keep some kind of a writer's diary, now might be an ideal time to start. A diary or journal can be a good, no-risk place to try out ideas for more formal essays, or just to stretch your writing muscles and ligaments, especially during a semester when you are focusing on improving your writing.

Time on Ice

Gretel Ehrlich

Gretel Ehrlich (b. 1946) is a poet, essayist, novelist, and filmmaker. She attended Bennington College, UCLA Film School, and the New School for Social Research. Her best known work, a collection of essays called The Solace of Open Spaces *(1985) evolved from a traumatic event in her own life. She had gone to Wyoming to film a documentary for the Public Broadcasting System, leaving her partner, David, who had just been pronounced terminally ill, behind in New York. When she finished work on the film she learned that David had died. She began traveling, seeking solace in nature, and ended up back in Wyoming, where she began a new life as a sheepherder. The journal entries she wrote during this period were eventually revised to become the essays in her book.*

Ehrlich's other publications include three books of poetry, collections of short stories, and the novel Heart Mountain *(1988), which takes up the lives of those living in the Japanese American relocation camps in Wyoming during World War II. This book, like* Solace of Open Spaces, *received a warm critical reception. In the essay that follows, you can witness one of the qualities that brings praise to Ehrlich's work: her powerful descriptions of landscapes that might seem featureless to the less practiced and observant eye.*

The reading we just took says the wind has stiffened to twenty knots. Fog comes and goes. It was a hole in the fog through which my plane descended this afternoon; now, at midnight, I'm looking up from seven-foot-thick ice and see sun circling like a necklace, a halo, a drawstring that pulls tight entrances to the body of sky and earth.

Later, I press my face into an *aglu,* which is what the Inuit call a seal's breathing hole. I peer down past the lair—a snow cave where a seal bears her pups in spring—and past empires of turquoise ice into black, into the 500-foot-deep universe of the Arctic Ocean.

I'm in the north Canadian Arctic, ten miles from Cornwallis Island on the frozen waters of Barrow Strait—1,000 miles from the North Pole—at the camp of my friend Brendan Kelly, an American research biologist affiliated with the University of Alaska. Brendan is completing a doctorate at Purdue University, studying and writing about the evolution and behavior of ringed seals, the most common type of seal found in the Arctic. When Brendan came here in March, on a National Science Foundation grant, the nights were forty, fifty below zero. Now, in May, it's balmy at ten above, and when snow comes it's so icy it sounds like sugar scouring the 16′ × 20′ Parcoll tent Brendan shares with his assistant, William Stortz—a carpenter in Alaska when he's not pursuing ringed seals—and two black labradors Brendan has trained to sniff out seals under the snow.

Here, at the top of the world, clouds sweep down so low the landscape appears flattened, as if Earth were clamped by a vise. I sleep on water, walk on water, dream on water—albeit frozen. The top seven or eight feet of Barrow Strait freeze each September and stay frozen until mid-June. To the north of us are the numerous Queen Elizabeth Islands—brown, rocky outcrops in a world of ephemeral ice.

5   In the Arctic, one day is six months long followed by one night. Time as we know it—divided into darkness and light, sleep and wakefulness—does not exist here. Rather, it keeps stretching from brightness to brightness, shuttered out only by occasional, arbitrary human sleep.

At 2:00 AM we eat dinner: steaks, Brie, pilot bread, and mushy potatoes that have frozen, thawed, and refrozen several times. Our dinner music, courtesy of numerous microphones set on the ice, is the sound of seals breathing as they come up from the cold Arctic waters to rest in their lairs. Near us as we eat, one of the five laptop computers powered by a photovoltaic panel calculates and diagrams the depth and frequency of seals' dives—ultrasonic pulses transmitted from seal to laptop via "pingers" (acoustic transmitters) that Brendan has attached to their fur and hydrophones he has set in the water.

Outside, fog is followed by frost fall. At 6:00 AM the sun is in the northwest. Clouds come from the west, then the south. Planes of light break ice into dazzling white lines, gray troughs, blue mirages in which distant island cliffs rise double-decked.

After breakfast William and Brendan start working on a new net design. The idea is to live-catch seals in their lairs, bring them to the tent, attach pingers to them, and release them into the water where they were found. Tall, big-boned, with a curly head of hair and deep-set Arctic blue eyes, Brendan is one of the few researchers who retrieve seals this way.

But all week, Brendan tells me, the seals have been coming up into the nets and escaping. Back to the drawing board: Brendan designs, William executes. Two new nets with hoopskirts hang from the ceiling and, needle and thread in hand, William sews an intricate, revised set of pulleys and alarms into the white folds.

10   Brendan has studied ice-breeding seals in the Bering Sea, in the Beaufort Sea, and in Barrow Strait, as well as walruses in the Chukchi Sea. Fifteen years ago he began coming to the Arctic in the spring to study ringed seals. "So little is known about them because they spend most of their lives under the ice," he says.

Late one afternoon we leave the tent to set one of the new nets, packing it gently in a komatik—a long sled—pulled behind a snowmobile. The black labs race ahead of our machines, veering off suddenly wherever the whiff of seal lures them but coming back to show us the way.

The entrance to this *aglu* is vagina-shaped; we squeeze the net in, careful not to set off any triggers that would cause the purse string at the bottom to draw tight. A hydrophone is lowered down, and we head back to the tent to wait until a seal swims in.

Before reaching camp, somewhere out on the expanse of ice, we stop and walk: clear sky, rising temperature, blocks of rough ice sticking up like great blue crystals or teeth that have been knocked out and left behind. Snow under our feet glitters in cold sun. Griffith Island is a lean arm of white against miles of powder blue. Brendan tells me that this blue is the result of the Tyndall effect: short wavelengths of light that have been scattered by air bubbles or particles.

Another midnight dinner listening to seals' deep breathing. If a seal swims up into the net, she'll set off an alarm that we'll hear. Nothing yet. Only the intimate sounds of a mother seal, then her baby, and the sound of scratching as they abrade ice at the edge of the breathing hole to keep it open. All night in sleep there is the white noise of receivers and the sounds of seals mixing with our human sounds; all night the sun shines.

On my fourth day in camp Brendan and William cut a large hole in the ice with chain saws, pulling blocks out with giant tongs. Eighty-four inches down through ice, then the black Arctic sea. A tent goes over it. "This is the poolside suite," Brendan announces, hoping a seal will use it as a breathing hole and visit us while we're in bed. Near dawn we lay sleeping bags around the hole. A jellyfish rises to the surface. Looking down, I can see where ice ends and darkness begins: It's like looking past the edge of our universe, and I wonder what kind of seeing this is. We sleep lightly, but no seal comes.

In the morning it is so warm the meat in the food cache is in danger of thawing, so William and I build an icebox using blocks lifted from the seal hole. It's an arduous task, like building an igloo, mortaring ice with snow. Around us surface ice begins to melt: All the blue of the world is here, even if there isn't any such thing as blue.

From time to time I stop in the middle of a small task and glass the horizon with binoculars. North of here a big chunk of ice calved off Ellesmere Island floats in a southwestern arc; it is big enough to be inhabited by a research team that simply goes with the flow and reports back where that current takes them. In this way, too, I follow the wayward arc my thoughts make and see how easily they are lost—ephemeral on ephemeral ice.

Sleep again, then an alarm sewn into one of the nets is triggered by a seal. We leap up, fumbling our clothes; put on overalls, caps, gloves; jump into snowmobiles; and race to the lair. (There are at this time four nets set—four lairs among hundreds being monitored.) "It would kill me if I drown a seal in one of my nets," Brendan says. (It happened one time.) He probes the *aglu* with a blunt, long-handled pole: no seal. Blocking the hole with his face, he peers in: The bottom of the net is open. The seal has come and gone; the purse line didn't close.

The temperature plummets. Our fingers and feet are numb. Back at camp, disappointed, we eat bacon, potatoes, and cheese biscuits, drink coffee, and redesign the net. Brendan's silences—perhaps born of so many years on the ice—seem sad. I read Chukchi shaman tales (beautifully translated by Howard Norman) about ghost-laden kayaks, seal hunts that go badly, caribou skins that talk in the night. As the wind picks up everything talks, everything is alive. The walls of our tent talk over our talking, everything living talks to everything dead, and polar-bear skins walk at night on red ice where they hunted seals.

20 The next day Brendan and I set out for the Inuit village of Resolute, on Cornwallis Island. Scooting fast across ice, we come to a three-foot crack—a flaw or lead where shore-fast ice has broken from ice that moves with the tides. I get off and Brendan "jumps" the snowmobile over the opening, but when I jump, one leg slides in and there is that terrible moment when I know I've done something stupid. As Brendan turns to see what's wrong, I claw my way to safety. He merely grins and we ride on.

I spot sled dogs—huskies—chained to posts and gnawing on seal and dog carcasses. We weave through them, Brendan's labs peering bashfully from the komatik. Up through the boneyard into the village: maybe fifty houses newly sided with bright vinyl. It's late afternoon and the young men are packing up their sleds to go seal hunting: caribou skins for warmth, food, gasoline for the snowmobiles, and rifles which replace the harpoons they once used.

In 1953 seventeen Inuit—mostly caribou hunters from Baffin Island and Inoucdjouac in northern Quebec—were brought to Cornwallis Island to plant the Canadian flag and live on its barren slopes and frozen seas. They were the first inhabitants of the island since the Thule people had been driven out by the Little Ice Age 500 years before. It is not a hospitable place: Almost nothing grows except for the lichen that grinds away at sedimentary rock. The new settlers were 1,000 miles north of their previous home, and while they had volunteered to move some later asked to be sent home. Now 770,000 square miles of the Northwest Territories, including Cornwallis, have been given over to the Inuit, who are calling the area Nunavut, meaning "our land." It is theirs, except they will hold mineral rights to only 14,000 square miles.

We drive through rows of small clapboard houses. In one yard polar-bear skins are stretched from wooden frames, and in another two whalebone jaws rest against a wall. There's a clinic, a school, a general store. Two children, their faces hidden behind their dog-ruff hoods, want to ride in the komatik with the dogs, and we let them. Women in long dresses pass, carrying babies on their backs, flashing their beautiful ear-to-ear smiles. Looking back at Resolute from the top of a hill, I'm astonished that any peoples have survived at all in this realm.

Prevailing winds circle with the sun. I feel gusts in my face, then behind me, and the clouds take the sky from all sides like a flower closing at the end of the day; snowflakes drift, sun makes long shadows lean out of ice floes. Brendan locks his legs around me as we fly across the landscape, then we stop at a sizable chunk of multiyear ice (ice that formed two or more winters ago, ice that has not melted seasonally) and chip blocks to take home and melt for drinking water. I look for polar bears. Three weeks before, Brendan tells me, one strolled by with her cub and took a bite out of his tent. Now three eider ducks fly by, low to the ground, and far out where our tent is but a tiny orange speck, the mirage of a blue lagoon shimmers.

Wash dishes, empty slop bucket, melt ice, heat water for tea, bake[25] cookies in our tiny, unevenly heated propane oven, feed the beloved dogs. Brendan logs in data: the time and duration of a seal coming into a lair, its position under the ice, the length and duration of dives. But what does this tell us about a seal's life? What is the seal thinking, dreaming? "How to understand what we know, how to find the patterns that connect, that's a question too infrequently asked—especially by scientists," Brendan says ruefully. "We're so backward. Some of my colleagues are still arguing over whether animals even have a consciousness."

Late one night, after a dinner of roast lamb, rice tinted yellow with bottled lemon juice, and watery wine out of a cardboard box, the weather changes. Low clouds to the south undulate over Somerset Island, thickly amassed, like the notation of some unearthly music. Heat waves shiver upward from the ice. Where cracks have appeared, the sky darkens, reflecting water. "Water sky" it is called, used by the Inuit to find leads in ice where seals will be basking.

The wind comes while we are asleep: Toolboxes and books falling off shelves wake us. The whole tent shudders, the windward side collapsing into the room. Brendan runs outside in underwear to pee and jumps back in quickly, blasted white with snow. "Life in the 'attic,' ain't it grand!" he says gleefully. The laces that pull the tent panels together begin to stretch apart. Wind intensifies, snow drifts against us. We put on more layers of clothes and huddle around mugs of coffee.

The alarm goes off; seal in hole number three. Brendan and William dig out a snowmobile while I gather equipment, and we race into the wind. Snow has turned to ice; it cuts our faces as we fly.

A small seal, which Brendan identifies as a male yearling, sticks his nose into the air, greeting us. "Hi, sweetheart," Brendan coos, picking him up under the pectoral flippers and laying him on the snow. "How about a little ride in the komatik?" The seal is frightened. Brendan and William struggle to lift him into the box on the sled.

30   A seal's nose is shaped like a Y; the nostrils close watertight after intakes of breath. His whiskers are translucent and beaded. Puffy cheeks, wet gray rings around soft eyes—no tear ducts. As his coat dries, he is silvery with black rings spotting the fur. A pungent smell fills the tent. "He's been eating cod," Brendan says.

When we try to attach the pinger by dabbing a small circle of fur with glue, the yearling seal gets scrappy. Brendan gets bitten on the thigh. William and I stop everything to clean the wound—seal bites are known to cause infections.

"What do their mothers do to calm them?" I ask.

"They scratch the baby's back with their claws," Brendan says, so I rake my fingernails across his back; he flips over and I scratch his chest too. His eyes close; he shoves his head into one corner of the box and sleeps, front flippers twitching once in a while like a sleeping baby's hands.

By 6:00 PM the young seal is back in the water, pinger attached. The storm has worsened. To get back from the lair to the tent I walk in front of the snowmobile following what I think are tracks, though I'm not sure. "That's where dogs come in handy," Brendan says. "They leave their mark along the trail and it shows up even in blizzards."

35   Now our readings tell us that the wind is at forty-five knots and gusting to sixty. The nylon lacings that hold the tent panels together are tearing. We draw them tighter. All the shelves—with tools, five laptop computers, receivers, transmitters, charged batteries, books, charts, and maps—have to be pulled into the center of the room. And the tall antenna toenailed to the tent's wooden floor and sticking up through the ceiling is listing perilously. It could bring the whole tent down if it goes, William says, so Brendan climbs the curved outside wall of the tent and lowers the metal pole.

The noise makes sleep impossible. "What will happen if the wind gets worse?" I ask as we lie side by side on the floor—dogs and humans, all in sleeping bags. "The tent will blow away and we might die of exposure," Brendan says, then smiles. "But we probably won't."

Then we sleep. In the morning the landscape is totally changed. Snow has buried all traces of life and topography; snowmobiles, komatiks, food caches, skis, ice floes—all gone. Snow drifts in wide fans like sand dunes. The wind ebbs, then gusts to sixty-five knots again.

The plane I was supposed to take to Montreal does not land. Our two-way radio goes dead. Contact with Jerry McEachern, who calls faithfully every evening from Shelf—shorthand for the Polar Continental Shelf Project, a research base set up by the Canadian government—is lost. I can't see Cornwallis or the buildings at Shelf when I go out to pee. Turning away from the wind, my backside is sandblasted by flying ice crystals.

Three days go by. The tent breathes in and out. It is like living in someone else's lung. Finally the wind subsides. I walk far away from the tent to see what I can see. Snow has drifted in steep, smooth walls streaming back from rough ice, and where ice is blown clear of snow, it is pale blue. We poke in drifted snow to find things, then digging begins. The engines and cowlings of the snowmobiles we unearth have to be thoroughly cleaned.

Brendan drives me to Shelf to see about getting a plane out. It is so warm suddenly that we don't bother with jackets. The skis of the snowmobile splash through meltwater. Jerry has arranged for me to get on the first flight that can get in up here. I'm shocked, when I look at the calendar, to see we are well into the first week of June. After a much-cherished shower we start back to camp. Looking out over Barrow Strait past Cape Matyr, around Sheringham Point toward Allen Bay, I see the floor of the world has turned blue; only the islands are white.

By afternoon many small cracks have appeared in the ice beneath[40] us, some straight, some zigzagging. The dogs approach cautiously, then leap wide. The white massifs of grounded ice floes, which from a distance look like tall masted schooners, shelter cerulean ponds. Blue earth merges with blue sky, every hue pale and delicate. We pass two kill sites where polar bears not long ago feasted on seals: circles of blood and fur and a bashed-in lair. Bear scats are topped off with Arctic fox scats. The glory of ice becoming a sea again fills my eyes: It is like skating over the blue iris of an eye.

Two days later, at the tiny, crowded airport, Brendan and I sit wordlessly. Inuit women wait with their babies encircled by fur. They are going to other islands to visit relatives and once again live among caribou. Brendan's eyes blaze blue as ice. He will stay on until the meltwater reaches his knees and life on the frozen sea becomes impossible. "It seems as if I just get to know my way around when it all melts again," he says, and the old sadness comes back into his voice. There is nothing else to say. Then the plane, half cargo, half people, takes me away.

Two weeks later I hear from him. It has been raining in Resolute. Magnetic storms on the sun have disturbed radio contacts, and the planes are not able to land because their instruments don't work. The ice is going fast, he says. He's had to move onto the island. When I ask him what the landscape looks like now, there is a pause, then he says: "Yesterday a ship passed through the middle of the strait pushing ice with its bow. I watched it demolish what was left of the ice; it went right through where our tent used to be; where we lived is gone."

Additional Rhetorical Strategies

Definition (paragraph 5); Analogy and Metaphor (throughout); Narration (throughout).

Discussion Questions

1. Why is this essay titled "Time on Ice"? What is the significance of time in the essay? Why does the author periodically note the time at which a particular event occurred?
2. Who seems to be the intended audience for this essay: readers who have visited the Arctic, or readers who have not? How can you tell? How has Ehrlich adapted her language to describe the frozen landscape so that her intended audience will likely be able not only to envision but also to comprehend it?
3. Look at the metaphors Ehrlich uses. Several of them refer to parts of a human or animal's body: "vagina" (paragraph 12), "teeth" (paragraph 13), "lungs" (paragraph 38), and "iris of an eye" (paragraph 40), for instance. In several, if not all cases, these body parts are immense in scale. What is the accumulated effect of this network of metaphors?
4. How would you characterize the relationship between the scientist (Brendan Kelly) and the nonscientist (Gretel Ehrlich), in terms of their knowledge and concerns? What about the relationship between the visiting researcher and the Inuit who live in the region all year? What kinds of knowledge are the special province of each of these groups? How would you characterize the biologist's relationship with the natural creatures he studies? How would you characterize the writer's relationship with the people and objects she describes?

Essay Questions

1. Write an essay in which you describe the indescribable. Take on a challenge similar to Ehrlich's, in that the subject of your essay is something that few have seen and few can imagine. If you have never been to any places that are off the beaten path, you might choose to describe a landscape that exists only in your imagination, or one inspired by a painting or a photograph you have seen, or a

place described to you by a grandparent or an acquaintance from a foreign land.

2. Ehrlich's senses are subjected to a wholly unfamiliar set of stimuli when she visits the Canadian Arctic. Choose one or more of the human senses—sight, sound, touch, smell, taste—and examine the ways Ehrlich conveys the stimuli that affect these senses. Would you say that the stimuli are more or less various than the stimuli she would encounter on a given day in the contiguous United States? How might her sensitivity to stimuli change in response to the setting in which she finds herself? What are the inherent challenges in describing the sights, sounds, tactile sensations, smells, and tastes she encounters in the Arctic?

Thematic Pair: What We Wear

▲▼Biography of a Dress

Jamaica Kincaid

Jamaica Kincaid (b. 1949) was born Elaine Potter Richardson, on the Caribbean island of Antigua. Her works of fiction, all of which draw heavily on her own experience, include a collection of short stories, At the Bottom of the River *(1983), and two novels that were originally published as series of short stories in the* New Yorker: Annie John *(1985) and* Lucy *(1990). When asked about the autobiographical roots of* Lucy, *Kincaid replied "I've never really written about anyone except myself and my mother." She has also published a book-length nonfiction essay on postcolonial Antigua,* A Small Place *(1988).*

Although Kincaid was raised in the Caribbean, she does not consider her writing a part of a tradition of Caribbean writers. The curriculum of the schools she attended on Antigua was determined by the British perspective on civilization, so she came to believe that all great writers were British—and dead: "I thought that all the great writing had been done before 1900 . . . I never wanted to be a writer because I didn't know that any such thing existed." After she moved to the United States, with the intention of becoming an au pair, *she began to develop her own trademark writing style, which you can sample in the following descriptive essay.*

The dress I am wearing in this black-and-white photograph [p. 135], taken when I was two years old, was a yellow dress made of cotton poplin (a fabric with a slightly unsmooth texture first manufactured in the French town of Avignon and brought to England by the Huguenots,[1] but I could not have known that at the time), and it was made for me by my mother. This shade of yellow, the color of my dress that I am wearing when I was two years old, was the same shade of yellow as boiled cornmeal, a food that my mother was always eager for me to eat in one form (as a porridge) or another (as fongie, the starchy part of my midday meal) because it was cheap and therefore easily available (but I did not know that at the time), and because she thought that foods bearing the colors yellow, green or orange were particularly rich in vitamins and so boiled cornmeal would be particularly rich in vitamins and so boiled cornmeal would be particularly good for me. But I was then (not so now) extremely particular about what I would eat, not knowing then (but I do now) of shortages and abundance, having no consciousness of the idea of rich and poor (but I know now that we were poor then), and would eat only boiled beef (which I required my mother to chew for me first and, after she had made it soft, remove it from her mouth and place it in mine), certain kinds of boiled fish (doctor or angel), hard-boiled eggs (from hens, not ducks), poached

---

[1]Huguenots: French Protestants of the 16th and 17th centuries—Eds.

calf's liver and the milk from cows, and so would not even look at the
boiled cornmeal (porridge or fongie). There was not one single thing
that I could isolate and say I did not like about the boiled cornmeal
(porridge or fongie) because I could not isolate parts of things then
(though I can and do now), but whenever I saw this bowl of trembling
yellow substance before me I would grow still and silent, I did not cry,
that did not make me cry. My mother told me this then (she did not tell
me this now, she does not remember this now, she does not remember
telling me this now): she knew of a man who had eaten boiled cornmeal
at least once a day from the time he was my age then, two years old,
and he lived for a very long time, finally dying when he was almost one
hundred years old, and when he died he had looked rosy and new,
with the springy wrinkles of the newborn, not the slack pleats of skin of
the aged: as he lay dead his stomach was cut open, and all his insides
were a beautiful shade of yellow, the same shade of yellow as boiled
cornmeal. I was powerless then (though not so now) to like or dislike
this story; it was beyond me then (though not so now) to understand
the span of my lifetime then, two years old, and it was beyond me then
(though not so now), the span of time called almost one hundred years
old; I did not know then (though I do now) that there was such a thing
as an inside to anybody, and that this inside would have a color, and
that if the insides were the same shade of yellow as the yellow of boiled
cornmeal my mother would want me to know about it.

On a day when it was not raining (that would have been unusual,
that would have been out of the ordinary, ruining the fixed form of the
day), my mother walked to one of the Harneys' stores (there were
many Harneys who owned stores, and they sold the same things, but I
did not know then and I do not know now if they were all of the same
people) and bought one-and-a-half yards of this yellow cotton poplin to
make a dress for me, a dress I would wear to have my picture taken on
the day I turned two years old. Inside, the store was cool and dark, and
this was a good thing because outside was hot and overly bright. Someone named Harney did not wait on my mother, but someone named
Miss Verna did and she was very nice still, so nice that she tickled my
cheek as she spoke to my mother, and I reached forward as if to kiss
her, but when her cheek met my lips I opened my mouth and bit her
hard with my small child's teeth. Her cry of surprise did not pierce the
air, but she looked at me hard, as if she knew me very, very well; and
later, much later, when I was about twelve years old or so and she was
always in and out of the crazy house, I would pass her on the street and
throw stones at her, and she would turn and look at me hard, but she
did not know who I was, she did not know who anyone was at all, not
at all. Miss Verna showed my mother five flat thick bolts of cloth,
white, blue (sea), blue (sky), yellow and pink, and my mother chose the
yellow after holding it up against the rich copper color that my hair

was then (it is not so now); she paid for it with a one-pound note that had an engraving of the king George Fifth on it (an ugly man with a cruel, sharp, bony nose, not the kind, soft, fleshy noses I was then used to), and she received change that included crowns, shillings, florins and farthings.

My mother, carrying me and the just-bought piece of yellow poplin wrapped in coarse brown paper in her arms, walked out of Mr. Harney's store, up the street a few doors away, and into a store called Murdoch's (because the family who owned it were the Murdochs), and there my mother bought two skeins of yellow thread, the kind used for embroidering and a shade of yellow almost identical to the yellow poplin. My mother not only took me with her everywhere she went, she carried me, sometimes in her arms, sometimes on her back; for this errand she carried me in her arms; she did not complain, she never complained (but later she refused to do it anymore and never gave an explanation, at least not one that I can remember now); as usual, she spoke to me and sang to me in French patois (but I did not understand French patois then and I do not now and so I can never know what exactly she said to me then). She walked back to our house on Dickenson Bay Street, stopping often to hold conversations with people (men and women) she knew, speaking to them sometimes in English, sometimes in French; and if after they said how beautiful I was (for people would often say that about me then but they do not say that about me now), she would laugh and say I did not like to be kissed (and I don't know if that was really true then but it is not so now). And that night after we had eaten our supper (boiled fish in a butter-and-lemon-juice sauce) and her husband (who was not my father but I did not know that at the time, I know that now) had gone for a walk (to the jetty), she removed the yellow poplin from its brown wrapper and folded and made creases in it and with scissors made holes (for the arms and neck) and slashes (for an opening in the back and the shoulders); she then placed it along with some ordinary thread (yellow), the thread for embroidering, the scissors and a needle in a basket that she had brought with her from her home in Dominica when she first left it at sixteen years of age.

For days afterward, my mother, after she had finished her usual chores (clothes washing, dish washing, floor scrubbing, bathing me, her only child, feeding me a teaspoon of cod-liver oil), sat on the sill of the doorway, half in the sun, half out of the sun, and sewed together the various parts that would make up altogether my dress of yellow poplin; she gathered and hemmed and made tucks; she was just in the early stages of teaching herself how to make smocking and so was confined to making straight stitches (up-cable, down-cable, outline, stem, chain); the bodice of the dress appeared simple, plain, and the detail and pattern can only be seen close up and in real life, not from far away and not in a photograph; and much later, when she grew in confidence with this craft, the bodice of my dresses became overburdened with the stitches chevron, trellis, diamonds, Vandyke, and species of birds she had never seen (swan) and species of flowers she had never seen (tulip) and species of animals she had never seen (bear) in real life, only in a picture in a book.

5   My skin was not the color of cream in the process of spoiling, my hair was not the texture of silk and the color of flax, my eyes did not gleam like blue jewels in a crown, the afternoons in which I sat watching my mother make me this dress were not cool, and verdant lawns and pastures and hills and dales did not stretch out before me; but it was the picture of such a girl at two years old—a girl whose skin was the color of cream in the process of spoiling, whose hair was the texture of silk and the color of flax, a girl whose eyes gleamed like blue jewels in a crown, a girl whose afternoons (and mornings and nights) were cool, and before whom stretched verdant lawns and pastures and hills and dales—that my mother saw, a picture on an almanac advertising a particularly fine and scented soap (a soap she could not afford to buy then but I can now), and this picture of this girl wearing a yellow dress with smocking on the front bodice perhaps created in my mother the desire to have a daughter who looked like that or perhaps created the desire in my mother to try and make the daughter she already had look like that. I do not know now and I did not know then. And who was that girl really? (I did not ask then because I could not ask then but I ask now.) And who made her dress? And this girl would have had a mother; did the mother then have some friends, other women, and did they sit together under a tree (or sit somewhere else) and compare strengths of potions used to throw away a child, or weigh the satisfactions to be had from the chaos of revenge or the smooth order of forgiveness; and this girl with skin of cream on its way to spoiling and hair the color of flax, what did her insides look like, what did she eat? (I did not ask then because I could not ask then and I ask now but no one can answer me, really answer me.)

    My second birthday was not a major event in anyone's life, certainly not my own (it was not my first and it was not my last, I am now forty-three years old), but my mother, perhaps because of circumstances (I would not have known then and to know now is not a help), perhaps only because of an established custom (but only in her family, other people didn't do this), to mark the occasion of my turning two years old had my ears pierced. One day, at dusk (I would not have called it that then), I was taken to someone's house (a woman from Dominica, a woman who was as dark as my mother was fair, and yet they were so similar that I am sure now as I was then that they shared the same tongue), and two thorns that had been heated in a fire were pierced through my earlobes. I do not now know (and could not have known then) if the pain I experienced resembled in any way the pain my mother experienced while giving birth to me or even if my mother, in having my ears bored in that way, at that time, meant to express hostility or aggression toward me (but without meaning to and without knowing that it was possible to mean to). For days afterward my earlobes were swollen and covered with a golden crust (which might have glistened in the harsh sunlight, but I can only imagine that now), and the pain of my earlobes must have filled up all that made up my entire being then and the pain of my earlobes must have been unbearable, because it was then that was the first time that I separated myself from myself, and I became two people (two small children then, I was two years old), one having the experience, the other observing the one having the experience. And the observer, perhaps because it was an act of my own will (strong then, but stronger now), my first and only real act of self-invention, is the one of the two I most rely on, the one of the two whose voice I believe to be the true voice; and of course it is the observer who cannot be relied on as the final truth to be believed, for the observer has woven between myself and the person who is having an experience a protective membrane, which allows me to see but only feel as much as I can handle at any given moment. And so . . .

. . . On the day I turned two years old, the twenty-fifth of May 1951, a pair of earrings, small hoops made of gold from British Guiana (it was called that then, it is not called that now), were placed in the bored holes in my earlobes (which by then had healed); a pair of bracelets made of silver from someplace other than British Guiana (and that place too was called one thing then, something else now) was placed one on each wrist; a pair of new shoes bought from Bata's was placed on my feet. That afternoon, I was bathed and powdered, and the dress of yellow poplin, completed, its seams all stitched together with a certainty found only in the natural world (I now realize), was placed over my head, and it is quite possible that this entire act had about it the feeling of being draped in a shroud. My mother, carrying me in her arms (as usual), took me to the studio of a photographer, a man named Mr. Walker, to have my picture taken. As she walked along with me in her arms (not complaining), with the heat of the sun still so overwhelming that it, not gravity, seemed to be the force that kept us pinned to the earth's surface, I placed my lips against one side of her head (the temple) and could feel the rhythm of the blood pulsing through her body; I placed my lips against her throat and could hear her swallow saliva that had collected in her mouth; I placed my face against her neck and inhaled deeply a scent that I could not identify then (how could I, there was nothing to compare it to) and cannot now, because it is not of animal or place or thing, it was (and is) a scent unique to her, and it left a mark of such depth that it eventually became a part of my other senses, and even now (yes, now) that scent is also taste, touch, sight and sound.

    And Mr. Walker lived on Church Street in a house that was myste-
rious to me (then, not now) because it had a veranda (unlike my own
house) and it had many rooms (unlike my own house, but really Mr.
Walker's house had only four rooms, my own house had one) and the
windows were closed (the windows in my house were always open).
He spoke to my mother, I did not understand what they said, they did
not share the same tongue. I knew Mr. Walker was a man, but how I
knew that I cannot say (now, then, sometime to come). It is possible
that because he touched his hair often, smoothing down, caressing, the
forcibly straightened strands, and because he admired and said that he
admired my dress of yellow poplin with its simple smocking (giving to
me a false air of delicacy), and because he admired and said that he admired the plaid taffeta ribbon in my hair, I thought that he perhaps
wasn't a man at all, I had never seem a man do or say any of those
things, I had then only seen a woman do or say those things. He (Mr.
Walker) stood next to a black box which had a curtain at its back (this
was his camera but I did not know that at the time, I only know it now)
and he asked my mother to stand me on a table, a small table, a table
that made me taller, because the scene in the background, against
which I was to be photographed, was so vast, it overwhelmed my two-
year-old frame, making me seem a mere figurine, not a child at all; and
when my mother picked me up, holding me by the armpits with her
hands, her thumb accidentally (it could have been deliberate, how
could someone who loved me inflict so much pain just in passing?)
pressed deeply into my shoulder, and I cried out and then (and still
now) looked up at her face and couldn't find any reason in it, and could
find no malice in it, only that her eyes were full of something, a feeling
that I thought then (and am convinced now) had nothing to do with
me; and of course it is possible that just at that moment she had realized that she was exhausted, not physically, but just exhausted by this
whole process, celebrating my second birthday, commemorating an
event, my birth, that she may not have wished to occur in the first place
and may have tried repeatedly to prevent, and then, finally, in trying to
find some beauty in it, ended up with a yard and a half of yellow
poplin being shaped into a dress, teaching herself smocking and purchasing gold hoops from places whose names never remained the same
and silver bracelets from places whose names never remained the same.
And Mr. Walker, who was not at all interested in my mother's ups and
downs and would never have dreamed of taking in the haphazard
mess of her life (but there was nothing so unusual about that, every life,
I now know, is a haphazard mess), looked on for a moment as my
mother, belying the look in her eyes, said kind and loving words to me
in a kind and loving voice, and he then walked over to a looking glass
that hung on a wall and squeezed with two of his fingers a lump the
size of a pinch of sand that was on his cheek; the lump had a shiny

white surface and it broke, emitting a tiny plap sound, and from it came a long ribbon of thick, yellow pus that curled on Mr. Walker's cheek imitating, almost, the decoration on the birthday cake that awaited me at home, and my birthday cake was decorated with a series of species of flora and fauna my mother had never seen (and still has not seen to this day, she is seventy-three years old).

After that day I never again wore my yellow poplin dress with the smocking my mother had just taught herself to make. It was carefully put aside, saved for me to wear to another special occasion; but by the time another special occasion came (I could say quite clearly then what the special occasion was and can say quite clearly now what the special occasion was but I do not want to), the dress could no longer fit me, I had grown too big for it.

Additional Rhetorical Strategies

Comparison and Contrast (throughout); Narration (throughout).

Discussion Questions

1. The word *biography* nearly always refers to a person, not an object. What is the effect of using this word in her title? How does Kincaid use the biography of a dress as a vehicle to tell about the life of a little girl (i.e., her own autobiography)? Nowhere in the essay does Kincaid directly address the expression on the face of the little girl in the picture, or her stance. What details in the essay indirectly contribute to your understanding of the little girl's expression and stance?

2. How would you characterize the relationship between the forty-three-year-old Kincaid, who is narrating the piece, and the two-year-old Kincaid who is the subject of the photo and essay? What do the two have in common, and how do they differ? Do you notice any patterns in the statements (mostly parenthetical) pertaining to the similarities and differences between the two?

3. The ear piercing seems to have been a pivotal moment in the young girl's life. How might that moment relate to, or illuminate, the structure and narrative voice of Kincaid's essay?

4. Explore the theme of knowledge in this essay. Who has it; who loses it gradually; who gains it gradually?

5. How would you characterize the relationship between Jamaica Kincaid and her mother? Point to specific passages in the text to support your answer. How do you think cultural factors affected Kincaid's mother's attitude toward her child? What is the significance of the discussions among the hypothetical mother and her friends, as characterized in paragraph 6?

6. How would you describe the structure of this essay? What principle seems to guide the order of the parts, the beginnings and ends of paragraphs, the inclusion of some information and the exclusion of other information?

Essay Questions

1. Choose something about this essay—a sentence, a paragraph, related statements from throughout the essay—that confused you, and write an exploratory essay in which you test out various explanations. Despite the child-like tone and syntax of much of the essay, not all of the meaning lies right on the surface: this is an essay that will repay close attention and sustained thought.
2. Locate a photograph from your own life history, and describe it for an audience who cannot possibly see all you see when you look at it. You might choose a photograph of yourself, a family member, a friend, your home, and so on. Kincaid writes in paragraph 4 that the details of the embroidery on her dress "can only be seen close up and in real life"; of course, the physical limitations of looking at a photo instead of a real person are the least of the limitations for a stranger looking at this photo of her younger self. Write an essay that fills in both the physical and the emotional details that a casual observer would miss. Also consider including descriptions of things that did not happen (such as the man who did not wait on Kincaid's mother, or the cry that "did not pierce the air" [paragraph 2], along with things that did, just as Kincaid does in her essay.

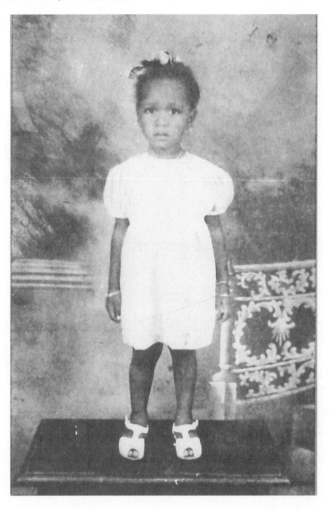

▲▼Overalls

James Agee

James Agee (1909–1955) was a poet, journalist, film critic, screenwriter, and novelist. His works include a volume of poetry titled Permit Me Voyage *(1934); screen adaptations of C. S. Forester's "The African Queen" (1952) and Stephen Crane's "The Bride Comes to Yellow Sky" (1952); and the semi-autobiographical novel* A Death in the Family, *which was unfinished at the time of his death and awarded a posthumous Pulitzer Prize in 1957.*

Agee is best known for the work from which the following description of overalls was excerpted. In 1936, Agee and the photographer Walker Evans were assigned by Fortune *magazine to do a feature story examining the lives of poor Alabama sharecroppers.* Fortune *found the passionate piece unacceptable, and it was not published until 1941, when it appeared as a book,* Let Us Now Praise Famous Men. *Too uncompromising to be well received at the time of its publication, the book has since achieved the status of a classic.*

The photographs by Evans were meant not just to accompany the text; indeed, Agee considered them more vital than the text he wrote. As he explained, "If I could do it, I'd do no writing here at all. It would be photographs; the rest would be fragments of cloth, bits of cotton, lumps of earth, records of speech, pieces of wood and iron, phials of odors, plates of food and of excrement." As you read the selection that follows, decide to what extent Agee's prose approximates the stark, unmediated contact with the substance of the sharecroppers' lives that he set as his ideal.

They are pronounced overhauls.

Try—I cannot write of it here—to imagine and to know, as against other garments, the difference of their feeling against your body; drawn-on, and bibbed on the whole belly and chest, naked from the kidneys up behind, save for broad crossed straps, and slung by these straps from the shoulders; the slanted pockets on each thigh, the deep square pockets on each buttock; the complex and slanted structures, on the chest, of the pockets shaped for pencils, rulers, and watches; the coldness of sweat when they are young, and their stiffness; their sweetness to the skin and pleasure of sweating when they are old; the thin metal buttons of the fly; the lifting aside of the straps and the deep slipping downward in defecation; the belt some men use with them to steady their middles; the swift, simple, and inevitably supine gestures of dressing and of undressing, which, as is less true of any other garment, are those of harnessing and of unharnessing the shoulders of a tired and hard-used animal.

They are round as stovepipes in the legs (though some wives, told to, crease them).

In the strapping across the kidneys they again resemble work harness, and in their crossed straps and tin buttons.

5   And in the functional pocketing of their bib, a harness modified to the convenience of a used animal of such high intelligence that he has use for tools.

And in their whole stature: full covering of the cloven strength of the legs and thighs and of the loins; then nakedness and harnessing behind, naked along the flanks; and in front, the short, squarely tapered, powerful towers of the belly and chest to above the nipples.

And on this façade, the cloven halls for the legs, the strong-seamed, structured opening for the genitals, the broad horizontal at the waist, the slant thigh pockets, the buttons at the point of each hip and on the breast, the geometric structures of the usages of the simpler trades—the complexed seams of utilitarian pockets which are so brightly picked out against darkness when the seam-threadings, double and triple stitched, are still white, so that a new suit of overalls has among its beauties those of a blueprint: and they are a map of a working man.

The shirts too; squarely cut, and strongly seamed; with big square pockets and with metal buttons: the cloth stiff, the sweat cold when it is new, the collar large in newness and standing out in angles under the ears; so that in these new workclothes a man has the shy and silly formal charm of a mail-order-catalogue engraving.

The changes that age, use, weather, work upon these.

10   They have begun with the massive yet delicate beauty of most things which are turned out most cheaply in great tribes by machines: and on this basis of structure they are changed into images and marvels of nature.

The structures sag, and take on the look, some of use; some, the pencil pockets, the pretty atrophies of what is never used; the edges of the thigh pockets become stretched and lie open, fluted, like the gills of a fish. The bright seams lose their whiteness and are lines and ridges. The whole fabric is shrunken to size, which was bought large. The whole shape, texture, color, finally substance, all are changed. The shape, particularly along the urgent frontage of the thighs, so that the whole structure of the knee and musculature of the thigh is sculptured there; each man's garment wearing the shape and beauty of his induplicable body. The texture and the color change in union, by sweat, sun, laundering, between the steady pressures of its use and age: both, at length, into realms of fine softness and marvel of draping and velvet plays of light which chamois and silk can only suggest, not touch,[1] and into a region and scale of blues, subtle, delicious, and deft beyond what

---

[1]The texture of old paper money.

I have ever seen elsewhere approached except in rare skies, the smoky light some days are filmed with, and some of the blues of Cézanne: one could watch and touch even one such garment, study it, with the eyes, the fingers, and the subtlest lips, almost illimitably long, and never fully learn it; and I saw no two which did not hold some world of exquisiteness of its own. Finally, too; particularly athwart the crest and swing of the shoulders, of the shirts: this fabric breaks like snow, and is stitched and patched: these break, and again are stitched and patched and ruptured, and stitches and patches are manifolded upon the stitches and patches, and more on these, so that at length, at the shoulders, the shirt contains virtually nothing of the original fabric and a man, George Gudger,[2] I remember so well, and many hundreds of others like him, wears in his work on the power of his shoulders a fabric as intricate and fragile, and as deeply in honor of the reigning sun, as the feather mantle of a Toltec prince.[3]

Gudger has three; it is perhaps four changes of overalls and workshirts. They are, set by set, in stages of age, and of beauty, distinctly apart from one another; and of the three I remember, each should at best be considered separately and at full length. I have room here to say only that they represent medium-early, middle, and medium-late stages, and to suggest a little more about these. The youngest are still dark; their seams are still visible; the cloth has not yet lost all of its hardness, nor the buttons their brightness. They have taken the shape of the leg, yet they are still the doing as much of machinery as of nature. The middle-aged are fully soft and elegantly textured, and are lost out of all machinery into a full prime of nature. The mold of the body is fully taken, the seams are those of a living plant or animal, the cloth's grain is almost invisible, the buttons are rubbed and mild, the blue is at the full silent, greatly restrained strength of its range; the patches in the overalls are few and strategic, the right[4] knee, the two bones of the rump, the elbows, the shoulders are quietly fledged: the garments are still wholly competent and at their fullness of comfort. The old: the cloth sleeps against all salients of the body in complete peace, and in its loose hangings, from the knee downward, is fallen and wandered in the first loss of form into foldings I believe no sculptor has ever touched. The blue is so vastly fainted and withdrawn it is discernible scarcely more as blue than as that most pacific silver which the bone wood of the houses and the visage of genius seem to shed, and is a color and cloth seeming ancient, veteran, composed, and patient to the source of being, as too the sleepings and the drifts of form. The shoulders are that

[2]George Gudger: Described at the opening of the book as "a one-mule halfcropper, aged thirty-one"—Eds.
[3]Toltec: Pre-Aztec Native American—Eds.
[4]The left knee is rubbed thin and has absorbed irreducibly the gold shadow of the blended colors of the clays of that neighborhood.

full net of sewn snowflakes of which I spoke. The buttons are blind as cataracts, and slip their soft holes. The whole of the seat and of the knees and elbows are broken and patched, the patches subdued in age almost with the original cloth, drawn far forward toward the feathering of the shoulders. There is a more youthful stage than the youngest of these; Ricketts . . . wears such overalls; there are many median modulations; and there is a stage later than the latest here, as I saw in the legs of Woods'[5] overalls, which had so entirely lost one kind of tendency to form that they had gained another, and were wrinkled minutely and innumerably as may best be paralleled by old thin oilskin crumpled, and by the skin of some aged faces.

Additional Rhetorical Strategies

Analogy (paragraphs 2, 4, 5); Process Analysis (paragraph 11); Example (paragraph 12).

Discussion Questions

1. Examine the first line closely. What does it tell you about the author's stance toward his subject? What does the passive voice tell you? Who is the implied agent of the act of pronunciation? Where does the author stand in relation to that agent? To what extent does the placement of this sentence privilege the voice (dialect) of the sharecroppers themselves? To what extent and for how long (in the essay) does Agee keep the sharecroppers on a generic, as opposed to an individual, level? To what effect?

2. In this essay, Agee explores a continuum between machinery and nature. To what extent are these two forces opposed, and where do they intersect? What are the larger implications, given the context of the working classes whose lives Agee is describing and Walker is photographing?

3. Underline all the references to parts of the body in this essay. To whose bodies do they refer? Look particularly at paragraphs 2 and 11. What is the effect of this intimate focus on the physical body? Does the effect differ in these two examples?

4. In his second sentence Agee writes "I cannot write of it here." This is an odd admission with which to open such a detailed descriptive essay. (You might note for comparison the opening line of Maxine Hong Kingston's essay on p. 67.) How does this essay express the inexpressible, and to what extent must it imply rather than express its subject? How do the references to artists and works of art, and

---

[5]Woods: Ricketts and Woods were other sharecroppers Agee got to know—Eds.

the artistic tone that crops up intermittently in this piece, relate to the problem of expressing the inexpressible?

Essay Questions

1. Compare and contrast Agee's use of literal and figurative language in this essay. How do the two kinds of language interact here? Look for instance at the first figure of speech he employs, the harness analogy that begins in paragraph 2. Does that figurative language stand in complete contrast to the literal language that came before? At what point does Agee make it clear that the figure is also meant literally? Trace the continuum between the two kinds of language. Look also at the other metaphors and analogies Agee employs throughout the essay and ponder their significance and effects.

2. In paragraph 7, Agee writes that overalls "are a map of the working man." Although his subject is the working class in general, it is clear that he is writing more specifically about the working *man*. Write an essay discussing the inferences about masculinity, and the expectations the culture imposes on men in particular, that one can make from reading Agee's description of this one article of masculine attire.

Exploring Connections: Questions Linking the Thematic Pair

1. Write a descriptive essay about an item of clothing or other everyday object. Explore the larger personal and/or social meanings that seem to inhere in the object. Draw on any relevant rhetorical strategies you have learned from reading Kincaid's and Agee's essays to strengthen the effect of your own essay.

2. Kincaid describes a dress worn by herself at a far younger age; Agee describes a pair of overalls worn by a man who is distanced from him in terms of class. How do the two kinds of distance affect the essays each writes? What tactics does each employ to bridge the distances? Where in each essay do you sense that the writer is drawn close to the subject of his or her essay, and where does each draw back?

Exemplification

Exemplification is a process through which writers select specific examples to represent, clarify, and support either general or abstract statements. Exemplification is such an indispensable feature of thinking and writing that it is difficult even to imagine a successful writer's doing without it. Yet exemplification is also such an accustomed part of our thinking that we may well take it for granted and not fully appreciate how it can work to strengthen our writing. The primary functions of exemplification in writing are to make abstractions concrete and to lend detail to generalization. But exemplification also clarifies our ideas, helps readers to follow the course of our thinking, heightens their interest in our subject, and, generally, adds substance to our prose.

Of all the methods of thinking in writing presented in this book, exemplification (sometimes called illustration) is undoubtedly the one with which we are most familiar. Our daily conversations are punctuated with such phrases as *for example, for instance,* and the like. When we use such phrases, we are explaining through examples. An example may be thought of as a part, a model, or a pattern of something. *Example* is often used interchangeably with such terms as *instance, case, sample,* and *specimen.* Each term helps explain something larger. Dictionary definitions regularly use examples. *The American Heritage Dictionary* defines *mixed metaphor* as a "succession of metaphors that produce an incongruous and ludicrous effect." The dictionary proceeds immediately to illustrate—to exemplify—this abstract statement with a concrete instance: "for example: *His mounting ambition was soon bridled by a wave of opposition.*" The example is offered to ensure that the precise meaning of the phrase is clearly understood. Such an illustration highlights the standard way in which an example carries thinking from the abstract to the concrete.

Examples Help Make Ideas Clear and Convincing

For most writers, exemplification is an instinctive process: we sense the need for an example each time we discuss a subject in abstract or general terms. If we decided to talk about America in the 1960s as a "rebellious decade," we would immediately be aware that we ought to supply examples to support our contention. While we might choose the

143

women's-liberation, the civil-rights, and the anti-war movements as our major examples, we would also need to develop each in enough detail to make our point convincing. If we were writing about the recurrence of organized abuses of civil rights in this country, we might substantiate our thesis with such examples as the excesses of nineteenth-century vigilante groups or the violent activities of the Ku Klux Klan today. Exemplification usually anticipates such questions as "Can you be more specific?" "What evidence can you provide to support this statement?" "What are some examples of the point you are making?" Examples offer concrete representations of general or abstract thinking. They make our ideas clearer.

Consider, for example, how the columnist and novelist William Safire draws on the principles of illustration to clarify and reinforce the controlling idea of his essay "On Keeping a Diary"—that each of us should keep a fairly regular written account of our personal observations:

> Diaries remind us of details that would otherwise fade from memory and make less vivid our recollection. Navy Secretary Gideon Welles, whose private journal is an invaluable source for Civil War historians, watched Abraham Lincoln die in a room across the street from Ford's Theater and later jotted down a detail that puts the reader in the room: "The giant sufferer lay extended diagonally across the bed, which was not long enough for him. . . ."
>
> Diaries can be written in psychic desperation, intended to be burned, as a hold on sanity: "I won't give up the diary again," wrote novelist Franz Kafka. "I must hold on here, it is the only place I can." Or written in physical desperation, intended to be read, as in the last entry in Arctic explorer Robert Scott's diary: "For God's sake look after our people. . . ."

As this passage demonstrates, exemplification adds a great deal of detail to our writing. Consider the alternative: Safire's point would not be nearly as convincing if he had simply given us reasons for keeping a diary without also illustrating each of those reasons. In effect, illustration adds texture to our sentences and paragraphs as well as substance to each of the points we want to make in our essays.

Exemplification invariably adds detail to our writing. Particular examples may appear in individual sentences or paragraphs, or they may even constitute an entire essay. If you were to write an essay in which you developed the thesis that the image of African Americans in advertising has changed significantly during the past two decades, you would have to support this thesis with an analysis of several examples. A single example may not prove sufficient to support a generalization. So, too, each example requires an adequate number of details to be convincing. If you wanted to discuss, say, the most significant recent directions in American popular music, you might well choose R.E.M., U2, and Alanis Morissette as your examples. It would then be appropriate to move on to consider in some detail each of their latest albums. One example may well lead to a series of others. In this instance, perhaps you would want to go on to discuss the lyrics of their music or the nature of their performances in concert—depending, of course, on your announced purpose, audience, and space limitations.

Selecting Examples

The choice of examples depends on the demands of a clearly stated thesis. Our essays should include only those examples that have a direct bearing on the thesis. So, too, the examples to be included should, taken together, touch on all aspects of the thesis or the general points that we intend to make. If, for example, you were writing about the economic effects of a national health care plan, you could draw on any number of examples, including the plan's consequences for patients, insurance companies, doctors, nurses, and other professionals in the health services and related fields. Yet in an essay dealing with, say, the effectiveness of the United Nations as a peacekeeping force in international crises, the gradual and detailed unfolding of one or two extended examples—the ongoing Arab-Israeli border disputes or the Soviet invasion of Afghanistan—may be the most appropriate way to assemble sufficient details to establish a clear and convincing thesis. We ought to remember, however, that as we reduce the number of examples to be discussed, we increase the need for treating each with greater specificity. It is not the number of examples that makes an essay successful but rather how well each is integrated into the writer's presentation, how pertinent each is to the point being made.

Exemplification may also take the form of an anecdote, fable, parable, or analogy that displays the general point being made. As in all other cases of exemplification, care must be exercised to ensure that each example is finally precise enough to be entirely clear to all of our readers.

When we select an example, we choose a part to represent the whole. One important thing to remember when using exemplification is that what can be said about one example can be said about any other in the group to which it belongs. When writing about, say, the second-class status of women in American professional sports, you would do well to cite as an example the discrepancies in tennis-tournament prize money. The point illustrated by this example could also be applied to other professional sports: basketball, golf, baseball, squash, and softball. In this case, tennis would be a fair and representative example for the proposed thesis: namely, that the material and psychological rewards of athletics remain fewer for women than men. Yet it would be unreasonable to compare the salaries of male and female professional basketball players, since the women's professional league is still in its formative stages. In sum, the examples we choose to support the points we make should be at once typical and striking: they must be vivid enough to attract and hold the reader's attention and yet representative enough to be taken seriously.

Organizing Examples

Considerable importance should be attached to the positioning and timing of exemplification in our writing. Each point should be illustrated fully, one at a time. the confusion of mixing one example with another must be avoided. Perhaps the best way to eliminate such potential disorder in our writing is to place each example as near as possible to the point being made. But should a series of examples be called for, we ought to remember that the positions of greatest emphasis are at the beginning and the end.

Exemplification is an integral part of nearly every method of thinking in writing. It appears frequently, as we will see in other sections of this book, in description and narration, and it enhances all other rhetorical techniques. Whether we use it within the confines of a single sentence or throughout an entire essay, exemplification helps tighten loose generalizations and effectively prevents us from jumping to conclusions—that is, from basing generalizations on a single example. But most important, exemplification makes abstract ideas concrete and, in doing so, makes our thinking in writing more lucid and persuasive.

America: The Multinational Society

Ishmael Reed

Ishmael Reed (b. 1938) began his college education at night school, but soon his writing skills and his gift for parody brought him to the attention of one of his English professors, who encouraged Reed to become a full-time student at the State University of New York at Buffalo. His first novel, The Freelance Pallbearers *(1968) received a warm critical reception. His prolific output since that time includes novels, poetry, songs, essays, and plays. The piece below comes from his collection of essays* Writin' is Fightin' *(1988). Many of Reed's written works satirize or attack the vices and excesses of the contemporary American middle and upper classes.*

One of Reed's most important contributions has taken the form of nurturing and promoting other minority authors. In 1971, Reed cofounded Yardbird Publishing Company; in 1973 he founded the Reed, Cannon, and Johnson Communications Company; and in 1976 he cofounded the Before Columbus Foundation. The mission of each of these publishing companies is to expand the canon of American literature to include all the different voices that make up our multinational society.

Ishmael Reed has taught at Harvard, Yale, and Dartmouth, and he currently teaches creative writing at the University of California at Berkeley.

At the annual Lower East Side Jewish Festival yesterday, a Chinese woman ate a pizza slice in front of Ty Thuan Duc's Vietnamese grocery store. Beside her a Spanish-speaking family patronized a cart with two signs: "Italian Ices" and "Kosher by Rabbi Alper." And after the pastrami ran out, everybody ate knishes.

—*New York Times,* 23 June 1983

On the day before Memorial Day, 1983, a poet called me to describe a city he had just visited. He said that one section included mosques, built by the Islamic people who dwelled there. Attending his reading, he said, were large numbers of Hispanic people, forty thousand of whom lived in the same city. He was not talking about a fabled city located in some mysterious region of the world. The city he'd visited was Detroit.

A few months before, as I was leaving Houston, Texas, I heard it announced on the radio that Texas's largest minority was Mexican-American, and though a foundation recently issued a report critical of bilingual education, the taped voice used to guide the passengers on the air trams connecting terminals in Dallas Airport is in both Spanish and English. If the trend continues, a day will come when it will be difficult to travel through some sections of the country without hearing commands in both English and Spanish; after all, for some western states, Spanish was the first written language and the Spanish style lives on in the western way of life.

Shortly after my Texas trip, I sat in an auditorium located on the campus of the University of Wisconsin at Milwaukee as a Yale professor—whose original work on the influence of African cultures upon those of the Americas has led to his ostracism from some monocultural intellectual circles—walked up and down the aisle, like an old-time southern evangelist, dancing and drumming the top of the lectern, illustrating his points before some serious Afro-American intellectuals and artists who cheered and applauded his performance and his mastery of information. The professor was "white." After his lecture, he joined a group of Milwaukeeans in a conversation. All of the participants spoke Yoruban, though only the professor had ever traveled to Africa.

One of the artists told me that his paintings, which included African and Afro-American mythological symbols and imagery, were hanging in the local McDonald's restaurant. The next day I went to McDonald's and snapped pictures of smiling youngsters eating hamburgers below paintings that could grace the walls of any of the country's leading museums. The manager of the local McDonald's said, "I don't know what you boys are doing, but I like it," as he commissioned the local painters to exhibit in his restaurant.

5   Such blurring of cultural styles occurs in everyday life in the United States to a greater extent than anyone can imagine and is probably more prevalent than the sensational conflict between people of different backgrounds that is played up and often encouraged by the media. The result is what the Yale professor, Robert Thompson, referred to as a cultural bouillabaisse, yet members of the nation's present educational and cultural Elect still cling to the notion that the United States belongs to some vaguely defined entity they refer to as "Western civilization," by which they mean, presumably, a civilization created by the people of Europe, as if Europe can be viewed in monolithic terms. Is Beethoven's Ninth Symphony, which includes Turkish marches, a part of Western civilization, or the late nineteenth- and twentieth-century French paintings, whose creators were influenced by Japanese art? And what of the cubists, through whom the influence of African art changed modern painting, or the surrealists, who were so impressed with the art of the Pacific Northwest Indians that, in their map of North America, Alaska dwarfs the lower forty-eight in size?

Are the Russians, who are often criticized for their adoption of "Western" ways by Tsarist dissidents in exile, members of Western civilization? And what of the millions of Europeans who have black African and Asian ancestry, black Africans having occupied several countries for hundreds of years? Are these "Europeans" members of Western civilization, or the Hungarians, who originated across the Urals in a place called Greater Hungary, or the Irish, who came from the Iberian Peninsula?

Even the notion that North America is part of Western civilization because our "system of government" is derived from Europe is being challenged by Native American historians who say that the founding fathers, Benjamin Franklin especially, were actually influenced by the system of government that had been adopted by the Iroquois hundreds of years prior to the arrival of large numbers of Europeans.

Western civilization, then, becomes another confusing category like Third World, or Judeo-Christian culture, as man attempts to impose his small-screen view of political and cultural reality upon a complex world. Our most publicized novelist recently said that Western civilization was the greatest achievement of mankind, an attitude that flourishes on the street level as scribbles in public restrooms: "White Power," "Niggers and Spics Suck," or "Hitler was a prophet," the latter being the most telling, for wasn't Adolph Hitler the archetypal monoculturalist who, in his pigheaded arrogance, believed that one way and one blood was so pure that it had to be protected from alien strains at all costs? Where did such an attitude, which has caused so much misery and depression in our national life, which has tainted even our noblest achievements, begin? An attitude that caused the incarceration of Japanese-American citizens during World War II, the persecution of Chicanos and Chinese-Americans, the near-extermination of the Indians, and the murder and lynchings of thousands of Afro-Americans.

Virtuous, hard-working, pious, even though they occasionally would wander off after some fancy clothes, or rendezvous in the woods with the town prostitute, the Puritans are idealized in our schoolbooks as "a hardy band" of no-nonsense patriarchs whose discipline razed the forest and brought order to the New World (a term that annoys Native American historians). Industrious, responsible, it was their "Yankee ingenuity" and practicality that created the work ethic. They were simple folk who produced a number of good poets, and they set the tone for the American writing style, of lean and spare lines, long before Hemingway. They worshiped in churches whose colors blended in with the New England snow, churches with simple structures and ornate lecterns.

The Puritans were a daring lot, but they had a mean streak. They₁₀ hated the theater and banned Christmas. They punished people in a cruel and inhuman manner. They killed children who disobeyed their parents. When they came in contact with those whom they considered heathens or aliens, they behaved in such a bizarre and irrational manner that this chapter in the American history comes down to us as a late-movie horror film. They exterminated the Indians, who taught them how to survive in a world unknown to them, and their encounter with the calypso culture of Barbados resulted in what the tourist guide in Salem's Witches' House refers to as the Witchcraft Hysteria.

The Puritan legacy of hard work and meticulous accounting led to the establishment of a great industrial society; it is no wonder that the

American industrial revolution began in Lowell, Massachusetts, but there was the other side, the strange and paranoid attitudes toward those different from the Elect.

The cultural attitudes of that early Elect continue to be voiced in everyday life in the United States: the president of a distinguished university, writing a letter to the *Times*, belittling the study of African civilizations; the television network that promoted its show on the Vatican art with the boast that this art represented "the finest achievements of the human spirit." A modern up-tempo state of complex rhythms that depends upon contacts with an international community can no longer behave as if it dwelled in a "Zion Wilderness" surrounded by beasts and pagans.

When I heard a schoolteacher warn the other night about the invasion of the American educational system by foreign curriculums, I wanted to yell at the television set, "Lady, they're already here." It has already begun because the world is here. The world has been arriving at these shores for at least ten thousand years from Europe, Africa, and Asia. In the late nineteenth and early twentieth centuries, large numbers of Europeans arrived, adding their cultures to those of the European, African, and Asian settlers who were already here, and recently millions have been entering the country from South America and the Caribbean, making Yale Professor Bob Thompson's bouillabaisse richer and thicker.

One of our most visionary politicians said that he envisioned a time when the United States could become the brain of the world, by which he meant the repository of all of the latest advanced information systems. I thought of that remark when an enterprising poet friend of mine called to say that he had just sold a poem to a computer magazine and that the editors were delighted to get it because they didn't carry fiction or poetry. Is that the kind of world we desire? A humdrum homogeneous world of all brains and no heart, no fiction, no poetry; a world of robots with human attendants bereft of imagination, of culture? Or does North America deserve a more exciting destiny? To become a place where the cultures of the world crisscross. This is possible because the United States is unique in the world: The world is here.

Additional Rhetorical Strategies

Narration (paragraphs 4–5); Argument (paragraph 6 and following); Analogy (paragraph 14).

Discussion Questions

1. Examine the structure of Reed's essay. Where does he put his many examples, in relation to the generalizations they support? Which

points does he illustrate before explicitly stating them, and which examples does he line up after he has stated the point they illustrate? What are the relative merits of each approach?

2. How would you characterize Reed's style? Cite specific lines to support your impressions. What are the effects of his stylistic choices?

3. What is Reed's opinion of the Puritans? How does he back it up? From what perspective or perspectives is he viewing them? What is the relevance of a critique of the Puritans to an essay about contemporary America?

4. Read this essay in conjunction with Mary Gordon's essay, "More Than Just a Shrine" (p. 97). Both authors examine the melting pot of American culture, and draw attention to the many ethnicities of the Europeans who settled here in the nineteenth century. How are the two authors' views similar, and where do they part company?

Essay Questions

1. Do you agree or disagree with Reed's main points? If you disagree, write an argumentative essay taking an opposing stance. If you agree, write an essay reinforcing the same or a similar main point, but using an entirely different rhetorical mode—narration, perhaps, or comparison and contrast. If you agree with his general point, but find some of Reed's strategies counterproductive, write an essay on the same topic while paying close attention to the potential effects of your rhetorical strategies on your audience.

2. Write an essay in which you open with multiple examples before explicitly discussing the point these examples are meant to illustrate. Construct the examples so that the reader can begin to infer your thesis statement before you infer it. Think about the advantages to this unorthodox essay structure so that you can use it as effectively as possible.

The Word Police

Michiko Kakutani

Michiko Kakutani (b. 1955) was born in New Haven, Connecticut and earned her B.A. from Yale University in 1976. She started working in the culture department of the New York Times in 1979; her writing assignments included book reviews and feature stories on cultural and literary events. While working for the Times, Kakutani had occasion to interview many famous writers, actors, and directors; she collected these interviews in the book titled The Poet at the Piano: Portraits of Writers, Filmmakers, Playwrights, and Other Artists at Work *(1988).*

In the following essay, which first appeared in the New York Times in January 1993, Kakutani uses her position as a book reviewer and cultural commentator to launch an attack on political correctness.

This month's inaugural festivities, with their celebration, in Maya Angelou's words, of "humankind"—"the Asian, the Hispanic, the Jew / The African, the Native American, the Sioux, / The Catholic, the Muslim, the French, the Greek / The Irish, the Rabbi, the Priest, the Sheik, / The Gay, the Straight, the Preacher, / The privileged, the homeless, the Teacher"—constituted a kind of official embrace of multiculturalism and a new politics of inclusion.

The mood of political correctness, however, has already made firm inroads into popular culture. Washington boasts a store called Politically Correct that sells pro-whale, anti-meat, ban-the-bomb T-shirts, bumper stickers and buttons, as well as a local cable television show called *Politically Correct Cooking* that features interviews in the kitchen with representatives from groups like People for the Ethical Treatment of Animals. The Coppertone suntan lotion people are planning to give their longtime cover girl, Little Miss (Ms?) Coppertone, a male equivalent, Little Mr. Coppertone. And even Superman (Superperson?) is rumored to be returning this spring, reincarnated as four ethnically diverse clones: an African-American, an Asian, a Caucasian and a Latino.

Nowhere is this P.C. mood more striking than in the increasingly noisy debate over language that has moved from university campuses to the country at large—a development that both underscores Americans' puritanical zeal for reform and their unwavering faith in the talismanic power of words.

Certainly no decent person can quarrel with the underlying impulse behind political correctness: a vision of a more just, inclusive society in which racism, sexism and prejudice of all sorts have been erased. But the methods and fervor of the self-appointed language police can lead to a rigid orthodoxy—and unintentional self-parody—opening the movement to the scorn of conservative opponents and the mockery of cartoonists and late-night television hosts.

It's hard to imagine women earning points for political correctness 5
by saying *ovarimony* instead of *testimony*—as one participant at the recent Modern Language Association convention was overheard to suggest. It's equally hard to imagine people wanting to flaunt their lack of
prejudice by giving up such words and phrases as *bull market, kaiser roll,
Lazy Susan,* and *charley horse.*

Several books on bias-free language have already appeared, and the
1991 edition of the Random House *Webster's College Dictionary* boasts an
appendix titled "Avoiding Sexist Language." The dictionary also includes such linguistic mutations as *womyn* (women, "used as an alternative spelling to avoid the suggestion of sexism perceived in the sequence
m-e-n") and *waitron* (a gender-blind term for waiter or waitress).

Many of these dictionaries and guides not only warn the reader
against offensive racial and sexual slurs, but also try to establish and
enforce a whole new set of usage rules. Take, for instance, *The Bias-Free
Word Finder, a Dictionary of Nondiscriminatory Language* by Rosalie Maggio (Beacon Press)—a volume often indistinguishable, in its meticulous
solemnity, from the tongue-in-cheek *Official Politically Correct Dictionary
and Handbook* put out last year by Henry Beard and Christopher Cerf
(Villard Books). Ms. Maggio's book supplies the reader intent on using
kinder, gentler language with writing guidelines as well as a detailed
listing of more than 5,000 "biased words and phrases."

Whom are these guidelines for? Somehow one has a tough time picturing them replacing *Fowler's Modern English Usage* in the classroom, or
being adopted by the average man (sorry, individual) in the street.

The "pseudogeneric *he,*" we learn from Ms. Maggio, is to be
avoided like the plague, as is the use of the word *man* to refer to humanity. *Fellow, king, lord* and *master* are bad because they're "male-
oriented words," and *king, lord* and *master* are especially bad because
they're also "hierarchical, dominator society terms." The politically correct lion becomes the "monarch of the jungle," new-age children play
"someone on the top of the heap," and the *Mona Lisa* goes down in history as Leonardo's "acme of perfection."

As for the word *black,* Ms. Maggio says it should be excised from 10
terms with a negative spin: She recommends substituting words like
mouse for *black eye, ostracize* for *blackball, payola* for *blackmail,* and *outcast* for
black sheep. Clearly, some of these substitutions work better than others:
Somehow the "sinister humor" of Kurt Vonnegut or *Saturday Night Live*
doesn't quite make it; nor does the "denouncing" of the Hollywood 10.

For the dedicated user of politically correct language, all these rules
can make for some messy moral dilemmas. Whereas *battered wife* is a
gender-biased term, the gender-free term *battered spouse,* Ms. Maggio
notes, incorrectly implies "that men and women are equally battered."

On one hand, say Francine Wattman Frank and Paula A. Treichler in
their book *Language, Gender, and Professional Writing* (Modern Language

Association), *he or she* is an appropriate construction for talking about an individual (like a jockey, say) who belongs to a profession that's predominantly male—it's a way of emphasizing "that such occupations are not barred to women or that women's concerns need to be kept in mind." On the other hand, they add, using masculine pronouns rhetorically can underscore ongoing male dominance in those fields, implying the need for change.

And what about the speech codes adopted by some universities in recent years? Although they were designed to prohibit students from uttering sexist and racist slurs, they would extend, by logic, to blacks who want to use the word *nigger* to strip the term of its racist connotations, or homosexuals who want to use the word *queer* to reclaim it from bigots.

In her book, Ms. Maggio recommends applying bias-free usage retroactively: She suggests paraphrasing politically incorrect quotations, or replacing "the sexist words or phrases with ellipsis dots and/or bracketed substitutes," or using *sic* "to show that the sexist words come from the original quotation and to call attention to the fact that they are incorrect."

15   Which leads the skeptical reader of *The Bias-Free Word Finder* to wonder whether *All the King's Men* should be retitled *All the Ruler's People*; *Pet Sematary*, *Animal Companion Graves*; *Birdman of Alcatraz*, *Birdperson of Alcatraz*; and *The Iceman Cometh*, *The Ice Route Driver Cometh*?

Will making such changes remove the prejudice in people's minds? Should we really spend time trying to come up with non-male-based alternatives to *Midas touch*, *Achilles' heel*, and *Montezuma's revenge*? Will tossing out Santa Claus—whom Ms. Maggio accuses of reinforcing "the cultural male-as-norm system"—in favor of Belfana, his Italian female alter ego, truly help banish sexism? Can the avoidance of "violent expressions and metaphors" like *kill two birds with one stone*, *sock it to 'em* or *kick an idea around* actually promote a more harmonious world?

The point isn't that the excesses of the word police are comical. The point is that their intolerance (in the name of tolerance) has disturbing implications. In the first place, getting upset by phrases like *bullish on America* or *the City of Brotherly Love* tends to distract attention from the real problems of prejudice and injustice that exist in society at large, turning them into mere questions of semantics. Indeed, the emphasis currently put on politically correct usage has uncanny parallels with the academic movement of deconstruction—a method of textual analysis that focuses on language and linguistic pyrotechnics—which has become firmly established on university campuses.

In both cases, attention is focused on surfaces, on words and metaphors; in both cases, signs and symbols are accorded more importance than content. Hence, the attempt by some radical advocates to remove *The Adventures of Huckleberry Finn* from curriculums on the grounds that Twain's use of the word *nigger* makes the book a racist text—never mind the fact that this American classic (written in 1884) depicts the spiritual kinship achieved between a white boy and a runaway slave, never mind the fact that the "nigger" Jim emerges as the novel's most honorable, decent character.

Ironically enough, the P.C. movement's obsession with language is accompanied by a strange Orwellian willingness to warp the meaning of words by placing them under a high-powered ideological lens. For instance, the *Dictionary of Cautionary Words and Phrases*—a pamphlet issued by the University of Missouri's Multicultural Management Program to help turn "today's journalists into tomorrow's multicultural newsroom managers"—warns that using the word *articulate* to describe members of a minority group can suggest the opposite, "that 'those people' are not considered well educated, articulate and the like."

The pamphlet patronizes minority groups, by cautioning the reader[20] against using the words *lazy* and *burly* to describe any member of such groups; and it issues a similar warning against using words like *gorgeous* and *petite* to describe women.

As euphemism proliferates with the rise of political correctness, there is a spread of the sort of sloppy, abstract language that Orwell said is "designed to make lies sound truthful and murder respectable, and to give an appearance of solidity to pure wind." *Fat* becomes *big boned* or *differently sized; stupid* becomes *exceptional; stoned* becomes *chemically inconvenienced.*

Wait a minute here! Aren't such phrases eerily reminiscent of the euphemisms coined by the government during Vietnam and Watergate? Remember how the military used to speak of "pacification," or how President Richard M. Nixon's press secretary, Ronald L. Ziegler, tried to get away with calling a lie an "inoperative statement"?

Calling the homeless "the underhoused" doesn't give them a place to live; calling the poor "the economically marginalized" doesn't help them pay the bills. Rather, by playing down their plight, such language might even make it easier to shrug off the seriousness of their situation.

Instead of allowing free discussion and debate to occur, many gung-ho advocates of politically correct language seem to think that simple suppression of a word or concept will magically make the problem disappear. In the *Bias-Free Word Finder*, Ms. Maggio entreats the reader not to perpetuate the negative stereotype of Eve. "Be extremely cautious in referring to the biblical Eve," she writes; "this story has profoundly contributed to negative attitudes toward women throughout history, largely because of misogynistic and patriarchal interpretations that labeled her evil, inferior, and seductive."

The story of Bluebeard, the rake (whoops!—the libertine) who[25] killed his seven wives, she says, is also to be avoided, as is the biblical story of Jezebel. Of Jesus Christ, Ms. Maggio writes: "There have been few individuals in history as completely androgynous as Christ, and it does his message a disservice to overinsist on his maleness." She doesn't give the reader any hints on how this might be accomplished; presumably, one is supposed to avoid describing him as the Son of God.

Of course the P.C. police aren't the only ones who want to proscribe what people should say or give them guidelines for how they may use an idea; Jesse Helms and his supporters are up to exactly the same thing when they propose to patrol the boundaries of the permissible in art. In each case, the would-be censor aspires to suppress what he or she finds distasteful—all, of course, in the name of the public good.

In the case of the politically correct, the prohibition of certain words, phrases and ideas is advanced in the cause of building a brave new world free of racism and hate, but this vision of harmony clashes with the very ideals of diversity and inclusion that the multicultural movement holds dear, and it's purchased at the cost of freedom of speech.

In fact, the utopian world envisioned by the language police would be bought at the expense of the ideals of individualism and democracy articulated in the "Gettysburg Address": "Four score and seven years ago our fathers brought forth on this continent a new nation, conceived in liberty and dedicated to the proposition that all men are created equal."

Of course, the P.C. police have already found Lincoln's words hopelessly "phallocentric." No doubt they would rewrite the passage: "Four score and seven years ago our foremothers and forefathers brought forth on this continent a new nation, formulated with liberty, and dedicated to the proposition that all humankind is created equal."

Additional Rhetorical Strategies

Cause and Effect (paragraphs 3, 4, 23); Analogy (paragraphs 17, 18); Argument (throughout).

Discussion Questions

1. Kakutani builds an argument through the extensive use of examples. Which ones do you find most and least compelling? Why? Were there points in the essay when you found yourself thinking of objections or counter-examples? If so, consider writing a rebuttal to Kakutani's essay. In this regard, you may want to consult Alleen Pace Nilsen's essay (p. 231).
2. How would you characterize Kakutani's tone? How might it affect her audience? How did it affect you as a reader? How might the tone be modified, and with what effect?
3. In paragraph 16, Kakutani asks the following rhetorical question about suggested changes in English usage to combat sexism and

racism: "Will making such changes remove the prejudice in people's minds?" The question of whether changing language will bring about larger social changes is a hotly debated one. Where in the essay does Kakutani actually address this question? What rhetorical strategies does she use? Ironically enough, the Orwell essay from which she quotes, "Politics and the English Language" posits an opposing viewpoint on this topic: Orwell writes, for instance, that "one can probably bring about some improvement by starting at the verbal end." Orwell's essay is widely available; you might seek it out in order to see how he plays out the idea of the efficacy of language change.

4. One of Kakutani's main points is that politically correct language "might even make it easier to shrug off the seriousness" of such plights as poverty and homelessness (paragraph 23). Do you agree or disagree with this statement? Support your answer with examples drawn from your own experience and knowledge. In your experience, which does the most damage: insensitivity about language or an oversensitivity to language?

Essay Questions

1. In paragraph 18, Kakutani alludes to the "attempt by some radical advocates to remove *The Adventures of Huckleberry Finn*" from school curricula. Do a research project on censorship. Which groups advocate censorship of literary works? What kinds of works does each group try to ban, and what reasons do they give? Does your research bear out the argument Kakutani makes about the convergence of the left and the right on the issue of censorship (paragraph 26)?

2. Do you think that changes in language bring about social change, or that social change brings about changes in language, or both, or neither? Be sure to support your argument with compelling examples drawn from your own experience and/or from written sources.

Less Work for Mother?

Ruth Schwartz Cowan

Ruth Schwartz Cowan (b. 1941) is a professor of history and Director of Women's Studies at the State University of New York at Stony Brook. Her written work springs from the conjunction of her academic interests and personal experience. She writes, "I have always believed that scholarship and life should be and are inseparable from each other, so that, several years ago, when I was casting about for an interesting research topic, I decided to explore the history of household technology; at that time I was spending just as many hours of the day being a housewife as being a scholar. The book resulting from this effort, More Work for Mother *[1983], is as much personal testament to the point of view that I had developed over the years of doing research as it is a report of the research itself." In "Less Work for Mother?", Cowan makes effective use of examples to debunk the seemingly commonsense notion that laborsaving appliances necessarily save labor.*

Things are never what they seem. Skimmed milk masquerades as cream. And laborsaving household appliances often do not save labor. This is the surprising conclusion reached by a small army of historians, sociologists, and home economists who have undertaken, in recent years, to study the one form of work that has turned out to be most resistant to inquiry and analysis—namely, housework.

During the first half of the twentieth century, the average American household was transformed by the introduction of a group of machines that profoundly altered the daily lives of housewives; the forty years between 1920 and 1960 witnessed what might be aptly called the "industrial revolution in the home." Where once there had been a wood- or coal-burning stove there now was a gas or electric range. Clothes that had once been scrubbed on a metal washboard were now tossed into a tub and cleansed by an electrically driven agitator. The dryer replaced the clothesline; the vacuum cleaner replaced the broom; the refrigerator replaced the icebox and the root cellar; an automatic pump, some piping, and a tap replaced the hand pump, the bucket, and the well. No one had to chop and haul wood any more. No one had to shovel out ashes or beat rugs or carry water; no one even had to toss egg whites with a fork for an hour to make an angel food cake.

And yet American housewives in 1960, 1970, and even 1980 continued to log about the same number of hours at their work as their grandmothers and mothers had in 1910, 1920, and 1930. The earliest time studies of housewives date from the very same period in which time studies of other workers were becoming popular—the first three decades of the twentieth century. The sample sizes of these studies were usually quite small, and they did not always define housework in precisely the same way (some counted an hour spent taking children to the playground as "work," while others called it "leisure"), but their results were more or less consistent: whether rural or urban, the average American housewife performed fifty to sixty hours of unpaid work in her home every week, and the only variable that significantly altered this was the number of small children.

A half century later not much had changed. Survey research had become much more sophisticated, and sample sizes had grown considerably, but the results of the time studies remained surprisingly consistent. The average American housewife, now armed with dozens of motors and thousands of electronic chips, still spends fifty to sixty hours a week doing housework. The only variable that significantly altered the size of that number was full-time employment in the labor force; "working" housewives cut down the average number of hours that they spend cooking and cleaning, shopping, and chauffeuring, to a not insignificant thirty-five—virtually the equivalent of another full-time job.

How can this be true? Surely even the most sophisticated advertis- 5 ing copywriter of all times could not fool almost the entire American population over the course of at least three generations. Laborsaving devices must be saving something, or Americans would not continue, year after year, to plunk down their hard-earned dollars for them.

And if laborsaving devices have not saved labor in the home, then what is it that has suddenly made it possible for more than 70 percent of the wives and mothers in the American population to enter the workforce and stay there? A brief glance at the histories of some of the technologies that have transformed housework in the twentieth century will help us answer some of these questions.

The portable vacuum cleaner was one of the earliest electric appliances to make its appearance in American homes, and reasonably priced models appeared on the retail market as early as 1910. For decades prior to the turn of the century, inventors had been trying to create a carpet-cleaning system that would improve on the carpet sweeper with adjustable rotary brushes (patented by Melville Bissell in 1876), or the semiannual ritual of hauling rugs outside and beating them, or the practice of regularly sweeping the dirt out of a rug that had been covered with dampened, torn newspapers. Early efforts to solve the problem had focused on the use of large steam, gasoline, or electric motors attached to piston-type pumps and lots of hoses. Many of these "stationary" vacuum-cleaning systems were installed in apartment houses or hotels, but some were hauled around the streets in horse-drawn carriages by entrepreneurs hoping to establish themselves as "professional house-cleaners."

In the first decade of the twentieth century, when fractional-horsepower electric motors became widely—and inexpensively—available, the portable vacuum cleaner intended for use in an individual household was born. One early model—invented by a woman, Corrine Dufour—consisted of a rotary brush, an electrically driven fan, and a wet sponge for absorbing the dust and dirt. Another, patented by David E. Kenney in 1907, had a twelve-inch nozzle, attached to a metal tube, attached to a flexible hose that led to a vacuum pump and separating devices. The Hoover, which was based on a brush, a fan, and a collecting bag, was on the market by 1908. The Electrolux, the first of the canister types of cleaner, which could vacuum something above the level of the floor, was brought over from Sweden in 1924 and met with immediate success.

These early vacuum cleaners were hardly a breeze to operate. All were heavy, and most were extremely cumbersome to boot. One early home economist mounted a basal metabolism machine on the back of one of her hapless students and proceeded to determine that more energy was expended in the effort to clean a sample carpet with a vacuum cleaner than when the same carpet was attacked with a hard broom. The difference, of course, was that the vacuum cleaner did a better job, at least on carpets, because a good deal of what the broom stirred up simply resettled a foot or two away from where it had first been lodged. Whatever the liabilities of the early vacuum cleaners may have been, Americans nonetheless appreciated their virtues; according to a market survey done in Zanesville, Ohio, in 1926, slightly more than half the households owned one. Eventually improvements in the design made these devices easier to operate. By 1960 vacuum cleaners could be found in 70 percent of the nation's homes.

10   When the vacuum cleaner is viewed in a historical context, however, it is easy to see why it did not save housewifely labor. Its introduction coincided almost precisely with the disappearance of the domestic servant. The number of persons engaged in household service dropped from 1,851,000 in 1910 to 1,411,000 in 1920, while the number of households enumerated in the census rose from 20.3 million to 24.4 million. Moreover, between 1900 and 1920 the number of household servants per thousand persons dropped from 98.9 to 58.0, while during the 1920s the decline was even more precipitous as the restrictive immigration acts dried up what had once been the single most abundant source of domestic labor.

For the most economically comfortable segment of the population, this meant just one thing: the adult female head of the household was doing more housework than she had ever done before. What Maggie had once done with a broom, Mrs. Smith was now doing with a vacuum cleaner. Knowing that this was happening, several early copywriters for vacuum cleaner advertisements focused on its implications. The vacuum cleaner, General Electric announced in 1918, is better than a maid: it doesn't quit, get drunk, or demand higher wages. The switch from Maggie to Mrs. Smith shows up, in time-study statistics, as an increase in the time that Mrs. Smith is spending at her work.

For those—and they were the vast majority of the population—who were not economically comfortable, the vacuum cleaner implied something else again: not an increase in the time spent in housework but an increase in the standard of living. In many households across the country, acquisition of a vacuum cleaner was connected to an expansion of living space, the move from a small apartment to a small house, the purchase of wall-to-wall carpeting. If this did not happen during the difficult 1930s, it became more possible during the expansive 1950s. As living quarters grew larger, standards for their upkeep increased; rugs had to be vacuumed every week, in some households every day, rather than semiannually, as had been customary. The net result, of course, was that when armed with a vacuum cleaner, housewives whose parents had been poor could keep more space cleaner than their mothers and grandmothers would have ever believed possible. We might put this everyday phenomenon in language that economists can understand: The introduction of the vacuum cleaner led to improvements in productivity but not to any significant decrease in the amount of time expended by each worker.

The history of the washing machine illustrates a similar phenomenon. "Blue Monday" had traditionally been, as its name implies, the bane of a housewife's existence—especially when Monday turned out to be "Monday . . . and Tuesday to do the ironing." Thousands of patents for "new and improved" washers were issued during the nineteenth century in an effort to cash in on the housewife's despair. Most of these early washing machines were wooden or metal tubs combined with some kind of hand-cranked mechanism that would rub or push or twirl laundry when the tub was filled with water and soap. At the end of the century, the Sears catalog offered four such washing machines, ranging in price from $2.50 to $4.25, all sold in combination with hand-cranked wringers.

These early machines may have saved time in the laundering process (four shirts could be washed at once instead of each having to be rubbed separately against a washboard), but they probably didn't save much energy. Lacking taps and drains, the tubs still had to be filled and emptied by hand, and each piece still had to be run through a wringer and hung up to dry.

Not long after the appearance of fractional-horsepower motors,[15] several enterprising manufacturers had the idea of hooking them up to the crank mechanisms of washers and wringers—and the electric washer was born. By the 1920s, when mass production of such machines began, both the general structure of the machine (a central-shaft agitator rotating within a cylindrical tub, hooked up to the household water supply) and the general structure of the industry (oligopolistic—with a very few firms holding most of the patents and controlling most of the market) had achieved their final form. By 1926 just over a quarter of the families in Zanesville had an electric washer, but by 1941 fully 52 percent of all American households either owned or had interior access (which means that they could use coin-operated models installed in the basements of apartment houses) to such a machine. The automatic washer, which consisted of a vertically rotating washer cylinder that could also act as a centrifugal extractor, was introduced by the Bendix Home Appliance Corporation in 1938, but it remained expensive, and therefore inaccessible, until after World War II. This machine contained timing devices that allowed it to proceed through its various cycles automatically; by spinning the clothes around in the extractor phase of its cycle, it also eliminated the wringer. Although the Bendix subsequently disappeared from the retail market (versions of this sturdy machine may still be found in Laundromats), its design principles are replicated in the agitator washers that currently chug away in millions of American homes.

Both the early wringer washers and their more recent automatic cousins have released American women from the burden of drudgery. No one who has ever tried to launder a sheet by hand, and without the benefits of hot running water, would want to return to the days of the scrubboard and tub. But "labor" is composed of both "energy expenditure" and "time expenditure," and the history of laundry work demonstrates that the one may be conserved while the other is not.

The reason for this is, as with the vacuum cleaner, twofold. In the early decades of the century, many households employed laundresses to do their wash; this was true, surprisingly enough, even for some very poor households when wives and mothers were disabled or employed full time in field or factory. Other households—rich and poor—used commercial laundry services. Large, mechanized "steam" laundries were first constructed in this country in the 1860s, and by the 1920s they could be found in virtually every urban neighborhood and many rural ones as well.

But the advent of the electric home washer spelled doom both for the laundress and for the commercial laundry; since the housewife's labor was unpaid, and since the washer took so much of the drudgery out of washday, the one-time expenditure for a machine seemed, in many families, a more sensible arrangement than continuous expenditure for domestic services. In the process, of course, the time spent on laundry work by the individual housewife, who had previously employed either a laundress or a service, was bound to increase.

For those who had not previously enjoyed the benefits of relief from washday drudgery, the electric washer meant something quite different but equally significant: an upgrading of household cleanliness. Men stopped wearing removable collars and cuffs, which meant that the whole of their shirts had to be washed and then ironed. Housewives began changing two sheets every week, instead of moving the top sheet to the bottom and adding only one that was fresh. Teenagers began changing their underwear every day instead of every weekend. In the early 1960s, when synthetic no-iron fabrics were introduced, the size of the household laundry load increased again; shirts and skirts, sheets and blouses that had once been sent out to the dry cleaner or the corner laundry were now being tossed into the household wash basket. By the 1980s the average American housewife, armed now with an automatic washing machine and an automatic dryer, was processing roughly ten times (by weight) the amount of laundry that her mother had been accustomed to. Drudgery had disappeared, but the laundry hadn't. The average time spent on this chore in 1925 had been 5.8 hours per week; in 1964 it was 6.2.

And then there is the automobile. We do not usually think of our[20] cars as household appliances, but that is precisely what they are since housework, as currently understood, could not possibly be performed without them. The average American housewife is today more likely to be found behind a steering wheel than in front of a stove. While writing this article I interrupted myself five times: once to take a child to field-hockey practice, then a second time, to bring her back when practice was finished; once to pick up some groceries at the supermarket; once to retrieve my husband, who was stranded at the train station; once for a trip to a doctor's office. Each time I was doing housework, and each time I had to use my car.

Like the washing machine and the vacuum cleaner, the automobile started to transform the nature of housework in the 1920s. Until the introduction of the Model T in 1908, automobiles had been playthings for the idle rich, and although many wealthy women learned to drive early in the century (and several participated in well-publicized auto races), they were hardly the women who were likely to be using their cars to haul groceries.

But by 1920, and certainly by 1930, all this had changed. Helen and Robert Lynd, who conducted an intensive study of Muncie, Indiana, between 1923 and 1925 (reported in their famous book *Middletown*), estimated that in Muncie in the 1890s only 125 families, all members of the "elite," owned a horse and buggy, but by 1923 there were 6,222 passenger cars in the city, "roughly one for every 7.1 persons, or two for every three families." By 1930, according to national statistics, there were roughly 30 million households in the United States—and 26 million registered automobiles.

What did the automobile mean for the housewife? Unlike public transportation systems, it was convenient. Located right at her doorstep, it could deposit her at the doorstep that she wanted or needed to visit. And unlike the bicycle or her own two feet, the automobile could carry bulky packages as well as several additional people. Acquisition of an automobile therefore meant that a housewife, once

she had learned how to drive, could become her own door-to-door delivery service. And as more housewives acquired automobiles, more
businessmen discovered the joys of dispensing with delivery services—
particularly during the Depression.

To make a long story short, the iceman does not cometh anymore.
Neither does the milkman, the bakery truck, the butcher, the grocer, the
knife sharpener, the seamstress, or the doctor. Like many other businessmen, doctors discovered that their earnings increased when they
stayed in their offices and transferred the responsibility for transportation to their ambulatory patients.

25   Thus a new category was added to the housewife's traditional job
description: chauffeur. The suburban station wagon is now "Mom's
Taxi." Children who once walked to school now have to be transported
by their mothers; husbands who once walked home from work now
have to be picked up by their wives; groceries that once were dispensed
from pushcarts or horse-drawn wagons now have to be packed into
paper bags and hauled home in family cars. "Contemporary women,"
one time-study expert reported in 1974, "spend about one full working
day per week on the road and in stores compared with less than two
hours per week for women in the 1920s." If everything we needed to
maintain our homes and sustain our families were delivered right to
our doorsteps—and every member of the family had independent
means for getting where she or he wanted to go—the hours spent on
housework by American housewives would decrease dramatically.

The histories of the vacuum cleaner, the washing machine, and the
automobile illustrate the varied reasons why the time spent in housework has not markedly decreased in the United States during the last
half century despite the introduction of so many ostensibly laborsaving
appliances. But these histories do not help us understand what has
made it possible for so many American wives and mothers to enter the
labor force full time during those same years. Until recently, one of the
explanations most often offered for the startling increase in the participation of married women in the workforce (up from 24.8 percent in
1950 to 50.1 percent in 1980) was household technology. What with mi-
crowave ovens and frozen foods, washer and dryer combinations and
paper diapers, the reasoning goes, housework can now be done in no
time at all, and women have so much time on their hands that they find
they must go out and look for a job for fear of going stark, raving mad.

As every "working" housewife knows, this pattern of reasoning is
itself stark, raving mad. Most adult women are in the workforce today
quite simply because they need the money. Indeed, most "working"
housewives today hold down not one but two jobs; they put in what
has come to be called a "double day." Secretaries, lab technicians, jani-
tors, sewing machine operators, teachers, nurses, or physicians for eight
(or nine or ten) hours, they race home to become chief cook and bottle

washer for another five, leaving the cleaning and the marketing for Saturday and Sunday. Housework, as we have seen, still takes a lot of time, modern technology notwithstanding.

Yet household technologies have played a major role in facilitating (as opposed to causing) what some observers believe to be the most significant social revolution of our time. They do it in two ways, the first of which we have already noted. By relieving housework of the drudgery that it once entailed, washing machines, vacuum cleaners, dishwashers, and water pumps have made it feasible for a woman to put in a double day without destroying her health, to work full time and still sustain herself and her family at a reasonably comfortable level.

The second relationship between household technology and the participation of married women in the workforce is considerably more subtle. It involves the history of some technologies that we rarely think of as technologies at all—and certainly not as household appliances. Instead of being sheathed in stainless steel or porcelain, these devices appear in our kitchens in little brown bottles and bags of flour; instead of using switches and buttons to turn them on, we use hypodermic needles and sugar cubes. They are various forms of medication, the products not only of modern medicine but also of modern industrial chemistry: polio vaccines and vitamin pills; tetanus toxins and ampicillin; enriched breads and tuberculin tests.

Before any of these technologies had made their appearance, nurs-30 ing may well have been the most time-consuming and most essential aspect of housework. During the eighteenth and nineteenth centuries and even during the first five decades of the twentieth century, it was the woman of the house who was expected (and who had been trained, usually by *her* mother) to sit up all night cooling and calming a feverish child, to change bandages on suppurating wounds, to clean bed linens stained with excrement, to prepare easily digestible broths, to cradle colicky infants on her lap for hours on end, to prepare bodies for burial. An attack of the measles might mean the care of a bedridden child for a month. Pneumonia might require six months of bed rest. A small knife cut could become infected and produce a fever that would rage for days. Every summer brought the fear of polio epidemics, and every polio epidemic left some group of mothers with the perpetual problem of tending to the needs of a handicapped child. Cholera, diphtheria, typhoid fever—if they weren't fatal—could mean weeks of sleepless nights and hard-pressed days. "Just as soon as the person is attacked," one experienced mother wrote to her worried daughter during a cholera epidemic in Oklahoma in 1885, "be it ever so slightly, he or she ought to go to bed immediately and stay there; put a mustard [plaster] over the bowels and if vomiting over the stomach. See that the feet are kept warm, either by warm iron or brick, or bottles of hot water. If the disease progresses the limbs will begin to cramp, which must be prevented by applying cloths wrung out of hot water and wrapping round them. When one is vomiting so terribly, of course, it is next to impossible to keep medicine down, but in cholera it must be done."

These were the routines to which American women were once accustomed, routines regarded as matters of life and death. To gain some sense of the way in which modern medicines have altered not only the routines of housework but also the emotional commitment that often accompanies such work, we need only read out a list of the diseases for which most American children are unlikely to succumb today, remembering how many of them once were fatal or terribly disabling: diphtheria, whooping cough, tetanus, pellagra, rickets, measles, mumps, tuberculosis, smallpox, cholera, malaria, and polio.

And many of today's ordinary childhood complaints, curable within a few days of the ingestion of antibiotics, once might have entailed weeks, or even months, of full-time attention: bronchitis; strep throat; scarlet fever; bacterial pneumonia; infections of the skin, or the eyes, or the ears, or the airways. In the days before the introduction of modern vaccines, antibiotics, and vitamin supplements, a mother who was employed full time was a serious, sometimes life-endangering threat to the health of her family. This is part of the reason why life expectancy was always low and infant mortality high among the poorest segment of the population—those most likely to be dependent upon a mother's wages.

Thus modern technology, especially modern medical technology, has made it possible for married women to enter the workforce by releasing housewives not just from drudgery but also from the dreaded emotional equation of female employment with poverty and disease. She may be exhausted at the end of her double day, but the modern "working" housewife can at least fall into bed knowing that her efforts have made it possible to sustain her family at a level of health and comfort that not so long ago was reserved only for those who were very rich.

Additional Rhetorical Strategies

Comparison and Contrast (paragraphs 2–4, 26, 34); Description (paragraphs 2, 8); Definition (paragraphs 3, 17, 28); Process Analysis (paragraph 9); Classification (paragraphs 29–30); Cause and Effect (throughout).

Discussion Questions

1. What myth or myths does Cowan set out to debunk in this essay? How does she go about it? Why does she use the example of the vacuum cleaner *and* the example of the washing machine, if they both end up proving similar points? What does she gain from the

near repetition? What explanation for women's presence in the workforce does she offer instead of the old explanation? Can you think of any other explanations for this phenomenon?

2. Early in the essay Cowan touches on some rather appalling statistics about the virtual second (unpaid) shift worked by women in the home (paragraphs 3–4). But by the end of the essay she is able to end on a more positive note: "the modern 'working' housewife can at least fall into bed knowing that her efforts have made it possible to sustain her family at a level of health and comfort that not so long ago was reserved only for those who were very rich" (paragraph 33). Re-examine the essay to identify the site at which she makes a transition from the negative to the positive perspective on women's work. How do the issues of gender and class function throughout the essay?

3. Who is the intended audience for this essay? How can you tell? What is the intended effect on that audience?

4. Where are the men in Cowan's account? Look at the places where men are referred to. Why don't they play a larger role in her analysis? How might the essay be developed further if the changing roles of men were taken into account?

Essay Questions

1. Write an essay in which you propose a solution to the old adage "a woman's work is never done" that will not fall prey to the disadvantages of the technological solutions Cowan critiques. What are some alternatives to the second shift that many women put in at home in addition to their paying jobs?

2. Consider some aspect of Americans' behavior—our dating, drinking, eating, or smoking habits, for instance. Go to the library and examine the ways in which that aspect of behavior is depicted in advertisements during the first three decades of this century. Then compare these early representations to contemporary advertisements depicting the same activity. Based on your observations, what general conclusions can you give about the perceptible changes in the ways in which this activity was and is presented to the American people? Be sure to present specific examples to verify your claims.

In Search of Our Mothers' Gardens

Alice Walker

Alice Walker (b. 1944) is perhaps best known for her novel The Color Purple, *which won both the Pulitzer Prize and the American Book Award in 1983. Her other novels include* The Third Life of Grange Copeland *(1970), which chronicles three generations of a black sharecropping family;* Meridian *(1976), which treats the civil rights movement;* The Temple of My Familiar *(1989), which spans half a million years of human history; and* Possessing the Secret of Joy *(1992), about female circumcision. She is also an accomplished poet, short story writer, and essayist. The following piece, "In Search of Our Mothers' Gardens," is the title essay in a collection she published in 1983.*

Although an inspiration to feminists of every ethnicity, Walker prefers to refer to herself as a "womanist": "'Womanist' encompasses 'feminist' as it is defined in Webster's, but also means instinctively pro-woman. . . . *it has a strong root in black women's culture. It comes (to me) from the word "womanish," a word our mothers used to describe, and attempt to inhibit, strong, outrageous, or outspoken behavior when we were children: 'You're acting* womanish!' *A labeling that failed, for the most part, to keep us from acting 'womanish' whenever we could, that is to say, like our mothers themselves, and like other women we admired." Again and again in her writing, Walker turns to this source of strength and inspiration. In the essay that follows, Walker's womanist philosophy and its roots are readily apparent.*

I described her own nature and temperament. Told how they needed a larger life for their expression. . . . I pointed out that in lieu of proper channels, her emotions had overflowed into paths that dissipated them. I talked, beautifully I thought, about an art that would be born, an art that would open the way for women the likes of her. I asked her to hope, and build up an inner life against the coming of that day. . . . I sang, with a strange quiver in my voice, a promise song.

—*"Avey," Jean Toomer,*[1] Cane
The poet speaking to a prostitute who
falls asleep while he's talking.

When the poet Jean Toomer walked through the South in the early twenties, he discovered a curious thing: black women whose spirituality was so intense, so deep, so *unconscious*, they were themselves unaware of the richness they held. They stumbled blindly through their lives: creatures so abused and mutilated in body, so dimmed and confused by pain, that they considered themselves

---

[1] Jean Toomer (1894–1967): A black poet, novelist, and major figure of the Harlem Renaissance; he wrote *Cane* in 1923.

unworthy even of hope. In the selfless abstractions their bodies became to the men who used them, they became more than "sexual objects," more even than mere women: They became "Saints." Instead of being perceived as whole persons, their bodies became shrines: What was thought to be their minds became temples suitable for worship. These crazy Saints stared out at the world, wildly, like lunatics—or quietly, like suicides; and the "God" that was in their gaze was as mute as a great stone.

Who were these Saints? These crazy, loony, pitiful women?

Some of them, without a doubt, were our mothers and grandmothers.

In the still heat of the post-Reconstruction South, this is how they seemed to Jean Toomer: exquisite butterflies trapped in an evil honey, toiling away their lives in an era, a century, that did not acknowledge them, except as "the *mule* of the world." They dreamed dreams that no one knew—not even themselves, in any coherent fashion—and saw visions no one could understand. They wandered or sat about the countryside crooning lullabies to ghosts, and drawing the mother of Christ in charcoal on courthouse walls.

They forced their minds to desert their bodies and their striving ₅ spirits sought to rise, like frail whirlwinds from the hard red clay. And when those frail whirlwinds fell, in scattered particles, upon the ground, no one mourned. Instead, men lit candles to celebrate the emptiness that remained, as people do who enter a beautiful but vacant space to resurrect a God.

Our mothers and grandmothers, some of them: moving to music not yet written. And they waited.

They waited for a day when the unknown thing that was in them would be made known; but guessed, somehow in their darkness, that on the day of their revelation they would be long dead. Therefore to Toomer they walked, and even ran, in slow motion. For they were going nowhere immediate, and the future was not yet within their grasp. And men took our mothers and grandmothers, "but got no pleasure from it." So complex was their passion and their calm.

To Toomer, they lay vacant and fallow as autumn fields, with harvest time never in sight: and he saw them enter loveless marriages, without joy; and become prostitutes, without resistance; and become mothers of children, without fulfillment.

For these grandmothers and mothers of ours were not Saints, but Artists; driven to a numb and bleeding madness by the springs of creativity in them for which there was no release. They were Creators, who lived lives of spiritual waste, because they were so rich in spirituality—which is the basis of Art—that the strain of enduring their unused and unwanted talent drove them insane. Throwing away this spirituality was their pathetic attempt to lighten the soul to a weight their work-worn, sexually abused bodies could bear.

10   What did it mean for a black woman to be an artist in our grandmothers' time? In our great-grandmothers' day? It is a question with an
answer cruel enough to stop the blood.

Did you have a genius of a great-great-grandmother who died
under some ignorant and depraved white overseer's lash? Or was she
required to bake biscuits for a lazy backwater tramp, when she cried
out in her soul to paint watercolors of sunsets, or the rain falling on the
green and peaceful pasturelands? Or was her body broken and forced
to bear children (who were more often than not sold away from her)—
eight, ten, fifteen, twenty children—when her one joy was the thought
of modeling heroic figures of rebellion, in stone or clay?

How was the creativity of the black woman kept alive, year after
year and century after century, when for most of the years black people
have been in America, it was a punishable crime for a black person to
read or write? And the freedom to paint, to sculpt, to expand the mind
with action did not exist. Consider, if you can bear to imagine it, what
might have been the result if singing, too, had been forbidden by law.
Listen to the voices of Bessie Smith, Billie Holiday, Nina Simone,
Roberta Flack, and Aretha Franklin, among others, and imagine those
voices muzzled for life. Then you may begin to comprehend the lives of
our "crazy," "Sainted" mothers and grandmothers. The agony of the
lives of women who might have been Poets, Novelists, Essayists, and
Short-Story Writers (over a period of centuries), who died with their
real gifts stifled within them.

And, if this were the end of the story, we would have cause to cry
out in my paraphrase of Okot p'Bitek's great poem:

> *O, my clanswomen*
> *Let us all cry together!*
> *Come,*
> *Let us mourn the death of our mother,*
> *The death of a Queen*
> *The ash that was produced*
> *By a great fire!*
> *O, this homestead is utterly dead*
> *Close the gates*
> *With* lacari *thorns,*
> *For our mother*
> *The creator of the Stool is lost!*
> *And all the young men*
> *Have perished in the wilderness!*

But this is not the end of the story, for all the young women—our
mothers and grandmothers, *ourselves*—have not perished in the wilderness. And if we ask ourselves why, and search for and find the answer,
we will know beyond all efforts to erase it from our minds, just exactly
who, and of what, we black American women are.

One example, perhaps the most pathetic, most misunderstood one,[15] can provide a backdrop for our mothers' work: Phillis Wheatley,[2] a slave in the 1700s.

Virginia Woolf, in her book *A Room of One's Own*, wrote that in order for a woman to write fiction she must have two things, certainly: a room of her own (with key and lock) and enough money to support herself.

What then are we to make of Phillis Wheatley, a slave, who owned not even herself? This sickly, frail black girl who required a servant of her own at times—her health was so precarious—and who, had she been white, would have been easily considered the intellectual superior of all the women and most of the men in the society of her day.

Virginia Woolf wrote further, speaking of course not of our Phillis, that "any woman born with a great gift in the sixteenth century [insert "eighteenth century," insert "black woman," insert "born or made a slave"] would certainly have gone crazed, shot herself, or ended her days in some lonely cottage outside the village, half witch, half wizard [insert "Saint"], feared and mocked at. For it needs little skill and psychology to be sure that a highly gifted girl who had tried to use her gift of poetry would have been so thwarted and hindered by contrary instincts [add "chains, guns, the lash, the ownership of one's body by someone else, submission to an alien religion"], that she must have lost her breath and sanity to a certainty."

The key words, as they relate to Phillis, are "contrary instincts." For when we read the poetry of Phillis Wheatley—as when we read the novels of Nella Larsen or the oddly false-sounding autobiography of that freest of all black women writers, Zora Hurston—evidence of "contrary instincts" is everywhere. Her loyalties were completely divided, as was, without question, her mind.

But how could this be otherwise? Captured at seven, a slave of[20] wealthy, doting whites who instilled in her the "savagery" of the Africa they "rescued" her from . . . one wonders if she was even able to remember her homeland as she had known it, or as it really was.

Yet, because she did try to use her gift for poetry in a world that made her a slave, she was "so thwarted and hindered by . . . contrary instincts, that she . . . lost her health. . . ." In the last years of her brief life, burdened not only with the need to express her gift but also with a penniless, friendless "freedom" and several small children for whom she was forced to do strenuous work to feed, she lost her health, certainly. Suffering from malnutrition and neglect and who knows what mental agonies, Phillis Wheatley died.

---

[2]Phillis Wheatley (ca. 1754–1784): A slave in a rich Boston family. Though she published her first poems at the age of thirteen and enjoyed an international reputation, she died poor and obscure.

So torn by "contrary instincts" was black, kidnapped, enslaved Phillis that her description of "the Goddess"—as she poetically called the Liberty she did not have—is ironically, cruelly humorous. And, in fact, has held Phillis up to ridicule for more than a century. It is usually read prior to hanging Phillis's memory as that of a fool. She wrote:

> *The Goddess comes, she moves divinely fair,*
> *Olive and laurel binds her golden hair.*
> *Wherever shines this native of the skies,*
> *Unnumber'd charms and recent graces rise.* [My emphasis]

It is obvious that Phillis, the slave, combed the "Goddess's" hair every morning; prior, perhaps, to bringing in the milk, or fixing her mistress's lunch. She took her imagery from the one thing she saw elevated above all others.

With the benefit of hindsight we ask, "How could she?"

25   But at last, Phillis, we understand. No more snickering when your stiff, struggling, ambivalent lines are forced on us. We know now that you were not an idiot or a traitor; only a sickly little black girl, snatched from your home and country and made a slave; a woman who still struggled to sing the song that was your gift, although in a land of barbarians who praised you for your bewildered tongue. It is not so much what you sang, as that you kept alive, in so many of our ancestors, *the notion of song.*

Black women are called, in the folklore that so aptly identified one's status in society, "the *mule* of the world," because we have been handed the burdens that everyone else—*everyone* else—refused to carry. We have also been called "Matriarchs," "Superwomen," and "Mean and Evil Bitches." Not to mention "Castraters" and "Sapphire's Mama." When we have pleaded for understanding, our character has been distorted; when we have asked for simple caring, we have been handed empty inspirational appellations, then stuck in the farthest corner. When we have asked for love, we have been given children. In short, even our plainer gifts, our labors of fidelity and love, have been knocked down our throats. To be an artist and a black woman, even today, lowers our status in many respects, rather than raises it: And yet, artists we will be.

Therefore we must fearlessly pull out of ourselves and look at and identify with our lives the living creativity some of our great-grandmothers were not allowed to know. I stress *some* of them because it is well known that the majority of our great-grandmothers knew, even without "knowing" it, the reality of their spirituality, even if they didn't recognize it beyond what happened in the singing at church—and they never had any intention of giving it up.

How they did it—those millions of black women who were not Phillis Wheatley, or Lucy Terry or Frances Harper or Zora Hurston or Nella Larsen or Bessie Smith; or Elizabeth Catlett, or Katherine Dunham, either—brings me to the title of this essay, "In Search of Our Mothers' Gardens," which is a personal account that is yet shared, in its theme and its meaning, by all of us. I found, while thinking about the far-reaching world of the creative black woman, that often the truest answer to a question that really matters can be found very close.

In the late 1920s my mother ran away from home to marry my father. Marriage, if not running away, was expected of seventeen-year-old girls. By the time she was twenty, she had two children and was pregnant with a third. Five children later, I was born. And this is how I came to know my mother: She seemed a large, soft, loving-eyed woman who was rarely impatient in our home. Her quick, violent temper was on view only a few times a year, when she battled with the white landlord who had the misfortune to suggest to her that her children did not need to go to school.

She made all the clothes we wore, even my brothers' overalls. She30 made all the towels and sheets we used. She spent the summers canning vegetables and fruits. She spent the winter evenings making quilts enough to cover our beds.

During the "working" day, she labored beside—not behind—my father in the fields. Her day began before sunup, and did not end until late at night. There was never a moment for her to sit down, undisturbed, to unravel her own private thoughts; never a time from interruption—by work or the noisy inquiries of her many children. And yet, it is to my mother—and all our mothers who were not famous—that I went in search of the secret of what has fed that muzzled and often mutilated, but vibrant, creative spirit that the black woman has inherited, and that pops out in wild and unlikely places to this day.

But when, you will ask, did my overworked mother have time to know or care about feeding the creative spirit?

The answer is so simple that many of us have spent years discovering it. We have constantly looked high, when we should have looked high—and low.

For example: In the Smithsonian Institution in Washington, D.C., there hangs a quilt unlike any other in the world. In fanciful, inspired, and yet simple and identifiable figures, it portrays the story of the Crucifixion. It is considered rare, beyond price. Though it follows no known pattern of quilt-making, and though it is made of bits and pieces of worthless rags, it is obviously the work of a person of powerful imagination and deep spiritual feeling. Below this quilt I saw a note that says it was made by "an anonymous Black woman in Alabama, a hundred years ago."

35   If we could locate this "anonymous" black woman from Alabama, she would turn out to be one of our grandmothers—an artist who left her mark in the only materials she could afford, and in the only medium her position in society allowed her to use.

As Virginia Woolf wrote further, in *A Room of One's Own:*

> Yet genius of a sort must have existed among women as it must have existed among the working class. [Change this to "slaves" and "the wives and daughters of sharecroppers."] Now and again an Emily Brontë or a Robert Burns [change this to "a Zora Hurston or a Richard Wright"] blazes out and proves its presence. But certainty it never got itself on to paper. When, however, one reads of a witch being ducked, of a woman possessed by devils [or "Sainthood"], of a wise woman selling herbs [our root workers], or even a very remarkable man who had a mother, then I think we are on the track of a lost novelist, a suppressed poet, or some mute and inglorious Jane Austen. . . . Indeed, I would venture to guess that Anon, who wrote so many poems without signing them, was often a woman. . . .

And so our mothers and grandmothers have, more often than not anonymously, handed on the creative spark, the seed of the flower they themselves never hoped to see: or like a sealed letter they could not plainly read.

And so it is, certainly, with my own mother. Unlike "Ma" Rainey's songs, which retained their creator's name even while blasting forth from Bessie Smith's mouth, no song or poem will bear my mother's name. Yet so many of the stories that I write, that we all write, are my mother's stories. Only recently did I fully realize this: That through years of listening to my mother's stories of her life, I have absorbed not only the stories themselves, but something of the manner in which she spoke, something of the urgency that involves the knowledge that her stories—like her life—must be recorded. It is probably for this reason that so much of what I have written is about characters whose counterparts in real life are so much older than I am.

But the telling of these stories, which came from my mother's lips as naturally as breathing, was not the only way my mother showed herself as an artist. For stories, too, were subject to being distracted, to dying without conclusion. Dinners must be started, and cotton must be gathered before the big rains. The artist that was and is my mother showed itself to me only after many years. This is what I finally noticed:

40   Like Mem, a character in *The Third Life of Grange Copeland*, my mother adorned with flowers whatever shabby house we were forced to live in. And not just your typical straggly country stand of zinnias, either. She planted ambitious gardens—and still does—with over fifty different varieties of plants that bloom profusely from early March until late November. Before she left home for the fields, she watered her flowers, chopped up the grass, and laid out new beds. When she

returned from the fields, she might divide clumps of bulbs, dig a cold pit, uproot and replant roses, or prune branches from her taller bushes or trees—until night came and it was too dark to see.

Whatever she planted grew as if by magic, and her fame as a grower of flowers spread over three counties. Because of her creativity with her flowers, even my memories of poverty are seen through a screen of blooms—sunflowers, petunias, roses, dahlias, forsythia, spirea, delphiniums, verbena . . . and on and on.

And I remember people coming to my mother's yard to be given cuttings from her flowers; I hear again the praise showered on her because whatever rocky soil she landed on, she turned into a garden. A garden so brilliant with colors, so original in its design, so magnificent with life and creativity, that to this day people drive by our house in Georgia—perfect strangers and imperfect strangers—and ask to stand or walk among my mother's art.

I notice that it is only when my mother is working in her flowers that she is radiant, almost to the point of being invisible—except as Creator: hand and eye. She is involved in work her soul must have. Ordering the universe in the image of her personal conception of Beauty.

Her face, as she prepares the Art that is her gift, is a legacy of respect she leaves to me, for all that illuminates and cherishes life. She has handed down respect for the possibilities—and the will to grasp them.

For her, so hindered and intruded upon in so many ways, being[45] an artist has still been a daily part of her life. This ability to hold on, even in very simple ways, is work black women have done for a very long time.

This poem is not enough, but it is something, for the woman who literally covered the holes in our walls with sunflowers:

> They were women then
> My mama's generation
> Husky of voice — Stout of
> Step
> With fists as well as
> Hands
> How they battered down
> Doors
> And ironed
> Starched white
> Shirts
> How they led
> Armies
> Headragged Generals
> Across mined
> Fields
> Booby-trapped

Kitchens
To discover books
Desks
A place for us
How they knew what we
Must *know*
Without knowing a page
Of it
Themselves

Guided by my heritage of a love of beauty and a respect for strength—in search of my mother's garden, I found my own.

And perhaps in Africa over two hundred years ago, there was just such a mother; perhaps she painted vivid and daring decorations in oranges and yellows and greens on the walls of her hut; perhaps she sang—in a voice like Roberta Flack's—*sweetly* over the compounds of her village; perhaps she wove the most stunning mats or told the most ingenious stories of all the village storytellers. Perhaps she was herself a poet—though only her daughter's name is signed to the poems that we know.

Perhaps Phillis Wheatley's mother was also an artist.

50   Perhaps in more than Phillis Wheatley's biological life is her mother's signature made clear.

Additional Rhetorical Strategies

Analogy (paragraphs 1, 4, 5); Definition (paragraph 9); Cause and Effect (paragraph 25); Narration (paragraph 40).

Discussion Questions

1. Look closely at Walker's use of other authors' work. How do the passages from Toomer, Woolf, and others function in her essay? How does Walker provide a corrective to each author whom she quotes? Why do you think she decided to draw so heavily on other authors, despite the fact that she finds them so in need of correction and modification? Is there a sense in which Walker's essay itself resembles the quilt made by the "anonymous Black woman in Alabama" (paragraph 34)?

2. The quotation by Jean Toomer begins with the word *I.* How long does it take Walker to refer to herself in the first person in this essay? In the meantime, do you have a hard time determining where she stands? What positive effect might come from her less-than-direct approach? In what ways does her approach resemble the approach of the women she admires and takes as her role models?

3. In this essay, Walker redefines the word *art*, saying "We have constantly looked high, when we should have looked high—and low" (paragraph 33). What is this "art"—the gardens, quilts, songs, stories, and mats—usually called? What kinds of scholars, if any, examine it, and what kinds of features do they recognize? Why is this the case? Can you imagine a different approach to this material, one suggested by Walker's essay?

4. Examine the analogies and metaphors Walker employs in this essay, both those she borrows from earlier writers and those she creates herself, both those she critiques and those she endorses. Look both at the ways that the metaphors allow the reader to see the actual historical women in a new light, and also the ways in which the women allow the reader to see the metaphors in a new light. The "Saint" metaphor (paragraphs 1–2), for instance, was no doubt originally meant to convey a sense of worshipful respect. How do the actual lives of the women as Walker describes them complicate and ultimately discredit that metaphor? Trace all of the religious analogies and references in the subsequent paragraphs to help you discover Walker's strategies.

Essay Questions

1. What or whom do you consider your main source of strength and inspiration? Do you tend to trace your identity to particular ancestors, to particular historical figures, to characters in books you read as a child? How might you express the values you hold most dear? How many other people's examples feed into your sense of who you are and what you believe? Write an essay in which you explore the sources of your identity and beliefs.

2. Write an essay in which you explore the figure of the artist in Walker's essay. How does the concept of art relate to the concept of spirituality? To the concept of insanity? How is art affected by the social conditions of the artist, and to what extent and in what forms can it transcend those conditions? These are just some of the questions to consider while exploring the topic of art for your expository essay.

Thematic Pair: Negotiating Public Space

▲▼The Arab World

Edward T. Hall

Edward T. Hall (b. 1914) received his A.B. at the University of Denver, his M.A. at the University of Arizona, and his Ph.D. at Columbia University. He has conducted field research in Micronesia, the southwestern United States, and Europe, among other places. After a long academic career teaching anthropology at several universities, Hall became a consultant to business and government agencies, which draw on his expertise regarding intercultural relations and communication.

Hall has devoted much of his career as an anthropologist to understanding cultural differences, and explaining the practical implications of these differences to a reading public. Several of his books, including Sensitivity and Empathy at Home and Abroad *(1962) and* Hidden Differences: Doing Business with the Japanese *(1987), are of direct interest to the international businessman or woman; others, such as* The Fourth Dimension in Architecture: The Impact of Building on Man's Behavior *(1975) and* The Anthropology of Everyday Life: An Autobiography *(1992), take a more general approach to understanding human behavior. As you read Hall's essay below, note the way he looks at phenomena we normally don't notice, uncovering worlds of meaning that those who take human behavior for granted invariably miss.*

In spite of over two thousand years of contact, Westerners and Arabs still do not understand each other. Proxemic research reveals some insights into this difficulty. Americans in the Middle East are immediately struck by two conflicting sensations. In public they are compressed and overwhelmed by smells, crowding, and high noise levels; in Arab homes Americans are apt to rattle around, feeling exposed and often somewhat inadequate because of too much space! (The Arab houses and apartments of the middle and upper classes which Americans stationed abroad commonly occupy are much larger than the dwellings such Americans usually inhabit.) Both the high sensory stimulation which is experienced in public places and the basic insecurity which comes from being in a dwelling that is too large provide Americans with an introduction to the sensory world of the Arab.

Behavior in Public

Pushing and shoving in public places is characteristic of Middle Eastern culture. Yet it is not entirely what Americans think it is (being pushy and rude), but stems from a different set of assumptions concerning not only the relations between people but how one experiences the body as well. Paradoxically, Arabs consider northern Europeans and Americans pushy, too. This was very puzzling to me when I started investigating these two views. How could Americans who stand aside and avoid touching be considered pushy? I used to ask Arabs to explain this paradox. None of my subjects was able to tell me specifically what particulars of American behavior were responsible, yet they all agreed that the impression was widespread among Arabs. After repeated unsuccessful attempts to gain insight into the cognitive world of the Arab on this particular point, I filed it away as a question that only time would answer. When the answer came, it was because of a seemingly inconsequential annoyance.

While waiting for a friend in a Washington, D.C., hotel lobby and wanting to be both visible and alone, I had seated myself in a solitary chair outside the normal stream of traffic. In such a setting most Americans follow a rule, which is all the more binding because we seldom think about it, that can be stated as follows: as soon as a person stops or is seated in a public place, there balloons around him a small sphere of privacy which is considered inviolate. The size of the sphere varies with the degree of crowding, the age, sex, and the importance of the person, as well as the general surroundings. Anyone who enters this zone and stays there is intruding. In fact, a stranger who intrudes, even for a specific purpose, acknowledges the fact that he has intruded by beginning his request with "Pardon me, but can you tell me . . . ?"

To continue, as I waited in the deserted lobby, a stranger walked up to where I was sitting and stood close enough so that not only could I easily touch him but I could even hear him breathing. In addition, the dark mass of his body filled the peripheral field of vision on my left side. If the lobby had been crowded with people, I would have understood his behavior, but in an empty lobby his presence made me exceedingly uncomfortable. Feeling annoyed by this intrusion, I moved my body in such a way as to communicate annoyance. Strangely enough, instead of moving away, my actions seemed only to encourage him, because he moved even closer. In spite of the temptation to escape the annoyance, I put aside thoughts of abandoning my post, thinking, "To hell with it. Why should I move? I was here first and I'm not going to let this fellow drive me out even if he is a boor." Fortunately, a group of people soon arrived whom my tormentor immediately joined. Their mannerisms explained his behavior, for I knew from both speech and gestures that they were Arabs. I had not been able to make this crucial identification by looking at my subject when he was alone because he wasn't talking and he was wearing American clothes.

5   In describing the scene later to an Arab colleague, two contrasting patterns emerged. My concept and my feelings about my own circle of privacy in a "public" place immediately struck my Arab friend as strange and puzzling. He said, "After all, it's a public place, isn't it?" Pursuing this line of inquiry, I found that in Arab thought I had no

rights whatsoever by virtue of occupying a given spot; neither my place nor my body was inviolate! For the Arab, there is no such thing as an intrusion in public. Public means public. With this insight, a great range of Arab behavior that had been puzzling, annoying, and sometimes even frightening began to make sense. I learned, for example, that if *A* is standing on a street corner and *B* wants his spot, *B* is within his rights if he does what he can to make *A* uncomfortable enough to move. In Beirut only the hardy sit in the last row in a movie theater, because there are usually standees who want seats and who push and shove and make such a nuisance that most people give up and leave. Seen in this light, the Arab who "intruded" on my space in the hotel lobby had apparently selected it for the very reason I had: it was a good place to watch two doors and the elevator. My show of annoyance, instead of driving him away, had only encouraged him. He thought he was about to get me to move.

Another silent source of friction between Americans and Arabs is in an area that Americans treat very informally—the manners and rights of the road. In general, in the United States we tend to defer to the vehicle that is bigger, more powerful, faster, and heavily laden. While a pedestrian walking along a road may feel annoyed he will not think it unusual to step aside for a fast-moving automobile. He knows that because he is moving he does not have the right to the space around him that he has when he is standing still (as I was in the hotel lobby). It appears that the reverse is true with the Arabs who apparently *take on rights to space as they move.* For someone else to move into a space an Arab is also moving into is a violation of his rights. It is infuriating to an Arab to have someone else cut in front of him on the highway. It is the American's cavalier treatment of moving space that makes the Arab call him aggressive and pushy.

Concepts of Privacy

The experience described above and many others suggested to me that Arabs might actually have a wholly contrasting set of assumptions concerning the body and the rights associated with it. Certainly the Arab tendency to shove and push each other in public and to feel and pinch women in public conveyances would not be tolerated by Westerners. It appeared to me that they must not have any concept of a private zone outside the body. This proved to be precisely the case.

In the Western world, the person is synonymous with an individual inside a skin. And in northern Europe generally, the skin and even the clothes may be inviolate. You need permission to touch either if you are a stranger. This rule applies in some parts of France, where the mere touching of another person during an argument used to be legally defined as assault. For the Arab the location of the person in relation to the body is quite different. The person exists somewhere down inside the body. The ego is not completely hidden, however, because it can be reached very easily with an insult. It is protected from touch but not from words. The dissociation of the body and the ego may explain why the public amputation of a thief's hand is tolerated as standard punishment in Saudi Arabia. It also sheds light on why an Arab employer living in a modern apartment can provide his servant with a room that is a boxlike cubicle approximately 5 by 10 by 4 feet in size that is not only hung from the ceiling to conserve floor space but has an opening so that the servant can be spied on.

As one might suspect, deep orientations toward the self such as the one just described are also reflected in the language. This was brought to my attention one afternoon when an Arab colleague who is the author of an Arab-English dictionary arrived in my office and threw himself into a chair in a state of obvious exhaustion. When I asked him what had been going on, he said: "I have spent the entire afternoon trying to find the Arab equivalent of the English word 'rape.' There is no such word in Arabic. All my sources, both written and spoken, can come up with no more than an approximation, such as 'He took her against her will.' There is nothing in Arabic approaching your meaning as it is expressed in that one word."

10 Differing concepts of the placement of the ego in relation to the body are not easily grasped. Once an idea like this is accepted, however, it is possible to understand many other facets of Arab life that would otherwise be difficult to explain. One of these is the high population density of Arab cities like Cairo, Beirut, and Damascus. According to the animal studies described in the earlier chapters, the Arabs should be living in a perpetual behavioral sink. While it is probable that Arabs are suffering from population pressures, it is also just as possible that continued pressure from the desert has resulted in a cultural adaptation to high density which takes the form described above. Tucking the ego down inside the body shell not only would permit higher population densities but would explain why it is that Arab communications are stepped up as much as they are when compared to northern European communication patterns. Not only is the sheer noise level much higher, but the piercing look of the eyes, the touch of the hands, and the mutual bathing in the warm moist breath during conversation represent stepped-up sensory inputs to a level which many Europeans find unbearably intense.

The Arab dream is for lots of space in the home, which unfortunately many Arabs cannot afford. Yet when he has space, it is very different from what one finds in most American homes. Arab spaces inside their upper middle-class homes are tremendous by our standards. They avoid partitions because Arabs *do not like to be alone.* The form of the home is such as to hold the family together inside a single protective shell, because Arabs are deeply involved with each other. Their personalities are intermingled and take nourishment from each other like the roots and soil. If one is not with people and actively involved in some way, one is deprived of life. An old Arab saying reflects this value: "Paradise without people should not be entered because it is Hell." Therefore, Arabs in the United States often feel socially and sensorially deprived and long to be back where there is human warmth and contact.

Since there is no physical privacy as we know it in the Arab family, not even a word for privacy, one could expect that the Arabs might use some other means to be alone. Their way to be alone is to stop talking. Like the English, an Arab who shuts himself off in this way is not indicating that anything is wrong or that he is withdrawing, only that he wants to be alone with his own thoughts or does not want to be intruded upon. One subject said that her father would come and go for days at a time without saying a word, and no one in the family thought anything of it. Yet for this very reason, an Arab exchange student visiting a Kansas farm failed to pick up the cue that his American hosts were mad at him when they gave him the "silent treatment." He only discovered something was wrong when they took him to town and tried forcibly to put him on a bus to Washington, D.C., the headquarters of the exchange program responsible for his presence in the U.S.

Arab Personal Distances

Like everyone else in the world, Arabs are unable to formulate specific rules for their informal behavior patterns. In fact, they often deny that there are any rules, and they are made anxious by suggestions that such is the case. Therefore, in order to determine how the Arab sets distances, I investigated the use of each sense separately. Gradually, definite and distinctive behavioral patterns began to emerge.

Olfaction occupies a prominent place in the Arab life. Not only is it one of the distance-setting mechanisms, but it is a vital part of a complex system of behavior. Arabs consistently breathe on people when they talk. However, this habit is more than a matter of different manners. To the Arab good smells are pleasing and a way of being involved with each other. To smell one's friend is not only nice but desirable, for to deny him your breath is to act ashamed. Americans, on the other hand, trained as they are not to breathe in people's faces, automatically communicate shame in trying to be polite. Who would expect that when our highest diplomats are putting on their best manners they are also communicating shame? Yet this is what occurs constantly, because diplomacy is not only "eyeball to eyeball" but breath to breath.

15   By stressing olfaction, Arabs do not try to eliminate all the body's odors, only to enhance them and use them in building human relationships. Nor are they self-conscious about telling others when they don't like the way they smell. A man leaving his house in the morning may be told by his uncle, "Habib, your stomach is sour and your breath doesn't smell too good. Better not talk too close to people today." Smell is even considered in the choice of a mate. When couples are being matched for marriage, the man's go-between will sometimes ask to smell the girl, who may be turned down if she doesn't "smell nice." Arabs recognize that smell and disposition may be linked.

In a word, the olfactory boundary performs two roles in Arab life. It enfolds those who want to relate and separates those who don't. The Arab finds it essential to stay inside the olfactory zone as a means of keeping tab on changes in emotion. What is more, he may feel crowded as soon as he smells something unpleasant. While not much is known about "olfactory crowding," this may prove to be as significant as any other variable in the crowding complex because it is tied directly to the body chemistry and hence to the state of health and emotions. . . . It is not surprising, therefore, that the olfactory boundary constitutes for the Arabs, an informal distance-setting mechanism in contrast to the visual mechanisms of the Westerner.

Facing and Not Facing

One of my earliest discoveries in the field of intercultural communication was that the position of the bodies of people in conversation varies with the culture. Even so, it used to puzzle me that a special Arab friend seemed unable to walk and talk at the same time. After years in the United States, he could not bring himself to stroll along, facing forward while talking. Our progress would be arrested while he edged ahead, cutting slightly in front of me and turning sideways so we could see each other. Once in this position, he would stop. His behavior was explained when I learned that for Arabs to view the other person peripherally is regarded as impolite, and to sit or stand back-to-back is considered very rude. You must be involved when interacting with Arabs who are friends.

One mistaken American notion is that Arabs conduct all conversations at close distances. This is not the case at all. On social occasions, they may sit on opposite sides of the room and talk across the room to each other. They are, however, apt to take offense when Americans use what are to them ambiguous distances, such as the four- to seven-foot social-consultative distance. They frequently complain that Americans are cold or aloof or "don't care." This was what an elderly Arab diplomat in an American hospital thought when the American nurses used "professional" distance. He had the feeling that he was being ignored, that they might not take good care of him. Another Arab subject remarked, referring to American behavior, "What's the matter? Do I smell bad? Or are they afraid of me?"

Arabs who interact with Americans report experiencing a certain flatness traceable in part to a very different use of the eyes in private and in public as well as between friends and strangers. Even though it is rude for a guest to walk around the Arab home eyeing things, Arabs look at each other in ways which seem hostile or challenging to the American. One Arab informant said that he was in constant hot water with Americans because of the way he looked at them without the slightest intention of offending. In fact, he had on several occasions barely avoided fights with American men who apparently thought their masculinity was being challenged because of the way he was looking at them. As noted earlier, Arabs look each other in the eye when talking with an intensity that makes most Americans highly uncomfortable.

Involvement

As the reader must gather by now, Arabs are involved with each other[20] on many different levels simultaneously. Privacy in a public place is foreign to them. Business transactions in the bazaar, for example, are not just between buyer and seller, but are participated in by everyone. Anyone who is standing around may join in. If a grownup sees a boy breaking a window, he must stop him even if he doesn't know him. Involvement and participation are expressed in other ways as well. If two men are fighting, the crowd must intervene. On the political level, *to fail to intervene* when trouble is brewing is to take sides, which is what our State Department always seems to be doing. Given the fact that few people in the world today are even remotely aware of the cultural mold that forms their thoughts, it is normal for Arabs to view *our* behavior as though it stemmed from *their* own hidden set of assumptions.

Feelings about Enclosed Spaces

In the course of my interviews with Arabs the term "tomb" kept cropping up in conjunction with enclosed space. In a word, Arabs don't mind being crowded by people but hate to be hemmed in by walls. They show a much greater overt sensitivity to architectural crowding than we do. Enclosed space must meet as least three requirements that I know of if it is to satisfy the Arabs: there must be plenty of unobstructed space in which to move around (possibly as much as a thousand square feet); very high ceilings—so high in fact that they do not normally impinge on the visual field; and, in addition, there must be an unobstructed view. It was spaces such as these in which the Americans referred to earlier felt so uncomfortable. One sees the Arab's need for a view expressed in many ways, even negatively, for to cut off a neighbor's view is one of the most effective ways of spiting him. In Beirut one can see what is known locally as the "spite house." It is nothing more than a thick, four-story wall, built at the end of a long fight between neighbors, on a narrow strip of land for the express purpose of denying a view of the Mediterranean to any house built on the land behind. According to one of my informants, there is also a house on a small plot of land between Beirut and Damascus which is completely surrounded by a neighbor's wall built high enough to cut off the view from all windows.

Boundaries

Proxemic patterns tell us other things about Arab culture. For example, the whole concept of the boundary as an abstraction is almost impossible to pin down. In one sense, there are no boundaries. "Edges" of town, yes, but permanent boundaries out in the country (hidden lines), no. In the course of my work with Arab subjects I had a difficult time translating our concept of a boundary into terms which could be equated with theirs. In order to clarify the distinctions between the two very different definitions, I thought it might be helpful to pinpoint acts which constituted trespass. To date, I have been unable to discover anything even remotely resembling our own legal concept of trespass.

Arab behavior in regard to their own real estate is apparently an extension of, and therefore consistent with, their approach to the body. My subjects simply failed to respond whenever trespass was mentioned. They didn't seem to understand what I meant by this term. This may be explained by the fact that they organize relationships with each other according to closed systems rather than spatially. For thousands of years Moslems, Marinites, Druses, and Jews have lived in their own villages, each with strong kin affiliations. Their hierarchy of loyalties is: first to one's self, then to kinsman, townsman, or tribesman, co-religionist and/or countryman. Anyone not in these categories is a stranger. Strangers and enemies are very closely linked, if not synonymous, in Arab thought. Trespass in this context is a matter of who you are, rather than a piece of land or a space with a boundary that can be denied to anyone and everyone, friend and foe alike.

In summary, proxemic patterns differ. By examining them it is possible to reveal cultural frames that determine the structure of a given people's perceptual world. Perceiving the world differently leads to differential definitions of what constitutes crowded living, different interpersonal relations, and a different approach to both local and international politics. . . .

Additional Rhetorical Strategies

Cause and Effect (paragraph 10); Comparison and Contrast (throughout).

Discussion Questions

1. Look at Hall's use of examples. Which examples follow the point being made, and which lead up to it? What kinds of examples does he use to support his argument? When he uses an isolated incident from his personal experience to support a given point (as he does, for example, in paragraphs 3–4), what, if anything, causes the reader to accept that example as representative rather than unique?
2. What are some of the unspoken rules for American behavior in public, as outlined by Hall? Can you think of other unspoken rules that we follow but never consciously learn or teach? What are some of the assumptions that lie behind such patterns of behavior?
3. Hall describes a servant's room in an Arab employer's house (paragraph 8). How does this servant's living quarters compare and contrast with the descriptions Hall gives of Arabs' living space elsewhere in the essay? To what extent does the information about the servant's living quarters contradict or undermine his overall points about Arab culture? What larger implications might you draw?
4. Look at the English words for which Hall finds no Arab equivalents. What are the implications of these linguistic differences? Are there any linguistic differences that you might interpret differently from Hall?

Essay Questions

1. Who is Hall's intended audience? How can you tell? Does he spend more time describing Arab behavior and preconceptions or American behavior and preconceptions? Pretend you are an anthropologist from a country other than the United States, and write an essay exploring the strange behavior and unconscious rules obeyed by Americans.
2. Throughout his essay, Hall implies that Americans are a homogeneous group. Given the actual ethnic makeup of U.S. citizens, see if you can critique Hall's assumptions about Americans. You might base your arguments on a manageable sample of the American population, for instance a classroom in which the students come from several different backgrounds. How might these different backgrounds, and the accompanying preconceptions, create the same level of misunderstanding that Hall describes between Americans and Arabs?

▲▼Just Walk on By: A Black Man Ponders His Ability to Alter Public Space

Brent Staples

Brent Staples (b. 1951) received his B.A. from Widener University in 1973 and his Ph.D. in psychology from the University of Chicago in 1982. He is a prolific journalist who has written for Chicago Magazine, *the* Chicago Reader, Down Beat Magazine, Harper's, New York Woman, *the* New York Times Magazine, *and* Ms., *for which "Just Walk on By" was written.*

In 1985 Staples joined the staff of the New York Times, *writing on literature, culture, and politics, and in 1990 he became a member of the* Times *editorial board. His autobiography,* Parallel Time: Growing Up in Black and White, *came out in 1994.*

My first victim was a woman—white, well dressed, probably in her early twenties. I came upon her late one evening on a deserted street in Hyde Park, a relatively affluent neighborhood in an otherwise mean, impoverished section of Chicago. As I swung onto the avenue behind her, there seemed to be a discreet, uninflammatory distance between us. Not so. She cast back a worried glance. To her, the youngish black man—a broad six feet two inches with a beard and billowing hair, both hands shoved into the pockets of a bulky military jacket—seemed menacingly close. After a few more quick glimpses, she picked up her pace and was soon running in earnest. Within seconds she disappeared into a cross street.

That was more than a decade ago. I was twenty-two years old, a graduate student newly arrived at the University of Chicago. It was in the echo of that terrified woman's footfalls that I first began to know the unwieldy inheritance I'd come into—the ability to alter public space in ugly ways. It was clear that she thought herself the quarry of a mugger, a rapist, or worse. Suffering a bout of insomnia, however, I was stalking sleep, not defenseless wayfarers. As a softy who is scarcely able to take a knife to a raw chicken—let alone hold it to a person's throat—I was surprised, embarrassed, and dismayed all at once. Her flight made me feel like an accomplice in tyranny. It also made it clear that I was indistinguishable from the muggers who occasionally seeped into the area from the surrounding ghetto. That first encounter, and those that followed, signified that a vast, unnerving gulf lay between nighttime pedestrians—particularly women—and me. And I soon gathered that being perceived as dangerous is a hazard in itself. I only needed to turn a corner into a dicey situation, or crowd some frightened, armed person in a foyer somewhere, or make an errant move after being pulled over by a policeman. Where fear and weapons meet—and they often do in urban America—there is always the possibility of death.

In that first year, my first away from my hometown, I was to become thoroughly familiar with the language of fear. At dark, shadowy intersections in Chicago, I could cross in front of a car stopped at a traffic light and elicit the *thunk, thunk, thunk, thunk* of the driver—black, white, male, or female—hammering down the door locks. On less traveled streets after dark, I grew accustomed to but never comfortable with people who crossed to the other side of the street rather than pass me. Then there were the standard unpleasantries with police, doormen, bouncers, cabdrivers, and others whose business is to screen out troublesome individuals *before* there is any nastiness.

I moved to New York nearly two years ago and I have remained an avid night walker. In central Manhattan, the near-constant crowd cover minimizes tense one-on-one street encounters. Elsewhere—visiting friends in SoHo,[1] where sidewalks are narrow and tightly spaced buildings shut out the sky—things can get very taut indeed.

Black men have a firm place in New York mugging literature. Norman Podhoretz[2] in his famed (or infamous) 1963 essay, "My Negro Problem—And Ours," recalls growing up in terror of black males; they "were tougher than we were, more ruthless," he writes—and as an adult on the Upper West Side of Manhattan, he continues, he cannot constrain his nervousness when he meets black men on certain streets. Similarly, a decade later, the essayist and novelist Edward Hoagland extols a New York where once "Negro bitterness bore down mainly on other Negroes." Where some see mere panhandlers, Hoagland sees "a mugger who is clearly screwing up his nerve to do more than just *ask* for money." But Hoagland has "the New Yorker's quick-hunch posture for broken-field maneuvering," and the bad guy swerves away.

I often witness that "hunch posture," from women after dark on the warrenlike streets of Brooklyn where I live. They seem to set their faces on neutral and, with their purse straps strung across their chests bandolier style, they forge ahead as though bracing themselves against being tackled. I understand, of course, that the danger they perceive is not a hallucination. Women are particularly vulnerable to street violence, and young black males are drastically overrepresented among the perpetrators of that violence. Yet these truths are no solace against the kind of alienation that comes of being ever the suspect, against being set apart, a fearsome entity with whom pedestrians avoid making eye contact.

---

[1]SoHo: A section of lower Manhattan known for its art galleries.
[2]Norman Podhoretz: An influential neo-conservative critic and former editor of *Commentary* magazine.

It is not altogether clear to me how I reached the ripe old age of twenty-two without being conscious of the lethality nighttime pedestrians attributed to me. Perhaps it was because in Chester, Pennsylvania, the small, angry industrial town where I came of age in the 1960s, I was scarcely noticeable against a backdrop of gang warfare, street knifings, and murders. I grew up one of the good boys, had perhaps a half-dozen fistfights. In retrospect, my shyness of combat has clear sources.

Many things go into the making of a young thug. One of those things is the consummation of the male romance with the power to intimidate. An infant discovers that random flailings send the baby bottle flying out of the crib and crashing to the floor. Delighted, the joyful babe repeats those motions again and again, seeking to duplicate the feat. Just so, I recall the points at which some of my boyhood friends were finally seduced by the perception of themselves as tough guys. When a mark cowered and surrendered his money without resistance, myth and reality merged—and paid off. It is, after all, only manly to embrace the power to frighten and intimidate. We, as men, are not supposed to give an inch of our lane on the highway; we are to seize the fighter's edge in work and in play and even in love; we are to be valiant in the face of hostile forces.

Unfortunately, poor and powerless young men seem to take all this nonsense literally. As a boy, I saw countless tough guys locked away; I have since buried several, too. They were babies, really—a teenage cousin, a brother of twenty-two, a childhood friend in his mid-twenties—all gone down in episodes of bravado played out in the streets. I came to doubt the virtues of intimidation early on. I chose, perhaps even unconsciously, to remain a shadow—timid, but a survivor.

10   The fearsomeness mistakenly attributed to me in public places often has a perilous flavor. The most frightening of these confusions occurred in the late 1970s and early 1980s when I worked as a journalist in Chicago. One day, rushing into the office of a magazine I was writing for with a deadline story in hand, I was mistaken for a burglar. The office manager called security and, with an ad hoc posse, pursued me through the labyrinthine halls, nearly to my editor's door. I had no way of proving who I was. I could only move briskly toward the company of someone who knew me.

Another time I was on assignment for a local paper and killing time before an interview. I entered a jewelry store on the city's affluent Near North Side. The proprietor excused himself and returned with an enormous red Doberman pinscher straining at the end of a leash. She stood, the dog extended toward me, silent to my questions, her eyes bulging nearly out of her head. I took a cursory look around, nodded, and bade her good night. Relatively speaking, however, I never fared as badly as another black male journalist. He went to nearby Waukegan, Illinois, a couple of summers ago to work on a story about a murderer who was born there. Mistaking the reporter for the killer, police hauled him from his car at gunpoint and but for his press credentials would probably have tried to book him. Such episodes are not uncommon. Black men trade tales like this all the time.

In "My Negro Problem—And Ours," Podhoretz writes that the hatred he feels for blacks makes itself known to him through a variety of avenues—one being his discomfort with that "special brand of paranoid touchiness" to which he says blacks are prone. No doubt he is speaking here of black men. In time, I learned to smother the rage I felt at so often being taken for a criminal. Not to do so would surely have led to madness—via that special "paranoid touchiness" that so annoyed Podhoretz at the time he wrote the essay.

I began to take precautions to make myself less threatening. I move about with care, particularly late in the evening. I give a wide berth to nervous people on subway platforms during the wee hours, particularly when I have exchanged business clothes for jeans. If I happen to be entering a building behind some people who appear skittish, I may walk by, letting them clear the lobby before I return, so as not to seem to be following them. I have been calm and extremely congenial on those rare occasions when I've been pulled over by the police.

And on late-evening constitutionals along streets less traveled by, I employ what has proved to be an excellent tension-reducing measure: I whistle melodies from Beethoven and Vivaldi and the more popular classical composers. Even steely New Yorkers hunching toward nighttime destinations seem to relax, and occasionally they even join in the tune. Virtually everybody seems to sense that a mugger wouldn't be warbling bright, sunny selections from Vivaldi's *Four Seasons*. It is my equivalent of the cowbell that hikers wear when they know they are in bear country.

Additional Rhetorical Strategies

Narration (paragraphs 1, 10, 11); Process Analysis (paragraphs 8–9); Analogy (paragraph 14).

Discussion Questions

1. Look at the opening of the essay. Why does Staples refer to the young woman as his "first victim"? How does this intentionally misleading gambit relate to Staples' thesis? What is the effect on the reader?
2. Staples published this essay in *Ms.* magazine, whose audience is largely female. What indications does he give that he has tailored his essay to a female audience? How and where does he signal the fact that he has taken the point of view of the young woman on the

street into account? Explore the double awareness he displays in this essay: an awareness of both the causes of others' fear of him and a simultaneous awareness of the alienating effects of that fear. To whom does the last sentence of the essay seem to be addressed, and with what intended effect?

3. What kinds of examples does Staples provide to support his thesis? Which kinds of examples do you find most effective? What is the effect of the examples taken from Norman Podhoretz's and Edward Hoagland's writing? What would Staples' essay sacrifice if he were to omit these examples and rely solely on his own experiences and those he has heard from other black men, who "trade tales like this all the time" (paragraph 11)?

4. In paragraph 2, the essay takes a turn: whereas at first it seems that the degree of danger to white women is at stake, suddenly we realize that it is actually the black men who are in danger ("being perceived as dangerous is a hazard in itself"). What is Staples' reason for introducing this reversal? How compelling is his argument in this section of the essay? Why?

Essay Questions

1. Read George Orwell's essay, "Shooting an Elephant" (p. 83), and compare Staples' predicament with that faced by Orwell. How might Staples' observation that the woman's "flight made [him] feel like an accomplice in tyranny" (paragraph 2) also apply to and illuminate Orwell's essay? What are some of the larger social forces and inequities that mold each writer's situation?

2. Explore the twin issues of power and powerlessness as they appear in Staples' essay. In the course of your analysis, you might consider the relative positions of women and men, blacks and whites, for instance. Look too at Staples' analysis of the role powerlessness plays in the making of a criminal. What kind of statement can you come to that would account for the role of power in the realm of public safety, and how would you support that statement?

Exploring Connections: Questions Linking the Thematic Pair

1. Both Hall and Staples discuss misunderstandings and misinterpretations between people whose often unconscious preconceptions differ. How might each essay help to improve communications between the groups discussed? [You might also want to look at Deborah Tannen's essay (p. 308) in this regard.] Is each author equally attentive to each perspective he discusses in his respective essay? Is each equally fair minded?

2. Write an essay in which you examine some aspect of human behavior, exploring both its intended and received message. How, for instance might a man view the act of opening a door for a woman? How might the woman for whom he opened the door interpret the action? How might a difference of interpretation be successfully negotiated if each party were to be informed of the other's intent? Feel free to use any other example you find revealing.

Definition

S
o fundamental is definition to the activities of thinking and writing that we too often take its procedures entirely for granted. As the vocabulary we slowly and sometimes painfully acquired in childhood and early adolescence becomes an almost unconscious part of our nature, we may begin to overlook the rock-bottom significance of many of our most common words. Worse, we may even begin to think their meanings so settled that we need never reconsider them at all. In fact, as our educations become more formalized we may tend to worry more about all the words we don't know than about all the words we do know. We bone up on vocabulary lists so we can pass tests that demonstrate our mastery of words like *lugubrious, acerbic, myopic,* and *obfuscate.* Yet what kind of tests would examine our grasp of such familiar words as *friend, grief, honor, wrong, violence, courage, sex, community, time,* or *love*—words that form the emotional and intellectual contours of most of our conscious and even unconscious lives? In our writing, we should be able to perform well with both vocabularies—the common and the uncommon—but we need to remember that the most familiar words will probably require the most attention.

As we think and write, we should keep a close watch on the words we use most frequently. Such words make up the vital part of our vocabulary and are the ones we tend to be most careless about. Words like *time, love, right, male,* or *female* look and feel simple, but they can be tricky and elusive. We can't assume that people will always interpret such words—no matter how ordinary-sounding they seem—exactly as we expect them to. An everyday word like *time,* for instance, may have radically different meanings and associations to a physicist, a terminally ill patient, a jazz musician, an Olympic runner, and a prisoner. Legal cases, diplomatic negotiations, political movements, and even medical decisions (for example, that someone is, or is not, to be pronounced dead) can, as we well know, hang on the precise definition of a word. Even the way we define our own proper names can have a vital bearing on how we conduct our lives.

Definition is basic to communication. We don't really know what we are talking about unless we know what our words mean. This isn't to say that we must always have at hand a precise definition for every word we use, but we do need to know, especially when we write, just when our use of a word requires the support of a careful definition. At a rough football game in which there are injuries and fights, for example, you might think that college sports are getting violent and not feel it necessary to ask yourself what exactly you mean by "violent." But if you decided to make that observation the basis for a composition about college sports, you could not construct a convincing case for your idea unless you made your notion of violence sufficiently precise. Just when does rough play become violent play? What looks like violence to you may be exciting play to another spectator and well-executed play to the winning coach. Though at first it may seem obvious, the meaning of a common word like *violence* needs to be thought out carefully once you decide to make it one of the principal words of your composition. To do this, you need to understand some of the ways in which words are defined.

Ever since Socrates and Plato, philosophers who virtually invented definition as a conceptual and rhetorical instrument, thinkers have tried to explain precisely what definition is and how it works. There are probably as many types of definition as there are intellectual disciplines. For the practical purposes of composition, however, three types of definition are essential: lexical, stipulative, and extended.

Lexical Definitions

Lexical definition—the definition we find when we consult a dictionary— is the simplest and most commonly used type of definition. It can be the means by which we learn a new word or clarify a familiar one. When we use a word without really thinking about its use, it is because we are probably in agreement with its lexical definition. There is nothing at all wrong with this practice, since verbal communication would come to a grinding halt if we had to stop to define each word we used each time we used it. Lexical definitions are rarely cited in writing; when they are, it is to show that the writer believes there is a need to call attention to the way a word is commonly used.

When working with lexical definitions, it is important to remember one thing: a lexical definition does not give us the complete meaning of the word. Instead, it gives us the word's accepted usage along with other basic information about the term's practical management. A good dictionary, for example, will generally supply us with the following: first, the range of a term's commonly accepted usages (for example, that *prejudice* can mean "any preconceived opinion or feeling, either favorable or unfavorable," not just unfavorable); second, the range of terms close in meaning to the word we are looking up (for example, that *rustic* can sometimes be synonymous with the terms *simple, artless, uncouth, rude,* or *boorish*); third, a brief notation on the word's roots (that *camera* derives from the Latin word for *vaulted room* or *vault*); and, fourth, the general class and distinguishing characteristics of a term (that a *whale* is "any of the larger marine mammals of the order Cetacea"). Such information about past and present usage, synonyms, etymology, and classification may, at times, be valuable knowledge, but it seldom gives us insight into the complete meaning of a word. If we look up, for example, a fairly complex everyday word like *adult*, we find that its primary definition is "having attained maturity," a phrase that, unless we know how to define the equally complex word *mature* tells us very little. To understand a word fully we need to think beyond its dictionary synonyms. Looking up words like *oil* and *water* in a dictionary will yield little vital knowledge concerning the powerful political or cultural dimensions of those terms. And without a consideration of a word's wider context, its meaning cannot be fully understood. This is one reason why we should cite dictionary definitions rarely and why we should never begin essays with "Webster defines X as . . . " when we intend our discussion to be a serious exploration into the meaning of X.

Stipulative Definitions

We use *stipulative definitions* when we deliberately want to alter in some way the customary lexical sense of a word. We may want to give a word a new shading or a sharper interpretation. We may find ourselves disagreeing with accepted usage and wanting to stipulate a new denotation. For example, you may decide that *adult* as defined by most dictionaries is too vague for your purposes, and so you make clear that in your essay you will use it in a more specific sense: "anyone regardless of sex or mental competence who is eighteen or over." We are also stipulating a definition when we want to focus on only one aspect of the lexical definition and not another. For example, in a paper you may want the term *classic* to refer only to the style or thought of ancient Greece or Rome, and not to the notion of lasting significance or recognized worth.

When using stipulative definitions in our writing, we should always be sure to announce clearly the first time we use a word what our special definition of it is. We should then remain consistent in our use of the word and not drift back to its lexical definition. For example, here is how the noted social critic Ivan Illich begins a discussion of the wasteful use of energy in modern transportation:

> The discussion of how energy is used to move people requires a formal distinction between transport and transit as the two components of traffic. By *traffic* I mean any movement of people from one place to another when they are outside their homes. By *transit* I mean those movements that put human metabolic energy to use, and by *transport*, that mode of movement which relies on other sources of energy. These energy sources will henceforth be mostly motors, since animals

compete fiercely with men for their food in an overpopulated world, unless they are thistle eaters like donkeys and camels.

Note that the writer's definitions are not precisely those we'd find in a dictionary. But neither are they so different from their normal dictionary entries as to cause undue trouble for readers. Stipulative definitions, as this brief excerpt clearly shows, can be extremely useful in our writing when we need to make careful distinctions between words that our readers have little reason to regard as essentially different. For example, if in a paper you wanted to make a distinction between *maturity* and *adulthood*, you would have to develop stipulative definitions for these closely related words. Given the similar dictionary usages of these terms, you could not as a writer expect your readers to be alert to any important shades of meaning you may find between them without the extra help of one or more stipulative definitions.

Clearly formed stipulative definitions can play a crucial role in accurate and forceful writing, but they do present dangers. By letting your special sense of a word stray too far from accepted usage—if you define *maturity*, say, as "the ability to read and write"—you risk confusing or losing readers who will naturally find it hard to shake off the weight of the word's ordinary lexical sense. It is a good idea when stipulating a definition to retain enough of a word's customary lexical usage to ensure comprehensibility. Try to avoid the communication impasse Humpty Dumpty gets himself into with Alice when he belligerently declares that words can mean whatever he chooses them to mean, "neither more nor less."

Extended Definitions

Lexical and stipulative definitions are usually concise, tending toward specification and clarification rather than elaboration. *Extended definition*, on the other hand, is a method of defining in greater detail. We usually reserve extended definition for words that are complex because of their evaluative, abstract, or emotional dimensions. It allows us to put a key term or concept on exhibit, to look at it in a network of relations and through a variety of perspectives. Complex words like *equality, fear*, or *anxiety* can be defined penetratingly and comprehensively by tying in the defining process to other rhetorical strategies, such as controlling metaphor or comparison and contrast. Extended definitions may run for a paragraph or two, or, as is often the case, constitute the main topic of a composition (see, for example, Perri Klass's "Ambition," on p. 208). In one sense, extended definition resembles stipulative definition: it is advisable when constructing an extended definition not to set our sense of the word at odds with its accepted usage. An effective extended definition expands and improves the common usage rather than contradicts it.

As some of the following selections show, extended definition is a common feature of expository writing. It is the type of definition we will use most frequently in our writing. We may, as Perri Klass does with the word *ambition,* explore the essential meaning of a word in order to learn more about some aspect of our culture; or we may, as Karen Horney does with the terms *fear* and *anxiety* (see p. 294), need to sharpen accepted definitions as a foundation for other concepts. To return to an earlier example, your observations on "violence" at a football game could lead to a carefully formulated essay on what violence means in our culture or to a few sentences or paragraphs on what violence means in college football. In either case, you'd need to take the word beyond the minimal definition provided by your dictionary and discuss it within the wider context of your information and experience.

In addition to its practical compositional use, definition can play a central role in the formation of concepts. As we have seen, definition involves more than merely looking up the established meanings of words. It can be in itself a rewarding intellectual activity, a process indispensable to every area of human inquiry: as the economist Karl Marx searched for an accurate definition of *commodity,* he developed an entirely new way of thinking about the value of human labor; attempting to construct a precise definition of *hysteria,* Sigmund Freud found himself confronted with a radically new conception of the mind. As you think through your compositions, you should try to remain particularly sensitive to the definitions of the words you are working with, their margins of accuracy, their opportunities for refinement or expansion. It is one of the best ways to transform old knowledge into new.

The Underclass

Herbert Gans

Herbert Gans (b. 1927) was born in Germany and emigrated to the United States in 1940. He earned his B.A. and M.A. at the University of Chicago, and his Ph.D. at the University of Pennsylvania. He has worked extensively as an urban planner and a researcher in the fields of sociology and planning, and he has been on the faculty at a number of universities, including the Massachusetts Institute of Technology and Columbia University. His many honors and awards include a Ford Foundation Fellowship, a grant from the National Endowment for the Humanities, and a Guggenheim Fellowship.

He is the author of several books, including The Urban Villagers: Groups and Class in the Life of Italian Americans *(1962),* People and Plans: Essays on Urban Problems and Solutions *(1968),* More Equality *(1973), and* Popular Culture and High Culture *(1974), and has contributed chapters to over 50 books. He is best known for his participant-observer method of research, in which he immerses himself in the life of the community that he is studying.*

Sticks and stones may break my bones, but names can never hurt me goes the old proverb. But like many old proverbs, this one is patent nonsense, as anyone knows who has ever been hurt by ethnic, racist or sexist insults and stereotypes.

The most frequent victims of insults and stereotypes have been the poor, especially those thought to be undeserving of help because someone decided—justifiably or not—that they had not acted properly. America has a long history of insults for the "undeserving" poor. In the past they were bums, hoboes, vagrants and paupers; more recently they have been culturally deprived and the hard-core poor. Now they are "the underclass."

Underclass was originally a 19th-century Swedish term for the poor. In the early 1960s, the Swedish economist Gunnar Myrdal revived it to describe the unemployed and unemployables being created by the modern economy, people who, he predicted, would soon be driven out of that economy unless it was reformed. Twenty years later, in Ronald Reagan's America, the word sprang to life again, this time not only to describe but also to condemn. Those normally consigned to the underclass include: women who start their families before marriage and before the end of adolescence, youngsters who fail to finish high school or find work, and welfare "dependents"—whether or not the behavior of any of these people is their own fault. The term is also applied to low-income delinquents and criminals—but not to affluent ones.

"Underclass" has become popular because it seems to grab people's attention. What grabs is the image of a growing horde of beggars, muggers, robbers and lazy people who do not carry their part of the economic load, all of them threatening nonpoor Americans and the stability of American society. The image may be inaccurate, but then insults and pejoratives don't have to be accurate. Moreover, underclass sounds technical, academic, and not overtly pejorative, so it can be used without anyone's biases showing. Since it is now increasingly applied to blacks and Hispanics, it is also a respectable substitute word with which to condemn them.

There are other things wrong with the word underclass. For one, it [5] lumps together in a single term very diverse poor people with diverse problems. Image all children's illnesses being described with the same word, and the difficulties doctors would have in curing them.

For example, a welfare recipient often requires little more than a decent paying job—and a male breadwinner who also has such a job—to make a normal go of it, while a high school dropout usually needs both a better-equipped school, better teachers and fellow students—and a rationale for going to school when he or she has no assurance that a decent job will follow upon graduation. Neither the welfare recipient nor the high school dropout deserves to be grouped with, or described by, the same word as muggers or drug dealers.

Labeling poor people as underclass is to blame them for their poverty, which enables the blamers to blow off the steam of self-righteousness. That steam does not, however, reduce their poverty. Unfortunately, underclass, like other buzzwords for calling the poor undeserving, is being used to avoid starting up needed antipoverty programs and other economic reforms.

Still, the greatest danger of all lies not in the label itself but in the possibility that the underclass is a symptom of a possible, and dark, American future: they we are moving toward a "post-post-industrial" economy in which there may not be enough decent jobs for all. Either too many more jobs will move to Third World countries where wages are far lower or they will be performed by ever more efficient computers and other machines.

If this happens, the underclass label may turn out to be a signal that the American economy, and our language, are preparing to get ready for a future in which some people are going to be more or less permanently jobless—and will be blamed for their joblessness to boot.

Needless to say, an American economy with a permanently job-[10] less population would be socially dangerous, for all of the country's current social problems, from crime and addiction to mental illness would be sure to increase considerably. America would then also become politically more dangerous, for various kinds of new protests have to be expected, not to mention the rise of quasi-fascist movements. Such movements can already be found in France and other European countries.

Presumably, Americans—the citizenry and elected officials both—will not let any of this happen here and will find new sources of decent jobs, as they have done in past generations, even if today this requires a new kind of New Deal. Perhaps there will be another instance of what always saved America in the past: new sources of economic growth that cannot even be imagined now.

The only problem is that in the past, America ruled the world economically, and now it does not—and it shows in our lack of economic growth. Consequently, the term underclass could become a permanent entry in the dictionary of American pejoratives.

Additional Rhetorical Strategies

Cause and Effect (paragraphs 5, 10); Example (paragraph 6); Argument (throughout).

Discussion Questions

1. Look at Gans's first paragraph. What is the effect of opening with a proverb and then immediately refuting it? What kind of expectations does this opening set up in the mind of the reader?
2. In paragraph 3, Gans traces the history of the word *underclass*. According to Gans, what did the word mean to Gunnar Myrdal? What did it come to mean in America under Ronald Reagan? How does Gans support his assertion that Americans use this word "not only to describe but also to condemn"? How does the intent of each speaker (Myrdal, modern-day Americans) affect Gans's interpretation of the word? How does he determine each speaker's intent?
3. As a reader, which of the dangers of the word *underclass* do you find most compelling? Why? Critique the dangers you find least compelling.
4. In paragraph 8, Gans makes a transition from pointing out the dangers of the label to exploring factors in our national economy that might be contributing to the widespread use of the word. Whereas in the first half of the essay, the word *underclass* seems to express widespread paranoia and lack of knowledge, now the same word expresses a real problem—and not only for those labeled the underclass. What is the effect on you as a reader to experience this shift in his argument? When he says in paragraph 10 that America will be "socially dangerous" and "politically more dangerous," what kinds of dangers is he alluding to? Who might be affected by these anticipated dangers?
5. In paragraph 11 the author sheds a ray of hope on the situation. How specific are the solutions he foresees? How compelling are they? What is the overall effect of reading the essay—optimism,

pessimism, or something else? How does his last paragraph affect the overall impression you take away from the essay?

Essay Questions

1. Among the people who use the word *underclass,* Gans (with good reason) never mentions the poor themselves. Choose a word that is often applied to one group by another. Write an essay in which you tease out the intentions of those who use the word. Look, too, at the word you have chosen from the perspective of a member of the group being so labeled. Explore the different connotations and repercussions that might pertain to the object, as well as the subject, of the utterance.

2. Several essays in this collection deal with the issue of "ethnic, racist, or sexist insults and stereotypes" (Gans, paragraph 1). Other examples include the essays by Kakutani, Naylor, Nilsen, Hentoff, and Gregorian. How do you assess the power of racist or sexist speech to wound its victims, and how do you measure the ill effects of such speech against the ill effects of suppressing speech? Write an essay in which you propose and argue in favor of a reasonable response to racist, sexist, and classist speech.

We're Not Really "Equal"

Thomas Sowell

The author of Ethnic America *(1981), from which the following selection is excerpted, Thomas Sowell (b. 1930) is a senior fellow at Stanford University's Hoover Institute and a member of the Economic Policy Advisory Board. A high-school dropout, Sowell attended Howard and Harvard Universities on the G.I. Bill and then earned a Ph.D. in economics from the University of Chicago. As a prominent black scholar in the largely white field of political economy, Sowell has had a long and deeply personal concern with the term, and the concept of, equality. He has written numerous books, including* Pink and Brown People *(1981),* Inside American Education: The Decline, the Deception, the Dogmas *(1993), and* Race and Culture: A World View *(1994).*

In "We're Not Really 'Equal'," Sowell not only emphasizes the necessity of systematic definition, but he also demonstrates two thinking processes by which we can arrive at systematic definitions in our writing. One process is to define a term by eliminating everything that it is not; the other is to describe something similar to the subject of our definition and then to delineate the differences between them.

As a teacher I have learned from sad experience that nothing so bores students as being asked to define their terms systematically before discussing some exciting issue. They want to get on with it, without wasting time on petty verbal distinctions.

Much of our politics is conducted in the same spirit. We are for "equality" or "the environment," or against an "arms race," and there is no time to waste on definitions and other Mickey Mouse stuff. This attitude may be all right for those for whom political crusades are a matter of personal excitement, like rooting for your favorite team and jeering the opposition. But for those who are serious about the consequences of public policy, nothing can be built without a solid foundation.

"Equality" is one of the great undefined terms underlying much current controversy and antagonism. This one confused word might even become the rock on which our civilization is wrecked. It should be worth defining.

Equality is such an easily understood concept in mathematics that we may not realize it is a bottomless pit of complexities anywhere else. That is because in mathematics we have eliminated the concreteness and complexities of real things. When we say that two plus two equals four, we either don't say two *what* or we say the same what after each number. But if we said that two apples plus two apples equals four oranges, we would be in trouble.

Sense

Yet that is what we are saying in our political reasoning. And we are in 5 trouble. Nothing is more concrete or complex than a human being. Beethoven could not play center field like Willie Mays, and Willie never tried to write a symphony. In what sense are they equal—or unequal? The common mathematical symbol for inequality points to the smaller quantity. But which is the smaller quantity—and in whose eyes—when such completely different things are involved?

When women have children and men don't, how can they be either equal or unequal? Our passionate desire to reduce things to the simplicity of abstract concepts does not mean that it can be done. Those who want to cheer their team and boo the visitors may like to think that the issue is equality versus inequality. But the real issue is whether or not we are going to talk sense. Those who believe in inequality have the same confusion as those who believe in equality. The French make better champagne than the Japanese, but the Japanese make better cameras than the French. What sense does it make to add champagne to cameras to a thousand other things and come up with a grand total showing who is "superior"?

When we speak of "equal justice under law," we simply mean applying the same rules to everybody. That has nothing whatsoever to do with whether everyone performs equally. A good umpire calls balls and strikes by the same rules for everyone, but one batter may get twice as many hits as another.

In recent years we have increasingly heard it argued that if outcomes are unequal, then the rules must have been applied unequally. It would destroy my last illusion to discover that Willie Mays didn't really play baseball any better than anybody else, but that the umpires and sportswriters just conspired to make it look that way. Pending the uncovering of intricate plots of this magnitude, we must accept the fact that performances are very unequal in different aspects of life. And there is no way to add up these apples, oranges and grapes to get one sum total of fruit.

Anyone with the slightest familiarity with history knows that rules have often been applied very unequally to different groups. (A few are ignorant or misguided enough to think that this is a peculiarity of American society.) The problem is not in seeing that unequal rules can lead to unequal outcomes. The problem is in trying to reason backward from unequal outcomes to unequal rules as the sole or main cause.

There are innumerable places around the world where those who 10 have been the victims of unequal rules have nevertheless vastly outperformed those who are favored. Almost nowhere in Southeast Asia have the Chinese minority had equal rights with the native peoples, but the average Chinese income in these countries has almost invariably been much higher than that of the general population. A very similar story could be told from the history of the Jews in many countries of Europe, North Africa and the Middle East. To a greater or lesser extent, this has also been the history of the Ibos in Nigeria, the Italians in Argentina, the Armenians in Turkey, the Japanese in the United States—and on and on.

Confused Terms

It would be very convenient if we could infer discriminatory rules whenever we found unequal outcomes. But life does not always accommodate itself to our convenience.

Those who are determined to find villains but cannot find evidence often resort to "society" as the cause of all our troubles. What do they mean by "society" or "environment"? They act as if these terms were self-evident. But environment and society are just new confused terms introduced to save the old confused term, equality.

The American environment or society cannot explain historical behavior patterns found among German-Americans if these same patterns can be found among Germans in Brazil, Australia, Ireland and elsewhere around the world. These patterns may be explained by the history of German society. But if the words "environment" or "society" refer to things that may go back a thousand years, we are no longer talking about either the causal or the moral responsibility of American society. If historic causes include such things as the peculiar geography of Africa or of southern Italy, then we are no longer talking about human responsibility at all.

This does not mean that there are no problems. There are very serious social problems. But that means that serious attention will be required to solve them—beginning with defining our terms.

Additional Rhetorical Strategies

Illustration (paragraphs 5, 10); Example (paragraph 9); Cause and Effect (paragraphs 9–12).

Discussion Questions

1. How would you describe Sowell's tone in the opening paragraphs of this essay? What effect does his tone have on you, as a student reading his work? Does the tone change over the course of the essay or does it remain the same?

2. Locate Sowell's thesis. Is his main purpose in writing this essay to define the word *equality?* If not, how does the definition of equality function in his essay?

3. The position Sowell is arguing against in this essay is implied throughout. How would you characterize this position? For what purpose and to what effect does Sowell invoke the mathematical concept of equality (paragraph 4)? Does it seem to be a fair critique of the people on the opposing side of the debate around equality?

4. Which of Sowell's supporting examples and analogies do you find most compelling, and which seem most flawed? Why? Where in the essay does he seem most logical, and where does he stray from that ideal?

Essay Questions

1. Why does Sowell bring up the issue of human responsibility in paragraph 13? How does this concept relate to equality? The excerpt reprinted here is part of a larger work. How might Sowell pursue the issue of responsibility and its relation to equality further if he were quoted at greater length? Write an essay exploring the relation between responsibility and the issue of equality. Feel free to diverge from the path you assume Sowell would take.

2. Instead of considering all the things equality is not, think of all the things it is. Then write a brief essay challenging Sowell's negative definition with a positive one. A good way to tackle this assignment would be to devise an answer to Sowell's rhetorical question in paragraph 6: "When women have children and men don't, how can they be either equal or unequal?"

Ambition

Perri Klass

Perri Klass (b. 1958) earned her A.B. and M.D. at Harvard University. She is currently a resident pediatrician at Boston Children's Hospital. The difficulties of juggling a career in medicine, motherhood, and the rigors of writing fiction and nonfiction frequently inform her written work. She was already writing stories before she decided to be a doctor, and managed not to give up the writing even throughout her years in medical school, an experience she captured in her book Not Entirely a Benign Procedure: Four Years as a Medical Student *(1987). She has also written short stories, some of which are collected in* I Am Having an Adventure *(1986) and a novel,* Recombinations *(1985). She has been a columnist for the* New York Times *(where she wrote the "Hers" column) and for* Discover, *and has contributed articles to such magazines as* Vogue, Esquire, Ms., Massachusetts Medicine, Self, Mademoiselle, Antioch, Christopher Street, *and* Berkeley Fiction Review.*

Speaking about the difference between writing fiction and nonfiction, and the difficulty of finding time to write, Klass said, "I can't do the fiction in those one- and two-hour blocks around the edges the way I can the nonfiction. I can't plan the fiction out in my head during the day in odd minutes in the hospital the way I can with nonfiction. I need a little more time." In the essay that follows, Klass touches on the pressures of fulfilling several of her life's ambitions at once.

In college, my friend Beth was very ambitious, not only for herself but for her friends. She was interested in foreign relations, in travel, in going to law school. "I plan to be secretary of state someday," she would say matter-of-factly. One mutual friend was studying literature, planning to go to graduate school; he would be the chairman of the Yale English department. Another friend was interested in political journalism and would someday edit *Time* magazine. I was a biology major, which was a problem: Beth's best friend from childhood was also studying biology, and Beth had already decided *she* would win the Nobel Prize. This was resolved by my interest in writing fiction. I would win *that* Nobel, while her other friend would win for science.

It was a joke; we were all smart-ass college freshmen, pretending the world was ours for the asking. But it was not entirely a joke. We were *smart* college freshmen, and why should we limit our ambitions?

I've always liked ambitious people, and many of my closest friends have had grandiose dreams. I like such people, not because I am desperate to be buddies with a future secretary of state but because I find ambitious people entertaining, interesting to talk to, fun to watch. And, of course, I like such people because I am ambitious myself, and I would rather not feel apologetic about it.

Ambition has gotten bad press. Back in the seventeenth century, Spinoza thought ambition and lust were "nothing but species of madness, although they are not enumerated among diseases." Especially in women, ambition has often been seen as a profoundly dislikable quality; the word "ambitious" linked to a "career woman" suggested that she was ruthless, hard as nails, clawing her way to success on top of the bleeding bodies of her friends.

Then, in the late seventies and the eighties, ambition became desir- 5 able, as books with titles like *How to Stomp Your Way to Success* became bestsellers. It was still a nasty sort of attribute, but nasty attributes were good because they helped you look out for number one.

But what I mean by ambition is dreaming big dreams, putting no limits on your expectations and your hopes. I don't really like very specific, attainable ambitions, the kind you learn to set in the career-strategy course taught by the author of *How to Stomp Your Way to Success*. I like big ambitions that suggest that the world could open up at any time, with work and luck and determination. The next book could hit it big. The next research project could lead to something fantastic. The next bright idea could change history.

Of course, eventually you have to stop being a freshman in college. You limit your ambitions and become more realistic, wiser about your potential, your abilities, the number of things your life can hold. Sometimes you get close to something you wanted to do, only to find it looks better from far away. Back when I was a freshman, to tell the truth, I wanted to be Jane Goodall, go into the jungle to study monkeys and learn things no one had ever dreamed of.[1] This ambition was based on an interest in biology and several *National Geographic* television specials; it turned out that wasn't enough of a basis for a life. There were a number of other early ambitions that didn't pan out either. I was not fated to live a wild, adventurous life, to travel alone to all the most exotic parts of the world, to leave behind a string of broken hearts. Oh well, you have to grow up, at least a little.

One of the worst things ambition can do is tell you you're a failure. The world is full of measuring tapes, books and articles to tell you where you should be at your age, after so-and-so many years of doing what you do.

Almost all of us have to deal with the tremendous success of friends (or enemies), with those who somehow started out where we did but are now way in front. My college-alumni magazine arrives

---

[1]Jane Goodall, a leading expert on the behavior of chimpanzees, has lived in Tanzania for more than 30 years—Eds.

every two months without fail, so I can find out who graduated two years *after* I did but is now running a groundbreaking clinic at a major university hospital (and I'm only just finishing my residency!). Who is restoring a fabulous mansion in a highly desirable town by the sea. Who got promoted yet again, due to natural brilliance and industry.

10   I read an article recently about how one's twenties are the decade for deciding on a career and finishing your training, and the thirties are for consolidating your success and rising within your chosen job (and here I am in my thirties, not even sure what I want to do yet!). With all these external yardsticks, the last thing anyone needs is an internal voice as well, whispering irritably that you were supposed to do it better, get further and that all you've actually accomplished is mush, since you haven't met your own goals.

The world is full of disappointed people. Some of them probably never had much ambition to start with; they sat back and waited for something good and feel cheated because it never happened. Some of them had very set, specific ambitions and, for one reason or another, never got what they wanted. Others got what they wanted but found it wasn't exactly what they'd expected it to be. Disappointed ambition provides fodder for both drama and melodrama: aspiring athletes (who coulda been contenders), aspiring dancers (all they ever needed was the music and the mirror).

The world is also full of people so ambitious, so consumed by drive and overdrive that nothing they pass on the way to success has any value at all. Life becomes one long exercise in delayed gratification; everything you do, you're doing only because it will one day get you where you want to be. Medical training is an excellent example of delayed gratification. You spend years in medical school doing things with no obvious relationship to your future as a doctor, and then you spend years in residency, living life on a miserable schedule, staying up all night and slogging through the day, telling yourself that one day all this will be over. It's what you have to do to become a doctor, but it's a lousy model for life in general. There's nothing wrong with a little delayed gratification every now and then, but a job you do only because of where it will get you—and not because you like it—means a life of muttering to yourself, "Someday this will be over." This is bad for the disposition.

As you grow up, your ambitions may come into conflict. Most prominently nowadays, we have to hear about Women Torn Between Family and Career, about women who make it to the top only to realize they left their ovaries behind. Part of growing up, of course, is realizing that there is only so much room in one life, whether you are male or female. You can do one thing wholeheartedly and single-mindedly and give up some other things. Or you can be greedy and grab for something new without wanting to give up what you already have. This leads to a chaotic and crowded life in which you are always late, always overdue, always behind, but rarely bored. Even so, you have to come to terms with limitations; you cannot crowd your life with occupations and then expect to do each one as well as you might if it were all you had to do. I realize this when I race out of the hospital, offending a senior doctor who had offered to explain something to me, only to arrive late at the day care center, annoying the people who have been taking care of my daughter.

People consumed by ambition, living with ambition, get to be a little humorless, a little one-sided. On the other hand, people who completely abrogate their ambition aren't all fun and games either. I've met a certain number of women whose ambitions are no longer for themselves at all; their lives are now dedicated to their offspring. I hope my children grow up to be nice people, smart people, people who use good grammar; and I hope they grow up to find things they love to do, and do well. But my ambitions are still for *me*.

Of course, I try to be mature about it all. I don't assign my friends15 Nobel Prizes or top government posts. I don't pretend that there is room in my life for any and every kind of ambition I can imagine. Instead, I say piously that all I want are three things: I want to write as well as I can, I want to have a family, and I want to be a good pediatrician. And then, of course, a voice inside whispers . . . to write a bestseller, to have ten children, to do stunning medical research. Fame and fortune, it whispers, fame and fortune. Even though I'm not a college freshman anymore, I'm glad to find that little voice still there, whispering sweet nothings in my ear.

Additional Rhetorical Strategies

Example (paragraphs 1, 9, 11, 12, 13); Cause and Effect (paragraph 3); Comparison and Contrast (paragraph 14).

Discussion Questions

1. Look at the opening and closing paragraphs of this essay. What do they have in common? How do they differ? How does the device of circling back with a difference demonstrate the progress in her thinking, and the progression of ideas in her essay from start to finish?
2. Ambition is often viewed as a negative trait; as Klass says, "Ambition has gotten bad press" (paragraph 4). In this essay the author freely admits to being ambitious. How successfully does she appeal to her readers despite their possible preconceptions about ambitious people, especially ambitious women? Analyze her tone in the essay. Are there places where she makes statements that might be alienating, but her tone or style help to turn your usual response on its head?

3. How does Klass define ambition? What are the "worst things" (paragraph 8) about ambition? To what extent would these negative consequences disappear if the ambitious people were following Klass's definition or implied guidelines?
4. Klass uses a lot of clichés in this essay. Some examples would be "hard as nails" (paragraph 4), "look out for number one" (paragraph 5), and "whispering sweet nothings in my ear" (paragraph 15). What is the effect of these clichés? Why do you think her editor did not ask her to revise those phrases? If some of the clichés seem to work for you, try to analyze the ways in which she transforms them from a negative feature to an asset.

Essay Questions

1. Think of a character trait that (like ambition) can be either positive or negative. Some possibilities would include generosity, simplicity, and self-control, but there are countless others. Write an essay in which you explore the range of behavior that might arise in conjunction with that character trait. You might want to end by addressing the following question: Is an excess of any good trait a potential problem?
2. Make a list of character traits that can have either positive or negative connotations depending on the gender of the person being described. Just as ambition is looked on in a less favorable light if the person in question is a woman, daintiness, for example, would likely be an insult if applied to a man, but probably a compliment if applied to a woman. There are countless other examples. Write an essay in which you explore the implications of the different connotations of one or more of the words on your list.

When Is It Rape?

Nancy Gibbs

Nancy Gibbs joined the staff of Time *in 1985 as a reporter for the maga-*
zine's International and Business and Economy sections. She began writ-
ing feature articles in 1988, and has covered such issues as child labor
laws, racism on campus, and separation of church and state. She is cur-
rently a senior editor at the magazine, and she also continues to write on
national affairs and domestic policy. In 1996 she collaborated with several
colleagues from Time *to publish the book* Mad Genius: The Odyssey,
Pursuit, and Capture of the Unabomber Suspect.

B e careful of strangers and hurry home, says a mother to her
daughter, knowing that the world is a frightful place but not
wishing to swaddle a child in fear. Girls grow up scarred by caution and enter adulthood eager to shake free of their parents' worst
nightmares. They still know to be wary of strangers. What they don't
know is whether they have more to fear from their friends.

Most women who get raped are raped by people they already
know—like the boy in biology class, or the guy in the office down the
hall, or their friend's brother. The familiarity is enough to make them let
down their guard, sometimes even enough to make them wonder afterward whether they were "really raped." What people think of as "real
rape"—the assault by a monstrous stranger lurking in the shadows—
accounts for only one out of five attacks.

So the phrase "acquaintance rape" was coined to describe the rest,
all the cases of forced sex between people who already knew each
other, however casually. But that was too clinical for headline writers,
and so the popular term is the narrower "date rape," which suggests an
ugly ending to a raucous night on the town.

These are not idle distinctions. Behind the search for labels is the
central mythology about rape: that rapists are always strangers, and
victims are women who ask for it. The mythology is hard to dispel because the crime is so rarely exposed. The experts guess—that's all they
can do under the circumstances—that while one in four women will be
raped in her lifetime, less than 10 percent will report the assault, and
less than 5 percent of the rapists will go to jail.

When a story of the crime lodges in the headlines, the myths have a s
way of cluttering the search for the truth. The tale of Good Friday in
Palm Beach landed in the news because it involved a Kennedy, but it
may end up as a watershed case, because all the mysteries and passions
surrounding date rape are here to be dissected. William Kennedy Smith
met a woman at a bar, invited her back home late at night and apparently had sex with her on the lawn. She says it was rape, and the police
believed her story enough to charge him with the crime. Perhaps it was

the bruises on her leg; or the instincts of the investigators who found her, panicked and shaking, curled up in the fetal position on a couch; or the lie-detector tests she passed.

On the other side, Smith has adamantly protested that he is a man falsely accused. His friends and family testify to his gentle nature and moral fiber and insist that he could not possibly have committed such a crime. Maybe the truth will come out in court—but regardless of its finale, the case has shoved the debate over date rape into the minds of average men and women.[1] Plant the topic in a conversation, and chances are it will ripen into a bitter argument or a jittery sequence of pale jokes.

Women charge that date rape is the hidden crime; men complain it is hard to prevent a crime they can't define. Women say it isn't taken seriously; men say it is a concept invented by women who like to tease but not take the consequences. Women say the date-rape debate is the first time the nation has talked frankly about sex; men say it is women's unconscious reaction to the excesses of the sexual revolution. Meanwhile, men and women argue among themselves about the "gray area" that surrounds the whole murky arena of sexual relations, and there is no consensus in sight.

In court, on campus, in conversation, the issue turns on the elasticity of the word *rape,* one of the few words in the language with the power to summon a shared image of a horrible crime.

At one extreme are those who argue that for the word to retain its impact, it must be strictly defined as forced sexual intercourse: a gang of thugs jumping a jogger in Central Park, a psychopath preying on old women in a housing complex, a man with an ice pick in a side street. To stretch the definition of the word risks stripping away its power. In this view, if it happened on a date, it wasn't rape. A romantic encounter is a context in which sex *could* occur, and so what omniscient judge will decide whether there was genuine mutual consent?

10   Others are willing to concede that date rape sometimes occurs, that sometimes a man goes too far on a date without a woman's consent. But this infraction, they say, is not as ghastly a crime as street rape, and it should not be taken as seriously. The *New York Post,* alarmed by the Willy Smith case, wrote in a recent editorial, "If the sexual encounter, *forced or not,* has been preceded by a series of consensual activities—drinking, a trip to the man's home, a walk on a deserted beach at three in the morning—the charge that's leveled against the alleged offender

---

[1]In December 1991 a Florida jury found William Kennedy Smith not guilty of rape. As Gibbs predicted, the high-profile trial—which included testimony from Smith's uncle, Senator Edward Kennedy—stimulated widespread discussion about date rape—Eds.

should, it seems to us, be different than the one filed against, say, the youths who raped and beat the jogger."[2]

This attitude sparks rage among women who carry scars received at the hands of men they knew. It makes no difference if the victim shared a drink or a moonlit walk or even a passionate kiss, they protest, if the encounter ended with her being thrown to the ground and forcibly violated. Date rape is not about a misunderstanding, they say. It is not a communications problem. It is not about a woman's having regrets in the morning for a decision she made the night before. It is not about a "decision" at all. Rape is rape, and any form of forced sex—even between neighbors, co-workers, classmates, and casual friends—is a crime.

A more extreme form of that view comes from activists who see rape as a metaphor, its definition swelling to cover any kind of oppression of women. Rape, seen in this light, can occur not only on a date but also in a marriage, not only by violent assault but also by psychological pressure. A Swarthmore College training pamphlet once explained that acquaintance rape "spans a spectrum of incidents and behaviors, ranging from crimes legally defined as rape to verbal harassment and inappropriate innuendo."

No wonder, then, that the battles become so heated. When innuendo qualifies as rape, the definitions have become so slippery that the entire subject sinks into a political swamp. The only way to capture the hard reality is to tell the story.

A thirty-two-year-old woman was on business in Tampa last year for the Florida supreme court. Stranded at the courthouse, she accepted a lift from a lawyer involved in her project. As they chatted on the ride home, she recalls, "he was saying all the right things, so I started to trust him." She agreed to have dinner, and afterward, at her hotel door, he convinced her to let him come in to talk. "I went through the whole thing about being old-fashioned," she says. "I was a virgin until I was twenty-one. So I told him talk was all we were going to do."

But as they sat on the couch, she found herself falling asleep. "By now, I'm comfortable with him, and I put my head on his shoulder. He's not tried anything all evening, after all." Which is when the rape came. "I woke up to find him on top of me, forcing himself on me. I didn't scream or run. All I could think about was my business contacts and what if they saw me run out of my room screaming rape.

"I thought it was my fault. I felt so filthy, I washed myself over and over in hot water. Did he rape me? I kept asking myself. I didn't consent. But who's gonna believe me? I had a man in my hotel room

[2]In 1989 a 28-year-old woman was savagely beaten and raped while jogging through New York's Central Park. The attack received national media coverage both because of its extreme brutality and because of the cavalier attitude expressed by the group of teenagers convicted of the crime.—Eds.

after midnight." More than a year later, she still can't tell the story without a visible struggle to maintain her composure. Police referred the case to the state attorney's office in Tampa, but without more evidence it decided not to prosecute. Although her attacker has admitted that he heard her say no, maintains the woman, "he says he didn't know that I meant no. He didn't feel he'd raped me, and he even wanted to see me again."

Her story is typical in many ways. The victim herself may not be sure right away that she has been raped, that she had said no and been physically forced into having sex anyway. And the rapist commonly hears but does not heed the protest. "A date rapist will follow through no matter what the woman wants because his agenda is to get laid," says Claire Walsh, a Florida-based consultant on sexual assaults. "First comes the dinner, then a dance, then a drink, then the coercion begins." Gentle persuasion gives way to physical intimidation, with alcohol as the ubiquitous lubricant. "When that fails, force is used," she says. "Real men don't take no for an answer."

The Palm Beach case serves to remind women that if they go ahead and press charges, they can expect to go on trial along with their attacker, if not in a courtroom then in the court of public opinion. The *New York Times* caused an uproar on its own staff not only for publishing the victim's name but also for laying out in detail her background, her high-school grades, her driving record, along with an unattributed quote from a school official about her "little wild streak." A freshman at Carleton College in Minnesota, who says she was repeatedly raped for four hours by a fellow student, claims that she was asked at an administrative hearing if she performed oral sex on dates. In 1989 a man charged with raping at knifepoint a woman he knew was acquitted in Florida because his victim had been wearing lace shorts and no underwear.

From a purely legal point of view, if she wants to put her attacker in jail, the survivor had better be beaten as well as raped, since bruises become a badge of credibility. She had better have reported the crime right away, before taking the hours-long shower that she craves, before burning her clothes, before curling up with the blinds down. And she would do well to be a woman of shining character. Otherwise the strict constructionist definitions of rape will prevail in court. "Juries don't have a great deal of sympathy for the victim if she's a willing participant up to the nonconsensual sexual intercourse," says Norman Kinne, a prosecutor in Dallas. "They feel that many times the victim has placed herself in the situation." Absent eyewitnesses or broken bones, a case comes down to her word against his, and the mythology of rape rarely lends her the benefit of the doubt.

20   She should also hope for an all-male jury, preferably composed of fathers with daughters. Prosecutors have found that women tend to be harsh judges of one another—perhaps because to find a defendant

guilty is to entertain two grim realities: that anyone might be a rapist, and that every woman could find herself a victim. It may be easier to believe, the experts muse, that at some level the victim asked for it. "But just because a woman makes a bad judgment, does that give the guy a moral right to rape her?" asks Dean Kilpatrick, director of the Crime Victim Research and Treatment Center at the Medical University of South Carolina. "The bottom line is, Why does a woman's having a drink give a man the right to rape her?"

Last week [on May 20, 1991] the Supreme Court waded into the debate with a 7-to-2 ruling that protects victims from being harassed on the witness stand with questions about their sexual history. The justices, in their first decision on "rape shield laws," said an accused rapist could not present evidence about a previous sexual relationship with the victim unless he notified the court ahead of time. In her decision, Justice Sandra Day O'Connor wrote that "rape victims deserve heightened protection against surprise, harassment, and unnecessary invasions of privacy."

That was welcome news to prosecutors who understand the reluctance of victims to come forward. But there are other impediments to justice as well. An internal investigation of the Oakland police department found that officers ignored a quarter of all reports of sexual assaults or attempts, though 90 percent actually warranted investigation. Departments are getting better at educating officers in handling rape cases, but the courts remain behind. A New York City task force on women in the courts charged that judges and lawyers were routinely less inclined to believe a woman's testimony than a man's.

The present debate over degrees of rape is nothing new: all through history, rapes have been divided between those that mattered and those that did not. For the first few thousand years, the only rape that was punished was the defiling of a virgin, and that was viewed as a property crime. A girl's virtue was a marketable asset, and so a rapist was often ordered to pay the victim's father the equivalent of her price on the marriage market. In early Babylonian and Hebrew societies, a married woman who was raped suffered the same fate as an adulteress—death by stoning or drowning. Under William the Conqueror, the penalty for raping a virgin was castration and loss of both eyes—unless the violated woman agreed to marry her attacker, as she was often pressured to do. "Stealing an heiress" became a perfectly conventional means of taking— literally—a wife.

It may be easier to prove a rape case now, but not much. Until the 1960s it was virtually impossible without an eyewitness; judges were often required to instruct jurors that "rape is a charge easily made and hard to defend against; so examine the testimony of this witness with caution." But sometimes a rape was taken very seriously, particularly if it involved a black man attacking a white woman—a crime for which black men were often executed or lynched.

25   Susan Estrich, author of *Real Rape,* considers herself a lucky victim. This is not just because she survived an attack seventeen years ago by a stranger with an ice pick, one day before her graduation from Wellesley. It's because police, and her friends, believed her. "The first thing the Boston police asked was whether it was a black guy," recalls Estrich, now a University of Southern California law professor. When she said yes and gave the details of the attack, their reaction was, "So, you were really raped." It was an instructive lesson, she says, in understanding how racism and sexism are factored into perceptions of the crime.

A new twist in society's perception came in 1975, when Susan Brownmiller published her book *Against Our Will: Men, Women, and Rape.* In it she attacked the concept that rape was a sex crime, arguing instead that it was a crime of violence and power over women. Throughout history, she wrote, rape has played a critical function. "It is nothing more or less than a conscious process of intimidation, by which *all men* keep *all women* in a state of fear."

Out of this contention was born a set of arguments that have become politically correct wisdom on campus and in academic circles. This view holds that rape is a symbol of women's vulnerability to male institutions and attitudes. "It's sociopolitical," insists Gina Rayfield, a New Jersey psychologist. "In our culture men hold the power, politically, economically. They're socialized not to see women as equals."

This line of reasoning has led some women, especially radicalized victims, to justify flinging around the term *rape* as a political weapon, referring to everything from violent sexual assaults to inappropriate innuendos. Ginny, a college senior who was really raped when she was sixteen, suggests that false accusations of rape can serve a useful purpose. "Penetration is not the only form of violation," she explains. In her view, rape is a subjective term, one that women must use to draw attention to other, nonviolent, even nonsexual forms of oppression. "If a woman did falsely accuse a man of rape, she may have had reasons to," Ginny says. "Maybe she wasn't raped, but he clearly violated her in some way."

Catherine Comins, assistant dean of student life at Vassar, also sees some value in this loose use of "rape." She says angry victims of various forms of sexual intimidation cry rape to regain their sense of power. "To use the word carefully would be to be careful for the sake of the violator, and the survivors don't care a hoot about him." Comins argues that men who are unjustly accused can sometimes gain from the experience. "They have a lot of pain, but it is not a pain that I would necessarily have spared them. I think it ideally initiates a process of self-exploration. 'How do I see women?' 'If I didn't violate her, could I have?' 'Do I have the potential to do to her what they say I did?' Those are good questions."

Taken to extremes, there is an ugly element of vengeance at work[30] here. Rape is an abuse of power. But so are false accusations of rape, and to suggest that men whose reputations are destroyed might benefit because it will make them more sensitive is an attitude that is sure to backfire on women who are seeking justice for all victims. On campuses where the issue is most inflamed, male students are outraged that their names can be scrawled on a bathroom-wall list of rapists and they have no chance to tell their side of the story.

"Rape is what you read about in the *New York Post* about seventeen little boys raping a jogger in Central Park," says a male freshman at a liberal-arts college, who learned that he had been branded a rapist after a one-night stand with a friend. He acknowledges that they were both very drunk when she started kissing him at a party and ended up back in his room. Even through his haze, he had some qualms about sleeping with her: "I'm fighting against my hormonal instincts, and my moral instincts are saying, 'This is my friend and if I were sober, I wouldn't be doing this.' " But he went ahead anyway. "When you're drunk, and there are all sorts of ambiguity, and the woman says 'Please, please' and then she says no sometime later, even in the middle of the act, there still may very well be some kind of violation, but it's not the same thing. It's not rape. If you don't hear her say no, if she doesn't say it, if she's playing around with you—oh, I could get squashed for saying it—there is an element of say no, mean yes."

The morning after their encounter, he recalls, both students woke up hung over and eager to put the memory behind them. Only months later did he learn that she had told a friend that he had torn her clothing and raped her. At this point in the story, the accused man starts using the language of rape. "I felt violated," he says. "I felt like she was taking advantage of me when she was very drunk. I never heard her say 'No!' 'Stop!' anything." He is angry and hurt at the charges, worried that they will get around, shatter his reputation, and force him to leave the small campus.

So here, of course, is the heart of the debate. If rape is sex without consent, how exactly should consent be defined and communicated, when and by whom? Those who view rape through a political lens tend to place all responsibility on men to make sure that their partners are consenting at every point of a sexual encounter. At the extreme, sexual relations come to resemble major surgery, requiring a signed consent form. Clinical psychologist Mary P. Koss of the University of Arizona in Tucson, who is a leading scholar on the issue, puts it rather bluntly: "It's the man's penis that is doing the raping, and ultimately he's responsible for where he puts it."

Historically, of course, this has never been the case, and there are some who argue that it shouldn't be—that women too must take responsibility for their behavior, and that the whole realm of intimate encounters defies regulation from on high. Anthropologist Lionel Tiger has little patience for trendy sexual politics that make no reference to biology. Since the dawn of time, he argues, men and women have always gone to bed with different goals. In the effort to keep one's genes in the gene pool, "it is to the male advantage to fertilize as many females as possible, as quickly as possible and as efficiently as possible." For the female, however, who looks at the large investment she will have to make in the offspring, the opposite is true. Her concern is to "select" who "will provide the best setup for their offspring." So, in general, "the pressure is on the male to be aggressive and on the female to be coy."

35   No one defends the use of physical force, but when the coercion involved is purely psychological, it becomes hard to assign blame after the fact. Journalist Stephanie Gutmann is an ardent foe of what she calls the date-rape dogmatists. "How can you make sex completely politically correct and completely safe?" she asks. "What a horribly bland, unerotic thing that would be! Sex is, by nature, a risky endeavor, emotionally. And desire is a violent emotion. These people in the date-rape movement have erected so many rules and regulations that I don't know how people can have erotic or desire-driven sex."

Nonsense, retorts Cornell professor Andrea Parrot, coauthor of *Acquaintance Rape: The Hidden Crime.* Seduction should not be about lies, manipulation, game playing, or coercion of any kind, she says. "Too bad that people think that the only way you can have passion and excitement and sex is if there are miscommunications, and one person is forced to do something he or she doesn't want to do." The very pleasures of sexual encounters should lie in the fact of mutual comfort and consent: "You can hang from the ceiling, you can use fruit, you can go crazy and have really wonderful sensual erotic sex, if both parties are consenting."

It would be easy to accuse feminists of being too quick to classify sex as rape, but feminists are to be found on all sides of the debate, and many protest the idea that all the onus is on the man. It demeans women to suggest that they are so vulnerable to coercion or emotional manipulation that they must always be escorted by the strong arm of the law. "You can't solve society's ills by making everything a crime," says Albuquerque attorney Nancy Hollander. "That comes out of the sense of overprotection of women, and in the long run that is going to be harmful to us."

What is lost in the ideological debate over date rape is the fact that men and women, especially when they are young, and drunk, and aroused, are not very good at communicating. "In many cases," says Estrich, "the man thought it was sex, and the woman thought it was rape, and they are both telling the truth." The man may envision a celluloid seduction, in which he is being commanding, she is being coy. A woman may experience the same event as a degrading violation of her will. That some men do not believe a woman's protests is scarcely surprising in a society so drenched with messages that women have rape fantasies and a desire to be overpowered.

By the time they reach college, men and women are loaded with cultural baggage, drawn from movies, television, music videos, and "bodice-ripper" romance novels. Over the years they have watched Rhett sweep Scarlett up the stairs in *Gone with the Wind;* or Errol Flynn, who was charged twice with statutory rape, overpower a protesting heroine who then melts in his arms; or Stanley rape his sister-in-law Blanche du Bois while his wife is in the hospital giving birth to a child in *A Streetcar Named Desire.* Higher up the cultural food chain, young people can read of date rape in Homer or Jane Austen, watch it in *Don Giovanni* or *Rigoletto.*

The messages come early and often, and nothing in the feminist[40] revolution has been able to counter them. A recent survey of sixth- to ninth-graders in Rhode Island found that a fourth of the boys and a sixth of the girls said it was acceptable for a man to force a woman to kiss him or have sex if he has spent money on her. A third of the children said it would not be wrong for a man to rape a woman who had had previous sexual experiences.

Certainly cases like Palm Beach, movies like *The Accused* and novels like Avery Corman's *Prized Possessions* may force young people to reexamine assumptions they have inherited. The use of new terms, like acquaintance rape and date rape, while controversial, has given men and women the vocabulary they need to express their experiences with both force and precision. This dialogue would be useful if it helps strip away some of the dogmas, old and new, surrounding the issue. Those who hope to raise society's sensitivity to the problem of date rape would do well to concede that it is not precisely the same sort of crime as street rape, that there may be very murky issues of intent and degree involved.

On the other hand, those who downplay the problem should come to realize that date rape is a crime of uniquely intimate cruelty. While the body is violated, the spirit is maimed. How long will it take, once the wounds have healed, before it is possible to share a walk on a beach, a drive home from work, or an evening's conversation without always listening for a quiet alarm to start ringing deep in the back of the memory of a terrible crime?

The Clamor on Campus

Universities have always been America's approximate monasteries, embracing codes of behavior too stringent for the outside world. Deans aim to enforce a set of rules that will guide young people from the safety of their family to the freedom of the rest of their life. Some students arrive barely knowing how to drink and sleep, much less drink and sleep together; they have little sense of what is appropriate and what is expected of them. So with a pitcher of beer in one hand and a dorm key in the other, society's children set out to discover who they are.

What many learn first is that within a cloistered courtyard, rape is an easy crime: doors are left unlocked, visitors come and go, and female students give classmates the benefit of the doubt. College officials have led the effort to raise consciousness about the problem through rape-awareness weeks, video series, pamphlets, training manuals, and posters: DATE RAPE IS VIOLENCE, NOT A DIFFERENCE OF OPINION. But when a really nasty incident occurs, the instinct too often is to handle it quietly and try to make it go away.

45   Katie Koestner was a virgin when she was allegedly raped by a student she had been dating at William and Mary College. The dean took her to the campus police, but steered her away from the outside authorities, she says. When she asked for an internal investigation, the accused man got to question her first, and then she had her turn. At 2:30 AM after seven-and-a-half hours, he was found guilty of sexual assault. Days later she learned his penalty: he was barred from entering any dorm or fraternity house other than his own for four years, but he was allowed to stay on campus. "The hearing officer told me that this is an educational institution, not a penitentiary," she recalls. "He even said, 'Maybe you guys can get back together next year.' I couldn't believe it."

The man later wrote in the campus newspaper that he had suffered the "terrible consequences of being falsely accused." He said he had been dating Koestner for three weeks; one night they slept together, without having sex, and then early the next morning, "without any protest or argument on the part of Ms. Koestner, we engaged in intercourse." He was found guilty, he said, not for physically forcing Koestner to have sex but for applying emotional pressure.

The debate grew more heated when Koestner went public with her story. Since then she has received stacks of letters and calls of support. Women raped decades ago phone and thank her for saving their daughters. Though the school defends its procedures, Vice President W. Samuel Sadler says that "Katie's coming forward has personalized the issue and led to a more intensive discussion, and frankly improved input."

That discussion goes on at colleges everywhere. "It seems like date and acquaintance rape is the rule rather than the exception on campuses today," says Frank Carrington, a consultant for Security on Campus, a nonprofit group based in Gulph Mills, Pennsylvania. "And the way the universities treat it is to cover up and protect their image while a tremendous outrage is building."

Nowhere is it building faster than at Carleton College, Minnesota's prestigious private liberal-arts school and, in 1983, one of the first in the nation to establish a sexual-harassment policy. In the language of the university's judicial code, "rape" doesn't officially exist. School administrators call it "sexual harassment" or "advances without sanction." But those phrases don't seem very useful when Julie, Amy, Kristene, and Karen try to describe what happened to them.

In October 1987, Amy had been on campus just five weeks when₅₀ she joined some friends to watch a video in the room of a senior. One by one the other students went away, leaving her alone with a student whose full name she didn't even know. "It ended up with his hands around my throat," she recalls. In a lawsuit she has filed against the college, she charges that he locked the door and raped her again and again for the next four hours. "I didn't want him to kill me. I just kept trying not to cry." Only afterward did he tell her, almost defiantly, his name. It was near the top of the "castration list" posted on women's bathroom walls around campus to warn other students about college rapists.

Amy went to the dean of students, whom she had been told she could trust. "He told me it was my word against my attacker's, and that if I went for a criminal prosecution, the victim was basically put on trial." So instead she picked the gentler alternative—an internal review, at which she ended up being grilled about her sexual habits and experiences. Her attacker was found guilty of sexual assault but was only suspended, because of a dean's assurance that he had no "priors" other than "advances without sanction."

Julie started dating a fellow cast member in a Carleton play. They had never slept together, she charges in a civil suit, until he came to her dorm room one night, uninvited, and raped her. Weeks later, she says, he ripped her dress at a play rehearsal and grabbed her exposed breast. Still she told no one. "If I had been raped by a stranger, I would have told someone. But to be raped by a friend—I began to wonder, Whom do you trust?" She struggled to hold her life and education together, but finally could manage no longer and left school. Only later did Julie learn that her assailant was the same man who had attacked Amy.

Two other students, Kristene and Karen, claim to have suffered similar experiences at the hands of another student; all four of the Carleton women have filed suit against the college. They claim the school knew these men had a history of sexual abuse and did nothing to prevent their attacking again. Even after the men were found guilty of sexual harassment, they were allowed to remain on campus, and the victims were barred from warning their dorm mates under the college's privacy policy. The local police chief says that in the past six years, no Carleton official has brought an assault victim to the department.

Carleton President Stephen Lewis Jr. explains that he is acutely aware of the problem of rape on campus, which is why the sexual-harassment policy was created in the first place. He believes the four students objected not so much to the procedures as to the outcome. All were advised of the option of going to the police. "These women chose to go to the university hearing board but didn't like the result, and now they're suing," says Lewis, who arrived on campus in the fall of 1987, after two of the alleged rapes took place. "We understand they're upset, but that doesn't mean they're right. I accept fully that Amy and Kristene believe they were raped, but the hearing boards concluded that they hadn't been." If the men, who were found guilty of lesser charges, had committed forced sexual intercourse, he says, they would have been expelled. "It's like a court of law. When the accused is acquitted, you can't then sue the jury."

55   This month [June 1991] Representative Jim Ramstad of Minnesota filed a bill in Congress—the "campus sexual-assault victims' bill of rights"—that guarantees students the right to have assaults investigated by police and to live in housing "free from sexual or physical intimidation." Under a law already passed, beginning in 1992 colleges will be required to make campus crime statistics public. That will give parents and prospective students a chance to make informed decisions about the risks they are willing to take with their safety. More important, the law may encourage colleges to be more vigilant about crime in their midst and more protective of young people in their care.

Additional Rhetorical Strategies

Comparison and Contrast (paragraph 7); Example (paragraphs 14–16, 50–54); Process Analysis (paragraph 17); Cause and Effect (paragraph 20); Argument (throughout).

Discussion Questions

1. Why, according to Gibbs, is it important to define the word *rape* carefully? Why does she say that the differences between "acquaintance rape" and "date rape" are "not idle distinctions" (paragraph 4)? What is at stake? Why does she draw attention to the judicial code at Carleton College (paragraphs 49 and following)? How will the definitions of rape affect the law she describes in her final paragraph, requiring colleges to make campus crime statistics public?

2. Beginning with paragraph 9, Gibbs outlines several different views of rape, from one extreme to the other. Can you tell where Gibbs herself might fall on this continuum? Where does the supporting evidence for your answer come from: the section in which she outlines the different views, or elsewhere in the essay? Do you think she gives each of the perspectives a fair hearing in paragraphs 9–12? Look closely at the language Gibbs uses, in these paragraphs

and elsewhere in the essay, to help you determine Gibbs' own stance.

3. Gibbs reports that at least one faction believes that "to stretch the definition of the word risks stripping away its power." Look through the essay and find examples of ways in which the word's definition might be said to have been stretched. Is it always the same faction who is stretching it? What, for instance, do you make of the accused man in paragraph 32 who "starts using the language of rape" to describe the violation he feels at being accused? Can you think of instances or reasons that might justify a stretching of the word beyond cases of stranger rape?

4. What is Gibbs' attitude toward politicizing the issue of rape? How would you read her tone when she speaks of "politically correct wisdom on campus" (paragraph 27)? What other alternatives does she posit for a political perspective? In what ways might her own view be seen as political? What is the function of the paragraphs on the role of race in the perception and prosecution of rape (paragraphs 24–25), for instance? And how would you characterize the cultural critique of movies, television, and so on, that she performs in paragraphs 39 and following?

5. Characterize the point of view of anthropologist Lionel Tiger (paragraph 34). What factors in contemporary American life might mitigate against his model of biological determinism?

Essay Questions

1. Gibbs reports that "On campuses where the issue is most inflamed, male students are outraged that their names can be scrawled on a bathroom-wall list of rapists and they have no chance to tell their side of the story." Write an essay proposing a fair and rational policy for such lists at your own college or university, and justify your decision to outlaw or legalize these lists.

2. Gibbs refers to Susan Brownmiller's theory that rape is a crime of violence and power, rather than a sex crime (paragraph 26). Write an essay in which you argue for or against Brownmiller's stance. What do you see as the primary motivation, reason, and meaning behind rape? What would be the consequences of your stance if you were asked to design a strategy for combating rape in your neighborhood, campus, or town?

Thematic Pair: Language and Prejudice

▲▼A Question of Language

Gloria Naylor

Gloria Naylor (b. 1950) explains, "I wanted to become a writer because I felt that my presence as a black woman and my perspective as a woman in general had been underrepresented in American literature." Her first novel, The Women of Brewster Place *(1982), won an American Book Award. Since that time, she has published three more novels,* Linden Hills *(1985),* Mama Day *(1988), and* Bailey's Cafe *(1992), in addition to numerous nonfiction essays. In all of her work, Naylor draws not only on her own experiences but on the Western literary tradition, broadly defined to include not only Shakespeare and Dante but also African American folklore.*

Naylor has criticized both the black and the white literary establishment for assuming "that a black writer's work should be 'definitive' of black experience. This type of critical stance denies the vast complexity of black existence, even if we were to limit that experience solely to America." In the essay that follows, which was first published in the New York Times *in 1986, Naylor explores a small but significant part of that vast complexity.*

Language is the subject. It is the written form with which I've managed to keep the wolf away from the door and, in diaries, to keep my sanity. In spite of this, I consider the written word inferior to the spoken, and much of the frustration experienced by novelists is the awareness that whatever we manage to capture in even the most transcendent passages falls far short of the richness of life. Dialogue achieves its power in the dynamics of a fleeting moment of sight, sound, smell, and touch.

I'm not going to enter the debate here about whether it is language that shapes reality or vice versa. That battle is doomed to be waged whenever we seek intermittent reprieve from the chicken and egg dispute. I will simply take the position that the spoken word, like the written word, amounts to a nonsensical arrangement of sounds or letters without a consensus that assigns "meaning." And building from the meanings of what we hear, we order reality. Words themselves are innocuous; it is the consensus that gives them true power.

I remember the first time I heard the word *nigger.* In my third-grade class, our math tests were being passed down the rows, and as I handed the papers to a little boy in back of me, I remarked that once again he had received a much lower mark than I did. He snatched his test from me and spit out that word. Had he called me a nymphomaniac or a necrophiliac, I couldn't have been more puzzled. I didn't know what a nigger was, but I knew that whatever it meant, it was something he shouldn't have called me. This was verified when I raised my hand, and in a loud voice repeated what he had said and watched the teacher scold him for using a "bad" word. I was later to go home and ask the inevitable question that every black parent must face— "Mommy, what does 'nigger' mean?"

And what exactly did it mean? Thinking back, I realize that this could not have been the first time the word was used in my presence. I was part of a large extended family that had migrated from the rural South after World War II and formed a close-knit network that gravitated around my maternal grandparents. Their ground-floor apartment in one of the buildings they owned in Harlem was a weekend mecca for my immediate family, along with countless aunts, uncles, and cousins who brought along assorted friends. It was a bustling and open house with assorted neighbors and tenants popping in and out to exchange bits of gossip, pick up an old quarrel or referee the ongoing checkers game in which my grandmother cheated shamelessly. They were all there to let down their hair and put up their feet after a week of labor in the factories, laundries, and shipyards of New York.

5   Amid the clamor, which could reach deafening proportions—two or three conversations going on simultaneously, punctuated by the sound of a baby's crying somewhere in the back rooms or out on the street—there was still a rigid set of rules about what was said and how. Older children were sent out of the living room when it was time to get into the juicy details about "you-know-who" up on the third floor who had gone and gotten herself "p-r-e-g-n-a-n-t!" But my parents, knowing that I could spell well beyond my years, always demanded that I follow the others out to play. Beyond sexual misconduct and death, everything else was considered harmless for our young ears. And so among the anecdotes of the triumphs and disappointments in the various workings of their lives, the word *nigger* was used in my presence, but it was set within contexts and inflections that caused it to register in my mind as something else.

In the singular, the word was always applied to a man who had distinguished himself in some situation that brought their approval for his strength, intelligence, or drive:

"Did Johnny really do that?"

"I'm telling you, that nigger pulled in $6,000 of overtime last year. Said he got enough for a down payment on a house."

When used with a possessive adjective by a woman—"my nigger"—it became a term of endearment for husband or boyfriend. But it could be more than just a term applied to a man. In their mouths it became the pure essence of manhood—a disembodied force that channeled their past history of struggle and present survival against the odds into a victorious statement of being: "Yeah, that old foreman found out quick enough—you don't mess with a nigger."

In the plural, it became a description of some group within the[10] community that had overstepped the bounds of decency as my family defined it: Parents who neglected their children, a drunken couple who fought in public, people who simply refused to look for work, those with excessively dirty mouths or unkempt households were all "trifling niggers." This particular circle could forgive hard times, unemployment, the occasional bout of depression—they had gone through all of that themselves—but the unforgivable sin was lack of self-respect.

A woman could never be a *nigger* in the singular, with its connotation of confirming worth. The noun *girl* was its closest equivalent in that sense, but only when used in direct address and regardless of the gender doing the addressing. *Girl* was a token of respect for a woman. The one syllable word was drawn out to sound like three in recognition of the extra ounce of wit, nerve or daring that the woman had shown in the situation under discussion.

"G-i-r-l, stop. You mean you said that to his face?"

But if the word was used in a third-person reference or shortened so that it almost snapped out of the mouth, it always involved some element of communal disapproval. And age became an important factor in these exchanges. It was only between individuals of the same generation, or from an older person to a younger (but never the other way around), that "girl" would be considered a compliment.

I don't agree with the argument that use of the word *nigger* at this social stratum of the black community was an internalization of racism. The dynamics were the exact opposite: the people in my grandmother's living room took a word that whites used to signify worthlessness or degradation and rendered it impotent. Gathering there together, they transformed *nigger* to signify the varied and complex human beings they knew themselves to be. If the word was to disappear totally from the mouths of even the most liberal of white society, none in that room was naïve enough to believe it would disappear from white minds. Meeting the word head-on, they proved it had absolutely nothing to do with the way they were determined to live their lives.

So there must have been dozens of times that the word *nigger* was[15] spoken in front of me before I reached the third grade. But I didn't "hear" it until it was said by a small pair of lips that had already learned it could be a way to humiliate me. That was the word I went home and asked my mother about. And since she knew that I had to grow up in America, she took me in her lap and explained.

Additional Rhetorical Strategies

Comparison and Contrast (paragraph 1); Narration (paragraph 3); Cause and Effect (paragraph 14); Example (throughout).

Discussion Questions

1. What is the connection between the first two paragraphs and the rest of the essay? What are the abstract points about language that Naylor makes in her opening paragraphs, and how are they borne out in the more concrete examples that follow?
2. What is Naylor's purpose in defining the word *nigger?* Are these the definitions you were previously aware of? If you had never used the word in these ways, what did you learn? If you had used the word in these ways, was there anything that Naylor's dissection of the word added to your understanding?
3. What can you infer about the values of a community by its use of language? What specifically do you learn about this group of African Americans living in Harlem after having migrated from the South after World War II, just from learning the four different definitions of one word, as they used it? What other clues could you pick up about this culture and its values from the paragraphs preceding the definitions themselves (paragraphs 4–5)?
4. How would you characterize Naylor's style in this essay? How is it like and unlike the styles of the people she quotes throughout? How does she convey the fact that the language used by her family had a "rigid set of rules" (paragraph 5)? How does she show that she herself is sensitive to different "contexts and inflections" (paragraph 5)?

Essay Questions

1. Naylor closes the essay just before her mother explains racism to young Gloria. What is the effect of this ending? What does it suggest about the relative importance of the little white boy's definition and the definitions of Naylor's family? Extrapolate from the rest of the essay the explanation Naylor's mother is about to give, or at least the explanation the adult Naylor herself would probably give to a young child who had just been called "nigger" for the first time by a white classmate, and write a new, expanded conclusion for Naylor's essay.
2. Compare and contrast spoken and written language. What are the relative advantages and disadvantages of each? What can the purveyors of written language learn from the masters of spoken language that can enrich their writing? Use the language Naylor uses in this essay as an example.

▲▼Sexism in Language

Alleen Pace Nilsen

Alleen Pace Nilsen (b. 1936) is on the faculty at Arizona State University at Tempe, where she specializes in sexist language and literature for young adults. She has written several books, including Language Play: An Introduction to Linguistics *(1983) and* Changing Words in a Changing World *(1980). She is co-editor (with her husband, Don Nilsen) and contributor to* The Language of Humor/The Humor of Language *(1983). The essay reprinted below was first published in* Sexism and Language *(1977), published by the National Council of Teachers of English.*

Alleen Pace Nilsen tells of an argument she had while living in Afghanistan with her husband over the relative importance of their respective work: "This was the moment that I became a feminist. I decided that I too would do something more important than housework. But when we returned 'home' to the University of Michigan campus in Ann Arbor, the feminists frightened me with their militancy and their anger against men. I wasn't that angry, so I decided to stay home and read the dictionary. I thought I could study how the English language reflected different cultural attitudes toward men and women and still not get involved in controversial social issues. I was mistaken. Language and culture are so closely related that it was impossible to really understand one without also giving a great deal of thought to the other."

Over the last hundred years, American anthropologists have travelled to the corners of the earth to study primitive cultures. They either became linguists themselves or they took linguists with them to help in learning and analyzing languages. Even if the culture was one that no longer existed, they were interested in learning its language because besides being tools of communication, the vocabulary and structure of a language tell much about the values held by its speakers.

However, the culture need not be primitive, nor do the people making observations need to be anthropologists and linguists. Anyone living in the United States who listens with a keen ear or reads with a perceptive eye can come up with startling new insights about the way American English reflects our values.

Animal Terms for People—Mirrors of the Double Standard

If we look at just one semantic area of English, that of animal terms in relation to people, we can uncover some interesting insights into how our culture views males and females. References to identical animals can have negative connotations when related to a female, but positive or neutral connotations when related to a male. For example, a *shrew* has come to mean "a scolding, nagging, evil-tempered woman," while *shrewd* means "keen-witted, clever, or sharp in practical affairs; astute . . . businessman, etc." (*Webster's New World Dictionary of the American Language*, 1964).

A *lucky dog* or a *gay dog* may be a very interesting fellow, but when a woman is a *dog*, she is unattractive, and when she's a *bitch* she's the personification of whatever is undesirable in the mind of the speaker. When a man is self-confident, he may be described as *cocksure* or even *cocky*, but in a woman this same self-confidence is likely to result in her being called a *cocky bitch*, which is not only a mixed metaphor, but also probably the most insulting animal metaphor we have. *Bitch* has taken on such negative connotations—children are taught it is a swear word—that in everyday American English, speakers are hesitant to call a female dog a *bitch*. Most of us feel that we would be insulting the dog. When we want to insult a man by comparing him to a dog, we call him a *son of a bitch*, which quite literally is an insult to his mother rather than to him.

5   If the female is called a *vixen* (a female fox), the dictionary says this means she is "an ill-tempered, shrewish, or malicious woman." The female seems both to attract and to hold on longer to animal metaphors with negative connotations. A *vampire* was originally a corpse that came alive to suck the blood of living persons. The word acquired the general meaning of an unscrupulous person such as a blackmailer and then, the specialized meaning of "a beautiful but unscrupulous woman who seduces men and leads them to their ruin." From this latter meaning we get the word *vamp*. The popularity of this term and of the name *vampire bat* may contribute to the idea that a female being is referred to in a phrase such as *the old bat*.

Other animal metaphors do not have definitely derogatory connotations for the female, but they do seem to indicate frivolity or unimportance, as in *social butterfly* and *flapper*. Look at the differences between the connotation of participating in a *hen party* and in a *bull session*. Male metaphors, even when they are negative in connotation, still relate to strength and conquest. Metaphors related to aggressive sex roles, for example, *buck, stag, wolf*, and *stud*, will undoubtedly remain attached to males. Perhaps one of the reasons that in the late sixties it was so shocking to hear policemen called *pigs* was that the connotations of *pig* are very different from the other animal metaphors we usually apply to males.

When I was living in Afghanistan, I was surprised at the cruelty and unfairness of a proverb that said, "When you see an old man, sit down and take a lesson; when you see an old woman, throw a stone." In looking at Afghan folk literature, I found that young girls were pictured as delightful and enticing, middle-aged women were sometimes interesting but more often just tolerable, while old women were always grotesque and villainous. Probably the reason for the negative connotation of old age in women is that women are valued for their bodies while men are valued for their accomplishments and their wisdom. Bodies deteriorate with age but wisdom and accomplishments grow greater.

When we returned home from Afghanistan, I was shocked to discover that we have remnants of this same attitude in America. We see it in our animal metaphors. If both the animal and the woman are young, the connotation is positive, but if the animal and the woman are old, the connotation is negative. Hugh Hefner might never have made it to the big time if he had called his girls *rabbits* instead of *bunnies.* He probably chose *bunny* because he wanted something close to, but not quite so obvious as *kitten* or *cat*—the all-time winners for connoting female sexuality. Also *bunny,* as in the skiers' *snow bunny,* already had some of the connotations Hefner wanted. Compare the connotations of *filly* to *old nag; bird* to *old crow* or *old bat;* and *lamb* to *crone* (apparently related to the early modern Dutch *kronje, old ewe* but now *withered old woman*).

Probably the most striking examples of the contrast between young and old women are animal metaphors relating to cats and chickens. A young girl is encouraged to be *kittenish,* but not *catty.* And though most of us wouldn't mind living next door to a *sex kitten,* we wouldn't want to live next door to a *cat house.* Parents might name their daughter *Kitty* but not *Puss* or *Pussy,* which used to be a fairly common nickname for girls. It has now developed such sexual connotations that it is used mostly for humor, as in the James Bond movie featuring Pussy Galore and her flying felines.

In the chicken metaphors, a young girl is a *chick.* When she gets old[10] enough she marries and soon begins feeling *cooped up.* To relieve the boredom she goes to *hen parties* and *cackles* with her friends. Eventually she has her *brood,* begins to *henpeck* her husband, and finally turns into an *old biddy.*

How English Glorifies Maleness

Throughout the ages physical strength has been very important, and because men are physically stronger than women, they have been valued more. Only now in the machine age, when the difference in strength between males and females pales into insignificance in comparison to the strength of earth-moving machinery, airplanes, and guns, males no longer have such an inherent advantage. Today a man of intellect is more valued than a physical laborer, and since women can compete intellectually with men, their value is on the rise. But language lags far behind cultural changes, so the language still reflects this emphasis on the importance of being male. For example, when we want to compliment a male, all we need to do is stress the fact that he is male by saying he is a *he-man*, or he is *manly*, or he is *virile*. Both *virile* and *virtuous* come from Latin *vir*, meaning *man*.

The command or encouragement that males receive in sentences like "Be a man!" implies that *to be a man* is to be honorable, strong, righteous, and whatever else the speaker thinks desirable. But in contrast to this, a girl is never told to be a *woman*. And when she is told to be a *lady*, she is simply being encouraged to "act feminine," which means sitting with her knees together, walking gracefully, and talking softly.

The armed forces, particularly the Marines, use the positive masculine connotation as part of their recruitment psychology. They promote the idea that to join the Marines (or the Army, Navy, or Air Force) guarantees that you will become a man. But this brings up a problem, because much of the work that is necessary to keep a large organization running is what is traditionally thought of as *women's work*. Now, how can the Marines ask someone who has signed up for a *man-sized job* to do *women's work?* Since they can't, they euphemize and give the jobs titles that either are more prestigious or, at least, don't make people think of females. Waitresses are called *orderlies*, secretaries are called *clerk-typists*, nurses are called *medics*, assistants are called *adjutants*, and cleaning up an area is called *policing* the area. The same kind of word glorification is used in civilian life to bolster a man's ego when he is doing such tasks as cooking and sewing. For example, a *chef* has higher prestige than a *cook* and a *tailor* has higher prestige than a *seamstress*.

Little girls learn early in life that the boy's role is one to be envied and emulated. Child psychologists have pointed out that experimenting with the role of the opposite sex is much more acceptable for little girls than it is for little boys. For example, girls are free to dress in boys' clothes, but certainly not the other way around. Most parents are amused if they have a daughter who is a *tomboy*, but they are genuinely distressed if they have a son who is a *sissy*. The names we give to young children reflect this same attitude. It is all right for girls to have boys' names, but pity the boy who has a girl's name! Because parents keep giving boys' names to girls, the number of acceptable boys' names keeps shrinking. Currently popular names for girls include *Jo, Kelly, Teri, Chris, Pat, Shawn, Toni,* and *Sam* (short for *Samantha*). *Evelyn, Carroll, Gayle, Hazel, Lynn, Beverley, Marion, Francis,* and *Shirley* once were acceptable names for males. But as they were given to females, they became less and less acceptable. Today, men who are stuck with them selfconsciously go by their initials or by abbreviated forms such as *Haze, Shirl, Frank,* or *Ev*. And they seldom pass these names on to their sons.

15   Many common words have come into the language from people's names. These lexical items again show the importance of maleness compared to the triviality of the feminine activities being described. Words derived from the names of women include *Melba toast*, named for the Australian singer Dame Nellie Melba; *Sally Lunn cakes*, named after an

eighteenth-century woman who first made them; *pompadour,* a hair style named after Madame Pompadour; and the word *maudlin,* as in *maudlin sentiment,* from Mary Magdalene, who was often portrayed by artists as displaying exaggerated sorrow.

There are trivial items named after men—*teddy bear* after Theodore Roosevelt and *sideburns* after General Burnside—but most words that come from men's names relate to significant inventions or developments. These include *pasteurization* after Louis Pasteur, *sousaphone* after John Philip Sousa, *mason jar* after John L. Mason, *boysenberry* after Rudolph Boysen, *pullman car* after George M. Pullman, *braille* after Louis Braille, *franklin stove* after Benjamin Franklin, *diesel engine* after Rudolf Diesel, *ferris wheel* after George W. G. Ferris, and the verb *to lynch* after William Lynch, who was a vigilante captain in Virginia in 1780.

The latter is an example of a whole set of English words dealing with violence. These words have strongly negative connotations. From research using free association and semantic differentials, with university students as subjects, James Ney concluded that English reflects both an anti-male and an anti-female bias because these biases exist in the culture (*Etc.: A Review of General Semantics,* March 1976, pp. 67–76). The students consistently marked as masculine such words as *killer, murderer, robber, attacker, fighter, stabber, rapist, assassin, gang, hood, arsonist, criminal, hijacker, villain,* and *bully,* even though most of these words contain nothing to specify that they are masculine. An example of bias against males, Ney observed, is the absence in English of a pejorative term for women equivalent to *rapist.* Outcomes of his free association test indicated that if "English speakers want to call a man something bad, there seems to be a large vocabulary available to them but if they want to use a term which is good to describe a male, there is a small vocabulary available. The reverse is true for women."

Certainly we do not always think positively about males; witness such words as *jerk, creep, crumb, slob, fink,* and *jackass.* But much of what determines our positive and negative feelings relates to the roles people play. We have very negative feelings toward someone who is hurting us or threatening us or in some way making our lives miserable. To be able to do this, the person has to have power over us and this power usually belongs to males.

On the other hand, when someone helps us or makes our life more pleasant, we have positive feelings toward that person or that role. *Mother* is one of the positive female terms in English, and we see such extensions of it as *Mother Nature, Mother Earth, mother lode, mother superior,* etc. But even though a word like *mother* is positive it is still not a word of power. In the minds of English speakers being female and being powerless or passive are so closely related that we use the terms *feminine* and *lady* either to mean female or to describe a certain kind of quiet and unobtrusive behavior.

Words Labeling Women as Things

20Because of our expectations of passivity, we like to compare females to items that people acquire for their pleasure. For example, in a recent commercial for the television show "Happy Days," one of the characters announced that in the coming season they were going to have not only "cars, motorcycles, and girls," but also a band. Another example of this kind of thinking is the comparison of females to food since food is something we all enjoy, even though it is extremely passive. We describe females as such delectable morsels as a *dish,* a *cookie,* a *tart, cheesecake, sugar and spice,* a *cute tomato, honey,* a *sharp cookie,* and *sweetie pie.* We say a particular girl has a *peaches and cream complexion* or "she looks good enough to eat." And parents give their daughters such names as *Candy* and *Cherry.*

Other pleasurable items that we compare females to are toys. Young girls are called *little dolls* or *China dolls,* while older girls—if they are attractive—are simply called *dolls.* We might say about a woman, "She's pretty as a picture," or "She's a fashion plate." And we might compare a girl to a plant by saying she is a *clinging vine,* a *shrinking violet,* or a *wallflower.* And we might name our daughters after plants such as *Rose, Lily, Ivy, Daisy, Iris,* and *Petunia.* Compare these names to boys' names such as *Martin* which means warlike, *Ernest* which means resolute fighter, *Nicholas* which means victory, *Val* which means strong or valiant, and *Leo* which means lion. We would be very hesitant to give a boy the name of something as passive as a flower although we might say about a man that he is a *late-bloomer.* This is making a comparison between a man and the most active thing a plant can do, which is to bloom. The only other familiar plant metaphor used for a man is the insulting *pansy,* implying that he is like a woman.

Additional Rhetorical Strategies

Cause and Effect (paragraphs 11, 14, 18–19); Argument (throughout); Comparison and Contrast (throughout); Example (throughout).

Discussion Questions

1. Pace Nilsen writes that "American English reflects our values" (paragraph 2). What strategies does she use to convince the reader of the truth of this statement, and the seriousness of its implications? Which of her examples and arguments do you find most compelling? Which seem questionable to you? Articulate your challenges to the latter, and provide supporting examples of your own.
2. This essay was first published in 1977, so some of the examples it contains might seem dated to contemporary readers. Make a list of

newer nouns and adjectives currently used to describe people of either gender. Do the built-in biases Pace Nilsen notices hold true for your generation?

3. In her opening paragraphs Pace Nilsen refers to the work of anthropologists and linguists, and then points out that one need not be an expert studying so-called primitive people in order to make fruitful observations of language and its implications. What is the effect of these two paragraphs? How would the essay be different if one were to omit one or the other of them?

4. What are the main categories of sexist language Pace Nilsen examines? In what ways are they analogous? How does each successive one add to the strength of her argument? How might you explain the strategy that caused her to choose these three categories and explore them in this particular order?

5. In paragraph 17, Pace Nilsen cites a study by James Ney. What were the results of this study? How do they support Pace Nilsen's overall argument? In what ways does the Ney study contradict Pace Nilsen's thesis? What might have been her reason for including this study?

Essay Questions

1. Choose a linguistic artifact—any spoken or written text—from your own time, and examine it for its assumptions about gender. You might choose to examine the words spoken by the characters on your favorite television program, the words of a popular song, the text of your school's affirmative action statement, a leaflet from your school's health center . . . the possibilities are limitless. Write an essay critiquing the subtle implications about gender you find in the text you have chosen.

2. Nilsen notes an Afghanistani proverb that advises "When you see an old man, sit down and take a lesson; when you see an old woman, throw a stone" (paragraph 6). Make a list of proverbs from your own culture of origin, and then examine the implications. You need not concentrate on proverbs that address gender issues. How do proverbs work to transmit a culture's values? What do the proverbs that you have listed tell you about the culture's values?

Exploring Connections: Questions Linking the Thematic Pair

1. Alleen Pace Nilsen writes that language "reflects [an] emphasis on the importance of being male" (paragraph 11). Gloria Naylor does not specifically say that the examples of speech she examines in her essay favor one gender over the other, although she does point out differences between the words applied to black men and the words

applied to black women. Reread Naylor's essay with the issue of gender in mind: do you see a significant discrepancy? What are the ways that a woman's strength could be signaled for a woman of Naylor's time and race? What are the words that can express the strength or power of a woman of your generation and ethnic and geographic origins?

2. Both Naylor and Nilsen find that power inheres in language, though Naylor is careful to point out that "Words themselves are innocuous; it is the consensus that gives the true power" (paragraph 2). Write an essay that defines and illustrates this principle.

Classification

As a method of thinking in writing, classification helps us sort out information about a subject into logically related categories. Its uses in writing range from the simple division of a general subject for the sake of clarity and convenience (for example, contact versus noncontact sports) to the complex build-up or unraveling of complete systems of knowledge (as in zoology). Classification offers writers both procedures for identifying fully all the parts of a subject as well as structures for organizing our thoughts about that subject.

Classification is often closely connected with definition in our thinking and writing. Definition establishes, in a brief or intensive way, exactly what a particular term does and does not mean. Classification presupposes that writers and readers agree on a term's general meaning and are more interested in identifying and understanding completely the various specific parts that make up the whole term. Classification therefore operates in a much broader field than that of definition. Writers working with classification begin with a subject, analyze it carefully, divide it into categories, and then classify each of its components into one of these categories according to some specifically shared quality.

The principles of classification can be used to enrich our understanding of even the most familiar subjects. Consider for a moment the ways lips can meet:

> If one wants to classify the kiss, then one must consider several principles of classification. One may classify kissing with respect to sound. Here the language is not sufficiently elastic to record all my observations. I do not believe that all the languages in the world have an adequate supply of onomatopoeia to denote the different sounds I have heard at my uncle's house. Sometimes it was smacking, sometimes hissing, sometimes crackling, sometimes explosive, sometimes squeaky, and so on forever. One may also classify kissing with regard to contact, as in the close kiss, or the passing kiss, and the clinging kiss. One may classify them with reference to the time element, as the brief and the prolonged. With reference to time, there is still another classification, and this is the only one I really care about. There is an enormous difference between the first kiss and all the others. The first kiss is incommensurable with everything which is included in the other classifications; it is indifferent to sound, touch, time in general. The first kiss is, however, qualitatively different from all others. There

are only a few people who consider this; it would really be a pity if there was but one who had thought about it.

This passage, drawn from *Either/Or* (1843), the first major work by the Danish philosopher Søren Kierkegaard, is part of a thorough analysis of the conflict between aesthetics (the sense of the beautiful) and ethics (the principles of right conduct). Kierkegaard demonstrates in the passage just how handy classification can be when writers are looking for an easy way into their subjects and trying to chart out a clear course for developing their thinking and writing. In effect, this passage reveals that the very process of classifying can give both shape and substance to our sentences. So too, as we can readily see here, classification works especially well when writers want to focus on refining related terms or ideas. By using classification simply and directly (signaled here by the repetition of "One may classify"), Kierkegaard also makes it easy for his audience to follow his train of thought. And along the way, the word choices he makes to classify the kiss reveal how onomatopoetic such distinctions can be. It is, in fact, the process of carefully thinking through the classification of the kiss that leads to his stating so ardent a conclusion: "There is an enormous difference between the first kiss and all the others."

When to Use Classification

We most often use classification when we deal with a subject that is extensive or complicated, or both. Scientists, for example, rely on classification to create order out of the enormous amount of information generated by their observations and analyses. Given the intricacy of their subjects and the need to be exact in their thinking, scientists could hardly function without classification. On another level, it is standard procedure for government officials to classify, say, the documents they produce, the armed forces they employ, and the citizens they tax. Corporate executives also depend on classification: of sales, profits, personnel, stockholders, and inventories. In a similar manner, university administrators regularly classify students each semester by, among other factors, grades, credits carried, credits earned, and financial status.

Perhaps more so than we realize, classification is also a feature of our own daily academic and personal routines. Consider what it would be like to find the one book needed to finish a research paper if the library had not organized its holdings according to some readily understood principle of classification. Or take an activity as commonplace as shopping in a supermarket. Think of the mass confusion that would result on a crowded Saturday afternoon if the store manager hadn't grouped similar products and put signs up over each aisle, classifying its contents. We group together the courses we have enjoyed, the teachers we have admired. We also classify the foods we have eaten, the restaurants we have been to, and so on. (For an example of the classification of such an everyday activity as reading, see Donald Hall's essay on p. 258.) In all these instances, classification helps us analyze and control our experience and, thereby, serves as an invaluable aid to memory and a means of clarification. But ordinarily, we do not normally carry classification through to the minute, exhaustive stages expected of scientists and other professionals. Nonetheless, the fundamental operations of classification are governed by the same principles in all forms of thinking and writing.

How to Use Classification

The normal procedure to follow in classification begins when we analyze a subject carefully in order to divide it into all of its parts. This initial activity, called either *analysis* or *division*, arranges the subject into clear-cut and manageable categories. Once these parts have been identified, we then should group—classify—each of the individual aspects of the subject into clusters around a shared quality. If, for example, the subject were modern transportation, a topic far too cumbersome to begin writing about immediately, you could make the subject easier to handle by breaking it down into its parts: land vehicles, sea vehicles, and aircraft. The goal of this analysis or division would be to identify all the subject's components. You would then classify—that is, group together—sleds, bicycles, motorcycles, automobiles, buses, trains, and monorails in the first category; various sail and power boats in the second; and airplanes, helicopters, gliders, dirigibles, and any other machine capable of flight in the third. Depending on your interests, each individual element in a subdivision could, in turn, be defined and classified further. Automobiles could be broken down into additional subclasses according to manufacturer, size, price, gas mileage, repair estimates, and the like. Your purpose would determine the nature and extent of the classification.

Effective classification depends on several related principles. In the initial stage, when we analyze the subject in order to divide it into subclasses, we should take care that these divisions are distinct enough to prevent any overlap. If, for example, you were asked to clarify automobiles based on their size, you might reasonably and accurately establish such subclasses as—to use the curious language of automotive advertising—subcompact, compact, intermediate, and full-sized. But it would be inaccurate to create such categories as front-wheel drive or antilocking brake systems (ABS). These last two subdivisions are neither consistent with the prevailing factor of size nor mutually exclusive; that is, front-wheel drive and ABS could well be a feature of a car of any size, and many models are now promoted as having both front-wheel drive and ABS. Had you introduced such categories, you would have mistakenly shifted the basis for classification during the course of your thinking. At each level of classification, only one principle should be applied, and consistently, to all the elements being considered—in this case, size.

The automobile example also touches another essential point about using classification in thinking and writing. Since we have established that all subdivisions should be mutually exclusive, we might expect that significant differences would distinguish one category from another. But, in the case presented in the preceding paragraphs, it would be fair to question the distinction in size between a subcompact and a compact car. You would need to determine whether these categories are sufficiently different or are simply examples of advertisers' lapsing into the fallacy of classification known as *hairsplitting*. To prevent this in our own thinking and writing, we should base our subdivisions on a clearly articulated principle of classification.

Partition/Binary Classification

In its simplest form, called *partition* or *binary*, classification divides a subject in two: one positive category, one negative. The assumption here is that *non-* can be prefixed to any term in the second category, as in *athletic–nonathletic*. This form of classification also requires that all subsequent classes be split in two. For example, the athletic director of a college may want to identify likely candidates for a newly formed varsity volleyball team. The first step would be to classify the student body into athletes and nonathletes. Next, those athletes who have played the sport would be isolated from those who have not. This procedure would establish a suitable group of candidates for the team. Partition or binary classification is most appropriate for narrow, very limited purposes. It is most often simply a matter of convenience. It is obviously inexact; it tells us, for example, nothing more about the college's students than whether or not they have played volleyball. In this, as in all other instances when we classify, the thoroughness of the classification should be consistent with our purpose and with the complexity of the subject.

Classification as Structure

Classification also creates larger, far more intricate structures for thinking and writing. The chemist's periodic table of elements is, for example, the result of an elaborate, painstakingly precise system of classification. It is, in fact, a model of one of the great classificatory systems of modern thought. Each discipline has something analogous to it: an outline of essential components. That classification approximates the goal and work of an outline may be its chief value to us when we are thinking in writing. It can help organize our thoughts and conveniently group related words and ideas before we actually set out to write. Once we've begun writing, classification can help structure our thinking at the level of both the paragraph and the whole essay. As soon as we've identified the components in the classification, we can take each up fully, one at a time, with say, a paragraph devoted to each. This may take the form of naming the subclass to be considered at the beginning of the paragraph and proceeding to describe each of its members in detail and to say something important about it. Progressing from one distinct subclass to the next helps readers to understand the subjects being discussed and to follow the points being made about it. Classification also minimizes the risk of oversimplifying the subject and reducing it to little more than a stereotype. Because we are used to following through completely on our thinking, we are more alert to the potential complexity and divisions of a subject. But most important, with classification the general statements we make about a subject will be more solidly grounded in specific evidence and therefore more convincing.

Through classification, the most prominent aspects of a subject come more sharply into focus, and our dominant ideas about it become easier for readers to understand. Classification is both a procedure and a structure for thinking and writing. It enables us to present our ideas about a subject clearly, thoroughly, and convincingly.

Friends, Good Friends—and Such Good Friends

Judith Viorst

Judith Viorst (b. 1931) is a poet, journalist, and author of books for adults and children. Her collection of poems include It's Hard to Be Hip over Thirty and Other Tragedies of Married Life *(1968) and* How Did I Get to Be Forty and Other Atrocities *(1976). Even though her verse is light and humorous, it is not easy to write. Speaking of her poems she has said, "I slave over them. It always makes me feel ashamed to say how hard I work on them because they are 'light verse' and yet it took me four years to write the twenty-four poems in* How Did I Get to Be Forty and Other Atrocities." *Her books for children, which are inspired by life with her three sons, include* I'll Fix Anthony *(1969) and* Alexander and the Terrible, Horrible, No Good, Very Bad Day *(1972).*

After her youngest son left for college, Viorst enrolled in classes at the Washington Psychoanalytic Institute. Her studies there contributed to the book Serious Losses *(1986). Viorst's husband, Milton Viorst, is also a writer, and she finds the arrangement works out well: "We read each other's work, help each other think of synonyms when we can't think of a word, and all the rest of it." The essay below first appeared in* Redbook, *where Viorst's monthly column has appeared since 1968.*

Women are friends, I once would have said, when they totally love and support each other, and bare to each other the secrets of their souls, and run—no questions asked—to help each other, and tell harsh truths to each other (no, you can't wear that dress unless you lose ten pounds first) when harsh truths must be told.

Women are friends, I once would have said, when they share the same affection for Ingmar Bergman, plus train rides, cats, warm rain, charades, Camus, and hate with equal ardor Newark and Brussels sprouts and Lawrence Welk[1] and camping.

In other words, I once would have said that a friend is a friend all the way, but now I believe that's a narrow point of view. For the friendships I have and the friendships I see are conducted at many levels of intensity, serve many different functions, meet different needs, and range from those as all-the-way as the friendship of the soul sisters mentioned above to that of the most nonchalant and casual playmates.

Consider these varieties of friendship:

5   1. Convenience friends. These are women with whom, if our paths weren't crossing all the time, we'd have no particular reason to be

[1]Ingmar Bergman, Swedish filmmaker; Albert Camus, French writer; Lawrence Welk, a television band leader—Eds.

friends: a next-door neighbor, a woman in our car pool, the mother of one of our children's closest friends or maybe some mommy with whom we serve juice and cookies each week at the Glenwood Co-op Nursery.

Convenience friends are convenient indeed. They'll lend us their cups and silverware for a party. They'll drive our kids to soccer when we're sick. They'll take us to pick up our car when we need a lift to the garage. They'll even take our cats when we go on vacation. As we will for them.

But we don't, with convenience friends, ever come too close or tell too much; we maintain our public face and emotional distance. "Which means," says Elaine, "that I'll talk about being overweight but not about being depressed. Which means I'll admit being mad but not blind with rage. Which means that I might say that we're pinched this month but never that I'm worried sick over money."

But which doesn't mean that there isn't sufficient value to be found in these friendships of mutual aid, in convenience friends.

2. Special-interest friends. These friendships aren't intimate, and they needn't involve kids or silverware or cats. Their value lies in some interest jointly shared. And so we may have an office friend or a yoga friend or a tennis friend or a friend from the Women's Democratic Club.

"I've got one woman friend," says Joyce, "who likes, as I do, to take₁₀ psychology courses. Which makes it nice for me—and nice for her. It's fun to go with someone you know and it's fun to discuss what you've learned, driving back from the classes." And for the most part, she says, that's all they discuss.

"I'd say that what we're doing is *doing* together, not being together," Suzanne says of her Tuesday-doubles friends. "It's mainly a tennis relationship, but we play together well. And I guess we all need to have a couple of playmates."

I agree.

My playmate is a shopping friend, a woman of marvelous taste, a woman who knows exactly *where* to buy *what,* and furthermore is a woman who always knows beyond a doubt what one ought to be buying. I don't have the time to keep up with what's new in eyeshadow, hemlines and shoes and whether the smock look is in or finished already. But since (oh, shame!) I care a lot about eyeshadow, hemlines and shoes, and since I don't *want* to wear smocks if the smock look is finished, I'm very glad to have a shopping friend.

3. Historical friends. We all have a friend who knew us when . . . maybe way back in Miss Meltzer's second grade, when our family lived in that three-room flat in Brooklyn, when our dad was out of work for seven months, when our brother Allie got in that fight where they had to call the police, when our sister married the endodontist from Yonkers and when, the morning after we lost our virginity, she was the first, the only, friend we told.

15   The years have gone by and we've gone separate ways and we've little in common now, but we're still an intimate part of each other's past. And so whenever we go to Detroit we always go to visit this friend of our girlhood. Who knows how we looked before our teeth were straightened. Who knows how we talked before our voice got un-Brooklyned. Who knows what we ate before we learned about artichokes. And who, by her presence, puts us in touch with an earlier part of ourself, a part of ourself it's important never to lose.

"What this friend means to me and what I mean to her," says Grace, "is having a sister without sibling rivalry. We know the texture of each other's lives. She remembers my grandmother's cabbage soup. I remember the way her uncle played the piano. There's simply no other friend who remembers those things."

4. Crossroads friends. Like historical friends, our crossroads friends are important for *what was*—for the friendship we shared at a crucial, now past, time of life. A time, perhaps, when we roomed in college together; or worked as eager young singles in the Big City together; or went together, as my friend Elizabeth and I did, through pregnancy, birth and that scary first year of new motherhood.

Crossroads friends forge powerful links, links strong enough to endure with not much more contact than once-a-year letters at Christmas. And out of respect for those crossroads years, for those dramas and dreams we once shared, we will always be friends.

5. Cross-generational friends. Historical friends and crossroads friends seem to maintain a special kind of intimacy—dormant but always ready to be revived—and though we may rarely meet, whenever we do connect, it's personal and intense. Another kind of intimacy exists in the friendships that form across generations in what one woman calls her daughter–mother and her mother–daughter relationships.

20   Evelyn's friend is her mother's age—"but I share so much more than I ever could have with my mother"—a woman she talks to of music, of books and of life. "What I get from her is the benefit of her experience. What she gets—and enjoys—from me is a youthful perspective. It's a pleasure for both of us."

I have in my own life a precious friend, a woman of 65 who has lived very hard, who is wise, who listens well; who has been where I am and can help me understand it; and who represents not only an ultimate ideal mother to me but also the person I'd like to be when I grow up.

In our daughter role we tend to do more than our share of self-revelation; in our mother role we tend to receive what's revealed. It's another kind of pleasure—playing wise mother to a questing younger person. It's another very lovely kind of friendship.

6. Part-of-a-couple friends. Some of the women we call our friends we never see alone—we see them as part of a couple at couples' parties. And though we share interests in many things and respect each other's

views, we aren't moved to deepen the relationship. Whatever the reason, a lack of time or—and this is more likely—a lack of chemistry, our friendship remains in the context of a group. But the fact that our feeling on seeing each other is always, "I'm *so* glad she's here" and the fact that we spend half the evening talking together says that this too, in its own way, counts as a friendship.

(Other part-of-a-couple friends are the friends that came with the marriage, and some of these friends we could live without. But sometimes, alas, she married our husband's best friend; and sometimes, alas, she *is* our husband's best friend. And so we find ourself dealing with her, somewhat against our will, in a spirit of what I'll call *reluctant friendship*.)

7. Men who are friends. I wanted to write just of women friends,[25] but the women I've talked to won't let me—they say I must mention man–woman friendships too. For these friendships can be just as close and as dear as those that we form with women. Listen to Lucy's description of one such friendship:

"We've found we have things to talk about that are different from what he talks about with my husband and different from what I talk about with his wife. So sometimes we call on the phone or meet for lunch. There are similar intellectual interests—we always pass on to each other the books that we love—but there's also something tender and caring too."

In a couple of crises, Lucy says, "he offered himself for talking and for helping. And when someone died in his family he wanted me there. The sexual, flirty part of our friendship is very small, but *some*—just enough to make it fun and different." She thinks—and I agree—that the sexual part, though small, is always *some*, is always there when a man and a woman are friends.

It's only in the past few years that I've made friends with men, in the sense of a friendship that's *mine*, not just part of two couples. And achieving with them the ease and the trust I've found with women friends has value indeed. Under the dryer at home last week, putting on mascara and rouge, I comfortably sat and talked with a fellow named Peter. Peter, I finally decided, could handle the shock of me minus mascara under the dryer. Because we care for each other. Because we're friends.

8. There are medium friends, and pretty good friends, and very good friends indeed, and these friendships are defined by their level of intimacy. And what we'll reveal at each of these levels of intimacy is calibrated with care. We might tell a medium friend, for example, that yesterday we had a fight with our husband. And we might tell a pretty good friend that this fight with our husband made us so mad that we slept on the couch. And we might tell a very good friend that the reason we got so mad in that fight that we slept on the couch had something to

do with that girl who works in his office. But it's only to our very best friends that we're willing to tell all, to tell what's going on with that girl in his office.

30   The best of friends, I still believe, totally love and support and trust each other, and bare to each other the secrets of their souls, and run—no questions asked—to help each other, and tell harsh truths to each other when they must be told.

But we needn't agree about everything (only 12-year-old girl friends agree about *everything*) to tolerate each other's point of view. To accept without judgment. To give and to take without ever keeping score. And to *be* there, as I am for them and as they are for me, to comfort our sorrows, to celebrate our joys.

Additional Rhetorical Strategies

Comparison and Contrast (paragraph 19); Definition (throughout); Example (throughout).

Discussion Questions

1. What is the effect of opening her essay with a couple of paragraphs expressing a definition of friendship that the author no longer believes in? Can you infer the cause of her shift in perspective? How has the definition changed by the closing paragraphs? (You might want to look at Perri Klass's essay "Ambition" (p. 208) for an example of a similar rhetorical strategy.)

2. Do you think the word *friend* suffers at all from being stretched to include so many categories of relationships, from the very casual to the very intimate? Or do you think the word benefits from the flexibility Viorst has ascribed to it? Do you see a reason for restricting the use of the word *friend* only for the kind of "soul sisters" she describes in the opening paragraphs, or do you find that such distinctions cause problems? Are there any categories that Viorst includes that stretch the definition *too* far, in your estimation? Where, if anywhere, would you draw the line?

3. This essay first appeared in *Redbook* in 1977. What features within the essay are typical of that time and that audience? If you were to rewrite the essay to appeal to modern women of your own age, what examples might you change? How might your word choices differ from Viorst's?

4. How would you characterize Viorst's tone in this essay? If you find her style humorous, identify the sources of the humor. How, for instance, would it affect the tone of the essay if you were to replace the word *artichoke* in paragraph 15 with a different food item? How

would the tone be affected if you were to change the pronouns in paragraph 14 from "we" to "I" or "you"?

5. Until she reaches the seventh category, Viorst doesn't seem to consider male friends an option. Even then, she confesses that she included them only at the insistence of some of the women she interviewed; that is, it was not her idea. How does her decision not to consider male friendships until late in the essay affect you as a reader? Do you agree with her (and her friend Lucy) that male–female friendships always include sexual tension? Can you think of exceptions?

Essay Questions

1. Write an essay in which you classify male friendships—friendships among males, and friendships men form with women. Explore what you see as the typically male ways of relating with others.

2. Write an essay on friendship using a different rhetorical form. You might try narration, comparison and contrast, or definition. In the latter two cases, you will probably want to rely on examples to make your points concrete for your reader.

The Plot Against People

Russell Baker

Russell Baker (b. 1925) began his writing career in 1947, when he was hired as a reporter by the Baltimore Sun. *He quickly earned a reputation as a fast, accurate reporter, and was rewarded by a promotion to the position of London bureau chief. He later covered the White House and the Senate for the* Sun *and then the* New York Times, *until 1962, when he got bored "wearing out my hams waiting for somebody to come out and lie to me." At this point the* Times *offered him a column, which came to be called the "Observer." His syndicated column is filled with wry political satire and witty observations on everyday life. Many of his columns have been collected in books, including* No Cause for Panic *(1964),* Baker's Dozen *(1964),* Poor Russell's Almanac *(1972),* So This Is Depravity *(1980), and* There's a Country in my Cellar *(1990).*

Baker is also the author of two autobiographies, Growing Up *(1982), which won the Pulitzer Prize, and* The Good Times *(1989).*

Inanimate objects are classified into three major categories—those that don't work, those that break down and those that get lost.

The goal of all inanimate objects is to resist man and ultimately to defeat him, and the three major classifications are based on the method each object uses to achieve its purpose. As a general rule, any object capable of breaking down at the moment when it is most needed will do so. The automobile is typical of the category.

With the cunning typical of its breed, the automobile never breaks down while entering a filling station with a large staff of idle mechanics. It waits until it reaches a downtown intersection in the middle of the rush hour, or until it is fully loaded with family and luggage on the Ohio Turnpike.

Thus it creates maximum misery, inconvenience, frustration and irritability among its human cargo, thereby reducing its owner's life span.

5   Washing machines, garbage disposals, lawn mowers, light bulbs, automatic laundry dryers, water pipes, furnaces, electrical fuses, television tubes, hose nozzles, tape recorders, slide projectors—all are in league with the automobile to take their turn at breaking down whenever life threatens to flow smoothly for their human enemies.

Many inanimate objects, of course, find it extremely difficult to break down. Pliers, for example, and gloves and keys are almost totally incapable of breaking down. Therefore, they have had to evolve a different technique for resisting man.

They get lost. Science has still not solved the mystery of how they do it, and no man has ever caught one of them in the act of getting lost. The most plausible theory is that they have developed a secret method of locomotion which they are able to conceal the instant a human eye falls upon them.

It is not uncommon for a pair of pliers to climb all the way from the cellar to the attic in its single-minded determination to raise its owner's blood pressure. Keys have been known to burrow three feet under mattresses. Women's purses, despite their great weight, frequently travel through six or seven rooms to find hiding space under a couch.

Scientists have been struck by the fact that things that break down virtually never get lost, while things that get lost hardly ever break down.

A furnace, for example, will invariably break down at the depth of$_{10}$ the first winter cold wave, but it will never get lost. A woman's purse, which after all does have some inherent capacity for breaking down, hardly ever does; it almost inevitably chooses to get lost.

Some persons believe this constitutes evidence that inanimate objects are not entirely hostile to man, and that a negotiated peace is possible. After all, they point out, a furnace could infuriate a man even more thoroughly by getting lost than by breaking down, just as a glove could upset him far more by breaking down than by getting lost.

Not everyone agrees, however, that this indicates a conciliatory attitude among inanimate objects. Many say it merely proves that furnaces, gloves and pliers are incredibly stupid.

The third class of objects—those that don't work—is the most curious of all. These include such objects as barometers, car clocks, cigarette lighters, flashlights and toy-train locomotives. It is inaccurate, of course, to say that they never work. They work once, usually for the first few hours after being brought home, and then quit. Thereafter, they never work again.

In fact, it is widely assumed that they are built for the purpose of not working. Some people have reached advanced ages without ever seeing some of these objects—barometers, for example—in working order.

Science is utterly baffled by the entire category. There are many$_{15}$ theories about it. The most interesting holds that the things that don't work have attained the highest state possible for an inanimate object, the state to which things that break down and things that get lost can still only aspire.

They have truly defeated man by conditioning him never to expect anything of them, and in return they have given man the only peace he receives from inanimate society. He does not expect his barometer to work, his electric locomotive to run, his cigarette lighter to light or his flashlight to illuminate, and when they don't it does not raise his blood pressure.

He cannot attain that peace with furnaces and keys and cars and women's purses as long as he demands that they work for their keep.

Additional Rhetorical Strategies

Process Analysis (paragraph 7); Cause and Effect (paragraph 16); Example (throughout).

Discussion Questions

1. What is Baker's main reason for writing this essay? How does the rhetorical form of classification further his purpose?
2. Several times in the essay Baker refers to scientists and scientific theories, debates, and so on. What is the effect of these references? At what or whom does his humor seem to be directed?
3. Look closely at Baker's use of detail for humorous effect. Try substituting other details for the ones Baker has chosen and see if the effect diminishes. How can one go about selecting details that will enhance the humor of a piece of writing?
4. What negative or positive experiences have you had with household objects? Can you think of a category of inanimate objects that Baker has not thought of? How might that category be seen as part of the "Plot Against People?" Or is it a category that people might enlist on their side in this war between humans and their possessions?

Essay Questions

1. Choose a trivial object of everyday human experience and elevate it to a ridiculous degree by writing a psuedo-scientific paper explaining the given phenomenon. You might choose the classification mode or any other rhetorical form that suits your purpose.
2. Write an essay with a title such as "The Plot Against Inanimate Objects," as a response, from the point of view of any one of the objects Baker writes about, to Baker's essay. Use your imagination to put yourself in the place of the lawn mower, keys, pliers, or purse that you have chosen as the narrator of your essay.

Five Myths about Immigration

David Cole

David Cole (b. 1958) is Professor of Law at the Georgetown University Law Center. He earned his B.A. and J.D. at Yale University, and served as a clerk on the Third Circuit of the United States Court of Appeals. From 1985–1990 he worked as a staff attorney for the Center for Constitutional Rights, and while there litigated several important First Amendment cases. He continues to work as a volunteer staff attorney at the Center for Constitutional Rights in addition to teaching at Georgetown.

Professor Cole has published widely in the areas of law and literature, civil rights, criminal justice, and constitutional law, and is also a frequent contributor to the Washington Post, *the* Los Angeles Times, *and the* New York Times. *The essay reprinted here was originally published in the* Nation.

For a brief period in the mid-nineteenth century, a new political movement captured the passions of the American public. Fittingly labeled the "Know-Nothings," their unifying theme was nativism. They liked to call themselves "Native Americans," although they had no sympathy for people we call Native Americans today. And they pinned every problem in American society on immigrants. As one Know-Nothing wrote in 1856: "Four-fifths of the beggary and three-fifths of the crime spring from our foreign population; more than half the public charities, more than half the prisons and almshouses, more than half the police and the cost of administering criminal justice are for foreigners."

At the time, the greatest influx of immigrants was from Ireland, where the potato famine had struck, and Germany, which was in political and economic turmoil. Anti-alien and anti-Catholic sentiments were the order of the day, especially in New York and Massachusetts, which received the brunt of the wave of immigrants, many of whom were dirt-poor and uneducated. Politicians were quick to exploit the sentiment: There's nothing like a scapegoat to forge an alliance.

I am especially sensitive to this history: My forebears were among those dirt-poor Irish Catholics who arrived in the 1860s. Fortunately for them, and me, the Know-Nothing movement fizzled within fifteen years. But its pilot light kept burning, and is turned up whenever the American public begins to feel vulnerable and in need of an enemy.

Although they go by different names today, the Know-Nothings have returned. As in the 1850s, the movement is strongest where immigrants are most concentrated: California and Florida. The objects of prejudice are of course no longer Irish Catholics and Germans; 140 years later, "they" have become "us." The new "they"—because it

seems "we" must always have a "they"—are Latin Americans (most recently, Cubans), Haitians and Arab-Americans, among others.

5   But just as in the 1850s, passion, misinformation and shortsighted
fear often substitute for reason, fairness and human dignity in today's
immigration debates. In the interest of advancing beyond know-
nothingism, let's look at five current myths that distort public debate
and government policy relating to immigrants.

America is being overrun with immigrants   In one sense, of course, this is true, but
in that sense it has been true since Christopher Columbus arrived. Except for the real Native Americans, we are a nation of immigrants.

It is not true, however, that the first-generation immigrant share of
our population is growing. As of 1990, foreign-born people made up
only 8 percent of the population, as compared with a figure of about 15
percent from 1870 to 1920. Between 70 and 80 percent of those who immigrate every year are refugees or immediate relatives of U.S. citizens.

Much of the anti-immigrant fervor is directed against the undocumented, but they make up only 13 percent of all immigrants residing in
the United States, and only 1 percent of the American population. Contrary to popular belief, most such aliens do not cross the border illegally but enter legally and remain after their student or visitor visa ex-
pires. Thus, building a wall at the border, no matter how high, will not
solve the problem.

Immigrants take jobs from U.S. citizens   There is virtually no evidence to support
this view, probably the most widespread misunderstanding about immigrants. As documented by a 1994 A.C.L.U. Immigrants' Rights
Project report, numerous studies have found that immigrants actually
create more jobs than they fill. The jobs immigrants take are of course
easier to see, but immigrants are often highly productive, run their own
businesses and employ both immigrants and citizens. One study found
that Mexican immigration to Los Angeles County between 1970 and
1980 was responsible for 78,000 new jobs. Governor Mario Cuomo reports that immigrants own more than 40,000 companies in New York,
which provide thousands of jobs and $3.5 billion to the state's economy
every year.

10*Immigrants are a drain on society's resources*   This claim fuels many of the recent
efforts to cut off government benefits to immigrants. However, most
studies have found that immigrants are a net benefit to the economy because, as a 1994 Urban Institute report concludes, "immigrants generate
significantly more in taxes paid than they cost in services received."
The Council of Economic Advisers similarly found in 1986 that "immigrants have a favorable effect on the overall standard of living."

Anti-immigrant advocates often cite studies purportedly showing
the contrary, but these generally focus only on taxes and services at the
local or state level. What they fail to explain is that because most taxes

go to the federal government, such studies would also show a net loss when applied to U.S. citizens. At most, such figures suggest that some redistribution of federal and state monies may be appropriate; they say nothing unique about the costs of immigrants.

Some subgroups of immigrants plainly impose a net cost in the short run, principally those who have most recently arrived and have not yet "made it." California, for example, bears substantial costs for its disproportionately large undocumented population, largely because it has on average the poorest and least educated immigrants. But that has not been true of every wave of immigrants that has ever reached our shores; it was as true of the Irish in the 1850s, for example, as it is of Salvadorans today. From a long-term perspective, the economic advantages of immigrations are undeniable.

Some have suggested that we might save money and diminish incentives to immigrate illegally if we denied undocumented aliens public services. In fact, undocumented immigrants are already ineligible for most social programs, with the exception of education for schoolchildren, which is constitutionally required, and benefits directly related to health and safety, such as emergency medical care and nutritional assistance to poor women, infants and children. To deny such basic care to people in need, apart from being inhumanly callous, would probably cost us more in the long run by exacerbating health problems that we would eventually have to address.

Aliens refuse to assimilate, and are depriving us of our cultural and political unity. This claim has been made about every new group of immigrants to arrive on U.S. shores. Supreme Court Justice Stephen Field wrote in 1884 that the Chinese "have remained among us a separate people, retaining the original peculiarities of dress, manners, habits, and modes of living, which are as marked as their complexion and language." Five years later, he upheld the racially based exclusion of Chinese immigrants. Similar claims have been made over different periods of our history about Catholics, Jews, Italians, Eastern Europeans and Latin Americans.

In most instances, such claims are simply not true; "American cul-15 ture" has been created, defined and revised by persons who for the most part are descended from immigrants once seen as anti-assimilationist. Descendants of the Irish Catholics, for example, a group once decried as separatist and alien, have become presidents, senators and representatives (and all of these in one family, in the case of the Kennedys). Our society exerts tremendous pressure to conform, and cultural separatism rarely survives a generation. But more important, even if this claim were true, is this a legitimate rationale for limiting immigration in a society built on the values of pluralism and tolerance?

Noncitizen immigrants are not entitled to constitutional rights Our government has long declined to treat immigrants as full human beings, and nowhere is that more clear than in the realm of constitutional rights. Although the Constitution literally extends the fundamental protections in the Bill of Rights to all people, limiting to citizens only the right to vote and run for federal office, the federal government acts as if this were not the case.

In 1893 the executive branch successfully defended a statute that required Chinese laborers to establish their prior residence here by the testimony of "at least one credible white witness." The Supreme Court ruled that this law was constitutional because it was reasonable for Congress to presume that nonwhite witnesses could not be trusted.

The federal government is not much more enlightened today. In a pending case I'm handling in the Court of Appeals for the Ninth Circuit, the Clinton Administration has argued that permanent resident aliens lawfully living here should be extended no more First Amendment rights than aliens applying for first-time admission from abroad—that is, none. Under this view, students at a public university who are citizens may express themselves freely, but students who are not citizens can be deported for saying exactly what their classmates are constitutionally entitled to say.

Growing up, I was always taught that we will be judged by how we treat others. If we are collectively judged by how we have treated immigrants—those who appear today to be "other" but will in a generation be "us"—we are not in very good shape.

Additional Rhetorical Strategies

Definition (paragraphs 1, 4); Cause and Effect (paragraphs 3, 8, 9, 10, 11, 14, 17); Comparison and Contrast (paragraphs 4, 5, 11); Example (throughout).

Discussion Questions

1. What is the principle upon which Cole bases his classification of the myths about immigration? How many basic categories of immigrants does he describe? Of these, which does he seem most interested in discussing? How comprehensive do you think Cole's classification of myths about immigration is? What is Cole's stated purpose for talking about the myths about immigration? What is his attitude toward each of these myths? Point to specific words and phrases to support your response.

2. As you re-read Cole's essay, consider the sequence of myths he presents. What noticeable order—or sense of priority—is evident in his presentation of these five myths? Cole's classification is supported by a series of details. As you review his paragraphs, select one detail from each and explain how this detail helps make his classification more effective.

3. Think of another issue that has become the focal point of recent political attention and debate. What myths are associated with that issue? How would you classify those myths? Identify specific examples of the ways in which politicians draw on these popular myths to elicit favorable responses from their constituents. What do you perceive to be the consequences of those political efforts?

Essay Questions

1. The fourth myth critiqued by Cole is that "immigrants refuse to assimilate." Write an essay in which you explore the advantages and disadvantages of assimilation from the point of view of both the new immigrants and the more established immigrants who consider themselves Americans. You may want to include a discussion of the concept "cultural . . . unity" (paragraph 14) in your essay.
2. If you disagree with Cole, write an essay arguing against one or more of his main points. Like Cole, you will want to cite studies and statistics to support your argument. Be selective when choosing your sources; do not cite any that would not stand up to the scrutiny of an unbiased reader.

Four Kinds of Reading

Donald Hall

Reading first-rate writers and attempting to write like them is one very useful way to develop our ability to express ourselves. Even the most expert writers learn a great deal from reading the work of others. Donald Hall (b. 1928)—a highly accomplished poet, playwright, editor, teacher and freelance writer—offers the following incisive analogy: "A good way to learn to write well is to read good prose. Gradually we acquire the manners that make the good writing we admire. It's like learning a foreign language by living with a family that speaks it, by shopping in it, and by listening to shows with dialogue in it."

The clarity and simplicity of Hall's advice mark all of his writing. Educated at Harvard, Oxford, and Stanford, Hall taught at the University of Michigan from 1957 until 1975, when he began devoting himself exclusively to writing and tending the family farm in Durham, New Hampshire. He has also lectured on literature and read his poetry at more than 400 colleges.

The following essay, in which Hall divides reading into four basic categories, was first published in the New York Times *in 1969.*

Everywhere one meets the idea that reading is an activity desirable in itself. It is understandable that publishers and librarians—and even writers—should promote this assumption, but is strange that the idea should have general currency. People surround the idea of reading with piety, and do not take into account the purpose of reading or the value of what is being read. Teachers and parents praise the child who reads, and praise themselves, whether the text be *The Reader's Digest* or *Moby Dick*. The advent of TV has increased the false values ascribed to reading, since TV provides a vulgar alternative. But this piety is silly; and most reading is no more cultural nor intellectual nor imaginative than shooting pool or watching *What's My Line*.[1]

It is worth asking how the act of reading became something to value in itself, as opposed for instance to the act of conversation or the act of taking a walk. Mass literacy is a recent phenomenon, and I suggest that the aura which decorates reading is a relic of the importance of reading to our great-great-grandparents. Literacy used to be a mark of social distinction, separating a small portion of humanity from the rest. The farm laborer who was ambitious for his children did not daydream that they would become schoolteachers or doctors; he daydreamed that they would learn to read, and that a world would therefore open up to them

---

[1] A popular television game show broadcast by CBS from 1950–1967—Eds.

in which they did not have to labor in the fields fourteen hours a day for six days a week in order to buy salt and cotton. On the next rank of society, ample time for reading meant that the reader was free from the necessity to spend most of his waking hours making a living. This sort of attitude shades into the contemporary man's boost of his wife's cultural activities. When he says that his wife is interested in books and music and pictures, he is not only enclosing the arts in a female world, he is saying that he is rich enough to provide her with the leisure to do nothing. Reading is an inactivity, and therefore a badge of social class. Of course, these reasons for the piety attached to reading are never acknowledged. They show themselves in the shape of our attitudes toward books; reading gives off an air of gentility.

It seems to me possible to name four kinds of reading, each with a characteristic manner and purpose. The first is reading for information—reading to learn about a trade, or politics, or how to accomplish something. We read a newspaper this way, or most textbooks, or directions on how to assemble a bicycle. With most of this material, the reader can learn to scan the page quickly, coming up with what he needs and ignoring what is irrelevant to him, like the rhythm of the sentence, or the play of metaphor. Courses in speed reading can help us read for this purpose, training the eye to jump quickly across the page. If we read the *New York Times* with the attention we should give a novel or a poem, we will have time for nothing else, and our mind will be cluttered with clichés and dead metaphor. Quick eye-reading is a necessity to anyone who wants to keep up with what's happening, or learn much of what has happened in the past. The amount of reflection, which interrupts and slows down the reading, depends on the material.

But it is not the same activity as reading literature. There ought to be another word. If we read a work of literature properly, we read slowly, and we *hear* all the words. If our lips do not actually move, it's only laziness. The muscles in our throat move, and come together when we see the word *squeeze*. We hear the sounds so accurately that if a syllable is missing in a line of poetry we hear the lack, though we may not know what we are lacking. In prose we accept the rhythms, and hear the adjacent sounds. We also register a track of feeling through the metaphors and associations of words. Careless writing prevents this sort of attention, and becomes offensive. But the great writers reward it. Only by the full exercise of our powers to receive language can we absorb their intelligence and their imagination. This kind of reading goes through the ear—though the eye takes in the print, and decodes it into sound—to the throat and the understanding, and it can never be quick. It is slow and sensual, a deep pleasure that begins with touch and ends with the sort of comprehension that we associate with dream.

Too many intellectuals read in order to reduce images to abstrac- 5 tions. One reads philosophy slowly, as if it were literature, but much time must be spent with the eyes turned away from the page, reflecting on the text. To read literature this way is to turn it into something it is not—to concepts clothed in character, or philosophy sugar-coated. I think that most literary intellectuals read this way, including brighter professors of English, with the result that they miss literature completely, and concern themselves with a minor discipline called the history of ideas. I remember a course in Chaucer at my University in which the final exam required the identification of a hundred or more fragments of Chaucer, none as long as a line. If you like poetry, and read Chaucer through a couple of times slowly, you found yourself knowing them all. If you were a literary intellectual, well-informed about the great chain of being, chances are you had a difficult time. To read literature is to be intimately involved with the words on the page, and never to think of them as the embodiments of ideas which can be expressed in other terms. On the other hand, intellectual writing— closer to mathematics on a continuum that has at its opposite pole lyric poetry—requires intellectual reading, which is slow because it is reflective and because the reader must pause to evaluate concepts.

But most of the reading which is praised for itself is neither literary nor intellectual. It is narcotic. Novels, stories, and biographies—historical sagas, monthly regurgitations of book clubs, four- and five-thousand word daydreams of the magazines—these are the opium of the suburbs. The drug is not harmful except to the addict himself, and is no more injurious to him than Johnny Carson or a bridge club, but it is nothing to be proud of. This reading is the automated daydream, the mild trip of the housewife and the tired businessman, interested not in experience and feeling but in turning off the possibilities of experience and feeling. Great literature, if we read it well, opens us up to the world, and makes us more sensitive to it, as if we acquired eyes that could see through walls and ears that could hear the smallest sounds. But by narcotic reading, one can reduce great literature to the level of *The Valley of the Dolls*.[2] One can read *Anna Karenina* passively and inattentively, and float down the river of lethargy as if one were reading a confession magazine: "I Spurned My Husband for a Count."

I think that everyone reads for narcosis occasionally, and perhaps most consistently in late adolescence, when great readers are born. I remember reading to shut the world out, away at a school where I did not want to be; I invented a word for my disease: "bibliolepsy," on the analogy of narcolepsy. But after a while the books became a window on the world, and not a screen against it. This change doesn't always happen. I think that late adolescent narcotic reading accounts for some of the badness of English departments. As a college student, the boy loves read-

---

[2]A film made in 1967 considered so bad that it has become a camp/trash classic—Eds.

ing and majors in English because he would be reading anyway. Deciding on a career, he takes up English teaching for the same reason. Then in graduate school he is trained to be a scholar, which is painful and irrelevant, and finds he must write papers and publish them to be a Professor—and at about that time he no longer requires reading for narcosis, and he is left with nothing but a Ph.D. and the prospect of fifty years of teaching literature; and he does not even like literature.

Narcotic reading survives the impact of television, because this type of reading has even less reality than melodrama; that is, the reader is in control; once the characters reach into the reader's feelings, he is able to stop reading, or glance away, or superimpose his own daydream. The trouble with television is that it embodies its own daydream. Literature is often valued precisely because of its distance from the tangible. Some readers prefer looking into the text of a play to seeing it performed. Reading a play, it is possible to stage it oneself by an imaginative act; but it is also possible to remove it from real people. Here is Virginia Woolf, who was lavish in her praise of the act of reading, talking about reading a play rather than seeing it: "Certainly there is a good deal to be said for reading *Twelfth Night* in the book if the book can be read in a garden, with no sound but the thud of an apple falling to the earth, or of the wind ruffling the branches of the trees." She sets her own stage; the play is called *Virginia Woolf Reads Twelfth Night in a Garden.* Piety moves into narcissism, and the high metaphors of Shakespeare's lines dwindle into the flowers of an English garden; actors in ruffles wither, while the wind ruffles branches.

Additional Rhetorical Strategies

Example (paragraphs 2, 3, 8); Cause and Effect (paragraphs 2, 7); Comparison and Contrast (paragraphs 3, 4, 8); Process Analysis (paragraphs 3–6).

Discussion Questions

1. On what criteria does Hall divide reading into four categories? Are the distinguishing features found within the books or material being read, or within the people doing the reading, or both? Could the same person conceivably read the same book in two different ways on two different days? Give an example to support your answer.

2. Hall opens his essay on a provocative note: he questions the widespread assumption that "reading is an activity desirable in itself." In the first two paragraphs, how does Hall encourage his readers to re-examine their attitudes toward the value of reading? How does he make so disputable a contention seem reasonable? What is his ultimate goal in making this argument?

3. Even though Hall critiques the practice of surrounding "the idea of reading with piety" (paragraph 1), it's clear that he does think rather highly of at least some forms of reading. Which of the four kinds of reading described in this essay does Hall seem to value most? Which one seems to serve as the yardstick against which each of the others is measured? Where does he place this category in his essay? What is the effect of placing it there? What other logical arrangements can you think of, and how would the essay be different if you were to rearrange his categories?

4. In this essay, Hall compares and contrasts reading and watching television. Read Marie Winn's essay elsewhere in this collection (p. 349) on the same subject. Which essay do you find more compelling? Why?

Essay Questions

1. Consider some common activity—say, grocery shopping, viewing films, choosing clothes to wear. Write an essay in which you create categories for these activities. Classify the activity rather than the subject; that is, make the mind's activity the focus of your essay.

2. In paragraph 7 Hall tells the tragicomic tale of the biblioleptic college student who majors in English, only to find himself years later stuck in a career that doesn't suit his personality in the least. Think of some of the reasons that you and your classmates have for choosing your own majors. What conceivable changes in personality might render these choices irrelevant as you mature? Write an essay in which you set forth a reasoned approach to choosing a major, an approach that circumvents some of the traps that you see your friends falling into.

Thematic Pair: Understanding Human Behavior

▲▼ Territorial Behavior

Desmond Morris

Desmond Morris (b. 1928) earned his B.S. at Birmingham University and his Ph.D. at Oxford. Over the course of his career, Morris has won both academic respectability and the hearts of the general reading public. His activities have ranged from hosting the television show Zootime, *whose animal guests were known for their unpredictable antics, to serving as curator of mammals at the London Zoo. He resigned as curator when the royalties from* The Naked Ape *(1968) allowed him to devote himself full time to writing and research. In* The Naked Ape, *he brings the methods of observation he learned when studying animals to bear upon his fellow human beings. Much of his work since that time—including* The Human Zoo *(1969),* Manwatching: A Field Guide to Human Behavior *(1977), and* Bodywatching: A Field Guide to the Human Species *(1985)—has focused on human behavior.*

Morris's background, skills, and knowledge combine to produce highly informative and readable prose. As he explains, "A lot of statements I make have this huge backup of quantified field work . . . [Some] do not and are simply based on intuition and anecdotal observation. The agony of writing a pop book is that you can't sort of say which is which. The text has got to flow." As you read the essay below, which was originally a chapter from Manwatching, *notice how Morris walks the line between scholarship and popular writing.*

A territory is a defended space. In the broadest sense, there are three kinds of human territory: tribal, family, and personal.

It is rare for people to be driven to physical fighting in defense of these "owned" spaces, but fight they will, if pushed to the limit. The invading army encroaching on national territory, the gang moving into a rival district, the trespasser climbing into an orchard, the burglar breaking into a house, the bully pushing to the front of a queue, the driver trying to steal a parking space, all of these intruders are liable to be met with resistance varying from the vigorous to the savagely violent. Even if the law is on the side of the intruder, the urge to protect a territory may be so strong that otherwise peaceful citizens abandon all their usual controls and inhibitions. Attempts to evict families from their homes, no matter how socially valid the reasons, can lead to siege conditions reminiscent of the defense of a medieval fortress.

The fact that these upheavals are so rare is a measure of the success of Territorial Signals as a system of dispute prevention. It is sometimes cynically stated that "all property is theft," but in reality it is the opposite. Property, as owned space which is displayed as owned space, is a specil kind of sharing system which reduces fighting much more than it causes. Man is a cooperative species, but he is also competitive, and

his struggle for dominance has to be structured in some way if chaos is
to be avoided. The establishment of territorial rights is one such structure. It limits dominance geographically. I am dominant in my territory
and you are dominant in yours. In other words, dominance is shared
out spatially, and we all have some. Even if I am weak and unintelli-
gent and you can dominate me when we meet on neutral ground, I can
still enjoy a thoroughly dominant role as soon as I retreat to my private
base. Be it ever so humble, there is no place like a home territory.

Of course, I can still be intimidated by a particularly dominant individual who enters my home base, but his encroachment will be dangerous for him and he will think twice about it, because he will know that
here my urge to resist will be dramatically magnified and my usual
subservience banished. Insulted at the heart of my own territory, I may
easily explode into battle—either symbolic or real—with a result that
may be damaging to both of us.

In order for this to work, each territory has to be plainly advertised
as such. Just as a dog cocks its leg to deposit its personal scent on the 5
trees in its locality, so the human animal cocks its leg symbolically all
over his home base. But because we are predominantly visual animals
we employ mostly visual signals, and it is worth asking how we do this
at the three levels: tribal, family, and personal.

First: the Tribal Territory. We evolved as tribal animals, living in
comparatively small groups, probably of less than a hundred, and we
existed like that for millions of years. It is our basic social unit, a group
in which everyone knows everyone else. Essentially, the tribal territory
consisted of a home base surrounded by extended hunting grounds.
Any neighboring tribe intruding on our social space would be repelled
and driven away. As these early tribes swelled into agricultural super-
tribes, and eventually into industrial nations, their territorial defense
systems became increasingly elaborate. The tiny, ancient home base of
the hunting tribe became the great capital city, the primitive warpaint
became the flags, emblems, uniforms, and regalia of the specialized military, and the war chants became national anthems, marching songs, and
bugle calls. Territorial boundary lines hardened into fixed borders, often
conspicuously patrolled and punctuated with defensive structures—
forts and lookout posts, checkpoints and great walls, and, today, customs barriers.

Today each nation flies its own flag, a symbolic embodiment of its
territorial status. But patriotism is not enough. The ancient tribal hunter
lurking inside each citizen finds himself unsatisfied by membership in
such a vast conglomeration of individuals, most of whom are totally
unknown to him personally. He does his best to feel that he shares a
common territorial defense with them all, but the scale of the operation
has become inhuman. It is hard to feel a sense of belonging with a tribe
of fifty million or more. His answer is to form sub-groups, nearer to his

ancient pattern, smaller, and more personally known to him—the local club, the teenage gang, the union, the specialist society, the sports association, the political party, the college fraternity, the social clique, the protest group, and the rest. Rare indeed is the individual who does not belong to at least one of these splinter groups, and take from it a sense of tribal allegiance and brotherhood. Typical of all these groups is the development of Territorial Signals—badges, costumes, headquarters, banners, slogans, and all the other displays of group identity. This is where the action is, in terms of tribal territorialism, and only when a major war breaks out does the emphasis shift upwards to the higher group level of the nations.

Each of these modern pseudo-tribes sets up its own special kind of home base. In extreme cases nonmembers are totally excluded, in others they are allowed in as visitors with limited rights and under a control system of special rules. In many ways they are like miniature nations, with their own flags and emblems and their own border guards. The exclusive club has its own "customs barrier": the doorman who checks your "passport" (your membership card) and prevents strangers from passing in unchallenged. There is a government: the club committee; and often special displays of the tribal elders: the photographs or portraits of previous officials on the walls. At the heart of the specialized territories there is a powerful feeling of security and importance, a sense of shared defense against the outside world. Much of the club chatter, both serious and joking, directs itself against the rottenness of everything outside the club boundaries—in that "other world" beyond the protected portals.

In social organizations which embody a strong class system, such as military units and large business concerns, there are many territorial rules, often unspoken, which interfere with the official hierarchy. High-status individuals, such as officers or managers, could in theory enter any of the regions occupied by the lower levels in the peck order, but they limit this power in a striking way. An officer seldom enters a sergeant's mess or a barrack room unless it is for a formal inspection. He respects those regions as alien territories even though he has the power to go there by virtue of his dominant role. And in businesses, part of the appeal of unions, over and above their obvious functions, is that with their officials, headquarters, and meetings they add a sense of territorial power for the staff workers. It is almost as if each military organization and business concern consists of two warring tribes: the officers versus the other ranks, and the management versus the workers. Each has its special home base within the system, and the territorial defense pattern thrusts itself into what, on the surface, is a pure social hierarchy. Negotiations between managements and unions are tribal battles fought out over the neutral ground of a boardroom table, and

are as much concerned with territorial display as they are with resolv-
ing problems of wages and conditions. Indeed, if one side gives in too
quickly and accepts the other's demands, the victors feel strangely
cheated and deeply suspicious that it may be a trick. What they are
missing is the protracted sequence of ritual and counter-ritual that
keeps alive their group territorial identity.

Likewise, many of the hostile displays of sports fans and teenage[10]
gangs are primarily concerned with displaying their group image to
rival fan-clubs and gangs. Except in rare cases, they do not attack one
another's headquarters, drive out the occupants, and reduce them to
a submissive, subordinate condition. It is enough to have scuffles on
the borderlands between the two rival territories. This is particularly
clear at football matches, where the fan-club headquarters becomes
temporarily shifted from the clubhouse to a section of the stands, and
where minor fighting breaks out at the unofficial boundary line between the massed groups of rival supporters. Newspaper reports
play up the few accidents and injuries which do occur on such occasions, but when these are studied in relation to the total numbers of
displaying fans involved it is clear that the serious incidents represent only a tiny fraction of the overall group behavior. For every actual punch or kick there are a thousand war cries, war dances, chants,
and gestures.

Second: the Family Territory. Essentially, the family is a breeding
unit and the family territory is a breeding ground. At the center of this
space there is the nest—the bedroom—where tucked up in bed, we feel
at our most territorially secure. In a typical house the bedroom is up-
stairs, where a safe nest should be. This puts it farther away from the
entrance hall, the area where contact is made, intermittently, with the
outside world. The less private reception rooms, where intruders are allowed access, are the next line of defense. Beyond them, outside the
walls of the building, there is often a symbolic remnant of the ancient
feeding grounds—a garden. Its symbolism often extends to the plants
and animals it contains, which cease to be nutritional and become
merely decorative—flowers and pets. But like a true territorial space it
has a conspicuously displayed boundary line, the garden fence, wall, or
railings. Often no more than a token barrier, this is the outer territorial
demarcation, separating the private world for the family from the public world beyond. To cross it puts any visitor or intruder at an immediate disadvantage. As he crosses the threshold, his dominance wanes,
slightly but unmistakably. He is entering an area where he senses that
he must ask permission to do simple things that he would consider a
right elsewhere. Without lifting a finger, the territorial owners exert
their dominance. This is done by all the hundreds of small ownership
"markers" they have deposited on their family territory: the ornaments,
the "possessed" objects positioned in the rooms and on the walls; the

furnishings, the furniture, the colors, the patterns, all owner-chosen and all making this particular home base unique to them.

It is one of the tragedies of modern architecture that there has been a standardization of these vital territorial living units. One of the most important aspects of a home is that it should be similar to other homes only in a general way, and that in detail it should have many differences, making it a *particular* home. Unfortunately, it is cheaper to build a row of houses, or a block of flats, so that all the family living units are identical, but the territorial urge rebels against this trend and houseowners struggle as best they can to make their mark on their mass-produced properties. They do this with garden-design, with front-door colors, with curtain patterns, with wallpaper and all the other decorative elements that together create a unique and different family environment. Only when they have completed this nest-building do they feel truly "at home" and secure.

When they venture forth as a family unit they repeat the process in a minor way. On a day trip to the seaside, they load the car with personal belongings and it becomes their temporary, portable territory. Arriving at the beach they stake out a small territorial claim, marking it with rugs, towels, baskets, and other belongings to which they can return from their seaboard wanderings. Even if they all leave it at once to bathe, it retains a characteristic territorial quality and other family groups arriving will recognize this by setting up their own "home" bases at a respectful distance. Only when the whole beach has filled up with these marked spaces will newcomers start to position themselves in such a way that the inter-base distance becomes reduced. Forced to pitch between several existing beach territories they will feel a momentary sensation of intrusion, and the established "owners" will feel a similar sensation of invasion, even though they are not being directly inconvenienced.

The same territorial scene is being played out in parks and fields and on riverbanks, wherever family groups gather in their clustered units. But if rivalry for spaces creates mild feelings of hostility, it is true to say that, without the territorial system of sharing and space-limited dominance, there would be chaotic disorder.

15   Third: the Personal Space. If a man enters a waiting room and sits at one end of a long row of empty chairs, it is possible to predict where the next man to enter will seat himself. He will not sit next to the first man, nor will he sit at the far end, right away from him. He will choose a position about halfway between these two points. The next man to enter will take the largest gap left, and sit roughly in the middle of that, and so on, until eventually the latest newcomer will be forced to select a seat that places him right next to one of the already seated men. Similar patterns can be observed in cinemas, public urinals, airplanes, trains, and buses. This is a reflection of the fact that we all carry with us, everywhere we go, a portable territory called a Personal Space. If peo-

ple move inside this space, we feel threatened. If they keep too far out-side it, we feel rejected. The result is a subtle series of spatial adjust-ments, usually operating quite unconsciously and producing ideal com-promises as far as this is possible. If a situation becomes too crowded, then we adjust our reactions accordingly and allow our personal space to shrink. Jammed into an elevator, a rush-hour compartment, or a packed room, we give up altogether and allow body-to-body contact, but when we relinquish our Personal Space in this way, we adopt cer-tain special techniques. In essence, what we do is to convert these other bodies into "nonpersons." We studiously ignore them, and they us. We try not to face them if we can possibly avoid it. We wipe all expressive-ness from our faces, letting them go blank. We may look up at the ceil-ing or down at the floor, and we reduce body movements to a mini-mum. Packed together like sardines in a tin, we stand dumbly still, sending out as few social signals as possible.

Even if the crowding is less severe, we still tend to cut down our social interactions in the presence of large numbers. Careful observa-tions of children in play groups revealed that if they are high-density groupings there is less social interaction between the individual chil-dren, even though there is theoretically more opportunity for such con-tacts. At the same time, the high-density groups show a higher fre-quency of aggressive and destructive behavior patterns in their play. Personal Space—"elbow room"—is a vital commodity for the human animal, and one that cannot be ignored without risking serious trouble.

Of course, we all enjoy the excitement of being in a crowd, and this reaction cannot be ignored. But there are crowds and crowds. It is pleasant enough to be in a "spectator crowd," but not so appealing to find yourself in the middle of a rush-hour crush. The difference be-tween the two is that the spectator crowd is all facing in the same direc-tion and concentrating on a distant point of interest. Attending a the-ater, there are twinges of rising hostility toward the stranger who sits down immediately in front of you or the one who squeezes into the seat next to you. The shared armrest can become a polite, but distinct, terri-torial boundary-dispute region. However, as soon as the show begins, these invasions of Personal Space are forgotten and the attention is fo-cused beyond the small space where the crowding is taking place. Now, each member of the audience feels himself spatially related, not to his cramped neighbors, but to the actor on the stage, and this dis-tance is, if anything, too great. In the rush-hour crowd, by contrast, each member of the pushing throng is competing with his neighbors all the time. There is no escape to a spatial relation with a distant actor, only the pushing, shoving bodies all around.

Those of us who have to spend a great deal of time in crowded conditions become gradually better able to adjust, but no one can ever become completely immune to invasions of Personal Space. This is because they remain forever associated with either powerful hostile or equally powerful loving feelings. All through our childhood we will have been held to be loved and held to be hurt, and anyone who invades our Personal Space when we are adults is, in effect, threatening to extend his behavior into one of these two highly charged areas of human interaction. Even if his motives are clearly neither hostile nor sexual, we still find it hard to suppress our reactions to his close approach. Unfortunately, different countries have different ideas about exactly how close is close. It is easy enough to test your own "space reaction": when you are talking to someone in the street or in any open space, reach out with your arm and see where the nearest point on his body comes. If you hail from western Europe, you will find that he is at roughly fingertip distance from you. In other words, as you reach out, your fingertips will just about make contact with his shoulder. If you come from eastern Europe you will find you are standing at "wrist distance." If you come from the Mediterranean region you will find that you are much closer to your companion, at little more than "elbow distance."

Trouble begins when a member of one of these cultures meets and talks to one from another. Say a British diplomat meets an Italian or an Arab diplomat at an embassy function. They start talking in a friendly way, but soon the fingertips man begins to feel uneasy. Without knowing quite why, he starts to back away gently from his companion. The companion edges forward again. Each tries in his way to set up a Personal Space relationship that suits his own background. But it is impossible to do. Every time the Mediterranean diplomat advances to a distance that feels comfortable for him, the British diplomat feels threatened. Every time the Briton moves back, the other feels rejected. Attempts to adjust this situation often lead to a talking pair shifting slowly across a room, and many an embassy reception is dotted with western-Europe fingertip-distance men pinned against the walls by eager elbow-distance men. Until such differences are fully understood and allowances made, these minor differences in "body territories" will continue to act as an alienation factor which may interfere in a subtle way with diplomatic harmony and other forms of international transaction.

20   If there are distance problems when engaged in conversation, then there are clearly going to be even bigger difficulties where people must work privately in a shared space. Close proximity of others, pressing against the invisible boundaries of our personal body territory, makes it difficult to concentrate on nonsocial matters. Flat mates, students sharing a study, sailors in the cramped quarters of a ship, and office staff in crowded workplaces, all have to face this problem. They solve it by "cocooning." They use a variety of devices to shut themselves off from the others present. The best possible cocoon, of course, is a small private room—a den, a private office, a study, or a studio—which physically obscures the presence of other nearby territory owners. This is the ideal

solution for nonsocial work, but the space sharers cannot enjoy this luxury. Their cocooning must be symbolic. They may, in certain cases, be able to erect small physical barriers, such as screens and partitions, which give substance to their invisible Personal Space boundaries, but when this cannot be done, other means must be sought. One of these is the "favored object." Each space sharer develops a preference, repeatedly expressed until it becomes a fixed pattern, for a particular chair, or table, or alcove. Others come to respect this, and friction is reduced. This system is often formally arranged (this is my desk, that is yours), but even where it is not, favored places soon develop. Professor Smith has a favorite chair in the library. It is not formally his, but he always uses it and others avoid it. Seats around a mess room table, or a boardroom table, become almost personal property for specific individuals. Even in the home, father has his favorite chair for reading the newspaper or watching television. Another device is the blinkers posture. Just as a horse that overreacts to other horses and the distractions of the noisy race course is given a pair of blinkers to shield its eyes, so people studying privately in a public place put on pseudo-blinkers in the form of shielding hands. Resting their elbows on the table, they sit with their hands screening their eyes from the scene on either side.

A third method of reinforcing the body-territory is to use personal markers. Books, papers, and other personal belongings are scattered around the favored site to render it more privately owned in the eyes of companions. Spreading out one's belongings is a well-known trick in public transport situations, where a traveler tries to give the impression that seats next to him are taken. In many contexts carefully arranged personal markers can act as an effective territorial display, even in the absence of the territory owners. Experiments in a library revealed that placing a pile of magazines on the table in one seating position successfully reserved that place for an average of 77 minutes. If a sports-jacket was added, draped over the chair, then the "reservation effect" lasted for over two hours.

In these ways, we strengthen the defenses of our Personal Spaces, keeping out intruders with the minimum of open hostility. As with all territorial behavior, the object is to defend space with signals rather than with fists and at all three levels—the tribal, the family, and the personal—it is a remarkably efficient system of space-sharing. It does not always seem so, because newspapers and newscasts inevitably magnify the exceptions and dwell on those cases where the signals have failed and wars have broken out, gangs have fought, neighboring families have feuded, or colleagues have clashed, but for every territorial signal that has failed, there are millions of others that have not. They do not rate a mention in the news, but they nevertheless constitute a dominant feature of human society—the society of a remarkably territorial animal.

Additional Rhetorical Strategies

Analogy (paragraph 5); Process Analysis (paragraphs 6, 19); Cause and Effect (paragraphs 7, 15); Example (paragraphs 13, 20, 21); Definition (paragraph 15); Comparison and Contrast (paragraph 17).

Discussion Questions

1. Analyze the structure of Morris's essay. He names the three kinds of territory he will discuss, but he doesn't get started immediately on the task of discussing them. How do the intervening paragraphs function? Once he starts explicating each of the three categories, he occasionally includes subcategories. Make an outline, map, or other visual representation to capture and study the structure of this essay.
2. To what or whom are contemporary humans being compared in this essay? Where do the comparisons appear? How do they help the author to defamiliarize everyday occurrences, that is, allow us to see them as if with a fresh pair of eyes?
3. Defamiliarization is also achieved through the point of view of the narrator. How would you characterize Morris's stance or voice in this essay? How does his particular perspective help you to see the seemingly commonplace in a new light?

Essay Questions

1. Morris begins his essay with the claim that people will fight to defend their territory. Can you remember a time when you resisted someone from encroaching on your personal space? What about your "tribal" and family territory? Write an essay in which you define when physical resistance is called for to defend personal or other kinds of space. Alternatively, if you disagree with Morris, write an essay in which you explain why physical force is not justified in the defense of personal or group territory.
2. How would you react if you were in an elevator with a stranger who looked at you rather than at the elevator door? How would you react if you were riding in a nearly empty bus and a stranger sat down in the seat next to you? Have you ever broken the unstated rules about respecting space that Morris describes in his essay? If you have had any experiences along these lines, write an essay in which you describe the situation and the reactions of the people involved. See if you can classify these reactions—perhaps classification will help structure the form of your essay.

▲▼Three Kinds of Discipline

John Holt

John Holt (1923–1985) was born in New York City and attended Yale University. After serving in World War II, he became an elementary and later a high school teacher. His experiences in the private and public schools led to a lifelong interest in school reform. He wrote numerous books, including two bestsellers based on his teaching journals: How Children Fail *(1964) and* How Children Learn *(1967). His other books include* Freedom and Beyond *(1972), from which the essay below is taken,* Instead of Education: Helping People to Do Things Better *(1976), and* Teach Your Own *(1981). He was an early advocate of home schooling, and he founded the magazine* Growing Without Schooling *in 1977 as a resource for parents who pursued that option.*

A child, in growing up, may meet and learn from three different kinds of discipline. The first and most important is what we might call the Discipline of Nature or of Reality. When he is trying to do something real, if he does the wrong thing or doesn't do the right one, he doesn't get the result he wants. If he doesn't pile one block right on top of another, or tries to build on a slanting surface, his tower falls down. If he hits the wrong key, he hears the wrong note. If he doesn't hit the nail squarely on the head, it bends, and he has to pull it out and start with another. If he doesn't measure properly what he is trying to build, it won't open, close, fit, stand up, fly, float, whistle, or do whatever he wants it to do. If he closes his eyes when he swings, he doesn't hit the ball. A child meets this kind of discipline every time he tries to *do* something, which is why it is so important in school to give children more chances to do things, instead of just reading or listening to someone talk (or pretending to). This discipline is a good teacher. The learner never has to wait long for his answer, it usually comes quickly, often instantly. Also it is clear, and very often points toward the needed correction; from what happened he can not only see that what he did was wrong, but also why, and what he needs to do instead. Finally, and most important, the giver of the answer, call it Nature, is impersonal, impartial, and indifferent. She does not give opinions, or make judgments: she cannot be wheedled, bullied, or fooled; she does not get angry or disappointed; she does not praise or blame; she does not remember past failures or hold grudges; with her one always gets a fresh start, this time is the one that counts.

The next discipline we might call the Discipline of Culture, of Society, or What People Really Do. Man is a social, cultural animal. Children sense around them this culture, this network of agreements, customs, habits, and rules binding the adults together. They want to understand it and be a part of it. They watch very carefully what people around them are doing and want to do the same. They want to do right, unless they become convinced they can't do right. Thus children rarely misbehave seriously in church, but sit as quietly as they can. The example of all those grownups is contagious. Some mysterious ritual is going on, and children, who like rituals, want to be part of it. In the same way, the little children that I see at concerts or operas, though they may fidget a little, or perhaps take a nap now and then, rarely make any disturbance. With all those grownups sitting there, neither moving nor talking, it is the most natural thing in the world to imitate them. Children who live among adults who are habitually courteous to each other, and to them, will soon learn to be courteous. Children who live surrounded by people who speak a certain way will speak that way, however much we may try to tell them that speaking that way is bad or wrong.

The third discipline is the one most people mean when they speak of discipline—the Discipline of Superior Force, of sergeant to private, of "you do what I tell you or I'll make you wish you had." There is bound to be some of this in a child's life. Living as we do surrounded by things that can hurt children, or that children can hurt, we cannot avoid it. We can't afford to let a small child find out from experience the danger of playing in a busy street, or of fooling with the pots on the top of a stove, or of eating up the pills in the medicine cabinet. So, along with other precautions, we say to him, "Don't play in the street, or touch things on the stove, or go into the medicine cabinet, or I'll punish you." Between him and the danger too great for him to imagine we put a lesser danger, but one he can imagine and maybe therefore wants to avoid. He can have no idea of what it would be like to be hit by a car, but he can imagine being shouted at, or spanked, or sent to his room. He avoids these substitutes for the greater danger until he can understand it and avoid it for its own sake. But we ought to use this discipline only when it is necessary to protect the life, health, safety, or well-being of people or other living creatures, or to prevent destruction of things that people care about. We ought not to assume too long, as we usually do, that a child cannot understand the real nature of the danger from which we want to protect him. The sooner he avoids the danger, not to escape our punishment, but as a matter of good sense, the better. He can learn that faster than we think. In Mexico, for example, where people drive their cars with a good deal of spirit, I saw many children no older than five or four walking unattended on the streets. They understood about cars, they knew what to do. A child whose life is full of the threat and fear of punishment is locked into babyhood. There is no way for him to grow up, to learn to take responsibility for his life and acts. Most important of all, we should not assume that having to yield to the threat of our superior force is good for the child's character. It is never good for *anyone's* character. To bow to superior force makes us feel impotent and cowardly for not having had the strength or courage to resist. Worse, it makes us resentful and vengeful. We can hardly wait to make someone pay for our humiliation, yield to us as we were once made to yield. No, if we cannot always avoid using the Discipline of Superior Force, we should at least use it as seldom as we can.

There are places where all three disciplines overlap. Any very demanding human activity combines in it the disciplines of Superior Force, of Culture, and of Nature. The novice will be told, "Do it this way, never mind asking why, just do it that way, that is the way we always do it." But it probably *is* just the way they always do it, and usually for the very good reason that it is a way that has been found to work. Think, for example, of ballet training. The student in a class is told to do this exercise, or that; to stand so; to do this or that with his head, arms, shoulders, abdomen, hips, legs, feet. He is constantly corrected. There is no argument. But behind these seemingly autocratic demands by the teacher lie many decades of custom and tradition, and behind that, the necessities of dancing itself. You cannot make the moves of classical ballet unless over many years you have acquired, and renewed every day, the needed strength and suppleness in scores of muscles and joints. Nor can you do the difficult motions, making them look easy, unless you have learned hundreds of easier ones first. Dance teachers may not always agree on all the details of teaching these strengths and skills. But no novice could learn them all by himself. You could not go for a night or two to watch the ballet and then, without any other knowledge at all, teach yourself how to do it. In the same way, you would be unlikely to learn any complicated and difficult human activity without drawing heavily on the experience of those who know it better. But the point is that the authority of these experts or teachers stems from, grows out of their greater competence and experience, the fact that what they do *works,* not the fact that they happen to be the teacher and as such have the power to kick a student out of the class. And the further point is that children are always and everywhere attracted to that competence, and ready and eager to submit themselves to a discipline that grows out of it. We hear constantly that children will never do anything unless compelled to by bribes or threats. But in their private lives, or in extracurricular activities in school, in sports, music, drama, art, running a newspaper, and so on, they often submit themselves willingly and wholeheartedly to very intense disciplines, simply because they want to learn to do a given thing well. Our Little-Napoleon football coaches, of whom we have too many and hear far too much, blind us to the fact that millions of children work hard every year getting better at sports and games without coaches barking and yelling at them.

Additional Rhetorical Strategies

Argument/Persuasion (paragraph 3); Cause and Effect (paragraph 3); Example (throughout).

Discussion Questions

1. Holt jumps right into a discussion of the first kind of discipline in his second sentence, without explaining why he has ordered the three kinds in this particular sequence. Look at the overall organization of the essay and see if you can articulate a principle underlying Holt's decision to present his points in this order.
2. Who is Holt's implied audience for this piece? What kind of behavior does he hope to produce in his audience? What strategies does he use to convince his audience? Do any of his strategies mirror any of the three kinds of discipline?
3. Look at the kinds of examples Holt uses in each of his four paragraphs. How do they differ from one another? How is each example suited to the classification it is meant to exemplify? Explain how all three kinds of discipline are evident in the example of the ballet dancer.
4. What is Holt's most convincing argument against an overreliance on the Discipline of Superior Force? Can you construct a counterargument to his case against that form of discipline?
5. What are the limitations of the second type of discipline, the Discipline of Culture? To what extent do you agree that children want to be a part of the "network of agreements, customs, habits, and rules binding the adults together" (paragraph 2)? What are the best solutions in cases in which this principle proves to be inadequate?

Essay Questions

1. Write an essay on the same topic as Holt has chosen—discipline—but employ a different rhetorical strategy. You may want to compare and contrast two forms of discipline, argue for or against a certain approach to discipline, narrate an episode in which discipline figures prominently, and so on. Your essay should be informed by your own philosophy on discipline, which may of course differ from Holt's.
2. The people meting out the discipline in Holt's essay include parents, teachers, coaches, and sergeants, among others. How might the kinds of disciplines ideally used by each, and by others in a position to mete out discipline, differ? Where, for instance, would you draw the line between the kinds of discipline a child should rightfully expect to encounter at home and at school? Why? You might choose to write your essay in the form of guidelines for

teachers at a specific school (real or imaginary), or for drill sergeants, or for any other group for whom a clear set of guidelines would be useful.

Exploring Connections: Questions Linking the Thematic Pair

1. Both John Holt and Desmond Morris classify and describe patterns of human behavior, but their main purposes in doing so differ dramatically. How would you characterize the authorial intent of each of the authors in this pair? What effect does each hope to have on his intended audience?
2. Discuss the relative importance of nature and culture in each of the realms of behavior analyzed by Holt and by Morris. What role does nature play for each author, and to what extent does culture affect the behavior of the humans they discuss in their essays?

Comparison and Contrast

W
e use comparison to explore the similarities that seem to link subjects. Many of our everyday decisions are actually simple instances of comparison: what clothes to wear, what to eat, which brands to buy, whether we should write a letter, read a book, make a call, or watch television. We repeatedly—however subtly or even unconsciously—rely on comparison to map out our options and to help us get through the choices we make each day. So, too, more consequential decisions—where to go to college, what to do after graduation, how best to raise a family—are most often the result of thinking comparatively.

As a method of thinking and writing, comparison establishes similarities between subjects drawn from the same class or general category. Comparison is inseparable from contrast. We use contrast to highlight differences. When considering how any two things are similar, we undoubtedly will also discover more exactly how they are different. For example, the decision to buy a cassette tape deck is based, for most of us, on a good deal of comparative shopping. We check the prices of the leading brands and examine the performance features of the models we can afford: all the ones we are considering offer Dolby noise reduction and push-button controls for recording, playing, and ejecting a cassette. But one has memory, the other does not; one shuts off automatically, the other does not; and so on. When we think or write in comparative terms, we invariably touch upon contrasts.

As a structure for writing, comparison is often used in conjunction with other rhetorical strategies, particularly when writers want to establish underlying or supporting causes, narratives, or descriptions of points to be made later in the essay. But comparison can also be extremely effective when writers make it the principal mode of their exposition. It can help us to discover more salient points to make about a subject. For example, Bruce Catton's comparison of Generals Grant and Lee (see p. 286) adds another, and more personal, dimension to

our understanding of the Civil War and of "the strengths of two conflicting currents that, through them, had come into final collision."
Comparison is also a useful method for making abstract or remote subjects more concrete and readily accessible. By comparing everyday examples of "fear" and "anxiety," Karen Horney (see p. 294) makes her
analysis of neurosis more accessible to a wide range of readers. And,
perhaps most importantly, comparison helps us sort out experience.
For example, John Mack Faragher's comparison of pioneer diaries (see
p. 315) makes it easier to understand the different roles of men and
women in settling the American West. Training in discovering similarities and making distinctions—both qualitatively and quantitatively—
better prepares us to express convincingly our understanding of complex subjects.

Determining a Basis for Comparison

Comparison involves two basic operations: first, considering two categories of the same subject, and second, examining the common features
of those two categories. A diagram of these relationships may be
charted as follows:

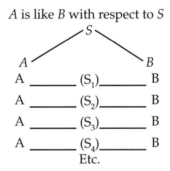

A is like B with respect to S

In this structure, A is the first component in the comparison, B the
second. S designates the subject about which an idea, a tentative conclusion, is developed. This controlling statement in turn determines
the bases (S_1–S_4) for establishing similarities (and differences) between A and B.

Now let us look at the diagram in operation. Suppose that you
want to write an essay about the relative merits of nuclear and solar energy. You've come to the conclusion that solar energy is the safest, most
abundant, and least expensive source of energy for the future. You rec-

ognize that advocates of nuclear energy might disagree, so you decide to organize your essay by comparing the two. Within that framework, the structure of the comparison might look something like this:

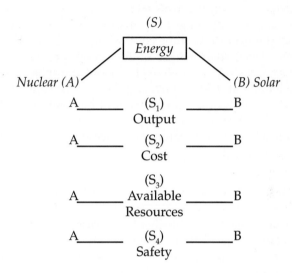

This diagram should make clear that the points to be compared must normally be stated in the same set of terms. They must be drawn from roughly similar categories of experience or levels of abstraction and share at least several characteristics. It would be appropriate to compare, for example, one city, restaurant, sport, college, or politician with another; but it would be inappropriate to compare, say, a dormitory room with a textbook. In the preceding diagram, nuclear and solar energy can be appropriately compared because they are both forms of energy. So too, "output," "cost," "available resources," and "safety" are suitable points to consider in nearly any proposed discussion of energy.

Selecting Points of Comparison

When writing essays of comparison, we ought to remember that the points of comparison are related to the subject but not necessarily to each other: each point can be thought of as a *discrete* factor in our comparison. In this diagram, for example, "output" has no necessary or logical connection to "cost," nor "available resources" to "safety."

Establishing a Main Idea

Yet all of these points are related by virtue of their contribution to your main idea about energy. The diagram also suggests just how careful you must be when developing an essay of comparison. Determining the relative emphasis of comparison and contrast depends on what you want to say about your subject. In this instance, you would be more likely to spend most of your time contrasting nuclear and solar energy, trying to prove that solar energy offers a more promising alternative source of future energy. It is your idea about the subject—your tentative conclusion about it—to which all points in the comparison (in this case "output," "safety," and so on) should be connected. Having this dominant idea control the quality, quantity, and order of the points to be compared will ensure greater coherence for the essay and keep it from being a meaningless *list*.

Planning an Essay of Comparison

The process of developing an essay of comparison begins when we settle on a specific subject, discovering exactly how it is like or unlike something else. An effective comparison establishes a clear purpose and a limited frame of reference. It would be unmanageable, for example, to compare capitalism with socialism. You ought to narrow the focus to, say, production, and then proceed to develop a specific, and hence manageable, idea about production in relation to the general concepts of capitalism and socialism. Let's say that you wanted to establish that production is far greater in a capitalist economy. Each of the points then selected for comparison should be related to this main idea: worker incentive, equipment, organization, markets, and so on. These points, in turn, should be unfolded fully and given sufficient attention.

Comparison can be a particularly strong method for shaping expository essays, especially when writers are confident that they know both sides of their subject well enough to draw an accurate, detailed, and balanced account of each side. Comparison is even more effective when writers present differences in what are normally regarded as similar subjects or when they uncover similarities that were not previously apparent. Consider, for example, the following opening paragraph from "A Report on the New Feminism," an essay by Ellen Willis, a music and film critic and an early and influential voice in the women's movement in America:

> Like the early feminist movement, which grew out of the campaign to end slavery, the present-day women's movement has been inspired and influenced by the black liberation struggle. The situation of women and blacks is similar in many ways. Just as blacks live in a

world defined by whites, women live in a world defined by males. (The generic term of human being is "man"; "woman" means "wife of man.") To be female or black is to be peculiar; whiteness and maleness are the norm. Newspapers do not have "men's pages," nor would anyone think of discussing the "man problem." Racial and sexual stereotypes also resemble each other: women, like blacks, are said to be childish, incapable of abstract reasoning, innately submissive, biologically suited for menial tasks, emotional, close to nature.

Willis's paragraph clearly highlights the principles of comparison and contrast. She quickly establishes a series of striking comparisons between the struggle for "black liberation" and the feminist movement. Notice, too, that Willis refines her comparison as she develops the paragraph: she first states that the situation of women and African Americans is similar, defines that similarity by saying that both women and African Americans are outsiders, then provides examples that prove her point. She also makes her paragraph much more interesting to read for her audience by varying her sentence structure. She presents background information, notes the norms against which women and African Americans are regarded as "peculiar," and illustrates the sexual and racial stereotypes that have contributed to the second-class status of both groups. Willis manages to develop these comparisons within seven sentences and to organize them into a brief but effective paragraph. Her paragraph also demonstrates that a writer's focus should always be on developing perceptive comparisons, avoiding those that are obvious or little more than clever.

Developing an Essay of Comparison: Three Methods

The organization of an essay of comparison depends on the complexity of the subject and the length needed to make a convincing presentation of both sides. There are three standard methods for organizing a comparison. The first, what we may call the *whole-subject-by-whole-subject* design, presents all of the features of one side (*A*), in relation to the subject (*S*), and then presents all of the features of the other side (*B*) in the same sequence. Suzanne Britt's comparison of neat and sloppy people (see p. 291) is a particularly vivid example of whole-subject-by-whole-subject comparison. Following this pattern, an outline of the essay comparing nuclear and solar energy would look like this:

Controlling Idea, or Thesis

   I. Introduction
  II. Nuclear Energy
     A. Output
     B. Cost
     C. Available Resources

D. Safety
III. Solar Energy
    A. Output
    B. Cost
    C. Available Resources
    D. Safety
IV. Summary

This organization is best suited to relatively short essays, ones in which readers will have no difficulty remembering each of the points about nuclear energy until each is compared with solar power. In such instances, the writer is concerned more with the overall comparative effect than with any one of the details involved. This whole-subject-by-whole-subject design offers the writer a simple, easily handled structure for organizing points of comparison that are *limited in number and complexity.* One of the risks of the design, however, is that the writer will produce what are in effect separate essays—one on nuclear energy, the other on solar energy. Yet the writer may minimize this possibility by consistently focusing on the specific points of comparison (S_1–S_4) rather than on the general terms *nuclear* and *solar* (*A* and *B*).

For longer, more complex essays, writers normally adapt for their particular purpose the *point-by-point comparison.* Using the same example, the outline of a point-by-point comparison would look like this:

Controlling Idea, or Thesis

   I. Introduction
  II. Output
    A. Nuclear Energy
    B. Solar Energy
III. Cost
    A. Nuclear Energy
    B. Solar Energy
IV. Available Resources
    A. Nuclear Energy
    B. Solar Energy
  V. Safety
    A. Nuclear Energy
    B. Solar Energy
VI. Summary

Depending on the complexity of the issues involved, each of the points of comparison could be unfolded in either a single paragraph or a series of paragraphs. And the amount of space given to each of the two sides within each point should be roughly the same. One advantage of this method is that it allows writers to make any number of finely drawn connections between subjects. (See, for example, E. J. Dionne, Jr's essay on "How Liberals and Conservatives are Failing America," p. 297.)

A third possible method of organization—the *sentence-by-sentence* comparison—occurs less frequently in writing. It usually appears in isolated paragraphs, very brief essays, or in the especially intense circumstances of an examination, when time restraints may demand that we restrict ourselves to a sentence-by-sentence comparison. This method of organizing a comparison adapts the basic procedures of a point-by-point comparison to the level of a limited series of sentences.

As we have seen, comparison and contrast can organize our thinking in writing—from single paragraphs to long expository essays. Long expository essays frequently draw on two or more forms of comparison. (See, for example, Bruce Catton's essay on p. 286.) Whatever the length or the particular method of comparison we are working with, we should remember that our essay will have far greater potential for succeeding if we organize carefully the sequence of points to be compared. In essays of comparison, the final point commands the most emphasis.

Comparison helps us to write more imaginatively and authoritatively. Discovering and developing similarities or differences is one way, for example, to simplify complex thoughts and make them more accessible to ourselves and others. Yet, in addition to what it literally says, a well-formulated comparison reinforces the reader's sense that we are particularly knowledgeable and in command of both our subject and our idea about it. To develop a comparison is to demonstrate that we know and can write about *A*; that we know and can write about *B*; that we know and can write about the precise relationship that exists between *A* and *B*; and that we can marshal this knowledge in support of a distinctive idea about the subject in question. In general, a comparison or contrast structure for an essay helps us establish and maintain control over a series of points throughout the process of composition— a control that increases the confidence of both writers and readers of expository prose.

Grant and Lee: A Study in Contrasts

Bruce Catton

Bruce Catton (1899–1978) attended Oberlin College until his studies were interrupted by service in World War I. Afterwards, he worked as a reporter for various newspapers, and as a speechwriter and information director for various government agencies, including the War Production Board. He edited the American Heritage *magazine from 1954 until his death in 1978. Catton became the foremost authority on the Civil War; his books on the subject include* Mr. Lincoln's Army *(1951);* A Stillness at Appomattox *(1953), for which he won both a Pulitzer Prize and a National Book Award; and* Gettysburg: The Final Fury *(1974). President Gerald Ford awarded him a Medal of Freedom for his life's accomplishments.*

The following essay, a model of the comparison and contrast form, was first published in a collection of essays titled The American Story *(1956).*

W hen Ulysses S. Grant and Robert E. Lee met in the parlor of a modest house at Appomattox Court House, Virginia, on April 9, 1865, to work out the terms for the surrender of Lee's Army of Northern Virginia, a great chapter in American life came to a close, and a great new chapter began.

These men were bringing the Civil War to its virtual finish. To be sure, other armies had yet to surrender, and for a few days the fugitive Confederate government would struggle desperately and vainly, trying to find some way to go on living now that its chief support was gone. But in effect it was all over when Grant and Lee signed the papers. And the little room where they wrote out the terms was the scene of one of the poignant, dramatic contrasts in American history.

They were two strong men, these oddly different generals, and they represented the strengths of two conflicting currents that, through them, had come into final collision.

Back of Robert E. Lee was the notion that the old aristocratic concept might somehow survive and be dominant in American life.

5 Lee was tidewater Virginia, and in his background were family, culture, and tradition . . . the age of chivalry transplanted to a New World which was making its own legends and its own myths. He embodied a way of life that had come down through the age of knighthood and the English country squire. America was a land that was beginning all over again, dedicated to nothing much more complicated than the rather hazy belief that all men had equal rights and should have an equal chance in the world. In such a land Lee stood for the feeling that it was somehow of advantage to human society to have a pronounced inequality in the social structure. There should be a leisure class, backed by ownership of land; in turn, society itself should be

keyed to the land as the chief source of wealth and influence. It would bring forth (according to this ideal) a class of men with a strong sense of obligation to the community; men who lived not to gain advantage for themselves, but to meet the solemn obligations which had been laid on them by the very fact that they were privileged. From them the country would get its leadership; to them it could look for the higher values—of thought, of conduct, of personal deportment—to give it strength and virtue.

Lee embodied the noblest elements of this aristocratic ideal. Through him, the landed nobility justified itself. For four years, the Southern states had fought a desperate war to uphold the ideals for which Lee stood. In the end, it almost seemed as if the Confederacy fought for Lee; as if he himself was the Confederacy . . . the best thing that the way of life for which the Confederacy stood could ever have to offer. He had passed into legend before Appomattox. Thousands of tired, underfed, poorly clothed Confederate soldiers, long since past the simple enthusiasm of the early days of the struggle, somehow considered Lee the symbol of everything for which they had been willing to die. But they could not quite put this feeling into words. If the Lost Cause, sanctified by so much heroism and so many deaths, had a living justification, its justification was General Lee.

Grant, the son of a tanner on the Western frontier, was everything Lee was not. He had come up the hard way and embodied nothing in particular except the eternal toughness and sinewy fiber of the men who grew up beyond the mountains. He was one of a body of men who owed reverence and obeisance to no one, who were self-reliant to a fault, who cared hardly anything for the past but who had a sharp eye for the future.

These frontier men were the precise opposites of the tidewater aristocrats. Back of them, in the great surge that had taken people over the Alleghenies and into the opening Western country, there was a deep, implicit dissatisfaction with a past that had settled into grooves. They stood for democracy, not from any reasoned conclusion about the proper ordering of human society, but simply because they had grown up in the middle of democracy and knew how it worked. Their society might have privileges, but they would be privileges each man had won for himself. Forms and patterns meant nothing. No man was born to anything, except perhaps to a chance to show how far he could rise. Life was competition.

Yet along with this feeling had come a deep sense of belonging to a national community. The Westerner who developed a farm, opened a shop, or set up in business as a trader, could hope to prosper only as his own community prospered—and his community ran from the Atlantic to the Pacific and from Canada down to Mexico. If the land was settled, with towns and highways and accessible markets, he could better himself. He saw his fate in terms of the nation's own destiny. As its horizons expanded, so did his. He had, in other words, an acute dollars-and-cents stake in the continued growth and development of his country.

10   And that, perhaps, is where the contrast between Grant and Lee becomes most striking. The Virginia aristocrat, inevitably, saw himself in relation to his own region. He lived in a static society which could endure almost anything except change. Instinctively, his first loyalty would go to the locality in which that society existed. He would fight to the limit of endurance to defend it, because in defending it he was defending everything that gave his own life its deepest meaning.

The Westerner, on the other hand, would fight with an equal tenacity for the broader concept of society. He fought so because everything he lived by was tied to growth, expansion, and a constantly widening horizon. What he lived by would survive or fall with the nation itself. He could not possibly stand by unmoved in the face of an attempt to destroy the Union. He would combat it with everything he had, because he could only see it as an effort to cut the ground out from under his feet.

So Grant and Lee were in complete contrast, representing two diametrically opposed elements in American life. Grant was the modern man emerging; beyond him, ready to come on the stage, was the great age of steel and machinery, of crowded cities and a restless burgeoning vitality. Lee might have ridden down from the old age of chivalry, lance in hand, silken banner fluttering over his head. Each man was the perfect champion of his cause, drawing both his strengths and his weaknesses from the people he led.

Yet it was not all contrast, after all. Different as they were—in background, in personality, in underlying aspiration—these two great soldiers had much in common. Under everything else, they were marvelous fighters. Furthermore, their fighting qualities were really very much alike.

Each man had, to begin with, the great virtue of utter tenacity and fidelity. Grant fought his way down the Mississippi Valley in spite of acute personal discouragement and profound military handicaps. Lee hung on in the trenches at Petersburg after hope itself had died. In each man there was an indomitable quality . . . the born fighter's refusal to give up as long as he can still remain on his feet and lift his two fists.

15   Daring and resourcefulness they had, too; the ability to think faster and move faster than the enemy. These were the qualities which gave Lee the dazzling campaigns of Second Manassas and Chancellorsville and won Vicksburg for Grant.

Lastly, and perhaps greatest of all, there was the ability, at the end, to turn quickly from war to peace once the fighting was over. Out of the way these two men behaved at Appomattox came the possibility of a peace of reconciliation. It was a possibility not wholly realized, in the years to come, but which did, in the end, help the two sections to become one nation again . . . after a war whose bitterness might have seemed to make such a reunion wholly impossible. No part of either man's life became him more than the part he played in this brief meeting in the McLean house at Appomattox. Their behavior there put all succeeding generations of Americans in their debt. Two great Americans, Grant and Lee—very different, yet under everything very much alike. Their encounter at Appomattox was one of the great moments of American history.

Additional Rhetorical Strategies

Definition (paragraphs 5, 8); Analogy (paragraph 12).

Discussion Questions

1. Examine the structure of Catton's essay. How much space does he devote to comparing the two historical figures, and how much to contrasting them? When do the two figures appear in the same paragraph, and when do they have one or more paragraphs devoted wholly to them? What is the effect of each of these decisions, and of the decision to treat the contrasts before the comparisons? Which of Catton's main points are reinforced by his structural choices, and in what specific ways?

2. What is Catton's purpose in contrasting Grant and Lee? His purpose in comparing them? Are both equally relevant to his larger points about American history? How?

3. How does Catton achieve a sense of even-handedness in this essay? Even though history resulted in winners and losers, how does Catton give them both equal and fair treatment in this essay? What were the motives and ideals of each man (and his soldiers)? Did either side have the monopoly on right thinking or goodwill?

4. Are there points in this essay that you find disputable, or observations that you might have interpreted differently? For instance, do you agree with Catton's inference that "thousands of tired, underfed, poorly clothed Confederate soldiers" shared the same aristocratic ideals as Lee, even though they would never be aristocrats (paragraph 6)? What other motives might they have had? Also, do you agree with Catton's final comparison, when he lauds their mutual ability to "turn quickly from war to peace once the fighting was over" (paragraph 16), especially given their "refusal to give up," mentioned in paragraph 14? How might you explain this seeming inconsistency?

Essay Questions

1. Write an essay in which you compare and contrast two people you know, or two fictional characters. What broader repercussions or implications can you draw from the exercise of comparing and contrasting them?

2. Although Grant and Lee lived and fought in the same time period—the Civil War—and the same general geographical area—North America—the ways of life they were defending differed both temporally and spatially. Write an essay in which you explore the differences between the two war heroes in terms of the spatial and temporal orientations that Catton mentions or alludes to in his essay.

Neat People versus Sloppy People

Suzanne Britt

Suzanne Britt is a freelance writer and editor who also teaches writing. Her essays have appeared in the Baltimore Sun, Newsday, *the* New York Times, *and* Newsweek, *among other periodicals. Her essays can also be found in* Show and Tell *and* Skinny People Are Dull and Crunchy Like Carrots, *both published in 1982. Britt received her education at Salem College and Washington University, and she has taught writing at Meredith College and at the Divinity School at Duke University. She has also published a textbook for writing classes called* A Writer's Rhetoric *(1988).*

I've finally figured out the difference between neat people and sloppy people. The distinction is, as always, moral. Neat people are lazier and meaner than sloppy people.

Sloppy people, you see, are not really sloppy. Their sloppiness is merely the unfortunate consequence of their extreme moral rectitude. Sloppy people carry in their mind's eye a heavenly vision, a precise plan, that is so stupendous, so perfect, it can't be achieved in this world or the next.

Sloppy people live in Never-Never Land. Someday is their métier. Someday they are planning to alphabetize all their books and set up home catalogs. Someday they will go through their wardrobes and mark certain items for tentative mending and certain items for passing on to relatives of similar shape and size. Someday sloppy people will make family scrapbooks into which they will put newspaper clippings, postcards, locks of hair, and the dried corsage from their senior prom. Someday they will file everything on the surface of their desks, including the cash receipts from coffee purchases at the snack shop. Someday they will sit down and read all the back issues of the *New Yorker*.

For all these noble reasons and more, sloppy people never get neat. They aim too high and wide. They save everything, planning someday to file, order, and straighten out the world. But while these ambitious plans take clearer and clearer shape in their heads, the books spill from the shelves onto the floor, the clothes pile up in the hamper and closet, the family mementos accumulate in every drawer, the surface of the desk is buried under mounds of paper and the unread magazines threaten to reach the ceiling.

Sloppy people can't bear to part with anything. They give loving 5 attention to every detail. When sloppy people say they're going to tackle the surface of a desk, they really mean it. Not a paper will go unturned; not a rubber band will go unboxed. Four hours or two weeks into the excavation, the desk looks exactly the same, primarily because the sloppy person is meticulously creating new piles of papers with new headings and scrupulously stopping to read all the old book catalogs before he throws them away. A neat person would just bull-doze the desk.

Neat people are bums and clods at heart. They have cavalier atti-tudes toward possessions, including family heirlooms. Everything is just another dust-catcher to them. If anything collects dust, it's got to go and that's that. Neat people will toy with the idea of throwing the chil-dren out of the house just to cut down on the clutter.

Neat people don't care about process. They like results. What they want to do is get the whole thing over with so they can sit down and watch the rasslin' on TV. Neat people operate on two unvarying princi-ples: Never handle any item twice, and throw everything away.

The only thing messy in a neat person's house is the trash can. The minute something comes to a neat person's hand, he will look at it, try to decide if it has immediate use and, finding none, throw it in the trash.

Neat people are especially vicious with mail. They never go through their mail unless they are standing directly over a trash can. If the trash can is beside the mailbox, even better. All ads, catalogs, pleas for charitable contributions, church bulletins and money-saving coupons go straight into the trash can without being opened. All letters from home, postcards from Europe, bills and paychecks are opened, immediately responded to, then dropped in the trash can. Neat people keep their receipts only for tax purposes. That's it. No sentimental sal-vaging of birthday cards or the last letter a dying relative ever wrote. Into the trash it goes.

10   Neat people place neatness above everything, even economics. They are incredibly wasteful. Neat people throw away several toys every time they walk through the den. I knew a neat person once who threw away a perfectly good dish drainer because it had mold on it. The drainer was too much trouble to wash. And neat people sell their furniture when they move. They will sell a La-Z-Boy recliner while you are reclining in it.

Neat people are no good to borrow from. Neat people buy every-thing in expensive little single portions. They get their flour and sugar in two-pound bags. They wouldn't consider clipping a coupon, saving a leftover, reusing plastic nondairy whipped cream containers or rinsing off tin foil and draping it over the unmoldy dish drainer. You can never borrow a neat person's newspaper to see what's playing at the movies. Neat people have the paper all wadded up and in the trash by 7:05 AM.

Neat people cut a clean swath through the organic as well as the in-organic world. People, animals, and things are all one to them. They are so insensitive. After they've finished with the pantry, the medicine cab-inet, and the attic, they will throw out the red geranium (too many leaves), sell the dog (too many fleas), and send the children off to boarding school (too many scuff-marks on the hardwood floors).

Additional Rhetorical Strategies

Cause and Effect (paragraph 4); Example (throughout).

Discussion Questions

1. How would you characterize Britt's purpose in writing this essay? Given that purpose, does it matter that the essay lacks a formal conclusion? If you were to write a conclusion, in keeping with the tone and content of the essay as it now stands, how would it go?

2. Britt intentionally works against her readers' expectations in this essay: most people upon reading the title would expect to find an essay criticizing sloppy people for being inconsiderate. How effective is this strategy? Does she end up winning you over to a point of view you would not have considered before reading her essay? Or does the lesson for the reader have less to do with neatness and sloppiness *per se* than with a larger point, and if so, how might you express that point?

3. Pick out phrases and sentences that you found humorous and then analyze the source of the humor. Most of the time when we read or hear something funny, we just laugh and feel no compulsion to take the joke apart to see how it works, but humor actually is susceptible to analysis, and people who would like to add humor to their writing would do well to analyze the strategies used by successful humorists.

4. Where and to what effect does Britt use generalizations? What are the benefits and risks of generalizing? Where does she use very concrete details for examples or as evidence? What are the benefits and risks of piling on the details? Analyze the mixture of generalization and specificity that Britt uses in this essay. What is the effect of this mixture?

Essay Questions

1. Choose two categories of human beings—for example, liberals and conservatives, shy people and outgoing people, givers and takers . . . the possibilities are limited only by your observation and imagination. Write an essay comparing and contrasting the two types. You may choose to present only the contrasting features, as Britt does, or to present both, depending on the demands of your chosen subject matter. You may choose either a light or a serious tone, or anything in between.

2. Write an essay in which your thesis is the opposite from what the average person would expect. Support your thesis by taking a fresh—even paradoxical—perspective on the topic, as Britt does when she claims that "Neat people are lazier and meaner than sloppy people."

Fear and Anxiety

Karen Horney

*Born in Germany and trained as a Freudian psychoanalyst, **Karen Horney** (1885–1952) grew critical of Freud's view of women and skeptical of his contention that sexual and aggressive instincts are the motivating forces in human beings. She became an outspoken doubter at a time when the Freudian faithful were particularly intolerant of heretics. At a meeting in New York City, Karen Horney was interrogated about her differences with Freud and judged unqualified to teach psychoanalysis. The following week she and 20 of her supporters founded a rival institute of psychological study, which continues to flourish.*

In the following excerpt from her famous study, The Neurotic Personality of Our Time *(1937), she carefully examines the differences between two closely related words, fear and anxiety, words of special importance for her work with neurotic patients and for her study of neurosis.*

When a mother is afraid that her child will die when it has only a pimple or a slight cold we speak of anxiety; but if she is afraid when the child has a serious illness we call her reaction fear. If someone is afraid whenever he stands on a height or when he has to discuss a topic he knows well, we call his reaction anxiety; if someone is afraid when he loses his way high up in the mountains during a heavy thunderstorm we would speak of fear. Thus far we should have a simple and neat distinction: fear is a reaction that is proportionate to the danger one has to face, whereas anxiety is a disproportionate reaction to danger, or even a reaction to imaginary danger.

This distinction has one flaw, however, which is that the decision as to whether the reaction is proportionate depends on the average knowledge existing in the particular culture. But even if that knowledge proclaims a certain attitude to be unfounded, a neurotic will find no difficulty in giving his action a rational foundation. In fact, one might get into hopeless arguments if one told a patient that his dread of being attacked by some raving lunatic is neurotic anxiety. He would point out that his fear is realistic and would refer to occurrences of the kind he fears. The primitive would be similarly stubborn if one considered certain of his fear reactions disproportionate to the actual danger. For instance, a primitive man in a tribe which has taboos on eating certain animals is mortally frightened if by any chance he has eaten the tabooed meat. As an outside observer you would call this a disproportionate reaction, in fact an entirely unwarranted one. But knowing the tribe's beliefs concerning forbidden meat you would have to realize that the situation represents a real danger to the man, danger that the hunting or fishing grounds may be spoiled or danger of contracting an illness.

There is a difference, however, between the anxiety we find in primitives and the anxiety we consider neurotic in our culture. The content of neurotic anxiety, unlike that of the primitive, does not conform with commonly held opinions. In both the impression of a disproportionate reaction vanishes once the meaning of the anxiety is understood. There are persons, for example, who have a perpetual anxiety about dying; on the other hand, because of their sufferings they have a secret wish to die. Their various fears of death, combined with their wishful thinking with regard to death, create a strong apprehension of imminent danger. If one knows all these factors one cannot help but call their anxiety about dying an adequate reaction. Another, simplified example is seen in persons who become terrified when they find themselves near a precipice or a high window or on a high bridge. Here again, from without, the fear reaction seems to be disproportionate. But such a situation may present to them, or stir up in them, a conflict between the wish to live and the temptation for some reason or another to jump down from the heights. It is this conflict that may result in anxiety.

All these considerations suggest a change in the definition. Fear and anxiety are both proportionate reactions to danger, but in the case of fear the danger is a transparent, objective one and in the case of anxiety it is hidden and subjective. That is, the intensity of the anxiety is proportionate to the meaning the situation has for the person concerned, and the reasons why he is thus anxious are essentially unknown to him.

The practical implication of the distinction between fear and anxiety is that the attempt to argue a neurotic out of his anxiety—the method of persuasion—is useless. His anxiety concerns not the situation as it stands actually in reality, but the situation as it appears to him. The therapeutic task, therefore, can be only that of finding out the meaning certain situations have for him.

Additional Rhetorical Strategies

Definition (paragraphs 1, 4); Example (throughout).

Discussion Questions

1. Since Horney later qualifies the clear distinction between fear and anxiety that she makes in paragraph 1, why does she offer the distinction in the first place? How is it necessary to her revised definition? How might her final definition have suffered if she had offered it at the outset instead?
2. In paragraph 2, Horney explains that "the decision as to whether the reaction is proportionate depends on the average knowledge

existing in the particular culture." Her example is taken from what she calls a "primitive" culture. Can you think of any examples from your own culture? Since it is hard to step outside your own culture, you might consider examples from an earlier era in American history, or in the history of your country of origin.

3. Horney contrasts anxiety among primitives with the anxiety of neurotics in our own culture (paragraph 3). Why does she persist in labeling the primitive's reaction "anxiety," even though by her own earlier definition, it is fear?

4. After reading this selection, do you think some of your anxieties may actually be fears? Do you think that some of what you thought were fears are actually anxieties? Why? What conflicts might be behind some of your anxieties?

Essay Questions

1. Write an essay in which you compare and contrast two different but frequently related terms, such as courage and bravery, cowardice and caution, love and lust, loyalty and servility. Use examples to make all distinctions clear and to keep your reader aware of the complexities of your chosen terms.

2. Horney's primary audience seems to be the psychiatric community. Write an essay on fear and anxiety that is aimed at a different specific audience. Some options might include mountain climbers, soldiers, agoraphobic people, and so on.

How Liberals and Conservatives Are Failing America

E. J. Dionne, Jr.

Eugene J. Dionne, Jr. (b. 1952) combines the academic credentials of a Ph.D. with the experience of a career journalist. Previously a reporter for the New York Times, *he is presently employed by the* Washington Post. *He has also contributed to several periodicals, including* Commonweal, *the* New York Times Book Review, *and the* Utne Reader. *His book* Why Americans Hate Politics: The Death of the Democratic Process *(1992) won the* Los Angeles Times *Book Prize in the current interest category. The following essay is excerpted from the introduction to that book.*

At the very moment when democracy is blossoming in Eastern Europe, it is decaying in the United States. Over the last three decades, the faith of the American people in their democratic institutions has declined, and Americans have begun to doubt their ability to improve the world through politics. After two centuries in which the United States stood proudly as an example of what an engaged citizenry could accomplish through public life, Americans view politics with boredom and detachment. For most of us, politics is increasingly abstract, a spectator sport barely worth watching. Election campaigns generate less excitement than ever and are dominated by television commercials, direct mailing, polling, and other approaches that treat individual voters not as citizens deciding their nation's fate, but as mere collections of impulses to be stroked and soothed.

True, we still praise democracy incessantly and recommend democracy to the world. But at home, we do little to promote the virtues that self-government requires or to encourage citizens to believe that public engagement is worth the time. Our system has become one long-running advertisement against self-government. For many years, we have been running down the public sector and public life. Voters doubt that elections give them any real control over what the government does, and half of them don't bother to cast ballots.

Because of our flight from public life, our common citizenship no longer fosters a sense of community or common purpose. Social gaps, notably the divide between blacks and whites, grow wider. The very language and music heard in the inner city is increasingly estranged from the words and melodies of the affluent suburbs. We have less and less to do with each other, meaning that we feel few obligations to each other and are less and less inclined to vindicate each other's rights.

The abandonment of public life has created a political void that is increasingly filled by the politics of attack and by issues that seem unimportant or contrived. In 1988, George Bush made the pollution of Boston Harbor and the furloughing of a convicted murderer central issues in his campaign for the presidency. Neither Boston Harbor nor prison furloughs mattered once Bush took office.[1] The issues that will matter most in the nineties—the challenges to America's standard of living from global competition, the dangers in the Middle East, the impending collapse of Communist power—were hardly discussed at all in 1988.

5   The 1988 campaign was just a sign of things to come. In the 1990s, politicians themselves seem as fed up with the process as even their angriest constituents. "We're getting better at symbolism," Sen. Pete Domenici, a New Mexico Republican, told *Washington Post* reporter Helen Dewar in late 1991. "You need more symbols when you don't have much substance." Sen. Joseph R. Biden, Jr., a Delaware Democrat, spoke with equal candor about the tyranny of symbolic politics. "You have to answer symbols," Biden said, "with symbols." Thus did politicians claim that a federal crime bill was battling street violence by subjecting murderers of federal egg inspectors, meat inspectors, and horse inspectors to the death penalty. Did the egg inspectors, let alone anyone else in the country, suddenly feel safe? The 1991 confrontation between Justice Clarence Thomas and Prof. Anita Hill transfixed the nation. It also left partisans on both sides of the battle lines furious and frustrated, and average citizens aghast.

We are even uncertain about the meaning of America's triumph in the Cold War. We worry that the end of the Cold War will mean a diminished role for the United States in world history. Economic power is passing not only to Japan but also to a new Europe, which is finally recovering from the self-inflicted wounds of two world wars. The categories that have dominated our thinking for so long are utterly irrelevant to the new world we face. The international alliance that President Bush assembled against Iraq would have been inconceivable just two years earlier. Indeed, the very weapons we used against Saddam's forces were built for a different conflict in a different place against a different enemy—a conflict we happily avoided. And much of the debate over Iraq was shaped by the Vietnam conflict, as if the use of American force always means the same thing in every part of the world and against every adversary.

Most of the problems of our political life can be traced to the failure of the dominant ideologies of American politics, liberalism and conservatism. My central argument . . . is that liberalism and conservatism

---

[1]George Bush highlighted issues that reflected poorly on the leadership of his opponent Michael Dukakis, who was governor of Massachusetts at the time. Many commentators felt that the Bush campaign catered to public fear rather than providing a fair discussion of policy issues—Eds.

are framing political issues as a series of false choices. Wracked by con-tradiction and responsive mainly to the needs of their various con-stituencies, liberalism and conservatism *prevent* the nation from settling the questions that most trouble it. On issue after issue, there is consen-sus on where the country should move or at least on what we should be arguing about; liberalism and conservativism make it impossible for that consensus to express itself.

To blame our problems on the failure of "ideologies" would seem a convenient way to avoid attaching responsibility to individuals. But to hold ideologies responsible for our troubles is, in fact, to place a burden on those who live by them and formulate them. It is also a way of say-ing that ideas matter, and that ideas, badly formulated, interpreted, and used, can lead us astray. We are suffering from a false polarization in our politics, in which liberals and conservatives keep arguing about the same things when the country wants to move on.

The cause of this false polarization is the cultural civil war that broke out in the 1960s. Just as the Civil War dominated American polit-ical life for decades after it ended, so is the cultural civil war of the 1960s, with all its tensions and contradictions, shaping our politics today. We are still trapped in the 1960s.

The country still faces three major sets of questions left over from[10] the old cultural battles: Civil rights and the full integration of blacks into the country's political and economic life; the revolution in values involving feminism and changed attitudes toward child-rearing and sexuality; and the ongoing debate over the meaning of the Vietnam War, which is less a fight over whether it was right to do battle in that Southeast Asian country than an argument over how Americans see their nation, its leaders, and its role in the world.

It is easy to understand why conservatives would like the cultural civil war to continue. It was the *Kulturkampf* of the 1960s that made them so powerful in our political life.[2] Conservatives were able to destroy the dominant New Deal coalition by using cultural and social issues—race, the family, "permissiveness," crime—to split New Deal constituencies. The cultural issues, especially race, allowed the conservatives who took control of the Republican Party to win over what had been the most loy-ally Democratic group in the nation, white Southerners, and to peel off millions of votes among industrial workers and other whites of modest incomes.

The new conservative majority that has dominated presidential pol-itics since 1968 is inherently unstable, since it unites upper-income

---

[2]*Kulturkampf* is a German word meaning "cultural struggle" that has come into English to designate political conflict waged in the cultural arena—Eds.

groups whose main interest is in smaller government and lower taxes, and middle-to-lower income groups, who are culturally conservative but still support most of the New Deal and a lot of the Great Society. The lower-income wing of the conservative coalition has tended to vote Republican for President, to express its cultural values, but Democratic for Congress, to protect its economic interests. Conservative politicians are uneasy about settling the cultural civil war because they fear that doing so would push their newfound supporters among the less well-to-do back toward the Democrats in presidential contests.

The broad political interests of liberals lie in settling the cultural civil war, but many liberals have an interest in seeing it continue. The politics of the 1960s shifted the balance of power within the liberal coalition away from working-class and lower-middle-class voters, whose main concerns were economic, and toward upper-middle-class reformers mainly interested in cultural issues and foreign policy. Increasingly, liberalism is defined not by its support for energetic government intervention in the economy, but by its openness to cultural change and its opposition to American intervention abroad. The rise of the cultural issues made the upper-middle-class reformers the dominant voices within American liberalism. The reformers, no less than the conservatives, have a continuing interest in seeing the cultural civil war continue.

Indeed, what is striking about political events in the 1960s is that they allowed both of the nation's dominant ideologies, and both parties, to become vehicles for upper-middle-class interests. Both the Goldwater campaign and the antiwar forces associated with George McGovern's candidacy were movements of the upper middle class imbued with a moral (or in the eyes of their critics, moralistic) vision.[3] These constituencies were *not* primarily concerned with the political issues that matter to less well-to-do voters—notably the performance of the nation's economy, the distribution of economic benefits, the availability of health care, and the efficacy of the most basic institutions of government, including schools, roads, and the criminal justice system. While upper-middle-class reformers, left and right, argued about morality, anticommunism, imperialism, and abstract rights, a large chunk of the electorate was confined to the sidelines, wondering why the nation's political discussion had become so distant from their concerns. And as the 1980s became the 1990s, many who had become accustomed to middle-class living standards suddenly found their own well-being threatened and worried about how their children would manage to make their way in an increasingly competitive world economy.

---

[3]Barry Goldwater ran for president as the Republican nominee in 1964; George McGovern ran for president as the Democratic nominee in 1972—Eds.

By continuing to live in the 1960s, conservatives and liberals have distorted their own doctrines and refused to face up to the contradictions within their creeds. Both sides constantly invoke individual "rights," then criticize each other for evading issues involving individual and collective responsibility. Each side claims to have a communitarian vision but backs away from community whenever its demands come into conflict with one of its cherished doctrines.

Conservatives claim to be the true communitarians because of their support for the values of "family, work, and neighborhood." Unlike liberals, conservatives are willing to assert that "community norms" should prevail on such matters as sex, pornography, and the education of children. Yet the typical conservative is unwilling to defend the interests of traditional community whenever its needs come into conflict with those of the free market. If shutting down a plant throws thousands in a particular community out of work, conservatives usually defend this assault on "family, work, and neighborhood" in the name of efficiency. Many of the things conservatives bemoan about modern society—a preference for short-term gratification over long-term commitment, the love of things instead of values, a flight from responsibility toward selfishness—result at least in part from the workings of the very economic system that conservatives feel so bound to defend. For conservatives, it is much easier to ignore this dilemma and blame "permissiveness" on "big government" or "the liberals."

The liberals often make that easy. Liberals tout themselves as the real defenders of community. They speak constantly about having us share each other's burdens. Yet when the talk moves from economic issues to culture or personal morality, liberals fall strangely mute. Liberals are uncomfortable with the idea that a virtuous community depends on virtuous individuals. Liberals defend the welfare state, but are uneasy when asked what moral values the welfare state should promote—as if billions of federal dollars can be spent in a "value-free" way. Liberals rightly defend the interests of children who are born into poverty through no choice of their own. Yet when conservatives suggest that society has a vital interest in how the parents of these poor children behave, many liberals accuse the conservatives of "blaming the victim." When conservatives suggest that changing teenage attitudes toward premarital sex might reduce teen pregnancy, many liberals end the conversation by accusing the conservatives of being "prudes" or "out of touch."

Not all conservatives and liberals fall into the neat categories I have just described, and the questions each side raises about the other's proposals are often legitimate. It often *is* more efficient and socially beneficial to shut down a loss-making plant. It *is* unfair to condemn the poor for sexual practices that we celebrate when those engaging in them live in Hollywood or make millions in business.

way in which liberals and conservatives approach the community is a good example of what I mean by false truth, America's cultural values are a rich and not necessarily ctory mix of liberal instincts and conservative values. Polls own intuitions) suggest that Americans believe in helping those w.... fall on hard times, in fostering equal opportunity and equal rights in providing broad access to education, housing, health care, and child care. Polls (and our intuitions) also suggest that Americans believe that intact families do the best job at bringing up children, that hard work should be rewarded, that people who behave destructively toward others should be punished, that small institutions close to home tend to do better than big institutions run from far away, that private moral choices usually have social consequences. Put another way, Americans believe in social concern and self-reliance; they want to match rights and responsibilities; they think public moral standards should exist but are skeptical of too much meddling in the private affairs of others.

20   One fair reaction to the above is to call it a catalogue of the obvious. But that is precisely the point: The false choices posed by liberalism and conservatism make it extremely difficult for the perfectly obvious preferences of the American people to express themselves in our politics. We are encouraging an "either/or" politics based on ideological preconceptions rather than a "both/and" politics based on ideas that broadly unite us.

To be sure, free elections in a two-party system inevitably encourage polarization; voters who like some things about liberals or Democrats and some things about conservatives or Republicans end up having to choose one package or the other. In free elections, each side will always try to polarize the electorate in a way that will leave a majority standing on its side. But if free elections leave so many in the electorate dissatisfied with where they have to stand, and push large numbers out of the electorate entirely, then it is fair to conclude that the political process is badly defective.

Moreover, after the election is over, parties have to govern. But putting such a premium on false choices and artificial polarization, our electoral process is making it harder and harder for electoral winners to produce what they were elected for: good government. The false polarization that may be inevitable at election time is carrying over into the policy debates that take place afterward. Political "positioning" may be necessary in an electoral campaign; when it becomes part of the intellectual debate, the talk becomes dishonest. Our intellectual life, which is supposed to clear matters up, produces only more false choices.

In recent years, much has been written about the rise of "negative campaigning" and of the "killer" television spots that instantly bury a political candidate's chances. Much has also been said about the rise of the "character issue" and the seemingly incessant interest of the press in the private lives of politicians. A candidate's sex life or his draft record dominate the public discussion. What were once called "issues" are cast to one side. Taken together, these developments suggest that politics is destined to become ever more seamy. Democracy takes on all the dignity of mud-wrestling. When American political consultants descended upon Eastern Europe to help "guide" newcomers to democracy in the ways of modern politics, there was much alarm. Why should newly founded democracies be "guided" toward the dismal stuff that we Americans call politics?

In explaining these sorry developments, we have tended, I believe, to focus too narrowly on the political *process* and not enough on the *content* of politics.

The focus on process is perfectly sensible as far as it goes. By allow-25 ing the paid, thirty-second television spot to become our dominant means of political communication, we have shaped our political life in certain directions. In a thirty-second spot, candidates and parties can only give impressions, appeal to feelings, arouse emotions. Wedged in the midst of ads for all manner of products, the political spot needs to grab its audience. This tends to rule out even thirty seconds of sober discussion of the issues. Sobriety rarely grabs anyone. Most democracies offer political parties and candidates significant blocks of time in which they can tell their stories. And most provide the time free. The fact that our spots must be paid for raises the cost of American campaigns far above the levels in most other democracies. Raising the cost of campaigns has heightened the importance of fund-raising. This forces politicians to spend an untoward amount of time raising money. It also gives lobbyists and political action committees undo influence on our politics and gives average voters much less. The strong and the wealthy tend to have the most money to give away.

Reformers have many good ideas on how the system can be improved. Allocating free or cheap television time to candidates and parties would help. Offering the time in blocks larger than thirty seconds would help, too. There is no shortage of ideas on how to reduce the influence of money on politics, including a variety of limitations on the size and kind of contribution that can be made, and various schemes for total or partial public financing of campaigns. All these things would improve our politics.

But they would not, finally, cure our underlying political problems. The real problem is not the spots themselves but what is said in them. Why is it that they focus so insistently on either character assassination or divisive social issues that leave the electorate so angry and dissatisfied? This is not a technical question, but a political issue. Once upon a time, most of the thirty-second spots that ran on television were *positive*. They sought to mobilize voters behind causes and candidates they could believe in, not in opposition to ideas and constituencies they loathed. The content of political advertising suggested that, on balance, politicians were more concerned with getting things done than with foiling the nasty designs of others.

At its best, democratic politics is about what Arthur Schlesinger, Jr., calls "the search for remedy." The purpose of democratic politics is to solve problems and resolve disputes. But since the 1960s, the key to winning elections has been to reopen the same divisive issues over and over again. The issues themselves are not reargued. No new light is shed. Rather, old resentments and angers are stirred up in an effort to get voters to cast yet one more ballot of angry protest. Political consultants have been truly ingenious in figuring out endless creative ways of tapping into popular anger about crime. Yet their spots do not solve the problem. Endless arguments about whether the death penalty is a good idea do not put more cops on the street, streamline the criminal justice system, or resolve some of the underlying causes of violence.

The decline of a "politics of remedy" creates a vicious cycle. Campaigns have become negative in large part because of a sharp decline in popular faith in government. To appeal to an increasingly alienated electorate, candidates and their political consultants have adopted a cynical stance that, they believe with good reason, plays into popular cynicism about politics and thus wins them votes. But cynical campaigns do not resolve issues. They do not lead to "remedies." Therefore, problems get worse, the electorate becomes *more* cynical—and so does the advertising. At the end of it all, the governing process, which is supposed to be about real things, becomes little more than a war over symbols.

30   Politicians engage in symbolic rather than substantive politics for another reason: Liberals and conservatives alike are uncertain about what remedies they can offer without blowing their constituencies apart. The two broad coalitions in American political life—liberal and Democratic, conservative and Republican—have become so unstable that neither side can afford to risk very much. That is because the ties that bind Americans to each other, to their communities, and thus to their political parties have grown ever weaker.

The party system of the New Deal era was relatively stable because definable groups voted together and largely held together, even in bad times. Now, almost everything else conspires against group solidarity. Unions are in trouble—and conservatives have done everything they could to weaken them. The new jobs in the service industries promote individualism. The decline of the small town and the old urban ethnic enclaves and the rise of new suburbs, exurbs, and condominium developments further weakens social solidarity. Old urban neighborhoods feel abandoned by the liberal politicians whom they once counted on for support.

In the new politics, each voter is studied and appealed to as an *individual*. This is both the cause and effect of the rise of polling and television advertising. It also explains the increasing harshness of political attack and counterattack. In the old politics, voters felt real loyalties, which could be appealed to in a positive way. Political loyalties were reinforced by other forms of group solidarity. Now, insofar as voters identify with groups, it is often with abstract national groups rather than concrete local ones. An Italian machinist in a Detroit suburb may identify himself more with his fellow gun owners than with his ethnic group, his neighborhood, or his fellow workers. Since he believes that politics will do little to improve his life or that of his community, he votes defensively. If the government won't do anything *for* him, he damn well won't let it do anything *against* him, such as tax him more heavily or take away his gun. It is not an irrational response, given the current state of our politics.

It does no good to yearn for an America that no longer exists, especially since pluralism and geographical and social mobility have created much that we love about the United States. But if our politics is to get better, it is crucial that we recognize that the fragmentation of American society has made our public life much more difficult. We need to find ways to tie citizens back into public life, not to turn them off even more. Above all, we need to end the phony polarization around the issues of the 1960s that serves only to carry us ever further from a deliberative, democratic public life.

Additional Rhetorical Strategies

Cause and Effect (paragraphs 3, 9, 14, 21, 25, 29–31); Classification (paragraph 10); Analogy (paragraph 23); Argument (throughout).

Discussion Questions

1. To what does Dionne attribute current American apathy about politics and loss of faith in democracy? Examine each of the causal arguments he makes throughout this essay. Which comes first for Dionne, a loss of a sense of community or a flight from public life, for instance? Analyze the other cause-and-effect statements he makes as well.

2. In paragraph 7, Dionne states that "liberalism and conservatism are framing political issues as a series of false choices." To which false choices is he referring? What are the real choices that the politicians are avoiding?

3. According to Dionne, how are the liberals and conservatives alike? How do they differ? Does he focus more on comparison or contrast? Can you tell which party he belongs to? Look at the critiques

of each party in paragraphs 16 and 17. How might you defend either party from his charges? Is he equally fair in his representations of each party's position? What do such phrases as "liberal instincts and conservative values" (paragraph 19) reveal about Dionne's own values?

4. Near the end of his essay, Dionne laments the fact that group identification often functions on a national rather than a local level; he uses the example of the gun owner who votes with his fellow gun owners rather than with his "ethnic group, his neighborhood, or his fellow workers" (paragraph 32). What are the advantages and disadvantages of Americans forming affinity groups that cut across race, class, and geographic lines?

5. What kinds of solutions does he propose or imply to the problems he describes? How workable are these solutions? Can you propose additional solutions and approaches?

Essay Questions

1. In paragraph 27, Dionne points out that "Once upon a time, most of the thirty-second spots that ran on television were *positive*." Do a research project in which you test this hypothesis. Has the tenor of political advertising really changed? Since what point? Does the shift coincide with the 60s, the historical moment from which Dionne times the change in America's relationship to politics?

2. Do a close analysis of the language of Dionne's essay. What might be the deeper implications of the words he chooses? What, for instance, might qualify as an "intact family" (paragraph 19) in Dionne's world view? What might he refer to when he talks of conservatives' suggestions "that changing teenage attitudes toward premarital sex might reduce teen pregnancy" (paragraph 17)? How bland and generalized must he make his summary of what Americans believe in (paragraph 19) in order not to alienate any of his readers whose perspectives might differ from his own?

Thematic Pair: Language and Gender

▲▼How Male and Female Students Use Language Differently

Deborah Tannen

Deborah Tannen (b. 1945) is a linguist who, in her own words, has developed a "humanistic approach to linguistic analysis." Although many of her books, including her recent publication, Gender and Discourse *(Oxford University Press, 1994), are aimed at an audience of her scholarly peers, she also finds value in reaching a wider reading audience. "I see one of my missions—a presentation of linguistic research to a general audience—as a means of understanding human communication and improving it."*

Much of her work has been done in an area called interactional sociolinguistics: she analyzes language in its everyday social contexts. In 1986 she published the best-selling That's Not What I Meant!: How Conversational Style Makes or Breaks Your Relations with Others. *Soon she turned her attention to communication and miscommunication between the genders, producing* You Just Don't Understand: Women and Men in Conversation *(1990). In this work, rather than placing the blame for miscommunication on one gender or the other, she clarifies how socialization tends to produce differences not only in the ways men and women express themselves, but—perhaps more importantly—in the ways in which they understand the words spoken by others. More recently, she has narrowed her focus to women's and men's (often unexamined) communication strategies in the workplace; this latest book is titled* Talking from Nine to Five: How Women's and Men's Conversational Styles Affect Who Gets Heard, Who Gets Credit, and What Gets Done at Work *(1994).*

The essay that follows was originally published in the Chronicle of Higher Education *in 1991. In this essay she treats a subject you might find especially relevant.*

When I researched and wrote my latest book, *You Just Don't Understand: Women and Men in Conversation,* the furthest thing from my mind was reevaluating my teaching strategies. But that has been one of the direct benefits of having written the book.

The primary focus of my linguistic research always has been the language of everyday conversation. One facet of this is conversational style: how different regional, ethnic, and class backgrounds, as well as age and gender, result in different ways of using language to communicate. *You Just Don't Understand* is about the conversational styles of women and men. As I gained more insight into typically male and female ways of using language, I began to suspect some of the causes of the troubling facts that women who go to single-sex schools do better in later life, and that when young women sit next to young men in classrooms, the males talk more. This is not to say that all men talk in class, nor that no women do. It is simply that a greater percentage of discussion time is taken by men's voices.

The research of sociologists and anthropologists such as Janet Lever, Marjorie Harness Goodwin, and Donna Eder has shown that girls and boys learn to use language differently in their sex-separate peer groups. Typically, a girl has a best friend with whom she sits and talks, frequently telling secrets. It's the telling of secrets, the fact and the way that they talk to each other, that makes them best friends. For boys, activities are central: their best friends are the ones they do things with. Boys also tend to play in larger groups that are hierarchical. High-status boys give orders and push low-status boys around. So boys are expected to use language to seize center stage: by exhibiting their skill, displaying their knowledge, and challenging and resisting challenges.

These patterns have stunning implications for classroom interaction. Most faculty members assume that participating in class discussion is a necessary part of successful performance. Yet speaking in a classroom is more congenial to boys' language experience than to girls', since it entails putting oneself forward in front of a large group of people, many of whom are strangers and at least one of whom is sure to judge speakers' knowledge and intelligence by their verbal display.

Another aspect of many classrooms that makes them more hos- 5 pitable to most men than to most women is the use of debate-like formats as a learning tool. Our educational system, as Walter Ong argues persuasively in his book *Fighting for Life* (Cornell University Press, 1981), is fundamentally male in that the pursuit of knowledge is believed to be achieved by ritual opposition: public display followed by argument and challenge. Father Ong demonstrates that ritual opposition—what he calls "adversativeness" or "agonism"—is fundamental to the way most males approach almost any activity. (Consider, for example, the little boy who shows he likes a little girl by pulling her braids and shoving her.) But ritual opposition is antithetical to the way most females learn and like to interact. It is not that females don't fight, but they don't fight for fun. They don't *ritualize* opposition.

Anthropologists working in widely disparate parts of the world have found contrasting verbal rituals for women and men. Women in completely unrelated cultures (for example, Greece and Bali) engage in ritual laments: spontaneously produced rhyming couplets that express their pain, for example, over the loss of loved ones. Men do not take part in laments. They have their own, very different verbal ritual: a contest, a war of words in which they vie with each other to devise clever insults.

When discussing these phenomena with a colleague, I commented that I see these two styles in American conversation: many women bond by talking about troubles, and many men bond by exchanging playful insults and put-downs, and other sorts of verbal sparring. He exclaimed: "I never thought of this, but that's the way I teach: I have students read an article, and then I invite them to tear it apart. After we've torn it to shreds, we talk about how to build a better model."

This contrasts sharply with the way I teach: I open the discussion of readings by asking, "What did you find useful in this? What can we use in our own theory building and our own methods?" I note what I see as weaknesses in the author's approach, but I also point out that the writer's discipline and purposes might be different from ours. Finally, I offer personal anecdotes illustrating the phenomena under discussion and praise students' anecdotes as well as their critical acumen.

These different teaching styles must make our classrooms wildly different places and hospitable to different students. Male students are more likely to be comfortable attacking the readings and might find the inclusion of personal anecdotes irrelevant and "soft." Women are more likely to resist discussion they perceive as hostile, and, indeed, it is women in my classes who are most likely to offer personal anecdotes.

10   A colleague who read my book commented that he had always taken for granted that the best way to deal with students' comments is to challenge them; this, he felt it was self-evident, sharpens their minds and helps them develop debating skills. But he had noticed that women were relatively silent in his classes, so he decided to try beginning discussions with relatively open-ended questions and letting comments go unchallenged. He found, to his amazement and satisfaction, that more women began to speak up.

Though some of the women in his class clearly liked this better, perhaps some of the men liked it less. One young man in my class wrote in a questionnaire about a history professor who gave students questions to think about and called on people to answer them: "He would then play devil's advocate . . . i.e., he debated us. . . . That class really sharpened me intellectually. . . . We as students do need to know how to defend ourselves." This young man valued the experience of being attacked and challenged publicly. Many, if not most, women would shrink from such "challenge," experiencing it as public humiliation.

A professor at Hamilton College told me of a young man who was upset because he felt his class presentation had been a failure. The professor was puzzled because he had observed that class members had listened attentively and agreed with the student's observations. It turned out that it was this very agreement that the student interpreted as failure: since no one had engaged his ideas by arguing with him, he felt they had found them unworthy of attention.

So one reason men speak in class more than women is that many of them find the "public" classroom setting more conducive to speaking, whereas most women are more comfortable speaking in private to a small group of people they know well. A second reason is that men are more likely to be comfortable with the debate-like form that discussion may take. Yet another reason is the different attitudes toward speaking in class that typify women and men.

Students who speak frequently in class, many of whom are men, assume that it is their job to think of contributions and try to get the floor to express them. But many women monitor their participation not only to get the floor but to avoid getting it. Women students in my class tell me that if they have spoken up once or twice, they hold back for the rest of the class because they don't want to dominate. If they have spoken a lot one week, they will remain silent the next. These different ethics of participation are, of course, unstated, so those who speak freely assume that those who remain silent have nothing to say, and those who are reining themselves in assume that the big talkers are selfish and hoggish.

When I looked around my classes, I could see these differing ethics[15] and habits at work. For example, my graduate class in analyzing conversation had twenty students, eleven women and nine men. Of the men, four were foreign students: two Japanese, one Chinese, and one Syrian. With the exception of the three Asian men, all the men spoke in class at least occasionally. The biggest talker in the class was a woman, but there were also five women who never spoke at all, only one of whom was Japanese. I decided to try something different.

I broke the class into small groups to discuss the issues raised in the readings and to analyze their own conversational transcripts. I devised three ways of dividing the students into groups: one by the degree program they were in, one by gender, and one by conversational style, as closely as I could guess it. This meant that when the class was grouped according to conversational style, I put Asian students together, fast talkers together, and quiet students together. The class split into groups six times during the semester, so they met in each grouping twice. I told students to regard the groups as examples of interactional data and to note the different ways they participated in the different groups. Toward the end of the term, I gave them a questionnaire asking about their class and group participation.

I could see plainly from my observation of the groups at work that women who never opened their mouths in class were talking away in the small groups. In fact, the Japanese woman commented that she found it particularly hard to contribute to the all-woman group she was in because "I was overwhelmed by how talkative the female students were in the female-only group." This is particularly revealing because it highlights that the same person who can be "oppressed" into silence in one context can become the talkative "oppressor" in another. No one's conversational style is absolute; everyone's style changes in response to the context and others' styles.

Some of the students (seven) said they preferred the same-gender groups; others preferred the same-style groups. In answer to the question "Would you have liked to speak in class more than you did?" six of the seven who said yes were women; the one man was Japanese. Most startlingly, this response did not come only from quiet women; it came from women who had indicated they had spoken in class never, rarely, sometimes, and often. Of the eleven students who said the amount they had spoken was fine, seven were men. Of the four women who checked "fine," two added qualifications indicating it wasn't completely fine: One wrote in "maybe more," and one wrote, "I have an urge to participate but often feel I should have something more interesting/relevant/wonderful/intelligent to say!"

I counted my experiment a success. Everyone in the class found the small groups interesting, and no one indicated he or she would have preferred that the class not break into groups. Perhaps most instructive, however, was the fact that the experience of breaking into groups, and of talking about participation in class, raised everyone's awareness about classroom participation. After we had talked about it, some of the quietest women in the class made a few voluntary contributions, though sometimes I had to insure their participation by interrupting the students who were exuberantly speaking out.

20   Americans are often proud that they discount the significance of cultural differences: "We are all individuals," many people boast. Ignoring such issues as gender and ethnicity becomes a source of pride: "I treat everyone the same." But treating people the same is not equal treatment if they are not the same.

The classroom is a different environment for those who feel comfortable putting themselves forward in a group than it is for those who find the prospect of doing so chastening, or even terrifying. When a professor asks, "Are there any questions?" students who can formulate statements the fastest have the greatest opportunity to respond. Those who need significant time to do so have not really been given a chance at all, since by the time they are ready to speak, someone else has the floor.

In a class where some students speak out without raising hands, those who feel they must raise their hands and wait to be recognized do not have equal opportunity to speak. Telling them to feel free to jump in will not make them feel free; one's sense of timing, of one's rights and obligations in a classroom, are automatic, learned over years of interaction. They may be changed over time, with motivation and effort, but they cannot be changed on the spot. And everyone assumes his or her own way is best. When I asked my students how the class could be changed to make it easier for them to speak more, the most talkative woman said she would prefer it if no one had to raise hands, and a foreign student said he wished people would raise their hands and wait to be recognized.

My experience in this class has convinced me that small-group interaction should be part of any class that is not a small seminar. I also am convinced that having the students become observers of their own interaction is a crucial part of their education. Talking about ways of talking in class makes students aware that their ways of talking affect other students, that the motivations they impute to others may not truly reflect others' motives, and that the behaviors they assume to be self-evidently right are not universal norms.

The goal of complete equal opportunity in class may not be attainable, but realizing that one monolithic classroom-participation structure is not equal opportunity is itself a powerful motivation to find more-diverse methods to serve diverse students—and every discussion is diverse.

Additional Rhetorical Strategies

Cause and Effect (paragraph 12); Narration (paragraphs 15, 16); Example (throughout).

Discussion Questions

1. According to Tannen, why do girls thrive in single-sex schools? What might the teachers and administrators in co-ed schools learn from the successes of single-sex schools, and how might they modify their practices to take advantage of the insights gained from studying same-sex schools for girls?

2. In paragraph 19, Tannen writes that "treating people the same is not equal treatment if they are not the same." Tease out the larger implications of this statement. Does it suggest, for instance, a rationale for affirmative action programs in universities and colleges? Or does it suggest that if the boys and girls had been treated alike from the start, then by the time they reached the college classroom they might be more nearly "the same"? Or does it suggest to you an *essential* difference between males and females that ensures they will never be the same? Look elsewhere in the essay for evidence to back up your argument about Tannen's stance on these issues. Do you agree or disagree with Tannen? Why?

3. Tannen is "convinced that having the students become observers of their own interaction is a crucial part of their education" (paragraph 23). Think of an example *besides* conversation style that students might

do well to become more self-conscious about. How might a teacher facilitate this act of reflection? How might the students benefit?

4. Whenever one generalizes about gender differences, one risks alienating one's readers. To what extent is Tannen successful in reaching both male and female readers? Are there specific passages you found yourself rejecting, because you felt your own gender was being unfairly characterized? Were there any passages that made you wonder how people of the opposite gender might react? Identify strategies Tannen employs in an attempt to avoid alienating her readers. Can you suggest further strategies to improve the reception of an essay such as this one?

Essay Questions

1. In paragraph 5, Tannen agrees that patterns of male communication versus female communication are similar in "widely disparate parts of the world." But in paragraphs 14 and following, she tells a story of a class she taught in which the students' conversational styles seemed to depend at least as much upon race as upon gender. Write an essay in which you explore your own conversational style, in contrast to or in comparison with the styles of other members of your extended family. Which factor seems to be more compelling: your family's ethnicity or your gender?

2. Deborah Tannen has been criticized for suggesting, through her model of "cultural difference," that men don't dominate women in our culture; they just misunderstand them. Tannen's response is that to pit "difference" against "dominance" is to create a false dichotomy. Instead, cultural difference "provides a model for explaining how dominance can be created in face-to-face interaction." In "How Male and Female Students Use Language Differently," does Tannen seem to be setting up a model of difference or of dominance, or does she manage to illustrate how the two intersect? Support your answer with specific examples from the text.

▲▼Pioneer Diaries of Women and Men

John Mack Faragher

John Mack Faragher (b. 1945) is an American historian, educator, and author. He taught at Yale University and the University of Hartford before joining the American history faculty at Mount Holyoke College in 1978. The following essay comes from his first book, Women and Men on the Overland Trail *(1979), which was based on his dissertation. More recently, Faragher has authored* Sugar Creek: Life on the Illinois Prairie *(1986) and* Daniel Boone: The Life and Legend of an American Pioneer *(1992). He served as the general editor for the* Encyclopedia of Colonial and Revolutionary America *(1990).*

The long, dangerous trek of pioneers across the overland trails remains one of the great American adventure stories of the nineteenth century. But unlike most of the fictional adventure tales of that time, this was one experience that involved the arduous cooperation of both sexes. As one emigrant woman put it, "They talk of the times that tried men's souls but this was the time [that tried] both men's and women's souls." In the essay that follows, Faragher compares and contrasts the diaries kept by male and female pioneers during that seven-month trip.

Differences between the worlds of men and women are reflected in the emigrant diaries. Despite similarity in content, there was a notable difference in the style of men's and women's writing. Women usually wrote with a pervasive personal presence, most often using the first person. "I am now sitting on a hill side on a stone, a little distant from the camp," Rebecca Ketcham wrote in her diary late one afternoon. "After I commenced writing Mrs Dix called to me to come to her to see a beautiful bunch of verbena she had found. I went and looked about with her a little, then sat down again to my writing. Very soon Camela called to me to see how the wild peas grow." Even in less fluently written women's diaries, the subject "I" tended to be the ultimate standard of perception. "Met yesterday a very long and steep road coming out of Grande River bottom. I never saw as crooked a road in my life." Men, on the contrary, typically employed the more impersonal "we."[1] Sometimes the referent of this pronoun was hard to specify, shifting with the context. Usually the "we" most clearly referred to the men as a group.

> [May 4, 1851] We traveled 16 miles this day over very hilly road.
> [May 6] This day we left camp at 8 o'clock and traveled 12 miles, camped where we found but little wood and poor water.

---

[1]Sixty-three percent of the women diarists consistently used the *I*, but only 46 percent of the men.

> [May 7] This day we gathered up and started after traveling five or six miles it commenced blowing and raining very hard. We all got very wet.
>
> [May 8] This morning some of our women washed. We gathered up afternoon and traveled ten miles and camped on an open prairie, where we had no wood and but little grass.

The subject of these passages is not clear until the women are introduced; then the "we" seems to be masculine. Another man wrote, "We drove up and turned out our stock to grass while the girls got busy getting supper."

Women diarists typically located themselves in relation to space and time—often taking care to note where they were sitting, what they had been doing, and what was going on around them as they wrote. "The sun is shining bright and warm, and a cool breeze blowing makes it very nice indeed, and it seems very much like home. . . . Oh, they are starting, so I must stop for today. . . . Trying to write walking, but it won't do." Most women did not go into quite the detail Agnes Stewart included in this passage, but men, by contrast, were likely not to bother with any of these, content to assume that the fact of writing itself established a sufficient identifying framework.[2]

Men's writing was usually plain, unadorned, and terse.

> Fri 10 made this day 14 and encamped at the Willow Springs good water but little grass 3 Buffaloes killed the Main Spring 1-½ miles above
>
> Sat 11 Made this day 20 Miles to Independence Rock Camped below the Rock good water ½ way
>
> Sun 12 Lay by this day.

Women, on the other hand, frequently employed a range of stylistic elaborations. They took care to identify names of people and places and specify dates and times, while men regularly left names out, neglected to record dates, and abbreviated their words and phrases, sometimes beyond recognition.[3] Most women used extended description: colorful adjectives, qualifying phrases, long passages of explanation and summary. Elizabeth Dixon Smith, who often wrote long passages, commented that "I would have written a great deal more if I had the opportunity. Sometimes I would not get the chance to write for two or three days, and then would have to rise in the night when my babe and all hands were asleep, light a candle and write." It was a rare man, however, who regularly employed elaborating devices in his diary writing.[4]

---

[2]Ninety-four percent of the women diarists and 44 percent of the men explicitly placed themselves in relation to time and space at least once in their accounts.

[3]Seventy-five percent of women and 39 percent of men used exact names, dates, and places in their accounts.

[4]Seventy-nine percent of women and 22 percent of men used one or more forms of extended description at least once.

In general, men and women were concerned with different orders of meaning. There was an almost inverse relationship in the way most men wrote about objects and things, most women about people.[5] The following two passages—both written somewhat more elaborately than the mode for either sex—illustrate the differences:

> [September 23, 1843] We went up to the ford & fastened our waggons to gether as we did at the upper crossing & drove over. This ford is better than the upper one, tho it is a bout 8 or 10 inches deeper than the upper one. Tho we went strate a craws, & in camped on the bank. Grazing indifferent.
> [September 24] We struck through the hill & struck a creek & in camped Grazing indifferent. Dist 12.
> [September 25] We continued through the hills & struck a smawl spring in nine miles Grazing indifferent. Then we struck a nonther one in 5 or 6 miles. Tolerable incampement. Then we struck a smaller branch at nite. Grazing indifferent. Distance 19.

> [June 16, 1853] Frank and a number of young friends are amusing themselves with the "Mansions of Happiness" and judging from their merry laugh, I should think they were enjoying it very much indeed. Father has taken his pillow under the wagon and is having his daily siesta. Willie is watching the horses and I am in the wagon, spending an hour with you, my dear children.

These differences in writing style conform to the differences be- 5 tween the social and cultural worlds of men and women. Speech patterns, it is known, can reflect such cultural differences. "Different social structures may generate different speech systems or linguistic codes. The latter entail for the individual specific principles of choice which regulate the selections he makes from the totality of options represented in a given language."[6] In other words, groups enjoying different social and cultural relations but sharing the same language will make use of different syntactic and lexical selections for everyday communication in a given social situation; these language choices in use are known as codes.

The connections between speech and written language are complicated, the latter mediated by formal conventions that do not apply to everyday speech. But as Arthur Ponsonby notes in his study of diaries, diary writing may be the closest of all written forms to speech. The effort to conform to a stylistic convention requires too much of a person making daily entries. "You have no time to think, you do not want to

[5]Twenty-nine percent of men diarists wrote primarily about people, versus 64 percent of women diarists.
[6]Basil Bernstein, "Elaborated and Restricted Codes: Their Social Origins and Consequences," in Alfred G. Smith, ed., *Communication and Culture* (New York: Holt, Rinehart, and Winston, 1966), p. 429.

think, you want to remember, you cannot consciously adopt any particular artifice; you jot down the day's doings either briefly or burst out impulsively here and there into detail; and without being conscious of it, you yourself emerge and appear out of the sum total of those jottings, however brief they be."[7] The overland diaries fit Ponsonby's characterization precisely; lacking in formalities, they are probably good, though limited, representations of the speech codes employed by men and women.

Basil Bernstein has distinguished between two general types of language codes in contemporary English speech that correspond remarkably well to the contrasting styles in the diary writings of these mid-nineteenth-century men and women. Men's diaries may be characterized by their use of a "restrictive" code, that is, a code drawn from a narrow range of choices: unelaborated prose, written in apparent haste, emphasizing the how rather than the why, with implicit as distinguished from explicit meanings. Such a code typically appears among people in close behavioral connection, sharing common assumptions and expectations. In this context, group members can assume that their fellows understand without having everything stated explicitly. The "we" dominates the "I," because people assume a common identity. Restrictive codes are part of communal situation; the communication of gesture, motion, and physical interaction often substitutes for language and discourages the development of expressive skills.

Women's writing best fits the contrasting designation of "elaborated" code: the use of extended description, modifying words and phrases, and explicit statement. Elaborated codes are required in situations where social connections are weak or lacking and language is employed to bridge the gap between individuals. In these circumstances people cannot assume a common understanding but must use language quite explicitly to inquire and inform. Consequently rather less is taken for granted; clarification, elucidation, and discovery are the primary tasks of verbal communication. This code, then, takes as its subject not a group but individuals (the "I" and the other), places a premium upon empathy, and is in general most often associated with a people-oriented content.

The analysis of the diary writing suggests again that essentially different social situations of men and women were associated with different cultural phenomena. The men's world was made of the stuff of action, a world of closely shared identifications, expectations, and assumptions. In the standardized and even ritualized behavior of men lay the ability to communicate without verbal expression. "The men generally," William Oliver reported, "are not very talkative." For

---

[7]Arthur Ponsonby, *English Diaries*, 2nd ed. (London: Methuen, 1923), p. 5.

women, however, articulation was at the very heart of their world, for verbal expression could achieve an interpersonal closeness that was socially denied by the exclusion of women from the public world and their isolation at home. In contradistinction to his silent men, Oliver remarked that he had overheard women "unfasten the sluices of their eloquence, and fairly maintain the character of their sex." A large part of women's rich cultural heritage was verbal—women's voluminous lore. And women were required to learn the cultural art of conversation and communication, including letter and diary writing, to make up for the social isolation of the farm.

Psychologically this analysis further suggests that the meek femi-10 nine character assumed that she needed to explain and elaborate her feelings in order to make herself understood. Women's empathy for others was the other side of women's concern that their true selves be truly communicated by taking time and care with language. Masculine characters, on the other hand, assumed that they were understood and saw no need to articulate things that seemed perfectly obvious to them. The face men presented to the world, however, was held rigid; no tears were allowed to soften the harsh exterior to reveal the emotional essence within. Men assumed that their public faces, silent and brooding, represented their true selves, but they were fooling themselves. Men hid their feelings from themselves, understood themselves in an incomplete way, but found comfort in the company of their similarly repressed brothers. These were men, in Avery Craven's well-chosen words, "with homely vices and virtues and with more than their share of half-starved emotions."

Additional Rhetorical Strategies

Definition (paragraphs 5, 7, 8); Classification (paragraphs 7, 8); Cause and Effect (paragraphs 9, 10); Example (throughout).

Discussion Questions

1. How are the male and female diaries alike? How are they different? Why does Faragher emphasize the differences to such a large extent? Analyze the structure of the essay. How do the first four paragraphs differ from the rest of the essay? How are the first four paragraphs structured? What is the function of each of the remaining paragraphs?
2. Why does Faragher go to such great lengths in paragraph 6 to establish that diaries are closer than most other forms of writing to everyday speech? What objection is Faragher anticipating, and how might his argument be less convincing had he not anticipated it?

3. What does Faragher explicitly say, and what do the excerpts from the diaries say, about the respective intended audiences for the men's and women's diaries? Strictly speaking, of course, diaries are often kept private, so that the writer and the reader are one and the same. But what can you tell about the larger audiences whom these diarists might have had in mind?

4. In paragraph 10, Faragher ventures to make a psychological analysis of the women and men, based on their stylistic choices as diarists. To what extent do these inferences seem to be justified by the texts he has quoted and discussed? Are there alternative interpretations you might make, given the same evidence? Were some of the psychological inferences less compelling than others? Why? You might look at Deborah Tannen's essay (p. 308) for further ideas on this topic.

Essay Questions

1. In paragraph 9, Faragher quotes William Oliver's remarks on women who "unfasten the sluices of their eloquence, and fairly maintain the character of their sex." What kind of image of women's speech is painted by Oliver's words? What kinds and categories of speech are typically considered women's speech? What relative value is ascribed to these categories of speech?

2. If you have access to primary materials in your school's library (or in a relative's attic), read through a batch of letters or diaries, and make a tally indicating the frequency of the distinguishing features you observe. Base a comparison and contrast essay on this data. You need not compare and contrast writers of different genders; you might choose instead to look at writers of different ages (letters exchanged between grandparents and grandchildren, for instance) or writers in different eras (diaries of nineteenth century women versus diaries of twentieth century women, for instance).

Exploring Connections: Questions Linking the Thematic Pair

1. In her essay, Tannen focuses on the spoken word; in his essay, Faragher focuses on the informal written word. What difference, if any, might this make in their analyses? How might a comparative analysis of men's and women's language differ from the two examples given if the researcher were to study formal written samples?

2. Considering that Faragher and Tannen differ in terms of their disciplines (history and sociolinguistics, respectively) and in their genders, and considering that they are examining language samples from different centuries, how consistent are their results? Do the psychological portraits of women and of men that emerge from their studies suggest that little has changed since the 1850s, or can you detect significant shifts in gender roles and expectations based on these analyses of language usage?

Analogy and Extended Metaphor

When we find a number of point-by-point resemblances between the features of two different things—like the heart and a pump or the human brain and a computer—we are thinking with the help of analogy. In expository writing, analogy is particularly useful for making abstract or hard-to-follow subjects easier to visualize and understand. Analogy also plays an important organizing role in such narrative forms as fables and allegories. In descriptive writing it can help make our observations more vivid and concrete. In argument, analogy is a method of reasoning in which we infer *possible* similarities between two things on the basis of *established* similarities. In general, analogy works in our writing and thinking in two ways: first, as a means of illustration by which we make difficult topics easier to understand; and, second, as a means of reasoning by which we can draw conclusions for an argument.

Analogy often is loosely used to describe many types of comparison. For clear thinking and writing, however, it seems best to stay close to the term's original mathematical sense of *proportion*: one thing is to another as a third thing is to a fourth. This form of analogy shows up frequently on aptitude tests. A simple illustration would be:

Head : Hat :: Foot : χ
χ is
(A) Book   (C) Shoe
(B) Sweater   (D) Ankle

We should have no trouble coming up with "(C) Shoe" as our answer. Quite clearly, a shoe bears the same relationship to a foot that a hat does to a head. To supply the missing part of the analogy, we first determined the relationship between the two given parts of our equation, then found the term that made the relationship between the second pair equivalent to the first.

The key word here is *relationship*. The above analogy (admittedly, a simple one) works as all analogies do—by establishing an equivalency of relationships. Shoes and hats are similar here not because they are both objects of clothing but because as objects of clothing they bear similar relations to corresponding parts of the body, a relation that a sweater—also an article of clothing—does not bear to foot. We can keep our root analogy going quite easily in this case by extending the equation so that it eventually covers all body parts and their corresponding articles of clothing.

Explaining by Means of Analogy

One reason that the hat–shoe analogy looks so simple is that it draws all of its comparisons from the same class of objects. But not all analogies work in such an elementary fashion. In fact, the kinds of analogies that require the most thought (and that we can learn the most from) work by demonstrating similar relations between different classes of phenomena. Analogies of this type are often used in scientific explanation—for example, the customary comparisons of the heart to a pump or the brain to a computer. Consider the brain–computer resemblance. The brain is said to be like a computer because some of the parts and functions of the brain are related to the brain in ways that certain parts and functions of a computer are related to the computer. Unlike our earlier example, the similarity is one of relations within two objects belonging to two entirely different classes (one a part of the body, the other a human invention).

Yet, despite the intellectual attraction of analogies and the working models they can lead to, we should approach argument by analogy with a good deal of caution. No matter how legitimately constructed, analogies frequently suppress as many dissimilarities as they express similarities. A computer, for example, bears a resemblance only to the cognitive areas of the brain. Vast resources of the brain affecting emotions, perceptions, sensations, balance, and spatial orientation are overlooked by the analogy. And even with respect to cognition it is potentially troublesome to compare a completely input-dependent machine to an organism that still gives every indication of being at least partially "self-programming." No psychiatrist has yet had to analyze a computer's dreams.

These limitations should not discourage us from using analogy in our thinking and writing. Carefully worked-out analogies can be of enormous value in helping us organize and express our ideas. Subjects especially abstract or difficult to grasp can be more readily comprehended or more easily visualized when referred analogically to more familiar or more easily understood structures. Speaking of the brain *as if* it were a computer or the heart *as if* it were a pump helps us to grasp concretely some of the functions of those complex organs in ways we might not be able to do if we thought about them directly.

The Visual Impact of Analogy

Though analogies can be enormously useful in helping us construct forceful arguments and explain complicated matters clearly, they also can give our writing pictorial vitality and emphasis. For example, here is a passage in which Henry David Thoreau uses an analogy for visual impact:

> Cape Cod is the bared and bended arm of Massachusetts! the shoulder is at Buzzard's Bay; the elbow, or crazy-bone, at Cape Mallebarre; the wrist at Truro; and the sandy fist at Provincetown,—behind which the State stands on her guard, with her back to the Green Mountains, and her feet planted on the floor of the ocean, like an athlete protecting her Bay,—boxing with northeast storms, and, ever and anon, heaving up her Atlantic adversary from the lap of earth,—ready to thrust forward her other fist, which keeps guard the while upon her breast at Cape Ann.

Note that Thoreau doesn't merely state that his native Massachusetts is a rugged land; he makes us *see* that ruggedness by means of an effective analogy. Notice, too, how Thoreau enhances the visual power of his analogy by comparing Massachusetts not just to the human body but to the human body in a fighter's stance.

Analogy as a Means of Discovery

When used imaginatively, analogy can be far more than a rhetorical strategy for simplification or emphasis: it can be a stimulus to creative thinking. By linking together two separate conceptual or physical entities, we may begin to perceive new implications and new connections that may lead to an entirely altered understanding of our subject. An analogy between the relation of God the Father to the Trinity and the relation of the sun to the solar system led the German astronomer Johannes Kepler (1571–1630) to a radically new conception of planetary motion. The English physician William Harvey (1578–1657) reported that the notion of the circulation of blood in the body first occurred to him when he noticed that the "flaps" inside the veins behaved as valves and that the heart was essentially a pump. Other kinds of analogies have left an indelible mark on human consciousness. We see the passage of human life as a pilgrimage or voyage, the world as a stage, time as a river, largely because of deep-rooted analogies sustained by myth and literature throughout the ages.

In all analogies, we should expect to find some nonanalogical elements, areas that do not correspond exactly. Consequently, a potentially vital analogy will always involve a conflict between its logical limitations and its rhetorical usefulness. When we work with an analogy, we should try beforehand to sketch out the full range of its correspondences. Our "blueprint" will then help us discover precisely how much strain our comparison will bear. It will also help us decide how many points of similarity our composition actually requires. The "extendibility" of an analogy will play a key part in determining the range and organization of our ideas, but the effect of a potentially rich analogy can be virtually negated if we drag out resemblances to the point of triviality.

In the selections that follow, we will see how various writers have put analogy to work effectively, making the abstract concrete, the unobservable observable, the remote near, the strange familiar.

For a discussion of extended metaphor, see the Introduction, "Learning to Write Is Learning to Think," p. 14–17.

The Attic of the Brain

Lewis Thomas

"We have language and can build metaphors as skillfully and precisely as ribosomes make proteins," wrote Lewis Thomas (1913–1993), a man who moved through language and the laboratory with energy and eloquence. Thomas was a doctor, researcher, professor, and director of the Memorial Sloane-Kettering Cancer Center in New York City, as well as a National Book Award winner in Arts and Letters.

Although he began writing poetry during his college days at Prince-ton and published over 200 scientific papers, Thomas did not begin his ca-reer as an essayist until he was in his late 50s, when he began contribut-ing a popular column, "Notes of a Biology Watcher," to the prestigious New England Journal of Medicine. *Some of these essays were collected and published in his first book,* The Lives of a Cell *(1974), which has sold well over 300,000 copies, making it one of the most popular works of its kind. His subsequent books include* The Medusa and the Snail *(1979),* Late Thoughts on Listening to Mahler's Ninth Symphony *(1982), from which the following essay was taken, and* The Fragile Species *(1992).*

My parents' house had an attic, the darkest and strangest part of the building, reachable only by placing a stepladder beneath the trapdoor and filled with unidentifiable articles too impor-tant to be thrown out with the trash but no longer suitable to have at hand. This mysterious space was the memory of the place. After many years all the things deposited in it became, one by one, lost to con-sciousness. But they were still there, we knew, safely and comfortably stored in the tissues of the house.

These days most of us live in smaller, more modern houses or in apartments, and attics have vanished. Even the deep closets in which we used to pile things up for temporary forgetting are rarely designed into new homes.

Everything now is out in the open, openly acknowledged and dis-played, and whenever we grow tired of a memory, an old chair, a trunkful of old letters, they are carted off to the dump for burning.

This has seemed a healthier way to live, except maybe for the smoke—everything out to be looked at, nothing strange hidden under the roof, nothing forgotten because of no place left in impenetrable darkness to forget. Openness is the new lifestyle, no undisclosed be-longings, no private secrets. Candor is the rule in architecture. The house is a machine for living, and what kind of a machine would hide away its worn-out, obsolescent parts?

But it is in our nature as human beings to clutter, and we hanker for 5 places set aside, reserved for storage. We tend to accumulate and outgrow possessions at the same time, and it is an endlessly discomforting mental task to keep sorting out the ones to get rid of. We might, we think, remember them later and find a use for them, and if they are gone for good, off to the dump, this is a source of nervousness. I think it may be one of the reasons we drum our fingers so much these days.

We might take a lesson here from what has been learned about our brains in this century. We thought we discovered, first off, the attic, although its existence has been mentioned from time to time by all the people we used to call great writers. What we really found was the trapdoor and a stepladder, and off we clambered, shining flashlights into the corners, vacuuming the dust out of bureau drawers, puzzling over the names of objects, tossing them down to the floor below, and finally paying around fifty dollars an hour to have them carted off for burning.

After several generations of this new way of doing things we took up openness and candor with the febrile intensity of a new religion, everything laid out in full view, and as in the design of our new houses it seemed a healthier way to live, except maybe again for smoke.

And now, I think, we have a new kind of worry. There is no place for functionless, untidy, inexplicable notions, no dark comfortable parts of the mind to hide away the things we'd like to keep but at the same time forget. The attic is still there, but with the trapdoor always open and the stepladder in place we are always in and out of it, flashing lights around, naming everything, unmystified.

I have an earnest proposal for psychiatry, a novel set of therapeutic rules, although I know it means waiting in line.

10   Bring back the old attic. Give new instructions to the patients who are made nervous by our times, including me, to make a conscious effort to hide a reasonable proportion of thought. It would have to be a gradual process, considering how far we have come in the other direction talking, talking all the way. Perhaps only one or two thoughts should be repressed each day, at the outset. The easiest, gentlest way might be to start with dreams, first by forbidding the patient to mention any dream, much less to recount its details, then encouraging the outright forgetting that there was a dream at all, remembering nothing beyond the vague sense that during sleep there had been the familiar sound of something shifting and sliding, up under the roof.

We might, in this way, regain the kind of spontaneity and zest for ideas, things popping into the mind, uncontrollable and ungovernable thoughts, the feel that this notion is somehow connected unaccountably with that one. We could come again into possession of real memory, the kind of memory that can come only from jumbled forgotten furniture, old photographs, fragments of music.

It has been one of the great errors of our time to think that by thinking about thinking, and then talking about it, we could possibly straighten out and tidy up our minds. There is no delusion more damaging than to get the idea in your head that you understand the functioning of your own brain. Once you acquire such a notion, you run the danger of moving in to take charge, guiding your thoughts, shepherding your mind from place to place, *controlling* it, making lists of regulations. The human mind is not meant to be governed, certainly not by any book of rules yet written; it is supposed to run itself, and we are obliged to follow it along, trying to keep up with it as best we can. It is all very well to be aware of your awareness, even proud of it, but never try to operate it. You are not up to the job.

I leave it to the analysts to work out the techniques for doing what now needs doing. They are presumably the professionals most familiar with the route, and all they have to do is turn back and go the other way, session by session, step by step. It takes a certain amount of hard swallowing and a lot of revised jargon, and I have great sympathy for their plight, but it is time to reverse course.

If after all, as seems to be true, we are endowed with unconscious minds in our brains, these should be regarded as normal structures, installed wherever they are for a purpose. I am not sure what they are built to contain, but as a biologist, impressed by the usefulness of everything alive, I would take it for granted that they are useful, probably indispensable organs of thought. It cannot be a bad thing to own one, but I would no more think of meddling with it than trying to exorcise my liver, an equally mysterious apparatus. Until we know a lot more, it would be wise, as we have learned from other fields in medicine, to let them be, above all not to interfere. Maybe, even—and this is the notion I wish to suggest to my psychiatric friends—to stock them up, put more things into them, make *use* of them. Forget whatever you feel like forgetting. From time to time, practice *not* being open, discover new things *not* to talk about, learn reserve, hold the tongue. But above all, develop the human talent for forgetting words, phrases, whole unwelcome sentences, all experiences involving wincing. If we should ever lose the loss of memory, we might lose as well that most attractive of signals ever flashed from the human face, the blush. If we should give away the capacity for embarrassment, the touch of fingertips might be the next to go, and then the suddenness of laughter, the unaccountable sure sense of something gone wrong, and, finally, the marvelous conviction that being human is the best thing to be.

Attempting to operate one's own mind, powered by such a magical instrument as the human brain, strikes me as rather like using the world's biggest computer to add columns of figures, or towing a Rolls-Royce with a nylon rope.

I have tried to think of a name for the new professional activity, but each time I think of a good one I forget it before I can get it written down. Psychorepression is the only one I've hung on to, but I can't guess at the fee schedule.

Additional Rhetorical Strategies

Comparison and Contrast (paragraphs 1–4); Process Analysis (paragraph 10).

Discussion Questions

1. Compare and contrast paragraphs 1 and 6. Is the attic literal or metaphorical or some implicit combination of the two in Thomas's opening paragraph? What becomes of it in paragraph 6? What are the literal equivalents of the things—the trapdoor and stepladder, the dusk, and all the rest—that he mentions in this paragraph?
2. Thomas utilizes the metaphor of the attic to critique candor and psychotherapy. How does he construct the connection between the language of architecture and the language of psychology throughout the essay?
3. How is the reader meant to take Thomas's suggested solution, "psychorepression"? Look closely at his language in the section of the essay in which he lays out his proposals; how would you characterize his tone? If he cannot seriously expect the psychiatric establishment to take up his suggestions, what more realistic solutions might be implied by his essay?
4. Parts of Thomas's essay might be characterized as antiscientific. For instance, in paragraph 14 he refers to the liver as a "mysterious apparatus," with which he would prefer not to interfere. At other times he identifies with a scientific frame of mind; for instance, in the same paragraph just quoted, he writes that "as a biologist [he is] impressed with the usefulness of everything alive." How would you characterize the typical scientific approach to the world around us? Compare and contrast Thomas's approach with the usual approach. What does he gain and lose by his idiosyncratic approach? (You might profitably compare "The Attic of the Brain" to Mark Twain's "Reading the River" in this regard.)

Essay Questions

1. Analyze Thomas's use of the extended architectural metaphor to represent memory. Don't stop at the opening paragraphs; where else does the metaphorical language appear? To what effect?
2. In this essay, Lewis Thomas considers some of the ways that changes in architecture resemble fashionable changes in lifestyle.

Think about the house or apartment where you grew up (or one of the houses or apartments where you lived as you were growing up) and discuss the ways in which the structure of the dwelling reflected your family's lifestyle. In some cases, of course, we inherit the relics of an earlier generation. If your family did not quite fit in (figuratively) to its house, write of the discrepancies between the two.

Reading the River

Mark Twain

*One of America's outstanding novelists and humorists, Samuel Lang-
horne Clemens (Mark Twain) was born near the Mississippi River in
1835. Widely read and admired in his own time, Twain's classic novels,*
The Adventures of Tom Sawyer *(1876) and* The Adventures of
Huckleberry Finn *(1885), have secured him a prominent place in American literary history.*

*Twain was also a prolific journalist and essayist. He published a se-
ries of articles on his years as an apprentice pilot on the Mississippi in the*
Atlantic *in 1875. In 1882, Twain's publisher suggested that he use these
essays as the basis for a book and urged Twain to revisit the scenes of his
earlier adventures. But times—and life on the Mississippi—had changed
greatly since his years as a cub pilot; the river had lost much of its antebel-
lum "romance and beauty." Twain published his youthful and seasoned
views of life on the river in a book-length autobiographical narrative,* Life
on the Mississippi *(1883). In the following selection, Twain creates a series of striking analogies to express a vivid sense of the wisdom he acquired while learning his trade.*

T he face of the water, in time, became a wonderful book—a
book that was a dead language to the uneducated passenger but which told its mind to
me without reserve, delivering its most cherished secrets as clearly as
if it uttered them with a voice. And it was not a book to be read once
and thrown aside, for it had a new story to tell every day. Throughout
the long twelve hundred miles there was never a page that was void
of interest, never one that you could leave unread without loss, never
one that you would want to skip, thinking you could find higher enjoyment in some other thing. There never was so wonderful a book
written by man, never one whose interest was so absorbing, so unflag-
ging, so sparklingly renewed with every reperusal. The passenger
who could not read it was charmed with a peculiar sort of faint dim-
ple on its surface (on the rare occasions when he did not overlook it
altogether) but to the pilot that was an *italicized* passage; indeed it was
more than that, it was a legend of the largest capitals with a string of
shouting exclamation points at the end of it, for it meant that a wreck
or a rock was buried there that could tear the life out of the strongest
vessel that ever floated. It is the faintest and simplest expression the
water ever makes, and the most hideous to a pilot's eye. In truth, the
passenger who could not read this book saw nothing but all manner
of pretty pictures in it, painted by the sun and shaded by the clouds,
whereas to the trained eye these were not pictures at all, but the
grimmest and most dead-earnest of reading matter.

Now when I had mastered the language of this water, and had come to know every trifling feature that bordered the great river as familiarly as I knew the letters of the alphabet, I had made a valuable acquisition. But I had lost something, too. I had lost something which could never be restored to me while I lived. All the grace, the beauty, the poetry, had gone out of the majestic river! I still kept in mind a certain wonderful sunset which I witnessed when steamboating was new to me. A broad expanse of the river was turned to blood; in the middle distance the red hue brightened into gold, through which a solitary log came floating, black and conspicuous; in one place a long, slanting mark lay sparkling upon the water; in another the surface was broken by boiling, tumbling rings, that were as many-tinted as an opal; where the ruddy flush was faintest, was a smooth spot that was covered with graceful circles and radiating lines, ever so delicately traced; the shore on our left was densely wooded, and the somber shadow that fell from this forest was broken in one place by a long, ruffled trail that shone like silver; and high above the forest wall a clean-stemmed dead tree waved a single leafy bough that glowed like a flame in the unobstructed splendor that was flowing from the sun. There were graceful curves, reflected images, woody heights, soft distances; and over the whole scene, far and near, the dissolving lights drifted steadily, enriching it every passing moment with new marvels of coloring.

I stood like one bewitched. I drank it in, in a speechless rapture. The world was new to me, and I had never seen anything like this at home. But as I have said, a day came when I began to cease from noting the glories and the charms which the moon and the sun and the twilight wrought upon the river's face; another day came when I ceased altogether to note them. Then, if that sunset scene had been repeated, I should have looked upon it without rapture, and should have commented upon it, inwardly, after this fashion: "This sun means that we are going to have wind to-morrow; that floating log means that the river is rising, small thanks to it; that slanting mark on the water refers to a bluff reef which is going to kill somebody's steamboat one of these nights, if it keeps on stretching out like that; those tumbling 'boils' show a dissolving bar and a changing channel there; the lines and circles in the slick water over yonder are a warning that that troublesome place is shoaling up dangerously; that silver streak in the shadow of the forest is the 'break' from a new snag, and he has located himself in the very best place he could have found to fish for steamboats; that tall dead tree, with a single living branch, is not going to last long, and then how is a body ever going to get through this blind place at night without the friendly old landmark?"

No, the romance and beauty were all gone from the river. All the value any feature of it had for me now was the amount of usefulness it could furnish toward compassing the safe piloting of a steamboat. Since those days, I have pitied doctors from my heart. What does the lovely flush in a beauty's cheek mean to a doctor but a "break" that ripples above some deadly disease? Are not all her visible charms sown thick with what are to him the signs and symbols of hidden decay? Does he ever see her beauty at all, or doesn't he simply view her professionally and comment upon her unwholesome condition all to himself? And doesn't he sometimes wonder whether he has gained most or lost most by learning his trade?

Additional Rhetorical Strategies

Comparison and Contrast (paragraph 1); Description (paragraph 2); Cause and Effect (paragraph 3).

Discussion Questions

1. According to Twain, in what sense is the river like a book? What is gained by being able to read the river? What is lost? How is this dual effect—both pleasure and problem—relevant to the book analogy?
2. How is each paragraph related to the ones that precede and follow it in this brief essay? How does paragraph 1, for instance, prepare us for paragraphs 2 and 3? How does paragraph 3 prepare us for paragraph 4? Discuss the internal coherence of this essay and the specific ways in which Twain achieves it.
3. In this essay Twain not only compares the river to a book, but he also compares himself with other people, first with the casual passengers who see "pretty pictures" in the water (paragraph 1), and later with the physician (paragraph 4). What is his attitude toward each of these people?
4. How does Twain's attitude toward the casual passengers and the physician compare and contrast to this attitude toward his own younger and older self, and how is he revealed by the things he says about them?

Essay Questions

1. Think of something that you see differently now from the way you viewed it when you were younger. Write an essay comparing the two different perspectives on the same thing, using appropriate language to convey your shift in perception. Was the change purely positive, or have you, like Twain, lost something in the transition? You may want to look also at "Once More to the Lake" (p. 52) for a different take on the kinds of shift in perspective that can come with age.

2. Compare Twain's two descriptions of the river scene. How would you characterize the differences between them? What attitude toward the river and the surrounding scenery is conveyed by each? Pay special attention to the ways in which Twain's style and diction change in order to communicate these different impressions.

The Allegory of the Cave

Plato

The writings of Plato (ca. 426–347 BC) have bequeathed a rich intellectual vision which has remained the foundation for much of subsequent philosophical inquiry in Western civilization. Born of aristocratic Athenian parents, Plato traveled widely in Egypt, Italy, and Sicily after the death of his mentor, Socrates, in 399 BC Sometime after 387 BC, Plato founded his Academy, in which he taught until his death. The most famous student at the Academy was Aristotle, who studied with Plato for 20 years.

The following selection from Plato's Republic—*a dialogue between Socrates and Glaucon—dramatizes his belief in a hierarchy of knowledge. As is evident in his recounting of our plight in the allegory of the cave, Plato believes that we are trapped by the deception of our senses. He envisions us as prisoners in a cave, able to see only the shadows of reality. Philosophical education, expressed in the dialectical form of argument (what he calls* dialogue*), can best free us from the constraints of our limited view of the world and enable us to know the most profound meaning of good, beauty, truth.*

And now, I said, let me show in a figure how far our nature is enlightened or unenlightened: Behold! human beings living in an underground den, which has a mouth open toward the light and reaching all along the den; here they have been from their childhood, and have their legs and necks chained so that they cannot move, and can only see before them, being prevented by the chains from turning round their heads. Above and behind them a fire is blazing at a distance, and between the fire and the prisoners there is a raised way; and you will see, if you look, a low wall built along the way, like the screen which marionette-players have in front of them, over which they show the puppets.

I see.

And do you see, I said, men passing along the wall carrying all sorts of vessels, and statues and figures of animals made of wood and stone and various materials, which appear over the wall? Some of them are talking, others silent.

You have shown me a strange image, and they are strange prisoners.

5   Like ourselves, I replied; and they see only their own shadows, or the shadows of one another, which the fire throws on the opposite wall of the cave?

True, he said; how could they see anything but the shadows if they were never allowed to move their heads?

And of the objects which are being carried in like manner they would only see the shadows?

Yes, he said.

And if they were able to converse with one another, would they not suppose that they were naming what was actually before them?

Very true.   10

And suppose further that the prison had an echo which came from the other side, would they not be sure to fancy when one of the passers-by spoke that the voice which they heard came from the passing shadow?

No question, he replied.

To them, I said, the truth would be literally nothing but the shadows of the images.

That is certain.

And now look again, and see what will naturally follow if the 15 prisoners are released and disabused of their error. At first, when any of them is liberated and compelled suddenly to stand up and turn his neck round and walk and look toward the light, he will suffer sharp pains; the glare will distress him, and he will be unable to see the realities of which in his former state he had seen the shadows; and then conceive someone saying to him, that what he saw before was an illusion, but that now, when he is approaching nearer to being and his eye is turned toward more real existence, he has a clearer vision— what will be his reply? And you may further imagine that his instructor is pointing to the objects as they pass and requiring him to name them—will he not be perplexed? Will he not fancy that the shadows which he formerly saw are truer than the objects which are now shown to him?

Far truer.

And if he is compelled to look straight at the light, will he not have a pain in his eyes which will make him turn away to take refuge in the objects of vision which he can see, and which he will conceive to be in reality clearer than the things which are now being shown to him?

True, he said.

And suppose once more, that he is reluctantly dragged up a steep and rugged ascent, and held fast until he is forced into the presence of the sun himself, is he not likely to be pained and irritated? When he approaches the light his eyes will be dazzled, and he will not be able to see anything at all of what are now called realities.

Not all in a moment, he said.   20

He will require to grow accustomed to the sight of the upper world. And first he will see the shadows best, next the reflections of men and other objects in the water, and then the objects themselves; then he will gaze upon the light of the moon and the stars and the spangled heaven; and he will see the sky and the stars by night better than the sun or the light of the sun by day?

Certainly.

Last of all he will be able to see the sun, and not mere reflections of him in the water, but he will see him in his own proper place, and not in another; and he will contemplate him as he is.

Certainly.

25 He will then proceed to argue that this is he who gives the season and the years, and is the guardian of all that is in the visible world, and in a certain way the cause of all things which he and his fellows have been accustomed to behold?

Clearly, he said, he would first see the sun and then reason about him.

And when he remembered his old habitation, and the wisdom of the den and his fellow prisoners, do you not suppose that he would felicitate himself on the change, and pity them?

Certainly, he would.

And if they were in the habit of conferring honors among themselves on those who were quickest to observe the passing shadows and to remark which of them went before, and which followed after, and which were together; and who were therefore best able to draw conclusions as to the future, do you think that he would care for such honors and glories, or envy the possessors of them? Would he not say with Homer,

"Better to be the poor servant of a poor master,"

and to endure anything, rather than think as they do and live after their manner?

30 Yes, he said, I think that he would rather suffer anything than entertain these false notions and live in this miserable manner.

Imagine once more, I said, such a one coming suddenly out of the sun to be replaced in his old situation; would he not be certain to have his eyes full of darkness?

To be sure, he said.

And if there were a contest, and he had to compete in measuring the shadows with the prisoners who had never moved out of the den, while his sight was still weak, and before his eyes had become steady (and the time which would be needed to acquire this new habit of sight might be very considerable), would he not be ridiculous? Men would say of him that up he went and down he came without his eyes; and that it was better not even to think of ascending; and if anyone tried to loose another and lead him up to the light, let them only catch the offender, and they would put him to death.

No question, he said.

35 This entire allegory, I said, you may now append, dear Glaucon, to the previous argument; the prison-house is the world of sight, the light of the fire is the sun, and you will not misapprehend me if you interpret the journey upward to be the ascent of the soul into the intellectual world according to my poor belief, which, at your desire, I have expressed—whether rightly or wrongly, God knows. But, whether true or false, my opinion is that in the world of knowledge the idea of good ap-

pears last of all, and is seen only with an effort; and, when seen, is also inferred to be the universal author of all things beautiful and right, parent of light and of the lord of light in this visible world, and the immediate source of reason and truth in the intellectual; and that this is the power upon which he who would act rationally either in public or private life must have his eye fixed.

I agree, he said, as far as I am able to understand you.

Moreover, I said, you must not wonder that those who attain to this beatific vision are unwilling to descend to human affairs; for their souls are ever hastening into the upper world where they desire to dwell, which desire of theirs is very natural, if our allegory may be trusted.

Yes, very natural.

And is there anything surprising in one who passes from divine contemplations to the evil state of man, misbehaving himself in a ridiculous manner; if, while his eyes are blinking and before he has become accustomed to the surrounding darkness, he is compelled to fight in courts of law, or in other places, about the images or the shadows of images of justice, and is endeavoring to meet the conceptions of those who have never yet seen absolute justice?

Anything but surprising, he replied.   40

Anyone who has common sense will remember that the bewilderments of the eyes are of two kinds, and arise from two causes, either from coming out of the light or from going into the light, which is true of the mind's eye, quite as much as of the bodily eye; and he who remembers this when he sees anyone whose vision is perplexed and weak, will not be too ready to laugh; he will first ask whether that soul of man has come out of the brighter life, and is unable to see because unaccustomed to the dark, or having turned from darkness to the day is dazzled by excess of light. And he will count the one happy in his condition and state of being, and he will pity the other; or, if he have a mind to laugh at the soul which comes from below into the light, there will be more reason in this than in the laugh which greets him who returns from above out of the light into the den.

That, he said, is a very just distinction.

Additional Rhetorical Strategies

Description (paragraph 1); Classification (paragraph 40); Argument (throughout); Cause and Effect (throughout).

Discussion Questions

1. Identify the series of part-by-part resemblances that Plato creates in this selection from the *Republic*. At what point does he explicitly introduce the analogy? How does he develop this analogy?

2. How does the newly released prisoner of the cave respond if he is forced into the light? How can he come to see the light? What does this suggest about Plato's views about the nature of learning?

3. What is the effect of presenting his lesson in the form of a dialogue? What role does each interlocutor play? What principles of argument underpin the structure of this dialogue?

4. What happens to the liberated prisoner who then returns to the cave? How does he regard the actions of the other prisoners? To what do the contests and honors conferred among the prisoners correspond allegorically? Why do you suppose that Plato does not simply conclude *when* the person has "seen the light"?

5. This excerpt not only provides an allegory for the search for knowledge; it also dramatizes the enlightenment of a student by means of a dialogue with his teacher. Given Plato's account of the coming into knowledge, why do you think he communicated his lesson by means of an allegory rather than by some more straightforward method?

Essay Questions

1. In a sense, this selection from the *Republic* could be seen as a process analysis, an analysis of the way by which a person comes into knowledge. Write a process analysis in which you illuminate an abstract process by means of an analogy with something more concrete.

2. Try your hand at writing an essay in which you create an analogy to critique some aspect of contemporary American culture. Feel free to model your essay on Plato's, in terms of creating an imaginary world that parallels and thereby illuminates your own.

Feminism at the Crossroads

Katha Pollitt

Katha Pollitt (b. 1949) publishes widely in such periodicals as the Na-
tion, Mother Jones, the New York Times Book Review, and Dissent,
where the following article, based on a talk given at the New School for So-
cial Research in New York City in 1993, was first published. Her collec-
tion of essays, Reasonable Creatures: Essays on Women and Feminism, *was published in 1994.*

Pollitt is also an accomplished poet. She has received, among other
awards, the National Book Critics Circle Award for best poetry, for her
book Antarctic Traveller. *Readers of her poetry agree that one of her most*
impressive skills is her ability to use visual imagery to explore human
thought and emotion. As you read the essay that follows, keep in mind
Pollitt's other life as a poet, and note the ways in which her facility with
imagery informs her nonfiction writing.

Feminism, like Broadway, the novel, and God, has been declared dead many times. Indeed, unlike those other items, it has been de-clared dead almost since its birth—by which I mean its modern re-birth in the 1960s. Feminism has also, as Susan Faludi demonstrated so cleverly in *Backlash*, been blamed for making women miserable, for causing everything from infertility—see? you waited too long to get pregnant because you were hell-bent on a fancy career and didn't settle for that nice boy next door twenty years ago, and now look—to poverty and divorce, which in this version of life is always initiated by men. And if that line doesn't work, there are always children, as in: feminism is all right for *women,* but what about the kids, foisted off on day care centers run by child molesters and deprived of paternal authority by di-vorce, which in this version of life is always initiated by women.

So it's with great pleasure and some relief that I observe that we are not gathered here tonight to debate whether feminism is actively bad or just irrelevant, but to discuss its future direction.[1] "Feminism at the Crossroads"—that sounds dramatic, doesn't it, full of promise, or is it threat?—of challenge at any rate, opportunities to be seized or missed, or signposts that if rightly read will send women onto the broad main highway of civic life and personal happiness but if misread or wrongly chosen will send them down some ill-lit alley, or even up the proverbial garden path. I will quarrel a bit with that metaphor later, but first I'd like to observe that a crossroads is a much more exciting place to be than a graveyard, so clearly we are making progress!

[1]This essay was delivered as a speech at the New School for Social Research in New York City in the autumn of 1993—Eds.

What are the street signs on the feminist crossroads? Women today are enjoying a lively debate on a number of issues, although perhaps "enjoying" is not the *mot juste* here, given how acrimonious these debates can become.[2] There's a debate around sexuality issues, which tends to be played out over pornography. And there's a debate about gender roles in marriage, which is expressed around issues of, say, the "mommy track" at work, whereby women would trade professional advancement for a schedule that would make it easier for them to fulfill a modified version of traditional domestic roles at home: you'll notice that nobody calls it the "parent track." There's a debate about work itself: should women enter the male-dominated professions on terms already laid down, or change them? Or fight for the upward valuation of the traditional female jobs? Grade school teacher or college professor? Nurse or doctor? Fight for the right of women soldiers to enter combat, or fight the military itself?

What all these debates have in common is that they tend to divide into two broad camps: In one fall those who would shore up and protect some notion of women as different than men—whether by nature, nurture, or more or less immutable social function—who, because of that difference, need special protections in order not to be disadvantaged by a male-dominant social order. And in the other, we find those who see gender as a more fluid social construction, with the sexes sharing a broad range of traits and ways of life, and who see their feminist task as opening every social possibility/opportunity to women. To oversimplify greatly, one can pose the question as, which do women need, more freedom or more protection? More respect for individual variations among women or more respect for traditional feminine traits and roles?

But if one street sign reads freedom and another protection, we can see that there are problems with our crossroads metaphor. In the first place, if standing at the crossroads means having to choose a direction, it will immediately become apparent that American feminism has been divided over which path to take for over a century. Although I'm sure Andrea Dworkin would take issue with me here, I see important continuities between the antipornography movement and, say, the Women's Christian Temperance Union (WCTU): both use powerful Puritan energies already present in American society in order to mount a challenge to male domestic irresponsibility and violence: men will be tamed by being deprived of their evil pleasures (rather than: women will be empowered by confronting inequality head-on); both mistake a symbol for a cause; both share a certain sense of women as pure and nonsexual and better than men: Frances Willard, the head of the WCTU, even espoused the ideal of marriage without sex entirely.[3] And today's pro-sex feminists can trace their lineage back to Frances Wright, Victoria Woodhull, the Utopian feminists of the Oneida community, and other early nineteenth-century social experiments. Similarly, the debate over whether women need more protection or more equality at work has a long history, with surprising people lining up on both sides of the issue: Eleanor Roosevelt, for example, opposed the Equal Rights Amendment because she believed it would expose women to increased exploitation in the workplace, and supported so-called protective legislation that limited the hours of working women.

A second problem with our crossroads metaphor is that it assumes that, along the special/equal or protection/freedom divide women will line up on one side or the other. As Ann Snitow suggested in "Pages from a Gender Diary" (*Dissent,* spring 1989) this is a misleading picture, which better fits hardened crusaders of the movement than it does most women. It may be true that at some deep philosophical level there is a contradiction between wanting more sexual freedom and wanting less pornography, or wanting to see women's experience reflected across the academic board and wanting independent women's studies departments, or wanting to break down the gender-segregated workforce and wanting comparable worth for the historically underpaid jobs in which women predominate. But at the practical level of lived daily life, one finds surprisingly few women who feel compelled to take a hard and consistent line. In her interesting book, *Feminism Without Illusions,* Elizabeth Fox-Genovese argues that there is a contradiction between the individualism at the heart of the modern American women's movement and the demands it also makes, or ought to make, for more collective responsibility for the disadvantaged. But many women, including myself, don't see it as an either/or situation. Last year, to give an example from my own work, I wrote an article attacking the wing of feminism I called "difference feminism," that is, the notion that women are more or less immutably different than men in ways that have important moral consequences. For example, that women are kinder, gentler, more harmonious, and less competitive than men. I argued that the different social styles of the two sexes are more apparent than real and do not, in any case, translate into moral and political differences in the public realm, and that it was a great mistake to base claims to political power on, for example, the supposed superior altruism and honesty of female politicians. I still think I was right, despite the suspicious fact

---

[3]Andrea Dworkin is a prominent contemporary leader in the antipornography movement. The WCTU, founded in 1874, advocated wholesale prohibition of alcohol as a remedy for a variety of social problems—Eds.

that of all the essays I've written for the *Nation*, this was the one that got the most favorable comment from men. But the fact is, many women have no trouble at all believing simultaneously that women are morally superior to men and that they are also equal to men. In the same way, women can both admire Hillary Rodham Clinton because she is a smart, powerful, working mother, and live with the unfortunate fact that her current political position was achieved through marriage.

A very good example of how close the two different strains of feminism can be is the response to Anita Hill. Now there's certainly a way to read Hill's charges that fits in with protectionist, women-are-better feminism: as many pointed out at the time of the Thomas hearings, not every woman would be disgusted, bowled over and physically upset by off-color remarks of the sort she claimed Thomas made to her—plenty of women, indeed, have been known to make such remarks themselves. Her ten-year silence also fits a certain vision of women as unable to defend themselves, thus needing lots of extra help from the law and the state. But the political effect of Hill's testimony could not have been more activist: women, the lesson was, must win political power in order for their concerns to be addressed.[4]

It should not, perhaps, surprise us that in daily life, and in the political realm as well, feminists, and many women who resist the label too, should find themselves traveling all roads at once rather than marching firmly down one path or the other. This reflects women's real condition: most women work *and* have children; are married *and* know that marriage these days may well not be for life. Women who have abortions also have babies; women who resent men's interest in pornography *also* have forced Harlequin romances to include semi-explicit sex scenes. They want to have sexual adventures *and* not to be raped or abused. To be both women *and* human beings. It's not so surprising, then, that we find women who consider themselves to be feminists shifting back and forth between these two camps. And historically, indeed, both have achieved some success.

On the whole, however, I would say that feminism's best hope lies with equality, because although equality has the defect of sometimes seeming rather counter-intuitive—why legally treat pregnancy like an illness when we all know very well it *isn't* an illness—it has the great advantage of being open-ended. Protectionist or difference feminism says, in effect: this is what women are like, this is the kind of life they lead, so let's shape social policy and the law to acknowledge and reflect

---

[4]In 1991 law professor Anita Hill accused Clarence Thomas of sexual harassment. In testimony before the Senate committee considering Thomas's confirmation to the Supreme Court she described incidents of verbal and physical harassment that she had experienced 10 years earlier—Eds.

it. For example, the "mommy track" says, look, we all know women do most of the child care and most of the housework, so let's make it easier for them to get through the double day of paid employment and domestic responsibilities. In the short run, this might even genuinely help women—but it also assumes that gender roles in the family aren't going to change, even though they are rapidly doing so, even as we speak, and throws its weight behind keeping those roles the same. Protectionist policies of the past have a way of outdating themselves. When the Soviet Union, in its early days, instituted a policy whereby women could take off from work while they had their menstrual periods, that probably seemed the height of compassion, common sense, and enlightened social policy. But what it really did was ensure that women would do all the domestic labor—after all, they had those days off, free for the asking—and enshrine in law ideas about menstruation that seem fairly fantastic today.

If I had to predict which road feminism will take, I would have to say that the material conditions for protectionist or "difference" feminism seem to be steadily eroding. Fewer and fewer women can afford to make stay-at-home motherhood the basis for a full identity; you will notice that stay-at-home childless wifehood, once also a common lifestyle, is no longer even discussed as a rational choice. Families are small and not very stable; that seems likely to remain the case, even if the family-values crowd succeeds in making abortion harder to achieve or divorce more difficult to obtain. In the workplace, gender barriers are slowly breaking down: that women are naturally more caring than men may suit the self-image of nurses and social workers, but doesn't really do much for, say, bartenders and marines. Little by little, the genders are converging: they are educated more alike and raised more alike than ever before, and out of economic necessity as much as anything else, their roles within marriage are converging too. Consider the recent census report that 20 percent of fathers care for children while their wives are working.

The idea that men and women are radically different species of being, which not so long ago struck so many as an indisputable fact of nature, is more and more coming to be revealed as a historical construct, connected to the rise of the bourgeois industrial household, a social form whose end we are living through. In that sense, then, protectionist or difference feminism is at bottom a nostalgic project, which I think today appeals to women at least partly because it seems to protect them against new and uncertain social forms and understandings—the sexually predatory behavior, for example of many male college students, which in previous situations was directed toward women of inferior social class rather than those of their own. The truth is, though, that it can't protect them, it can only make them feel better for a little while, like praying in a foxhole.

So perhaps the real way feminism will resolve its indecisiveness at the crossroads is that it will continue to debate and hesitate and try both roads at once until one day it sees that in fact the crossroads has disappeared. And then, of course, being feminists, we'll all congratulate ourselves over how right we were to choose what was, in fact, the only possible path—equality, which will at that point be understood to mean not women being the same as men, but both sexes sharing a more or less common life.

Additional Rhetorical Strategies

Classification (paragraph 4); Definition (paragraph 11); Comparison and Contrast (throughout); Example (throughout).

Discussion Questions

1. Trace the course of the extended metaphor of the crossroads throughout the essay. In what ways does Pollitt find the metaphor apt, and in what ways does it fall short of that ideal for metaphors? What is the effect of the author's quarrels with the guiding metaphor of her essay?

2. Which of the "two broad camps" Pollitt first defines in paragraph 4 do you think Pollitt finds most compatible with her own feminist views? At what point in the essay did you realize that Pollitt had a preference? Were there any word choices in the initial characterization of the two camps that gave you an early hint as to her stance? What is the effect of her withholding a direct statement of her own opinion until late in the essay?

3. In many essays on feminism you may have read, the opposition lies between men and women; this essay, on the other hand, is one of a growing number that treats debates within feminism. Where are the men in this essay? From the few mentions of them, can you infer Pollitt's stance toward men? Look, among other places, at paragraph 11, in which Pollitt refers to the "sexually predatory behavior of many male college students." How are we meant to interpret this phrase? How does the context, a paragraph discussing gender as a "historical construct," affect your interpretation of that line?

4. In paragraph 6, Pollitt briefly outlines the argument made by Elizabeth Fox-Genovese, who sees a contradiction between "the individualism at the heart of the modern American women's movement and the demands it also makes, or ought to make, for more collective responsibility for the disadvantaged." How do Fox-Genovese's terms align with Pollitt's terms, "special/equal or protection/freedom" (paragraph 6)? To what extent do they overlap, and what unique features does each set of terms bring to the debate?

Essay Questions

1. Write an essay in the form of an extended metaphor, and then follow Pollitt's lead: critique the metaphor in the body of your essay, in order to reach a more complex and nuanced view of your topic. You might draw your initial metaphor from the realm of public discourse; that is, choose a cliché that is in the air, and then test its limitations.

2. Reread paragraph 9, in which Pollitt outlines the difference between short- and long-term benefits. In light of this, and in light of other parts of her argument that you find pivotal, suggest a metaphor that would more accurately capture the situation of feminism today. In the final paragraph, Pollitt recommends that we "try both roads at once." Since this is a physical impossibility, see if you can come up with a metaphor that does not contain an inherent contradiction. Write an essay based on the metaphor you propose.

Thematic Pair:
Television as a Drug

▲▼TV Addiction

Marie Winn

Marie Winn (b. 1936) was born in Prague, Czechoslovakia, and moved to the United States in 1939. She is a freelance writer who specializes mainly in children's literature. In addition to writing dozens of books for children, she has published books for parents and teachers on issues related to child rearing and education. The essay below was taken from her book The Plug-In Drug: Television, Children, and the Family *(1977), which was selected as a notable book by the American Library Association. Her most recent books are* Children Without Childhood *(1983) and* Unplugging the Plug-In Drug *(1987). Winn also contributes articles to such periodicals as the* New York Times Magazine, New York Times Book Review, *and* Parade.

The word "addiction" is often used loosely and wryly in conversation. People will refer to themselves as "mystery book addicts" or "cookie addicts." E. B. White writes of his annual surge of interest in gardening: "We are hooked and are making an attempt to kick the habit." Yet nobody really believes that reading mysteries or ordering seeds by catalogue is serious enough to be compared with addictions to heroin or alcohol. The word "addiction" is here used jokingly to denote a tendency to overindulge in some pleasurable activity.

People often refer to being "hooked on TV." Does this, too, fall into the lighthearted category of cookie eating and other pleasures that people pursue with unusual intensity, or is there a kind of television viewing that falls into the more serious category of destructive addiction?

When we think about addiction to drugs or alcohol, we frequently focus on negative aspects, ignoring the pleasures that accompany drinking or drug-taking. And yet the essence of any serious addiction is a pursuit of pleasure, a search for a "high" that normal life does not supply. It is only the inability to function without the addictive substance that is dismaying, the dependence of the organism upon a certain experience and an increasing inability to function normally without it. Thus a person will take two or three drinks at the end of the day not merely for the pleasure drinking provides, but also because he "doesn't feel normal" without them.

An addict does not merely pursue a pleasurable experience and need to experience it in order to function normally. He needs to *repeat* it again and again. Something about that particular experience makes life without it less than complete. Other potentially pleasurable experiences are no longer possible, for under the spell of the addictive experience, his life is peculiarly distorted. The addict craves an experience and yet he is never really satisfied. The organism may be temporarily sated, but soon it begins to crave again.

5   Finally a serious addiction is distinguished from a harmless pursuit of pleasure by its distinctly destructive elements. A heroin addict, for instance, leads a damaged life: his increasing need for heroin in increasing doses prevents him from working, from maintaining relationships, from developing in human ways. Similarly an alcoholic's life is narrowed and dehumanized by his dependence on alcohol.

Let us consider television viewing in the light of the conditions that define serious addictions.

Not unlike drugs or alcohol, the television experience allows the participant to blot out the real world and enter into a pleasurable and passive mental state. The worries and anxieties of reality are as effectively deferred by becoming absorbed in a television program as by going on a "trip" induced by drugs or alcohol. And just as alcoholics are only inchoately aware of their addiction, feeling that they control their drinking more than they really do ("I can cut it out any time I want—I just like to have three or four drinks before dinner"), people similarly overestimate their control over television watching. Even as they put off other activities to spend hour after hour watching television, they feel they could easily resume living in a different, less passive style. But somehow or other while the television set is present in their homes, the click doesn't sound. With television pleasures available, those other experiences seem less attractive, more difficult somehow.

A heavy viewer (a college English instructor) observes: "I find television almost irresistible. When the set is on, I cannot ignore it. I can't turn it off. I feel sapped, will-less, enervated. As I reach out to turn off the set, the strength goes out of my arms. So I sit there for hours and hours."

The self-confessed television addict often feels he "ought" to do other things—but the fact that he doesn't read and doesn't plant his garden or sew or crochet or play games or have conversations means that those activities are no longer as desirable as television viewing. In a way a heavy viewer's life is as imbalanced by his television "habit" as a drug addict's or an alcoholic's. He is living in a holding pattern, as it were, passing up the activities that lead to growth or development or a sense of accomplishment. This is one reason people talk about their television viewing so ruefully, so apologetically. They are aware that it is an unproductive experience, that almost any other endeavor is more worthwhile by any human measure.

10   Finally it is the adverse effect of television viewing on the lives of so many people that defines it as a serious addiction. The television habit distorts the sense of time. It renders other experiences vague and curiously unreal while taking on a greater reality for itself. It weakens relationships by reducing and sometimes eliminating normal opportunities for talking, for communicating.

And yet television does not satisfy, else why would the viewer continue to watch hour after hour, day after day? "The measure of health," writes Lawrence Kubie, "is flexibility . . . and especially the freedom to cease when sated." But the television viewer can never be sated with his television experiences—they do not provide the true nourishment that satiation requires—and thus he finds that he cannot stop watching.

Additional Rhetorical Strategies

Definition (paragraphs 3–5); Argument (throughout); Comparison and Contrast (throughout).

Discussion Questions

1. Discuss the function of the first paragraph of Winn's essay. Why does she begin by bringing up what she considers less trivial uses of the addiction analogy before introducing an addiction analogy of her own: television addiction? Do you have any reservations about her characterizations of some addictions as more serious than others? Might "cookie addicts," for instance, in some cases have serious eating disorders? How does excessive television viewing compare to bulimia, in terms of the criteria Winn sets out in this essay or in terms of other criteria you find more relevant?

2. Although Winn mentions the pleasurable aspects of addiction, she focuses mainly on the destructive aspects in this essay. What are the destructive features she chooses to highlight? Can you think of other terms in which to describe the destructive side of addiction? Does television also meet these additional criteria?

3. In her final paragraph, Winn argues that the television viewer is never sated no matter how much television she or he watches. How does this idea compare with other models of desire? Is desire automatically killed when it is satisfied? Is unattainable satisfaction more alluring than that which is easily sated? Can you think of desires other than television that are satisfied in what Winn (or you) might consider a more "healthy" way, to borrow the terminology Winn invokes in this paragraph?

4. The two genuine addictions Winn draws on throughout her essay for purposes of her analogy are drugs and alcohol. The former are illegal and the latter is legal for adults. Does this contrast, or any other contrast between drugs and alcohol, make a difference in the validity of the two similar analogies? How might her argument have been different if she had used, for example, cigarettes?

5. What kinds of evidence does Winn use to bolster her argument that television addiction resembles drug addiction? What other kinds of evidence might she profitably have employed?

Essay Questions

1. Winn argues in this essay not against the quality of television, but rather against the nature of the experience itself, which can be seen as fundamentally passive. Could her argument be mustered against other, more respected activities? Consider, for example, such activities as attending a lecture or a concert. Write an essay comparing and contrasting two such activities, ones that at times seem in danger of lulling the spectator into passivity. Explain why each activity prompts passive behavior, and suggest possible ways to render such experiences more active.

2. If you watch television and you think the effects can be more beneficial than Winn suggests, create a different analogy for television viewing, one that brings to light the more positive aspects of the activity. Develop your analogy in an essay.

▲▼Crack and the Box

Pete Hamill

Pete Hamill (b. 1935) was educated at the Pratt Institute and Mexico City College. He was a sheet metal worker and later an advertising designer before beginning a career in journalism, as a reporter for the New York Post *from 1960–63. He has been a columnist for* Newsday, *the* New York Daily News, *the* Village Voice, *and* Esquire, *where "Crack and the Box" first appeared in 1990. Highlights from his columns are collected in two volumes:* Irrational Ravings *(1971) and* The Invisible City: A New York Sketchbook *(1980).*

Hamill also writes screenplays, short stories, and novels. His novels include The Gift *(1973),* Flesh and Blood *(1977),* Dirty Laundry *(1978), and* Loving Women: A Novel of the Fifties *(1989). His novels benefit from his years as a journalist, both in their realistic settings and true-to-life dialogue. In 1994 he published his memoir,* A Drinking Life.

One sad rainy morning last winter, I talked to a woman who was addicted to crack cocaine. She was twenty-two, stiletto-thin, with eyes as old as tombs. She was living in two rooms in a welfare hotel with her children, who were two, three, and five years of age. Her story was the usual tangle of human woe: early pregnancy, dropping out of school, vanished men, smack and then crack, tricks with johns in parked cars to pay for the dope. I asked her why she did drugs. She shrugged in an empty way and couldn't really answer beyond "makes me feel good." While we talked and she told her tale of squalor, the children ignored us. They were watching television.

Walking back to my office in the rain, I brooded about the woman, her zombielike children, and my own callous indifference. I'd heard so many versions of the same story that I almost never wrote them anymore; the sons of similar women, glimpsed a dozen years ago, are now in Dannemora or Soledad or Joliet;[1] in a hundred cities, their daughters are moving into the same loveless rooms. As I walked, a series of homeless men approached me for change, most of them junkies. Others sat in doorways, staring at nothing. They were additional casualties of our time of plague, demoralized reminders that although this country holds only 2 percent of the world's population, it consumes 65 percent of the world's supply of hard drugs.

Why, for God's sake? Why do so many millions of Americans of all ages, races, and classes choose to spend all or part of their lives stupefied? I've talked to hundreds of addicts over the years; some were my

---

[1]Three U.S. prisons—Eds.

friends. But none could give sensible answers. They stutter about the pain of the world, about despair or boredom, the urgent need for magic or pleasure in a society empty of both. But then they just shrug. Americans have the money to buy drugs; the supply is plentiful. But almost nobody in power asks, *Why?* Least of all, George Bush and his drug warriors.

William Bennett talks vaguely about the heritage of sixties permissiveness, the collapse of Traditional Values, and all that. But he and Bush offer the traditional American excuse: It Is Somebody Else's Fault. This posture set the stage for the self-righteous invasion of Panama, the bloodiest drug arrest in world history. Bush even accused Manuel Noriega of "poisoning our children." But he never asked *why* so many Americans demand the poison.[2]

5   And then, on that rainy morning in New York, I saw another one of those ragged men staring out at the rain from a doorway. I suddenly remembered the inert postures of the children in that welfare hotel, and I thought: *television.*

Ah, no, I muttered to myself: too simple. Something as complicated as drug addiction can't be blamed on television. Come on. . . . but I remembered all those desperate places I'd visited as a reporter, where there were no books and a TV set was always playing and the older kids had gone off somewhere to shoot smack, except for the kid who was at the mortuary in a coffin. I also remembered when I was a boy in the forties and early fifties, and drugs were a minor sideshow, a kind of dark little rumor. And there was one major difference between that time and this: television.

We had unemployment then; illiteracy, poor living conditions, racism, governmental stupidity, a gap between rich and poor. We didn't have the all-consuming presence of television in our lives. Now two generations of Americans have grown up with television from their earliest moments of consciousness. Those same American generations are afflicted by the pox of drug addiction.

Only thirty-five years ago, drug addiction was not a major problem in this country. There were drug addicts. We had some at the end of the nineteenth century, hooked on the cocaine in patent medicines. During the placid fifties, Commissioner Harry Anslinger pumped up the budget of the old Bureau of Narcotics with fantasies of reefer madness. Heroin was sold and used in most major American cities, while the bebop generation of jazz musicians got jammed up with horse.

---

[2]William Bennett was the director of drug policy—the Bush administration's so-called "Drug Czar"—from 1989–1990. In 1989 President Bush ordered U.S. troops to invade Panama and arrest that country's leader, General Manuel Noriega, based on evidence that he was involved in drug trafficking. Noriega was convicted of the charges in a U.S. court in 1992—Eds.

But until the early sixties, narcotics were still marginal to American life; they weren't the $120-billion market they make up today. If anything, those years have an eerie innocence. In 1955 there were 31,700,000 TV sets in use in the country (the number is now past 184 million). But the majority of the audience had grown up without the dazzling new medium. They embraced it, were diverted by it, perhaps even loved it, but they weren't *formed* by it. That year, the New York police made a mere 1,234 felony drug arrests; in 1988 it was 43,901. They confiscated ninety-seven *ounces* of cocaine for the entire year; last year it was hundreds of pounds. During each year of the fifties in New York, there were only about a hundred narcotics-related deaths. But by the end of the sixties, when the first generation of children *formed* by television had come to maturity (and thus to the marketplace), the number of such deaths had risen to 1,200. The same phenomenon was true in every major American city.

In the last Nielsen survey of American viewers, the average family10 was watching television seven hours a day. This has never happened before in history. No people has ever been entertained for seven hours a *day.* The Elizabethans didn't go to the theater seven hours a day. The pre-TV generation did not go to the movies seven hours a day. Common sense tells us that this all-pervasive diet of instant imagery, sustained now for forty years, must have changed us in profound ways.

Television, like drugs, dominates the lives of its addicts. And though some lonely Americans leave their sets on without watching them, using them as electronic companions, television usually absorbs its viewers the way drugs absorb their users. Viewers can't work or play while watching television; they can't read; they can't be out on the streets, falling in love with the wrong people, learning how to quarrel and compromise with other human beings. In short they are asocial. So are drug addicts.

One Michigan State University study in the early eighties offered a group of four- and five-year-olds the choice of giving up television or giving up their fathers. Fully one third said they would give up Daddy. Given a similar choice (between cocaine or heroin and father, mother, brother, sister, wife, husband, children, job), almost every stoned junkie would do the same.

There are other disturbing similarities. Television itself is a consciousness-altering instrument. With the touch of a button, it takes you out of the "real" world in which you reside and can place you at a basketball game, the back alleys of Miami, the streets of Bucharest, or the cartoony living rooms of Sitcom Land. Each move from channel to channel alters mood, usually with music or a laugh track. On any given evening, you can laugh, be frightened, feel tension, thump with excitement. You can even tune in *MacNeil/Lehrer* and feel sober.

But none of these abrupt shifts in mood is *earned.* They are attained as easily as popping a pill. Getting news from television, for example, is simply not the same experience as reading it in a newspaper. Reading is *active.* The reader must decode little symbols called words, then create images or ideas and make them connect; at its most basic level, reading is an act of the imagination. But the television viewer doesn't go through that process. The words are spoken to him by Dan Rather or Tom Brokaw or Peter Jennings. There isn't much decoding to do when watching television, no time to think or ponder before the next set of images and spoken words appears to displace the present one. The reader, being active, works at his or her own pace; the viewer, being passive, proceeds at a pace determined by the show. Except at the highest levels, television never demands that its audience take part in an act of imagination. Reading always does.

15   In short, television works on the same imaginative and intellectual level as psychoactive drugs. If prolonged television viewing makes the young passive (dozens of studies indicate that it does), then moving to drugs has a certain coherence. Drugs provide an unearned high (in contrast to the earned rush that comes from a feat accomplished, a human breakthrough earned by sweat or thought or love).

And because the television addict and the drug addict are alienated from the hard and scary world, they also feel they make no difference in its complicated events. For the junkie, the world is reduced to him and the needle, pipe, or vial; the self is absolutely isolated, with no desire for choice. The television addict lives the same way. Many Americans who fail to vote in presidential elections must believe they have no more control over such a choice than they do over the casting of *L.A. Law.*

The drug plague also coincides with the unspoken assumption of most television shows: Life should be *easy.* The most complicated events are summarized on TV news in a minute or less. Cops confront murder, chase the criminals, and bring them to justice (usually violently) within an hour. In commercials, you drink the right beer and you get the girl. *Easy!* So why should real life be a grind? Why should any American have to spend years mastering a skill or a craft, or work eight hours a day at an unpleasant job, or endure the compromises and crises of a marriage? Nobody *works* on television (except cops, doctors, and lawyers). Love stories on television are about falling in love or breaking up; the long, steady growth of a marriage—its essential *dailiness*—is seldom explored, except as comedy. Life on television is almost always simple: good guys and bad, nice girls and whores, smart guys and dumb. And if life in the real world isn't that simple, well, hey, man, have some dope, man, be happy, feel good.

The doper always whines about how he *feels;* drugs are used to enhance his feelings or obliterate them, and in this the doper is very American. No other people on earth spend so much time talking about their feelings; hundreds of thousands go to shrinks, they buy self-help books by the millions, they pour out intimate confessions to virtual strangers in bars or discos. Our political campaigns are about emotional issues now, stated in the simplicities of adolescence. Even alleged statesmen can start a sentence, "I feel that the Sandinistas should . . ." when they once might have said, "I *think* . . . ." I'm convinced that this exaltation of cheap emotions over logic and reason is one by-product of hundreds of thousands of hours of television.

Most Americans under the age of fifty have now spent their lives absorbing television; that is, they've had the structures of drama pounded into them. Drama is always about conflict. So news shows, politics, and advertising are now all shaped by those structures. Nobody will pay attention to anything as complicated as the part played by Third World debt in the expanding production of cocaine; it's much easier to focus on Manuel Noriega, a character right out of *Miami Vice*, and believe that even in real life there's a Mister Big.

What is to be done? Television is certainly not going away, but its[20] addictive qualities can be controlled. It's a lot easier to "just say no" to television than to heroin or crack. As a beginning, parents must take immediate control of the sets, teaching children to watch specific television *programs*, not "television," to get out of the house and play with other kids. Elementary and high schools must begin teaching television as a subject, the way literature is taught, showing children how shows are made, how to distinguish between the true and the false, how to recognize cheap emotional manipulation. All Americans should spend more time reading. And thinking.

For years, the defenders of television have argued that the networks are only giving the people what they want. That might be true. But so is the Medellín cartel.[3]

Additional Rhetorical Strategies

Narration (paragraph 1); Cause and Effect (paragraphs 5–6, 15, 18); Comparison and Contrast (paragraphs 7–9); Example (paragraph 13).

Discussion Questions

1. What is the effect of beginning this essay with an anecdote drawn from personal experience? How does the anecdote set the audience

---

[3]During the 1980s the "Medellín cartel" became a symbol of the profitable and vicious international drug trade. Based in the Colombian city of Medellín, the cartel supplied a large percentage of the U.S. cocaine market until its leader was killed by Colombian police in 1993—Eds.

up for Hamill's thesis? Describe the progression from paragraph 1 to paragraph 2, then paragraph 3. How does Hamill gradually expand the scope of his topic? Analyze the comparative effectiveness of an example of one family, versus addicts in 100 cities, versus millions of addicts. Pinpoint the personal epiphany for Hamill; at what point in the essay does he describe the moment when everything fell into place and suddenly made sense to him?

2. How does Hamill differentiate his approach from that of George Bush and William Bennett? What does Hamill gain from focusing on the demand for narcotics rather than on suppliers such as Noriega?

3. At what point in the essay does Hamill begin to explore the similarities between drug addiction and television addiction? Besides extended analogy, what would you identify as Hamill's main rhetorical strategy? Where in the essay do the two primary strategies come together?

4. In paragraph 6, Hamill identifies the "one major difference between that time and this: television." Can you think of other major differences between the two time periods in question? Are there other ways you might critique Hamill's thesis? What, for instance, was the role of radio in American culture before the advent of television? How would the picture Hamill paints change—how might the statistics shift—if he were to include statistics on alcohol consumption along with the data on the consumption of illegal drugs?

5. Look at Donald Hall's essay, "Four Kinds of Reading" (p. 258). How might he react to the contrasts Hamill draws between television viewing and reading (paragraph 14), or to the part of Hamill's solution that involves reading (paragraph 20)? With which author are you more inclined to agree? Why?

Essay Questions

1. What do you think about Hamill's suggestion that television be taught as a subject in school, just the way that literature is taught? Write an essay agreeing or disagreeing with that proposal, keeping in mind the fact that more and more university syllabi now include television programs, and the fact that certain segments of the society are vehemently opposed to such changes in the curriculum.

2. Implied in Hamill's essay is a more healthy, nonaddictive way of life, the opposite of the self-destructive life of the addict. Write an essay in which you explore the factors that add up to a fulfilling life. If your ideal differs from the one implied by Hamill, you may choose to compare and contrast your ideal with his.

Exploring Connections: Questions Linking the Thematic Pair

1. Compare and contrast Winn's essay and Hamill's essay. How do their rhetorical approaches differ? What are the relative strengths and weaknesses of each approach? Which essay do you find more compelling? Why?

2. Write an essay in which you argue against a view of television as destructive and addictive. What are the possible beneficial effects of television? How has the world changed for the better thanks to the advent of television? Alternatively, if you believe that television, like food, can be used or abused, write an essay arguing for a more complicated, subtle view of television.

3. Keep a television-viewing journal for one week. Write not only what you watched, but also what you noticed about your television-watching habits, and what you analyzed about the messages promoted by the programs you watched. At the end of the week, reread your journal entries and choose one entry or a constellation of related entries, and base a short formal essay on this informal material. Remember that although the journal, being exploratory, is not expected to have a thesis, your formal paper is.

Cause and Effect

Something happens and we want to find out *why*. In many ordinary situations we do not have to look very far to find an answer: the CD skips because it is dirty; the parking lot is full because of a rock concert. But understanding why something happens in other situations can be far more complicated: Is the baby crying because he is tired, uncomfortable, or sick? Did we fail to make the interview on time because of heavy traffic or an unconscious desire to miss it? Did the nuclear reactor shut down because of instrument failure or human error? In all of these examples we are dealing with a phenomenon that is at the heart of much of our empirical knowledge: the relation of cause and effect.

Because it seems so basic to human perception and reason, causal explanation is usually thought of as a fairly obvious mental procedure. We believe that every effect must have a cause; that the cause can be discovered by retracing the sequence of events that led to it; that similar causes will produce similar effects. But such beliefs, though they play an influential role in everyday life, have long been discredited in many areas of physics, philosophy, and psychology, where belief in causation is considered, as British philosopher Bertrand Russell put it, "a relic of a bygone era." It would be, of course, wholly impractical to adopt the same attitude toward causation in our daily affairs as physicists adopt in their investigation of subatomic particles, but it is, nevertheless, a good rule of thinking and writing to interpret and construct causal explanations cautiously.

When working with causal explanations in our compositions, we may proceed by moving either backward, from effect to cause, or forward, from cause to effect. We observe event or phenomenon B and show what caused it; or we observe event or phenomenon A and show what effect it will have. Whether we progress from A to B or from B to A will depend on our evidence and the kind of case we want to make— for example, do we want to explain or to predict? But whichever direction we decide to go in, it is important to remember that nothing becomes a cause or an effect merely by our calling it one. We must establish solid grounds for a causal sequence. If we can determine no causal explanation for event B, we have no valid reason to think of it as an "effect," nor should we think of A as a "cause" if we can calculate no possible consequences that would result from it. To call something an effect presupposes the existence of a cause, and vice versa.

361

In our casual thinking we tend to consider mainly single causes and single effects. But seldom are events so simple. When thinking hard about cause-and-effect relationships, we would do best to outline an entire set of causal possibilities (some immediate, some remote, some coexistent with effects, and some merely contributory), all of which are in some way connected with the effect or effects we are examining. Then, once we have systematically assembled a set of possible causes, we may proceed to select and isolate a few of the most significant and examine in detail their relation to the effect(s). The very selection of causes and effects can reveal much about our methods and predispositions. What a drug company, for example, may see as the harmless side-effects of one of its products, a government regulatory agency may find deadly. Whereas one historian would base a causal analysis of the American involvement in Vietnam almost exclusively upon world economic factors, another might lean toward an explanation based upon the power drives of high-level political figures. In fact, cause-and-effect reasoning—whether explicit or implicit, valid or invalid—occurs quite frequently as a strategy in many forms of persuasion, from political propaganda to toothpaste commercials.

Four Ways to Organize a Cause-and-Effect Essay

The complexity of our subject and our purpose, the depth of our information, and the angle of our interpretation will usually determine our method of causal exposition. Suppose you are a reporter analyzing the crash of a jetliner. The following four rhetorical patterns will suggest possible ways to organize a cause-and-effect essay.

A Single Cause Leading to a Single Effect This is quite clearly the easiest pattern to work with, though it is often open to the charge of oversimplification. You determine that the crash was caused by the fracture of a pylon bolt that holds the engine in place. The single-cause–single-effect procedure is commonly used to establish blame: "Who or what caused X?" can usually be rephrased as "Who or what is to blame for X?" It can be represented thus:

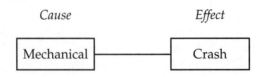

A Single Cause Leading to Multiple Effects　You pinpoint the fractured bolt as being responsible for the crash and then show how the crash was not a single event but a spectrum of interrelated tragedies and losses—all the consequence of a tiny bit of metal. This pattern frequently is used dramatically to show how small events can have enormous consequences. It can be shown figuratively in this way:

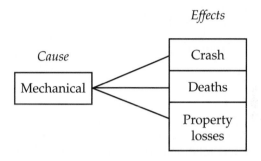

Multiple Causes Leading to a Single Effect　Since we usually perceive effects singly and since most significant effects can be traced to a number of causes, this is perhaps the most common cause-and-effect pattern. You see the crash as the consequence of many interlocking factors: the fractured bolt, unexpected damage to the plane's hydraulic system, inadequate maintenance standards, poor aerodynamic design, an inattentive ground crew, and so on. That pattern of cause and effect would look like this:

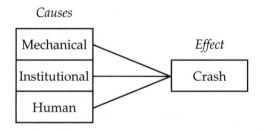

Multiple Causes Leading to Multiple Effects　This pattern demands the coordination of two groups of information—an analytical breakdown of causes and of effects. It is best used when trying to deal judiciously with highly complex matters. You would analyze the crash as a number of separate effects (deaths, property loss, recriminations, disruptions), produced by a number of causes, as in the following representation:

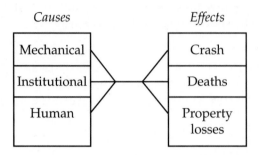

The above examples are intended to give an idea of how to manage cause-and-effect relationships in composition. For the sake of illustration, one topic was looked at in all four ways. In practice, however, a single, primary rhetorical procedure will usually be determined by the subject we are examining and the information we have at our disposal. In the case of the plane crash, the most satisfactory explanation would probably result from retracing a single effect back to its multiple causes. But in cases that have more far-reaching or lasting effects, such as wars, cultural movements, or political revolutions, we might do better to examine the subject with respect to multiple causes leading to multiple effects.

Seven Common Errors

Cause-and-effect explanations are particularly susceptible to erroneous reasoning. We can easily fall into traps when constructing causal explanations because of confusions stemming from the similarity of cause-and-effect relationships to other types of relationships.

What follows are seven common sources of confusion:

1. *Confusing a cause with an effect:* One of the first things we need to do in a causal analysis is make sure we distinguish between causes and effects— was the cracked steering column the principal cause of the accident or was it simply one of the effects of the crash?

2. *Confusing a cause with an antecedent:* That *A* occurs *before B* is no reason to think *A* causes *B*. A sore throat may precede a fever, but it does not produce the fever. This is one of the most prevalent fallacies (it goes by the name *post hoc, ergo propter hoc*—"after this, therefore because of this")

and is often used as the basis for commercial and political propaganda: President X is elected, the economy improves, and President X promotes himself as the *cause* of that improvement.

3. *Confusing a cause with a necessary condition:* A necessary condition is a condition without which something could not have occurred. It is closely connected to causal sequences, but should not be mistaken for a cause. The jetliner didn't crash *because* it took off, but its having taken off was a necessary condition of the crash. A boy struck by a car while crossing a street was not hit *because* he crossed the street (to think so would be superstitious), but his crossing was a necessary condition for the accident.

4. *Confusing a cause with a sign or symptom:* An ache or pain is not in itself the cause of our illness, but rather a symptom of it; sexual impotence may be a sign of marital problems, not necessarily a cause. Signs and symptoms are often closely associated with causal sequences and need to be examined carefully to make sure we do not mistake a peripheral event for a pivotal one.

5. *Confusing cause with correlation:* Statistics may show that 99 percent of the people who use Sparkle toothpaste have no cavities; but that figure may not signify any causal connection, for those who use Sparkle may rely on any number of dental aids, all of which may be causal factors in helping to eliminate decay. When examining statistical information, we should investigate all the relevant facts surrounding a case or claim. A high degree of correlation between two sets of data may strongly suggest a causal relationship, but it alone does not conclusively demonstrate that relationship.

6. *Confusing a cause with the whole of which it is but a part:* Sometimes an important causal factor may be only one element of a larger aggregate of elements. We may loosely speak of candy (a whole) as causing acne, but to establish precisely a cause-and-effect relationship between the two, we would need to specify which ingredient (which part) of a particular type of candy produces the physiological reaction that gives rise to pimples.

7. *Confusing a cause with a purpose:* A purpose may sometimes be similar to a cause ("Upton Sinclair wrote *The Jungle* to expose the evils of the meatpacking industry"), but not always. We have eyes to see with—that is their purpose—but seeing did not cause us to have eyes. Whenever we are tracing a chain of causes back to a first cause, we need to be clear about our use of *purpose* and *cause*. In general, it is convenient to think of a purpose as connected with the future, a cause as connected with the past.

Tightly linked cause-and-effect sequences are not easily established. Causal analysis is one of the toughest and most challenging types of thinking required in composition. In the following selections, we'll see how different writers with different purposes construct causal connections to help explain why things happen (or have happened) in many different areas of study: sociology, psychology, biology, politics, and environmental science.

Why Women Smile

Amy Cunningham

Amy Cunningham (b. 1955) grew up in the suburbs of Chicago, although her family is originally from the South. She studied English at the University of Virginia and graduated with a bachelor's degree in 1977. Since that time she has been writing essays for magazines such as Redbook, Glamour, *and* Washington Post Magazine. *The essay reprinted here first appeared in* Lear's *in 1993.*

Cunningham recalls that when writing this essay, "I was unhappy with myself for taking too long, for not being efficient the way I thought a professional writer should be—but the work paid off and now I think it is one of the best essays I've written." Reflecting on the work of a professional writer she notes, "When I was younger I thought if you had talent you would make it as a writer. I'm surprised to realize now that good writing has less to do with talent and more to do with the discipline of staying seated in the chair, by yourself, in front of the computer and getting the work done."

After smiling brilliantly for nearly four decades, I now find myself trying to quit. Or, at the very least, seeking to lower the wattage a bit.

Not everyone I know is keen on this. My smile has gleamed like a cheap plastic night-light so long and so reliably that certain friends and relatives worry that my mood will darken the moment my smile dims. "Gee," one says, "I associate you with your smile. It's the essence of you. I should think you'd want to smile more!" But the people who love me best agree that my smile—which springs forth no matter where I am or how I feel—hasn't been serving me well. Said my husband recently, "Your smiling face and unthreatening demeanor make people like you in a fuzzy way, but that doesn't seem to be what you're after these days."

Smiles are not the small and innocuous things they appear to be: Too many of us smile in lieu of showing what's really on our minds. Indeed, the success of the women's movement might be measured by the sincerity—and lack of it—in our smiles. Despite all the work we American women have done to get and maintain full legal control of our bodies, not to mention our destinies, we still don't seem to be fully in charge of a couple of small muscle groups in our faces.

We smile so often and so promiscuously—when we're angry, when we're tense, when we're with children, when we're being photographed, when we're interviewing for a job, when we're meeting candidates to employ—that the Smiling Woman has become a peculiarly American archetype. This isn't entirely a bad thing, of course. A smile lightens the load, diffuses unpleasantness, redistributes nervous tension. Women doctors smile more than their male counterparts, studies show, and are better liked by their patients.

5   Oscar Wilde's old saw that "a woman's face is her work of fiction" is often quoted to remind us that what's on the surface may have little connection to what we're feeling. What is it in our culture that keeps our smiles on automatic pilot? The behavior seems to be an equal blend of nature and nurture. Research has demonstrated that since females often mature earlier than males and are less irritable, girls smile more than boys from the very beginning. But by adolescence, the differences in the smiling rates of boys and girls are so robust that it's clear the culture has done more than its share of the dirty work. Just think of the mothers who painstakingly embroidered the words ENTER SMILING on little samplers, and then hung their handiwork on doors by golden chains. Translation: "Your real emotions aren't welcome here."

Clearly, our instincts are another factor. Our smiles have their roots in the greetings of monkeys, who pull their lips up and back to show their fear of attack, as well as their reluctance to vie for a position of dominance. And like the opossum caught in the light by the clattering garbage cans, we, too, flash toothy grimaces when we make major mistakes. By declaring ourselves nonthreatening, our smiles provide an extremely versatile means of protection.

Our earliest baby smiles are involuntary reflexes having only the vaguest connection to contentment or comfort. In short, we're genetically wired to pull on our parents' heartstrings. As Desmond Morris explains in *Babywatching*, this is our way of attaching ourselves to our caretakers, as truly as baby chimps clench their mothers' fur. Even as babies we're capable of projecting onto others (in this case, our parents) the feelings we know we need to get back in return.

Bona fide social smiles occur at two-and-a-half to three months of age, usually a few weeks after we first start gazing with intense interest into the faces of our parents. By the time we are six months old, we are smiling and laughing regularly in reaction to tickling, feedings, blown raspberries, hugs, and peekaboo games. Even babies who are born blind intuitively know how to react to pleasurable changes with a smile, though their first smiles start later than those of sighted children.

Psychologists and psychiatrists have noted that babies also smile and laugh with relief when they realize that something they thought might be dangerous is not dangerous after all. Kids begin to invite their parents to indulge them with "scary" approach-avoidance games; they love to be chased or tossed up into the air. (It's interesting to note that as adults, we go through the same gosh-that's-shocking-and-dangerous-but-it's-okay-to-laugh-and-smile cycles when we listen to raunchy stand-up comics.)

From the wilds of New Guinea to the sidewalks of New York,[10] smiles are associated with joy, relief, and amusement. But smiles are by no means limited to the expression of positive emotions: People of many different cultures smile when they are frightened, embarrassed, angry, or miserable. In Japan, for instance, a smile is often used to hide pain or sorrow.

Psychologist Paul Ekman, the head of the University of California's Human Interaction Lab in San Francisco, has identified 18 distinct types of smiles, including those that show misery, compliance, fear, and contempt. The smile of true merriment, which Dr. Ekman calls the Duchenne Smile, after the 19th century French doctor who first studied it, is characterized by heightened circulation, a feeling of exhilaration, and the employment of two major facial muscles: the zygomaticus major of the lower face, and the orbicularis oculi, which crinkles the skin around the eyes. But since the average American woman's smile often has less to do with her actual state of happiness than it does with the social pressure to smile no matter what, her baseline social smile isn't apt to be a felt expression that engages the eyes like this. Ekman insists that if people learned to read smiles, they could see the sadness, misery, or pain lurking there, plain as day.

Evidently, a woman's happy, willing deference is something the world wants visibly demonstrated. Woe to the waitress, the personal assistant or receptionist, the flight attendant, or any other woman in the line of public service whose smile is not offered up to the boss or client as proof that there are no storm clouds—no kids to support, no sleep that's been missed—rolling into the sunny workplace landscape. Women are expected to smile no matter where they line up on the social, cultural, or economic ladder: College professors are criticized for not smiling, political spouses are pilloried for being too serious, and women's roles in films have historically been smiling ones. It's little wonder that men on the street still call out, "Hey, baby, smile! Life's not *that* bad, is it?" to women passing by, lost in thought.

A friend remembers being pulled aside by a teacher after class and asked, "What is wrong, dear? You sat there for the whole hour looking so sad!" "All I could figure," my friend says now, "Is that I wasn't smiling. And the fact that *she* felt sorry for me for looking normal made me feel horrible."

Ironically, the social laws that govern our smiles have completely reversed themselves over the last 2,000 years. Women weren't always expected to seem animated and responsive; in fact, immoderate laughter was once considered one of the more conspicuous vices a woman could have, and mirth was downright sinful. Women were kept apart, in some cultures even veiled, so that they couldn't perpetuate Eve's seductive, evil work. The only smile deemed appropriate on a privileged woman's face was the serene, inward smile of the Virgin Mary at Christ's birth, and even that expression was best directed exclusively at young children. Cackling laughter and wicked glee were the kinds of sounds heard only in hell.

15   What we know of women's facial expressions in other centuries comes mostly from religious writings, codes of etiquette, and portrait paintings. In 15th century Italy, it was customary for artists to paint lovely, blank-faced women in profile. A viewer could stare endlessly at such a woman, but she could not gaze back. By the Renaissance, male artists were taking some pleasure in depicting women with a semblance of complexity, Leonardo da Vinci's Mona Lisa, with her veiled enigmatic smile, being the most famous example.

The Golden Age of the Dutch Republic marks a fascinating period for studying women's facial expressions. While we might expect the drunken young whores of Amsterdam to smile devilishly (unbridled sexuality and lasciviousness were *supposed* to addle the brain), it's the faces of the Dutch women from fine families that surprise us. Considered socially more free, these women demonstrate a fuller range of facial expressions than their European sisters. Frans Hals's 1622 portrait of Stephanus Geraerdt and Isabella Coymans, a married couple, is remarkable not just for the full, friendly smiles on each face, but for the frank and mutual pleasure the couple take in each other.

In the 1800s, sprightly, pretty women began appearing in advertisements for everything from beverages to those newfangled Kodak Land cameras. Women's faces were no longer impassive, and their willingness to bestow status, to offer, proffer, and yield, was most definitely promoted by their smiling images. The culture appeared to have turned the smile, originally a bond shared between intimates, into a socially required display that sold capitalist ideology as well as kitchen appliances. And female viewers soon began to emulate these highly idealized pictures. Many longed to be more like her, that perpetually smiling female. She seemed so beautiful. So content. So whole.

By the middle of the 19th century, the bulk of America's smile burden was falling primarily to women and African American slaves, providing a very portable means of protection, a way of saying, "I'm harmless. I won't assert myself here." It reassured those in power to see signs of gratitude and contentment in the faces of subordinates. As long ago as 1963, adman David Ogilvy declared the image of a woman smiling approvingly at a product clichéd, but we've yet to get the message. Cheerful Americans still appear in ads today, smiling somewhat less disingenuously than they smiled during the middle of the century, but smiling broadly nonetheless.

Other countries have been somewhat reluctant to import our "Don't worry, be happy" American smiles, When McDonald's opened in Moscow not long ago and when EuroDisney debuted in France last year, the Americans involved in both business ventures complained that they couldn't get the natives they'd employed to smile worth a damn.

Europeans visiting the United States for the first time are often sur-[20] prised at just how often Americans smile. But when you look at our history, the relentless good humor (or, at any rate, the pretense of it) falls into perspective. The American wilderness was developed on the assumption that this country had a shortage of people in relation to its possibilities. In countries with a more rigid class structure or caste system, fewer people are as captivated by the idea of quickly winning friends and influencing people. Here in the States, however, every stranger is a potential associate. Our smiles bring new people on board. The American smile is a democratic version of a curtsy or doffed hat, since, in this land of free equals, we're not especially formal about the ways we greet social superiors.

The civil rights movement never addressed the smile burden by name, but activists worked on their own to set new facial norms. African-American males stopped smiling on the streets in the 1960s, happily aware of the unsettling effect this action had on the white population. The image of the simpleminded, smiling, white-toothed black was rejected as blatantly racist, and it gradually retreated into the distance. However, like the women of Sparta and the wives of samurai, who were expected to look happy upon learning their sons or husbands had died in battle, contemporary American women have yet to unilaterally declare their faces their own property.

For instance, imagine a woman at a morning business meeting being asked if she could make a spontaneous and concise summation of a complicated project she's been struggling to get under control for months. She might draw the end of her mouth back and clench her teeth—*Eek!*—in a protective response, a polite, restrained expression of her surprise, not unlike the expression of a conscientious young schoolgirl being told to get out paper and pencil for a pop quiz. At the same time, the woman might be feeling resentful of the supervisor who sprang the request, but she fears taking that person on. So she holds back on comment. The whole performance resolves in a weird grin collapsing into a nervous smile that conveys discomfort and unpreparedness. A pointed remark by way of explanation or self-defense might've worked better for her—but her mouth was otherwise engaged.

We'd do well to realize just how much our smiles misrepresent us, and swear off for good the self-deprecating grins and ritual displays of deference. Real smiles have beneficial physiological effects, according to Paul Ekman. False ones do nothing for us at all.

"Smiles are as important as sound bites on television," insists producer and media coach Heidi Berenson, who has worked with many of Washington's most famous faces. "And women have always been better at understanding this than men. But the smile I'm talking about is not a cutesy smile. It's an authoritative smile. A genuine smile. Properly timed, it's tremendously powerful."

25   To limit a woman to one expression is like editing down an orchestra to one instrument. And the search for more authentic means of expression isn't easy in a culture in which women are still expected to be magnanimous smilers, helpmates in crisis, and curators of everybody else's morale. But change is already floating in the high winds. We see a boon in assertive female comedians who are proving that women can *dish out* smiles, not just wear them. Actress Demi Moore has stated that she doesn't like to take smiling roles. Nike is running ads that show unsmiling women athletes sweating, reaching, pushing themselves. These women aren't overly concerned with issues of rapport; they're not being "nice" girls—they're working out.

If a woman's smile were truly her own, to be smiled or not, according to how the *woman* felt, rather than according to what someone else needed, she would smile more spontaneously, without ulterior, hidden motives. As Rainer Maria Rilke[1] wrote in *The Journal of My Other Self*, "Her smile was not meant to be seen by anyone and served its whole purpose in being smiled."

That smile is my long-term aim. In the meantime, I hope to stabilize on the smile continuum somewhere between the eliciting grin of Farrah Fawcett and the haughty smirk of Jeane Kirkpatrick.

Additional Rhetorical Strategies

Analogy (paragraphs 1, 2, 6, 22, 27); Process Analysis (paragraphs 7–9); Narration (paragraph 14); Example (paragraphs 14, 24); Argument (throughout).

Discussion Questions

1. In this essay Cunningham draws on several different fields of inquiry—including physiology, psychology, sociology, and history—to construct a model of multiple causality. Locate and examine each of these different causes. Which seems most crucial to her overall argument? Why? What function do the additional causes serve?
2. Where does the author stand in relation to her essay? Where does she reveal her presence? Where does she step back to some degree?

[1]European poet (1875–1926)—Eds.

What is the effect of her presence and relative absence over the course of the essay?

3. In paragraph 5 Cunningham brings up the old nature versus nurture debate. Which of the causes for smiling posited in this essay can be attributed to nature, and which to nurture? On balance, where does Cunningham stand?

4. Cunningham goes to Japan for an example of a smile that indicates pain or sorrow (paragraph 10). See the essays by Hall and Tannen in this collection for other examples of cultural differences. Comment on the ways in which the cross-cultural comparisons affect your own stance on nature versus nurture questions raised in number 3 above.

Essay Question

1. Write an essay exploring the comparison Cunningham suggests between race and gender (paragraphs 19, 22). How compelling do you find this analogy? In what ways is the situation of women today analogous to the situation of blacks before the Civil Rights movement? In what ways are the two situations different? If it is true that blacks have succeeded in setting "new facial norms" (paragraph 22) and women have yet to liberate themselves from the old facial norms, posit some reasons for this difference. Are there other ways in which women might take blacks as their role models?

2. Look in magazines, newspapers, photography books, art catalogs, family albums, and so on and find two or more pictures of smiling people. Analyze the subtext behind the smiles. You may want to compare and contrast two pictures of smiles that shed light on each other from your perspective.

Bound to Bicker

Laurence Steinberg

Laurence Steinberg (b. 1952) earned his B.A. at Vassar College and his Ph.D. at Cornell University. He has taught at the University of California, Irvine, and the University of Wisconsin, Madison. He is currently a professor in the Department of Psychology at Temple University in Philadelphia, Pennsylvania. He has published several books about childhood, adolescence, and the teen years, including Adolescence *(1985, revised 1989 and 1993),* When Teenagers Work *(1986),* You and Your Adolescent *(1990), and* Childhood *(1995). In addition, he and his wife, writer Wendy Steinberg, co-authored* Crossing Paths *(1994).*

The following essay, which was first published in Psychology Today *in September 1987, proposes an answer to the question of why adolescents and their parents cannot seem to live in harmony.*

"It's like being bitten to death by ducks." That's how one mother described her constant squabbles with her eleven-year-old daughter. And she's hardly alone in the experience. The arguments almost always involve mundane matters—taking out the garbage, coming home on time, cleaning up the bedroom. But despite its banality, this relentless bickering takes its toll on the average parent's mental health. Studies indicate that parents of adolescents—particularly mothers—report lower levels of life satisfaction, less marital happiness, and more general distress than parents of younger children. Is this continual arguing necessary?

For the past two years, my students and I have been examining the day-to-day relationships of parents and young teenagers to learn how and why family ties change during the transition from childhood into adolescence. Repeatedly, I am struck by the fact that, despite considerable love between most teens and their parents, they can't help sparring. Even in the closest of families, parents and teenagers squabble and bicker surprisingly often—so often, in fact, that we hear impassioned recountings of these arguments in virtually every discussion we have with parents or teenagers. One of the most frequently heard phrases on our interview tapes is, "We usually get along but . . ."

As psychologist Anne Petersen notes, the subject of parent–adolescent conflict has generated considerable controversy among researchers and clinicians. Until about twenty years ago, our views of such conflict were shaped by psychoanalytic clinicians and theorists, who argued that spite and revenge, passive aggressiveness and rebelliousness toward parents are all normal, even healthy, aspects of adolescence. But studies conducted during the 1970s on samples of average teenagers and their parents (rather than those who spent Wednesday afternoons on analysts' couches) challenged the view that family storm and stress was inevitable or pervasive. These surveys consistently showed that three-fourths of all teenagers and parents, here and abroad, feel quite close to each other and report getting along very well. Family relations appeared far more pacific than professionals and the public had believed.

Had clinicians overstated the case for widespread storm and stress, or were social scientists simply off the mark? The answer, just now beginning to emerge, seems to be somewhere between the two extremes.

The bad news for parents is that conflict, in the form of nagging, ₅ squabbling, and bickering, is more common during adolescence than during any other period of development, except, perhaps, the "terrible twos." But the good news is that arguments between parents and teenagers rarely undo close emotional bonds or lead adolescents and their parents to reject one another. And, although most families with adolescents go through a period of heightened tension, the phase is usually temporary, typically ending by age fifteen or sixteen.

My own studies point to early adolescence—the years from ten to thirteen—as a period of special strain between parents and children. But more intriguing, perhaps, is that these studies reveal that puberty plays a central role in triggering parent–adolescent conflict. Specifically, as youngsters develop toward physical maturity, bickering and squabbling with parents increase. If puberty comes early, so does the arguing and bickering; if it is late, the period of heightened tension is delayed. Although many other aspects of adolescent behavior reflect the intertwined influences of biological and social factors, this aspect seems to be directly connected to the biological event of puberty; something about normal physical maturation sets off parent–adolescent fighting. It's no surprise that they argue about overflowing trash cans, trails of dirty laundry, and blaring stereos. But why should teenagers going through puberty fight with their parents more often than youngsters of the same age whose physical development is slower? More to the point: if puberty is inevitable, does this mean that parent–child conflict is, too?

It often helps to look closely at our evolutionary relatives when we are puzzled by aspects of human behavior, especially when the puzzle includes biological pieces. We are only now beginning to understand how family relations among monkeys and apes are transformed in adolescence, but one fact is clear: it is common, at puberty, for primates living in the wild to leave their "natal group," the group into which they were born. Among chimpanzees, who are our close biological relatives, but whose family structure differs greatly from ours, emigration is restricted to adolescent females. Shortly after puberty, the adolescent voluntarily leaves her natal group and travels on her own—often a rather treacherous journey—to find another community in which to mate.

In species whose family organization is more analogous to ours, such as gibbons, who live in small, monogamous family groups, both adolescent males and females emigrate. And if they don't leave voluntarily soon after puberty begins, they are thrown out. In both cases, adolescent emigration helps to increase reproductive fitness, since it minimizes inbreeding and increases genetic diversity.

Studies of monkeys and apes living in captivity show just what happens when such adolescent emigration is impeded. For many non-human primates, the consequences can be dire: among many species of monkeys, pubertal development is inhibited so long as youngsters remain in their natal group. Recent studies of monogamous or polyandrous monkeys, such as tamarins and marmosets, have shown that the sexual development of young females is inhibited specifically by their mothers' presence. When the mother is removed, so is her inhibitory effect, and the daughter's maturation can begin in a matter of a few days.

10   Taken together, these studies suggest that it is evolutionarily adaptive for most offspring to leave their family early in adolescence. The pressure on adolescents to leave their parents is most severe among primates such as gibbons, whose evolution occurred within the context of small family groups, because opportunities for mating within the natal group are limited and such mating may threaten the species' gene pool. It should come as no surprise, therefore, to find social and biological mechanisms that encourage the departure of adolescent primates—including, I think, humans—from the family group around puberty.

One such mechanism is conflict, which, if intense enough, drives the adolescent away. Squabbling between teenagers and their parents today may be a vestige of our evolutionary past, when prolonged proximity between parent and offspring threatened the species' genetic integrity.

According to psychologist Raymond Montemayor of Ohio State University, who studies the relationships of teenagers and their parents, accounts of conflict between adolescents and their elders date back virtually as far as recorded history. But our predecessors enjoyed an important advantage over today's parents: adolescents rarely lived at home much beyond puberty. Prior to industrialization in this country, high-school-aged youngsters often lived in a state of semiautonomy in which they were allowed to work and earn money but lived under the authority of adults other than their parents. Indeed, as historian Michael Katz of the University of Pennsylvania notes, many adolescents actually were "placed out" at puberty—sent to live away from their parents' household—a practice that strikingly resembles the forced emigration seen among our primate relatives living in the wild.

Most historians of adolescence have interpreted the practice of placing out in terms of its implications for youngsters' educational and vocational development. But did adolescents have to leave home to learn their trade? And is it just coincidental that this practice was synchronized with puberty? Historian Alan Macfarlane notes that placing out may have developed to provide a "mechanism for separating the generations at a time when there might otherwise have been considerable difficulty" in the family.

Dozens of nonindustrialized societies continue to send adolescents away at puberty. Separating children from their parents, known as "extrusion," has a great deal in common with the behavior of many nonhuman primates. In societies that practice extrusion, youngsters in late childhood are expected to begin sleeping in households other than their parents'. They may see their parents during the day but are required to spend the night with friends of the family, with relatives, or in a separate residence reserved for preadolescents. Even in traditional societies that do not practice extrusion formally, the rite of passage at puberty nevertheless includes rituals symbolizing the separation of the young person from his or her family. The widespread existence of these rituals suggests that adolescent emigration from the family at puberty may have been common in many human societies at some earlier time.

Conflict between parents and teenagers is not limited to family life in 15 the contemporary United States. Generally, parent–child conflict is thought to exist at about the same rate in virtually all highly developed, industrialized Western societies. The sociological explanation for such intergenerational tension in modern society is that the rapid social change accompanying industrialization creates irreconcilable and conflict-provoking differences in parents' and children's values and attitudes. But modernization may well have increased the degree and pervasiveness of conflict between young people and their parents for other reasons.

Industrialization hastened the onset of puberty, due to improvements in health, sanitation, and nutrition. (Youngsters in the United States go through puberty about four years earlier today than their counterparts did a hundred years ago.) Industrialization also has brought extended schooling, which has prolonged youngsters' economic dependence on their parents and delayed their entrance into full-time work roles. The net result has been a dramatic increase over the past century in the amount of time that physically mature youngsters and their parents must live in close contact.

A century ago, the adolescent's departure from home coincided with physical maturation. Today, sexually mature adolescents may spend seven or eight years in the company of their parents. Put a different way, industrialization has impeded the emigration of physically mature adolescents from their family of origin—the prescription for parent–adolescent conflict.

Puberty, of course, is just one of many factors that can exacerbate the level of tension in an adolescent's household. Inconsistent parenting, blocked communication channels, and extremes of strictness or permissiveness can all make a strained situation worse than it need be. An adolescent's family should seek professional help whenever fighting and arguing become pervasive or violent or when they disrupt family functioning, no matter what the adolescent's stage of physical development.

Given our evolutionary history, however, and the increasingly prolonged dependence of adolescents on their parents, some degree of conflict during early adolescence is probably inevitable, even within families that had been close before puberty began. Telling parents that fighting over taking out the garbage is related to the reproductive fitness of the species provides little solace—and doesn't help get the garbage out of the house, either. But parents need to recognize that quarreling with a teenager over mundane matters may be a normal—if, thankfully, temporary—part of family life during adolescence. Such squabbling is an atavism that ensures that adolescents grow up. If teenagers didn't argue with their parents, they might never leave home at all.

Additional Rhetorical Strategies

Analogy (paragraphs 1, 10, 12, 14); Comparison and Contrast (paragraphs 7–8).

Discussion Questions

1. Where is Steinberg's thesis statement? What is the central question answered by his essay: why do adolescents argue with their parents, or why do they argue more here and now than in previous generations and in other cultures? How (and where) does he answer each of these questions?
2. What competing theories does Steinberg address in his essay? How does he counter them? Are there any other explanations for the phenomena he describes that he does not anticipate and address?
3. In paragraph 4, Steinberg suggests that previous studies have either overestimated or underestimated the prevalence of bickering between adolescents and their parents, and that the real answer lies "somewhere between the two extremes." On what does he seem to be basing this conclusion?
4. Do you know of any differences between human and primate sociology or biology that might cause you to question the analogy Steinberg draws in paragraphs 7–10? In tamarins and marmosets, for instance, is the late onset of puberty a cause or an effect of family dynamics? Is this difference sufficient for you to discount the entire theory, or do you find it compelling nonetheless?
5. Steinberg draws not only on biology, but also on history and anthropology, to build his case. How effective do you find this interdisciplinary approach? What advantages does it have over studying a problem using the methodology and knowledge of only one discipline?

Essay Questions

1. At the very end of the essay, Steinberg offers some words of consolation to the beleaguered parents. (Or does he? Perhaps if the teenagers didn't argue so much, their parents would not be as eager to get rid of them, so their leaving home would not be greeted as a consolation.) Drawing on the information provided in this essay and your own experience, write an open letter to the parents of adolescents, explaining why their formerly personable offspring are now impossible to get along with, and offering advice for the duration of their stay in the parental home.

2. Write a causation essay of your own, in which you choose among competing explanations of a phenomenon in your own major field of study. Try modeling your essay after Steinberg's suspended structure: Consider each hypothesis and reject it before building a case for the theory you prefer. Don't forget to mention exceptions to the rule, as Steinberg does in his second-to-the-last paragraph.

Of Crime, Cause, and Correlation

Stephen Jay Gould

Stephen Jay Gould (b. 1941) earned his A.B. at Antioch College and his Ph.D. at Columbia University, and has since been awarded over 20 honorary degrees from colleges and universities. He is a professor of geology at Harvard and curator of invertebrate paleontology at the Museum of Comparative Zoology. He is renowned and beloved for his ability to translate difficult scientific theories into language that the nonscientist can understand. He has published several books with the subtitle Reflections on Natural History, *including* Hen's Teeth and Horses' Toes *(1983),* The Flamingo's Smile *(1985),* Bully for Brontosaurus *(1991) and* Eight Little Piggies *(1993). Each volume is a collection of essays originally written for his column "This View of Life," which appears monthly in the magazine* Natural History.

When asked about the difficulty of writing about science for an audience of lay readers, Gould responded: "Every field has its jargon. I think scientists hide behind theirs perhaps more than other people in other professions do—it's part of our mythology—but I don't think the concepts of science are intrinsically more difficult than the professional notions in any other field. The main reason why the impression may persist that it's more difficult in science is just that good writers are self-selected out of science. They tend to be channeled into other areas, so most scientists end up without skills in writing, without thinking about it very much."

Since sex can be gentle and a thing of great beauty, it may seem peculiar that so many animals are most touchy and aggressive during their mating seasons. Nonetheless, this apparent paradox makes sense in light of evolutionary theory. An organism's success in the evolutionary race may be measured by the number of offspring raised to carry its genes into future generations. For a male, more copulations with more females mean more offspring, and this biological imperative can engender severe competition among males and zealous defense of females within a male's orbit—hence the link of sex with aggression. Females may also struggle among themselves to win the attention of best fit males or to discourage inappropriate suitors.

In most mammals, sex is seasonal—and periods of nastiness and aggression therefore ebb and flow in correlation with mating activity throughout the year. Yet writings on human evolution usually cite a loss of seasonality in mating as a key feature of our biological history. Human females ovulate at regular intervals throughout the year and both males and females seem interested in and capable of indulging in sexual activity at any time. Indeed, the invention of adaptive reasons for this loss of seasonality forms a common theme in treatises on human evolution—the advantages of monogamy and a strong pair bond for raising children, for example, and the role of continual sexual receptivity among females in maintaining a male's interest in sticking around. I regard most of these scenarios as pretty silly and purely speculative, but they do attempt to explain a fact of evident importance—why humans are the most persistently sexy of primates.

Yet this very loss of evident seasonality has prompted many scientists to wonder whether some small or subtle remnant of our evolutionary past might still be preserved in modern humans. Does any vestigial seasonality of sexual behavior and its correlates in aggression still remain with us? Does the animal still lurk beneath a human guise?

Since we have no direct evidence for seasonality in human sexual behavior, scientists who seek some sign of it must search the dossier of human activity for conduct that cycles with the seasons and might be linked with sexuality. Various types of aggressive behavior form a promising area for investigation.

This style of research faces, unfortunately, one enormous and 5 daunting problem—it falls so easily into what is probably the most common error of human reasoning, the confusion of correlation with cause. We may illustrate the fallacy with some simple examples. Halley's comet is approaching the earth and has been steadily drawing nearer to us for many years. During the same time, my pet hamster has been ageing continually and the price of an ice cream cone has risen steadily in Boston. If I computed what scientists call a correlation coefficient between any two of these events (comet distances, hamster ages, and cone prices), I would get a nearly perfect relationship—a quantitative value near the maximum of 1. Yet everyone understands intuitively that none of these correlations has any causal meaning—lots of things are moving in the same direction independently.

Even more difficult to interpret are correlations between phenomena that seem to have some causal relationship, but in which the potential causal pathways are both great in number and varied in style. The simple existence of a correlation does not permit a distinction among these myriad pathways. Seasonality, for example, has numerous consequences—variation in temperature and length of daylight are the most direct and prominent. When we find a kind of human behavior that cycles with the seasons, and not by accident, how can we know which of the astronomical number of facets of seasonality it reflects? The causal pathways are often subtle, indirect, and complex. Why, for example, do we play baseball in the summer and football in the fall and winter? Nothing intrinsic to the games dictates such a custom, especially in our modern all-weather domed stadiums. The reason is linked with seasonality, but by a most indirect and historical route. Baseball has old and populist origins as a game of ordinary folk in rural and urban communities. Our great-grandfathers played it when they could, and when their families would enjoy watching—when it was warm enough, in summer. But football had its origin as a collegiate sport, and colleges (for reasons originally and indirectly linked to the warmth of seasons and the timing of agriculture) are not in session until the fall.

Thus the problem in using correlation with seasons as a method for making inferences about the vestigial existence of human sexual cycles: we may expect to find many seasonal fluctuations in potentially indirect correlates of sex—aggressive behavior most prominently—but we cannot infer cause, because the simple correlation cannot, by itself, tell us which of the numerous aspects of seasonality has engendered the behavioral cycle. The discovery of yearly cycles in aggressive behavior does not permit the inference that human biology still records a vestige of primate mating seasons, for two reasons: first, too many unrelated aspects of seasonality may be causing the correlation, and these must be identified and eliminated before we have any right to assert an evolutionary hypothesis; second, underlying sexual cycles are not (by far) the only cause of human aggression. Nonetheless, psychiatrist Richard Michael and ethologist Doris Zumpe recently published a study in the *American Journal of Psychiatry* that made just such a claim and elicited a flurry of press commentary about our vestigial animality (*Sexual Violence in the United States and the Role of Season,* July 1983). Michael and Zumpe fall right into the fallacy of confusing correlation with cause: they find a simple correlation of aggression to season and ascribe its cause to vestigial sexual cyclicism without any supporting evidence and without even discussing an old and sensible alternative explanation that fits the data far better.

Michael and Zumpe considered the frequency of four crimes— forcible rape, aggravated assault, murder, and robbery—throughout the year in sixteen American localities from Maine to Honolulu. They found that rape and assault showed nearly the same pattern in all but two localities for rape and all but four for assault: the greatest number occurred in summer, within an eight-week period between July 7 and September 8. They conclude: "Because of the close relationship between assault and rape, and because rapes are invariably less numerous than assaults, we postulate that rape comprises a subcategory of assaultive behavior." Robberies, on the other hand, tend to show a reverse pattern, with the greatest number in winter, while murders are scattered throughout the year and display no seasonal peaks. The authors also found no significant differences in frequencies of the various crimes among their sixteen places—especially no tendency toward more violence in hotter climates.

Michael and Zumpe's data provide nothing more than a correlation between frequency of some crimes (but not others) and seasonal fluctuations of climate. They clearly do not have enough information to make causal assertions—for the correlation of crime and season may have a host of potential reasons (or even no reason at all), and the correlation itself does not permit a distinction among numerous possibilities.

Nonetheless, Michael and Zumpe present a single hypothesis about[10] cause, providing no alternative at all, and implying that their data are sufficient to make such an assertion. They claim that seasonal fluctuations in hormone levels probably underlie cycles of crime—and suggest that these fluctuations record a vestige of primate mating cycles. They write: "The view that environmental factors may act via neuroendocrine pathways in the human to influence our behavior is consistent with the known role of these factors in socially living, nonhuman primates, which show increased aggressivity at the start of the mating season."

I believe that two debilitating objections can be raised against this far-fetched conclusion: first, some of the authors' own data contradict it (or at least fit uncomfortably within their hypothesis); second, an explanation that they never consider—the old and "classical" explanation for crime's well known seasonal cycles—fits all the data, and fits them better and more simply than the hormonal hypothesis.

If rape correlates with assault because it constitutes "a subcategory of assaultive behavior," and aggression cycles with the season as a result of environmentally entrained variation in hormone levels, then why does murder show no seasonal pattern? Surely murder is aggression. Moreover, though we may regard robbery as premeditated behavior for gain and not, therefore, as another category of aggression expected to cycle with rape and assault, we still cannot understand, on Michael and Zumpe's hypothesis, why robbery shows a reversed seasonal pattern. If their hypothesis has general merit, it should explain the cycles of all the crimes they consider. Michael and Zumpe's batting average, in short, is poor. Their speculation fits only half their data; a third crime (murder) does not show the expected pattern, while a fourth (robbery) displays a different cycle, which they do not attempt to explain at all.

Michael and Zumpe have discovered nothing new. The four patterns that they cite "have been known by criminologists and the beat cop for many years" (to quote Mark Fox, who outlined the same objections in a letter to *Science News,* September 24, commenting on a previous favorable report of Michael and Zumpe's article). The same criminologists and policemen have a standard explanation that fits all four patterns—not just two of them—and seems eminently direct and reasonable to me. It relies upon an immediate, nonbiological reason for correlations between seasons and crime. Quite simply, and to put it somewhat crudely, rapes and assaults peak in summer because winter is a hell of a time to lurk in alleyways—more contact and greater availability in summer provide more opportunity. Robberies show a reversed pattern because weapons are more easily concealed under winter attire. Murders show no pattern because most are unplanned acts of violence committed against friends and family members at moments of extreme stress. I do not assert that this classical explanation must be correct, but it explains everything simply and should not be omitted from discussion. Yet Michael and Zumpe ignored it in favor of exclusive speculations about evolutionary vestiges. The potential pathways from correlation to cause are always numerous.

Michael and Zumpe seem to think that their demonstration of similar peaks in rape and assault for their coldest (Maine) and warmest (Hawaii and Puerto Rico) regions argues for biology and against the idea that "higher temperatures facilitate increased social interaction." But this fact is irrelevant to the debate because both explanations predict it. In particular, the social hypothesis simply requires that summers be warm—and it is hot enough during a Maine summer to populate the alleyways. Similarly, Michael and Zumpe's demonstration that regions with greater seasonal change in temperature show greater annual fluctuations in frequency of rape and assault, if anything, fits the social hypothesis better—it really is too cold during a Maine winter, but quite possible in Honolulu.

15   I wrote this essay primarily to illustrate, by egregious example, the cardinal fallacy of confusing correlation with cause. But Michael and Zumpe's article raises two other interesting and general points about scientific explanation.

Why, first of all, do so many scientists show a preference for arcane, complex, indirect, and implausible causal pathways when simple (if less intriguing) explanations are so clearly available? (I have previously argued that the higher batting averages of lefties really can be explained by the unexciting and classical observation that lefties hit right-handed pitching better, and that most pitchers, like most of us, are right-handed—and not by newfangled, high-falutin notions about differences between left and right brains, as two overenthusiastic doctors have suggested.) We should start with the immediate and obvious (they usually work), and move to the complex and indirect when our initial efforts fail. Have a healthy respect for simple answers; the world is not always a deep conundrum fit only for consideration by certified scholars.

Second, why are we so fascinated by explanations that invoke innate and inherited biology (vestigial mating cycles in this case), when simpler hypotheses based upon the interaction of a flexible personality with the immediate environment explain things better and more fully? We seem drawn, in the absence of good evidence, to biological hypotheses for differences in social and intellectual behavior between men and women, or the activities of criminal and law-abiding citizens. I suspect that this preference reflects one of the oldest and most unfortunate biases of Western thought, dating back at least to Plato's search for essences. We want to know what we are "really" like, why we behave as we do. Somehow, we feel that a claim for something inborn and inherited must be more fundamental or essential than an undetermined response to an immediate environment. We prefer to believe that more men are driven to rape in summer by a rise in hormones reflecting an evolutionary past than by a simple increase in availability of targets. But if humans have an essence, it surely lies in the remarkable flexibility that permits such an enormous range of unprogrammed responses to environment. This flexibility defines us and makes us human. We should not only cherish and foster it, but also learn to recognize and take interest in its manifestations.

Additional Rhetorical Strategies

Example (paragraphs 5, 16); Argument (throughout).

Discussion Questions

1. What is the difference between cause and correlation? How many different kinds of causality does Gould mention or imply in this essay? How do they differ from one another, and from correlation?
2. Gould uses the study by Michael and Zumpe as an example of a confusion between cause and correlation. On what other counts does he critique these researchers? What larger principles might one take away from this essay, besides the critique of one particular study?
3. In paragraph 5, Gould provides a silly example involving Halley's comet, a hampster, and the price of an ice cream cone. He dismisses the seeming "correlation coefficient" among these three factors on the basis of intuition. What is the relationship between science and intuition? Did the stance taken by Gould, a renowned scientist, toward intuition surprise you? What is the relationship between intuition and common sense, or, as Gould calls it, "simple answers" (paragraph 16). What is Gould's attitude toward "certified scholars" (paragraph 16) as expressed in this essay, and how might he define the good scientist?
4. What evolutionary fact about humans emerges from this essay? To those who would like to reduce humanity to its essence, what answer does Gould supply?

Essay Questions

1. Write a paper critiquing any other essay in this book that makes a causal argument, based on Gould's clarification of the difference between cause and correlation. You need not choose an essay from this chapter; several other chapters also contain essays that employ causal reasoning. See the Additional Rhetorical Strategies lists for ideas of essays to examine.

2. Gould deplores the preference shown by many scientists for "arcane, complex, indirect, and implausible causal pathways when simple (if less intriguing) explanations are so clearly available" (paragraph 16). Write a satirical essay in which you offer a comically complex, needlessly laborious explanation for a straightforward phenomenon.

Hate Radio

Patricia Williams

Patricia J. Williams (b. 1951) is Professor of Law at Columbia University School of Law. She received her B.A. from Wellesley College and her J.D. from Harvard Law School, and has practiced law as a deputy city attorney for the city of Los Angeles and as a staff attorney for the Western Center on Law and Poverty. Before joining the law faculty at Columbia, Professor Williams taught at the University of Wisconsin School of Law, the Harvard University Women's Studies Program, and the City University of New York Law School at Queen's College. She has also held fellowships at centers for advanced research at Dartmouth College, the University of California at Irvine, and Stanford University.

Patricia Williams is a public intellectual and advocate for social justice, and has been a commentator and guest on numerous radio and television shows. Her many publications reach both scholarly and general audiences, and her 1993 book The Alchemy of Race and Rights *was greeted with widespread critical acclaim. In 1995 she published* The Rooster's Egg.

Three years ago I stood at my sink, washing the dishes and listening to the radio. I was tuned to rock and roll so I could avoid thinking about the big news from the day before—George Bush had just nominated Clarence Thomas to replace Thurgood Marshall on the Supreme Court. I was squeezing a dot of lemon Joy into each of the wineglasses when I realized that two smoothly radio-cultured voices, a man's and a woman's, had replaced the music.

"I think it's a stroke of genius on the president's part," said the female voice.

"Yeah," said the male voice, "Then those blacks, those African Americans, those Negroes—hey 'Negro' is good enough for Thurgood Marshall—whatever, they can't make up their minds [what] they want to be called. I'm gonna call them Blafricans. Black Africans. Yeah, I like it. Blafricans. Then they can get all upset because now the president appointed a Blafrican."

"Yeah, well, that's the way those liberals think. It's just crazy."   5

"And then after they turn down his nomination the president can say he tried to please 'em, and then he can appoint someone with some intelligence."

Back then, this conversation seemed so horrendously unusual, so singularly hateful, that I picked up a pencil and wrote it down. I was certain that a firestorm of protest was going to engulf the station and purge those foul radio mouths with the good clean soap of social outrage.

I am so naive. When I finally turned on the radio and rolled my dial to where everyone else had been tuned while I was busy watching

Cosby reruns, it took me a while to understand that there's a firestorm all right, but not of protest. In the two and a half years since Thomas has assumed his post on the Supreme Court, the underlying assumptions of the conversation I heard as uniquely outrageous have become commonplace, popularly expressed, and louder in volume. I hear the style of that snide polemicism everywhere, among acquaintances, on the street, on television in toned-down versions. It is a crude demagoguery that makes me heartsick. I feel more and more surrounded by that point of view, the assumptions of being without intelligence, the coded epithets, the "Blafrican"-like stand-ins for "nigger," the mocking angry glee, the endless tirades filled with nonspecific, nonempirically based slurs against "these people" or "those minorities" or "feminazis" or "liberals" or "scumbags" or "pansies" or "jerks" or "sleazeballs" or "loonies" or "animals" or "foreigners."

At the same time I am not so naive as to suppose that this is something new. In clearheaded moments I realize I am not listening to the radio anymore, I am listening to a large segment of white America think aloud in ever louder resurgent thoughts that have generations of historical precedent. It's as though the radio has split open like an egg, Morton Downey, Jr.'s clones and Joe McCarthy's[1] ghost spilling out, broken yolks, a great collective of sometimes clever, sometimes small, but uniformly threatened brains—they have all come gushing out. Just as they were about to pass into oblivion, Jack Benny and his humble black sidekick Rochester get resurrected in the ungainly bodies of Howard Stern and his faithful black henchwoman, Robin Quivers. The culture of Amos and Andy has been revived and reassembled in Bob Grant's radio minstrelry and radio newcomer Daryl Gates's sanctimonious imprecations on behalf of decent white people.[2] And in striking imitation of Jesse Helms's nearly forgotten days as a radio host the far Right has found its undisputed king in the personage of Rush Limbaugh—a polished demagogue with a weekly radio audience of at least 20 million, a television show that vies for ratings with the likes of Jay Leno, a newsletter with a circulation of 380,000, and two best-selling books whose combined sales are closing in on six million copies.

---

[1]Downey is a controversial radio and television commentator; during the early 1950s McCarthy (R–Wisconsin) used demagoguery to inflate paranoia about communism—Eds.

[2]The comedian Jack Benny—and his "sidekick" Rochester—performed on radio from 1932–1948 and on television from 1950–1965. The extremely popular "Amos and Andy" radio show employed white actors to represent negative stereotypes of African Americans throughout the 1930s and 1940s. In 1951 CBS transferred the show to television using black actors, but canceled production in 1953 after strong protests from the NAACP. Formerly the chief of police in Los Angeles, Daryl Gates resigned in 1992 after widespread racism in the department became public knowledge—Eds.

From Churchill to Hitler to the old Soviet Union, it's clear that₁₀ radio and television have the power to change the course of history, to proselytize, and to coalesce not merely the good and the noble, but the very worst in human nature as well. Likewise, when Orson Welles made his famous radio broadcast "witnessing" the landing of a space-ship full of hostile Martians, the United States ought to have learned a lesson about the power of radio to appeal to mass instincts and incite mass hysteria. Radio remains a peculiarly powerful medium even today, its visual emptiness in a world of six trillion flashing images allowing one of the few remaining playgrounds for the aural subconscious. Perhaps its power is attributable to our need for an oral tradition after all, some conveying of stories, feelings, myths of ancestors, epics of alienation, and the need to rejoin ancestral roots, even ignorant bigoted roots. Perhaps the visual quiescence of radio is related to the popularity of e-mail or electronic networking. Only the voice is made manifest, unmasking worlds that cannot—or dare not?—be seen. Just yet. Nostalgia crystallizing into a dangerous future. The preconscious voice erupting into the expressed, the prime time.

What comes out of the modern radio mouth could be the *Iliad*, the *Rubaiyat*, the griot's song of our times. If indeed radio is a vessel for the American "Song of Songs," then what does it mean that a manic, adolescent Howard Stern is so popular among radio listeners, that Rush Limbaugh's wittily smooth sadism has gone the way of prime-time television, and that both vie for the number one slot on all the best-selling book lists? What to make of the stories being told by our modern radio evangelists and their tragic unloved chorus of callers? Is it really just a collapsing economy that spawns this drama of grown people sitting around scaring themselves to death with fantasies of black feminist Mexican able-bodied gay soldiers earning $100,000 a year on welfare who are so criminally depraved that Hillary Clinton or the Antichrist-of-the-moment had no choice but to invite them onto the government payroll so they can run the country? The panicky exaggeration reminds me of a child's fear. . . . *And then, and then, a huge lion jumped out of the shadows and was about to gobble me up, and I can't ever sleep again for a whole week.*

As I spin the dial on my radio, I can't help thinking that this stuff must be related to that most poignant of fiber-optic phenomena, phone sex. Aural Sex. Radio Racism with a touch of S & M. High-priest hosts with the power and run-amok ego to discipline listeners, to smack with the verbal back of the hand, to smash the button that shuts you up once and for all. "Idiot!" shouts New York City radio demagogue Bob Grant and then the sound of droning telephone emptiness, the voice of dissent dumped out some trapdoor in aural space.

As I listened to a range of such programs what struck me as the most unifying theme was not merely the specific intolerance on such hot topics as race and gender, but a much more general contempt for the world, a verbal stoning of anything different. It is like some unusually violent game of "Simon Says," this mockery and shouting down of callers, this roar of incantations, the insistence on agreement.

But, ah, if you *will* but only agree, what sweet and safe reward, what soft enfolding by a stern and angry radio god. And as an added bonus, the invisible shield of an AM community, a family of fans who are Exactly Like You, to whom you can express, in anonymity, all the filthy stuff you imagine "them" doing to you. The comfort and relief of being able to ejaculate, to those who understand, about the dark imagined excess overtaking, robbing, needing to be held down and taught a good lesson, needing to put it in its place and before the ravenous demon enervates all that is true and good and pure in this life.

15   The audience for this genre of radio flagellation is mostly young, white, and male. Two thirds of Rush Limbaugh's audience is male. According to *Time* magazine, 75 percent of Howard Stern's listeners are white men. Most of the callers have spent their lives walling themselves off from any real experience with blacks, feminists, lesbians, or gays. In this regard, it is probably true, as former Secretary of Education William Bennett says, that Rush Limbaugh "tells his audience that what you believe inside, you can talk about in the marketplace." Unfortunately, what's "inside" is then mistaken for what's "outside," treated as empirical and political reality. The *National Review* extols Limbaugh's conservative leadership as no less than that of Ronald Reagan, and the Republican party provides Limbaugh with books to discuss, stories, angles, and public support. "People were afraid of censure by gay activists, feminists, environmentalists—now they are not because Rush takes them on," says Bennett.

U.S. history has been marked by cycles in which brands of this or that hatred come into fashion and go out, are unleashed and then restrained. If racism, homophobia, jingoism, and woman-hating have been features of national life in pretty much all of modern history, it rather begs the question to spend a lot of time wondering if right-wing radio is a symptom or a cause. For at least 400 years, prevailing attitudes in the West have considered African Americans less intelligent. Recent statistics show that 53 percent of people in the U.S. agree that blacks and Latinos are less intelligent than whites, and a majority believe that blacks are lazy, violent, welfare-dependent, and unpatriotic.

I think that what has made life more or less tolerable for "out" groups have been those moments in history when those "inside" feelings were relatively restrained. In fact, if I could believe that right-wing radio were only about idiosyncratic, singular, rough-hewn individuals thinking those inside thoughts, I'd be much more inclined to agree with Columbia University media expert Everette Dennis, who says that Stern's and Limbaugh's popularity represents the "triumph of the individual" or with *Time* magazine's bottom line that "the fact that either is seriously considered a threat . . . is more worrisome than Stern or Limbaugh will ever be." If what I were hearing had even a tad more to do with real oppressions, with real white *and* black levels of joblessness and homelessness, or with the real problems of real white men, then I wouldn't have bothered to slog my way through hours of Howard Stern's miserable obsessions.

Yet at the heart of my anxiety is the worry that Stern, Limbaugh, Grant, et al. represent the very antithesis of individualism's triumph. As the *National Review* said of Limbaugh's ascent, "It was a feat not only of the loudest voice but also of a keen political brain to round up, as Rush did, the media herd and drive them into the conservative corral." When asked about his political aspirations, Bob Grant gloated to the *Washington Post*, "I think I would make rather a good dictator."

The polemics of right-wing radio are putting nothing less than hate onto the airwaves, into the marketplace, electing it to office, teaching it in schools, and exalting it as freedom. What worries me is the increasing-to-constant commerce of retribution, control, and lashing out, fed not by fact but fantasy. What worries me is the reemergence, more powerfully than at any time since the institution of Jim Crow, of a socio-centered self that excludes "the likes of," well, me for example, from the civic circle, and that would rob me of my worth and claim and identity as a citizen. As the *Economist* rightly observes, "Mr. Limbaugh takes a mass market—white, mainly male, middle-class, ordinary America—and talks to it as an endangered minority."

I worry about this identity whose external reference is a set of be-[20] liefs, ethics, and practices that excludes, restricts, and acts in the world on me, or mine, as the perceived if not real enemy. I am acutely aware of losing *my* mythic individualism to the surface shapes of my mythic group fearsomeness as black, as female, as left wing. "I" merge not fluidly but irretrievably into a category of "them." I become a suspect self, a moving target of loathsome properties, not merely different but dangerous. And that worries me a lot.

What happens in my life with all this translated license, this permission to be uncivil? What happens to the social space that was supposedly at the sweet mountaintop of the civil rights movement's trail? Can I get a seat on the bus without having to be reminded that I *should* be standing? Did the civil rights movement guarantee us nothing more than to use public accommodations while surrounded by raving lunatic bigots? "They didn't beat this idiot [Rodney King] enough," says Howard Stern.

Not long ago I had the misfortune to hail a taxicab in which the driver was listening to Howard Stern undress some woman. After some blocks, I had to get out. I was, frankly, afraid to ask the driver to turn it off—not because I was afraid of "censoring" him, which seems to be the only thing people will talk about anymore, but because the driver was stripping me too, as he leered through the rearview mirror. "Something the matter?" he demanded, as I asked him to pull over and let me out well short of my destination. (I'll spare you the full story of what happened from there—trying to get another cab, as the cabbies stopped for all the white businessmen who so much as scratched their heads near the curb; a nice young white man, seeing my plight, giving me his cab, having to thank him, he hero, me saved-but-humiliated, cabdriver pissed and surly. I fight my way to my destination, finally arriving in bad mood, militant black woman, cranky feminazi.)

When Yeltsin blared rock music at his opponents holed up in the parliament building in Moscow, in imitation of the U.S. Marines trying to torture Manual Noriega in Panama, all I could think of was that it must be like being trapped in a crowded subway car when all the portable stereos are tuned to Bob Grant or Howard Stern. With Howard Stern's voice a tinny, screeching backdrop, with all the faces growing dreamily mean as though some soporifically evil hallucinogen were gushing into their bloodstreams, I'd start begging to surrender.

Surrender to what? Surrender to the laissez-faire resegregation that is the metaphoric significance of the hundreds of "Rush rooms" that have cropped up in restaurants around the country; rooms broadcasting Limbaugh's words, rooms for your listening pleasure, rooms where bigots can capture the purity of a Rush-only lunch counter, rooms where all those unpleasant others just "choose" not to eat? Surrender to the naughty luxury of a room in which a Ku Klux Klan meeting could take place in orderly, First Amendment fashion? Everyone's "free" to come in (and a few of you outsiders do), but mostly the undesirable nonconformists are gently repulsed away. It's a high-tech world of enhanced choice. Whites choose mostly to sit in the Rush room. Feminists, blacks, lesbians, and gays "choose" to sit elsewhere. No need to buy black votes, you just pay them not to vote; no need to insist on white-only schools, you just sell the desirability of black-only schools. Just sit back and watch it work, like those invisible shock shields that keep dogs cowering in their own backyards.

25   How real is the driving perception behind all the Sturm und Drang of this genre of radio-harangue—the perception that white men are an oppressed minority, with no power and no opportunity in the land that they made great? While it is true that power and opportunity are shrinking for all but the very wealthy in this country (and would that Limbaugh would take that issue on), the fact remains that while men are still this country's most privileged citizens and market actors. To give just a small example, according to the *Wall Street Journal*, blacks were the only racial group to suffer a net job loss during the 1990–91 economic downturn at the companies reporting to the Equal Employment Opportunity Commission. Whites, Latinos, and Asians, meanwhile, gained thousands of jobs. While whites gained 71,144 jobs at

these companies, Latinos gained 60,040, Asians gained 55,104, and blacks lost 59,479. If every black were hired in the United States tomorrow, the numbers would not be sufficient to account for white men's expanding balloon of fear that they have been specifically dispossessed by African Americans.

Given deep patterns of social segregation and general ignorance of history, particularly racial history, media remain the principal source of most American's knowledge of each other. Media can provoke violence or induce passivity. In San Francisco, for example, a radio show on KMEL called "Street Soldiers" has taken this power as a responsibility with great consequence: "Unquestionably," writes Ken Auletta in the *New Yorker*, "the show has helped avert violence. When a Samoan teenager was slain, apparently by Filipino gang members, in a drive-by shooting, the phones lit up with calls from Samoans wanting to tell [the hosts] they would not rest until they had exacted revenge. Threats filled the air for a couple of weeks. Then the dead Samoan's father called in, and, in a poignant exchange, the father said he couldn't tolerate the thought of more young men senselessly slaughtered. There would be no retaliation, he vowed. And there was none." In contrast, we must wonder at the phenomenon of the very powerful leadership of the Republican party, from Ronald Reagan to Robert Dole to William Bennett, giving advice, counsel, and friendship to Rush Limbaugh's passionate divisiveness.

The outright denial of the material crisis at every level of U.S. society, most urgently in black inner-city neighborhoods but facing us all, is a kind of political circus, dissembling as it feeds the frustrations of the moment. We as a nation can no longer afford to deal with such crises by *imagining* an excess of bodies, of babies, of job-stealers, of welfare mothers, of overreaching immigrants, of too-powerful (Jewish, in whispers) liberal Hollywood, of lesbians and gays, of gang members ("gangsters" remain white, and no matter what the atrocity, less vilified than "gang members," who are black), of Arab terrorists, and uppity women. The reality of our social poverty far exceeds these scapegoats. This right-wing backlash resembles, in form if not substance, phenomena like anti-Semitism in Poland: there aren't but a handful of Jews left in that whole country, but the giant balloon of heated anti-Semitism flourishes apace, Jews blamed for the world's evils.

The overwhelming response to right-wing excesses in the United States has been to seek an odd sort of comfort in the fact that the First Amendment is working so well that you can't suppress this sort of thing. Look what's happened in Eastern Europe. Granted. So let's not talk about censorship or the First Amendment for the next ten minutes. But in Western Europe, where fascism is rising at an appalling rate, suppression is hardly the problem. In Eastern and Western Europe as well as the United States, we must begin to think just a little bit about the fiercely coalescing power of media to spark mistrust, to fan it into forest fires of fear and revenge. We must begin to think about the levels of national and social complacence in the face of such resolute ignorance. We must ask ourselves what the expected result is, not of censorship or suppression, but of so much encouragement, so much support, so much investment in the fashionability of hate. What future is it that we are designing with the devotion of such tremendous resources to the disgraceful propaganda of bigotry?

Additional Rhetorical Strategies

Narration (paragraphs 1–5, 20); Analogy (paragraphs 11, 13); Argument (throughout).

Discussion Questions

1. In her opening paragraph Williams reveals her political orientation by implying that she found the nomination of Clarence Thomas disturbing. What is the effect of this revelation so early in the essay? How might it affect readers who agree with her politically? Readers who disagree with her politically? This essay was originally published in *Ms.* magazine. How would you characterize the audience she probably had in mind when she composed the essay?

2. In paragraph 9, Williams writes "In clearheaded moments I realize I am not listening to the radio anymore, I am listening to a large segment of white America think aloud. . . ." What seems more disturbing to her, the fact that white Americans are thinking hateful racist thoughts or that they are expressing them? Support your answer with quotations from her essay. What solution does Williams seem to be advocating?

3. Discuss the idea of individualism from the perspective of the purveyors of hate radio and from the perspective of Patricia Williams. How does she critique their position?

4. Look closely at the analogies that Williams employs in her discussion of hate radio, those who broadcast it, and those who listen to it. What effect does each analogy have? For instance, at least twice she highlights the childish nature of this phenomenon (paragraphs 11 and 13). To what extent does this analogy make hate radio seem less dangerous than it might otherwise be perceived? What other effect might this analogy produce, that might perhaps counterbalance the aforementioned effect?

5. In her final paragraph, Williams writes "let's not talk about censorship or the First Amendment for the next ten minutes." What seems to be Williams's stance on censorship? What does she find to be a more pressing concern?

Essay Questions

1. Listen to a broadcast that Williams might characterize as "hate radio." Analyze the intended audience and the rhetorical strategies used by the radio personality to move his or her audience.

2. In paragraph 10, Williams writes that "radio and television have the power to change the course of history, to proselytize, and to co-alesce not merely the good and noble, but the very worst inhuman nature as well." Her focus in this essay is on the latter, that is, the radio and television broadcasts that change the course of history by coalescing the "very worst in human nature." Think of an instance in which the media has changed the course of human history for the good instead, and write an essay in which you not only explain how that happened, but also how we might work toward a time when the beneficial effects of the media begin to outweigh the detrimental effects.

Thematic Pair: The Environmental Future

▲▼The Next Ice Age

Sir Frederick Hoyle

Analyzing chains of causality is essential to both the methods and aims of science, but while most scientists are content to pursue cause and effect in highly specialized areas, Sir Frederick Hoyle (b. 1915) has never shrunk from great schemes and ultimate questions. In 1950 he published The Nature of the Universe, *a book that advanced the now unfashionable steady-state hypothesis of an infinitely expanding universe. As ambitious as its title, the book was both attacked as an oversimplification and celebrated as "one of the finest pieces of scientific exposition for the layman which has appeared in recent years." Similar controversy has followed his other publications, which include* Frontiers of Astronomy *(1955),* Man and Materialism *(1956),* Of Men and Galaxies *(1966), and, in recent years,* The Origin of the Universe and the Origin of Religion *(1993) and an autobiography,* Home is Where the Wind Blows: Chapters from a Cosmologist's Life *(1994). He is also the author of countless essays and science fiction novels.*

Although he is both reviled and praised as a "popularizer" of science, Hoyle's academic and professional credentials are impressive. He graduated from Cambridge with distinction in mathematics in 1939 and later became the first director of that university's Institute of Theoretical Astronomy. Since then he has received countless other honors and appointments, including knighthood in 1972. The following essay finds him investigating, with characteristic meticulousness, a causal chain that leads to an ambitious conclusion: the prediction of another ice age.

More than three-quarters of all the ice in the world is in the southern polar continent of Antarctica, a conveniently distant place. Most of the rest of the world's ice lies in Greenland, also a remote place. So we are accustomed to thinking of the heavily populated lands of the Earth as being ice-free, except for the minute smears of the stuff we encounter in winter.

The Stone Age people who executed the magnificent cave paintings to be seen in southwest France and Spain did not enjoy such a pleasant situation. Twenty thousand years ago an ice sheet comparable to the one now in Greenland lay across Scandinavia. It had extensions reaching into Russia, Germany, and Britain. Another ice sheet of polar dimensions lay across the heartland of Canada, and its extensions reached beyond Chicago.

Nor was the grim situation of 20,000 years ago confined to the northern temperate latitudes. That ice age extended fingers even into the tropics. Substantial glaciers appeared on high tropical mountains such as those in Hawaii.

In the luxury of our present ice-free state we are apt to think that the ice age is over. But all the evidence is that the piling of vast quantities of ice onto the northern temperate latitudes (a belt of land running from the U.S.S.R. through Western Europe to Canada and the U.S.) has scarcely begun. To understand the overwhelming threat the future has in store for mankind, let us go back several tens of millions of years.

5   It is well known that the continents of the Earth are not in fixed positions; they drift about slowly in characteristic periods of 50 to 100 million years. About 40 million years ago the continent of Antarctica moved toward the South Pole. This caused the first glaciers there, and about 20 million years ago Antarctica was substantially ice covered.

A sinister process then set in, with its origin in the remarkable inability of the direct rays of the sun to melt either snow or ice. Most sunshine is reflected by snow, while it penetrates ice so deeply and diffusely that it has little melting effect at its surface. The sun does nothing directly to Antarctic ice, which would accumulate indefinitely from repeated snowfalls if icebergs did not break away into the sea at the outer edges of the ice sheet.

By about 20 million years ago a balance between the gain of new ice and the loss of old ice had been set up. The icebergs chilled the surrounding salty water. If this cooled water had remained at the ocean surface no harm would have been done. Despite its inability to melt ice and snow, sunlight is highly effective at warming the surface layers of the ocean, and would soon have resupplied the heat lost to the icebergs. This did not happen, however, because the dense, cool water sank from the surface to the ocean depths and the deep basins began to fill with water that was literally ice-cold.

This process eventually changed the warm world ocean of 50 million years ago into today's overwhelmingly ice-cold world ocean—with a thin skin of warmer water at its surface. Only this thin warm skin protects us from the next ice age.

As the chilling of the deep ocean occurred slowly and inexorably the Earth's climate worsened. By about 10 million years ago glaciers had appeared in Alaska. The first major intrusion of ice onto the lands of the northern temperate belt occurred about two million years ago. From time to time the ice would melt and for a while the land would be ice-free. Then the ice would come, again and again.

10   The ice-age periods became progressively longer than the intervening interglacials. In the past million years the situation has worsened, until the average interglacial period has now shrunk to no more than 10,000 years. Since this is just the length of time since the present warm interglacial period began, our ration of ice-free conditions is over. The next ice age is already due.

A sequence of ice ages continues for as long as the continent in question resides at the pole in question. Our present sequence of ice ages will therefore continue for as long as the continent of Antarctica remains at the South Pole, which will probably be for several more tens of millions of years. The conclusion is that the present sequence of ice ages has scarcely begun. There are hundreds of ice ages still to come.

Why should there be an alternating sequence of ice ages and inter-glacials? At present snow lies during the winter over most of the north-ern temperate region. Instead of accumulating year by year into conti-nental ice sheets, it melts each spring and summer. This is the essence of the interglacial condition. We are ice-free now, not because of a lack of snowfall but because of the spring thaw.

Melting comes from warmth in the air. Unlike the sun's direct rays, the longer-wave heat radiation generated by warm air is absorbed in snow or ice, which therefore melts almost immediately, thin surface layer after thin surface layer. The process is highly efficient and, given a sufficient supply of warm air, a whole winter's snow melts in a few days. Thus winter snow stays until warm air comes, and almost in a flash it is gone.

Where does the warm air get its heat? Mostly from the surface layer of warm ocean water that overlies the mass of ice-cold deeper water. Remove the surface layer of warm ocean water and there would then be no warm air. The snows of winter would not melt, ice sheets would begin to build, and the next ice age would have arrived.

The important surface layer of warm ocean water stores about ten₁₅ times more heat than is required by the air and the land each year, a ten-to-one margin of safety. That is enough to have prevented the next ice age for 10,000 years, but not sufficient to withstand every kind of ac-cident. The finest particles of ash thrown into the air by the recent erup-tion of the Mount St. Helens volcano will take about ten years to settle down to ground level. Fine particles of any electrically insulating mate-rial reflect sunlight back into space and so reduce the amount available to heat the ocean surface. The Mount St. Helens volcanic eruption was not remotely big enough to have produced such a reflecting layer around the Earth.

In 1815 Mount Tambora in the Dutch East Indies produced an explo-sion that threw a sufficient quantity of fine ash into the high atmosphere to have a noticeable effect on the Northern Hemisphere summer of 1816. It was a summer of agricultural disaster in New England, the coldest on record at places as widely separated as New Haven and Geneva.

As an astronomer, I prefer to consider the possibility of a similar but much more violent effect triggered from outside the Earth: the im-pact of a giant meteorite. There is no question that giant meteorites, half a mile long or more, must hit the Earth from time to time, and such col-lisions must throw a vast quantity of debris into the atmosphere.

The most notable meteoritic event of modern times occurred in July, 1908. Miss K. Stephens wrote to *The Times* from Godmanchester about a strange light she had seen in the midnight sky, commenting that "it would be interesting if anyone could explain the cause." It was not until 1927 that even the point of impact of the meteorite was discovered, by an expedition that penetrated to the Tunguska River region in Siberia. An enormous area of devastation was found, almost twice that caused by Mount St. Helens, showing that a comparatively minor meteoritic collision can be far more destructive than the explosion of a volcano.

Once in every 5,000 to 10,000 years a meteoritic collision occurs which projects sufficient fine dust into the high atmosphere to make the Earth into a temporarily reflective planet. The resulting cutoff of sunlight robs the surface waters of the terrestrial ocean of their protective store of heat, and the air that blows over the land from the sea is then no longer warm enough to melt the snows of winter.

20   How long will the snow accumulate? Within two or three decades at most, all the fine dust will have settled to the Earth's surface under gravity and sunlight will no longer be reflected back into space. Warm summer air will blow again over the land, and within only a further year or two the accumulated snows will be melted into lakes, streams, and rivers. Admittedly, there would have been a number of very bad years, enough to throw human society into a crisis beside which the multitudinous troubles which now dog our daily lives would seem like pinpricks. But after a half a century things would be back to normal— seemingly.

This apparent loophole in which had seemed an inexorable line of reasoning troubled me for a long time until the day I chanced on a description of the following simple experiment: If air that has not been thoroughly dried, that contains a number of very small water drops, is cooled progressively in a chamber, the droplets do not solidify into ice crystals as their temperature falls below the normal freezing point, but remain as a supercooled liquid down to a remarkably low temperature, close to –40 °C, when at last the liquid water goes into ice.

If a beam of light passes through the chamber, and if one looks at it from a direction at right angles to the beam, the chamber appears dark so long as the droplets stay liquid. Their transition to ice is signaled by a sudden radiance from the interior of the chamber. This means that whereas liquid droplets transmit light beams, ice crystals scatter them.

Even in the driest desert regions of the Earth there is always more than sufficient water in the air, if it is condensed from vapor into fine crystals of ice, to produce an almost perfectly reflective blanket. Does this happen anywhere? It does, particularly in the polar regions. The ice crystals are known to polar explorers as "diamond dust," a name that illustrates their brilliant reflective properties. Diamond dust is responsible for a bewildering range of optical effects—halos, mock suns, arcs, coronas, and iridescent clouds.

Why does diamond dust not form everywhere? Because except in the polar regions, water droplets in the atmosphere are kept above the critical temperature, near –40 °C, at which they would be transformed into ice. What prevents the temperature of water droplets from falling to –40 °C throughout much of the high atmosphere is heat from the oceans. Reduce the heat supplied by the oceans to the air by about 25 percent and diamond dust would form, not just in the polar regions but over much of the Earth.

But this is exactly what would happen in the situation I have de-[25] scribed: fine particles thrown up into the high atmosphere, either by an enormous volcano or by the collision of a giant meteorite, would cool the surface of the ocean and the ability of the ocean to supply heat to the air would be significantly reduced. Diamond dust would create an additional particle blanket around the Earth that would stay long after the first particles had fallen to ground level under gravity, and the diamond dust would then take over the job of reflecting sunlight, and so keep the ocean cool indefinitely.

Clearly, there are two distinct self-maintaining cycles of the world climate. If the surface layer of the ocean is warm, as it is at present, enough heat passes from the ocean to the air to prevent diamond dust forming, except in polar regions. Sunlight comes through to the ocean and keeps the surface warm. This is the first cycle.

The second goes exactly the opposite way. If the surface of the ocean is cool, insufficient heat goes into the air to prevent diamond dust forming. Significantly more sunlight is then reflected back into space and the surface of the ocean remains cool.

Both the first and second cycles are logically consistent. If the Earth happens to be in either of them it tends to stay in that cycle, unless a catastrophic incident causes a sudden jump from the one cycle to the other. Indeed, the two cycles are exactly those I have described as interglacial and ice ages, and the interlaced sequence of ice ages and the interglacials arises because of such catastrophic events as collisions of the Earth with giant meteorites or explosions of volcanoes.

Ice ages have exceedingly abrupt terminations. Something about the end of the last ice age took the mammoths by surprise. Along with the mastodon and woolly rhinoceros, they became extinct. Complete mammoths with surprisingly little degeneration have been recovered from present-day ice in Siberia. Either they died of hypothermia caused by freezing rain, or they blundered into bogs and pools of exceedingly cold water formed from melting permafrost.

When one considers the effect on mammoths of sudden heat from[30] a brassy sky caused by the absorbent particles thrown up by an iron meteorite, all the evidence falls into place. The frozen ground would soften and the mammoths would flounder. Frozen pools and lakes would partially melt. In the conditions of poor visibility, the mammoths and other animals would be likely to blunder to their deaths in the icy bogs.

The progression of catastrophic events controls the sequence of ice ages and interglacial periods. The grim aspect of this is that because of the suddenness of the catastrophic events, switches back and forth between interglacial cycles and ice-age cycles occur swiftly, in timespans of a few decades at most.

One may derive some consolation from the possibility that the switch to the next ice age may still be several thousand years into the future. On the other hand, the switch could have occurred in 1908, if the giant meteorite whose light was seen by Miss K. Stephens had happened to be larger. The switch could occur tomorrow, and if it were to do so there is no human being, young or old, who would escape its appalling consequences.

Additional Rhetorical Strategies

Definition (paragraph 23); Comparison and Contrast (paragraphs 26–28).

Discussion Questions

1. In what way does Hoyle set the stage for the "overwhelming threat . . . in store for mankind" (paragraph 4)? How does he dramatically use the fact that we are "apt to think that the ice age is over"? Where else in the essay do you see him building toward a dramatic effect? What resistance does he assume his audience will have toward his subject? How does he counter that resistance?
2. Because of its tightly connected causal chain, Hoyle's essay may require more than one reading. Reread the essay with pencil in hand and outline the causal sequence Hoyle has assembled. Start by considering the chain of events that leads to ice-free eras, and then look at what happens in that chain to produce ice ages.
3. After reading Hoyle's essay, are you left with any hope for the survival of our species? What possible loopholes or crumbs of hope does he offer, despite the rather grim conclusion he seems to find so inevitable?
4. Hoyle thinks and writes about events on a massive scale, and about time in almost unimaginable increments. Identify the strategies he uses to make the unimaginable not only imaginable to a lay reader, but even concrete enough to be frightening.

Essay Questions

1. Suppose you were an important government official and Hoyle's catastrophic predictions were brought to your attention. How would you handle the situation? You may choose among several approaches, including the following: a speech to Congress, promoting your solution; an open letter to the American people (or the United Nations), calming the masses with a more soothing perspective on the situation; or a policy statement addressed to the National Science Foundation, requesting funding or outlining any other strategy you deem most efficacious. Use the tone and diction appropriate to your imagined station and audience.

2. "The Next Ice Age," as described by Hoyle, is a theory, not a fact. What stake does Hoyle have in its accuracy? How can you tell? Can you identify any conflict between Hoyle, the astronomer, and Hoyle, the citizen of a planet doomed to freeze? If so, how does he resolve the conflict?

▲▼The Warming of the World

Carl Sagan

Carl Sagan (1934–1996) entered the University of Chicago at age 16 on a scholarship. He earned his A.B. with general and special honors and went on to complete his Ph.D. in astronomy at Chicago as well. Early on he gained a reputation for challenging the scientific orthodoxies. Among his theories that began by raising controversy but were later accepted by the scientific community is his explanation of the Venus greenhouse effect, which figures in the following essay.

Sagan is one of the most widely known scientists in America, largely due to his popular books (including The Dragons of Eden: Speculations on the Evolution of Human Intelligence *[1977] and* Broca's Brain: Reflections on the Romance of Science *[1979]) and his even more popular public television series* Cosmos. *Sagan had a gift for translating difficult scientific concepts into language the general public can not only understand, but also enjoy. This gift can be attributed in part to a genuine respect for and trust in his audience. As he noted, "the public is a lot brighter and more interested in science than they're given credit for. . . . They're not numbskulls. Thinking scientifically is as natural as breathing."*

W hen humans first evolved—in the savannahs of East Africa a few million years ago—our numbers were few and our powers feeble. We knew almost nothing about controlling our environment—even clothing had yet to be invented. We were creatures of the climate, utterly dependent upon it.

A few degrees hotter or colder on average, and our ancestors were in trouble. The toll taken much larger by the ice ages, in which average land temperatures dropped some 8°C (centigrade, or Celsius), must have been horrific. And yet, it is exactly such climatic change that pushed our ancestors to develop tools and technology, science and civilization. Certainly, skills in hunting, skinning, tanning, building shelters and refurbishing caves must owe much to the terrors of the deep ice age.

Today, we live in a balmy epoch, 10,000 years after the last major glaciation. In this climatic spring, our species has flourished; we now cover the entire planet and are altering the very appearance of our world. Lately—within the last century or so—humans have acquired, in more ways than one, the ability to make major changes in that climate upon which we are so dependent. The Nuclear Winter findings are one dramatic indication that we can change the climate—in this case, in the spasm of nuclear war. But I wish here to describe a different kind of climatic danger, this one slower, more subtle and arising from intentions that are wholly benign.

It is warm down here on Earth because the sun shines. If the sun were somehow turned off, the Earth would rapidly cool. The oceans would freeze, eventually the atmosphere itself would condense out and our planet would be covered everywhere by snowbanks of solid oxygen and nitrogen 10 meters (about 30 feet) high. Only the tiny trickle of heat from the Earth's interior and the faint starlight would save our world from a temperature of absolute zero.

We know how bright the sun is; we know how far from it we are; 5 and we know what fraction of the sunlight reaching the Earth is reflected back to space (about 30 percent). So we can calculate—with a simple mathematical equation—what the average temperature of the Earth should be. But when we do the calculation, we find that the Earth's temperature should be about 20°C below the freezing point of water, in stark contradiction to our everyday experience. What have we done wrong?

As in many such cases in science, what we've done wrong is to forget something—in this case, the atmosphere. Every object in the universe radiates some kind of light to space; the colder the object, the longer the wavelength of radiation it emits. The Earth—much colder than the sun—radiates to space mainly in the infrared part of the spectrum, not the visible. Were the sun turned off, the Earth would soon be indetectable in ordinary visible light, though it would be brilliantly illuminated in infrared light.

When sunlight strikes the Earth, part is reflected back into the sky; much of the rest is absorbed by the ground and heats it—the darker the ground, the greater the heating. The ground radiates back upward in the infrared. Thus, for an airless Earth, the temperature would be set solely by a balance between the incoming sunlight absorbed by the surface and the infrared radiation that the surface emits back to space.

When you put air on a planet, the situation changes. The Earth's atmosphere is, generally, still transparent to visible light. That's why we can see each other when we talk, glimpse distant mountains and view the stars.

But in the infrared, all that is different. While the oxygen and nitrogen in the air are transparent in both the infrared and the visible, minor constituents such as water vapor (H_2O) and carbon dioxide (CO_2) tend to be much more opaque in the infrared. It would be useless for us to have eyes that could see at a wavelength, say, of 15 microns in the infrared, because the air is murky black there.

Accordingly, if you add air to a world, you heat it: The surface now 10 has difficulty when it tries to radiate back to space in the infrared. The atmosphere tends to absorb the infrared radiation, keeping heat near the surface and providing an infrared blanket for the world. There is very little CO_2 in the Earth's atmosphere—only 0.03 percent. But that small amount is enough to make the Earth's atmosphere opaque in important regions of the infrared spectrum. CO_2 and H_2O are the reason the global temperature is not well below freezing. We owe our comfort—indeed, our very existence—to the fact that these gases are present and are much more transparent in the visible than in the infrared. Our lives depend on a delicate balance of invisible gases. Too much blanket, or too little, and we're in trouble.

This property of many gases to absorb strongly in the infrared but not in the visible, and thereby to heat their surroundings, is called the "greenhouse effect." A florist's greenhouse keeps its planty inhabitants warm. The phrase "greenhouse effect" is widely used and has an instructive ring to it, reminding us that we live in a planetary-scale greenhouse and recalling the admonition about living in glass houses and throwing stones. But, in fact, florists' greenhouses do not keep warm by the greenhouse effect; they work mainly by inhibiting the movement of air inside, another matter altogether.

We need look only as far as the nearest planet to see an example of an atmospheric greenhouse effect gone wild. Venus has in its atmosphere an enormous quantity of carbon dioxide (roughly as much as is buried as carbonates in all the rocks of the Earth's crust). There is an atmosphere of CO_2 on Venus 90 times thicker than the atmosphere of the Earth and containing some 200,000 times more CO_2 than in our air. With water vapor and other minor atmospheric constituents, this is enough to make a greenhouse effect that keeps the surface of Venus around 470°C (900°F)—enough to melt tin or lead.

When humans burn wood or "fossil fuels" (coal, oil, natural gas, etc.), they put carbon dioxide into the air. One carbon atom (C) combines with a molecule of oxygen (O_2) to produce CO_2. The development of agriculture, the conversion of dense forest to comparatively sparsely vegetated farms, has moved carbon atoms from plants on the ground to carbon dioxide in the air. About half of this new CO_2 is removed by plants or by the layering down of carbonates in the oceans. On human timescales, these changes are irreversible: Once the CO_2 is in the atmosphere, human technology is helpless to remove it. So the overall amount of CO_2 in the air has been growing—at least since the industrial revolution. If no other factors operate, and if enough CO_2 is put into the atmosphere, eventually the average surface temperature will increase perceptibly.

There are other greenhouse gases that are increasingly abundant in the Earth's atmosphere—halocarbons, such as the freon used in refrigerator cooling systems; or nitrous oxide (N_2O), produced by automobile exhausts and nitrogenous fertilizers; or methane (CH_4), produced partly in the intestines of cows and other ruminants.

15   But let's for the moment concentrate on carbon dioxide: How long, at the present rates of burning wood and fossil fuels, before the global climate becomes significantly warmer? And what would the consequences be?

It is relatively simple to calculate the immediate warming from a given increase in the CO_2 abundance, and all competent calculations seem to be in good agreement. More difficult to estimate are (1) the rate at which carbon dioxide will continue to be put into the atmosphere (it depends on population growth rates, economic styles, alternative energy sources and the like) and (2) feedbacks—ways in which a slight warming might produce other, more drastic, effects.

The recent increase in atmospheric CO_2 is well documented. Over the last century, this CO_2 buildup should have resulted in a few tenths of a degree of global warming, and there is some evidence that such a warming has occurred.

The National Academy of Sciences estimates that the present atmospheric abundance of CO_2 is likely to double by the year 2065, although experts at the academy predict a 1-in-20 chance that it will double before 2035—when an infant born today becomes 50 years old. Such a doubling would warm the air near the surface of the Earth by 2°C or 3°C—maybe by as much as 4°C. These are average temperature values; there would naturally be considerable local variation. High latitudes would be warmed much more, although a baked Alaska will be some time coming.

There would be precipitation changes. The annual discharge of rivers would be altered. Some scientists believe that central North America—including much of the area that is now the breadbasket of the world—would be parched in summer if the global temperature increases by a few degrees. There would be some mitigating effects; for example, where plant growth is not otherwise limited, more CO_2 should aid photosynthesis and make more luxuriant growth (of weeds as well as crops). If the present CO_2 injection into the atmosphere continued over a few centuries, the warming would be greater than from all other causes over the last 100,000 years.

As the climate warms, glacial ice melts. Over the last 100 years, the[20] level of the world's oceans has risen by 15 centimeters (6 inches). A global warming of 3°C or 4°C over the next century is likely to bring a further rise in the average sea level of about 70 centimeters (28 inches). An increase of this magnitude could produce major damage to ports all over the world and induce fundamental changes in the patterns of land development. A serious speculation is that greenhouse temperature increases of 3°C or 4°C could, in addition, trigger the disintegration of the West Antarctic Ice Sheet, with huge quantities of polar ice falling into the ocean. This would raise sea level by some 6 meters (20 feet) over a period of centuries, with the eventual inundation of all coastal cities on the planet.

There are many other possibilities that are poorly understood, including the release of other greenhouse gases (for example, methane from peat bogs) accelerated by the warming climate. The circulation of the oceans might be an important aspect of the problem. The scientific community is attempting to make an environmental-impact statement for the entire planet on the consequences of continued burning of fossil fuels. Despite the uncertainties, a kind of consensus is in: Over the next century or more, with projected rates of burning of coal, oil and gas, there is trouble ahead.

The problem is difficult for at least three different reasons:

(1) We do not yet fully understand how severe the greenhouse consequences will be.
(2) Although the effects are not yet strikingly noticeable in everyday life, to deal with the problem, the present generation might have to make sacrifices for the next.
(3) The problem cannot be solved except on an international scale: The atmosphere is ignorant of national boundaries. South African carbon dioxide warms Taiwan, and Soviet coal-burning practices affect productivity in America. The largest coal resources in the world are found in the Soviet Union, the United States and China, in that order. What incentives are there for a nation such as China, with vast coal reserves and a commitment to rapid economic development, to hold back on the burning of fossil fuels because the result might, decades later, be a parched American sunbelt or still more ghastly starvation in sub-Saharan Africa? Would countries that might benefit from a warmer climate be as vigorous in restraining the burning of fossil fuels as nations likely to suffer greatly?

Fortunately, we have a little time. A great deal can be done in decades. Some argue that government subsidies lower the price of fossil fuels, inviting waste; more efficient usage, besides its economic advantage, could greatly ameliorate the CO_2 greenhouse problem. Parts of the solution might involve alternative energy sources, where appropriate: solar power, for example, or safer nuclear fission reactors, which, whatever their other dangers, produce no greenhouse gases of importance. Conceivably, the long-awaited advent of commercial nuclear fusion power might happen before the middle of the next century.

However, any technological solution to the looming greenhouse problem must be worldwide. It would not be sufficient for the United States or the Soviet Union, say, to develop safe and commercially feasible fusion power plants: That technology would have to be diffused worldwide, on terms of cost and reliability that would be more attractive to developing nations than a reliance on fossil fuel reserves or imports. A serious, very high-level look at patterns of U.S. and world energy development in light of the greenhouse problem seems overdue.

25   During the last few million years, human technology, spurred in part by climatic change, has made our species a force to be reckoned with on a planetary scale. We now find, to our astonishment, that we

pose a danger to ourselves. The present world order is, unfortunately, not designed to deal with global-scale dangers. Nations tend to be concerned about themselves, not about the planet; they tend to have short-term rather than long-term objectives. In problems such as the increasing greenhouse effect, one nation or region might benefit while another suffers. In other global environmental issues, such as nuclear war, all nations lose. The problems are connected: Constructive international efforts to understand and resolve one will benefit the others.

Further study and better public understanding are needed, of course. But what is essential is a global consciousness—a view that transcends our exclusive identification with the generational and political groupings into which, by accident, we have been born. The solution to these problems requires a perspective that embraces the planet and the future. We are all in this greenhouse together.

Additional Rhetorical Strategies

Comparison and Contrast (paragraphs 12–13); Definition (paragraph 14); Argument (paragraphs 23–26).

Discussion Questions

1. Examine the strategies Sagan uses to make his topic comprehensible to lay people. What were the hardest concepts in this essay for you to grasp? What did Sagan do in each case to try to ease your difficulty?
2. Look at Sagan's use of abstract and concrete language. In the first paragraph, for instance, he is talking about an unimaginably large scale ("a few million years ago") in imprecise terms, then he brings in a very specific concrete detail (the clothing). Trace his use of each extreme throughout the essay. What is the effect of moving back and forth between the very large and the very small, the abstract and the concrete?
3. How would you characterize Sagan's tone in this essay? Where does he take on a humorous tone? Where does his tone become more grave? What is the reason and the effect of each of the tonal shifts in the essay?
4. What is Sagan's overarching purpose in writing this essay? What are the solutions he proposes? What kinds of sacrifices might be necessary? What kind of consciousness is he promoting? How does the fact that he writes for a wide general audience fit in with his ultimate goal?

Essay Questions

1. Look at Sagan's definition of the "greenhouse effect" (paragraph 11). In what ways does he suggest that the analogy with a greenhouse is accurate? In what ways is it misleading? Can you think of a more accurate term to describe the warming phenomenon that Sagan describes in the essay? Write an informal essay in which you brainstorm for other analogies, and test each to see how apt it might be to the phenomenon Sagan describes.

2. Sagan writes that "any technological solution to the looming greenhouse problem must be worldwide" (paragraph 24). How might the citizens of the world be convinced to take a global perspective, as a first step toward solving the problem? Do you advocate a grassroots approach, a summit among world leaders, more media attention (of what kind), or another approach? Write a persuasive essay proposing an effective approach that will get all the nations and peoples on earth working together to solve the problem of global warming.

Exploring Connections: Questions Linking the Thematic Pair

1. Sir Frederick Hoyle predicts that the fate of the earth will be shaped by a severe cooling trend, whereas Carl Sagan predicts the opposite catastrophe: an intense warming of the world. How might a lay person who has read both essays decide which to believe? Are there any points of overlap between the two predictions? Are there any indications that either scientist has taken into account the opposing possibility?

2. What is the role of mankind in each essay? Which model is more dependent on the actions of humans? What kinds of actions might humans take to help ward off each eventuality?

3. Compare and contrast the styles of Hoyle and Sagan. Each is a scientist appealing to a nonscientific audience. Where do their strategies for getting their points across to this general audience overlap, and in what ways do they differ? Did you prefer one style over the other? Why? Were you more inclined to believe the prediction made by the writer with the more compelling style, or were you able to keep matters of style and content separate in your mind?

CHAPTER 9

Process Analysis

Process analysis explains how to do something, how something works, or how something happened. As a procedure for developing sequences in thinking and writing, process analysis resembles narration and causal analysis in its attention to a series of related events. But its purpose and method distinguish it from these other rhetorical forms. Narration tells *what* happened. Cause and effect accounts for *why*. Process analysis explains *how*. If, for example, you wanted to write about automobiles, you could define, classify, illustrate, or compare them. You could also describe one in detail, narrate a story about it, and discuss it, say, as a factor in the increasing death rate on holiday weekends. But as soon as you consider how an automobile works, how it is made, how it can be repaired, or how it can be driven, you are engaged in process analysis. Process analysis examines a series of actions that bring about a particular result.

Two Kinds of Process Analysis

There are two basic kinds of process analysis: specified and informative. *Specified* process analysis explains how to do something (for example, how to get from one place to another, how to play lacrosse, how to prepare for a job interview, or how to build a skyscraper). *Informative* process analysis explains how something works or happened—that is, how something is or was done (for example, how a computer works, how oil is refined, how calculators are manufactured, or how a dictatorship was overthrown). In both forms of process analysis, the writer presents a brief overview of the subject to be covered, then divides the part of the whole operation into steps or stages, and proceeds to consider each in precise enough detail for readers either to perform the actions indicated or to understand them fully. The writer of a successful process analysis relies on simple language, accurate verbs, distinct transitions, and, most important, on a clear chronological sequence to explain or make a *single point:* say, how to take better notes in class or how a small group of citizens rallied to defeat a giant utility's proposal to build a nuclear reactor in their community.

We are all familiar with the many forms of *specified* process analysis. We commonly encounter it in cookbooks, instruction manuals, handbooks, rule books, and textbooks of various sorts. Specified process analysis is frequently written in the second person; the writer leads an audience through a series of moves to a predetermined end. The success of a specified process analysis depends on the clarity and completeness of our directions. Let's suppose, for example, that your neighbor wanted to know how you prepared an especially tasty spaghetti sauce. You might well begin your recipe with a brief general statement about how it saves time and money. You would then list the necessary ingredients and equipment, and follow up with a precise set of directions for preparing and serving it. But specified process analysis may be applied to *any* subject that calls for how-to-do-it guidance: writing an essay, putting an end to procrastination, managing personal finances, achieving success in business, or coping with gadgets. In each case, we examine the situation carefully, clarify our purpose, and identify our audience. We also need to consider the kind and amount of information required to complete the process, being careful not to overestimate what our audience knows about our subject. We would then move on to establish as simple a sequence as possible for the process. In effect, we must present information complete enough for anyone in our established audience to go through the process, carry out all the procedures, and produce the intended results. To that end, we may supplement our written instructions with graphics—especially when they simplify, clarify, or condense our words, thereby heightening reader responsiveness and comprehension.

Informative process analysis provides readers with a thorough understanding of a process that they would like to know something (or know more) about: how a friend saved several hundred dollars each year when shopping for clothes, how earthquakes get started, how an electric car works. (For a memorable account of starting a car, see Michael Anania's essay on p. 416.) The process may also be one that readers are unlikely or unable to perform themselves: how hang gliders stay aloft, how lasers are used in surgery, how a photographer shoots an underwater scene in shark-infested waters. In informative process, the emphasis shifts from how-to-do-it instruction to how-it-is-done explanation. Readers should come away from informative process writing with a general understanding of the principles involved in how something works or happened—whether it is a simple household appliance or a complex political crisis.

In order to understand how something works, we frequently need to understand how it is put together. For example, describing the interrelation of parts in a television set may be necessary before showing how the set functions. Informative process analysis may be classified as *mechanical* (how an instant camera works), *scientific* (how molecules are formed), *historical* (how the United States came to suffer in Vietnam what has been called its first defeat in war), *natural* (how rain clouds form), *social* (how women's roles in society are changing), *creative* (how novels are written), or *psychological* (how dreams can be interpreted).

Examine for a moment the opening paragraphs of a newspaper report on how helicopters fly:

> It is in the very nature of the helicopter that its great versatility is found. To begin with, the helicopter is the fulfillment of one of man's earliest and most fantastic dreams, the dream of flying—not just like a bird—but of flying as nothing else flies or has ever flown. To be able to fly straight up and straight down—to fly forward or back or sidewise, or to hover over one spot till the fuel supply is exhausted.
>
> To see how the helicopter can do things that are not possible for the conventional fixed-wing plane, let us first examine how a conventional plane "works." It works by its shape—by the shape of its wing, which deflects air when the plane is in motion. That is possible because air has density and resistance. It reacts to force. The wing is curved and set at an angle to catch the air and push it down; the air, resisting, pushes against the under surface of the wing, giving it some of its lift. At the same time the curved upper surface of the wing exerts suction, tending to create a lack of air at the top of the wing. The air, again resisting, sucks back, and this gives the wing about twice as much lift as the air pressure below the wing. This is what takes place when the wing is pulled forward by propellers or pushed forward by jet blasts. Without the motion the wing has no lift.
>
> Now the helicopter combines in its whirling rotor blades—which are merely long, thin wings—both the function of the conventional wing, which is lift, and the function of the propeller, which is thrust. As the blades whirl around the top of the helicopter fuselage the air passes over and under them, giving enough lift to hoist the plane up. By changing the angle of pitch of the whirling rotors, the pilot gives the plane direction. If he tilts the blades forward, the plane goes ahead; if he hauls them back, the craft flies backward. By tilting them to one side or the other he moves to his right or left, and when the angle of pitch is flattened the craft hovers over one spot. This tilting is accomplished by the most important part of the helicopter's moving mechanism—called the rotor head—which is mounted at or near the top of the drive shaft from the power plant.

This passage is an excellent example of informative process analysis because the writer tells us virtually everything we need to know in order to understand how helicopters fly. By comparing a helicopter with a conventional fixed-wing plane in nontechnical, easily understood language, the writer allows even those with no scientific training to understand a helicopter's basic operations. After reading this passage, many of us may not have completely overcome our fear of flying in such machines, but all of us should have an extremely clear sense of the aerodynamic principles that govern its flight. So, too, we should have a much better sense of how to organize a process analysis essay in which we might be asked to explain a seemingly complicated, highly technical operation.

Steps in Process Analysis

The writer of any process analysis essay typically follows a sequence of moves. First, he or she presents a general description of the process and its purpose. This makes the writer's next move more readily accessible to the audience: breaking the process down into its chief stages and then further down into particular steps. Each step in the process is then described in detail. In doing so, the writer needs to maintain a balance between presuming too little knowledge on the part of the audience (thus risking boredom) and presuming too much (thus nearly guaranteeing confusion). Along the way, the writer should define any unavoidable special terms and identify any ingredients crucial to completing the process, as Kurt Vonnegut does when writing about the process—and the benefits—of revising drafts of an essay. (See p. 442.) Finally, the writer may choose to conclude the essay by summarizing the main stages of the process and perhaps offering a general comment on it.

The most important factor in the success of a process analysis essay is a clear and systematic chronological sequence. Establishing a precise order for a series of actions or functions may be complicated by the fact that several things may happen at once. For example, explaining how a washing machine works would be more difficult than advising someone on how to assemble a model airplane: when a washing machine is in operation, several actions take place simultaneously. Perhaps the best way to deal with this predicament is to organize the process into several general operations (in this case, washing, rinsing, and spin-drying the laundry) and then to consider each in detail and in the clearest chronological sequence.

Three Stages in the Writing Process

Writing is another process marked by simultaneous activities. For the sake of clarity, writing is usually divided into three general chronological stages: pre-writing, writing, and rewriting. Yet most writers rarely follow such neat, discrete steps while composing. To be more precise, we literally think before, during, and after we put our pens to paper. Most of us, for example, are hardly even conscious of how much we rewrite as our hand moves across a page. We are writing to find out what it is we think. And as soon as we have discovered that, we are apt to make changes. Breaking down writing—and many other complicated processes—into separate stages is done primarily for pedagogical reasons: we want to unravel the process, to make it specific and simple enough to be understood, at least basically. We are thereby sacrificing precision for general understanding. (For an example of one writer's instructions on writing well, see Kurt Vonnegut's "How to Write with

Style," p. 442.) But whether we are trying to convey a basic or an exact sense of how either a sentence or a washing machine works, we must be confident that we know enough about our subject to determine which operation should be described first and to arrange the most easily understood sequence for our audience. So, too, we must create a sense of closure—a satisfying sense of completeness—for the process analyzed.

Process analysis can be applied to any number of actions, operations, functions, or changes—and each will require that a distinctive sequence be developed. The decision whether to use specified or informative process analysis depends, of course, on the subject: the process of repairing a motorcycle would necessitate specified; the process of explaining how a roommate passed math for the first time, informative. In each instance, there is a different set of principles underlying the sequence. But no matter whether it appears as one of several rhetorical features of an essay or as the dominant rhetorical strategy, process analysis is one of the most methodical—and instructive—ways to develop and order our compositions.

Starting

Michael Anania

Michael Anania (b. 1939) is a poet and critic who teaches at the University of Illinois at Chicago. Anania earned a B.A. from the University of Nebraska and a Ph.D. in literature from the State University of New York at Buffalo. In addition to teaching, Anania worked first as the poetry and then as the literary editor of the Swallow Press. *Besides his numerous essays on contemporary American culture and reviews of literature, Anania has published several volumes of poetry—including* The Color of Dust (1970), Riversongs (1978), The Sky at Ashland (1986), *and* Selected Poems (1994)—*and a novel titled* The Red Menace, *a portrait of American culture in the 1950s. In 1991 he published a collection of essays titled* In Plain Sight: Obsessions, Morals, and Domestic Laughter. *In addition to serving as a contributing editor for* TriQuarterly, *Anania writes frequently for* Chicago *magazine, where the following essay first appeared.*

Michael Anania reports that the most challenging and satisfying aspect of writing lies in the process of discovering—and making—relationships between and among our ideas. Engaged in the work of establishing connections in an essay, Anania usually reserves questions of technique for revision. When asked to explain the origins of "Starting," Anania said, "I enjoy any excuse to write about cars."

"First of all, I pat the gas, just once, with the key off. Then I turn the key on, push it all the way to the floor, and let up slowly. Halfway up and I start it."

"With mine, you gotta hold the pedal all the way down to the floor, crank it till it catches, and when it does, let it up about two-thirds of the way."

Five or six of us are stamping around the outer lobby of my apartment building in down parkas and ski gloves. It is January in Chicago, one of the mornings of the car. Outside, the bright sun gives the air a blue sheen like finely worked carbon steel. It scrapes against the glass front wall of the lobby and hones itself along the three-week mounds of snow layered like limestone beside the walk.

"Four times." It's Eddie leaning against the heater vents behind the mailboxes. His tone is canonical. "Four times. Just pump it four times, and it starts right up."

5   "I try to go out at night, you know, and start her up. And after the engine's hot, I rev it up real high, turn the key off, and push the gas all the way down. You can just hear her sucking gas up to the engine."

"Well, with my diesel, you have to wait for this light on the dash to go off. That means the glow plug's hot enough to start it, but by then on a day like today, you've used up too much of the battery, and it won't start anyway."

Diesel? Light on the dash? No wonder his car doesn't start. Cars that start have a system, a private ritual worked out by their owners on days like this one, sitting shivering and hopeful in their machines. They have, these devices, the force of private truth—how and when and how many times the pedal is pushed, how far the choke is pulled out and when, whether the key is turned on before or after the pedal is pushed. Some of this lore comes from tow-truck jump starters who bob up from under the hood and shout, "Keep it all the way to the floor," or "Get your foot off the gas," or "Pump it." How much of this really matters is impossible to know. It matters, obviously, to the way we live with cars, and standing around the lobby with the guys it has a curiously familiar and disquieting ring to it, a touch of early high-school locker-room sex education—vain, improbable, idiosyncratic, and just as indispensable.

There is something intimate, however painful, about trying to start your car on a bitter cold morning. After the little rituals of pedal pushing and precision choke pulling, the deepening, sad song of a slowing starter motor, the inside of the windshield hazed over with your own quickening breath, a haze eventually webbed with threads of self-propelled crystal that run at loony angles across the glass. Bits of advice, a lifetime of pseudo-mechanic's lore carols up out of the collective technological unconscious—to avoid flooding the engine put the gas pedal to the floor, or to avoid flooding the engine keep your foot off the pedal entirely, pump it, never pump it, add heat, crank it, don't crank it you'll wear down the battery, try it again, call the motor club.

The engine is nearing death, and the starter's grind reaches a slow, trembling note that is as much attuned to sadness and despair as the loneliest of Big Walter Horton's quavering train-whistle obligatos or the most mournful of B. B. King's spine-quivering chords. By now you're bowing into the steering wheel, your stomach tightening as the engine slows, the edge of the cold key cutting into your finger and your thumb. You try each contradictory piece of advice in turn—first slowly, punctuating each separate attempt with a moment of silence, then rapidly, in quick succession, until the dashboard warning lights darken and the last bit of energy from the overburdened battery clicks like ice on glass against the failing solenoid.

This is the zero point of your love of your car, your love of cars in[10] general, the moral retribution for every sin it has suffered on your account, punishment for a long string of specific failures beginning with the profligacies of the showroom and ending with last night's lack of concern for a full gas tank and for an even longer misguided faith in the efficacy of cars, all the way back to the first moment in late childhood when you knew, watching a Pontiac Catalina drift by like a cream-and-turquoise Beatrice,[1] that wheels were the way to freedom, love, and happiness. Neighbors slip by on the way to work. Old Chevys clamor to life, rust-bitten Fords, the painfully modest compact in the next parking stall, all of them kicking up white plumes of exhaust above the blackening snow. Just one rebuke after another.

Mea culpa, mea culpa, mea maxima culpa . . .[2] or hit the steering wheel in disgust . . . or stand outside in the cold, the hood up and your battery cables raised like a begging bowl. At 26 below help comes from all sides. Everyone's tragedy is no one's tragedy. But at a mere ten below, you are alone, a very special and conspicuous failure, leprous, unclean.

Nothing, except love and America, promises more than a car, so there are few disappointments more bitter. Remember when you saw it on television, swooning like a dancer through the curves of a mountain road as lushly green as any of the emerald visions of the Hudson River school or skimming the surface of Pacific Ocean water along the California coast or conquering the Baja or lasering toward the vanishing point of a crayon-colored Mohave sunset, irresistibly lustrous and fluid? They don't sell us cars with tires whitened with salt and salt streaks trailing like tears from the lash tips of their windshield wipers, this Lot's wife of a car, immovable, dead.

Additional Rhetorical Strategies

Analogy (paragraphs 7, 9, 12); Description (paragraphs 8, 12); Narrative (paragraph 9); Cause and Effect (paragraph 10).

Discussion Questions

1. When you have finished reading this essay, do you have a good idea of how to start your car on a day when the temperature is below zero? Why or why not? What do you consider Anania's main purpose in writing this essay? What do you make of all the contradictory bits of advice? What pattern, if any, do you notice among them? How does this pattern relate to the overall structure of the essay?

2. This essay contains a number of figurative comparisons. Reread the essay carefully and identify as many as possible. Characterize the nature of the figurative language used in this essay. What are the principle sources of Anania's metaphors and similes? How does his choice of figurative language contribute to the tone of this essay?

---

[1]The highest expression of feminine beauty (from Dante)—Eds.
[2]Latin phrase indicating the acknowledgment of personal fault or error—Eds.

3. How would you describe the author's relationship with his car? What, in effect, is his attitude toward his car? What words and phrases help you identify this relationship? How does Anania react to his car's failure to start? Whom does he blame? What other failures does this specific failure invoke?
4. In paragraph 7, Anania mocks the speaker who relies on the light on his dash. How are the mechanistic and the ritualistic set in opposition in this essay? Why does Anania tout the latter over the former? Look at the language of lore and ritual that permeates the essay. What is the effect?

Essay Questions

1. Choose one of your own rituals and write a process analysis essay. You need not describe it in such a way that your audience can follow it like a set of instructions; rather, convey the essence and the personal meaning of the ritual.
2. Anania's essay relies on the reader's familiarity with America's love affair with the automobile, and in his essay, as it often is elsewhere, this love is coded specifically as a male love for a female car. Clip some advertisements for automobiles out of a magazine and analyze the ways the car is feminized, and how the feeling of the love affair is invoked. If you can find advertisements in which the lover is female and the automotive object of desire is coded as male, you might want to focus your analysis on these advertisements, or compare and contrast two ads.

When You Camp Out, Do It Right

Ernest Hemingway

"No matter how good a phrase or a simile a writer may have," wrote **Ernest Hemingway** *(1899–1961) in* Death in the Afternoon, *"if he puts it where it is not absolutely necessary and irreplaceable he is spoiling his work for egotism." In his own distinctly terse prose style, Hemingway most frequently wrote about men leading dangerous or adventuresome lives—soldiers, bullfighters, hunters, and fishermen. With the publication of* The Sun Also Rises *in 1926, Hemingway became the leading public voice of a group of disillusioned expatriates living in Paris, which Gertrude Stein named the "lost generation."*

In the following selection, published originally in the Toronto Star *newspaper, Hemingway draws heavily on his own experience in the wilderness and provides detailed advice not on "roughing it in the woods" but rather on the process of ensuring that one is "really comfortable in the bush."*

Thousands of people will go into the bush this summer to cut the high cost of living. A man who gets his two weeks' salary while he is on vacation should be able to put those two weeks in fishing and camping and be able to save one week's salary clear. He ought to be able to sleep comfortably every night, to eat well every day and to return to the city rested and in good condition.

But if he goes into the woods with a frying pan, an ignorance of black flies and mosquitoes, and a great and abiding lack of knowledge about cookery the chances are that his return will be very different. He will come back with enough mosquito bites to make the back of his neck look like a relief map of the Caucasus. His digestion will be wrecked after a valiant battle to assimilate half-cooked or charred grub. And he won't have had a decent night's sleep while he has been gone.

He will solemnly raise his right hand and inform you that he has joined the grand army of never-agains. The call of the wild may be all right, but it's a dog's life. He's heard the call of the tame with both ears. Waiter, bring him an order of milk toast.

In the first place he overlooked the insects. Black flies, no-see-ums, deer flies, gnats and mosquitoes were instituted by the devil to force people to live in cities where he could get at them better. If it weren't for them everybody would live in the bush and he would be out of work. It was a rather successful invention.

5   But there are lots of dopes that will counteract the pests. The simplest perhaps is oil of citronella. Two bits' worth of this purchased at any pharmacist's will be enough to last for two weeks in the worst fly- and mosquito-ridden country.

Rub a little on the back of your neck, your forehead and your wrists before you start fishing, and the blacks and skeeters will shun you. The odor of citronella is not offensive to people. It smells like gun oil. But the bugs do hate it.

Oil of pennyroyal and eucalyptol are also much hated by mosquitoes, and with citronella they form the basis for many proprietary preparations. But it is cheaper and better to buy the straight citronella. Put a little on the mosquito netting that covers the front of your pup tent or canoe tent at night, and you won't be bothered.

To be really rested and get any benefit out of a vacation a man must get a good night's sleep every night. The first requisite for this is to have plenty of cover. It is twice as cold as you expect it will be in the bush, four nights out of five, and a good plan is to take just double the bedding that you think you will need. An old quilt that you can wrap up in is as warm as two blankets.

Nearly all outdoor writers rhapsodize over the browse bed. It is all right for the man who knows how to make one and has plenty of time. But in a succession of one-night camps on a canoe trip all you need is level ground for your tent floor and you will sleep all right if you have plenty of covers under you. Take twice as much cover as you think that you will need, and then put two-thirds of it under you. You will sleep warm and get your rest.

When it is clear weather you don't need to pitch your tent if you are only stopping for the night. Drive four stakes at the head of your made-up bed and drape your mosquito bar over that, then you can sleep like a log and laugh at the mosquitoes.

Outside of insects and bum sleeping the rock that wrecks most camping trips is cooking. The average tyro's idea of cooking is to fry everything and fry it good and plenty. Now, a frying pan is a most necessary thing to any trip, but you also need the old stew kettle and the folding reflector baker.

A pan of fried trout can't be bettered and they don't cost any more than ever. But there is a good and bad way of frying them.

The beginner puts his trout and his bacon in and over a brightly burning fire the bacon curls up and dries into a dry tasteless cinder and the trout is burned outside while it is still raw inside. He eats them and it is all right if he is only out for the day and going home to a good meal at night. But if he is going to face more trout and bacon the next morning and other equally well-cooked dishes for the remainder of two weeks he is on the pathway to nervous dyspepsia.

The proper way is to cook over coals. Have several cans of Crisco or Cotosuet or one of the vegetable shortenings along that are as good as lard and excellent for all kinds of shortening. Put the bacon in and when it is about half cooked lay the trout in the hot grease, dipping them in corn meal first. Then put the bacon on top of the trout and it will baste them as it slowly cooks.

15   The coffee can be boiling at the same time and in a smaller skillet pancakes being made that are satisfying the other campers while they are waiting for the trout.

With the prepared pancake flours you take a cupful of pancake flour and add a cup of water. Mix the water and flour and as soon as the lumps are out it is ready for cooking. Have the skillet hot and keep it well greased. Drop the batter in and as soon as it is done on one side loosen it in the skillet and flip it over. Apple butter, syrup or cinnamon and sugar go well with the cakes.

While the crowd have taken the edge from their appetites with flapjacks the trout have been cooked and they and the bacon are ready to serve. The trout are crisp outside and firm and pink inside and the bacon is well done—but not too done. If there is anything better than that combination the writer has yet to taste it in a lifetime devoted largely and studiously to eating.

The stew kettle will cook your dried apricots when they have resumed their predried plumpness after a night of soaking, it will serve to concoct a mulligan in, and it will cook macaroni. When you are not using it, it should be boiling water for the dishes.

In the baker, mere man comes into his own, for he can make a pie that to his bush appetite will have it all over the product that mother used to make, like a tent. Men have always believed that there was something mysterious and difficult about making a pie. Here is a great secret. There is nothing to it. We've been kidded for years. Any man of average office intelligence can make at least as good a pie as his wife.

20   All there is to a pie is a cup and a half of flour, one-half teaspoonful of salt, one-half cup of lard and cold water. That will make pie crust that will bring tears of joy into your camping partner's eyes.

Mix the salt with the flour, work the lard into the flour, make it up into a good workmanlike dough with cold water. Spread some flour on the back of a box or something flat, and pat the dough around a while. Then roll it out with whatever kind of round bottle you prefer. Put a little more lard on the surface of the sheet of dough and then slosh a little flour on and roll it up and then roll it out again with the bottle.

Cut out a piece of the rolled out dough big enough to line a pie tin. I like the kind with holes in the bottom. Then put in your dried apples that have soaked all night and been sweetened, or your apricots, or your blueberries, and then take another sheet of the dough and drape it gracefully over the top, soldering it down at the edges with your fingers. Cut a couple of slits in the top dough sheet and prick it a few times with a fork in an artistic manner.

Put it in the baker with a good slow fire for forty-five minutes and then take it out and if your pals are Frenchmen they will kiss you. The penalty for knowing how to cook is that the others will make you do all the cooking.

It is all right to talk about roughing it in the woods. But the real woodsman is the man who can be really comfortable in the bush.

Additional Rhetorical Strategies

Cause and Effect (paragraphs 1, 2, 4); Description (paragraphs 2, 17).

Discussion Questions

1. Who is Hemingway's intended audience for this piece? What is his attitude toward that audience? Does he consider himself essentially the same as his audience or essentially different? Point to specific rhetorical and stylistic strategies to support your answer.
2. Hemingway seems contemptuous of the man who "has heard the call of the tame with both ears" (paragraph 3). Why? What is Hemingway's ideal of masculinity? Is this the ideal you expected, given what you know of his other writing?
3. What is the role of women in camping, according to Hemingway? Why do women appear to be so tangential in his version of camping out? Can you infer an attitude toward women from the things he says and doesn't say?
4. How would you characterize the sound of Hemingway's voice in this essay? Point to specific lines to illustrate your response. Do you notice any changes in tone as the essay progresses? What is the effect of Hemingway's tone on you as a reader?

Essay Questions

1. Hemingway makes good use of sensory detail in this essay; it's used sparingly, but just at the right moments to provoke a response in the reader: we can almost taste the trout, for instance. Write a process analysis essay in which you simultaneously give detailed instructions for performing the task in question and also build in a motive for your reader to follow your instructions.
2. Draft an essay in which you present a specified process analysis of some knowledge (or creative ability) that you have. Use Hemingway's essay as a model of your relationship with your readers, especially in terms of their relative level of knowledge. Then prepare another draft, using the same topic but varying your audience: in this case imagine an audience of people who are as knowledgeable as you are. Compare and contrast the two drafts in terms of word choice and sentence structure. Then pick the draft you think is most effective, and polish it to hand in as a formal essay.

The Complete Breath

Yogi Ramacharaka

Yogi Ramacharaka is the pen name assumed by William Walker Atkinson (1862–1932), a writer and businessman who published numerous books on yoga and related topics in the early years of this century. Born in Baltimore, Atkinson studied law and was admitted to the bar in Pennsylvania and Illinois. Beginning in 1900, he worked as an editor for Suggestion *magazine and later edited the periodicals* New Thought *and* Advanced Thought. *He also wrote over two dozen books, both under his real name and his pseudonym. His* Advanced Course in Yogi Philosophy and Oriental Occultism *(1905) went through 30 editions, and he so skillfully described the philosophy and practice of yoga that even today he is sometimes mistaken for a South Asian authority on the subject.*

In addition to writing about yoga, Atkinson published such titles as Practical Psychomancy and Crystal Gazing; A Course of Lessons on the Psychic Phenomena of Distant Sensing, Clairvoyance, Psychometry, Crystal Gazing, Etc. *(1908) and* The Psychology of Salesmanship *(1913). The selection below is taken from* The Hindu-Yogi Science of Breath *(1904).*

Perhaps the best way to teach you how to develop the Yogi Complete Breath would be to give you simple directions regarding the breath itself, and then follow up the same with general remarks concerning it. Right here we wish to say that this Complete Breath is not a forced or abnormal thing, but on the contrary is a going back to first principles—a return to Nature. The healthy adult savage and the healthy infant of civilization both breathe in this manner, but civilized man has adopted unnatural methods of living, clothing, etc., and has lost his birthright. And we wish to remind the reader that the Complete Breath does not necessarily call for the complete filling of the lungs at every inhalation. One may inhale the average amount of air, using the Complete Breathing Method and distributing the air inhaled, be the quantity large or small, to all parts of the lungs. But one should inhale a series of full Complete Breaths several times a day, whenever opportunity offers, in order to keep the system in good order and condition.

The following simple exercise will give you a clear idea of what the Complete Breath is:

(1) Stand or sit erect. Breathing through the nostrils, inhale steadily, first filling the lower part of the lungs, which is accomplished by bringing into play the diaphragm, which descending exerts a gentle pressure on the abdominal organs, pushing forward the front walls of the abdomen. Then fill the middle part of the lungs, pushing out the lower ribs, breastbone and chest. Then fill the higher portion of the lungs, protruding the upper chest, thus lifting the

chest, including the upper six or seven pairs of ribs. In the final movement, the lower part of the abdomen will be slightly drawn in, which movement gives the lungs a support and also helps to fill the highest part of the lungs.

At first reading it may appear that this breath consists of three distinct movements. This, however, is not the correct idea. The inhalation is continuous, the entire chest cavity from the lower diaphragm to the highest point at the chest in the region of the collar-bone, being expanded with a uniform movement. Avoid a jerky series of inhalations, and strive to attain a steady continuous action. Practice will soon overcome the tendency to divide the inhalation into three movements, and will result in a uniform continuous breath. You will be able to complete the inhalation in a couple of seconds after a little practice.

(2) Retain the breath a few seconds.   5

(3) Exhale quite slowly, holding the chest in a firm position, and drawing the abdomen in a little and lifting it upward slowly as the air leaves the lungs. When the air is entirely exhaled, relax the chest and abdomen. A little practice will render this part of the exercise easy, and the movement once acquired will be afterward performed almost automatically.

It will be seen that by this method of breathing all parts of the respiratory apparatus are brought into action, and all parts of the lungs, including the most remote air cells, are exercised. The chest cavity is expanded in all directions. You will find it quite a help to you if you will practice this breath before a large mirror, placing the hands lightly over the abdomen so that you may feel the movements. At the end of the inhalation, it is well to occasionally slightly elevate the shoulders, thus raising the collarbone and allowing the air to pass freely into the small upper lobe of the right lung, which place is sometimes the breeding place of tuberculosis.

At the beginning of practice, you may have more or less trouble in acquiring the Complete Breath, but a little practice will make perfect, and when you have once acquired it you will never willingly return to the old methods.

The practice of the Complete Breath will make any man or woman immune to Consumption and other pulmonary troubles, and will do away with all liability to contract "colds," as well as bronchial and similar weaknesses. Consumption is due principally to lowered vitality attributable to an insufficient amount of air being inhaled. The impairment of vitality renders the system open to attacks from disease germs. Imperfect breathing allows a considerable part of the lungs to remain inactive, and such portions offer an inviting field for bacilli, which invading the weakened tissue soon produce havoc. Good healthy lung tissue will resist the germs, and the only way to have good healthy lung tissue is to use the lungs properly.

10 Consumptives are nearly all narrow-chested. What does this mean? Simply that these people were addicted to improper habits of breathing, and consequently their chests failed to develop and expand. The man who practices the Complete Breath will have a full broad chest and the narrow-chested man may develop his chest to normal proportions if he will but adopt this mode of breathing. Such people must develop their chest cavities if they value their lives. Colds may often be prevented by practicing a little vigorous Complete Breathing whenever you feel that you are being unduly exposed. When chilled, breathe vigorously a few minutes, and you will feel a glow all over your body. Most colds can be cured by Complete Breathing and partial fasting for a day.

The quality of the blood depends largely upon its proper oxygenation in the lungs, and if it is under-oxygenated it becomes poor in quality and laden with all sorts of impurities, and the system suffers from lack of nourishment, and often becomes actually poisoned by the waste products remaining uneliminated in the blood. As the entire body, every organ and every part, is dependent upon the blood for nourishment, impure blood must have a serious effect upon the entire system.

The stomach and other organs of nutrition suffer much from improper breathing. Not only are they ill nourished by reason of the lack of oxygen, but as the food must absorb oxygen from the blood and become oxygenated before it can be digested and assimilated, it is readily seen how digestion and assimilation is impaired by incorrect breathing. And when assimilation is not normal, the system receives less and less nourishment, the appetite fails, bodily vigor decreases, and energy diminishes, and the man withers and declines. All from the lack of proper breathing.

Even the nervous system suffers from improper breathing, inasmuch as the brain, the spinal cord, the nerve centers, and the nerves themselves, when improperly nourished by means of the blood, become poor and inefficient instruments for generating, storing, and transmitting the nerve currents.

The effect of the reproductive organs upon the general health is too well known to be discussed at length here, but we may be permitted to say that with the reproductive organs in a weakened condition the entire system feels the reflex action and suffers sympathetically. The Complete Breath produces a rhythm which is Nature's own plan for keeping this important part of the system in normal condition, and, from the first, it will be noticed that the reproductive functions are strengthened and vitalized, thus, by sympathetic reflex action, giving tone to the whole system.

15 In the practice of the Complete Breath, during inhalation, the diaphragm contracts and exerts a gentle pressure upon the liver, stomach and other organs, which in connection with the rhythm of the lungs acts as a gentle massage of these organs and stimulates their actions,

and encourages normal functioning. Each inhalation aids in this internal exercise, and assists in causing a normal circulation to the organs of nutrition and elimination.

The Western world is paying much attention to Physical Culture just now, which is a good thing.[1] But in their enthusiasm they must not forget that the exercise of the external muscles is not everything. The internal organs also need exercise, and Nature's plan for this exercise is proper breathing. The diaphragm is Nature's principal instrument for this internal exercise. Its motion vibrates the important organs of nutrition and elimination, and massages and kneads them at each inhalation and exhalation, forcing blood into them, and then squeezing it out, and imparting a general tone to the organs. Any organ or part of the body which is not exercised gradually atrophies and refuses to function properly, and lack of the internal exercise afforded by the diaphragmatic action leads to diseased organs. The Complete Breath gives the proper motion to the diaphragm, as well as exercising the middle and upper chest. It is indeed "complete" in its action.

From the standpoint of Western physiology alone, without reference to the Oriental philosophies and science, this Yogi system of Complete Breathing is of vital importance to every man, woman and child who wishes to acquire health and keep it. Its very simplicity keeps thousands from seriously considering it, while they spend fortunes in seeking health through complicated and expensive "systems." Health knocks at their door and they answer not. Verily the stone which the builders reject is the real cornerstone of the Temple of Health.

Additional Rhetorical Strategies

Definition (paragraph 1); Cause and Effect (paragraphs 9 and following); Comparison and Contrast (paragraph 16).

Discussion Questions

1. Did you find yourself following Yogi Ramacharaka's instructions for the complete breath as you read? What is it about this essay that gives it this effect on its readers?
2. What kind of tone does the author set up with his audience? Whom does he assume will make up his audience? How can you tell? What hints does he give that he might have written this differently if his audience had been different, say, for instance, an Eastern rather than a Western audience?

---

[1]Physical exercise and sporting activities became widely popular in the U.S. and parts of Europe at the turn of the century—Eds.

3. Look at the places in his essay where the author defines the complete breath by telling his reader what it is *not,* and the places in the instructions where he tells his reader what not to do. What seems to motivate these sentences phrased in the negative?
4. Where does this essay become vague? What do you sense that the author is leaving out in these instances? Why might he be vague about such things as what one might be "unduly exposed" to (paragraph 10), or about the benefits to the reproductive system (paragraph 14), for example?
5. This essay was written in 1904. Given current knowledge about physiology and health, how do you judge the claims Ramacharaka makes regarding the benefits of the complete breath? What might the knowledge that tuberculosis ("consumption") is caused by airborne bacteria, for instance, do to your reading of this essay? Or the knowledge that there is no oxygen in the stomach and intestines, and that oxygen plays a role in only the very last stages of digestion, when the food is converted to energy? To what extent do his opening and closing paragraphs serve to mitigate your instinctive response to his claims?

Essay Questions

1. This essay dissects a process that is nearly always unconscious, almost never analyzed by the conscious mird and expressed by the written word. Write an essay in which you analyze a process that you were never explicitly taught, and that you do now without thinking. Some examples might include kissing, walking, napping, eating.
2. On the other hand, to do this activity prope y, according to the author, one must practice. Think of another activity that requires practice, and write a process analysis essay in which you break the seemingly seamless process into its component steps. Some examples might include executing a dance step, swinging a bat or a tennis racket, tying a shoe, or taking off a turtleneck sweater.

On Dumpster Diving

Lars Eighner

*Lars Eighner (b. 1948) attended the University of Texas and worked,
among other places, in a state mental hospital and a drug-crisis program
before becoming homeless.* Travels with Lizbeth *in his account of surviv-
ing for three years on the streets. His manuscript caught the eye of an editor at* Threepenny Review, *where his essays on homelessness, including
"On Dumpster Diving," came out before they were published as a book in
1993. Eighner is also the author of* Lavender Blue *(1988) and* Bayou
Boy and Other Stories *(1993).*

   *Eighner began writing as a child, and he began publishing before he
became homeless. He says, "A writer needs talent, luck, and persistence.
You can make do with two out of three, and the more you have of one, the
less you need of the others. You can't do without training and practice."*

L ong before I began Dumpster diving I was impressed with
    Dumpsters, enough so that I wrote the Merriam–Webster re-
    search service to discover what I could about the word "Dump-
ster." I learned from them that "Dumpster" is a proprietary word belonging to the Dempster Dumpster company.

Since then I have dutifully capitalized the word although it was
lowercased in almost all of the citations Merriam–Webster photocopied
for me. Dempster's word is too apt. I have never heard these things
called anything but Dumpsters. I do not know anyone who knows the
generic name for these objects. From time to time, however, I hear a
wino or hobo give some corrupted credit to the original and call them
Dipsy Dumpsters.

I began Dumpster diving about a year before I became homeless.

I prefer the term "scavenging" and use the word "scrounging"
when I mean to be obscure. I have heard people, evidently meaning to
be polite, using the word "foraging," but I prefer to reserve the word
for gathering nuts and berries and such which I do also according to the
season and the opportunity. "Dumpster diving" seems to me to be a little too cute and, in my case, inaccurate because I lack the athletic ability
to lower myself into the Dumpsters as the true divers do, much to their
increased profit.

I like the frankness of the word "scavenging," which I can hardly 5
think of without picturing a big black snail on an aquarium wall. I live
from the refuse of others. I am a scavenger. I think it a sound and honorable niche, although if I could I would naturally prefer to live the
comfortable consumer life, perhaps—and only perhaps—as a slightly
less wasteful consumer owing to what I have learned as a scavenger.

While my dog Lizbeth and I were still living in the house on Avenue B in Austin, as my savings ran out, I put almost all my sporadic

income into rent. The necessities of daily life I began to extract from Dumpsters. Yes, we ate from Dumpsters. Except for jeans, all my clothes came from Dumpsters. Boom boxes, candles, bedding, toilet paper, medicine, books, a typewriter, a virgin male love doll, change sometimes amounting to many dollars: I acquired many things from the Dumpsters.

I have learned much as a scavenger. I mean to put some of what I have learned down here, beginning with the practical art of Dumpster diving and proceeding to the abstract.

What is safe to eat?

After all, the finding of objects is becoming something of an urban art. Even respectable employed people will sometimes find something tempting sticking out of a Dumpster or standing beside one. Quite a number of people, not all of them of the bohemian type, are willing to brag that they found this or that piece in the trash. But eating from Dumpsters is the thing that separates the dilettanti from the professionals.

10 Eating safely from the Dumpsters involves three principles: using the senses and common sense to evaluate the condition of the found materials, knowing the Dumpsters of a given area and checking them regularly, and seeking always to answer the question "Why was this discarded?"

Perhaps everyone who has a kitchen and a regular supply of groceries has, at one time or another, made a sandwich and eaten half of it before discovering mold on the bread or got a mouthful of milk before realizing the milk had turned. Nothing of the sort is likely to happen to a Dumpster diver because he is constantly reminded that most food is discarded for a reason. Yet a lot of perfectly good food can be found in Dumpsters.

Canned goods, for example, turn up fairly often in the Dumpsters I frequent. All except the most phobic people would be willing to eat from a can if it came from a Dumpster. Canned goods are among the safest of foods to be found in Dumpsters, but are not utterly foolproof.

Although very rare with modern canning methods, botulism is a possibility. Most other forms of food poisoning seldom do lasting harm to a healthy person. But botulism is almost certainly fatal and often the first symptom is death. Except for carbonated beverages, all canned goods should contain a slight vacuum and suck air when first punctured. Bulging, rusty, dented cans and cans that spew when punctured should be avoided, especially when the contents are not very acidic or syrupy.

Heat can break down the botulin, but this requires much more cooking than most people do to canned goods. To the extent that botulism occurs at all, of course, it can occur in cans on pantry shelves as well as in cans from Dumpsters. Need I say that home-canned goods found in Dumpsters are simply too risky to be recommended.

From time to time one of my companions, aware of the source of[15] my provisions, will ask, "Do you think these crackers are really safe to eat?" For some reason it is most often the crackers they ask about.

This question always makes me angry. Of course I would not offer my companion anything I had doubts about. But more than that I wonder why he cannot evaluate the condition of the crackers for himself. I have no special knowledge and I have been wrong before. Since he knows where the food comes from, it seems to me he ought to assume some of the responsibility for deciding what he will put in his mouth.

For myself I have few qualms about dry foods such as crackers, cookies, cereal, chips, and pasta if they are free of visible contaminates and still dry and crisp. Most often such things are found in the original packaging, which is not so much a positive sign as it is the absence of a negative one.

Raw fruits and vegetables with intact skins seem perfectly safe to me, excluding of course the obviously rotten. Many are discarded for minor imperfections which can be pared away. Leafy vegetables, grapes, cauliflower, broccoli, and similar things may be contaminated by liquids and may be impractical to wash.

Candy, especially hard candy, is usually safe if it has not drawn ants. Chocolate is often discarded only because it has become discolored as the cocoa butter de-emulsified. Candying after all is one method of food preservation because pathogens do not like very sugary substances.

All of these foods might be found in any Dumpster and can be eval-[20] uated with some confidence largely on the basis of appearance. Beyond these are foods which cannot be correctly evaluated without additional information.

I began scavenging by pulling pizzas out of the Dumpster behind a pizza delivery shop. In general prepared food requires caution, but in this case I knew when the shop closed and went to the Dumpster as soon as the last of the help left.

Such shops often get prank orders, called "bogus." Because help seldom stays long at these places pizzas are often made with the wrong topping, refused on delivery for being cold, or baked incorrectly. The products to be discarded are boxed up because inventory is kept by counting boxes: A boxed pizza can be written off; an unboxed pizza does not exist.

I never placed a bogus order to increase the supply of pizzas and I believe no one else was scavenging in this Dumpster. But the people in the shop became suspicious and began to retain their garbage in the shop overnight.

While it lasted I had a steady supply of fresh, sometimes warm pizza. Because I knew the Dumpster I knew the source of the pizza, and because I visited the Dumpster regularly I knew what was fresh and what was yesterday's.

25   The area I frequent is inhabited by many affluent college students. I am not here by chance; the Dumpsters in this area are very rich. Students throw out many good things, including food. In particular they tend to throw everything out when they move at the end of a semester, before and after breaks, and around midterm when many of them despair of college. So I find it advantageous to keep an eye on the academic calendar.

The students throw food away around the breaks because they do not know whether it has spoiled or will spoil before they return. A typical discard is a half jar of peanut butter. In fact nonorganic peanut butter does not require refrigeration and is unlikely to spoil in any reasonable time. The student does not know that, and since it is Daddy's money, the student decides not to take a chance.

Opened containers require caution and some attention to the question "Why was this discarded?" But in the case of discards from student apartments, the answer may be that the item was discarded through carelessness, ignorance, or wastefulness. This can sometimes be deduced when the item is found with many others, including some that are obviously perfectly good.

Some students, and others, approach defrosting a freezer by chucking out the whole lot. Not only do the circumstances of such a find tell the story, but also the mass of frozen goods stays cold for a long time and items may be found still frozen or freshly thawed.

Yogurt, cheese, and sour cream are items that are often thrown out while they are still good. Occasionally I find a cheese with a spot of mold, which of course I just pare off, and because it is obvious why such a cheese was discarded, I treat it with less suspicion than an apparently perfect cheese found in similar circumstances. Yogurt is often discarded, still sealed, only because the expiration date on the carton had passed. This is one of my favorite finds because yogurt will keep for several days, even in warm weather.

30   Students throw out canned goods and staples at the end of semesters and when they give up college at midterm. Drugs, pornography, spirits, and the like are often discarded when parents are expected— Dad's day, for example. And spirits also turn up after big party weekends, presumably discarded by the newly reformed. Wine and spirits, of course, keep perfectly well even once opened.

My test for carbonated soft drinks is whether they still fizz vigorously. Many juices or other beverages are too acid or too syrupy to cause much concern provided they are not visibly contaminated. Liquids, however, require some care.

One hot day I found a large jug of Pat O'Brien's Hurricane mix. The jug had been opened, but it was still ice cold. I drank three large glasses before it became apparent to me that someone had added the rum to the mix, and not a little rum. I never tasted the rum and by the time I began to feel the effects I had already ingested a very large quantity of the beverage. Some divers would have considered this a boon, but being suddenly and thoroughly intoxicated in a public place in the early afternoon is not my idea of a good time.

I have heard of people maliciously contaminating discarded food and even handouts, but mostly I have heard of this from people with vivid imaginations who have had no experience with the Dumpsters themselves. Just before the pizza shop stopped discarding its garbage at night, jalapeños began showing up on most of the discarded pizzas. If indeed this was meant to discourage me it was a wasted effort because I am native Texan.

For myself, I avoid game, poultry, pork, and egg-based foods whether I find them raw or cooked. I seldom have the means to cook what I find, but when I do I avail myself of plentiful supplies of beef which is often in very good condition. I suppose fish becomes disagreeable before it becomes dangerous. The dog is happy to have any such thing that is past its prime and, in fact, does not recognize fish as food until it is quite strong.

Home leftovers, as opposed to surpluses from restaurants, are very35 often bad. Evidently, especially among students, there is a common type of personality that carefully wraps up even the smallest leftover and shoves it into the back of the refrigerator for six months or so before discarding it. Characteristic of this type are the reused jars and margarine tubs which house the remains.

I avoid ethnic foods I am unfamiliar with. If I do not know what it is supposed to look like when it is good, I cannot be certain I will be able to tell if it is bad.

No matter how careful I am I still get dysentery at least once a month, oftener in warm weather. I do not want to paint too romantic a picture. Dumpster diving has serious drawbacks as a way of life.

I learned to scavenge gradually, on my own. Since then I have initiated several companions into the trade. I have learned that there is a predictable series of stages a person goes through in learning to scavenge.

At first the new scavenger is filled with disgust and self-loathing. He is ashamed of being seen and may lurk around, trying to duck behind things, or he may try to dive at night.

(In fact, most people instinctively look away from a scavenger. By40 skulking around, the novice calls attention to himself and arouses suspicion. Diving at night is ineffective and needlessly messy.)

Every grain of rice seems to be a maggot. Everything seems to stink. He can wipe the egg yolk off the found can, but he cannot erase the stigma of eating garbage out of his mind.

That stage passes with experience. The scavenger finds a pair of running shoes that fit and look and smell brand new. He finds a pocket calculator in perfect working order. He finds pristine ice cream, still frozen, more than he can eat or keep. He begins to understand: People do throw away perfectly good stuff, a lot of perfectly good stuff.

At this stage, Dumpster shyness begins to dissipate. The diver, after all, has the last laugh. He is finding all manner of good things which are his for the taking. Those who disparage his profession are the fools, not he.

He may begin to hang onto some perfectly good things for which he has neither a use nor a market. Then he begins to take note of the things which are not perfectly good but are nearly so. He mates a Walkman with broken earphones and one that is missing a battery cover. He picks up things which he can repair.

45 At this stage he may become lost and never recover. Dumpsters are full of things of some potential value to someone and also of things which never have much intrinsic value but are interesting. All the Dumpster divers I have known come to the point of trying to acquire everything they touch. Why not take it, they reason, since it is all free.

This is, of course, hopeless. Most divers come to realize that they must restrict themselves to items of relatively immediate utility. But in some cases the diver simply cannot control himself. I have met several of these pack-rat types. Their ideas of the values of various pieces of junk verge on the psychotic. Every bit of glass may be a diamond, they think, and all that glistens, gold.

I tend to gain weight when I am scavenging. Partly this is because I always find far more pizza and doughnuts than water-packed tuna, nonfat yogurt, and fresh vegetables. Also I have not developed much faith in the reliability of Dumpsters as a food source, although it has been proven to me many times. I tend to eat as if I have no idea where my next meal is coming from. But mostly I just hate to see food go to waste and so I eat much more than I should. Something like this drives the obsession to collect junk.

As for collecting objects, I usually restrict myself to collecting one kind of small object at a time, such as pocket calculators, sunglasses, or campaign buttons. To live on the street I must anticipate my needs to a certain extent: I must pick up and save warm bedding I find in August because it will not be found in Dumpsters in November. But even if I had a home with extensive storage space I could not save everything that might be valuable in some contingency.

I have proprietary feelings about my Dumpsters. As I have suggested, it is no accident that I scavenge from Dumpsters where good finds are common. But my limited experience with Dumpsters in other areas suggests to me that it is the population of competitors rather than the affluence of the dumpers that most affects the feasibility of survival by scavenging. The large number of competitors is what puts me off the idea of trying to scavenge in places like Los Angeles.

Curiously, I do not mind my direct competition, other scavengers,[50] so much as I hate the can scroungers.

People scrounge cans because they have to have a little cash. I have tried scrounging cans with an able-bodied companion. Afoot a can scrounger simply cannot make more than a few dollars a day. One can extract the necessities of life from the Dumpsters directly with far less effort than would be required to accumulate the equivalent value in cans.

Can scroungers, then, are people who *must* have small amounts of cash. These are drug addicts and winos, mostly the latter because the amounts of cash are so small.

Spirits and drugs do, like all other commodities, turn up in Dumpsters and the scavenger will from time to time have a half bottle of a rather good wine with his dinner. But the wino cannot survive on these occasional finds; he must have his daily dose to stave off the DTs. All the cans he can carry will buy about three bottles of Wild Irish Rose.

I do not begrudge them the cans, but can scroungers tend to tear up the Dumpsters, mixing the contents and littering the area. They become so specialized that they can see only cans. They earn my contempt by passing up change, canned goods, and readily hockable items.

There are precious few courtesies among scavengers. But it is a com-[55]mon practice to set aside surplus items: pairs of shoes, clothing, canned goods, and such. A true scavenger hates to see good stuff go to waste and what he cannot use he leaves in good condition in plain sight.

Can scroungers lay waste to everything in their path and will stir one of a pair of good shoes to the bottom of a Dumpster, to be lost or ruined in the muck. Can scroungers will even go through individual garbage cans, something I have never seen a scavenger do.

Individual garbage cans are set out on the public easement only on garbage days. On other days going through them requires trespassing close to a dwelling. Going through individual garbage cans without scattering litter is almost impossible. Litter is likely to reduce the public's tolerance of scavenging. Individual garbage cans are simply not as productive as Dumpsters; people in houses and duplexes do not move as often and for some reason do not tend to discard as much useful material. Moreover, the time required to go through one garbage can that serves one household is not much less than the time required to go through a Dumpster that contains the refuse of twenty apartments.

But my strongest reservation about going through individual garbage cans is that this seems to me a very personal kind of invasion to which I would object if I were a householder. Although many things in Dumpsters are obviously meant never to come to light, a Dumpster is somehow less personal.

I avoid trying to draw conclusions about the people who dump in the Dumpsters I frequent. I think it would be unethical to do so, although I know many people will find the idea of scavenger ethics too funny for words.

60   Dumpsters contain bank statements, bills, correspondence, and other documents, just as anyone might expect. But there are also less obvious sources of information. Pill bottles, for example. The labels on pill bottles contain the name of the patient, the name of the doctor, and the name of the drug. AIDS drugs and antipsychotic medicines, to name but two groups, are specific and are seldom prescribed for any other disorders. The plastic compacts for birth control pills usually have complete label information.

Despite all of this sensitive information, I have had only one apartment resident object to my going through the Dumpster. In that case it turned out the resident was a university athlete who was taking bets and who was afraid I would turn up his wager slips.

Occasionally a find tells a story. I once found a small paper bag containing some unused condoms, several partial tubes of flavored sexual lubricant, a partially used compact of birth control pills, and the torn pieces of a picture of a young man. Clearly she was through with him and planning to give up sex altogether.

Dumpster things are often sad—abandoned teddy bears, shredded wedding books, despaired-of sales kits. I find many pets lying in state in Dumpsters. Although I hope to get off the streets so that Lizbeth can have a long and comfortable old age, I know this hope is not very realistic. So I suppose when her time comes she too will go into a Dumpster. I will have no better place for her. And after all, for most of her life her livelihood has come from the Dumpster. When she finds something I think is safe that has been spilled from the Dumpster I let her have it. She already knows the route around the best Dumpsters. I like to think that if she survives me she will have a chance of evading the dog catcher and of finding her sustenance on the route.

Silly vanities also come to rest in the Dumpsters. I am a rather accomplished needleworker. I get a lot of materials from the Dumpsters. Evidently sorority girls, hoping to impress someone, perhaps themselves, with their mastery of a womanly art, buy a lot of embroider-by-number kits, work a few stitches horribly, and eventually discard the whole mess. I pull out their stitches, turn the canvas over, and work an original design. Do not think I refrain from chuckling as I make original gifts from these kits.

65   I find diaries and journals. I have often thought of compiling a book of literary found objects. And perhaps I will one day. But what I find is hopelessly commonplace and bad without being, even unconsciously, camp. College students also discard their papers. I am horrified to discover the kind of paper which now merits an A in an undergraduate course. I am grateful, however, for the number of good books and magazines the students throw out.

In the area I know best I have never discovered vermin in the Dumpsters, but there are two kinds of kitty surprise. One is alley cats which I meet as they leap, claws first, out of Dumpsters. This is especially thrilling when I have Lizbeth in tow. The other kind of kitty surprise is a plastic garbage bag filled with some ponderous, amorphous mass. This always proves to be used cat litter.

City bees harvest doughnut glaze and this makes the Dumpster at the doughnut shop more interesting. My faith in the instinctive wisdom of animals is always shaken whenever I see Lizbeth attempt to catch a bee in her mouth, which she does whenever bees are present. Evidently some birds find Dumpsters profitable, for birdie surprise is almost as common as kitty surprise of the first kind. In hunting season all kinds of small game turn up in Dumpsters, some of it, sadly, not entirely dead. Curiously, summer and winter, maggots are uncommon.

The worst of the living and near-living hazards of the Dumpsters are the fire ants. The food that they claim is not much of a loss, but they are vicious and aggressive. It is very easy to brush against some surface of the Dumpster and pick up half a dozen or more fire ants, usually in some sensitive area such as the underarm. One advantage of bringing Lizbeth along as I make Dumpster rounds is that, for obvious reasons, she is very alert to ground-based fire ants. When Lizbeth recognizes the signs of fire ant infestation around our feet she does the Dance of the Zillion Fire Ants. I have learned not to ignore this warning from Lizbeth, whether I perceive the tiny ants or not, but to remove ourselves at Lizbeth's first *pas de bourrée*.[1] All the more so because the ants are the worst in the months I wear flip-flops, if I have them.

(Perhaps someone will misunderstand the above. Lizbeth does the Dance of the Zillion Fire Ants when she recognizes more fire ants than she cares to eat, not when she is being bitten. Since I have learned to react promptly, she does not get bitten at all. It is the isolated patrol of fire ants that falls in Lizbeth's range that deserves pity. Lizbeth finds them quite tasty.)

By far the best way to go through a Dumpster is to lower yourself 70 into it. Most of the good stuff tends to settle at the bottom because it is usually weightier than the rubbish. My more athletic companions have often demonstrated to me that they can extract much good material from a Dumpster I have already been over.

To those psychologically or physically unprepared to enter a Dumpster, I recommend a stout stick, preferably with some barb or hook at one end. The hook can be used to grab plastic garbage bags. When I find canned goods or other objects loose at the bottom of a

---

[1]*pas de bourrée:* A transitional ballet step—Eds.

Dumpster I usually can roll them into a small bag that I can then hoist up. Much Dumpster diving is a matter of experience for which nothing will do except practice.

Dumpster diving is outdoor work, often surprisingly pleasant. It is not entirely predictable; things of interest turn up every day and some days there are finds of great value. I am always very pleased when I can turn up exactly the thing I most wanted to find. Yet in spite of the element of chance, scavenging more than most other pursuits tends to yield returns in some proportion to the effort and intelligence brought to bear. It is very sweet to turn up a few dollars in change from a Dumpster that has just been gone over by a wino.

The land is now covered with cities. The cities are full of Dumpsters. I think of scavenging as a modern form of self-reliance. In any event, after ten years of government service, where everything is geared to the lowest common denominator, I find work that rewards initiative and effort refreshing. Certainly I would be happy to have a sinecure again, but I am not heartbroken not to have one anymore.

I find from the experience of scavenging two rather deep lessons. The first is to take what I can use and let the rest go by. I have come to think that there is no value in the abstract. A thing I cannot use or make useful, perhaps by trading, has no value however fine or rare it may be. I mean useful in a broad sense—so, for example, some art I would think useful and valuable, but other art might be otherwise for me.

75   I was shocked to realize that some things are not worth acquiring, but now I think it is so. Some material things are white elephants that eat up the possessor's substance.

The second lesson is of the transience of material being. This has not quite converted me to a dualist, but it has made some headway in that direction. I do not suppose that ideas are immortal, but certainly mental things are longer-lived than other material things.

Once I was the sort of person who invests material objects with sentimental value. Now I no longer have those things, but I have the sentiments yet.

Many times in my travels I have lost everything but the clothes I was wearing and Lizbeth. The things I find in Dumpsters, the love letters and ragdolls of so many lives, remind me of this lesson. Now I hardly pick up a thing without envisioning the time I will cast it away. This I think is a healthy state of mind. Almost everything I have now has already been cast out at least once, proving that what I own is valueless to someone.

Anyway, I find my desire to grab for the gaudy bauble has been largely sated. I think this is an attitude I share with the very wealthy— we both know there is plenty more where what we have came from. Between us are the rat-race millions who have confounded their selves with the objects they grasp and who nightly scavenge the cable channels looking for they know not what.

I am sorry for them.   80

Additional Rhetorical Strategies

Classification (paragraphs 22, 31); Definition (paragraph 2); Example (throughout).

Discussion Questions

1. In paragraph 40, Eighner writes "most people instinctively look away from scavengers." If you are among those who look away, identify the preconceptions about homeless people you had before reading this essay. What are the most surprising things you learned about homeless people from reading this essay? Were there specific insights that seemed at first to be alien in the context of an analysis of the process of dumpster diving?

2. Analyze the structure of Eighner's essay. Where does he identify the steps one should take when dumpster diving? How does the remainder of the essay follow or deviate from that organizing principle? Identify the function of any seeming tangents from the task of straight process analysis.

3. It is unlikely that there will be many homeless people among the readers of Eighner's essay. Identify the strategies he employs to make his subject matter relevant to those who are not homeless. What lessons might you as a reader take away from this essay, and apply in your own life, even if you foresee no time when you will actually be compelled to eat from dumpsters? What lines in particular seem directed to the students in the audience?

4. How does Eighner approach the part of his topic that most readers will find most repellent: the idea of eating from dumpsters? Locate the first reference to this topic, then locate the subsequent references to this topic. What comes between the earlier and later references to eating from dumpsters, besides merely a break to allow the audience to become accustomed to the idea? How does Eighner's breakdown of the "stages that a person goes through in learning to scavenge" mirror the reader's experience of the act of reading this essay?

5. Examine Eighner's use of concrete details. How does the level of detail affect you as you read his essay? Can you tell from the level and frequency of detail in this essay what kind of audience Eighner expected? How familiar with his topic does Eighner seem to think his audience will be?

Essay Questions

1. Eighner's process analysis essay is likely to stretch the limits of the typical reader's sympathetic imagination, in this case by providing an insider's view of homelessness. Think of another stigmatized or outcast group (besides the homeless) and write an essay that helps your reader to put him or herself in the place of a member of that group. You might choose the process analysis mode, but don't limit your options. A narrative mode, comparison and contrast, or any of a number of other modes might suit your purpose better.

2. Write a process analysis of a process that your readers are unlikely to want to engage in. You don't necessarily have to make it sound so appealing that your readers will change their minds about the activity itself—although it's fine if you do—but you should use rhetorical strategies to keep them engaged in the reading.

Thematic Pair: On the Writing Process

▲▼How to Write with Style

Kurt Vonnegut

Kurt Vonnegut (b. 1922) is one of America's most popular contemporary novelists. The author of such campus favorites as Cat's Cradle *(1963),* Slaughterhouse Five *(1969),* Deadeye Dick *(1982),* Galapagos *(1985), and* Between Time and Timbuktu *(1986), Vonnegut has also written several plays and contributed short fiction to periodicals ranging from the* Saturday Evening Post *and* Ladies' Home Journal *to* Cosmopolitan *and* Playboy.

In 1979, the International Paper Company began sponsoring a series of advertisements on the "Power of the Printed Word." Designed to help young people "read better, write better, and communicate better," this advertising campaign featured such celebrities and writers as Steve Allen, Bill Cosby, James Michener and George Plimpton, discussing such topics as how to use a library and how to enjoy the classics. International Paper reports that the series has been an enormous success; at one point, the company received nearly 1,000 reprint requests a day. International Paper obviously realizes that the more readers there are of books, magazines, and newspapers, the more paper it will sell. In the following advertisements from the series sponsored by International Paper, Vonnegut offers some practical tips on how to write well.

Newspaper reporters and technical writers are trained to reveal almost nothing about themselves in their writings. This makes them freaks in the world of writers, since almost all of the other ink-stained wretches in that world reveal a lot about themselves to readers. We call these revelations, accidental and intentional, elements of style.

These revelations tell us as readers what sort of person it is with whom we are spending time. Does the writer sound ignorant or informed, stupid or bright, crooked or honest, humorless or playful—? And on and on.

Why should you examine your writing style with the idea of improving it? Do so as a mark of respect for your readers, whatever you're writing. If you scribble your thoughts any which way, your readers will surely feel that you care nothing about them. They will mark you down as an egomaniac or a chowderhead—or worse, they will stop reading you.

The most damning revelation you can make about yourself is that you do not know what is interesting and what is not. Don't you yourself like or dislike writers mainly for what they choose to show you or make you think about? Did you ever admire an empty-headed writer for his or her mastery of the language? No.

5   So your own winning style must begin with ideas in your head.

1. Find a Subject You Care about

Find a subject you care about and which you in your heart feel others should care about. It is this genuine caring, and not your games with language, which will be the most compelling and seductive element in your style.

I am not urging you to write a novel, by the way—although I would not be sorry if you wrote one, provided you genuinely cared about something. A petition to the mayor about a pothole in front of your house or a love letter to the girl next door will do.

2. Do Not Ramble, Though

I won't ramble on about that.

3. Keep It Simple

As for your use of language: Remember that two great masters of language, William Shakespeare and James Joyce, wrote sentences which were almost childlike when their subjects were most profound. "To be or not to be?" asks Shakespeare's Hamlet. The longest word is three letters long. Joyce, when he was frisky, could put together a sentence as intricate and as glittering as a necklace for Cleopatra, but my favorite sentence in his short story "Eveline" is this one: "She was tired." At that point in the story, no other words could break the heart of a reader as those three words do.

Simplicity of language is not only reputable, but perhaps even sa-10 cred. The *Bible* opens with a sentence well within the writing skills of a lively fourteen-year-old: "In the beginning God created the heaven and the earth."

4. Have the Guts to Cut

It may be that you, too, are capable of making necklaces for Cleopatra, so to speak. But your eloquence should be the servant of the ideas in your head. Your rule might be this: If a sentence, no matter how excellent, does not illuminate your subject in some new and useful way, scratch it out.

5. Sound Like Yourself

The writing style which is most natural for you is bound to echo the speech you heard when a child. English was the novelist Joseph Conrad's third language, and much that seems piquant in his use of English was no doubt colored by his first language, which was Polish. And lucky indeed is the writer who has grown up in Ireland, for the English spoken there is so amusing and musical. I myself grew up in

Indianapolis, where common speech sounds like a band saw cutting galvanized tin, and employs a vocabulary as unornamental as a monkey wrench.

In some of the more remote hollows of Appalachia, children still grow up hearing songs and locutions of Elizabethan times. Yes, and many Americans grow up hearing a language other than English, or an English dialect a majority of Americans cannot understand.

All these varieties of speech are beautiful, just as the varieties of butterflies are beautiful. No matter what your first language, you should treasure it all your life. If it happens not to be standard English, and if it shows itself when you write standard English, the result is usually delightful, like a very pretty girl with one eye that is green and one that is blue.

15   I myself find that I trust my own writing most, and others seem to trust it most, too, when I sound most like a person from Indianapolis, which is what I am. What alternatives do I have? The one most vehemently recommended by teachers has no doubt been pressed on you, as well: to write like cultivated Englishmen of a century or more ago.

6. Say What You Mean to Say

I used to be exasperated by such teachers, but am no more. I understand now that all those antique essays and stories with which I was to compare my own work were not magnificent for their datedness or foreignness, but for saying precisely what their authors meant them to say. My teachers wished me to write accurately, always selecting the most effective words, and relating the words to one another unambiguously, rigidly, like parts of a machine. The teachers did not want to turn me into an Englishman after all. They hoped that I would become understandable—and therefore understood. And there went my dream of doing with words what Pablo Picasso did with paint or what any number of jazz idols did with music. If I broke all the rules of punctuation, had words mean whatever I wanted them to mean, and strung them together higgledy-piggledy, I would simply not be understood. So you, too, had better avoid Picasso-style or jazz-style writing, if you have something worth saying and wish to be understood.

Readers want our pages to look very much like pages they have seen before. Why? This is because they themselves have a tough job to do, and they need all the help they can get from us.

7. Pity the Readers

They have to identify thousands of little marks on paper, and make sense of them immediately. They have to *read*, an art so difficult that most people don't really master it even after having studied it all through grade school and high school—twelve long years.

So this discussion must finally acknowledge that our stylistic options as writers are neither numerous nor glamorous, since our readers are bound to be such imperfect artists. Our audience requires us to be sympathetic and patient teachers, ever willing to simplify and clarify—whereas we would rather soar high above the crowd, singing like nightingales.

That is the bad news. The good news is that we Americans are gov-[20]erned under a unique Constitution, which allows us to write whatever we please without fear of punishment. So the most meaningful aspect of our styles, which is what we choose to write about, is utterly unlimited.

8. For Really Detailed Advice

For a discussion of literary style in a narrower sense, in a more technical sense, I commend to your attention *The Elements of Style,* by William Strunk, Jr., and E. B. White (Macmillan, 1979). E. B. White is, of course, one of the most admirable literary stylists this country has so far produced.

You should realize, too, that no one would care how well or badly Mr. White expressed himself, if he did not have perfectly enchanting things to say.

Additional Rhetorical Strategies

Definition (paragraph 1); Cause and Effect (paragraphs 3, 16); Example (paragraphs 7, 9, 10, 12, 13, 16); Analogy (paragraphs 11, 12, 16).

Discussion Questions

1. Reread the part of the introduction to this section that focuses on specified process analysis. How closely does Vonnegut follow the model outlined there? Does he draw on the features of informative process analysis at all? Why do you think Vonnegut chose to list his instructions in this particular order?
2. When you have finished Vonnegut's essay, do you feel you can follow his instructions and become a better writer? Which parts of the essay are easiest to put into action? Why?
3. How would you characterize Vonnegut's own style in this essay on style? Is he formal or informal? Is he primarily abstract or concrete? To what extent does Vonnegut follow his own rules when writing this essay?
4. Vonnegut implies that a sense of audience is a paramount concern for writers. How would you characterize Vonnegut's attitude toward *his* audience? Does he treat them, for example, as if they were ignorant or informed? Point to specific words and phrases to support your answer.

5. Comment on the effectiveness of Vonnegut's use of metaphor in this essay. What are the primary sources of his metaphors? How effectively does he use analogy? What are the keys to a successful analogy?

Essay Questions

1. Think of an activity that you are reasonably confident you do well. Using specified process analysis as your basic structure, write an essay in which you explain to someone less experienced how best to perform this activity. Remember to be, as Vonnegut says, a "sympathetic and patient" teacher, "ever willing to simplify and clarify."
2. The poet Robert Frost once defined style in these terms: "I am not satisfied to let it go with the aphorism that style is the man. The man's ideas would be some element then of the man's style. So would his deeds. But I would narrow the definition. His deeds are his deeds; his ideas are his ideas. His style is the way he carries himself towards his ideas and deeds." How compatible is Frost's definition with the one Vonnegut offers here? Be as specific as possible.

▲▼The Maker's Eye

Donald M. Murray

Donald Murray (b. 1924) earned his A.B. at the University of New Hampshire, where, after a stint as a reporter and editorial writer, he became a professor of English. He has written fiction, poetry, and nonfiction, including several textbooks, among them Writing for Your Readers *(1983),* Write to Learn *(1984) and* Read to Write *(1985). He has contributed hundreds of articles to various periodicals, including the following essay, which first appeared in the* Writer *in 1973. He was awarded the Pulitzer Prize for his editorials in the* Boston Herald.

Although "The Maker's Eye" was originally intended for an audience of professional writers, it can be profitably read by anyone who takes seriously the quest to improve his or her writing skill.

When students complete a first draft, they consider the job of writing done—and their teachers too often agree. When professional writers complete a first draft, they usually feel that they are at the start of the writing process. When a draft is completed, the job of writing can begin.

That difference in attitude is the difference between amateur and professional, inexperience and experience, journeyman and craftsman. Peter F. Drucker, the prolific business writer, calls his first draft "the zero draft"—after that he can start counting. Most writers share the feeling that the first draft, and all of those which follow, are opportunities to discover what they have to say and how best they can say it.

To produce a progression of drafts, each of which says more and says it more clearly, the writer has to develop a special kind of reading skill. In school we are taught to decode what appears on the page as finished writing. Writers, however, face a different category of possibility and responsibility when they read their own drafts. To them the words on the page are never finished. Each can be changed and rearranged, can set off a chain reaction of confusion or clarified meaning. This is a different kind of reading, which is possibly more difficult and certainly more exciting.

Writers must learn to be their own best enemy. They must accept the criticism of others and be suspicious of it; they must accept the praise of others and be even more suspicious of it. Writers cannot depend on others. They must detach themselves from their own pages so that they can apply both their caring and their craft to their own work.

Such detachment is not easy. Science fiction writer Ray Bradbury [5] supposedly puts each manuscript away for a year to the day and then rereads it as a stranger. Not many writers have the discipline or the time to do this. We must read when our judgment may be at its worst, when we are close to the euphoric moment of creation.

Then the writer, counsels novelist Nancy Hale, "should be critical of everything that seems to him most delightful in his style. He should excise what he most admires, because he wouldn't thus admire it if he weren't . . . in a sense protecting it from criticism." John Ciardi, the poet, adds, "The last act of the writing must be to become one's own reader. It is, I suppose, a schizophrenic process, to begin passionately and to end critically, to begin hot and to end cold; and, more important, to be passion-hot and critic-cold at the same time."

Most people think that the principal problem is that writers are too proud of what they have written. Actually, a greater problem for most professional writers is one shared by the majority of students. They are overly critical, think everything is dreadful, tear up page after page, never complete a draft, see the task as hopeless.

The writer must learn to read critically but constructively, to cut what is bad, to reveal what is good. Eleanor Estes, the children's book author, explains: "The writer must survey his work critically, coolly, as though he were a stranger to it. He must be willing to prune, expertly and hard-heartedly. At the end of each revision, a manuscript may look . . . worked over, torn apart, pinned together, added to, deleted from, words changed and words changed back. Yet the book must maintain its original freshness and spontaneity."

Most readers underestimate the amount of rewriting it usually takes to produce spontaneous reading. This is a great disadvantage to the student writer, who sees only a finished product and never watches the craftsman who takes the necessary step back, studies the work carefully, returns to the task, steps back, returns, steps back, again and again. Anthony Burgess, one of the most prolific writers in the English-speaking world, admits, "I might revise a page twenty times." Roald Dahl, the popular children's writer, states, "By the time I'm nearing the end of a story, the first part will have been reread and altered and corrected at least 150 times. . . . Good writing is essentially rewriting. I am positive of this."

10   Rewriting isn't virtuous. It isn't something that ought to be done. It is simply something that most writers find they have to do to discover what they have to say and how to say it. It is a condition of the writer's life.

There are, however, a few writers who do little formal rewriting, primarily because they have the capacity and experience to create and review a large number of invisible drafts in their minds before they approach the page. And some writers slowly produce finished pages, performing all the tasks of revision simultaneously, page by page, rather than draft by draft. But it is still possible to see the sequence followed by most writers most of the time in rereading their own work.

Most writers scan their drafts first, reading as quickly as possible to catch the larger problems of subject and form, then move in closer and closer as they read and write, reread and rewrite.

The first thing writers look for in their drafts is *information.* They know that a good piece of writing is built from specific, accurate, and interesting information. The writer must have an abundance of information from which to construct a readable piece of writing.

Next writers look for *meaning* in the information. The specifics must build a pattern of significance. Each piece of specific information must carry the reader toward meaning.

Writers reading their own drafts are aware of *audience.* They put [15] themselves in the reader's situation and make sure that they deliver information which a reader wants to know or needs to know in a manner which is easily digested. Writers try to be sure that they anticipate and answer the questions a critical reader will ask when reading the piece of writing.

Writers make sure that the *form* is appropriate to the subject and the audience. Form, or genre, is the vehicle which carries meaning to the reader, but form cannot be selected until the writer has adequate information to discover its significance and an audience which needs or wants that meaning.

Once writers are sure the form is appropriate, they must then look at the *structure,* the order of what they have written. Good writing is built on a solid framework of logic, argument, narrative, or motivation which runs through the entire piece of writing and holds it together. This is the time when many writers find it most effective to outline as a way of visualizing the hidden spine by which the piece of writing is supported.

The element on which writers may spend a majority of their time is *development.* Each section of a piece of writing must be adequately developed. It must give readers enough information so that they are satisfied. How much information is enough? That's as difficult as asking how much garlic belongs in a salad. It must be done to taste, but most beginning writers underdevelop, underestimating the reader's hunger for information.

As writers solve development problems, they often have to consider questions of *dimension.* There must be a pleasing and effective proportion among all the parts of the piece of writing. There is a continual process of subtracting and adding to keep the piece of writing in balance.

Finally, writers have to listen to their own voices. *Voice* is the force [20] which drives a piece of writing forward. It is an expression of the writer's authority and concern. It is what is between the words on the page, what glues the piece of writing together. A good piece of writing is always marked by a consistent, individual voice.

As writers read and reread, write and rewrite, they move closer and closer to the page until they are doing line-by-line editing. Writers read their own pages with infinite care. Each sentence, each line, each clause, each phrase, each word, each mark of punctuation, each section of white space between the type has to contribute to the clarification of meaning.

Slowly the writer moves from word to word, looking through language to see the subject. As a word is changed, cut, or added, as a construction is rearranged, all the words used before that moment and all those that follow that moment must be considered and reconsidered.

Writers often read aloud at this stage of the editing process, muttering or whispering to themselves, calling on the ear's experience with language. Does this sound right—or that? Writers edit, shifting back and forth from eye to page to ear to page. I find I must do this careful editing in short runs, no more than fifteen or twenty minutes at a stretch, or I become too kind with myself. I begin to see what I hope is on the page, not what actually is on the page.

This sounds tedious if you haven't done it, but actually it is fun. Making something right is immensely satisfying, for writers begin to learn what they are writing about by writing. Language leads them to meaning, and there is the joy of discovery, of understanding, of making meaning clear as the writer employs the technical skills of language.

25 Words have double meanings, even triple and quadruple meanings. Each word has its own potential for connotation and denotation. And when writers rub one word against the other, they are often rewarded with a sudden insight, an unexpected clarification.

The maker's eye moves back and forth from word to phrase to sentence to paragraph to sentence to phrase to word. The maker's eye sees the need for variety and balance, for a firmer structure, for a more appropriate form. It peers into the interior of the paragraph, looking for coherence, unity, and emphasis, which make meaning clear.

I learned something about this process when my first bifocals were prescribed. I had ordered a larger section of the reading portion of the glass because of my work, but even so, I could not contain my eyes within this new limit of vision. And I still find myself taking off my glasses and bending my nose towards the page, for my eyes unconsciously flick back and forth across the page, back to another page, forward to still another, as I try to see each evolving line in relation to every other line.

When does this process end? Most writers agree with the great Russian writer Tolstoy, who said, "I scarcely ever reread my published writings, if by chance I come across a page, it always strikes me: all this must be rewritten; this is how I should have written it."

The maker's eye is never satisfied, for each word has the potential to ignite new meaning. This article has been twice written all the way through the writing process, and it was published four years ago. Now it is to be republished in a book. The editors make a few small suggestions, and then I read it with my maker's eye. Now it has been re-edited, re-revised, re-read, re-re-edited, for each piece of writing to the writer is full of potential and alternatives.

A piece of writing is never finished. It is delivered to a deadline,30 torn out of the typewriter on demand, sent off with a sense of accomplishment and shame and pride and frustration. If only there were a couple more days, time for just another run at it, perhaps then. . . .

Additional Rhetorical Strategies

Comparison and Contrast (paragraphs 1–2, 7); Classification (paragraph 3); Analogy (paragraph 18).

Discussion Questions

1. Analyze the structure of Murray's essay. Where does the process analysis actually begin? What is the function of all of the paragraphs preceding that section of the essay?

2. By giving a numbered sequence of the steps taken by a writer revising his or her prose, Murray implies that everyone's revision process will take more or less the same shape. If you are revising a piece of prose you have written, pay special attention to the order in which you consider the various aspects (such as information, meaning, audience, etc.) that Murray names. Do you find that you consider the essay from each of these angles in this particular order? If not, how would you explain the process by which you revise your prose, and the rationale for so doing?

3. Throughout much of the process analysis, Murray refers to "the writer" in the third person, but in paragraph 23 he switches to the first person, and provides examples from his personal experience. What is the effect of this shift?

4. Why does Murray end his essay with ellipses? How does this stylistic decision relate to the content of his essay? What is the effect, in paragraph 29, of telling the reader about the ongoing revision of the very essay we are reading?

Essay Questions

1. Revise one of your own essays that you wrote earlier in the semester. Identify the pieces of advice, from Murray or any of the professional writers he quotes, that struck you as most useful or enlightening. Why did these particular suggestions stand out for you? If you have chosen pieces of practical advice (as opposed to more vague statements of philosophy), try to apply this newly acquired insight to the essay you have chosen to revise.

2. Throughout the essay, Murray refers both to student writers and professional writers, sometimes to compare them and sometimes to contrast them. Do you think student writers are more like or unlike professional writers, in terms of their writing process (as opposed to their products)? Write an essay defending your answer.

Exploring Connections: Questions Linking the Thematic Pair

1. Vonnegut writes that most writers "reveal a lot about themselves to readers" (paragraph 1). What does each writer in this thematic pair reveal about himself to you, the reader? Don't think merely in terms of what kind of a writer Murray or Vonnegut is, but also what kind of person.

2. Vonnegut deals in his essay primarily with the writing process, whereas Murray deals primarily with the process of revision. Still, their advice overlaps to a large extent. Which ideas and suggestions appear in some form in both essays? What can you infer about Vonnegut's stance on revision from the short essay you have here, which never explicitly mentions the word "revision"?

Argument and Persuasion

The Difference between Argument and Persuasion

The main business of an argument is to convince an audience by means of careful reasoning that a certain claim is true. As such, argument is ordinarily distinguished from another rhetorical means of convincing audiences—persuasion. Though no firm line can be drawn to mark off the boundaries between these two age-old rhetorical methods, critics customarily see argument largely as a rational appeal to the understanding, and persuasion largely as an emotional appeal to the will. Argument attempts to convince an audience of a truth; persuasion, of a course of action. Argument also relies less heavily on stylistic features than does persuasion and builds its case upon a tight network of logical connections rather than upon powerful oratorical techniques. Clear-cut distinctions may hold in some extreme cases, but in most thinking and writing we should expect to find argument mixed with some degree of persuasion and persuasion tinged with some elements of argument. As a working distinction, however, we could say that the overall purpose of argument is to obtain an audience's *assent* (that is, its acceptance of a statement or abstract proposition), whereas the overall purpose of persuasion is to obtain an audience's *consent* (that is, its voluntary agreement to or acquiescence in a plan or desire).

Argument

In one form or another, arguments take up a sizable portion of our everyday lives. We quarrel with a friend over a broken appointment, dispute a call in a close game, try to change our roommate's mind about dropping a course, disagree with a police officer about a parking ticket, argue with a salesperson about the correct price of a product. Argument is even an ongoing process of our consciousness. We frequently carry on debates inside our heads: "If she says that, then I'll just point out. . . ." We also conduct arguments with ourselves as a necessary aid to decision-making and problem-solving. Though our everyday arguments can range from highly abstract debates with a friend about the existence of God to such practical disputes as who gets to use the shower first, most of our arguments arise spontaneously and are usually worked out only to the degree necessary to win or to resolve the conflict.

When it comes to expressing arguments on paper, however, our everyday types of argument will not always stand up. They tend to be far too informally presented, loosely constructed, and undeveloped. In rhetoric, argument is a special form of discourse, one that attempts to convince an audience that a specific claim or proposition is true wholly because a supporting body of logically related statements is also true. In a well-constructed argument, once we establish the truth of statements *A*, *B*, and *C*, and so forth, then we can reasonably be expected to assent to the principal claim or assertion. In other words, the truth of a statement is entirely dependent on the previously acknowledged truth of other statements.

For example, suppose you want to argue that standardized admission tests represent an unfair criterion by which to evaluate college applicants. To win your audience's assent to that claim, you must present *reasons* for believing the tests to be inadequate. You might construct your argument around such relevant points as:

1. The tests are culturally biased against minorities and disadvantaged students.
2. They focus on isolated bits of knowledge.
3. They ignore taste and judgment.
4. They give insufficient attention to creativity.
5. They tend to reward quicker and more competitive students while penalizing those who prefer to take their time and consider problems thoroughly.
6. They fail to give proper attention to writing ability.

Your reasons should be relevant to the main point of the argument (to complain about the early-morning hour of some of the tests would not be convincing); they should also be supported by facts (you need to research such things as reliability of scores, which subject areas are tested, and how writing ability is evaluated). Once you had systematically demonstrated that your set of reasons—or other reasons like these—was true, or very likely true, then you could feel confident that your main proposition should also be accepted as true.

The ability to make claims confidently and support them with well-constructed arguments is one of the best indications of cognitive and verbal achievement. In many professions—especially in law, journalism, education, science, and business—the formulation of convincing arguments is a skill few can afford to do without. In order to learn the enormously useful and intellectually satisfying art of arguing well, we need to know the various components of a solidly designed argument. For practical purposes, we can divide an argument into three components: first, its *claim*, which may also be referred to as its assertion, statement, proposition, or thesis-statement; second, its *reasoning pattern*, which is the logical relation of premises—that is, the statements forming the basis of an argument—and conclusions; and third, its *organization*, which includes the positioning of evidence, the order of points or reasons, and the interrelation of additional rhetorical strategies. In this section, we will examine the main characteristics of these three elements and some of the ways they function in our thinking and writing.

Claims

The first important element to consider in an argument is its claim or proposition—the point of the argument. Though this sounds obvious, we need only recall how often we have listened to or read arguments and wondered, "What's the point?" We should make sure when constructing an argument that it is built around what can reasonably be called an arguable point. In our everyday lives we argue loosely about many topics that would not be considered legitimate subjects for an extended, formal argument. For example, in an essay, you cannot seriously present an argument about commands such as "Pass the mashed potatoes" or "Turn down the music," though you might get into heated arguments about such imperatives in your daily life. Assertions of taste, such as "Tea tastes better than coffee," also don't constitute a legitimate basis for argument (but if you changed the assertion to "Tea is better for one's health than coffee," you would have an arguable point, one that might be supported with appropriate medical documentation). Likewise, matters of fact constitute another area of nonarguable propositions. There is no point in constructing arguments in order to demonstrate information that is "findable"—the distance from the earth to the moon or Mickey Mantle's 1955 batting average.

Arguable claims generally fall into four categories:

1. *Claims about meaning:* "What is X?" These are propositions that center on how we define or interpret something. What do we mean by "pornography"? Is a defendant "sane" enough to stand trial?

2. *Claims about value:* "Is X good or bad, right or wrong, useful or useless?" Though propositions about the value of something can rarely be argued conclusively, they do constitute a large and vital part of what intelligent people argue about: "Is capital punishment morally wrong?" "Who is funnier, Jim Carrey or Eddie Murphy?" "Is *War and Peace* a better novel than *Anna Karenina?*" When we make ethical and aesthetic evaluations, we need to base our judgments on clear and consistent criteria.

3. *Claims about consequences:* "What will happen as a result of X?" "What is the upshot of our believing X?" We argue over consequences whenever we examine the causal patterns involved in certain ideas and actions. Such arguments usually take an "if X, then Y" form: "If an international law is passed that apportions the solar system to different

nations, then space will become a theater of war." "If America were suddenly plunged into another Great Depression, then there would be a vast resettlement of rural areas."

4. *Claims about policy:* "What should be done about X?" In arguments having to do with policy, the proposition is usually stated in the form of a proposal and the operative words are *ought* and *should.* "Gun control ought to be mandatory in every state." "Utility companies should be nationalized." "Advertising on children's television programs ought to be better regulated."

Though an argument may focus entirely on any one of these four types of claims, many extended arguments depend upon a mixture of all of them. You may decide, say, to draw up an argument defending the right of women to have abortions (a claim about value), and in the course of the argument define what you mean by abortion (a claim about meaning), discuss the social benefits of abortion (a claim about consequences), and recommend that abortions be covered by health insurance (a claim about policy).

Reasoning Pattern

An arguable claim may make a compelling assertion, but it is nothing without a sound argument to back it up. That is where the second component of argument—the reasoning process—comes in. Put simply, reasoning is a special kind of thinking in which pieces of information are used in such a way as to yield new pieces of information. There are basically two types of reasoning: deductive and inductive. Roughly speaking, *deductive* arguments proceed from the general to the particular; *inductive* arguments proceed from the particular to the general. Thus, "All dogs are carnivorous; Fido is a dog; therefore Fido is carnivorous" is a deductive argument in that it proceeds from a general truth about a class (all dogs) to a truth about a particular member of that class (Fido). An inductive argument would proceed like this: "Spot is carnivorous, Fido is carnivorous, Lassie is carnivorous; they are all dogs; therefore all dogs are carnivorous." From an enumeration of truths about particular members of a class (Spot, Fido, and Lassie), we move to a truth about the class as a whole (all dogs).

There are many exceptions to the simple inductive–deductive dichotomy outlined above. For a more precise distinction between the two types of reasoning we need to consider the relationship between premises and conclusions.

Deductive Reasoning A deductive argument leads to a *necessary* conclusion—that is, the conclusion is logically entailed by the premises. Once we accept the premises as true and the connection between the premises and conclusions as *valid*,[1] then we must accept the truth of the conclusion. If all dogs are carnivorous and Fido is a dog, then it must follow that "Fido is carnivorous." In such deductive arguments the conclusions are said to be logically necessary.

This particular structure of deductive reasoning—two premises and a conclusion—makes up what is known in logic as a *syllogism*. A typical syllogism may be outlined and illustrated as follows:

Major premise: All *P* is *Q*	All dogs are carnivorous
Minor premise: *R* is *P*	Fido is a dog
Conclusion: *R* is *Q*	Therefore, Fido is carnivorous

Syllogisms can take many different forms, however, and some of them can be quite tricky. You might, for example, argue that because two things are alike in some respects they are therefore identical. Such reasoning would lead to incorrectly constructed syllogisms, though both premises are true:

All dogs are carnivorous	true premise	
All cats are carnivorous	true premise	invalid
Therefore all cats are dogs	false conclusion	form

Or, a syllogism can contain two true premises, be invalidly drawn, but lead to a true conclusion:

All dogs are carnivorous	true premise	
Fido is carnivorous	true premise	
Therefore Fido is a dog (Fido		valid
might have been a carnivorous cat)	true conclusion	form

Or, a syllogism can be correctly drawn from a false premise and thus lead to a false conclusion:

All dogs have five legs	false premise	
Fido is a dog	true premise	valid
Therefore Fido has five legs	false conclusion	form

Syllogisms that are correctly formed but false are, it is important to remember, still accepted as *valid*. The validity of deductive reasoning is wholly a matter of correct syllogistic construction and is not related to the truth or falsity of the premises. Only true premises and a valid construction will yield a conclusion that is both true and logically necessary. In our thinking and writing, we should always make sure that

---

[1]*Validity* refers not to whether a statement expresses a true fact but to whether it is consistent with logic.

our premises are true, or at least probably true, and our conclusions are validly drawn.

If we find ourselves devising an argument to counter the argument of another, we must be concerned not only with the soundness of our own reasoning but with the *un*soundness of our opponent's. In logic, the term *fallacy* denotes any form of invalid, deceptive, or unfair reasoning. In the glossary of this book, under "ARGUMENT, Fallacies of," we have presented brief explanations of the most frequently occurring fallacies. A familiarity with them, and others, is necessary for anyone who hopes to attain competence in the art of argumentation.

Inductive Reasoning Unlike deductive reasoning, inductive reasoning does not yield logically necessary conclusions. Inductive premises may give us excellent reasons for believing that our conclusion is true, but they can never logically entail the truth. To return to our example: you observe that Fido is carnivorous, Lassie is carnivorous, Spot is carnivorous, and these observations may well incline you to the conclusion that all dogs are carnivorous. In other words, you reach your conclusion entirely by means of a generalization based on a limited number of instances. Induction is the process of reasoning by which we move from evidence about *some* members of a particular class to a proposition about *all* members of that class. The strength of that movement—the "inductive leap" as it is sometime called—from particular examples to general statement depends wholly on the unstated assumption that future instances will confirm our generalization: that the fifteenth, hundredth, thousandth, and millionth dog we observe will also be carnivorous. But no matter how many dogs in our sample, the conclusion will still be an inductive one. At no point will the sheer number of observations change the inductive argument into a deductive one—that is to say, one in which the conclusion is necessary.

This is not meant to discredit inductive reasoning. Induction is not a less useful form of reasoning than deduction; in many cases, it is the only kind possible. We need to rely on inductive arguments continually in our everyday lives. Scientific knowledge could not exist were it not for the reliability of solid inductive reasoning. In fact, the premises of deductive syllogisms are often formed out of the conclusions obtained from inductive processes. Certain premises, such as "Dogs are carnivorous" or "Human beings are mortal," are considered true not because of definition but because of the overwhelming number of confirmative instances. Using an inductive conclusion as the premise of deductive argument, however, does not mean we have magically transformed induction into deduction. The main difference, we should recall, between the two types of reasoning has to do with the way conclusions are drawn from premises and not at all with the truth-value of the premises alone.

In the argumentative prose of capable writers, inductive enumerations and deductive syllogisms rarely appear in the skeletal forms shown above. Even Aristotle, who considered the discovery of the syllogism his greatest achievement, realized that interesting, engaging prose could not easily incorporate syllogistic reasoning in its naked forms. For one thing, syllogisms quickly become tiresome to read; for another, it is not always necessary to provide a logically complete account of how we get from one point to another. Aristotle recognized that the language people actually use relies not on fully developed syllogisms but on abbreviated syllogisms, which he called "enthymemes." An *enthymeme* is a syllogism in which a premise or a conclusion is unexpressed: "Fido eats meat because he is a dog" is a compressed way of stating the syllogistic conclusion without spelling out the entire deductive process. Sometimes an argument can be expressed more emphatically if the conclusion is left out: "To win a pennant you need strong pitching, but strong pitching is just what the Angels don't have." Though the logical conclusion is obvious, it is all the more forceful for having the audience supply it itself.

Though enthymemes can help make argument less verbose and the reasoning process less tediously diagrammatic, they can also be the cause of ambiguity and inconsistency. The meaning of a missing premise or conclusion may not always be as clear to an audience as we think it is. Furthermore, the missing portion of the syllogism—the dropped premise or conclusion—is no less a part of the argument merely because it is left unstated. The person constructing the argument is equally responsible for the sense and consistency of its implicit as well as its explicit parts. In an extended argument which depends on many suppressed syllogisms, we can easily get ourselves tangled up in an invisible network of implied assumptions and conclusions that may not hang together logically if worked out point by point. In the next section, we will see how some types of persuasion strategically use enthymemes as a way of by-passing certain premises and conclusions that the speaker does not want the audience to consider. In reading and listening to arguments, it is always a good idea to make the implied assumptions—the unstated premises and conclusions—as explicit as we can. This is one of the best means of finding holes in arguments and discovering points for rebuttal. We need not make our assumptions always explicit in our writing, but we should carefully keep track of the implied portions of our argument so that our own claims can stand up to the same tough-minded logical criticism we should be bringing to the arguments of others.

Organization: Constructing an Argument

The reasoning process is, of course, the heart of the argument. As the philosopher Monroe Beardsley says, argument is "reasoning's verbal record." Regardless of the truth of our claim, however, an argument stands or falls on the strength of the organizational framework that ties together the reasons we assemble to support our claim. For the most part, reasons can be assembled in one of two ways: we can structure our argument upon a series of independent reasons or upon a closely linked chain of interdependent reasons. Whether linked or separate, the reasons we assemble must be related carefully to our claim. How they are related to each other often determines our principle of organization.

In the earlier case concerning the inadequacy of standardized examinations, for example, six points were raised to show why the tests do not provide fair criteria for admissions decisions. These six reasons, though generally related by subject, were not dependent on each other; each answered the claim with a separate instance of educational inadequacy. Given the nature of the reasons, the overall organization of your argument would most likely be the arrangement of reasons you thought would provide the most effective argumentative order (usually strongest reason first, followed by weaker reasons, and ending with a strong summarizing reason to conclude your argument pointedly). Another important part of your organization would be the connection of each reason to your central claim in such a way that your proposition would be continually reinforced in the course of your argument. This reinforcement can usually be done through such logical signal words and phrases as *therefore, hence, it follows that, proves that, allows us to conclude that, consequently, thus, so, indicates that,* and so on.

The other method of organizing an argument—the chain structure— can be used only when we have a set of interdependent points. Suppose you decided to argue that the standardized admission tests were especially unfair because they scored results against a norm that was no longer applicable. You could then demonstrate through a succession of closely linked reasons that test scores are based on past standards; that recent data indicate that the scores have dropped dramatically on a national basis; that this drop is best explained by decreased learning ability; that the statistical decrease in learning ability based on the test-score data correlates closely with environmental increases of atomic waste due to nuclear testing; that since this environmental change constitutes a drastic historical change, contemporary students should not be rated according to the older standards of a cleaner environment; that therefore, since the test norms are based on these older standards, the admission tests are especially unfair to today's applicants. As we can see from this example, the strength of the argument depends on the strength of the *chain* of reasons, the conclusions of one point becoming the premises of the next. The organization of chain-structured arguments depends less upon an arrangement of points according to their relative importance than it does upon an arrangement of points according to their logical sequence.

Of all the structure and strategies for thinking in writing examined in this book, argumentation probably relies on a greater variety of rhetorical features than any other. In order to formulate arguable claims, we need to sharpen our definitions, make accurate classifications, and be alert to causal connections. But these are just a few considerations. Well-constructed arguments also make ample use of relevant illustration, work in process analysis, and frequently rely on narration, description, and comparison to support their claims. Carefully reasoned, tightly constructed argumentative essays prove that rhetoric not only is the art of writing well, but is vitally and instrumentally related to the art of thinking straight and true.

Persuasion

Nearly all of us spend a good deal of time each day trying to deal with various kinds of appeals—personal, professional, and commercial attempts to influence our thinking and direct our behavior. We are repeatedly encouraged, flattered, seduced, badgered, warned, and even threatened to consider this, to believe that, to do this, to buy that. But just as we are the targets of such requests, we also make quite a few ourselves: we may, for example, try to induce the manager of the local bicycle shop to repair our bike today rather than tomorrow, to encourage our friends to register for a particular biology course, to prevail upon our parents to let us share an apartment off-campus. Such appeals, whether they concern our everyday routines or our most intricate decisions, invariably involve some element of persuasion.

What is Persuasion?

Persuasion is written or oral discourse aimed at disposing an audience to think and act in accordance with a speaker's[2] will. To persuade is to resolve, change, or re-form an individual's or a group's feelings, opinions, beliefs, and actions in any effective manner. For many of us, the word *persuasion* calls to mind the manipulative tricks of twentieth-century advertising, politics, and propaganda. The alluring promises of corporations, religious sects, and political factions, as well as the strident pleas of an increasing number of special-interest groups, have helped create an atmosphere in which a term like *persuasion* has come to be associated with deception and exploitation, as

[2]For the sake of convenience, the term *speaker* will be used in reference to all types of verbal presentation, both oral and written.

well as with more subtle forms of mass seduction and indoctrination. Yet, though persuasion can be a more emotional form of writing and speaking than exposition and argument, there is also no reason why persuasion cannot serve the equally sensible and honorable end of encouraging, as Aristotle maintains it did, some virtuous behavior. It is this more positive sense—persuasion without a dubious ulterior motive—that is worth exploring in detail as a procedure for structuring our thinking and writing.

The Three Types of Persuasion

Aristotle divides persuasion into rational, emotional, and ethical appeals. *Rational appeals* rely on the speaker's ability to summon logic and good sense to move an audience to a specific action. *Emotional appeals* aim at an audience's feelings, at arousing a nonintellectual response as a means to secure some determined course of action. *Ethical appeals* are based on the speaker's personal presence, character, and reputation. Aristotle maintains that the most persuasive writing blends all three. Determining what should be the most effective mixture of such appeals depends on several interrelated factors: the subject, the desired action, the audience addressed, and the speaker's relationship with that audience. The proposed action may be clear-cut and well within sight—as in political addresses, lobbying, and sermons. Yet, on such ceremonial occasions as inaugurations, commencements, and holidays, the action called for may be less specific, perhaps a resolution rather than an immediate action. Persuasion in such cases amounts to inspirational statements which people are expected to apply to their own individual circumstances. There may be occasions, however, when the need for action is apparent but the possibilities of doing something are restricted for the audience.

Rational Appeals   A rational appeal must conform to the basic principles of argument, including accurate information, logical development, and convincing evidence. Persuasion, when it employs the principles of logic to promote an action, takes an audience beyond the conventional boundaries of argument. Both seek to earn an audience's assent to a particular belief. Argument, in fact, closes when the speaker is sure of such assent. But persuasion continues to work with the evidence of an argument, using it as the motive for doing something. In this respect, persuasion appeals both to intelligence and will; it aims at not only conviction but also action. It seeks an audience's consent.

Suppose, for example, that you are asked to write an essay in which you argue on behalf of the claim that drug abuse has contributed substantially to the increase in urban crime. You will have written a successful argument when you have gathered sufficient evidence and carefully built it into a convincing case. But such an essay could be made persuasive by using the same evidence for a different purpose—to propose a specific course of action. In this instance, you might urge your city's legislators to mandate a two-pronged attack on drugs and crime—say, to order stiffer penalties for pushers and wider availability of detoxification and counseling services for users. As this example suggests, argument and persuasion are often closely allied. An essay dominated by one usually will also include elements of the other, the precise combination being determined by the anticipated response of the audience.

Composing a successful persuasive essay depends to a great extent on knowing our audience and how receptive it will be to what we have to say. We need to discover as much as possible about people's beliefs, prejudices, and interests before we can persuade them to follow a desired course of action. Persuasion is addressed, then, to a specific audience; whereas an argumentative essay is addressed to a general audience, which includes anyone interested in discovering the facts of an issue. Persuasive writing attempts to solidify the speaker's relationship with an audience, by frequently acknowledging the audience's presence. Political speeches, for example, nearly always include specific references to the audience present. There is a prevailing sense of intimacy in persuasive writing, of speaking directly to a specific audience, of guiding it toward belief and action. In this respect, the more an audience is brought into an essay—that is, acknowledged by having its special characteristics highlighted—the more likely the writing will be persuasive.

Identifying with Your Audience

Persuasion begins when we establish a common ground of belief with our audience. By identifying ourselves with a particular group and focusing on areas of agreement, we are more likely to persuade each member to follow our recommended course of action. One of the surest ways to dispose an audience favorably to our ideas is to start with what they already know, with what they would readily assent to. Thus persuasion first concentrates on reaffirmation, on reminding an audience of what it already believes. While argument must respond directly to anticipated objections, persuasion glosses over resistance. If, for example, you are writing a persuasive essay on the hardships of migrant workers, you might not want to refer to their status as illegal aliens. Persuasion is also less rigorous when it comes to dealing with implied assumptions. The key terms in a persuasive essay are rarely as carefully defined as in argument, and we need not be concerned about complete conformity to the technical requirements of logic. Whereas the conclusions drawn in argument are necessary (the evidence points insistently toward one conclusion), in persuasion they are important to the extent that they move the audience to a desired action. The crucial issue in persuasion remains just how far we can move our readers *beyond* the point to which they would readily agree.

For example, you are asked to write an essay designed to persuade your college's administrators that the physically handicapped deserve equal access to each floor in every building on campus. You would not need to spend a great deal of time arguing on behalf of the validity of such a principle. But you would need to gather convincing evidence that some students do not now enjoy easy access. You could then propose specific ways to remedy the problem—say, by installing additional ramps and elevators and by providing adequate reserved parking for the handicapped near the entrance to each building. Persuasion, in effect, fuses an argument and an agenda. It leads an audience, to quote St. Augustine on persuasion, "not merely to know what should be done, but to do what they know should be done." In this sense, persuasion, unlike argument, gradually turns into subtle forms of command.

Emotional Appeals   The persuasive writing we most often encounter is based on appeals to an audience's emotions: anger, fear, frustration, contentment, desires, and the like. In deciding which emotion to appeal to, we should take into account the appropriateness of such an appeal to both the subject and the proposed action as well as the knowledge we have of the audience's temperament. In an appeal to the emotions, we must establish a substantive connection between the course of action being urged and the particular emotion being aroused. Appeals to the emotions of an audience are usually put at the end of an essay.

The standard procedure for structuring a persuasive essay is to interest people through their intellectual curiosity and then to move them to action through an emotional appeal. Reversing the order weakens the likelihood of action. Starting with an appeal to reason also shows greater respect for the audience and its collective intelligence. Yet, finally, nothing is more important to the success of an emotional appeal than the speaker who makes the presentation. In the end, an audience is often persuaded nearly as much by the personality of the speaker as by the substance of what is said.

Ethical Appeals   The ethical appeal in persuasion is based on the sense of character the speaker projects: usually a combination of personal qualities and credibility. The speaker establishes the ethical appeal of an essay—what Aristotle called its *ethos*—by conveying an impression of himself or herself as someone with good sense and good will. The importance of an ethical appeal may be seen by contrasting the different roles the speaker plays in argument and persuasion. In argument, an intelligent, clear-headed person's assent to the facts and truth of a matter normally has very little, if anything, to do with his or her response to the speaker's character and personality. In persuasion, however, our consent to follow a particular course of action has a great deal to do with our feelings about the speaker. The ethical appeal in persuasion works rather simply: the audience identifies with the speaker and consequently considers seriously whatever that person has to say. And, if the speaker projects the image of being not only decent and well-meaning but also perceptive, well-informed, and sympathetic to the needs and desires of the audience, its members will all the more readily agree to the speaker's proposed course of action.

The writer of effective, reputable persuasion—unlike the speaker in much advertising and propaganda—sounds modest, reasonable, and candid. He or she takes into account the points of view of others, has a practical grasp of complex problems, and offers commonsense solutions. This is a person we have confidence in—someone we can trust and perhaps even emulate. For example, in response to as volatile a subject as the escalating tensions among ethnic groups in a community, such a person would resist both oversimplifying the issues involved and urging some precipitous action. Instead, such a person would demonstrate sensitivity to the perspectives and interests of each contending party and offer prudent measures to seal the rift and restore friendly relations. Such a person thinks, speaks, writes, and acts on the strength of personal conviction.

Our efforts to write persuasively ought to be guided by a few reminders. We should:

1. Hone down our subject so that we have a manageable idea with a clearly stated proposed course of action.
2. Introduce the issue in a way that enhances our credibility and disposes our audience both intellectually and emotionally to hear what we have to say.
3. State vigorously and develop fully the claim, the proposition itself.
4. Be certain that the proofs we summon to support the recommended action are tied directly to our announced purpose.
5. Make sure that the rational, emotional, and ethical appeals are evident throughout the essay.
6. Use the conclusion of the essay to recapitulate the important points and to reaffirm the necessity of the proposed action.

Following these procedures for structuring a persuasive essay will increase the likelihood that our audience will understand our claim, assent to its merit, and consent to a particular course of action.

The formal writing requirements of many academic disciplines call for less frequent practice in persuasion than in other forms of writing. This does not hold equally true, however, outside of college, where the ability to speak and write persuasively can make a decided difference in our careers and our communities.

Five Classics

A Modest Proposal

Jonathan Swift

*Jonathan Swift (1667–1745) is the greatest ironist in all of English liter-
ature. He was born in Ireland of English parents, and educated at Trinity
College, Dublin. He worked first as a secretary to Sir William Temple, a
retired diplomat living in London. Swift took advantage of Temple's large
library, and made good use of his time in London to write his first volume
of satire, which included* A Tale of a Tub *and* The Battle of the Books
*(1704). In 1713 he was appointed Dean of St. Patrick's Cathedral in
Dublin. His most famous work, the satirical novel* Gulliver's Travels,
was published in 1726.

*In 1729, when Swift published the essay that follows, the Irish people
were in crisis. A widespread famine was in its third year, and England,
which was exploiting Ireland as a source of cheap labor and materials, had
forbidden Ireland to trade independently with other countries. Furthermore, the British government had imposed burdensome taxes on the already overtaxed Irish populace. In "A Modest Proposal," Swift takes on a
fictional persona in order to propose a solution you might find startling.*

It is a melancholy object to those who walk through this great town[1]
or travel in the country, when they see the streets, the roads, and
cabin doors, crowded with beggars of the female sex, followed by
three, four, or six children, all in rags and importuning every passenger
for an alms. These mothers, instead of being able to work for their honest livelihood, are forced to employ all their time in strolling to beg sustenance for their helpless infants, who, as they grow up, either turn
thieves for want of work, or leave their dear native country to fight for
the Pretender in Spain,[2] or sell themselves to the Barbados.[3]

I think it is agreed by all parties that this prodigious number of
children in the arms, or on the backs, or at the heels of their mothers,
and frequently of their fathers, is in the present deplorable state of the
kingdom a very great additional grievance; and therefore whoever
could find out a fair, cheap, and easy method of making these children
sound, useful members of the commonwealth would deserve so well of
the public as to have his statue set up for a preserver of the nation.

But my intention is very far from being confined to provide only
for the children of professed beggars; it is of a much greater extent, and
shall take in the whole number of infants at a certain age who are born

---

[1]Dublin—Eds.
[2]James Stuart (1688–1766). Exiled in Spain, he claimed to be the legitimate king of England and was supported by many Irishmen—Eds.
[3]Many Irishmen "sold" themselves as indentured servants to work in the British colony
of Barbados in exchange for their passage to the Caribbean—Eds.

of parents in effect as little able to support them as those who demand our charity in the streets.

As to my own part, having turned my thoughts for many years upon this important subject, and maturely weighed the several schemes of other projectors,[4] I have always found them grossly mistaken in their computations. It is true, a child just dropped from its dam may be supported by her milk for a solar year, with little other nourishment; at most not above the value of two shillings,[5] which the mother may certainly get, or the value in scraps, by her lawful occupation of begging; and it is exactly at one year old that I propose to provide for them in such a manner as instead of being a charge upon their parents or the parish, or wanting food and raiment for the rest of their lives, they shall on the contrary contribute to the feeding, and partly to the clothing, of many thousands.

5   There is likewise another great advantage in my scheme, that it will prevent those involuntary abortions, and that horrid practice of women murdering their bastard children, alas, too frequent among us, sacrificing the poor innocent babes, I doubt, more to avoid the expense than the shame, which would move tears and pity in the most savage and inhuman breast.

The number of souls in this kingdom being usually reckoned one million and a half, of these I calculate there may be about two hundred thousand couples whose wives are breeders, from which number I subtract thirty thousand couples who are able to maintain their own children, although I apprehend there cannot be so many under the present distress of the kingdom; but this being granted, there will remain an hundred and seventy thousand breeders. I again subtract fifty thousand for those women who miscarry, or whose children die by accident or disease within the year. There only remain an hundred and twenty thousand children of poor parents annually born. The question therefore is, how this number shall be reared and provided for, which, as I have already said, under the present situation of affairs, is utterly impossible by all the methods hitherto proposed. For we can neither employ them in handicraft nor agriculture; we neither build houses (I mean in the country) nor cultivate land. They can very seldom pick up livelihood by stealing till they arrive at six years old, except where they are of towardly parts;[6] although I confess they learn the rudiments much earlier, during which time they can however be looked upon only

---

[4]Planners—Eds.
[5]A shilling in Swift's day was worth less than twenty-five cents. Later in the essay he refers to other monetary denominations: a pound was made of twenty shillings, a shilling of twelve pence, a crown was five shillings, and a groat was worth a few cents—Eds.
[6]Natural abilities—Eds.

as probationers, as I have been informed by a principal gentleman in the county of Cavan, who protested to me that he never knew above one or two instances under the age of six, even in a part of the kingdom so renowned for the quickest proficiency in that art.

I am assured by our merchants that a boy or a girl before twelve years old is no salable commodity; and even when they come to this age, they will not yield above three pounds, or three pounds and half a crown at most on the Exchange; which cannot turn to account either to the parents or the kingdom, the charge of nutriment and rags having been at least four times that value.

I shall now therefore humbly propose my own thoughts, which I hope will not be liable to the least objection.

I have been assured by a very knowing American of my acquaintance in London, that a young healthy child well nursed is at a year old a most delicious, nourishing, and wholesome food, whether stewed, roasted, baked, or boiled; and I make no doubt that it will equally serve in fricassee or a ragout.[7]

I do therefore humbly offer it to public consideration that of the10 hundred and twenty thousand children, already computed, twenty thousand may be reserved for breed, whereof only one fourth part to be males, which is more than we allow to sheep, black cattle, or swine; and my reason is that these children are seldom the fruits of marriage, a circumstance not much regarded by our savages, therefore one male will be sufficient to serve four females. That the remaining hundred thousand may at a year old be offered in sale to the persons of quality and fortune through the kingdom, always advising the mother to let them suck plentifully in the last month, so as to render them plump and fat for a good table. A child will make two dishes at an entertainment for friends; and when the family dines alone, the fore or hind quarter will make a reasonable dish, and seasoned with a little pepper or salt will be very good boiled on the fourth day, especially in winter.

I have reckoned upon a medium that a child just born will weigh twelve pounds, and in a solar year if tolerably nursed increaseth to twenty-eight pounds.

I grant this food will be somewhat dear, and therefore very proper for landlords, who, as they have already devoured most of the parents, seem to have the best title to the children.

Infant's flesh will be in season throughout the year, but more plentiful in March, and a little before and after. For we are told by a grave author, an eminent French physician,[8] that fish being a prolific diet,

---

[7]A stew—Eds.

[8]François Rabelais (c. 1494–1553), Renaissance writer who authored the comedy *Gargantua and Pantagruel*. Rabelais was far from "grave"—Swift is being ironic—Eds.

there are more children born in Roman Catholic countries about nine months after Lent, than at any other season; therefore, reckoning a year after Lent, the markets will be more glutted than usual, because the number of popish infants is at least three to one in this kingdom; and therefore it will have one other collateral advantage, by lessening the number of Papists among us.

I have already computed the charge of nursing a beggar's child (in which list I reckon all cottagers, laborers, and four fifths of the farmers) to be about two shillings per annum, rags included; and I believe no gentleman would repine to give ten shillings for the carcass of a good fat child, which, as I have said, will make four dishes of excellent nutritive meat, when he hath only some particular friend or his own family to dine with him. Thus the squire will learn to be a good landlord, and grow popular among the tenants; the mother will have eight shillings net profit, and be fit for work till she produces another child.

15   Those who are more thrifty (as I must confess the times require) may flay the carcass; the skin of which artificially[9] dressed will make admirable gloves for the ladies, and summer boots for fine gentlemen.

As to our city of Dublin, shambles[10] may be appointed for this purpose in the most convenient parts of it, and butchers we may be assured will not be wanting; although I rather recommend buying the children alive, and dressing them hot from the knife as we do roasting pigs.

A very worthy person, a true lover of his country, and whose virtues I highly esteem, was lately pleased in discoursing on this matter to offer a refinement upon my scheme. He said that many gentlemen of his kingdom, having of late destroyed their deer, he conceived that the want of venison might be well supplied by the bodies of young lads and maidens, not exceeding fourteen years of age nor under twelve, so great a number of both sexes in every country being now ready to starve for want of work and service; and these to be disposed of by their parents, if alive, or otherwise by their nearest relations. But with due deference to so excellent a friend and so deserving a patriot, I cannot be altogether in his sentiments; for as to the males my American acquaintance assured me from frequent experience that their flesh was generally tough and lean, like that of our schoolboys, by continual exercise, and their taste disagreeable; and to fatten them would not answer the charge. Then as to the females, it would, I think with humble submission, be a loss to the public, because they soon would become breeders themselves; and besides, it is not improbable that some scrupulous people might be apt to censure such a practice (although

[9]Artfully—Eds.
[10]Slaughterhouses—Eds.

indeed very unjustly) as a little bordering upon cruelty; which, I confess, hath always been with me the strongest objection against any project, how well soever intended.

But in order to justify my friend, he confessed that this expedient was put into his head by the famous Psalmanazar, a native of the island Formosa,[11] who came from thence to London above twenty years ago, and in conversation told my friend that in his country when any young person happened to be put to death, the executioner sold the carcass to the persons of quality as a prime dainty; and that in his time the body of a plump girl of fifteen, who was crucified for an attempt to poison the emperor, was sold to his Imperial Majesty's prime minister of state, and other great mandarins of the court, in joints from the gibbet, at four hundred crowns. Neither indeed can I deny that if the same use were made of several plump young girls in this town, who without one single groat to their fortunes cannot stir abroad without a chair,[12] and appear at the playhouse and assemblies in foreign fineries which they never will pay for, the kingdom would not be the worse.

Some persons of a desponding spirit are in great concern about that vast number of poor people who are aged, diseased, or maimed, and I have been desired to employ my thoughts what course may be taken to ease the nation of so grievous an encumbrance. But I am not in the least pain upon that matter, because it is very well known that they are every day dying and rotting by cold and famine, and filth and vermin, as fast as can be reasonably expected. And as to the younger laborers, they are now in almost as hopeful a condition. They cannot get work, and consequently pine away for want of nourishment to a degree that if any time they are accidentally hired to common labor, they have not strength to perform it; and thus the country and themselves are happily delivered from the evils to come.

I have too long digressed, and therefore shall return to my subject. I[20] think the advantages by the proposal which I have made are obvious and many, as well as of the highest importance.

For first, as I have already observed, it would greatly lessen the number of Papists, with whom we are yearly overrun, being the principal breeders of the nation as well as our most dangerous enemies; and who stay at home on purpose to deliver the kingdom to the Pretender, hoping to take their advantage by the absence of so many good Protestants, who have chosen rather to leave their country than to stay at home and pay tithes against their conscience to an Episcopal curate.

---

[11]George Psalmanazar (c. 1679–1763) was French, but he pretended to be from Formosa (now Taiwan) and managed to deceive many members of London society—Eds.
[12]A sedan chair used to carry an important or wealthy person—Eds.

Secondly, the poorer tenants will have something valuable of their own, which by law may be made liable to distress[13] and help to pay their landlord's rent, their corn and cattle being already seized and money a thing unknown.

Thirdly, whereas the maintenance of an hundred thousand children, from two years old and upwards, cannot be computed at less than ten shillings a piece per annum, the nation's stock will be thereby increased fifty thousand pounds per annum, besides the profit of a new dish introduced to the tables of all gentlemen of fortune in the kingdom who have any refinement in taste. And the money will circulate among ourselves, the goods being entirely of our own growth and manufacture.

Fourthly, the constant breeders, besides the gain of eight shillings sterling per annum by the sale of their children, will be rid of the charge for maintaining them after the first year.

25   Fifthly, this food would likewise bring great custom to taverns, where the vintners will certainly be so prudent as to procure the best receipts[14] for dressing it to perfection, and consequently have their houses frequented by all the fine gentlemen, who justly value themselves upon their knowledge in good eating; and a skillful cook, who understands how to oblige his guests, will contrive to make it as expensive as they please.

Sixthly, this would be a great inducement to marriage, which all wise nations have either encouraged by rewards or enforced by laws and penalties. It would increase the care and tenderness of mothers toward their children, when they were sure of a settlement for life to the poor babes, provided in some sort by the public, to their annual profit instead of expense. We should see an honest emulation among the married women, which of them could bring the fattest child to the market. Men would become as fond of their wives during the time of pregnancy as they are now of their mares in foal, their cows in calf, or sows when they are ready to farrow; nor offer to beat or kick them (as is too frequent a practice) for fear of a miscarriage.

Many other advantages might be enumerated. For instance, the addition of some thousand carcasses in our exportation of barreled beef, the propagation of swine's flesh, and improvements in the art of making good bacon, so much wanted among us by the great destruction of pigs, too frequent at our tables, which are no way comparable in taste or magnificence to a well-grown, fat, yearling child, which roasted whole will make a considerable figure at a lord mayor's feast or any other public entertainment. But this and many others I omit, being studious of brevity.

[13]Liable to seizure for payment of debt—Eds.
[14]Recipes—Eds.

Supposing that one thousand families in this city would be constant customers for infants' flesh, besides others who might have it at merry meetings, particularly weddings and christenings, I compute that Dublin would take off annually about twenty thousand carcasses, and the rest of the kingdom (where probably they will be sold somewhat cheaper) the remaining eighty thousand.

I can think of no one objection that will possibly be raised against this proposal, unless it should be urged that the number of people will be thereby much lessened in the kingdom. This I freely own, and it was indeed one principal design in offering it to the world. I desire the reader will observe; that I calculate my remedy for this one individual kingdom of Ireland and for no other that ever was, is, or I think ever can be upon earth. Therefore, let no man talk to me of other expedients: of taxing our absentees at five shillings a pound: of using neither clothes nor household furniture except what is of our own growth and manufacture: of utterly rejecting the materials and instruments that promote foreign luxury: of curing the expensiveness of pride, vanity, idleness, and gaming in our women: of introducing a vein of parsimony, prudence, and temperance: of learning to love our country, in the want of which we differ even from Laplanders and the inhabitants of Topinamboo:[15] of quitting our animosities and factions, nor acting any longer like the Jews,[16] who were murdering one another at the very moment their city was taken: of being a little cautious not to sell our country and conscience for nothing: of teaching landlords to have at least one degree of mercy toward their tenants: lastly, of putting a spirit of honesty, industry, and skill into our shopkeepers; who, if a resolution could now be taken to buy only our native goods, would immediately unite to cheat and exact upon us in the price, the measure, and the goodness, nor could ever yet be brought to make one fair proposal of just dealing, though often and earnestly invited to it.

Therefore, I repeat, let no man talk to me of these and the like expe-30 dients, till he hath at least some glimpse of hope that there will ever be some hearty and sincere attempt to put them in practice.

But as to myself, having been wearied out for many years with offering vain, ideal, visionary thoughts, and at length utterly despairing of success, I fortunately fell upon this proposal, which, as it is wholly new, so it hath something solid and real, of no expense and little trouble, full in our own power, and whereby we can incur no damage in disobliging England. For this kind of commodity will not bear

---

[15]Laplanders are the native inhabitants of the area of Scandinavia above the Arctic Circle. Topinamboo is in Brazil, and was thought during Swift's time to be a very savage place—Eds.
[16]Reference to the Roman conquest of Jerusalem in 70 AD—Eds.

exportation, the flesh being of too tender a consistence to admit a long continuance in salt, although perhaps I could name a country which would be glad to eat up our whole nation without it.

After all, I am not so violently bent upon my own opinion as to reject any offer proposed by wise men, which shall be found equally innocent, cheap, easy, and effectual. But before something of that kind shall be advanced in contradiction to my scheme, and offering a better, I desire the author or authors will be pleased maturely to consider two points. First, as things now stand, how they will be able to find food and raiment for an hundred thousand useless mouths and backs. And secondly, there being a round million of creatures in human figure throughout this kingdom, whose sole subsistence put into a common stock would leave them in debt two millions of pounds sterling, adding those who are beggars by profession to the bulk of farmers, cottagers and laborers, with their wives and children who are beggars in effect; I desire those politicians who dislike my overture, and may perhaps be so bold to attempt an answer, that they will first ask the parents of these mortals whether they would not at this day think it a great happiness to have been sold for food at a year old in this manner I prescribe, and thereby have avoided such a perpetual scene of misfortunes as they have since gone through by the oppression of landlords, the impossibility of paying rent without money or trade, the want of common sustenance, with neither house nor clothes to cover them from the inclemencies of the weather, and the most inevitable prospect of entailing the like or greater miseries upon their breed forever.

I profess, in the sincerity of my heart, that I have not the least personal interest in endeavoring to promote this necessary work, having no other motive than the public good of my country, by advancing our trade, providing for infants, relieving the poor, and giving some pleasure to the rich. I have no children by which I can propose to get a single penny; the youngest being nine years old, and my wife past childbearing.

Additional Rhetorical Strategies

Description (paragraph 1); Cause and Effect (paragraphs 5, 21–27); Process Analysis (paragraph 10); Narration (paragraph 18).

Discussion Questions

1. What is the narrator's thesis? What is the author's thesis? Where is the narrator's thesis stated? What is the function of the paragraphs preceding his statement of a thesis? Where is the author's thesis stated? If you believe that either or both theses are implied rather

than stated, then paraphrase the thesis or theses in question in your own words.

2. What is the effect of the gap between the narrator and the author? How would you describe the tone of this essay? In what ways, besides the creation of a fictional narrator, does Swift create this tone? Give specific examples from the text. Pay careful attention to the diction (word choices) he employs. Look also at the most horrific passages, in terms of content. How does Swift handle the style of these passages?

3. At what point in the essay did you realize this was a satire? On rereading the essay, do you find any earlier clues that you did not pick up on a first reading?

4. Much of the irony of this piece is directed at the British. To what extent is it also directed at the Irish? What are the traits in the Irish that have resulted from years of victimization at the hands of the British? How are these traits satirized in the essay?

5. Look closely at the structure of the essay. In paragraph 20, for instance, the speaker accuses himself of digressing. Are the preceding paragraphs actually digressions? What function do they serve? What are the objections that the narrator addresses in paragraph 29? Anticipating and addressing objections is a time-honored strategy in persuasive essays. How does Swift's use of this device differ from the norm? Look for other examples of Swift's strategic use of essay structure.

Essay Questions

1. Write a satirical essay, putting to use some of the strategies you have observed in Swift's writing. You might think of this assignment in terms of advocating one solution to a problem while pretending to advocate another. Or you might think of it in terms of playing the fool among knaves. Or you might think in terms of borrowing Swift's super-rational, at times mathematical reasoning for a cause that is utterly irrational—or so rational that it forgets to take feeling, morals, etc. into account.

2. Write an essay in which you infer the social problems of 18th century Ireland from the ironic solutions Swift proposes. It is clear that poverty and hunger are widespread, but what other social ills can you infer from the text?

The Declaration of Independence

Thomas Jefferson

Thomas Jefferson (1743–1826) served his country in many capacities, including governor of Virginia, minister to France, secretary of state, vice president, and the nation's third president. He also achieved success as a lawyer, farmer, philosopher, writer, architect, scientist, musician, and inventor. Among his accomplishments during his two terms as president was the negotiation of the Louisiana Purchase, which effectively doubled the size of the nation. The accomplishments that he valued most were inscribed, at his request, on his tombstone: "Here was buried Thomas Jefferson, Author of the Declaration of American Independence, Of the Statute of Virginia for Religious Freedom, and Father of the University of Virginia."

When the Continental Congress convened in Philadelphia in 1775, a five-man committee was chosen to draft a declaration of independence from the British crown. The other committee members, all older than Jefferson, deferred to his literary skill, and he drafted the document that, after three days of debate and revision, became the "Unanimous Declaration of the Thirteen United States of America." (The Continental Congress never officially called it by the title under which it has since become famous.) As you read the document reprinted below, you will notice the effect of Enlightenment principles in his reasoned approach, and you will see why Jefferson came to be one of the most quotable figures in American history.

Thomas Jefferson died on the fiftieth anniversary of the signing of the Declaration of Independence.

When in the course of human events, it becomes necessary for one people to dissolve the political bands which have connected them with another, and to assume among the Powers of the earth, the separate and equal station to which the Laws of Nature and of Nature's God entitle them, a decent respect to the opinions of mankind requires that they should declare the causes which impel them to the separation.

We hold these truths to be self-evident, that all men are created equal, that they are endowed by their Creator with certain unalienable Rights, that among these are Life, Liberty and the pursuit of Happiness.

That to secure these rights, Governments are instituted among Men, deriving their just powers from the consent of the governed.

That whenever any Form of Government becomes destructive of these ends, it is the Right of the People to alter or to abolish it, and to institute a new Government, laying its foundation on such principles and organizing its powers in such form, as to them shall seem most likely to effect their Safety and Happiness. Prudence, indeed, will dictate that Governments long established should not be changed for light and transient causes; and accordingly all experience hath shown that mankind are more disposed to suffer, while evils are sufferable, than to right themselves by abolishing the forms to which they are accustomed. But when a long train of abuses and usurpations pursuing invariably the same Object evinces a design to reduce them under absolute Despotism, it is their right, it is their duty, to throw off such government, and to provide new Guards for their future security.

Such has been the patient sufferance of these Colonies; and such is 5 now the necessity which constrains them to alter their former Systems of Government. The history of the present King of Great Britain is a history of repeated injuries and usurpations, all having in direct object the establishment of an absolute Tyranny over these States. To prove this, let Facts be submitted to a candid world.

He has refused his Assent to Laws, the most wholesome and necessary for the public good.

He has forbidden his Governors to pass Laws of immediate and pressing importance, unless suspended in their operation till his Assent should be obtained; and when so suspended, he has utterly neglected to attend to them.

He has refused to pass other Laws for the accommodation of large districts of people, unless those people would relinquish the right of Representation in the Legislature, a right inestimable to them and formidable to tyrants only.

He has called together legislative bodies at places unusual, uncomfortable, and distant from the depository of their Public Records, for the sole purpose of fatiguing them into compliance with his measures.

He has dissolved Representative Houses repeatedly, for opposing 10 with manly firmness his invasions on the rights of the people.

He has refused for along time, after such dissolutions, to cause others to be elected; whereby the Legislative Powers, incapable of Annihilation, have returned to the People at large for their exercise; the State remaining in the mean time exposed to all the dangers of invasion from without, and convulsions within.

He has endeavored to prevent the population of these States, for that purpose obstructing the Laws of Naturalization of Foreigners; refusing to pass others to encourage their migration hither, and raising the conditions of new Appropriations of Lands.

He has obstructed the Administration of Justice, by refusing his Assent to Laws for establishing Judiciary Powers.

He has made Judges dependent on his Will alone, for the tenure of their offices, and the amount and payment of their salaries.

He has erected a multitude of New Offices, and sent hither swarms 15 of Officers to harass our People, and eat out their substance.

He has kept among us, in time of peace, Standing Armies without the consent of our Legislature.

He has affected to render the Military independent of and superior to the Civil Power.

He has combined with others to subject us to jurisdictions foreign to our constitution, and unacknowledged by our laws; giving his Assent to their acts of pretended Legislation:

For quartering large bodies of armed troops among us:

20   For protecting them, by a mock Trial, from Punishment for any Murders which they should commit on the Inhabitants of these States:

For cutting off our Trade with all parts of the world:

For imposing Taxes on us without our Consent:

For depriving us in many cases, of the benefits of Trial by Jury:

For transporting us beyond Seas to be tried for pretended offenses:

25   For abolishing the free System of English Laws in a Neighbouring Province, establishing therein an Arbitrary government and enlarging its boundaries so as to render it at once an example and fit instrument for introducing the same absolute rule into these Colonies:

For taking away our Charters, abolishing our most valuable Laws, and altering fundamentally the Forms of our Governments.

For suspending our own Legislatures, and declaring themselves invested with Power to legislate for us in all cases whatsoever.

He has abdicated Government here, by declaring us out of his Protection and waging War against us.

He has plundered our seas, ravaged our Coasts, burnt our towns and destroyed the Lives of our people.

30   He is at this time transporting large Armies of foreign Mercenaries to compleat the works of death, desolation and tyranny, already begun with circumstances of Cruelty & perfidy scarcely paralleled in the most barbarous ages, and totally unworthy the Head of a civilized nation.

He has constrained our fellow Citizens taken Captive on the high Seas to bear Arms against their Country, to become the executioners of their friends and Brethren, or to fall themselves by their Hands.

He has excited domestic insurrections amongst us, and has endeavored to bring on the inhabitants of our frontiers, the merciless Indian Savages, whose known rule of warfare, is an undistinguished destruction of all ages, sexes and conditions.

In every stage of these Oppressions We Have Petitioned for Redress in the most humble terms: Our repeated petitions have been answered only by repeated injury. A Prince, whose character is thus marked by every act which may define a Tyrant, is unfit to be the ruler of a free People.

Nor have We been wanting in attention to our British brethren. We have warned them from time to time of attempts by their legislature to extend an unwarrantable jurisdiction over us. We have reminded them of the circumstances of our emigration and settlement here. We have appealed to their native justice and magnanimity and we have conjured them by the ties of our common kindred to disavow these usurpations, which would inevitably interrupt our connections and correspondence. They too have been deaf to the voice of justice and consanguinity. We must, therefore, acquiesce in the necessity, which denounces our Separation, and hold them, as we hold the rest of mankind, Enemies in War, in Peace Friends.

We, therefore, the Representatives of the United States of America,35 in General Congress, Assembled, appealing to the Supreme Judge of the world for the rectitude of our intentions, do, in the Name, and by Authority of the good People of these Colonies, solemnly publish and declare, That these United Colonies are, and of Right out to be, Free and Independent States; that they are Absolved from all Allegiance to the British Crown, and that all political connection between them and the State of Great Britain, is and ought to be totally dissolved; and that as Free and Independent States, they have full power to levy War, conclude Peace, contract Alliances, establish Commerce, and to do all other Acts and Things which Independent States may of right do. And for the support of this Declaration, with a firm reliance on the protection of Divine Providence, we mutually pledge to each other our lives, our Fortunes, and our sacred Honor.

Additional Rhetorical Strategies

Cause and Effect (paragraphs 2, 32); Example (throughout).

Discussion Questions

1. What is Jefferson's thesis in this essay? Does he state it directly? If so, where? If not, how might you paraphrase it?
2. Analyze the famous first sentence of paragraph 2. What truths does Jefferson hold to be "self-evident"? What does it mean, in terms of an argumentative essay, to declare certain premises self-evident? Can you imagine an audience that might require evidence to support any of the premises Jefferson includes among the self-evident truths? How might an author defend such truths to such an audience? Why might Jefferson have decided not to provide such a defense?
3. Now go on to analyze the logic of the remainder of paragraph 2. Note how each sentence leads clearly and succinctly to the next. Trace the course of the argument from the opening line to the point at which Jefferson begins to enumerate the "repeated injuries and usurpations" suffered by the colonists.
4. How would you characterize Jefferson's language in this essay? For instance, does he rely more on literal or on figurative language? What is the effect when he switches from one to the other? Does he

rely more on abstract or concrete language? Again, how do the effects differ?

5. Can you detect an organizing principle among the charges Jefferson levels against the British crown? Do the charges get progressively more or less serious, for instance? Do you detect other patterns? Also, explain (in terms of logic and syntax) the clauses (paragraphs 19–27) beginning with the word "For" instead of the word "He."

Essay Questions

1. From your 20th-century perspective, can you critique any of the assumptions or assertions contained in this document? You might consider, for instance, the point of view of women, of the "merciless Indian savages" (paragraph 32), and those who take a separation of church and state as a fundamental premise upon which our nation is based.

2. Jefferson, although a slave owner himself, was opposed to slavery. Obtain a copy of Jefferson's original draft of the "Declaration" and trace the evolution of language pertaining, directly or indirectly, to the practice of slavery. How does the final draft compare with the first draft in relation to this issue?

Declaration of Sentiments and Resolutions

Elizabeth Cady Stanton

Elizabeth Cady Stanton (1815–1902) was an orator, journalist, and prominent women's rights advocate. She and Susan B. Anthony collaborated on the campaign for universal suffrage. Together they published the journal Revolution *(1868–69) and the three-volume* History of Woman Suffrage *(1881–86). Stanton also published two volumes of Biblical interpretation under the title* A Woman's Bible *(1895, 1898). Her autobiography,* Eighty Years and More *was published in 1898.*

Stanton was one of the organizers of the history-making Seneca Falls Convention, held in 1848. Those who attended the convention amended and adopted Stanton's "Declaration of Sentiments and Resolutions," reprinted here. The document became the platform of the women's movement in the United States. Stanton later served as the president of the National Woman Suffrage Association.

When, in the course of human events, it becomes necessary for one portion of man to assume among the people of the earth a position different from that which they have hitherto occupied, but one to which the laws of nature and of nature's God entitle them, a decent respect to the opinions of mankind requires that they should declare the causes that impel them to such a course.

We hold these truths to be self-evident: that all men and women are created equal; that they are endowed by their Creator with certain inalienable rights; that among these are life, liberty, and the pursuit of happiness; that to secure these rights governments are instituted, deriving their just powers from the consent of the governed. Whenever any form of government becomes destructive of these ends, it is the right of those who suffer from it to refuse allegiance to it, and to insist upon the institution of a new government, laying its foundation on such principles, and organizing its powers in such form, as to them shall seem most likely to effect their safety and happiness. Prudence, indeed, will dictate that governments long established should not be changed for light and transient causes; and accordingly all experience hath shown that mankind are more disposed to suffer, while evils are sufferable, than to right themselves by abolishing the forms to which they were accustomed. But when a long train of abuses and usurpations, pursuing invariably the same object, evinces a design to reduce them under absolute despotism, it is their duty to throw off such government, and to provide new guards for their future security. Such has been the patient sufferance of the women under this government, and such is now the necessity which constrains them to demand the equal station to which they are entitled.

The history of mankind is a history of repeated injuries and usurpations on the part of man toward woman, having in direct object the establishment of an absolute tyranny over her. To prove this, let facts be submitted to a candid world.

He has never permitted her to exercise her inalienable right to the elective franchise.

5   He has compelled her to submit to laws, in the formation of which she had no voice.

He has withheld from her rights which are given to the most ignorant and degraded men—both natives and foreigners.

Having deprived her of this first right of a citizen, the elective franchise, thereby leaving her without representation in the halls of legislation, he has oppressed her on all sides.

He has made her, if married, in the eye of the law, civilly dead.

He has taken from her all right in property, even to the wages she earns.

10   He has made her, morally, an irresponsible being, as she can commit many crimes with impunity, provided they be done in the presence of her husband. In the covenant of marriage, she is compelled to promise obedience to her husband, he becoming to all intents and purposes, her master—the law giving him power to deprive her of her liberty, and to administer chastisement.

He has so framed the laws of divorce, as to what shall be the proper causes, and in case of separation, to whom the guardianship of the children shall be given, as to be wholly regardless of the happiness of women—the law, in all cases, going upon a false supposition of the supremacy of man, and giving all power into his hands.

After depriving her of all rights as a married woman, if single, and the owner of property, he has taxed her to support a government which recognizes her only when her property can be made profitable to it.

He has monopolized nearly all the profitable employments, and from those she is permitted to follow, she receives but a scanty remuneration. He closes against her all the avenues to wealth and distinction which he considers most honorable to himself. As a teacher of theology, medicine, or law, she is not known.

He has denied her the facilities for obtaining a thorough education, all colleges being closed against her.

15   He allows her in Church, as well as State, but a subordinate position, claiming Apostolic authority for her exclusion from the ministry, and, with some exceptions, from any public participation in the affairs of the Church.

He has created a false public sentiment by giving to the world a different code of morals for men and women, by which moral delinquencies which exclude women from society, are not only tolerated, but deemed of little account in man.

He has usurped the prerogative of Jehovah himself, claiming it as his right to assign for her a sphere of action, when that belongs to her conscience and to her God.

He has endeavored, in every way that he could, to destroy her confidence in her own powers, to lessen her self-respect, and to make her willing to lead a dependent and abject life.

Now, in view of this entire disfranchisement of one-half the people of this country, their social and religious degradation—in view of the aggrieved, oppressed, and fraudulently deprived of their most sacred rights, we insist that they have immediate admission to all the rights and privileges which belong to them as citizens of the United States.

In entering upon the great work before us, we anticipate no small[20] amount of misconception, misrepresentation, and ridicule; but we shall use every instrumentality within our power to effect our object. We shall employ agents, circulate tracts, petition the State and National legislatures, and endeavor to enlist the pulpit and the press in our behalf. We hope this Convention will be followed by a series of Conventions embracing every part of this country.

[The following resolutions were discussed by Lucretia Mott, Thomas and Mary Ann McClintock, Amy Post, Catharine A. F. Stebbins, and others, and were adopted:]

Whereas, The great precept of nature is conceded to be, that "man shall pursue his own true and substantial happiness." Blackstone in his Commentaries remarks, that this law of Nature being coeval with mankind, and dictated by God himself, is of course superior in obligation to any other. It is binding over all the globe, in all countries, and at all times; no human laws are of any validity if contrary to this, and such of them are as valid, derive all their force, and all their validity, and all their authority, mediately and immediately, from this original; therefore,

Resolved, That such laws as conflict, in any way, with the true and substantial happiness of woman, are contrary to the great precept of nature and of no validity, for this is "superior in obligation to any other."

Resolved, That all laws which prevent woman from occupying such a station in society as her conscience shall dictate, or which place her in a position inferior to that of man, are contrary to the great precept of nature, and therefore of no force or authority.

Resolved, That woman is man's equal—was intended to be so by the[25] Creator, and the highest good of the race demands that she should be recognized as such.

Resolved, That the women of this country ought to be enlightened in regard to the laws under which they live, that they may no longer publish their degradation by declaring themselves satisfied with their present position, nor their ignorance, by asserting that they have all the rights they want.

Resolved, That inasmuch as man, while claiming for himself intellectual superiority, does accord to woman moral superiority, it is preeminently his duty to encourage her to speak and teach, as she has an opportunity, in all religious assemblies.

Resolved, That the same amount of virtue, delicacy, and refinement of behavior that is required of woman in the social state, should also be required of man, and the same transgressions should be visited with equal severity on both man and woman.

Resolved, That the objection of indelicacy and impropriety, which is so often brought against woman when she addresses a public audience, comes with a very ill-grace from those who encourage, by their attendance, her appearance on the stage, in the concert, or in feats of the circus.

30   *Resolved,* That woman has too long rested satisfied in the circumscribed limits which corrupt customs and a perverted application of the Scriptures have marked out for her, and that it is time she should move in the enlarged sphere which her great Creator has assigned her.

Resolved, That it is the duty of the women of this country to secure to themselves their sacred right to the elective franchise.

Resolved, That the equality of human rights results necessarily from the fact of the identity of the race in capabilities and responsibilities.

Resolved, therefore, That, being invested by the Creator with the same capabilities, and the same consciousness of responsibility for their exercise, it is demonstrably the right and duty of woman, equally with man, to promote every righteous cause by every righteous means; and especially in regard to the great subjects of morals and religion, it is self-evidently her right to participate with her brother in teaching them, both in private and in public, by writing and by speaking, by any instrumentalities proper to be used, and in any assemblies proper to be held; and this being a self-evident truth growing out of the divinely implanted principles of human nature, any custom or authority adverse to it, whether modern or wearing the hoary sanction of antiquity, is to be regarded as a self-evident falsehood, and at war with mankind.

[At the last session Lucretia Mott offered and spoke to the following resolution:]

35   *Resolved,* That the speedy success of our cause depends upon the zealous and untiring efforts of both men and women, for the overthrow of the monopoly of the pulpit, and for the securing to woman an equal participation with men in the various trades, professions, and commerce.

Additional Rhetorical Strategies

Cause and Effect (paragraphs 1, 19); Comparison and Contrast (paragraphs 16, 27); Example (throughout).

Discussion Questions

1. Examine Stanton's "Declaration" in close comparison with Jefferson's, written 72 years earlier. How much of Jefferson's text is repeated verbatim in Stanton's? What is the effect of this close repetition? What does Stanton gain as a result of the echoes from the "Declaration of Independence"?
2. Identify the differences between the earlier and the later text. In the opening paragraphs, the changes are slight but significant. Discuss these, then move on to a more general comparison and contrast between the two lists of grievances. How were (or are) women like an emerging nation, and how are they different?
3. What is the effect of the title of Stanton's piece? Why "Sentiments and Resolutions" instead of "Independence"? What kinds of actions does Stanton advocate? What spheres of action were available to the women and the colonists, respectively?
4. Although Stanton's document was revolutionary in the mid-19th century, it is of course possible for those of us who live in the late 20th century to critique it from our vantage point. Can you point to indications that Stanton, for all her belief in equality, had still internalized some of the contemporary messages about a woman's place?
5. Examine Stanton's attitude towards men, as it is expressed and implied in this document. Is man the enemy, or is he also a comrade? Will the liberation of women be detrimental or beneficial to men, according to Stanton? Look also at her similarly complex attitude toward the church.

Essay Questions

1. It is apparent from paragraph 20 that Stanton anticipates "no small amount of misconception, misrepresentation, and ridicule" to result from the publication of her "Sentiments and Resolutions." Imagine you are one of her fellow countrymen or women, someone with a stake in the outcome of these early gender wars. Write a letter to the editor of your local newspaper responding to the document by Stanton.
2. Assess our nation's progress on the resolutions Stanton set forth in 1848. How far have we come in the struggle for women's rights? What tasks still remain?

On Being Inaugurated President of the United States

John F. Kennedy

John Fitzgerald Kennedy (1917–1963) was born into one of the wealthiest and most prominent families in Massachusetts. He attended Harvard, where his grades for the first three years were mostly mediocre, but in his senior year he wrote a thesis (later reworked into the best-selling Why England Slept *[1940]) that impressed the faculty to such an extent that they awarded him honors upon graduation. In World War II he proved to be a hero when the torpedo boat under his command was sunk by a Japanese destroyer: though wounded, Kennedy not only rescued survivors but also swam for help.*

Kennedy began his political career in 1947, as the U.S. representative from Massachusetts. From 1953–1960 he served as that state's U.S. senator. While serving as senator, he published Profiles in Courage *(1956), for which he was awarded a Pulitzer Prize. In 1961 he became the youngest man ever elected president of the United States. He represented a new generation in American politics, for whom World War II and the Cold War were the defining features. His primary focus during his presidency was foreign affairs; he won great praise for his handling of the crisis over Cuba in 1962 that came close to starting World War III. On the domestic front, perhaps his most lasting legacy was the creation of the Peace Corps.*

A blizzard had frozen the landscape of Washington D.C. on January 20, 1961, when Kennedy delivered the following speech, widely regarded as one of a handful of great inaugural addresses. He spoke of his vision for America and the world, admitting that this vision could not be realized "in the first one thousand days." These words came to bitterly ironic fruition on November 22, 1963, when John F. Kennedy was assassinated in Dallas. The entire country mourned his loss.

We observe today not a victory of party but a celebration of freedom, symbolizing an end as well as a beginning, signifying renewal as well as change. For I have sworn before you and Almighty God the same solemn oath our forebears prescribed nearly a century and three-quarters ago.

The world is very different now. For man holds in his mortal hands the power to abolish all forms of human poverty and all forms of human life. And yet the same revolutionary belief for which our forebears fought is still at issue around the globe, the belief that the rights of man come not from the generosity of the state but from the hand of God.

We dare not forget today that we are the heirs of that first revolution. Let the word go forth from this time and place, to friend and foe alike, that the torch has been passed to a new generation of Americans, born in this century, tempered by war, disciplined by a hard and bitter peace, proud of our ancient heritage, and unwilling to witness or permit the slow undoing of those human rights to which this nation has always been committed, and to which we are committed today at home and around the world.

Let every nation know, whether it wishes us well or ill, that we shall pay any price, bear any burden, meet any hardship, support any friend, oppose any foe, to assure the survival and the success of liberty.

This much we pledge—and more.

To those old allies whose cultural and spiritual origins we share, we 5 pledge the loyalty of faithful friends. United, there is little we cannot do in a host of co-operative ventures. Divided, there is little we can do, for we dare not meet a powerful challenge at odds and split asunder.

To those new states whom we welcome to the ranks of the free, we pledge our word that one form of colonial control shall not have passed away merely to be replaced by a far more iron tyranny. We shall not always expect to find them supporting our view. But we shall always hope to find them strongly supporting their own freedom, and to remember that, in the past, those who foolishly sought power by riding the back of the tiger ended up inside.

To those people in the huts and villages of half the globe struggling to break the bonds of mass misery, we pledge our best efforts to help them help themselves, for whatever period is required, not because the Communists may be doing it, not because we seek their votes, but because it is right. If a free society cannot help the many who are poor, it cannot save the few who are rich.

To our sister republics south of our border, we offer a special pledge: to convert our good words into good deeds in a new alliance for progress, to assist free men and free governments in casting off the chains of poverty. But this peaceful revolution of hope cannot become the prey of hostile powers. Let all our neighbors know that we shall join with them to oppose aggression or subversion anywhere in the Americas. And let every other power know that this hemisphere intends to remain the master of its own house.

To that world assembly of sovereign states, the United Nations, our 10 last best hope in an age where the instruments of war have far outpaced the instruments of peace, we renew our pledge of support: to prevent it from becoming merely a forum for invective, to strengthen its shield of the new and the weak, and to enlarge the area in which its writ may run.

Finally, to those nations who would make themselves our adversary, we offer not a pledge but a request: that both sides begin anew the quest for peace, before the dark powers of destruction unleashed by science engulf all humanity in planned or accidental self-destruction.

We dare not tempt them with weakness. For only when our arms are sufficient beyond doubt can we be certain beyond doubt that they will never be employed.

But neither can two great and powerful groups of nations take comfort from our present course—both sides over-burdened by the cost of modern weapons, both rightly alarmed by the steady spread of the deadly atom, yet both racing to alter that uncertain balance of terror that stays the hand of mankind's final war.

So let us begin anew, remembering on both sides that civility is not a sign of weakness and sincerity is always subject to proof. Let us never negotiate out of fear, but let us never fear to negotiate.

15   Let both sides explore what problems unite us instead of belaboring those problems which divide us.

Let both sides, for the first time, formulate serious and precise proposals for the inspection and control of arms, and bring the absolute power to destroy other nations under the absolute control of all nations.

Let both sides seek to invoke the wonders of science instead of its terrors. Together let us explore the stars, conquer the deserts, eradicate disease, tap the ocean depths and encourage the arts and commerce.

Let both sides unite to heed in all corners of the earth the command of Isaiah to "undo the heavy burdens . . . and let the oppressed go free."

And if a beachhead of co-operation may push back the jungle of suspicion, let both sides join in creating a new endeavor—not a new balance of power, but a new world of law, where the strong are just and the weak secure and the peace preserved.

20   All this will not be finished in the first one hundred days. Nor will it be finished in the first one thousand days, nor in the life of this Administration, nor even perhaps in our lifetime on this planet. But let us begin.

In your hands, my fellow citizens, more than mine, will rest the final success or failure of our course. Since this country was founded, each generation of Americans has been summoned to give testimony to its national loyalty. The graves of young Americans who answered the call to service surround the globe.

Now the trumpet summons us again—not as a call to bear arms, though arms we need; not as a call to battle, though embattled we are; but a call to bear the burden of a long twilight struggle, year in and year out "rejoicing in hope, patient in tribulation," a struggle against the common enemies of man: tyranny, poverty, disease, and war itself.

Can we forge against these enemies a grand and global alliance, North and South, East and West, that can assure a more fruitful life for all mankind? Will you join in that historic effort?

In the long history of the world only a few generations have been granted the role of defending freedom in its hour of maximum danger. I do not shrink from this responsibility; I welcome it. I do not believe that any of us would exchange places with any other people or any other generation. The energy, the faith, the devotion which we bring to this endeavor will light our country and all who serve it, and the glow from that fire can truly light the world.

And so, my fellow Americans, ask not what your country can do$_{25}$ for you; ask what you can do for your country.

My fellow citizens of the world, ask not what America will do for you, but what together we can do for the freedom of man.

Finally, whether you are citizens of America or citizens of the world, ask of us here the same high standards of strength and sacrifice which we ask of you. With a good conscience our only sure reward, with history the final judge of our deeds, let us go forth to lead the land we love, asking His blessing and His help, but knowing that here on earth God's work must truly be our own.

Additional Rhetorical Strategies

Cause and Effect (paragraph 12); Analogy (paragraphs 19, 22).

Discussion Questions

1. Look closely at the way Kennedy constructs his sentences. You don't need a fancy vocabulary in order to describe the sentence structures or their effect; just use your own words to describe his strategies. Look, for instance, at the second sentence of paragraph 2: "For man holds in his mortal hands the power to abolish all forms of human poverty and all forms of human life." The final two phrases are parallel—indeed almost identical but for the substitution of the very last word—in structure, but opposite in meaning. What is the effect of this strategy? Nearly every sentence in this inaugural address will repay close attention.
2. Does Kennedy focus more on domestic or foreign affairs in this speech? Point to specific evidence to support your answer. Given what you know of the context in which the speech was delivered, what might be the reason for his focus?
3. What principle does Kennedy seem to value above all others? Support your answer with specific evidence from the text.
4. What is Kennedy's attitude towards science, as expressed in his speech? What were the scientific advances of the day that prompted his remarks?
5. In paragraphs 19 and 22, Kennedy constructs a metaphor based on war and battle. This may be understandable in light of his own service during World War II and the specter of nuclear annihilation that loomed large at the time of his inauguration. What does he gain, and what does he lose, by couching the call for solutions to such things as "tyranny, poverty, and disease" in martial terms? What is the effect

of his suggestion that we battle war itself? Where else in the essay do you see Kennedy resorting to bellicose language?

Essay Questions

1. In the most oft-quoted passage in this speech, Kennedy says, "And so, my fellow Americans, ask not what your country can do for you; ask what you can do for your country" (paragraph 25). However, he gives precious little indication of the specific kinds of service to one's country he has in mind. Write an essay exploring one or more ways that an American citizen might translate Kennedy's call into action. Your essay might take the form of a report on an existing service organization or an everyday hero from your own community, or it might take a more general approach to community service.
2. Drawing on your analysis of Kennedy's rhetorical strategies, write a speech in which you exhort your audience to take action for a cause in which you strongly believe. You need not ask them to lay down their lives, but use language effectively to stir them to some significant action.

I Have a Dream

Martin Luther King, Jr.

Martin Luther King, Jr. (1929–1968) is recognized as the driving force of the civil rights movement. At the height of his career as an orator he delivered an average of 450 speeches a year, calling for racial equality and justice. He was born the son and grandson of preachers. He was educated at Morehouse College, the Crozer Theological Seminary, and Boston University, where he received his Ph.D. in systematic theology in 1955. The same year he led the protest following the arrest of Miss Rosa Parks, a black woman who had refused to give up her seat on the bus to a white man. The bus boycott King organized lasted over a year, and resulted in the Supreme Court declaring segregated buses illegal. In this action, as in all his subsequent actions, he adhered to the principles of nonviolence he learned from Mahatma Gandhi.

The speech reprinted below was delivered at a massive civil rights march on Washington, D.C. in 1963. Although King spent most of the night before writing his speech, he ended up deviating from his prepared text, and delivering a speech so powerful that thousands wept and cheered to hear it. In 1964 King was the first black man to be named "Man of the Year" by Time *magazine, and later that year he became the youngest recipient of the Nobel Peace Prize. He was assassinated on April 4, 1968, but his legacy lives on in the lives of millions of Americans who have benefited from his life's work and his inspiration.*

I am happy to join with you today in what will go down in history as the greatest demonstration for freedom in the history of our nation.

Five score years ago, a great American, in whose symbolic shadow we stand today, signed the Emancipation Proclamation. This momentous decree came as a great beacon light of hope to millions of Negro slaves who had been seared in the flames of withering injustice. It came as a joyous daybreak to end the long night of their captivity. But one hundred years later, the Negro still is not free. One hundred years later, the life of the Negro is still sadly crippled by the manacles of segregation and the chains of discrimination. One hundred years later, the Negro lives on a lonely island of poverty in the midst of a vast ocean of material prosperity. One hundred years later, the Negro is still anguished in the corners of American society and finds himself in exile in his own land. And so we have come here today to dramatize a shameful condition.

In a sense we have come to our nation's capital to cash a check. When the architects of our republic wrote the magnificent words of the Constitution and the Declaration of Independence, they were signing a promissory note to which every American was to fall heir. This note was the promise that all men—yes, black men as well as white men—would be guaranteed the inalienable rights of life, liberty, and the pursuit of happiness.

It is obvious today that America has defaulted on this promissory note insofar as her citizens of color are concerned. Instead of honoring this sacred obligation, America has given the Negro people a bad check, a check which has come back marked "insufficient funds." But we refuse to believe that the bank of justice is bankrupt. We refuse to believe that there are insufficient funds in the great vaults of opportunity of this nation; and so we have come to cash this check, a check that will give us upon demand the riches of freedom and the security of justice.

5   We have also come to this hallowed spot to remind America of the fierce urgency of *now*. This is not time to engage in the luxury of cooling off or to take the tranquilizing drug of gradualism. *Now* is the time to make real the promises of democracy. *Now* is the time to rise from the dark and desolate valley of segregation to the sunlit path of racial justice. *Now* is the time to lift our nation from the quicksands of racial injustice to the solid rock of brotherhood. *Now* is the time to make justice a reality for all of God's children.

It would be fatal for the nation to overlook the urgency of the moment. This sweltering summer of the Negro's legitimate discontent will not pass until there is an invigorating autumn of freedom and equality. Nineteen sixty-three is not an end, but a beginning. And those who hope that the Negro needed to blow off steam and will now be content will have a rude awakening if the nation returns to business as usual. There will be neither rest nor tranquility in America until the Negro is granted his citizenship rights. The whirlwinds of revolt will continue to shake the foundations of our nation until the bright day of justice emerges.

But there is something that I must say to my people who stand on the warm threshold which leads into the palace of justice. In the process of gaining our rightful place, we must not be guilty of wrongful deeds. Let us not seek to satisfy our thirst for freedom by drinking from the cup of bitterness and hatred. We must forever conduct our struggle on the high plane of dignity and discipline. We must not allow our creative protest to degenerate into physical violence. Again and again we must rise to the majestic heights of meeting physical force with soul force. And the marvelous new militancy which has engulfed the Negro community must not lead us to a distrust of all white people; for many of our white brothers, as evidenced by their presence here today, have come to realize that their destiny is tied up with our destiny, and they have come to realize that their freedom is inextricably bound to our freedom.

We cannot walk alone. And as we walk we must make the pledge that we shall always march ahead. We cannot turn back. There are those who are asking the devotees of civil rights, "When will you be satisfied?" We can never be satisfied as long as the Negro is the victim of the unspeakable horrors of police brutality. We can never be satisfied as long as our bodies, heavy with the fatigue of travel, cannot gain lodging in the motels of the highways and the hotels of the cities. We cannot be satisfied as long as the Negro's basic mobility is from a smaller ghetto to a larger one. We can never be satisfied as long as our children are stripped of their selfhood and robbed of their dignity by signs stating "For Whites Only." We cannot be satisfied as long as the Negro in Mississippi cannot vote and a Negro in New York believes he has nothing for which to vote. No, no, we are not satisfied, and we will not be satisfied until justice rolls down like waters and righteousness like a mighty stream.

I am not unmindful that some of you have come here out of great trials and tribulations. Some of you have come fresh from narrow jail cells. Some of you have come from areas where your quest for freedom left you battered by the storms of persecution and staggered by the winds of police brutality. You have been the veterans of creative suffering. Continue to work with the faith that unearned suffering is redemptive.

Go back to Mississippi, and go back to Alabama. Go back to South 10 Carolina. Go back to Georgia. Go back to Louisiana. Go back to the slums and ghettos of our Northern cities, knowing that somehow this situation can and will be changed. Let us not wallow in the valley of despair.

I say to you today, my friends, even though we face the difficulties of today and tomorrow, I still have a dream. It is a dream deeply rooted in the American dream. I have a dream that one day this nation will rise up and live out the true meaning of its creed: "We hold these truths to be self-evident, that all men are created equal." I have a dream that one day, on the red hills of Georgia, sons of former slaves and the sons of former slave owners will be able to sit down together at the table of brotherhood. I have a dream that one day even the state of Mississippi, a state sweltering with the heat of injustice, sweltering with the heat of oppression, will be transformed into an oasis of freedom and justice. I have a dream that my four little children will one day live in a nation where they will not be judged by the color of their skin, but by the content of their character.

I have a dream today. I have a dream that one day down in Alabama—with its vicious racists, with its governor's lips dripping with the words of interposition and nullification—one day right there in Alabama, little black boys and black girls will be able to join hands with little white boys and white girls as sisters and brothers.

I have a dream today. I have a dream that one day every valley shall be exalted and every hill and mountain shall be made low, the rough places will be made plain and the crooked places will be made straight, and the glory of the Lord shall be revealed, and all flesh shall see it together.

This our hope. This is the faith that I go back to the South with. And with this faith we will be able to hew out of the mountain of despair a stone of hope. With this faith we will be able to transform the jangling discords of our nation into a beautiful symphony of brotherhood. With this faith we will be able to work together, to play together, to struggle together, to go to jail together, to stand up for freedom together, knowing that we will be free one day.

15   And this will be the day—this will be the day when all of God's children will be able to sing with new meaning.

> My country, 'tis of thee,
> Sweet land of liberty,
> Of thee I sing;
> Land where my fathers died,
> Land of the Pilgrims' pride,
> From every mountainside
> Let freedom ring.

And if America is to be a great nation, this must become true.

And so let freedom ring from the prodigious hilltops of New Hampshire. Let freedom ring from the mighty mountains of New York. Let freedom ring from the heightening Alleghenies of Pennsylvania. Let freedom ring from the snow-capped Rockies of Colorado. Let freedom ring from the curvaceous slopes of California.

But not only that. Let freedom ring from Stone Mountain of Georgia. Let freedom ring from Lookout Mountain of Tennessee. Let freedom ring from every hill and molehill of Mississippi. "From every mountainside let freedom ring."

And when this happens—when we allow freedom to ring, when we let it ring from every village and every hamlet, from every state and every city—we will be able to speed up that day when all of God's children, black men and white men, Jews and Gentiles, Protestants and Catholics, will be able to join hands and sing in the words of the old Negro spiritual: "Free at last! Free at last! Thank God Almighty. We are free at last!"

Additional Rhetorical Strategies

Extended Metaphor (paragraphs 3–4); Example (throughout).

Discussion Questions

1. What features mark "I Have A Dream" as a speech as opposed to an essay to be read by solitary readers? What rhetorical strategies does King use to move the audience to whom the speech was originally addressed? What stylistic features mark this as a speech written by a preacher? How do these same strategies affect the solitary reader who peruses King's words? Pick out passages in which the style and content match perfectly. How does your inner ear respond to such passages?

2. Look closely at King's use of metaphor. The most sustained metaphor is drawn from finance: the "bad check," the "bank of justice," and the like in paragraphs 3–4. What is the connection between social and economic oppression? Look at the other metaphors he chooses. What larger implications do they contain?

3. In his speech, King quotes directly from at least two songs: "America" (paragraph 15) and "an old Negro spiritual" (paragraph 18). What is the "new meaning" (paragraph 15) that sounds forth from each song when each is sung in 1963? What is the effect of ending his speech with the words of a song?

4. One commentator has remarked that King devotes the first half of his speech "not to celebrating a dream, but to cataloging a nightmare." How does King convey the plight of African Americans in the 1960s? How does he make specific, concrete details and incidents stand in for the experience of the multitudes? Trace his skilled movement from concrete to abstract throughout the essay.

Essay Questions

1. Write a speech entitled "I Have a Dream," but describe your own dream for the future instead of King's. Be sure to clarify the current conditions that have prompted your dream of change, just as King does in his speech. Read your drafts aloud periodically as you write, so that you can check your cadences and the effect of your word choices, syntax, and so forth against the ear of a listening audience.

2. Look closely at King's use of allusion. His language echoes with the words of Thomas Jefferson, Abraham Lincoln, William Shakespeare, the Bible, and other sources. What is the effect of his highly allusive style? Trace one or two of the allusions to the source, and make a comparison between the original text and context and King's text and context.

Three Brief Arguments on Current Issues:

Free Speech on Campus

Should This Student Have Been Expelled?

Nat Hentoff

Nat Hentoff (b. 1925) earned his B.A. (with highest honors) from Northeastern University in 1946, and did graduate work at Harvard University and the Sorbonne. He is the author of well over a dozen works of fiction and nonfiction, many of which feature one of his two favorite topics: jazz music or social reform. Among his books are the novels Blues for Charlie Darwin *(1982) and* The Day they Came to Arrest the Book *(1982), and the nonfiction works* The First Freedom: The Tumultuous History of Free Speech in America *(1980), which won the Hugh M. Hefner First Amendment Award,* American Heroes: In and Out of School *(1987), and* Free Speech for Me—But Not for Thee: How the American Left and Right Relentlessly Censor Each Other *(1992). He has been a columnist for, among other publications,* Downbeat, *the* Village Voice, *and the* New Yorker.

As a student at Northeastern, Hentoff was forced to resign as editor of the university newspaper by a college president who did not agree with his views. Since that time, Hentoff has written extensively in favor of the First Amendment. He is a long-time member of the American Civil Liberties Union.

T he day that Brown denies any student freedom of speech is the day I give up my presidency of the university.

—Vartan Gregorian, president of Brown University, February 20

Doug Hann, a varsity football player at Brown, was also concentrating on organizational behavior and management and business economics. On the night of October 18, 1990, Hann, a junior, was celebrating his twenty-first birthday, and in the process had imbibed a considerable amount of spirits.

At one point, Hann shouted into the air, "Fuck you, niggers!" It was aimed at no one in particular but apparently at all black students at Brown. Or in the world. A freshman leaned out a dormitory window and asked him to stop being so loud and offensive.

Hann, according to reporters on the *Brown Daily Herald*, looked up and yelled, "What are you, a faggot?" Hann then noticed an Israeli flag in the dorm. "What are you, a Jew?" he shouted. "Fucking Jew!"

Hann had achieved the hat trick of bigotry. (In hockey, the hat trick is scoring three goals in a game.) In less than a minute, Hann had engaged in racist, anti-Semitic, and homophobic insults.

He wasn't through. As reported by Smita Nerula in the *Brown Daily* [5] *Herald*, the freshman who had asked Hann to cool it recruited a few people from his dorm "and followed Hann and his friends."

"This resulted in a verbal confrontation outside of Wayland Arch. At this time, [Hann] was said to have turned to one of the freshman's friends, a black woman, and shouted, `My parents own your people.' "

To the Jewish student, or the student he thought was Jewish, Hann said, "Happy Hanukkah."

There are reports that at this juncture Hann tried to fight some of the students who had been following him. But, the *Brown Daily Herald* reports, he "was held back by one of his friends, while [another] friend stretched his arm across the Wayland Gates to keep the students from following Hann."

John Howard Crouch—a student and Brown chapter secretary of the American Civil Liberties Union there—tells me that because Hann had friends restraining him, "nobody seriously expected fighting, regardless of anyone's words."

10   Anyway, there was no physical combat. Just words. Awful words, but nothing more than speech. (Nor were there any threats.)

This was not the first time Hann's graceful drunken language had surfaced at Brown. Two years before, in an argument with a black student at a fraternity bar, Hann had called the student a "nigger." Thereupon he had been ordered to attend a race relations workshop and to get counseling for possible alcohol abuse. Obviously, he has not been rehabilitated.

Months went by after Hann's notorious birthday celebration as Brown's internal disciplinary procedures cranked away. (To steal a phrase from Robert Sherrill, Brown's way of reaching decisions in these matters is to due process as military music is to music. But that's true of any college or university I know anything about.)

At last, the Undergraduate Disciplinary Council (five faculty or administration members and five students) ruled that Doug Hann was to leave the university forevermore. Until two years ago, it was possible for a Brown student to be dismissed, which meant that he or she could reapply after a decent period of penance. But now, Brown has enshrined the sentence of expulsion. You may go on to assist Mother Teresa in caring for the dying or you may teach a course in feminism to 2 Live Crew, but no accomplishments, no matter how noble, will get you back into Brown once you have been expelled.

Doug Hann will wander the earth without a Brown degree for the rest of his days.

15   The president of Brown, Vartan Gregorian—formerly the genial head of the New York Public Library—had the power to commute or even reverse the sentence. But the speech code under which Hann was thrown out had been proposed by Gregorian himself shortly after he was inaugurated in 1989, so he was hardly a detached magistrate.

On January 25 1991, Vartan Gregorian affirmed, with vigor, the expulsion decision by the Undergraduate Disciplinary Council.

Hann became a historic figure. Under all the "hate speech" codes enacted around the country in recent years, he is the first student to actually be expelled for violating one of the codes.

The *New York Times* (February 12) reported that "Howard Ehrlich, the research director of the National Institute Against Prejudice and Violence, said that he did not know of any other such expulsions, but that he was familiar with cases in which students who had harassed others were moved to other dormitories or ordered to undergo counseling."

But that takes place in *educational* institutions, whose presidents recognize that there are students who need help, not exile.

At first, there didn't seem to be much protest among the student[20] body at Brown on free speech grounds—except for members of the Brown chapter of the ACLU and some free thinkers on the student paper, as well as some unaffiliated objectors to expelling students for what they say, not for what they do. The number of these dissenters is increasing, as we shall see.

At the student paper, however, the official tone has changed from the libertarian approach of Vernon Silver, who was editor-in-chief last semester. A February 13 *Brown Daily Herald* editorial was headed: *"Good Riddance."*

It began: "Doug Hann is gone, and the university is well to be rid of him."

But President Gregorian has been getting a certain amount of flack and so, smiting his critics hip and thigh, we wrote a letter to the *New York Times*. Well, that letter (printed on February 21) was actually a press release, distributed by the Brown University News Bureau to all sorts of people, including me, on February 12. There were a few changes—and that *Brown Daily Herald* editorial was attached to it—but Gregorian's declaration was clearly not written exclusively for the *Times*.

Is this a new policy at the *Times*—taking public relations handouts for the letters page?

Next week I shall include a relentlessly accurate analysis of President[25] Gregorian's letter by the executive director of the Rhode Island ACLU. But first, an account of what Gregorian said in that letter to the *Times*.

President Gregorian indignantly denies that Brown has ever expelled "anyone for the exercise of free speech, nor will it ever do so." Cross his heart.

He then goes into self-celebration: "My commitment to free speech and condemnation of racism and homophobia are well known. . . .

"The university's code of conduct does not prohibit speech; it prohibits *actions*."

Now watch this pitiable curve ball:

"Offense III [of the Brown code]—which deals with harassment—[30] prohibits inappropriate, abusive, threatening, or demeaning actions based on race, religion, gender, handicap, ethnicity, national origin, or sexual orientation."

In the original press release, Gregorian underlined the word *actions*. There, and in the letter to the *Times*—lest a dozing reader miss the point—Gregorian emphasizes that "The rules do not proscribe words, epithets, or slanders, they proscribe behavior." Behavior that "shows flagrant disrespect for the well-being of others or is unreasonably disruptive of the University community."

Consider the overbreadth and vagueness of these penalty-bearing provisions. What are the definitions of "harassment," "inappropriate," "demeaning," "flagrant," "disrespect," "well-being," "unreasonably"?

Furthermore, with regard to Brown's termination of Doug Hann with extreme prejudice, Gregorian is engaging in the crudest form of Orwellian newspeak. Hann was kicked out for *speech*, and only speech—not for *actions*, as Gregorian huffily insists. As for behavior, the prickly folks whose burning of the American flag was upheld by the Supreme Court were indeed engaged in behavior. But that behavior was based entirely on symbolic speech. So was Hann's. He didn't punch anybody or vandalize any property. He brayed.

Art Spitzer, legal director of the ACLU's National Capital Area affiliate, wrote a personal letter to Gregorian:

35   "There is a very simple test for determining whether a person is being punished for his actions or his speech. You just ask whether he would have received the same punishment if he had spoken different words while engaging in the same conduct.

"Thus, would your student have been expelled if he had gotten drunk and stood in the same courtyard at the same hour of the night, shouting at the same decibel level, 'Black is Beautiful!' 'Gay is Good!' or 'Go Brown! Beat Yale!' or even 'Nuke Baghdad! Kill Saddam!'?

"I am confident," Spitzer said, that "he would not have been expelled for such 'actions.' If that is correct, it follows that *he was expelled for the unsavory content of his speech*, and not for his actions. I have no doubt that you can understand this distinction." (Emphasis added.)

"Now, you are certainly entitled to believe that it is appropriate to expel a student for the content of his speech when that content is sufficiently offensive to the 'university community.' . . .

"If that is your position, why can't you deliver it forthrightly? Then the university community can have an open debate about which opinions it finds offensive, and ban them. Perhaps this can be done once a year, so that the university's rules can keep pace with the tenor of the times—after all, it wouldn't do to have outmoded rules banning procommunist or blasphemous speech still on the books, now that it's 1991. Then students and teachers applying for admission or employment at Brown will know what they are getting into.

40   "Your recent statements, denying the obvious, are just hypocritical. . . ."

And what did the *New York Times*—in a stunningly fatuous February 21 editorial—say of Vartan Gregorian's sending Doug Hann into permanent exile? "A noble attempt both to govern and teach."

The *Times* editorials should really be signed, so that the rest of the editorial board isn't blamed for such embarrassments.

Additional Rhetorical Strategies

Narration (paragraphs 1–8, 12–13); Analogy (paragraph 12); Cause and Effect (paragraphs 35–36).

Discussion Questions

1. In paragraph 1, Hentoff records Doug Hann's status as a varsity football player, his major, and the fact that the incident in question occurred on his 21st birthday. What is the effect of this background information about Hann? How might it help further Hentoff's argument?
2. How would you characterize Hentoff's narration of the events of October 18, 1990? Does he try to whitewash Hann's actions or words? What seems to be his attitude toward Hann himself? Toward racism and homophobia?
3. Why does Hentoff draw attention to the difference between words and actions? According to Hentoff, how does Gregorian's letter deal with the distinction between words and actions? Why does he call Gregorian's citation of Offense III a "curve ball"?
4. What do you consider the most compelling parts of Hentoff's argument? What strategies does he use to convince you? Why do the less compelling parts of his argument fall short?
5. To what extent are the Mother Teresa and 2 Live Crew examples in paragraph 13 relevant to Hentoff's argument? To what extent are they a red herring? Do we know what Doug Hann has been doing since his expulsion? Does it matter?

Essay Questions

1. What do you think Hann's punishment should have been, if any? Would the fact that this was his second offense, and that a nonpunitive, educational solution had already been tried, weigh into the sentence you would impose? Do you think hate speech codes apply in this case? Are you in favor of or against codes that outlaw hate speech?
2. Hentoff critiques the "overbreadth and vagueness" of terms such as *"harassment, inappropriate, demeaning, flagrant, disrespect, well being, unreasonably"* (paragraph 32). Write a definition essay in which you define one or more of these terms in a way that sheds light on the hate speech issue.

Free Speech? Yes. Drunkenness? No.

Vartan Gregorian

Vartan Gregorian (b. 1935) was born in Tabriz, Iran, and educated at the College Armenian in Lebanon, where he concentrated on American studies, and at Stanford University, where he earned his Ph.D. He speaks and reads Turkish, Arabic, and French, in addition to his native Persian, English, and Armenian. He taught, among other places, at the University of California at Berkeley, San Francisco State University, UCLA, and the University of Pennsylvania, before becoming president of Brown University. He is the author of The Emergence of Modern Afghanistan: Politics of Reform and Modernization, 1880–1946 *(1969). His awards and fellowships include a Danforth Foundation Award for outstanding teaching and a Guggenheim fellowship.*

During the last several decades, our nation's colleges and universities have worked assiduously to develop America's potential talent and to reach out and educate the young without regard to religion, race or gender. Today's campuses are much different from those of the 1950s. Students who represent the broad spectrum of our nation now expect to be welcomed and supported, not merely accommodated or tolerated.

This is not a superficial change, nor has the process been an easy one. We are still striving to build communities where students can devote themselves to knowledge and personal growth without having to defend their racial or ethnic background or plead that their personal dignity or right to privacy be respected.

Today the leaders of American higher education are expected to set high academic standards and codes of conduct that reflect our universities' expectations and the rights and responsibilities of our students. Presidents of our universities are urged to protect the privacy of students, to fight against drug and alcohol abuse, sexual and racial harassment and to guarantee their physical safety. In addition, as educators they are supposed to speak out against intolerance of any kind. Our universities are asked to accomplish all the above objectives while safeguarding the principles of academic freedom, which are their hallmark.

Now come the tests. How does the public respond when our universities take appropriate action against harassment and intimidation?

5   Last year aggrieved students at Brown brought charges of harassment, intimidation and invasion of privacy against a fellow student. The University Disciplinary Council, composed of faculty, students and deans, found the student in question guilty of violating three major provisions of Brown University's 10-year-old code of conduct: disruptive behavior, harassment and drunkenness.

I upheld that expulsion on appeal. Because the university's disciplinary rulings are held in confidence, there was no public release of information. Press accounts, however, described the incident as one of loud drunkenness, of shouting anti-Semitic, anti-black, anti-homosexual obscenities at students in their dormitory rooms, of students driven from their rooms at 2 AM by disruption, of a confrontation during which the intoxicated student was physically restrained. It has even been noted that this was the second time the student had been found guilty of similar charges, the first incident having resulted in probation and counseling.

What has astonished me is how some members of the press have interpreted their own reports. Bouts of drunkenness and disruption have been excused as "sophomoric behavior," threats of physical violence and disruptive behavior have been rationalized or dismissed if no actual blows were struck, and the 2 AM abuse of fellow students in their dormitory rooms, through anti-Semitic, anti-black and anti-homosexual baiting, has been relabeled an exercise of "free speech." Obscenities have been transformed into "unpopular views."

Other voices operating on third-hand information have criticized the university for expelling a student under a so-called "hate speech" rule—the first such expulsion in the country, they say. It is not; and this is not a "free speech" issue. It does not seem to matter to them that Brown has no rule against "hate speech." Like a radioactive material, this canard about "hate speech" has a half-life; its contamination remains for a very long time.

It is ironic that those who have attempted to reconstruct this case as an infringement of "free speech" and defend without qualms the right of any student to shout racist or ethnic slanders at any hour, at any person, in any setting are unable or unwilling to publish the obscenities involved in this case for fear of offending their readers.

And a minor point: As a historian I am dismayed that only one of$_{10}$ those who have written so "authoritatively" about my own views had bothered to contact me.

The day when drunkenness was romanticized, when racial or sexual harassment could be winked at, condoned or considered merely in poor taste has long passed. In the nation's workplaces, a considerable corpus of federal and state law protects the rights and the dignity of employees.

The American Civil Liberties Union, which has opposed campus regulations that may "interfere with the freedom of professors, students and administrators to teach, learn, discuss and debate, or to express ideas, opinions or feelings in the classroom, public or private discourse," stated recently that colleges and universities are not prohibited from enacting "disciplinary codes aimed at restraining acts of harassment, intimidation and invasion of privacy. The fact that words may be used in connection with otherwise actionable conduct does not immunize such conduct from appropriate regulation."

Brown, the nation's seventh oldest college, was the only colonial college that did not exact a religious test for admission. Our tradition of openness, tolerance and intellectual freedom has extended over the two centuries since then and is vigorously sustained today. The exchange of ideas, public discourse and debate nurture in each succeeding generation a respect for the right of all individuals to form, espouse and defend their beliefs and thoughts. Imposed orthodoxies of all sorts, including that which is called "politically correct" speech, are anathema to our enterprise. So is the great silence between races, genders and ideologies. We must know what each other thinks.

However, as the First Amendment lawyer Floyd Abrams pointed out at Brown during a recent conference on free expression, there is a difference between unpopular ideas expressed in a public context and epithets delivered in the context of harassing, intimidating or demeaning behavior. At Brown, we expect our students to know the difference. For 10 years, Brown freshmen have received the university's "Tenets of Community Behavior" and have acknowledged in writing their understanding that the university will hold them to that standard of behavior. Indeed, the underlying principle of the "Tenets" is that "a socially responsible community provides a structure within which individual freedoms may flourish, but not so self-indulgently that they threaten the rights or freedoms of other individuals or groups." Intellectual independence and social responsibility are not mutually exclusive.

15   Today our nation's best campuses can be neither bastions of privilege nor enclaves of trendiness catering to the whims of clamorous and transitory groups. Our universities have been, are and must remain open intellectual communities. They also have an obligation to protect the safety and dignity of our students and their right to learn without intimidation or fear.

Additional Rhetorical Strategies

Narration (paragraph 5); Definition (paragraphs 7, 14); Analogy (paragraph 8).

Discussion Questions

1. How does Gregorian, a historian by discipline, open his essay? What is the effect of the historical overview that he gives? What impression does he give of the progress in American colleges and universities over the last few decades?
2. In paragraph 4, Gregorian asks, "How does the public respond when our universities take appropriate action against harassment

and intimidation?" Where does this shift the burden of the charge? What does it presuppose?

3. Look at the terms listed in paragraph 7, in which Gregorian accuses the press of interpreting key terms in such a way as to soften or rationalize Hann's actions. What is at stake in setting the terms, and how should the right to define the terms be established?

4. What do you consider the most compelling parts of Gregorian's argument? What strategies does he use to convince you? Why do the less compelling parts of his argument fall short?

5. According to Gregorian, Brown has no rule against hate speech (paragraph 8). What, according to Gregorian, was the infraction for which Hann was expelled? Does Gregorian quote the text of the rule Hann did violate anywhere in his essay? Does he imply the tenor of that rule? Given what you can tell about the rule from this essay, what, if anything, do you think Hann's punishment should have been?

6. Reread Gregorian's last paragraph. What are the values he espouses there? Does it seem possible to simultaneously uphold all these values? How successful do you think Gregorian has been in his attempt to do so?

Essay Questions

1. Go to the library and find the text of the letter to the *Times* (February 21, 1991) by Gregorian to which Hentoff refers. Compare and contrast that letter with the essay reprinted here, and with Hentoff's account of it in the essay on p. 497.

2. In paragraph 14, Gregorian writes "there is a difference between unpopular ideas expressed in a public context and epithets delivered in the context of harassing, intimidating, or demeaning behavior." If you agree with this statement, write an essay in which you explain the difference, with supporting examples. If you disagree, write an essay on the speciousness of the distinction.

Exploring Connections:
Questions Linking the Arguments on Free Speech on Campus

1. Compare and contrast Hentoff's and Gregorian's pieces on the basis of tone. To what kinds of audience is each most likely to appeal? What kind of audience is each most likely to alienate? How does each author try to seize the field by setting the terms for the debate himself? To what extent do the terms and issues each discusses overlap with the other's? To what extent is each taking his own route?

2. Hentoff makes good use of an ACLU lawyer's words (paragraph 35
    and following). Gregorian also makes good use of a quotation from
    the ACLU, as well as a quotation from a First Amendment lawyer.
    How is it possible that both can claim to be on the side of free
    speech, and that each can enlist the same forces on his side? Can
    you adjudicate between the competing claims in the area of free
    speech?

Gun Control

Armed and Safe

Sandra S. Froman

Sandra Froman (b. 1949) graduated from Stanford University in 1971. She is currently a trial lawyer with the firm of Snell and Wilmer in Tucson, Arizona. Froman is one of only twelve women on the 75-member board of directors of the National Rifle Association. She wrote the following argument against gun control at the invitation of her alumni magazine, Stanford *(March 1994).*

Emboldened by recent passage of the Brady Bill,[1] gun control proponents are calling for seven more severe firearms restrictions including registration, licensing and the banning and confiscation of certain firearms, including handguns. But there is little empirical evidence that more gun control laws will reduce crime or violence. On the contrary, to the extent to which gun control laws discourage lawful firearms ownership, they actually diminish public safety.

There are more than 200 million guns, of which about a third are handguns, in private hands in the United States. Approximately one-half of U.S. households have guns, and gun ownership is rising.

Proponents of gun control argue that since crime has risen along with gun ownership, guns must cause crime. This notion is like "proving" that police cause crime by the fact that during the 1960s crime increased and so did the number of police officers. In fact, from 1974 to 1988, handgun ownership increased 69 percent, but handgun murders declined 27 percent; further, a 47 percent increase in guns of all kinds was accompanied by a 31 percent decline in gun murder overall. As sociologists have found, the increase in the number of firearms in private hands is a response to fear of crime, rather than the cause of crime.

If guns "cause" violence, then how does one explain the rapid drop in Florida's murder rate following enactment of a law requiring the government to issue permits to carry concealed handguns to law-abiding citizens who pass criminal and mental background checks and a safety test? Florida's murder rate, which was 36 percent above the national average when the law was enacted, is now 4 percent below the national average. While there are still murders in Florida, the murderers now prefer unarmed tourists over residents who might be armed.

5   Another oft-repeated argument is "the more guns, the more gun accidents." The number of guns has nothing to do with the number

---

[1] The Brady Bill, enacted by Congress in 1993, provides for a five-day waiting period when purchasing a handgun so that law enforcement agencies can check the buyer's background. Named after Jim Brady, the presidential press secretary who was wounded during the 1981 assassination attempt on Ronald Reagan, the bill became law after seven years of Congressional debate—Eds.

of accidents. Since 1930, the number of fatal firearms accidents decreased 53 percent while the population doubled and the number of guns quadrupled. Safety programs implemented by the National Rifle Association, 4-H Clubs and other groups have played an important role in the lowering of the accident rate.

There is consensus among criminologists who have examined crime data that gun controls have little value in reducing crime. Indeed, there is persuasive evidence that widespread firearms possession among law-abiding citizens prevents and deters crime, and results in a lowering of the crime rate.

In a National Institute of Justice study, University of Massachusetts sociologist James D. Wright and two of his colleagues, Peter H. Rossi and Kathleen Daly, examined existing gun control research. Wright, a proponent of strict gun control when he began the research, stated in the 1981 report that, "The more deeply we have explored" that position, "the less plausible it has become." The report, published in 1983 as *Under the Gun: Weapons, Crime, and Violence in America,* found: "There appear to be no strong causal connections between private gun ownership and the crime rate. . . . It is commonly hypothesized that . . . homicide occurs simply because the means of lethal violence (firearms) are readily at hand, and . . . [many homicides] would not occur were firearms generally less available. There is no persuasive evidence that supports this view."

In a later NIJ study, Wright and Rossi interviewed more than 2,000 incarcerated felons to study the effect of various gun control laws on criminal behavior. Their study, published as *Armed and Considered Dangerous: A Survey of Felons and Their Firearms* (1986), found that gun control laws had no effect on the ability of criminals to obtain guns. Only 12 percent of criminals (and only 7 percent of "handgun predators") acquired the last handgun they used for a crime at a gun store, and of those many were stolen or obtained through other illegal means.

In addition, 56 percent of the felons said a criminal would not attack if he knew the victim was armed, and 74 percent agreed that one of the reasons burglars avoid occupied houses is that they fear being shot. When felons were asked whether they had personally decided not to commit a crime because of a belief that the victim might be armed, 39 percent said yes, and 8 percent said they had done this many times.

In a comprehensive study, Florida State University criminologist[10] Gary Kleck examined data for all 170 U.S. cities with a population in excess of 100,000, and analyzed 19 different types of gun controls to determine their effect on suicides, accidents and various crimes. Kleck, a liberal Democrat and member of the ACLU and Amnesty International, found that the majority of gun controls, including waiting periods, licensing systems and registration, had no measurable effect on crime. Kleck also found that handguns are used by law-abiding citizens to defend against crime about three times as often as they are misused by criminals committing crimes. Kleck's 1991 book, *Point Blank: Guns and Violence in America,* received the American Society of Criminology's Hindelang award as the most important contribution to criminology in the past several years. Yet, his research is generally ignored by the political officials whose gun control arguments are based on ideology, not criminology.

More recently, Kleck conducted a survey in which he concluded that there were roughly 2.5 million defensive uses of guns by civilians confronting criminals each year. This figure excluded use of guns by police, security guards and military personnel. It was estimated that approximately 1.9 million such uses involved handguns. Kleck's methodology was such as to ensure that each use being reported was a bona fide defensive use against a human being in connection with a crime where there was an actual confrontation between the civilian and the criminal.

Although 72 percent of the defensive uses occurred in or near the home, in 20 to 25 percent of the defensive uses (or up to half a million times a year), a civilian carrying a gun away from the home used it to defend against a criminal attack. In only 8 percent of the cases did the civilian actually kill or wound the offender. In the vast majority of cases, no shots were fired—the mere presence of the firearm prevented the crime from being completed.

These studies point out the danger of gun control laws that seek to deprive lawful Americans of the means of self-defense. In much of this country, the threat of criminal violence is a daily realty. Although many people are under the impression that the police exist to protect them, courts have ruled that the police have no legal obligation to protect the individual. And even if the police had such an obligation, there are simply not enough police to serve as personal bodyguards.

Women feel particularly vulnerable to crime and violence. For the average woman, a firearm is the only effective means of self-defense against a physically stronger male intent on raping or robbing, who may himself be armed. That may be why women are buying guns and taking firearms training in record numbers.

15   Despite the myth that a woman shouldn't own a gun because it might be turned against her, the truth is that in less than 1 percent of all defensive uses of firearms is the criminal able to take the gun away from the victim. As more women take responsibility for their own protection, the fear of crime will be replaced with skill, confidence and self-respect.

Jeffrey Snyder suggests in his thought-provoking article "A Nation of Cowards" (*The Public Interest,* Fall 1993) that law-abiding citizens allow and encourage crime by not fighting back, and that the intended victim has a moral responsibility to defend himself or herself. Whether a woman chooses to own a gun as a means to fight back is a deeply personal decision. But gun control laws that deprive women of this choice make them prisoners of their fear.

No matter how many gun control laws are enacted, criminals will always get guns. No matter how many guns are banned or confiscated, the supply is so large and guns are so durable, there will always be enough guns for criminals to use on their victims. The "crime" of gun control is that while the government cannot protect us from crime, it wants to restrict or take away altogether the means we have of protecting ourselves. Any gun control law that makes it illegal for the competent, law-abiding person to possess or carry a gun endangers public safety.

Senator Campbell's Rebuttal

Ms. Froman's arguments assert the right of self-defense. I agree with such a right. Now, can we get back to the actual kinds of gun control that are being discussed in Congress and in the state legislatures?

Let's get specific. Why not limit the number of guns an individual can purchase in a single day, month or year? Nothing in such a restriction would curb the right of the individual to purchase a gun to protect himself or herself, as Ms. Froman desires. Yet the NRA objects to such a law.

Why not outlaw the assault-style weapon? The defense of self and[20] home does not require a weapon meant for combat, capable of spraying 10 bullets per second in fully automatic mode and three bullets in semiautomatic mode. Yet the NRA wants to overturn the law that, since 1934, has restricted private ownership of fully automatic weapons. It is fighting to prevent any extension of that law to semiautomatic assault-style weapons.

Why not outlaw the large-capacity clip? Self-defense does not require a clip of 30, 29 or even 10 bullets. Such large-capacity clips make multiple killings by an insane person much more possible. Yet the NRA objects to bans on the size of clips.

Why not require a background check for those purchasing weapons? In California, 21,168 sales have been blocked since our 15-day waiting period went into effect in 1989. In Virginia, the number over the same period is 5,879. In Maryland, 3,647. In Florida, since 1991, the number is 16,513. Might some of these persons have obtained guns illegally anyway? Of course. But some also did not. Why does the NRA oppose a waiting period in which to perform this kind of background check that turned up so many ineligible persons (including the mentally ill) trying to purchase guns?

Why not tighten up what it takes to be a federally licensed gun dealer? There are more than a quarter of a million such dealers in the

United States right now. That's far more than the federal or state authorities can inspect in order to ensure they are reputable. Some of these dealers are simply fronts for gangs. The legitimate person's right to purchase a gun would not be infringed if there were 25,000 federally licensed gun dealers nationally instead of 280,000. Yet the NRA opposes tightening up the law on the gun dealers.

Ms. Froman presents the case that criminals are deterred by an armed citizenry. She may or may not be right. But what she has not proved is that to achieve this deterrence, citizens must carry large-capacity, semiautomatic and fully automatic weapons, equipped with expanding, flesh-tearing bullets, purchased on the spot, without background checks, purchased in huge volume from dealers who are not supervised.

25   To deter crime, we must do more than make dangerous guns less available. I believe criminals are deterred by sentences that mean something, handed out soon after the crime is committed. Punishment must be swift, sure and severe. Those who place the lives of others in jeopardy through the use of a firearm should receive stern punishment.

First offenders who use firearms must be given a taste of boot camp, not a commuted sentence. The death penalty, too, has a place. As a congressman, I voted for the death penalty on more than 30 instances. But—all this does not mean that we have solved the problem of violence. Weapons capable of mass destruction, far beyond their usefulness for personal defense, are killing us just as much as the people who use them are. If they weren't so available, there wouldn't be so many killings. Particularly for the poor trapped in the inner cities, who live in fear of a stray bullet, and for the families of those for whom it is already too late, let us enact reasonable, balanced gun control now.

Additional Rhetorical Strategies

Cause and Effect (throughout); Example (throughout).

Discussion Questions

1. What is Froman's thesis? Where does she state it? What kinds of evidence or arguments does she marshal in support of her thesis? What kinds of evidence or arguments does she avoid? How does her emphasis on safety determine the shape and content of her essay?
2. What does Froman tell us about the researchers whose work she cites? How do Wright's and Kleck's credentials, in particular, serve to support her thesis? To what extent is Wright held up as an implicit role model for the reader? How effective do you find this tactic?

3. What is the significance of the gender of the author? How might you react differently to this piece if it were written by a man? What advantages accrue from her gender? How, for instance, does she appeal to the women in the audience? In her essay and in her rebuttal, do you think she plays more on women's (and men's) fears or on the potential for empowerment? What is the effect of her borrowing, in paragraph 15, from the rhetoric of reproductive rights for her argument in favor of the freedom to bear arms?

4. Take a critical stance toward the arguments she makes in her essay and in her rebuttal to Campbell's essay. Can you think of other interpretations for the same data she presents? Do you find any places where she contradicts herself? Any places where she makes misleading points? Any places where the implications of her statements are offensive?

Essay Questions

1. Go the library and find one or more of the studies Froman cites. Read the studies for yourself, and decide if Froman accurately represented the findings. Also decide whether the methodologies used by the researchers seem sound, and whether other, more reasonable conclusions might be drawn from the same findings. Write an essay critiquing either the studies or Froman's use of them. Alternatively, go to the library and find other research studies on the topic, and see whether those findings support or undermine the findings cited by Froman.

2. If after reading the research for yourself, you find you agree with Froman's position on gun control, write an essay in which you advocate the right to bear arms, but use a different rhetorical form from the one chosen by Froman (who relies mainly on cause and effect).

Armed and Dangerous

Tom Campbell

Republican **Tom Campbell** *(b. 1952) earned his B.A., M.A., and Ph.D. at the University of Chicago, and his J.D. (magna cum laude) from Harvard University. He held several government posts in the White House and Supreme Court, culminating in a stint as a United States Representative for California in 1989–92. He is currently the state senator for California's 11th District. He has served as editor of the* Harvard Law Review, *and has published law review articles on topics such as employment discrimination, labor law and economics. He was a professor at the Stanford Law School from 1983–88.*

In Louisville, Ky.; Stockton, Calif.; Jacksonville, Fla.; Killeen, Tex.; and San Francisco, Calif., the same horrible story was repeated, all within the last five years. A mentally unstable person used a semiautomatic, large-capacity clip weapon to kill innocent people, then turned the weapon on himself. Men, women, children lay dead or maimed for life. In Louisville, eight were killed; in Stockton, five; in Jacksonville, nine; in Killeen, 22; in San Francisco, eight. In each instance, the murderer killed himself, after taking the lives of so many innocent others.

The threat of prison or even the death penalty will not deter in cases like this. The killing is done without consideration of arrest or punishment.

Some criminals, of course, can be deterred. For this reason, we need tougher criminal penalties for using a weapon in the commission of a crime. People who commit crimes with guns should go to jail or be put to death. The moral culpability of one who shoots a gun at another is the same whether someone is hit or not. For all this, however, not everyone is deterrable.

Would the San Francisco or Stockton massacres have occurred if large-capacity, semiautomatic weapons had not been available for easy purchase? Possibly. It could be that such a mentally unstable person would have smashed his car into the restaurant in Stockton, or into the office building in San Francisco. We can never know. But can we reduce the likelihood of such killings by limiting the accessibility of these weapons? Almost certainly. If the weapon is fast enough and the capacity of the cartridge clip is large enough, many will die before anything can be done to stop the killer. In the recent Long Island railway case, passengers found the opportunity to rush the killer as he attempted to change ammunition clips.

5   It is stultifyingly stupid to recite the mantra: "Guns don't kill, people do." The mentally unstable may have the urge to kill, but it is the

easy accessibility of guns capable of killing many people that makes it more likely that many people *will* be killed.

What is called for is a distinction. Weapons that are used for the protection of self or home or are used for hunting should be allowed, but weapons that carry the potential for mass killing should be banned. For protecting one's home or store, assuming one wants to use a gun, a shotgun is ideal. An AK-47 is not. A high-velocity, large-capacity, assault-style weapon has great potential for indiscriminate harm. Its high velocity bullets can pierce walls, at tremendous risk to innocent bystanders. A shotgun, by contrast, will not send its pellets beyond the immediate range; but within that range, its intimidation value is exceptionally high.

It is important to keep a clear view of this distinction between weapons used for self-protection and weapons that carry the potential for mass killing. Large-capacity clips are not necessary for self-protection. Only in war movies does a single individual hold off a horde with a sub-machine gun. And as for hunting, no hunter goes into the woods with a 30-round clip. Weapons that were built to produce rapid fire are likewise unnecessary. The key is not necessarily that a weapon is semiautomatic (that is, using some of the force of the previous shell to load the next round into the firing chamber). The key is whether the weapon is geared to rapid fire.

In like manner, neither a hunter nor a home protector needs a "Saturday Night Special"—a small, concealable weapon. Indeed, the ability of the homeowner to intimidate rests on the weapon being large and quite visible.

The arguments that revolve around the sale of various kinds of ammunition should also be couched in terms of what is necessary for self-defense. The NRA originally opposed banning the sale of the armor-piercing bullets and those that could pierce bullet-proof vests: the so-called "cop killers." Eventually, the NRA saw the weakness of its own argument, and that it was costing the organization credibility. The same poor judgment characterizes the opposition to banning shells that expand on contact, ravaging soft tissue. This kind of ammunition is even advertised, with express descriptions of its gruesome purpose and effect, in magazines appealing to would-be soldiers of fortune. The purpose of this communication is not to kill animals for food, and not simply to stop a threatening human. The purpose is to kill as horribly as possible.

For some kinds of weapons, all we need is a waiting period—to[10] prevent heat-of-an-argument killings, and to do a background check. Does a waiting period "interfere" with one's ability to obtain a weapon during a riot, such as the one in Los Angeles? Yes, it does. However, virtually every police chief and police officer skilled in riot control supports closing gun and liquor stores upon the start of a riot. If a waiting-period law is well publicized, storekeepers and others who feel they need a weapon can obtain one in advance, just as they obtain their insurance or door locks in advance.

What of the store owner who does buy a shotgun before there is any riot? Or the homeowner who wants to keep such a gun at hand to protect home and family? No reasonable adherent of gun control proposes taking away that right. However, given the statistics on accidental killings from keeping a gun in one's home or business, one should weigh the decision carefully. But having done so, the law should, and does, make possible legitimate ownership of such a weapon.

Sensible gun control, therefore, comes down to this: (1) a waiting period to reduce heat-of-passion killings; (2) a background check, to prevent at least those already certified as criminal or insane from obtaining guns; (3) a list of unavailable weapons, based on the capacity of clip, rapidity of fire, concealability, and velocity and characteristics of the bullet. Other weapons, for target sport, for hunting or for self-defense, would remain entirely legal after a waiting period. This analysis must be done by function, not simply by gun name and model number—since gun manufacturers can readily change either of those.

Some gun owners fear that "faceless bureaucrats" could use these criteria to ban all guns. That would be an abuse of the law, and courts have for many years now been available to prevent such abuses in other administrative law contexts. If an administrator oversteps his or her authority, an appeal to the judicial branch is a well-traveled, and quite successful, route in U.S. law.

Would criminals still get guns? Of course. Criminals obtain every substance of which society attempts to deprive them. All we can do is make such items harder to obtain. The more consistent our effort, the more likely we are to have a significant effect. Failure to achieve a perfect effect is no reason not to try for some positive effect. Would it seriously be argued that seat belts are a bad idea because they don't prevent all traffic deaths?

15   Does gun control mean that only criminals will have guns? No. Any responsible citizen wanting to protect himself or herself can have a gun suited to that purpose. (And it wouldn't be a bad idea if training in the use of guns and gun safety were required with every such legal purchase, to cut down on the possibility of accidental death at home.)

One of the NRA's most common and most deceptive arguments is its quoting only part of the Second Amendment to say "the right of the people to keep and bear arms shall not be infringed." The complete Second Amendment provides: "A well-regulated Militia, being necessary to the security of a free State, the right of the people to keep ad bear Arms, shall not be infringed." The courts have consistently held that this provision preserves the right to impose reasonable regulations on gun ownership and use, consistent with public safety. What is being urged here (waiting periods, registration, banning of certain weapons because of public safety concerns) certainly falls within the gambit of "well-regulated."

The case for reasonable gun control is compelling.

Why has reasonable gun control been so difficult? Because those who believe in it won't vote or donate on that basis, while those who oppose it will. The solution is as obvious as it is harsh, as it is necessary. Vote against a congressman or congresswoman who voted no on the Brady Bill or who voted against the pending assault-weapon bill. Vote against a state legislator who shies away from outlawing weapons capable of killing scores of humans. Until the rest of us, the potential victims of gun-supported violence, vote with the same conviction as the other side, they will win. Vote like your life depended upon it.

Ms. Froman's Rebuttal

Professor Campbell's arguments would be more convincing if he would get his facts straight. He reassuringly states, "No reasonable adherent of gun control proposes taking away" the right to own defensive firearms. But that is exactly what Handgun Control Inc. (HCI) in *Guns Don't Die, People Do* proposes, claiming that, if faced by a rapist or robber, "the best defense against injury is to put up no defense—give them what they want or run."

National data, analyzed by Professor Gary Kleck of Florida State[20] University, show that victims resisting with a gun are both far less likely to be raped or robbed and far less likely to be injured than those who follow HCI's advice and throw themselves on the mercy of violent felons. But HCI sees the Brady Bill as only the first step toward a national gun-licensing scheme to confine guns to sportsmen—self-defense would not be recognized as a legitimate purpose. Last October, in an interview in the *Tampa Tribune*, Sarah Brady stated, "To me, the only reason for guns in civilian hands is for sporting purposes."

Gun control proponents in Congress propose to follow the law currently in effect in Washington, D.C. (adopted at the behest of HCI), which makes it illegal for householders to own a handgun or keep any firearm assembled for self-defense. Under such a law, Bessie Jones, a 92-year-old wheelchair-bound Chicago woman who last November used a handgun in self-defense to kill a teenage robber in her home, would be a lawbreaker.

Professor Campbell would not recommend shotguns over handguns for in-home self-defense if he had ever held an attacker at bay while dialing 911. Or if he had considered how difficult it would have been for Bessie Jones to get to or use a shotgun from her wheelchair. It was a small-caliber, concealable revolver—the gun HCI wants to ban, and Professor Campbell says no one needs for self-defense—that saved Bessie Jones from being another helpless victim of crime.

Citing a few high-profile tragedies, Professor Campbell attempts to make a case for banning semiautomatic firearms. All his factual and technical errors aside, these incidents would have been completed with almost any type of firearm for one simple reason. There was no one there willing or capable of offering any resistance—the kind of responsible armed resistance that Professor Kleck says stops crime up to 2.5 million times per year.

Official government surveys show that so-called "assault weapons" are involved in only about 1 percent of gun crime. An article in *The Journal of California Law Enforcement* stated, "It is interesting to note, in the current hysteria over semiautomatic and military look-alike weapons, that the most common weapon used to murder peace officers was that of the .38 special and the .357 Magnum revolver." A New York City Police Department study found the average number of rounds fired at police per encounter was only 2.55.

25   Proposals to ban certain defensive pistol ammunition are likewise based on ignorance. Every law enforcement officer knows of incidents in which brutal attackers continued to maim and kill after being shot several times with traditional ammunition. Controlled expansion ammunition, like the Black Talon brand, was developed in response to such incidents. It is designed to stop the assailant quickly with the minimum number of hits. It is ideal as a defensive round because the fewer the rounds fired, the less likely that bystanders will be hit. Also, the way the metal jacket peels back keeps the round in the target so it does not pass through and injure someone else. Yet gun control advocates persist, on alleged humanitarian grounds, in trying to ban such ammunition. These misguided efforts, if successful, will result in police and law-abiding citizens using less effective ammunition at greater risk to themselves and innocent bystanders.

California's crime figures show that 70 percent of violent crime is committed by only 6 percent of the population, a small number of violent, repeat offenders passing through our revolving-door criminal justice system. Perhaps it is time to lock those doors and focus on controlling criminals, rather than on the rights of law-abiding citizens.

Additional Rhetorical Strategies

Cause and Effect (paragraphs 4–5, 12); Classification (paragraph 6); Analogy (paragraphs 10, 14); Example (throughout).

Discussion Questions

1. What is Campbell's thesis? Where does he state it? What comes before the thesis statement? To what effect? What kinds of evidence or arguments does he marshal in support of his thesis? What kinds

of evidence or arguments does he avoid? How does his emphasis on danger determine the shape and content of his essay?

2. Unlike Froman, Campbell does not rely on statistics or research to back up his claims, although he does at times allude to statistics. Look at paragraph 11, in which he states that "given the statistics on accidental killings from keeping a gun in one's home or business, one should weigh the decision carefully." What does he gain and lose by not citing the statistics to which he alludes? What larger point about statistics, and their usefulness when it comes to accidental deaths, might be implied by his strategy?

3. Campbell, a Republican, states that he has "voted for the death penalty on more than 30 instances" (rebuttal, paragraph 26). How do his party affiliation and his stance on the death penalty affect your reading of his essay? How might you react differently to this piece if it were written by a Democrat or someone who opposes the death penalty?

4. Take a critical stance toward the arguments he makes in his essay and in his rebuttal to Froman's essay. Can you think of other interpretations for the same examples he presents? Do you find any places where he contradicts himself? Any places where he makes misleading points? Any places where the implications of his statements are offensive?

Essay Questions

1. In paragraph 3, Campbell states, "The moral culpability of one who shoots a gun at another is the same whether someone is hit or not." Do you agree or disagree? Write an essay in which you explore the moral dimension of the gun control issue, a dimension that is largely ignored by the two authors included here.

2. Look up the text of the Brady Bill and other passed and pending legislation related to gun control. Does Campbell accurately represent the legislative efforts made to restrict the sale of firearms? Or do these bills, as Froman claims, limit the legitimate use of weapons for self defense? Use evidence from the language of the bills themselves as evidence for your argument.

Exploring Connections: Questions Linking the Arguments on Gun Control

1. The titles of these pieces, "Armed and Safe" and "Armed and Dangerous," suggest a reverse symmetry that does not materialize in the structure or content of the essays themselves. Which arguments does each author anticipate from the opposition, and which of these fail to materialize in the opposition's essay after all? Why does Campbell spend a large fraction of his allotted space distinguishing

among weapons (and kinds of ammunition) and describing their effects, whereas Froman does not distinguish among different types at all? To what extent do the two authors address each other's argument and concerns, and to what extent do they diverge from this task? To what purpose and with what effect?

2. Describe the intended audience for each piece. Does Froman seem to be addressing people who are already against gun control, or people who are in favor of it, or people who have not made up their minds? What indications can you find to support your impression? What about Campbell? What kind of audience is he addressing? How might you back up your answer?

3. Both authors play upon a feeling of fear among the citizenry: Froman mentions the vulnerability women feel in the face of crime and violence (paragraph 14), for instance, and Campbell speaks of the "poor trapped in the inner cities, who live in fear of a stray bullet" (rebuttal, paragraph 26). How is it that writers on opposing sides of this issue can each evoke a fearful response to the policy decision he or she opposes? How can each of them convince the reader that the world will be a safer place if only his or her side would prevail? Which do you find more convincing? Why?

The Death Penalty

Death and Justice:
How Capital Punishment Affirms Life

Edward I. Koch

Edward I. Koch (b. 1924) was born in the Bronx and attended City College and New York University, where he earned his law degree. In 1966, Koch was elected to the New York City Council; after that he served four terms in the U.S. House of Representatives. His voting record in the Congress was solidly liberal. In 1976, when he decided to run for mayor of New York, the city was in the throes of economic crisis and shaken by the Son of Sam murders. He shifted to the right politically and won the election. Koch served as mayor from 1977 to 1989. He was well loved by his constituents, who appreciated his candor and felt he was a good match for the spirit of the city. Roger Rosenblatt of Time *magazine wrote that "Koch has refined a combative style of oratory, which appeals strongly to a city where four-fifths of life is an argument."*

Koch is the author of two autobiographical works, Mayor *(1984) and* Politics *(1989). The following essay, which will give you a taste of his "combative style," was first published in the* New Republic *in 1985.*

Last December [1984] a man named Robert Lee Willie, who had been convicted of raping and murdering an 18-year-old woman, was executed in the Louisiana state prison. In a statement issued several minutes before his death, Mr. Willie said: "Killing people is wrong. . . . It makes no difference whether it's citizens, countries, or governments. Killing is wrong." Two weeks later in South Carolina, an admitted killer named Joseph Carl Shaw was put to death for murdering two teenagers. In an appeal to the governor for clemency, Mr. Shaw wrote: "Killing is wrong when I did it. Killing is wrong when you do it. I hope you have the courage and moral strength to stop the killing."

It is a curiosity of modern life that we find ourselves being lectured on morality by cold-blooded killers. Mr. Willie previously had been convicted of aggravated rape, aggravated kidnapping, and the murders of a Louisiana deputy and a man from Missouri. Mr. Shaw committed another murder a week before the two for which he was executed, and admitted mutilating the body of the 14-year-old girl he killed. I can't help wondering what prompted these murderers to speak out against killing as they entered the death-house door. Did their newfound reverence for life stem from the realization that they were about to lose their own?

Life is indeed precious, and I believe the death penalty helps to affirm this fact. Had the death penalty been a real possibility in the minds of these murderers, they might well have stayed their hand. They might have shown moral awareness before their victims died, and not after. Consider the tragic death of Rosa Velez, who happened to be home when a man named Luis Vera burglarized her apartment in Brooklyn. "Yeah, I shot her," Vera admitted. "She knew me, and I knew I wouldn't go to the chair."

During my 22 years in public service, I have heard the pros and cons of capital punishment expressed with special intensity. As a district leader, councilman, congressman, and mayor, I have represented constituencies generally thought of as liberal. Because I support the death penalty for heinous crimes of murder, I have sometimes been the subject of emotional and outraged attacks by voters who find my position reprehensible or worse. I have listened to their ideas. I have weighed their objections carefully. I still support the death penalty. The reasons I maintained my position can be best understood by examining the arguments most frequently heard in opposition.

1. The death penalty is "barbaric."   Sometimes opponents of capital punishment 5 horrify with tales of lingering death on the gallows, of faulty electric chairs, or of agony in the gas chamber. Partly in response to such protests, several states such as North Carolina and Texas switched to execution by lethal injection. The condemned person is put to death painlessly, without ropes, voltage, bullets, or gas. Did this answer the objections of death penalty opponents? Of course not. On June 22, 1984, the *New York Times* published an editorial that sarcastically attacked the new "hygienic" method of death by injection, and stated that "execution can never be made human through science." So it's not the method that really troubles opponents. It's the death itself they consider barbaric.

Admittedly, capital punishment is not a pleasant topic. However, one does not have to like the death penalty in order to support it any more than one must like radical surgery, radiation, or chemotherapy in order to find necessary these attempts at curing cancer. Ultimately we may learn how to cure cancer with a simple pill. Unfortunately, that day has not yet arrived. Today we are faced with the choice of letting the cancer spread or trying to cure it with the methods available, methods that one day will almost certainly be considered barbaric. But to give up and do nothing would be far more barbaric and would certainly delay the discovery of an eventual cure. The analogy between cancer and murder is imperfect, because murder is not the "disease" we are trying to cure. The disease is injustice. We may not like the death penalty, but it must be available to punish crimes of cold-blooded murder, cases in which any other form of punishment would be inadequate and, therefore, unjust. If we create a society in which injustice is not tolerated, incidents of murder—the most flagrant form of injustice—will diminish.

2. No other major democracy uses the death penalty.   No other major democracy—in fact, few other countries of any description—are plagued by a murder rate such as that in the United States. Fewer and fewer Americans can remember the days when unlocked doors were the norm and murder was a rare and terrible offense. In America the murder rate climbed 122 percent between 1963 and 1980. During that same period, the murder rate in New York City increased by almost 400 percent, and the statistics are even worse in many other cities. A study at M.I.T. showed that based on 1970 homicide rates a person who lived in a large American city ran a greater risk of being murdered than an American soldier in World War II ran of being killed in combat. It is not surprising that the laws of each country differ according to differing conditions and traditions. If other countries had our murder problem, the cry for capital punishment would be just as loud as it is here. And I daresay that any other major democracy where 75 percent of the people supported the death penalty would soon enact it into law.

3. *An innocent person might be executed by mistake.* Consider the work of Adam Bedau, one of the most implacable foes of capital punishment in this country. According to Mr. Bedau, it is "false sentimentality to argue that the death penalty should be abolished because of the abstract possibility that an innocent person might be executed." He cites a study of the 7,000 executions in this country from 1893 to 1971, and concludes that the record fails to show that such cases occur. The main point, however, is this: If government functioned only when the possibility of error didn't exist, government wouldn't function at all. Human life deserves special protections, and one of the best ways to guarantee that protection is to assure that convicted murderers do not kill again. Only the death penalty can accomplish this end. In a recent case in New Jersey, a man named Richard Biegenwald was freed from prison after serving 18 years for murder; since his release he has been convicted of committing four murders. A prisoner named Lemuel Smith, while serving four life sentences for murder (plus two life sentences for kidnapping and robbery) in New York's Green Haven Prison, lured a woman corrections officer into the chaplain's office and strangled her. He then mutilated and dismembered her body. An additional life sentence for Smith is meaningless. Because New York has no death penalty statute, Smith has effectively been given a license to kill.

But the problem of multiple murder is not confined to the nation's penitentiaries. In 1981, 91 police officers were killed in the line of duty in this country. Seven percent of those arrested in the cases that have been solved had a previous arrest for murder. In New York City in 1976 and 1977, 85 persons arrested for homicide had a previous arrest for murder. Six of these individuals had two previous arrests for murder, and one had four previous murder arrests. During those two years the New York police were arresting for murder persons with a previous arrest for murder on the average of one every 8.5 days. This is not surprising when we learn that in 1975, for example, the median time served in Massachusetts for homicide was less than two and a half years. In 1976 a study sponsored by the Twentieth Century Fund found that the average time served in the United States for first-degree murder is ten years. The median time served may be considerably lower.

4. Capital punishment cheapens the value of human life. On the contrary; it can be[10] easily demonstrated that the death penalty strengthens the value of human life. If the penalty for rape were lowered, clearly it would signal a lessened regard for the victims' suffering, humiliation, and personal integrity. It would cheapen their horrible experience, and expose them to an increased danger of recurrence. When we lower the penalty for murder, it signals a lessened regard for the value of the victim's life. Some critics of capital punishment, such as columnist Jimmy Breslin, have suggested that a life sentence is actually a harsher penalty for murder than death. This is sophistic nonsense. A few killers may decide not to appeal a death sentence, but the overwhelming majority make every effort to stay alive. It is by exacting the highest penalty for the taking of human life that we affirm the highest value of human life.

5. The death penalty is applied in a discriminatory manner. This factor no longer seems to be the problem it once was. The appeals process for a condemned prisoner is lengthy and painstaking. Every effort is made to see that the verdict and sentence were fairly arrived at. However, assertions of discrimination are no an argument for ending the death penalty but for extending it. It is not justice to exclude everyone from the penalty of the law if a few are found to be so favored. Justice requires that the law be applied equally to all.

6. Thou shalt not kill. The Bible is our greatest source of moral inspiration. Opponents of the death penalty frequently cite the sixth of the Ten Commandments in an attempt to prove that capital punishment is divinely proscribed. In the original Hebrew, however, the Sixth Commandment reads, "Thou Shalt Not Commit Murder," and the Torah specifies capital punishment for a variety of offenses. The biblical viewpoint has been upheld by philosophers throughout history. The greatest thinkers of the nineteenth century—Kant, Locke, Hobbes, Rousseau, Montesquieu, and Mill—agreed that natural law properly authorizes the sovereign to take life in order to vindicate justice. Only Jeremy Bentham was ambivalent. Washington, Jefferson, and Franklin endorsed it. Abraham Lincoln authorized executions for deserters in wartime. Alexis de Tocqueville, who expressed profound respect for American institutions, believed that the death penalty was indispensable to the support of social order. The United States Constitution, widely admired as one of the seminal achievements in the history of humanity, condemns cruel and inhuman punishment, but does not condemn capital punishment.

7. The death penalty is state-sanctioned murder. This is the defense with which Messrs. Willie and Shaw hoped to soften the resolve of those who sentenced them to death. By saying in effect, "You're no better than I am," the murderer seeks to bring his accusers down to his own level. It is also a popular argument among opponents of capital punishment, but a transparently false one. Simply put, the state has rights that the private individual does not. In a democracy, those rights are given to the state by the electorate. The execution of a lawfully condemned killer is no more an act of murder than is legal imprisonment an act of kidnapping. If an individual forces a neighbor to pay him money under threat of punishment, it's called extortion. If the state does it, it's called taxation. Rights and responsibilities surrendered by the individual are what give the state its power to govern. This contract is the foundation of civilization itself.

Everyone wants his or her rights, and will defend them jealously. Not everyone, however, wants responsibilities, especially the painful responsibilities that come with law enforcement. Twenty-one years ago a woman named Kitty Genovese was assaulted and murdered on a street in New York. Dozens of neighbors heard her cries for help but did nothing to assist her. They didn't even call the police. In such a climate the criminal understandably grows bolder. In the presence of moral cowardice, he lectures us on our supposed failings and tries to equate his crimes with our quest for justice.

15   The death of anyone—even a convicted killer—diminishes us all. But we are diminished even more by a justice system that fails to function. It is an illusion to let ourselves believe that doing away with capital punishment removes the murderer's deed from our conscience. The rights of society are paramount. When we protect guilty lives, we give up innocent lives in exchange. When opponents of capital punishment say to the state: "I will not let you kill in my name," they are also saying to murderers: "You can kill in your *own* name as long as I have an excuse for not getting involved."

It is hard to imagine anything worse than being murdered while neighbors do nothing. But something worse exists. When those same neighbors shrink back from justly punishing the murderer, the victim dies twice.

Additional Rhetorical Strategies

Cause and Effect (paragraphs 3, 7); Analogy (paragraph 6); Narration (paragraph 8).

Discussion Questions

1. What is the effect of Koch's opening paragraph? How else might the quotations from the two convicted murderers be glossed? Why does Koch risk the possibility that his reader will interpret the quo-

tations differently from him? What does he gain and lose by this strategy?

2. How, according to Koch, does "the death penalty help to affirm" the fact that "life is precious" (paragraph 3)? How convincing do you find his discussion of this point? What questions, if any, does it raise in your mind?

3. Koch chooses to structure his essay as a response to the most frequently heard arguments of the opposition. As you read the seven numbered points, did any other important points, which he neglected to mention, arise in your mind? Do you think he has done justice to his opposition's viewpoint, or do you find him disingenuous?

4. Examine each of his rebuttals to the standard arguments in turn. Which do you find most convincing? On which points does he seem to sidestep the central issue? What kinds of evidence and strategies does he use to persuade an audience? Which of these do you find most persuasive?

5. What is the function of the anecdote about Kitty Genovese (paragraph 14)? From Koch's point of view, how is it literally relevant to the issue of the death penalty, and how is it figuratively relevant? Note the last clause of the essay: "the victim dies twice." How are we meant to take this statement?

Essay Questions

1. In paragraph 9 Koch brings up the issue of multiple murder. A different solution to the problem of convicted murderers serving short sentences, only to be released and kill again, would be mandatory life sentencing. Write a comparison and contrast essay exploring these two alternatives, and weighing the respective merits of each.

2. Koch accuses opponents of capital punishment of wanting an "excuse for not getting involved" (paragraph 15). What other ways of getting involved in reducing crime can you envision? Write a persuasive paper in which you outline one or more alternative responses.

The Death Penalty

David Bruck

*David Bruck (b. 1949) is a lawyer who specializes in the defense of pris-
oners on death row. He often speaks out on the issue of capital punishment, both at public lectures and on television news programs. He has also
published analyses of related legal issues in such newspapers as the* New
York Times *and the* Washington Post. *The essay that follows was written in response to the essay by Ed Koch; both were published in the* New
Republic *in 1985.*

Mayor Ed Koch contends that the death penalty "affirms life."
By failing to execute murderers, he says, we "signal a lessened
regard for the value of the victim's life." Koch suggests that
people who oppose the death penalty are like Kitty Genovese's neighbors, who heard her cries for help but did nothing while an attacker
stabbed her to death.

This is the standard "moral" defense of death as punishment: even
if executions don't deter violent crime any more effectively than imprisonment, they are still required as the only means we have of doing justice in response to the worst of crimes.

Until recently, this "moral" argument had to be considered in the
abstract, since no one was being executed in the United States. But the
death penalty is back now, at least in the southern states, where every
one of the more than 30 executions carried out over the last two years
has taken place. Those of us who live in those states are getting to see
the difference between the death penalty in theory, and what happens
when you actually try to use it.

South Carolina resumed executing prisoners in January with the
electrocution of Joseph Carl Shaw. Shaw was condemned to death for
helping to murder two teenagers while he was serving as a military policeman at Fort Jackson, South Carolina. His crime, propelled by mental
illness and PCP, was one of terrible brutality. It is Shaw's last words
("Killing was wrong when I did it. It is wrong when you do it. . . .")
that so outraged Mayor Koch: he finds it "a curiosity of modern life that
we are being lectured on morality by cold-blooded killers." And so it is.

5   But is was not "modern life" that brought this curiosity into being.
It was capital punishment. The electric chair was J. C. Shaw's platform.
(The mayor mistakenly writes that Shaw's statement came in the form
of a plea to the governor for clemency: actually Shaw made it only seconds before his death, as he waited, shaved and strapped into the chair,
for the switch to be thrown.) It was the chair that provided Shaw with
celebrity and an opportunity to lecture us on right and wrong. What
made this weird moral reversal even worse is that J. C. Shaw faced his
own death with undeniable dignity and courage. And while Shaw died,

the TV crews recorded another "curiosity" of the death penalty—the crowd gathered outside the death-house to cheer on the executioner. Whoops of elation greeted the announcement of Shaw's death. Waiting at the penitentiary gates for the appearance of the hearse bearing Shaw's remains, one demonstrator started yelling, "Where's the beef?"

For those who had to see the execution of J. C. Shaw, it wasn't easy to keep in mind that the purpose of the whole spectacle was to affirm life. It will be harder still when Florida executes a cop-killer named Alvin Ford. Ford has lost his mind during his years of death-row confinement, and now spends his days trembling, rocking back and forth, and muttering unintelligible prayers. This has led to litigation over whether Ford meets a centuries-old legal standard for mental competency. Since the Middle Ages, the Anglo-American legal system has generally prohibited the execution of anyone who is too mentally ill to understand what is about to be done to him and why. If Florida wins its case, it will have earned the right to electrocute Ford in his present condition. If it loses, he will not be executed until the state has first nursed him back to some semblance of mental health.[1]

We can at least be thankful that this demoralizing spectacle involves a prisoner who is actually guilty of murder. But this may not always be so. The ordeal of Lenell Jeter—the young black engineer who recently served more than a year of a life sentence for a Texas armed robbery that he didn't commit—should remind us that the system is quite capable of making the very worst sort of mistake. That Jeter was eventually cleared is a fluke. If the robbery had occurred at 7 PM rather than 3 PM, he'd have had no alibi, and would still be in prison today. And if someone had been killed in that robbery, Jeter probably would have been sentenced to death. We'd have seen the usual execution-day interviews with state officials and the victim's relatives, all complaining that Jeter's appeals took too long. And Jeter's last words from the gurney would have taken their place among the growing literature of death-house oration that so irritates the mayor.

Koch quotes Hugo Adam Bedau, a prominent abolitionist, to the effect that the record fails to establish that innocent defendants have been executed in the past. But this doesn't mean, as Koch implies, that it hasn't happened. All Bedau was saying was that doubts concerning executed prisoners' guilt are almost never resolved. Bedau is at work now on an effort to determine how many wrongful death sentences may have been imposed: his list of murder convictions since 1900 in which the state eventually *admitted* error is some 400 cases long. Of course, very few of these cases involved actual executions: the mistakes that Bedau

---

[1]On June 26, 1986, the Supreme Court prohibited the execution of convicted murderers who are so insane they do not understand they will be executed. However, if Ford regains his sanity, Florida may execute him.

documents were uncovered precisely because the prisoner was alive and able to fight for his vindication. The cases where someone is executed are the very cases in which we're least likely to learn that we got the wrong man.

I don't claim that executions of entirely innocent people will occur very often. But they will occur. And other sorts of mistakes already have. Roosevelt Green was executed in Georgia two days before J. C. Shaw. Green and an accomplice kidnapped a young woman. Green swore that his companion shot her to death after Green had left, and that he knew nothing about the murder. Green's claim was supported by a statement that his accomplice made to a witness after the crime. The jury never resolved whether Green was telling the truth, and when he tried to take a polygraph examination a few days before his scheduled execution, the state of Georgia refused to allow the examiner into the prison. As the pressure for symbolic retribution mounts, the courts, like the public, are losing patience with such details. Green was electrocuted on January 9, while members of the Ku Klux Klan rallied outside the prison.

10   Then there is another sort of arbitrariness that happens all the time. Last October, Louisiana executed a man named Ernest Knighton. Knighton had killed a gas station owner during a robbery. Like any murder, this was a terrible crime. But it was not premeditated, and is the sort of crime that very rarely results in a death sentence. Why was Knighton electrocuted when almost everyone else who committed the same offense was not? Was it because he was black? Was it because his victim and all 12 members of the jury that sentenced him were white? Was it because Knighton's court-appointed lawyer presented no evidence on his behalf at his sentencing hearing? Or maybe there's no reason except bad luck. One thing is clear: Ernest Knighton was picked out to die the way a fisherman takes a cricket out of a bait jar. No one cares which cricket gets impaled on the hook.

Not every prisoner executed recently was chosen that randomly. But many were. And having selected these men so casually, so blindly, the death penalty system asks us to accept that the purpose of killing each of them is to affirm the sanctity of human life.

The death penalty states are also learning that the death penalty is easier to advocate than it is to administer. In Florida, where executions have become almost routine, the governor reports that nearly a third of his time is spent reviewing the clemency requests of condemned prisoners. The Florida Supreme Court is hopelessly backlogged with death cases. Some have taken five years to decide, and the rest of the Court's work waits in line behind the death appeals. Florida's death row currently holds more than 230 prisoners. State officials are reportedly considering building a special "death prison" devoted entirely to the isolation and electrocution of the condemned. The state is also considering the creation of a special public defender unit that will do nothing else but handle death penalty appeals. The death penalty, in short, is spawning death agencies.

And what is Florida getting for all of this? The state went through almost all of 1983 without executing anyone: its rate of intentional homicide declined by 17 percent. Last year Florida executed eight people— the most of any state, and the sixth highest total for any year since Florida started electrocuting people back in 1924. Elsewhere in the U.S. last year, the homicide rate continued to decline. But in Florida, it actually rose by 5.1 percent.

But these are just the tiresome facts. The electric chair has been a centerpiece of each of Koch's recent political campaigns, and he knows better than anyone how little the facts have to do with the public's support for capital punishment. What really fuels the death penalty is the justifiable frustration and rage of people who see that the government is not coping with violent crime. So what if the death penalty doesn't work? At least it gives us the satisfaction of knowing that we got one or two of the sons of bitches.

Perhaps we want retribution on the flesh and bone of a handful of[15] convicted murderers so badly that we're willing to close our eyes to all of the demoralization and danger that come with it. A lot of politicians think so, and they may be right. But if they are, then let's at least look honestly at what we're doing. This lottery of death both comes from and encourages an attitude toward human life that is not reverent, but reckless.

And that is why the mayor is dead wrong when he confuses such fury with justice. He suggests that we trivialize murder unless we kill murderers. By that logic, we also trivialize rape unless we sodomize rapists. The sin of Kitty Genovese's neighbors wasn't that they failed to stab her attacker to death. Justice does demand that murderers be punished. And common sense demands that society be protected from them. But neither justice nor self-preservation demands that we kill men whom we have already imprisoned.

The electric chair in which J. C. Shaw died earlier this year was built in 1912 at the suggestion of South Carolina's governor at the time, Cole Blease. Governor Blease's other criminal justice initiative was an impassioned crusade in favor of lynch law. Any lesser response, the governor insisted, trivialized the loathsome crimes of interracial rape and murder. In 1912 a lot of people agreed with Governor Blease that a proper regard for justice required both lynching and the electric chair. Eventually we are going to learn that justice requires neither.

Additional Rhetorical Strategies

Narration (paragraph 5); Analogy (paragraph 10); Cause and Effect (paragraphs 10, 13, 14); Process Analysis (paragraph 12).

Discussion Questions

1. Bruck wrote this essay in response to the essay by Edward Koch. Which of Koch's points does he choose to address? Which does he neglect? Which specific cases and studies from Koch's essay does Bruck shed a different light upon? Which interpretation do you find most compelling in each case?
2. Where does Bruck's authority come from? What passages in particular imply or demonstrate that he has extensive first-hand experience of the phenomenon of the death penalty and all its attendant problems?
3. What are Bruck's main points in his argument against the death penalty? How does he support each? Which main points and which kinds of supporting evidence do you find most compelling, and which least compelling? Why? In paragraph 14, he refers to some statistics that refute the idea of deterrence as "tiresome facts." Are they indeed tiresome? Are they more or less convincing than the stories about individual convicted murderers presented by both Koch and Bruck?
4. In paragraph 10, Bruck speaks of "another sort of arbitrariness." What is he referring to? How else might the example of Ernest Knighton, put forth in that paragraph, be explained and interpreted? What is the effect of Bruck's decision to present this point indirectly instead of directly?
5. What is the effect of the last paragraph? How, in Bruck's view, are lynching and the electric chair alike? What kind of vision of the past does Bruck present here? What kind of vision of the future?

Essay Question

1. Bruck posits that the segment of the American population that supports the death penalty does so not out of a belief that it's a real solution to crime, but rather out of frustration and a desire for retribution. What other evidence do you see to support the idea that the American people are frustrated with government's inability to solve problems? What kinds of repercussions do you see or foresee as a result of people acting on their frustration?

Exploring Connections:
Questions Linking the Arguments on the Death Penalty

1. Compare and contrast the stylistic choices of the two authors. Which uses more concrete detail when describing the murders? The murderers? The electric chair itself?, etc. Which of them prefers to

use the term "death penalty" and which prefers "capital punishment"? What is the difference in effect between these two terms?

2. Compare and contrast the implicit definitions of the word "moral,"
   as Koch and Bruck might define it. How does each claim the moral
   high ground? How might you choose between the two competing
   claims?

*A Case Study of Persuasion
in Contemporary America*

Pompeian BEAUTY POWDER

An Instant's Beauty May Mean Lasting Happiness

IT may take but an instant to capture love — an instant of flashing beauty, of healthful, glowing color — such as the "Complete Pompeian Beauty Toilette" gives. The woman who knows this secret looks confidently into the future and sees only happiness.

First, a touch of fragrant Pompeian DAY Cream (vanishing). It softens the skin and holds the powder. Work the cream well into the skin so the powder adheres evenly.

Then apply Pompeian BEAUTY Powder. It makes the skin beautifully fair and adds the charm of delicate fragrance.

Now a touch of Pompeian BLOOM for youthful color. Do you know that a bit of color in the cheeks makes the eyes sparkle with a new beauty?

Lastly, dust over again with the powder, in order to subdue the BLOOM. Presto! Such beauty and cool freshness in a few moments! *Note:* Don't use too much BLOOM. Get a natural result.

These three preparations may be used separately or together (as above), as the "Complete Pompeian Beauty Toilette." Pompeian DAY Cream (vanishing), removes face shine. Pompeian BEAUTY Powder, a powder that stays on — flesh, white, brunette. Pompeian BLOOM, a rouge that won't break—light, dark, medium. At all druggists, 50c each. Guaranteed by the makers of Pompeian MASSAGE Cream, Pompeian NIGHT Cream, Pompeian HAIR Massage.

"Don't Envy Beauty. Use Pompeian"

Very Special Offer (to Sept. 27th only)
To one person only in a family (and to September 27th only), we will send for a dime a special box of Pompeian BEAUTY Powder. It contains one-half of our regular 50c box and should be at least a month's supply. This offer is made so attractive that you simply cannot resist trying Pompeian BEAUTY Powder now. And once you try it we are sure you will buy it steadily. Samples of Pompeian DAY Cream and Pompeian BLOOM will be included, so that you can make many interesting beauty experiments. Clip the coupon now, before it is too late.

THE POMPEIAN COMPANY - - 2099 Superior Avenue, Cleveland, Ohio

GUARANTEE

The name Pompeian on any package is your guarantee of quality and safety. Should you not be completely satisfied, the purchase price will be gladly refunded by The Pompeian Co., at Cleveland, Ohio.

THE POMPEIAN CO., 2099 Superior Ave., Cleveland.
Gentlemen—I enclose a dime for the **Special** box powder. Neither I nor anyone in my family has tried Pompeian BEAUTY Powder.

Name.....................

Address...................

City......................

State.....................

Gaslight Advertising Archives, Inc.

Molly Pitcher, 1944

Molly Pitcher, Revolutionary heroine, symbolizes the spirit of America's women who take over the work of men at war.

Women are doing a big job on the Pennsylvania Railroad

More than 48,000 experienced Pennsylvania Railroad men have entered our armed forces. Yet, wartime's unusual needs for railroad service are being met . . . thanks in great part to more than 23,000 women who have rallied to the emergency. From colleges, high schools and homes, these women—after intensive training—are winning the wholehearted applause of the traveling public.

You see them working as trainmen, in ticket and station masters' offices and information bureaus, as platform ushers and train passenger representatives, in dining car service. Yes, even in baggage rooms, train dispatchers' offices, in shops and yards and as section hands. The Pennsylvania Railroad proudly salutes these "Molly Pitchers" who so gallantly fill the breach left by their fighting brothers-in-arms.

★ 48,769 in the Armed Forces
★ 317 have given their lives for their Country

Pennsylvania Railroad
Serving the Nation

BUY UNITED STATES
WAR BONDS AND STAMPS

I'm Margie.

I'm Margie.

Fly me.

I'm a girl. I'm an airplane.

I'm an airline.

I'm a fresh new way of getting you where you want to go (New York, Miami, New Orleans, Los Angeles, San Francisco—even London).

My name is Margie. Chances are you'll meet and fly Carol, Sally, Michelle and Gayle, too. Chances are you won't meet Leroy, Don, Peter or Lee, because they're working for you behind the scenes. But you'll be flying them all the same.

And soon you'll be able to fly Barbara, the first of our new fleet of DC-10's. She's this year's airplane. This winter she's joining her sister ships, National's 747's, with the only DC-10 service between New York and Florida and between Florida and California.

The idea is to make your next flight a nice personal experience, person-to-person.

So next time you're going someplace, give us a call. And call us by our first name: National.

Fly Margie. ❋ Fly National.

National honors American Express, BankAmericard, Carte Blanche, Diners Club, Master Charge/Interbank, UATP, our own card and cash.

Today's woman is in control. Demanding more because she deserves more. Daring because she wants more. ¶ She dreams about jeans that hug in the *right* places. A red silk teddy. A strapless, sequined cocktail dress. A mid-thigh mini. ¶ She *dares* to wear it. She *wants* to flaunt it. But those 15-20 extra lbs are begging to come off. ¶ Today's woman can make it happen with The Micro Diet. It's all the nutrition her body needs and everything she wants to slim down and slide into something sexy. ¶ The Micro Diet is low-calorie, low-fat, vitamin-packed, delicious meals — fiber-rich bars, shakes, chili, Italian entrees, European muesli and soups. ¶ The Micro Diet — maximum nutrients, micro calories — is tomorrow's technology for today's busy woman. ¶ The Micro Diet is Variety. Taste. Convenience. Affordability. It can make the difference between having just *any* body and *some* body.

*SOME*BODY

THE MICRO DIET

For free information in U.S. and Canada call toll-free
1-800-243-0707
or mail in coupon below.

☐ Send me complete details... I understand that there's no obligation.

Print Name _____

Address _____ Apt. No. _____

City _____ State _____ Zip _____

Telephone (_____) _____ CSR12

Mail coupon to: THE MICRO DIET, Dept. CSR12, 2440 Impala Drive, Carlsbad, CA 92008

© The Amazing Micro Diet

IF ROBIN MILLAGE paid much attention to conventional wisdom, she wouldn't be standing where she is today.

Petersburg, Alaska, is a tiny fishing village on an island off the coast of northern British Columbia. And for Robin Millage, it was nothing more than a vacation destination, until she saw it and decided to stay. You see, Robin's a bit of an adventurer.

Which may be why she recently bought a brand new Saturn, sight unseen, from a retailer in Spokane, Washington, and had it shipped 2500 miles to the village.

©1991 Saturn Corporation. Robin Millage is pictured with a 1992 Saturn SL2.

According to our records, not a lot of people do that. But Robin wanted a car she could trust. A car that was easy to service. Plus, a car that wasn't going to leave her alone in the woods. And everything she read pointed to a Saturn.

Of course, Robin's an exception. And we realize that everybody isn't going to just pick up and move to some pristine island in Alaska and buy a Saturn.

So why do you suppose there are two on the island now?

A DIFFERENT KIND OF COMPANY. A DIFFERENT KIND OF CAR.

If you'd like to know more about Saturn, and our new sedans and coupe, please call us at 1-800-522-5000.

SATURN.

Reprinted with permission of General Motors Corporation

Glossary

ALLITERATION: repetition of a consonant or vowel sound at the beginning or in the middle of words that are near enough to each other for the sound to draw attention: "through bogs and briers, barefooted and bareheaded" (Frederick Douglass).

ALLUSION: an indirect or casual reference to an event, person, place, and so on, that is generally familiar or expected to be known by the intended audience of the work in which it appears. Useful for its economy, for its ability to suggest much in few words, an allusion must be carefully chosen to fit its context and its audience. Peter Homans, for example, refers to the hero of Westerns as "this Galahad with a Colt .45 who stalks injustice on the dusty streets of Dodge" and thereby calls to mind the knight of Arthurian legend.

AMBIGUITY: the result of expressing an idea in words that have two or more possible meanings. Ambiguity is sometimes unintentional, as when a pronoun is used without a clear referent. Ambiguity can be intentionally used as a means of enhancing the meaning of a passage. When it adds to the meaning, ambiguity is effective. When it obscures the meaning, it is an error.

ANALOGY: a set of point-by-point resemblances between members of the same class or between different classes. See the introduction to "Analogy."

ANAPHORA: a device of repetition in which the same word or phrase occurs at the beginning of successive sentences or clauses. Anaphora is one of the more obvious schemes of repetition. It occurs most frequently at the end of an essay or when an attempt is being made to stir the emotions.

ANTICLIMAX: the arrangement of details so that the least important or incongruous follow the most important or appropriate. When used intentionally and with skill, anticlimax can have a humorous effect: "He has seen the ravages of war, he has known natural catastrophes, he has been to singles bars" (Woody Allen).

ANTITHESIS: a device in which contrasting ideas are juxtaposed, often in parallel structure. The balancing of unlike ideas in this way makes each more emphatic: "You have seen how a man was made a slave; you shall see how a slave was made a man" (Frederick Douglass).

ARGUMENT: a form of discourse that attempts to convince an audience that a specific claim or proposition is true wholly because a supporting body of logically related statements is also true. See the introduction to "Argument and Persuasion."

ARGUMENT: Fallacies of:

Ad hominem, a Latin phrase meaning "to the man," referring to arguments that turn away from the main issue in order to disparage individuals. *Ad hominem* arguments rely on intimidation and ignorance. Political campaign speeches often make use of this common but unethical tactic.

Bandwagon, an appeal that tries to get its audience to adopt an opinion that "everyone else" is said to hold. Popular with advertisers and political candidates, attempts to get us to jump on a bandwagon rely on our eagerness to be on the winning side. The candidate "everyone is voting for" and the jeans "everyone will be wearing" are promoted with bandwagon appeals.

Begging the question, a form of reasoning that asserts an unsupported premise and later restates that premise as a conclusion. We argue that the Bible is the Word of God because God says so in the Bible. Begging the question is sometimes referred to as arguing in a circle.

Red herring, a device used to avoid the central issue of an argument. The term comes from the old hunting practice of dragging a herring across the trail of an animal to confuse the dogs. Attempts to change the subject during the course of an argument introduce a "red herring" to sidetrack one's opponent.

CAUSE AND EFFECT: a pervasive aspect of daily thought which assumes that every action or state of being is the result of another action or state of being. The usefulness of cause-and-effect reasoning has been largely discredited in some areas of physics, philosophy, and psychology. See the introduction to "Cause and Effect."

CLASSIFICATION: a procedure for identifying all of the parts of a subject as well as a structure for organizing our thoughts about the subject. See the introduction to "Classification."

CLICHÉ: an expression used more often because it comes readily to mind than because it really suits the purpose. A cliché is an expression so weakened by repetition as not to be able to bear the weight of meaning: "hold your horses"; "don't put the cart before the horse."

CLIMACTIC ORDER: the arrangement of words, phrases, sentences, scenes, or episodes that proceeds from the least important to the most important.

COHERENCE: the quality of effective relations between all parts of a written work. When writing is coherent, there is a logical and expressive connection recognizable between sentences, paragraphs, and parts of a work. Cohesive writing presents a subject consistently, through a clear sequence of ideas.

COMPARISON AND CONTRAST: comparison establishes similarities between subjects drawn from the same class or general category; contrast highlights the differences between them. See the introduction to "Comparison and Contrast."

CONNOTATION: a word's range of associations and tonal qualities acquired through usage. See Introduction, "Exploring Words."

CONTROLLING OR STRUCTURAL METAPHOR: a form of comparison in which key resemblances between the principal subject and a subsidiary subject or image are used to organize a composition.

DEDUCTION: a strictly controlled form of reasoning which moves according to certain invariable rules from a premise to a logical conclusion. Deductive reasoning can produce valid arguments that are not necessarily true. See the introduction to "Argument and Persuasion."

DEFINITION: an explanation of the meaning of a term accomplished in one of the following ways:

lexical definition, a dictionary definition of accepted usage.

stipulative definition, an announced description of the limits of a term's meaning that either extends or limits the lexical definition.

extended definition, an expanded discussion of the meaning of a word. See the introduction to "Definition."

DENOTATION: the direct and explicit meaning of a particular word, as recorded in a dictionary. See Introduction, "Exploring Words."

DESCRIPTION: a detailed verbal picture of a person, place, object, or state of mind. *Objective* description is primarily factual and excludes mention of the writer's personal evaluation or response. *Subjective* description includes attention to both the subject described and the writer's response to it. See the introduction to "Description."

DICTION: the choice of words. Good diction is the result of choosing the most appropriate words for the purpose. Words are chosen from various levels of usage: slang, colloquial, technical, informal, and formal. Drawing words from one of these levels more frequently than from the others determines the level of diction in a piece of writing. The way the chosen words are combined is, however, a matter of style and not of diction.

DIGRESSION: a turning aside from the main subject to interrupt the development of an idea with unrelated or vaguely related material. In an informal essay an interesting digression is not a fault. In a work with a strong plot or in a formal essay, a digression is usually considered a flaw.

EMPHASIS: stress or attention given to particular words or ideas. Emphasis ought to be controlled so that the most important and least important points in an essay are given respectively the most and least emphasis. Repetition emphasizes a point, as does placing it at the end of a sentence, paragraph, or essay. There are also mechanical devices which add emphasis: italics (underlining), exclamation points, capital letters. Because mechanical devices are too often used in attempts to compensate a lack of real significance, readers tend to dismiss such ploys to gain their attention. Making what must be remembered most memorable is best done through repetition, proportion, and position.

ENTHYMEME: the rhetorical equivalent of the syllogism. An enthymeme states one premise, implies another, and contains a conclusion derived from both. A syllogism leads to a logically necessary conclusion; an enthymeme leads to a tentative conclusion. The formal syllogism is constructed of universally valid propositions, whereas the enthymeme is built upon probable premises; for example, "That car will fail inspection because its brakes are worn out." A conclusion is stated: "That car will fail inspection." One premise is stated: "Its brakes are worn out." And one premise is implied: "Any car with worn-out brakes will fail inspection." (See the introduction to "Argument and Persuasion.")

EUPHEMISM: use of a word or phrase less direct and considered less offensive than another word or phrase: as a military officer told a reporter, "You always write it's bombing, bombing, bombing. It's *not* bombing! It's *air support.*"

EXPOSITION: in nonfiction prose, the form of discourse that "puts forth" facts and ideas. Expository writing explains an idea about an object or abstraction. Most of the selections in this book make use of exposition.

HYPERBOLE: derived from the Greek meaning "to throw beyond." Hyperbole is an exaggeration used to increase the effect or emphasis of a statement. A characteristic of American speech, hyperbole is particularly pervasive in advertising. In expository prose, it is found more frequently in informal than in formal essays.

HYPOTHESIS: an unproved theory that is tentatively accepted as true in order to provide a basis for further investigation or argument. In an essay we often first state our idea about a subject as a hypothesis, and then examine, develop, support, and restate it as a conclusion.

ILLUSTRATION: a process in which writers select specific examples to represent, clarify, and support either general or abstract statements and principles. See the introduction to "Exemplification."

IMAGE: an image can be a verbal representation of any type (not just visual) of sensory experience. The creation of images is one of the ways writing, particularly poetry, is made more immediate and effective. In an essay, an appropriate image can do much to communicate the depth of one's idea about a subject.

INDUCTION: the process of reasoning by which we move from evidence about some members of a particular class to a proposition about all members of that class. The conclusions reached by induction are never logically conclusive. See the introduction to "Argument and Persuasion."

INFERENCE: a statement about what is still uncertain made on the basis of what is certain. See Introduction, "Observation and Inference."

IRONY: a kind of antithesis in which words or actions are seen as conveying the opposite of their surface significance. Of the many types of irony, verbal irony is most suited to the essay. In verbal irony, one's intended meaning is expressed in words that suggest an opposite literal meaning. The success of verbal irony depends upon the audience's ability to detect a difference between expression and intention.

METAPHOR: derived from the Greek word meaning *transfer*, it is the basic mental process by which we find resemblances between different kinds of things or ideas. See Introduction, "Making Metaphors."

METONOMY: derived from the Greek words meaning "other name." Metonomy substitutes some attribute or association of a thing in place of its name: the "White House" for the President, "cup" for the drink it holds, "paper" for the composition written on it. *Synecdoche,* a type of metonomy, substitutes the part for the whole, or the whole for the part: "strings" for violins, "wheels" for car; the "team" or "franchise" for the leading player.

NARRATION: a way of telling what happened by linking a succession of events together into a meaningful sequence. See the introduction to "Narration."

OBSERVATION: a deliberate mental activity in which we probe a subject in order to discover as much as possible about it. See Introduction, "Observation and Inference."

ONOMATOPOEIA: the use of words to echo the natural sound associated with the thing described or the formation of a single word, like *buzz* or *slap,* to represent the sound named. Although found more frequently in poetry, onomatopoeia occurs in expository prose on occasion: note the sound of kisses in the passage from Kierkegaard in the introduction to "Classification."

OXYMORON: a kind of compressed paradox that usually consists of a noun and its modifier. The modifier, however, seems to attribute to the noun a quality contradictory to its usual associations: *sweet sadness, deafening silence.* Used judiciously, an oxymoron can rise above its etymological meaning of "pointed foolishness" to focus attention sharply and convey a great deal in a few words. When used excessively, an oxymoron loses its point and appears only to be capricious word play.

PARADOX: a statement that seems contradictory but proves valid upon close inspection: "When my love swears that she is made of truth/I do believe her, though I know she lies" (Shakespeare, sonnet 138). Paradox creates temporary confusion in order to produce lasting clarity: "The single most important factor accounting for the doctrinal revival of ethnicity is the behavioral decline of ethnicity."

PARALLELISM: the arrangement of words, phrases, sentences, paragraphs, and sections of a composition so that elements of equal importance and function are given equal emphasis and form. Parallelism is one of the basic grammatical and rhetorical principles.

PERSONIFICATION: the attribution of human abilities or qualities to objects, animals, or abstractions. Helen Keller personifies imagination when she writes: "The silent worker is imagination which decrees reality out of chaos." Fables usually portray animals as if they were human; Aesop's Fables are classic examples of this type of personification.

PERSUASION: written or oral discourse aimed at disposing an audience to think and act in accordance with the speaker's will. See the introduction to "Argument and Persuasion."

POINT OF VIEW: the vantage point from which writing is presented. In expository prose, the author's point of view may be compared to a light illuminating an object: the strength, color, and position of that light determine what aspect of the object we see, and affect what kind of response we have to it. See the introduction to "Narration."

PREMISE: either of the two propositions in a syllogism from which a conclusion is drawn. Etymologically, "to go before," premises are the assumptions (either believed or entertained) from which deductive reasoning proceeds. In a more general sense, premises are the assumptions upon which an author bases an argument.

PURPOSE: the controlling intention of a composition. In an expository essay the general purpose might be to explain, convince, or describe, but the specific purpose would be, say, to convince the editors of the local newspaper that they had chosen to support the wrong candidate for mayor, or to explain to the readers of the college paper why the proposed tuition increase was passed without student opposition. When the purpose of an essay is stated directly, it is often called the thesis statement. Although the thesis statement expresses what you are trying to say, it does not fully explain your reason for saying it.

RHETORICAL QUESTION: a question posed not to provoke an answer but to assert or deny something indirectly. Rhetorical questions frequently occur in essays when the author is trying to disarm anticipated objections.

SIMILE: an explicit comparison of two things normally not considered alike, usually brought together by the words *like* or *as*. Thoreau compared grass to a ribbon: "The grass-blade, like a long green ribbon, streams from the sod into the summer." See also Introduction "Making Metaphors," or, as Maya Angelou writes, "Little children dashed by out of the dark like fireflies."

STYLE: in classical rhetoric, the choice of words and their arrangement. In contemporary usage, style generally refers to the relation between ideas and language. Robert Frost said that style is "the mind skating circles round itself as it moves forward." Diction, syntax, point of view, emphasis, figurative language all contribute to style. More difficult to define than to perceive, an author's style produces the recognizable individuality of a composition.

SYLLOGISM: a formal deductive argument composed of a major premise (All men are mortal), a minor premise (Socrates is a man), and a conclusion (therefore, Socrates is mortal). See the introduction to "Argument and Persuasion."

UNDERSTATEMENT: a form of irony in which something is said to be less than it is in order to emphasize its full meaning and significance. Understatement leaves it to the readers to build up what has been played down and therefore prompts them to engage actively in imaging the importance of what has been understated: "To say that he is ugly is nothing: to add that his figure is grotesque is to convey no adequate impression" (Edward Dicey on President Lincoln). When an offensive idea is understated, the result is a kind of euphemism. *Litotes* is a form of understatement in which the opposite of what is intended is denied: "This is no small matter."

Permissions
Acknowledgments

Cunningham, Amy. "Why Women Smile" by Amy Cunningham as appeared in *Lear's* 1993.

Didion, Joan. Excerpt from "On Morality" from *Slouching Towards Bethlehem* by Joan Didion. Copyright © 1968 and copyright renewed © 1996 by Joan Didion. Reprinted by permission of Farrar, Straus & Giroux, Inc.

Dillard, Annie. "The Stunt Pilot" by Annie Dillard, originally published in *Esquire*, 1989. Copyright © 1989 by Annie Dillard. Reprinted by permission of Blanche C. Gregory, Inc.

Dionne, E. J., Jr. Reprinted with the permission of Simon & Schuster from *Why Americans Hate Politics* by E. J. Dionne, Jr. Copyright © 1991 by E. J. Dionne, Jr. Afterword and Introduction copyright © 1992 by E. J. Dionne, Jr.

Edwards, Betty. Reprinted by permission of Jeremy P. Tarcher, Inc., a division of The Putnam Publishing Group, from *Drawing on the Right Side of the Brain* by Betty Edwards. Copyright © 1989 by Betty Edwards.

Ehrlich, Gretel. "Time on Ice" by Gretel Ehrlich. Reprinted by permission of Darhansoff and Verrill Literary Agency.

Eighner, Lars. Copyright © 1993 by Lars Eighner. From *Travels with Lizbeth: Three Years on the Road and on the Streets* by Lars Eighner. Reprinted by permission of St. Martin's Press Incorporated.

Faragher, John Mack. "Pioneer Diaries of Women and Men" from *Women and Men on the Overland Trail* by John Mack Faragher. Reprinted by permission of Yale University Press.

Frazier, Ian. "Making Marks" by Ian Frazier, *Audubon*, November/December 1996, Vol. 98, No. 6. Reprinted by permission of the author.

Froman, Sandra. "Armed and Safe" by Sandra S. Froman, orginally appeared in *Stanford Alumni* Magazine, March 1994. Reprinted by permission of the author.

Gans, Herbert. "The Underclass" by Herbert Gans as appeared in the *Washington Post*, September 10, 1990. © The Washington Post. Reprinted by permission.

Gibbs, Nancy. "When Is It Rape?" by Nancy Gibbs, *Time*, June 3, 1991. Copyright © 1991 Time Inc. Reprinted by permission.

Gordon, Mary. "More Than Just a Shrine: Paying Homage to the Ghosts of Ellis Island," by Mary Gordon, *The New York Times*, November 3, 1985. Copyright © 1985 by The New York Times Co. Reprinted by permission.

Gould, Stephen Jay. "Of Crime, Cause, and Correlation" by Stephen Jay Gould, *Discover*, December 1983. Copyright © 1983 by Stephen Jay Gould. Reprinted with permission of Discover Magazine.

Gregorian, Vartan. "Letter to the Editor" of *The New York Times* by Vartan Gregorian, February 21, 1991. Reprinted by permission of the author.

Sowell, Thomas. "We're Not Really Equal" by Thomas Sowell, originally published in *Newsweek,* September 7, 1981. Reprinted by permission of the author.

Staples, Brent. "Just Walk on By: A Black Man Ponders His Ability to Alter Public Space" by Brent Staples which originally appeared in *Ms.* Magazine. Reprinted by permission of the author.

Steinberg, Laurence. "Bound to Bicker" by Laurence Steinberg, *Psychology Today,* December 1989. Reprinted with permission from Psychology Today Magazine. Copyright © 1989 Sussex Publishers, Inc.

Tannen, Deborah. "How Male and Female Students Use Language Differently" by Deborah Tannen, *The Chronicle of Higher Education,* 1991, copyright Deborah Tannen. Reprinted by permission of the author.

Thomas, Lewis. "The Attic of the Brain" copyright © 1980 by Lewis Thomas from *Late Night Thoughts on Listening to Mahler's Ninth* by Lewis Thomas. Used by permission of Viking Penguin, a division of Penguin Books USA Inc.

Viorst, Judith. "Friends, Good Friends—and Such Good Friends" by Judith Viorst. Copyright © 1977 by Judith Viorst. Originally appeared in *Redbook.* Reprinted by permission of Lescher & Lescher, Ltd.

Vonnegut, Kurt. "How to Write with Style" by Kurt Vonnegut from "Power of the Printed Word" by International Paper. Reprinted by permission of International Paper Co.

Walker, Alice. "In Search of Our Mothers' Gardens" from *In Search of Our Mothers' Gardens: Womanists Prose* by Alice Walker. Copyright © 1974 by Alice Walker, reprinted by permission of Harcourt Brace & Company. "Women" from *Revolutionary Petunias And Other Poems,* copyright © 1970 by Alice Walker. Reprinted by permission of Harcourt Brace & Company.

White, E.B. "Once More to The Lake" from *One Man's Meat* by E.B. White. Copyright 1941 by E.B. White. Copyright renewed. Reprinted by permission of HarperCollins Publishers, Inc.

Williams, Patricia. "Hate Radio" by Patricia Williams, *Ms.* Magazine, March/April 1994. Reprinted by permission of Ms. Magazine, © 1994.

Winn, Marie. "Television Addiction" from *The Plug-In Drug, Revised Edition* by Marie Winn. Copyright © 1977, 1985 by Marie Winn Miller. Used by permission of Viking Penguin, a division of Penguin Books USA Inc.

Woolf, Virginia. "Death of a Moth" from *The Death of the Moth and Other Essays* by Virginia Woolf. Copyright 1942 by Harcourt Brace & Company and renewed 1970 by Marjorie T. Parsons, Executrix. Reprinted by permission of the publisher.

Index

A

Agee, James, "Overalls," 137–140

"The Allegory of the Cave" (Plato), 336–339

"Ambition" (Klass), 198, 208–211

"America: The Multinational Society" (Reed), 147–150

"American History" (Ortiz Cofer), 37, 59–65

Anania, Michael, "Starting," 412, 416–418

Angelou, Maya, "Graduation," 40–50

"The Arab World" (Hall), 179–188

Aristotle, 13, 459, 462, 464

"Armed and Dangerous" (Campbell), 514–518

"Armed and Safe" (Froman), 508–512

"The Attic of the Brain" (Thomas), 327–330

B

Baker, Carlos, 2

Baker, Russell, "The Plot Against People," 250–251

Beardsley, Monroe, 460

"Biography of a Dress" (Kincaid), 127–133

"Bound to Bicker" (Steinberg), 374–378

Britt, Suzanne, "Neat People versus Sloppy People," 283, 291–292

Bruck, David, "The Death
Penalty," 528–531

C

Campbell, Tom, "Armed and
Dangerous," 514–518
Catton, Bruce, "Grant and Lee: A
Study in Contrasts,"
279, 285, 286–289
Clemens, Samuel; *see* Mark
Twain
Cole, David, "Five Myths about
Immigration," 253–256
"The Complete Breath"
(Ramacharaka), 424–427
"Crack and the Box" (Hamill),
353–357
Crane, Stephen, 35
Cunningham, Amy, "Why
Women Smile," 367–372

D

"Death and Justice: How Capital
Punishment Affirms Life"
(Koch), 522–526
"Death of a Moth" (Woolf),
92, 113–115
"The Death Penalty" (Bruck),
528–531
"The Declaration of
Independence" (Jefferson),
476–479
"Declaration of Sentiments and
Resolutions" (Stanton),
481–484
Didion, Joan, "On Morality,"
29–31
Dillard, Annie, "The Stunt
Pilot," 15–17

Dionne, E. J., Jr., "How Liberals
and Conservatives Are Failing
America," 285, 297–305
Drawing on the Right Side of the
Brain (Edwards), 8

E

Edwards, Betty, "Left and
Right," 6, 8–9
Ehrlich, Gretel, "Time on Ice,"
95, 117–124
Eighner, Lars, "On Dumpster
Diving," 429–439
Either/Or (Kierkegaard), 240

F

Faragher, John Mack, "Pioneer
Diaries of Women and Men,"
280, 315–319
"Fear and Anxiety" (Horney),
294–295
"Feminism at the Crossroads"
(Pollitt), 341–346
"A First American Views His
Land" (Momaday), 94,
103–111
Fitzgerald, F. Scott, 37
"Five Myths about Immigration"
(Cole), 253–256
"Four Kinds of Reading"
(Hall), 258–261
Frazier, Ian, "Making
Marks," 22–26
"Free Speech? Yes. Drunkenness?
No." (Gregorian), 502–504
Freud, Sigmund, 199
"Friends, Good Friends, and Such
Good Friends" (Viorst),
244–248

Froman, Sandra S., "Armed and Safe," 508–512

G

Gans, Herbert, "The Underclass," 200–202

Gibbs, Nancy, "When Is It Rape?," 213–224

Gordon, Mary, "More Than Just a Shrine: Paying Homage to the Ghosts of Ellis Island," 97–101

Gould, Stephen Jay, "Of Crime, Cause, and Correlation," 380–385

"Graduation" (Angelou), 40–50

"Grant and Lee: A Study in Contrasts" (Catton), 286–289

The Great Gatsby (Fitzgerald), 37

Gregorian, Vartan, "Free Speech? Yes. Drunkenness? No.," 502–504

H

Hall, Donald, "Four Kinds of Reading," 241, 258–261

Hall, Edward T., "The Arab World," 179–186

Hamill, Pete, "Crack and the Box," 353–357

Harvey, William, 325

"Hate Radio" (Williams), 387–394

Hemingway, Ernest, "When You Camp Out, Do It Right," 420–423

Hentoff, Nat, "Should This Student Have Been Expelled?," 497–501

Hoagland, Edward, "Turtles," 13–14

Holt, John, "Three Kinds of Discipline," 273–275

Horney, Karen, "Fear and Anxiety," 6, 199, 280, 294–295

"How Liberals and Conservatives Are Failing America" (Dionne), 285, 297–305

"How Male and Female Students Use Language Differently" (Tannen), 308–313

"How to Write with Style" (Vonnegut), 414–415, 442–445

Hoyle, Frederick, "The Next Ice Age," 397–402

Hughes, Langston, "Salvation," 36, 80–82

I

"I Have a Dream" (King), 491–494

Illich, Ivan, 197

"In Search of Our Mothers' Gardens" (Walker), 168–176

J

James, William, 29

Jefferson, Thomas, "The Declaration of Independence," 476–479

Johnson, Mark, 12–13

The Jungle (Sinclair), 365

"Just Walk on By: A Black Man Ponders His Ability to Alter Public Space" (Staples), 188–191

K

Kakutani, Michiko, "The Word Police," 152–156

Kennedy, John F., "On Being Inaugurated President of the United States," 486–489

Kepler, Johannes, 325

Kierkegaard, Søren, 240

Kincaid, Jamaica, "Biography of a Dress," 127–133

King, Martin Luther, Jr., "I Have a Dream," 491–494

Kingston, Maxine Hong, "No Name Woman," 67–77

Klass, Perri, "Ambition," 198–199, 208–211

Koch, Edward I., "Death and Justice: How Capital Punishment Affirms Life," 522–526

L

Lakoff, George, 12–13

"Left and Right" (Edwards), 8–9

"Less Work for Mother?" (Schwartz Cowan), 158–166

M

Mairs, Nancy, "On Being a Cripple," 9–10

"The Maker's Eye" (Murray), 447–451

"Making Marks" (Frazier), 22–26

Marx, Karl, 199

Metaphors We Live By (Lakoff and Johnson), 12

"A Modest Proposal" (Swift), 467–474

Momaday, N. Scott, "A First American Views His Land," 13, 94, 103–111

"More Than Just a Shrine: Paying Homage to the Ghosts of Ellis Island" (Gordon), 97–101

Morris, Desmond, "Territorial Behavior," 264–271

Murray, Donald, "The Maker's Eye," 447–451

N

Naylor, Gloria, "A Question of Language," 227–229

"Neat People versus Sloppy People" (Britt), 291–292

"The Next Ice Age" (Hoyle), 397–402

"No Name Woman" (Kingston), 67–77

O

"Of Crime, Cause, and Correlation" (Gould), 380–385

"On Being a Cripple" (Mairs), 9–10

"On Being Inaugurated President of the United States" (Kennedy), 486–489

"On Dumpster Diving" (Eighner), 429–439

"On Keeping a Diary" (Safire), 144

"On Morality" (Didion), 29–31

"Once More to the Lake" (White), 52–57

Ortiz Cofer, Judith , "American History," 37, 59–65

Orwell, George, "Shooting an Elephant," 34, 83–89

"Overalls" (Agee), 137–140

P

Pace Nilsen, Alleen, "Sexism in Language," 231–236

"Pioneer Diaries of Women and Men" (Faragher), 315–319

Plato, "The Allegory of the Cave," 336–339

"The Plot Against People" (Baker), 250–251

Pollitt, Katha, "Feminism at the Crossroads," 341–346

Q

"A Question of Language" (Naylor), 227–229

R

Ramacharaka, Yogi, "The Complete Breath," 424–427

"Reading the River" (Twain), 332–334

The Red Badge of Courage (Crane), 35

Reed, Ishmael, "America: The Multinational Society," 147–150

"A Report on the New Feminism" (Willis), 282

Russell, Bertrand, 361

S

Safire, William, 144

Sagan, Carl, "The Warming of the World," 404–409

St. Augustine, 464

"Salvation" (Hughes), 80–82

Schwartz Cowan, Ruth, "Less Work for Mother?," 158–166

"Sexism in Language" (Pace Nilsen), 231–236

"Shooting an Elephant" (Orwell), 34, 83–89

"Should This Student Have Been Expelled?" (Hentoff), 497–501

Sinclair, Upton, 365

Sowell, Thomas, "We're Not Really 'Equal,' " 204–206

Stanton, Elizabeth Cady, "Declaration of Sentiments and Resolutions," 481–484

Staples, Brent, "Just Walk on By: A Black Man Ponders His Ability to Alter Public Space," 188–191

"Starting" (Anania), 416–418

Steinberg, Laurence, "Bound to Bicker," 374–378

"The Stunt Pilot" (Dillard), 15–17

Swift, Jonathan, "A Modest Proposal," 467–474

T

Tannen, Deborah, "How Male and Female Students Use Language Differently," 308–313

"Territorial Behavior" (Morris), 264–271

Thomas, Lewis, "The Attic of the Brain," 327–330

Thoreau, Henry David, 325

"Three Kinds of Discipline" (Holt), 273–275

"Time on Ice" (Ehrlich), 95, 117–124

"Turtles" (Hoagland), 13–14

"TV Addiction" (Winn), 349–351

Twain, Mark, "Reading the River," 332–334

U

"The Underclass" (Gans), 200–202

Updike, John, 13

V

Viorst, Judith, "Friends, Good Friends–and Such Good Friends," 244–248

Vonnegut, Kurt, "How to Write with Style," 414, 442–445

W

Walker, Alice, "In Search of Our Mothers' Gardens," 168–176

"The Warming of the World" (Sagan), 404–409

"We're Not Really 'Equal' " (Sowell), 204–206

"When Is It Rape?" (Gibbs), 213–224

"When You Camp Out, Do It Right" (Hemingway), 420–423

White, E. B., "Once More to the Lake," 52–57

"Why Women Smile" (Cunningham), 367–372

Williams, Patricia, "Hate Radio," 387–394

Willis, Ellen, 282–283

Winn, Marie, "TV Addiction," 349–351

Woolf, Virginia, "Death of a Moth," 92, 113–115

"The Word Police" (Kakutani), 152–156

lg 414

DATE DUE

DEC 16 2013		
DEC -3 2004	NOV 22 2013	
ILL		
ILL		
I LL		
JUN 6 2011		

Demco, Inc. 38-293